THE CAMBRIDGE COMPANION TO
THUCYDIDES

Thucydides' *History of the Peloponnesian*
influential works in the Western historio̧
unfinished account of the war between Ath،
her allies that lasted from 431 to 404 BCE an،
and of political analysis. The twenty chapters ،   ،، a wide
range of perspectives on different aspects of the   ـρretation and its
significance. The nature of the text is explorea   ،،etail, and problems of
Thucydides' historical and literary methodology are examined. Other chapters
analyse the ways in which Thucydides' work illuminates, or complicates, our
understanding of key historical questions for this period, above all those relating
to the nature and conduct of war, politics and empire. Finally, the book also
explores the continuing legacy of Thucydides, from antiquity to the present day.

POLLY A. LOW is a professor in the Department of Classics and Ancient
History at Durham University. Her publications include *Interstate Relations in
Classical Greece* (2007) and (as editor) *The Athenian Empire* (2008).

CAMBRIDGE
COMPANIONS TO
LITERATURE

A complete list of books in the series is at the back of this book.

THE CAMBRIDGE
COMPANION TO
THUCYDIDES

EDITED BY
POLLY A. LOW
Durham University

CAMBRIDGE
UNIVERSITY PRESS

Shaftesbury Road, Cambridge CB2 8EA, United Kingdom

One Liberty Plaza, 20th Floor, New York, NY 10006, USA

477 Williamstown Road, Port Melbourne, VIC 3207, Australia

314–321, 3rd Floor, Plot 3, Splendor Forum, Jasola District Centre, New Delhi – 110025, India

103 Penang Road, #05–06/07, Visioncrest Commercial, Singapore 238467

Cambridge University Press is part of Cambridge University Press & Assessment,
a department of the University of Cambridge.

We share the University's mission to contribute to society through the pursuit of
education, learning and research at the highest international levels of excellence.

www.cambridge.org
Information on this title: www.cambridge.org/9781107107052

DOI: 10.1017/9781316227442

First published 2023

A catalogue record for this publication is available from the British Library.

Library of Congress Cataloging-in-Publication Data
NAMES: Low, Polly, editor.
TITLE: The Cambridge companion to Thucydides / edited by Polly Low, University of Durham.
OTHER TITLES: Cambridge companions to literature.
DESCRIPTION: Cambridge, United Kingdom ; New York, NY : Cambridge University Press,
2023. | Series: Cambridge companions to literature | Includes bibliographical
references and index.
IDENTIFIERS: LCCN 2022030709 (print) | LCCN 2022030710 (ebook) | ISBN 9781107107052
(hardback) | ISBN 9781107514607 (paperback) | ISBN 9781316227442 (epub)
SUBJECTS: LCSH: Thucydides. | Thucydides–Themes, motives. | Thucydides–Influence. |
Greece–History–Peloponnesian War, 431-404 B.C.–Historiography.
CLASSIFICATION: LCC DF229.T6 C345 2023 (print) | LCC DF229.T6 (ebook) |
DDC 938/.05–dc23/eng/20220712
LC record available at https://lccn.loc.gov/2022030709
LC ebook record available at https://lccn.loc.gov/2022030710

ISBN 978-1-107-10705-2 Hardback
ISBN 978-1-107-51460-7 Paperback

To the memory of P. J. Rhodes

CONTENTS

List of Contributors   *page* xi
Preface   xv
List of Abbreviations   xvii

1   Introduction   1
     POLLY A. LOW

             PART I   CONTEXT AND METHODS

2   Establishing a New Genre: Thucydides and Non-historiographic
     Memory   17
     JONAS GRETHLEIN

3   Thucydidean Self-Presentation   31
     TOM BEASLEY

4   Thucydides' Use of Evidence and Sources   50
     P. J. RHODES

5   Rhetorical History: Speeches in Thucydides   63
     EMILY GREENWOOD

6   Prolegomena to the Peloponnesian War: Thucydides Book 1   77
     JEFFREY S. RUSTEN

7   Time and Foresight in Thucydides   89
     ROSARIA VIGNOLO MUNSON

8   Labouring for Truth in Thucydides   110
     ELIZABETH IRWIN

PART II   THEMES AND CONTENT

9   Thucydides and War   129
    JASON CROWLEY

10   Thucydides on Empire and Imperialism   143
     POLLY A. LOW

11   Ethnicity in Thucydides   160
     MARIA FRAGOULAKI

12   Thucydides and Leadership   177
     SARAH BROWN FERRARIO

13   Thucydides on Democracy and Other Regimes   198
     RYAN K. BALOT

14   Justice and Morality in Thucydides   215
     PAUL WOODRUFF

PART III   AFTER THUCYDIDES

15   Thucydides in Greek and Roman Historiography   233
     LUKE V. PITCHER

16   Thucydides in Byzantium   249
     SCOTT KENNEDY AND ANTHONY KALDELLIS

17   Thucydides in the Renaissance and Reformation   265
     KINCH HOEKSTRA

18   Narratives of Thucydides and the 19th-Century Discipline of
     (Ancient) History   282
     ALEXANDRA LIANERI

19   'What Really Happened': Varieties of Realism in Thucydides' *History*   301
     JOEL ALDEN SCHLOSSER

CONTENTS

20 Translating Thucydides   317
    JEREMY MYNOTT

    Bibliography   331
    Index Locorum   365
    Subject Index   373

CONTRIBUTORS

RYAN K. BALOT is Professor of Political Science and Classics at the University of Toronto. He is the author of *Greed and Injustice in Classical Athens* (2001), *Greek Political Thought* (2006) and *Courage in the Democratic Polis: Ideology and Critique in Classical Athens* (2014). He edited *A Companion to Greek and Roman Political Thought* (2009) and is co-editor of *The Oxford Handbook of Thucydides* (2017).

TOM BEASLEY's Yale PhD (2013) was a study of Thucydidean self-definition. He now works in the public humanities in Seattle, Washington.

JASON CROWLEY is Senior Lecturer in Ancient History at Manchester Metropolitan University. His main research interest is the psychology of combat, particularly the close-quarters close-order combat favoured by the classical Greeks. His first book, *The Psychology of the Athenian Hoplite: The Culture of Combat at Classical Athens*, which applies modern theories of combat motivation to the ancient world, was published in 2012, and subsequent publications have explored both the human experience of war and the effects war has on those who survive that experience.

SARAH BROWN FERRARIO is Associate Professor of Greek and Latin at the Catholic University of America. She is a specialist in Greek history, literature and politics, especially of the 5th and 4th centuries BCE. She is the author of *Historical Agency and the 'Great Man' in Classical Greece* (2014) and most recently of several chapters on the context and reception of tragedy and on the historical works of Xenophon. Her current research centres upon the rhetoric of leadership and democracy.

MARIA FRAGOULAKI is Senior Lecturer in Ancient Greek History at Cardiff University. Her research interests are ancient Greek historiography, especially Thucydides and Herodotus, kinship and international relations in antiquity, memory and performance studies. She is the author of *Kinship in Thucydides: Intercommunal Ties and Historical Narrative* (2013) and a co-editor of *Shaping*

Memory in Ancient Greece: Poetry, Historiography, and Epigraphy (2020). She is working on a monograph on Thucydides and Homer and co-editing a volume entitled *Doing Things with Thucydides: Politics, Education, Performance.*

EMILY GREENWOOD is Professor of Classics and Comparative Literature at Harvard University. She is the author of *Thucydides and the Shaping of History* (2006) and *Afro-Greeks: Dialogues between Anglophone Caribbean Literature and Classics in the Twentieth Century* (2010). She has guest edited a two-volume special issue of the *American Journal of Philology* entitled *Diversifying Classical Philology* (issues 143.2 and 143.4) and has co-edited *Reading Herodotus: A Study of the* Logoi *in Book 5 of Herodotus'* Histories (with Elizabeth Irwin, 2007) and *Homer in the Twentieth Century: Between World Literature and the Western Canon* (with Barbara Graziosi, 2007).

JONAS GRETHLEIN is Professor of Greek at Heidelberg University. His books include *The Greeks and Their Past: Poetry, Oratory and History in the Fifth Century* BCE (2010), *Experience and Teleology in Ancient Historiography: Futures Past from Herodotus to Augustine* (2013), *Aesthetic Experiences and Classical Antiquity: The Significance of Form in Narratives and Pictures* (2017) and *The Ancient Aesthetics of Deception: The Ethics of Enchantment from Gorgias to Heliodorus* (2021).

KINCH HOEKSTRA is Chancellor's Professor of Political Science and Law and Affiliated Professor of Classics and Philosophy at the University of California, Berkeley. His current projects include *The Thucydidean Renaissance*, based on his Carlyle Lectures, and co-editing Hobbes's translation of Thucydides for the *Clarendon Edition of the Works of Thomas Hobbes.*

ELIZABETH IRWIN has co-edited three books on Herodotus (most recently with Tom Harrison, *Interpreting Herodotus*) and authored numerous articles on Herodotus, Thucydides and 5th-century BCE Athenian imperialism. Her most recent work and current projects deal with a range of topics relevant to the late 5th century BCE, such as the intertextuality and relative chronology of the extant histories of Herodotus and Thucydides, religion in Thucydides, the engagement of Athenian drama with its historical and political contexts and the deployment of medical discourse in the political and ethical debates of late 5th-century BCE Athens.

ANTHONY KALDELLIS is Professor of Classics at the University of Chicago. He has written extensively on many aspects of Byzantine history, culture and literature, including on the transmission and reception of the classical tradition among the Byzantine historians. His most recent books include *The Byzantine Republic: People and Power at New Rome* (2015) and *Romanland: Ethnicity and Empire in Byzantium* (2019).

SCOTT KENNEDY is an assistant professor in the Program in Civilizations, Cultures, and Ideas at Bilkent University in Ankara, Turkey. He wrote his dissertation on the reception of Thucydides in the rhetorical tradition. He is interested in how classical texts were read and adapted by later readers and has published contributions on the afterlife of classical texts in late antiquity and Byzantium. He is currently at work on a monograph on how Thucydides and the Peloponnesian War were remembered from antiquity to Byzantium.

ALEXANDRA LIANERI is an assistant professor in the classics department of the Aristotle University of Thessaloniki. She is co-editor (with V. Zajko) of *Translation and the Classic* (2008) and editor of *The Western Time of Ancient History* (2011) and *Knowing Future Time in and through Greek Historiography* (2016). Her forthcoming books are *A Democracy of the Past: Translating Dēmokratia in Nineteenth-Century Britain, Edinburgh Critical History of Greek and Roman Philosophy* (co-edited with G. Cambiano) and the *Blackwell Companion to the Translation of Greek and Roman Epic* (co-edited with R. Armstrong).

POLLY A. LOW is a professor in the Department of Classics and Ancient History at Durham University. Her interests focus on the political history of the Greek world, particularly relations between states. Her publications include *Interstate Relations in Classical Greece* (2007) and (as editor) *The Athenian Empire* (2008).

ROSARIA VIGNOLO MUNSON is the J. Archer and Helen C. Turner Professor of Classics at Swarthmore College. She is the author of *Telling Wonders: Ethnographic and Political Discourse in the Work of Herodotus* (2001), *Black Doves Speak: Herodotus and the Language of Barbarians* (2005) and several articles on Herodotus and Thucydides. She has edited *Oxford Readings in Classical Studies: Herodotus* (2013). She has co-edited (with Carolyn Dewald) a commentary on Herodotus Book 1 for the Cambridge Greek and Latin Classics series (2022).

JEREMY MYNOTT published an edition and translation of *Thucydides* (2013) in the Cambridge Texts in the History of Political Thought series. He is an emeritus fellow of Wolfson College, Cambridge.

LUKE V. PITCHER is a fellow and tutor in Classics at Somerville College, Oxford. He has written numerous articles on the Greek historians from Polybius to Herodian and contributed several entries to *Brill's New Jacoby*.

†P. J. RHODES was Professor of Ancient History and subsequently an honorary professor and emeritus professor at Durham University. He worked particularly on Greek political history (both the formal structures and the behaviour of individuals within those structures) and on the literary and epigraphic sources for

Greek history; *inter alia* he edited Thucydides I–V.24 and wrote the notes for the Oxford World's Classics translation of Thucydides.

JEFFREY S. RUSTEN is Professor of Classics at Cornell University. His recent book-length publications include (for the Loeb Classical Library) *Philostratus, Heroicus, Gymnasticus, Discourses 1 and 2* (2014) and *The Birth of Comedy: Texts, Documents and Art from Athenian Comic Competitions, 486–280 BCE* (2011). His commentary on Thucydides Book 1 for the Cambridge Greek and Latin Classics series is in preparation.

JOEL ALDEN SCHLOSSER is Chair and Associate Professor of Political Science at Bryn Mawr College, where he teaches political theory. He has published articles and chapters on topics ranging from ancient figures such as Thucydides, Herodotus and Euripides to contemporary writers such as James Baldwin, Don DeLillo, Joan Didion and Claudia Rankine. He is the author of *What Would Socrates Do?* (2014) and *Herodotus in the Anthropocene* (2020).

PAUL WOODRUFF teaches philosophy and classics at The University of Texas at Austin. His main interest has been in making the ethical thinking of the ancient Greeks accessible to modern readers. He has translated a number of Platonic dialogues. He has translated and introduced all of Sophocles' surviving plays with Pete Meineck. He has also produced an abridged translation of Thucydides' *History* with connecting material and notes (2nd edition, 2021). His philosophical works include books on the virtues of reverence and justice, as well as one on the philosophy of theatre. His latest project is a book on practical virtue, building on a Socratic approach to the subject.

PREFACE

Thucydides' *History* is not the most obviously companionable of texts. Already in antiquity it was criticized (by Dionysius of Halicarnassus) for the bleakness of its subject matter. In more recent times, no one to my knowledge has ever chosen to take it with them to the BBC's Desert Island (Herodotus' *Histories*, on the other hand, have twice made it into a castaway's luggage).

However, the very difficulty of the work is one of the reasons for this *Companion*'s existence. One of the main goals of this volume (like others in this series) is to offer an accessible guide to Thucydides and his writing. Another key objective is to show why, in spite of its difficulty, this is a text worth grappling with, and also why it has remained so important to such a wide range of readers. The chapters in this book, therefore, deal not only with the way(s) in which Thucydides' work illuminates (and sometimes complicates) our understanding of his own time, but also with the various ways in which his text has influenced later writers, historians, theorists and others. This volume certainly does not claim to be comprehensive, but if it succeeds in giving a sense of the complexity, the importance and indeed the fascination of Thucydides, then it will have fulfilled its purpose.

I have incurred many debts in bringing this volume to completion. Students and colleagues, first at the University of Manchester and more recently at Durham University, have patiently endured my ongoing Thucydidean fixations. Parts of the work were undertaken at the Institute for Advanced Study, Princeton, and at the British School at Athens, both exceptionally supportive research environments. Daniel Tompkins, Peter Liddel and Christy Constantakopoulou have all (knowingly or unknowingly) generously helped me to clarify my thinking on various key problems. At Cambridge University Press, Michael Sharp and Katie Idle have offered careful and patient guidance, as too did the Press's anonymous readers. Pam Scholefield prepared the indexes with impeccable speed and skill. Naturally I am deeply indebted to all who agreed to contribute to this volume, but

I should single out two people in particular. Geoffrey Hawthorn enthusiastically offered to share his perspective on the experience of reading Thucydides as a political theorist, but he died before he was able to complete his chapter. P. J. Rhodes died very shortly after the volume was submitted to the Press, and although it is a pleasure and an honour that his work is included in this book, it is a great sadness that he will not see the final version in print. This volume is dedicated to his memory.

ABBREVIATIONS

Abbreviations of ancient authors and texts follow the conventions of the *Oxford Classical Dictionary*, and those of academic journals follow the conventions of *L'Année philologique*.

In addition, the following abbreviations are used:

C. Delphes: *Corpus des inscriptions de Delphes* (Paris, 1977–).

IGI³: D. M. Lewis, L. Jefferey and E. Erxleben, *Inscriptiones Graecae*. Vol. 1: *Inscriptiones Atticae Euclidis anno anteriores*, 3rd edition (Berlin, 1981–98).

K-A: R. Kassel and C. Austin, *Poetae Comici Graeci* (PCG), vol. 5 (Berlin, 1986).

ML: R. Meiggs and D. M. Lewis, *A Selection of Greek Historical Inscriptions, to the End of the Fifth Century* BC, revised edition (Oxford, 1988).

OR: R. G. Osborne and P. J. Rhodes, *Greek Historical Inscriptions, 478–404* BC (Oxford, 2017).

RO: P. J. Rhodes and R. G. Osborne, *Greek Historical Inscriptions, 404–323* BC (Oxford, 2003).

I

POLLY A. LOW

Introduction

Thucydides of Athens

Thucydides the Athenian wrote up the war fought between the
Peloponnesians and the Athenians ... (1.1.1)

It is, of course, a cliché to start an account of an author's work and its
significance with a potted biography (with the added danger, when we are
dealing with ancient authors, that this biography might be more or less
fanciful).[1] But in Thucydides' case, the author's biography has often been
seen as critical to the interpretation of his work.

One thing that we can say with confidence about Thucydides is that he
was an Athenian; that he mentions this in the opening words of his work
should alert us to the fact that this account of the 'war fought between the
Peloponnesians and the Athenians' is one produced from 'inside' the conflict.
We also know, from things Thucydides tells us elsewhere in his work, that he
was not just a first-hand observer of the war, and of the Athenian political
world that shaped and was shaped by it, but also a participant in it as a
general (4.104.4) and then (following military failure) an exile (5.26.5); it is
clear also that he lived to see the end of the war (5.26.1), even though his
narrative breaks off before the conflict reaches its conclusion.

Why does this matter? One consequence of Thucydides' close involvement
in the war that he narrates is that he was particularly well placed to investigate it (something he himself boasts of at 1.22.2 and 5.26.5). This is not
because he was an eyewitness to all (or indeed most) of the events of the war,
but because he had access to good sources of information and – we might
reasonably assume – the practical experience, especially of politics and of
warfare, required to make sense of what those sources told him.

---

[1] A danger that certainly applies to the ancient biographies of Thucydides: see Kennedy
and Kaldellis (Chapter 16).

Thucydides' status as 'participant-observer' in the events he describes is, therefore, seen by many as a distinct strength of his work. But it should be obvious that it is also a potential weakness, particularly if we want (or indeed need) to use this text as our principal source for the facts of the Peloponnesian War. (Thucydides is not our only source for this period, but his work is the only continuous contemporary narrative that survives.[2]) This is a history written by a politically active but ultimately politically unsuccessful Athenian, recounting a conflict in which both he and his city suffered humiliating military defeats. How could this experience not have some impact on the story that he chooses to tell us?

Assessing the extent of that impact is one of the recurring and ongoing challenges for readers and users of Thucydides – a challenge made greater by the very sophistication of Thucydides' narrative. Thucydides is a particularly elusive authorial presence,[3] and it is no straightforward matter to pin down his views on many of the most important themes of the work. Some of the factors that shaped his world view are, it is true, hardly surprising (nor, among extant authors from the ancient world, uncommon). Thucydides writes from the perspective of a socially and politically elite male, and no one would deny that this has an impact on his work: the world of his *History* is notably empty of women, for example;[4] and it is also a world in which the poor cannot (for the most part) be trusted to make sensible political decisions – a viewpoint that has obvious implications for Thucydides' representation of Athenian democratic governance.

Once we get beyond these rather obvious elements, however, there is much more scope for disagreement, both (as already noted) about what Thucydides' views were and about the extent to which they influenced his portrayal of the war. This disagreement has not, on the whole, centred on the accuracy of what Thucydides tells us: Thucydides' basic veracity – unlike, notably, that of his contemporary Herodotus – has been accepted by the overwhelming majority of commentators. However, few modern readers of Thucydides would be willing to go as far as the 1st-century BCE critic Dionysius of Halicarnassus, who claimed that 'Thucydides concerned

---

[2] We know of two other contemporary narrative historians whose works dealt with the Peloponnesian War (Hellanicus and Philistos of Syracuse), but no relevant parts of their texts have survived. The most complete non-Thucydidean narrative of this period is that of Diodorus Siculus: this was composed in the 1st century BCE and drew mostly on the works of the 4th-century BCE historian Ephorus, who in turn drew on Thucydides and other earlier sources. A useful (though often excessively critical) survey of these (and other non-Thucydidean) sources can be found in Gomme et al. 1945–81: vol. I. 29–84; see also Hose 2006.
[3] See Beasley (Chapter 3).   [4] Noted by Fragoulaki (Chapter 11).

himself above all with recording the truth, neither adding to nor subtracting from the facts unjustifiably, nor allowing himself any literary licence' (*On Thucydides*, 8). Although most readers of Thucydides continue to believe that he was interested in recording (his perception of) the truth, most would also accept that the process of writing up the history – for Thucydides as for any historian – inevitably involved a set of decisions about, as E. H. Carr put it, 'the selection and arrangement of the appropriate facts',[5] not to mention decisions about which 'facts' he considered 'appropriate' or, indeed, wholly factual.[6]

Where there is less consensus is on the question of how historically, politically or morally neutral (in the context of his own time) those decisions were. That is: should we see Thucydides as a historian who is, ultimately, striving to provide his readers with a non-partisan picture of the Peloponnesian War, one which largely (though not entirely) represses his personal stake in the events that he describes? Or should we suspect that the process of selection and arrangement has created a much more idiosyncratic – even distorted – account of the history of this period? Increasingly, readers of Thucydides have drawn attention to areas in which Thucydides' view of the world seems to diverge from what we can reconstruct (from other sources) as the typical perspectives of his time. To take a notorious case, his attitude to the causative role of religion in human affairs seems to have been a radical one, and this has a demonstrable impact not just on the way in which events (and characters' reactions to events) are depicted in the *History*, but also on the prominence given (or denied) to certain aspects of the conflict between Sparta and Athens (the significance of Ionian versus Dorian ethnicity, for example).[7] In this case, our non-Thucydidean evidence is full enough to allow us to build up a reasonably clear sense of how Thucydides' perspective might have affected his narrative; but this is much harder to do in those areas where we either lack really rich contemporary evidence for non-Thucydidean views (the ideology of Athenian imperialism, for example)[8] or where the reliability of our non-Thucydidean evidence is

---

[5] Carr 1987: 11. For surveys of more critical approaches to the ontological status of the historical 'fact' (an important question, but one beyond the scope of this Introduction), see (briefly) Jenkins 1991: 32–6; Evans 1997: 75–101 (the latter arguing for a more methodologically conservative position, the former for the more 'post-modern' position); see also Arnold 2000: 110–23.

[6] On Thucydides' selection and arrangement of his material, see further discussion later in this Introduction.

[7] On Thucydides and religion, see especially Hornblower 1992, and on ethnic identity in Thucydides, see Fragoulaki (Chapter 11).

[8] A problem addressed by Strasburger 2009 [1958].

open to question (as, for example, with depictions of Pericles' exercise of power).[9] And beyond that lie the 'unknown unknowns' – those areas where our reliance on the Thucydidean version is so complete that we cannot easily tell whether or not it needs to be challenged.

It is worth emphasizing that there is no established answer to the question of how much trust we should place in Thucydides' version of events. Nor does this volume adopt a single position on the problem: rather, the chapters which follow (particularly those in Part I) represent a variety of possible approaches. The reading argued for by Irwin (Chapter 8) – that Thucydides deliberately 'distort[s] by increments' – is probably at the most sceptical end of the current range of scholarly positions; as Rhodes shows (Chapter 4), it is also possible to argue for a Thucydides whose apparent lapses have a more innocent cause. Across this spectrum, no one is suggesting that we should not use Thucydides as a central witness to the events and to the wider mentality of 5th-century BCE Greek history; where there is disagreement – as the contributions to this volume illustrate – is on the question of exactly what sort of witness he was.

Thucydides beyond Athens

One way we might read Thucydides, therefore, is as a writer deeply embedded in 5th-century BCE Athens, informed by – albeit perhaps often reacting against – the political, social and moral ideas of that particular place and time. But Thucydides has often also been seen and used as a writer who transcends his own context, and his text as one that contains lessons that can be applied far beyond classical Greece.

The first person who seems to suggest this way of approaching the text was Thucydides himself, who claims early in his work that he intends it to be a *ktema es aiei*, a 'possession for all time' (1.22.4).[10] However, the comments that immediately precede this famous claim deserve some attention:

> I shall be content if it [i.e. this work] is judged useful by those who will want to have a clear understanding of what happened – and, such being the human

---

[9] The key alternative source for this question is Plutarch's *Pericles*, which preserves elements of a notably more critical interpretation of Pericles' activities, but whose reliability has traditionally been considered inferior to Thucydides' (though cf. Irwin, Chapter 8).

[10] Rawlings 2016 argues that this clause – usually interpreted (as in the translation offered here) as an assertion of perpetual relevance – should be associated with the verb *akouein* ('listen to'), which ends this sentence; that is, that Thucydides' key claim here is that his text is one that requires repeated study: on this aspect of his self-presentation, see further later in this chapter.

condition [*kata to anthrōpinon*] will happen again at some time in the same or a similar pattern. (1.22.4, trans. Hammond 2009)

First, we should note that Thucydides hopes that his work will be of permanent value as a historical record. In fact, his comments here can help us understand why the debates (discussed in the previous section) about Thucydides' historical objectivity have been so hard to resolve. If we take 1.22.4's promise of universal relevance at face value, then it is tempting to make a connection between this promised universality and historical objectivity; that is, to see in these lines an implied claim that Thucydides is able to separate himself from the day-to-day prejudices and biases – conscious or unconscious – that might have affected a lesser historian. However, as we have already seen, there are reasons to think that such a temptation should be resisted. Indeed, to the inevitable problems of subjectivity already discussed we could now add another concern: if Thucydides (as he claims at 1.22.4) wants his text to be useful as a guide to the future, will this have led him to focus on episodes from which he thinks wider, generalizable lessons might be learnt? If so (and there is wide agreement that this did indeed influence Thucydides' selection of material), how compatible is this goal with the task of setting down a complete history of the Peloponnesian War?[11]

Nonetheless, modern readers of Thucydides could reasonably conclude that Thucydides' wishes for the historical utility of his text did come true: his work has indeed become the fundamental point of reference for anyone wanting to understand the history of 5th-century BCE Greece. It is, though, worth remembering that this is a relatively recent phenomenon. Thucydides' earliest readers were, for the most part, not especially interested in the historical content of his work, because they were not especially interested in the history of the Peloponnesian War. Dionysius of Halicarnassus' position on the historical value of this event is unusually strongly expressed, but not otherwise atypical:

Thucydides, however, writes of a single war, and one which was neither glorious or fortunate, but which had best never happened at all or, failing that, should have been consigned to silence and oblivion and ignored by later generations. (*Letter to Gn. Pompeius*, 3.3–4; trans. Usher 1985)[12]

---

[11] On the balance (or tension) between comprehensiveness and selectivity in the *History*, see Hornblower 1987: ch. 2 (suggesting a distinction between 'Thucydides the tape-recorder and Thucydides the sociologist': 43); for an attempt to resolve this tension, see Ober 2009 [2001].

[12] On Dionysius' criticisms of Thucydides, see de Jonge 2017; for his readership (and non-readership) in Byzantium, see Kennedy and Kaldellis (Chapter 16). Burke 1966 analyses

When this period of ancient history did become more popular (something that becomes especially visible from the late 18th century onwards), it was Plutarch rather than Thucydides who was often drawn on as a key text; only gradually did Thucydides become established as the default ancient source for this period.[13]

This increased use of Thucydides' work as a historical source is closely associated with a parallel (though more long-standing) strand in his reception as a historical writer, one that focuses not so much on the content of his work as on the methods he used to discover and present that content. In other words: although Thucydides (at 1.22.4) expresses the hope that his work will be read for what it says about the Peloponnesian War, it has more consistently been read as an exemplar of the proper way to write history. As several chapters in Part III of this work show, not all responses to Thucydides' historical methodology have been positive, but many have – most influentially among those 19th-century readers who were responsible for shaping the dominant paradigms and methodologies of the modern discipline of History.

This matters not just for our understanding of Thucydidean reception, but also for the way we read the text today. To some modern readers, Thucydides can seem a reassuringly familiar text because he writes history in a way that, barring a few oddities (the inclusion of speeches, most notably), fits with some contemporary perceptions of how history should be written: a logically organised account, presented by an apparently detached author, avowedly committed to seeking out 'how it really happened'.[14] Until relatively recently, Thucydides' focus on political and military matters was equally in tune with dominant historiographical pre-occupations. This sense of familiarity is not coincidental, because these ideas of what history should look like were significantly influenced by, precisely, a particular way of understanding Thucydides' own methodology. And although most contemporary writers of history would not accept that this 'scientific' model of historiography is either attainable or, necessarily,

the relative popularity of ancient historians in the Renaissance and Early Modern periods (showing that Thucydides is consistently at the lower end of the league table).

[13] Morley 2014: ch. 1; Payen 2015. As Rusten 2009b: 6–7, notes, 'deference' to Thucydides was never absolute (Grote, for example, was at times a very critical reader), but his text nonetheless became the benchmark account of the period, to be tested (and, where necessary, corrected) against other sources.

[14] '*Wie es eigentlich gewesen*': Ranke 1824: vi, perhaps deliberately invoking (or quoting) Thuc. 2.48.3 (though cf. Stroud 1987). This is a very compressed (and oversimplified) account of modern historiography's relationship with Thucydidean methodology; for fuller discussion, see Lianeri (Chapter 18).

desirable, its legacy persists. It still often takes a deliberate effort to remind ourselves that, in the words of Nicole Loraux, 'Thucydides is not a colleague'.[15]

It is not only historians who have been keen to enlist Thucydides into their ranks. He has also been read – and continues to be read – as an author who can make a vital contribution to contemporary political and ideological debates. Such readings have surely been encouraged by Thucydides' manifesto at 1.22.4, and in particular by his claim that 'the human condition' (literally: 'the human thing') is a driving, consistent force in determining the shape of events. This claim, coupled with the promise that his text will aid the future reader to recognize (if not necessarily ameliorate) similar situations, both invites and legitimates attempts to see contemporary resonances in Thucydides' writing.

Some readers have taken Thucydides' suggestion that events will recur in 'the same or similar pattern' in a fairly literal sense and have looked for direct analogies between the events of the Peloponnesian War and those of their own times. Bernard Henderson, writing in 1927, found multiple parallels between 'The Great War between Athens and Sparta' and the 'Great War' of 1914–18.[16] Later in the century, analogies between the Atheno-Spartan conflict and the 'Cold War' between the USA and the USSR became popular; the use of such parallels (as Schlosser shows in Chapter 19) persists into our own times.[17] But Thucydides is not the only text (and the Peloponnesian War not the only conflict) that has provoked this sort of pattern-seeking. A more interesting phenomenon, because it is more specific to Thucydides, is the use of the work as the basis for more general theories of human behaviour, particularly in the realm of political and international theory: Thucydides has been recruited not just as the father of historiography, but also as a foundational figure in the history of political thought, as well as for a number of varieties of international relations theories (primarily, although not exclusively, those associated with the 'realist' school of thought).[18]

A question raised by this practice is: why? That is, what did and do people hope to gain by recruiting Thucydides into their theoretical schools? There is, of course, often a value to be had in finding ancient authority for one's

[15] Loraux 2011 [1980].

[16] Henderson 1927: the analogy is made explicit not just in his title, but in comparisons scattered throughout the work (e.g. the Megarian Decrees and the assassination of Archduke Franz-Ferdinand (10–11); the battles of Naupactus and Jutland (33); and the invasions of Plataea and Belgium (75–80)).

[17] See, e.g., Karp 1998 [1981].

[18] On this, see especially the chapters of Hoekstra (Chapter 17) and Schlosser (Chapter 19).

ideas, especially if those ideas might otherwise be thought to be somehow innovative or radical. But it is also worth considering whether Thucydides has been thought to be useful because he helps us formulate questions and problems or because he offers solutions to those problems. As we will see in this volume, this too is an area in which there is no established consensus. And even among the group of readers who have detected clear theoretical positions in Thucydides' work, there is no fixed agreement on what those messages are, nor indeed on why such agreement is so hard to reach. Some commentators (especially those associated with the 'Straussian' school) are committed to the proposition that Thucydides does indeed wish to set out a definite, coherent moral and political position; that (some) readers have been unable to reconstruct it is a failure of their understanding, not of Thucydides' text.[19] Others have preferred the picture of a 'post-modernist Thucydides',[20] who wishes to engage with the reader in a shared project of 'explor[ing] the ambiguities and limits of values';[21] or even a Thucydides whose lesson is, bluntly, that there are no lessons to be learnt: 'there can be no resolution and, for reasons we may never know, Thucydides was saved from any temptation to arrive at one'.[22]

Reading Thucydides

As we have seen, Thucydides intended his work to be useful, not just to contemporaries but also to future generations. A corollary of this – in Thucydides' eyes, at least – is that his work was not designed to be an entertaining or an easy read (or listen): the work, he claims, has no 'romantic element' and might therefore 'be less of a pleasure to the ear' (1.22.3); it was not composed 'as a showpiece for a single hearing' (1.22.3), but (as we have already noted) as a 'possession for all time'.[23]

It is worth reminding ourselves, again, that we are not obliged to take these authorial pronouncements entirely at face value, particularly since Thucydides here is clearly attempting to differentiate his work from that of his predecessors and contemporaries. (Many have seen a dig at Herodotus in Thucydides' disavowal of entertainment, though we should note that Herodotus is not named here.[24]) Moreover, although we have no firm

---

[19] On Straussian readings of Thucydides, see Jaffe 2015.
[20] The formulation of Connor 1977.   [21] Connor 1984b: 15.
[22] Hawthorn 2014: 239.
[23] See n. 10 for the significance of this phrase for understanding how Thucydides intended his work to be engaged with by contemporary audiences.
[24] As Thomas 2000: 267, suggests, we could read this criticism as one that is aimed at the wider practice of the 'agonistic, confrontational and rhetorical mode of intellectual

evidence about the original circulation or publication of Thucydides' work, it does seem very likely that at least parts of it were in fact performed orally, at symposia or festivals.[25] Nonetheless, Thucydides' assertion at 1.22.3 is not entirely groundless: from the outset, he insists on the fact that his is a carefully composed, 'written up' text (1.1.1) and (as Irwin shows in Chapter 8) that historical truth is something that his audience should expect to have to work hard to locate. And indeed, the proposition that this is not an 'easy' text is one with which most readers of Thucydides would (I suspect) agree.

Some of the difficulty of Thucydides' work derives from its prose style, the oddity of which struck even ancient readers. Dionysius of Halicarnassus' analysis is again worth quoting:

> In his choice of words he preferred those which were metaphorical, obscure, archaic and outlandish to those which were common and familiar to his contemporaries. ... In his arguments <and his sentences> there are often parentheses which delay the conclusion for a long time; and his style is generally tortuous, involved, difficult to unravel, and has other similar properties. (*On Thucydides*, 24, trans. Usher 1974)

As Dionysius notes, the difficulty of Thucydidean Greek lies both in its vocabulary and in its syntax. It is hard to assess fully the fairness of Dionysius' allegations that Thucydides' vocabulary was obscure and unusual because we are hampered by the lack of 5th-century BCE Attic prose texts with which he can be compared; we cannot, therefore, always be certain that a word that seems to us (on the basis of our extant evidence) to be very rare, or perhaps distinctly poetic or technical, would have seemed the same to its 5th-century BCE audience. One peculiarity of language that is very apparent, however, is Thucydides' great fondness for creating abstract nouns, often to express quite complex ideas.[26] Dionysius also drew attention to the lack of balance of Thucydides' sentence construction, and this is indeed often a feature of his style, as too is his tendency to distort word order and, perhaps most challenging of all (in terms of comprehension of the text, especially for non-native speakers of ancient Greek), his fondness for

discourse' (and, as such, one that includes, but is not limited to, Herodotus). For further discussion of Thucydides' contemporaries and rivals, see Grethlein (Chapter 2).

[25] Hornblower 1991–2008: vol. II, 26–8; vol. III, 31; more generally on performances of historical (and other prose) texts, see Thomas 2002: 249–69. Morrison 2006b offers an interpretation of the *History* that argues that it deliberately exploits its intermediate status between oral and written text.

[26] Some examples are usefully collected and discussed by Rusten 1989: 22–3; see also Parry 1970.

extreme compression. In the words of a modern commentator: 'since [Thucydides] often tries to say too much in too few words, the reading of him demands an unusual degree of concentration'.[27] This is a particular problem for translators of Thucydides (as Mynott notes in Chapter 20) and therefore also for readers of Thucydides in translation: the requirement for concentration applies here too, with the added obligation to be alert to ways in which translators will often have needed to fill in the gaps in Thucydides' Greek in order to make him comprehensible in English.

An issue that preoccupied many of Thucydides' readers for a period of around a hundred years (from the middle of the 19th century to the middle of the 20th century) was the apparently unfinished state of the work and the possible implications of this for the way it should be interpreted. Two broad schools of thought developed: 'separatists' or 'analysts', who believed that they could identify distinct layers of composition in the work, in which different Thucydidean perspectives on events could be detected, and 'unitarians', who argued that the text could (and should) be read as a coherent whole.[28]

The 'unitarian' approach to Thucydides has now largely won out, but it is worth being aware that the legacy of the separatist/analyst approach still informs some of the ways in which the work is read. In part, this is because the features of the text that provoked the 'separatist' readings in the first place are, of course, still there. How, for example, should we explain apparent inconsistencies in Thucydides' arguments, such as (to take a notorious example) the lack of fit between the explanation for the failure of the Sicilian Expedition offered at 2.65.11 (where lack of domestic unity is singled out as the primary cause of defeat) and the one that emerges from the narrative of Books 6 and 7? Is the fault here Thucydides' (or, more sympathetically, whatever it was that prevented him from undertaking the final, comprehensive revision of his work)?[29] Or does the problem lie with Thucydides' readers, who have over-interpreted his comments at 2.65.11

---

[27] Dover 1965: xviii. For further discussion of Thucydides' style, see Rusten 1989: 21–8, and for comparisons of Thucydides' style with that of his contemporaries, see Finley 1939; Denniston 1952: 8–22; Liberman 2017: 141–57. Hornblower 2004: ch. 12, offers a stimulating comparison of Thucydidean and Pindaric styles.

[28] The 'separatist' thesis was originally developed by Ullrich 1968 [1846], and importantly refined by Schwartz 1919. The development of the argument is helpfully summarized and explained by Rusten 2015: 62–6. Particularly significant in shaping the unitarian revival are Patzer 1937; Finley 1940; de Romilly 1963 [1947], 2012 [1956]. For a recent reading of Book 1 of Thucydides from a separatist or analyst viewpoint, see Liberman 2017.

[29] See, e.g., the note on this passage by the separatist-leaning Gomme et al. 1945–81: *ad loc.*: 'the natural conclusion is that the narrative [of Books 6 and 7] was written earlier than these comments'.

and tried too hard to generate a universal rule from a single aside?[30] On a larger scale: how should the – at least superficially – anomalous qualities of Books 5 and 8 (books that lack conventional speeches but include verbatim texts of treaty agreements) be understood? Might these books best be seen as some sort of preliminary draft,[31] or is their different appearance a deliberate choice, driven by and reflective of the distinctive nature of the events that they describe?[32] A final example: how should we interpret the fact that the work seems to end (one might say) without an end; that is, in the middle of a story – perhaps even in the middle of a sentence?[33] Should we follow the ancient biographers in assuming that Thucydides died while still working on his *History*? (Or that he simply abandoned the project?[34]) Could we have lost the final section of the work?[35] Or should we assume that the work ends precisely where Thucydides intended it to end, 'on perhaps the most optimistic note possible with regard to the fortunes of Athens',[36] and at a point that frees Thucydides from the responsibility (and the problem?) of narrating and explaining Athens' collapse and Sparta's victory.[37]

In other words: the questions that are now asked of Thucydides' text are sometimes not so very different from those that troubled the 'separatist' scholars. But if 'separatists' wanted to find ways to resolve the complexities and ambiguities of the work, the dominant trend among contemporary readers of the text is, rather, to show how those complexities are intrinsic

---

[30] See, e.g., Rusten 1989: *ad loc.*: 'here the difficulties of reducing T's work to a unity have seemed greatest. This is partly because the chapter has been given more authority than it was originally meant to possess.'

[31] Gomme et al. 1945–81: vol. V, 361–444 (two appendices, authored by Andrewes (Appendix 1: 'Indications of incompleteness') and Dover (Appendix 2: 'Strata of composition')).

[32] So, for example, Connor 1984a; Hornblower 1991–2008: vol. III, 1–4; Rood 1998b: esp. chs. 4 and 11.

[33] Hornblower 1991–2008: vol. III, 1053, noting that the *prōton* ('first') at the end of 8.109.1 requires (and lacks) a balancing and concluding clause.

[34] Death: Markellinos *Life of Thucydides* 45 (rejecting, at 43, claims that Book 8 was written by Thucydides' daughter or by Xenophon); Anon. *Life* 9. Project abandoned: e.g. Flory 1993: 116; Crane 1996: 256.

[35] The suggestion of Rusten 2015: 69–72.

[36] Forde 1989: 171 (reviving and expanding a possibility first raised by Dionysius of Halicarnassus, *On Thucydides*, 12).

[37] Irwin 2018: 323–34 (who also argues that the end of Herodotus' *History* should be read as alluding to the end of Thucydides' work – and indeed as a criticism of Thucydides' failure to finish his work properly). Hornblower 1991–2008: vol. III, 1053–4, also notes the parallels between Thucydides' ending and that of Herodotus, but argues (a more conventional position) that the process of allusion operates the other way round (i.e. that Thucydides is invoking Herodotus). For more discussion of the ending of the work and the interpretive challenges this creates, see Munson (Chapter 7).

to Thucydides' historical (and historiographical) task and to our understanding of it.[38] The application of narratological theory to Thucydides' text has been particularly productive in revealing the ways in which compression, expansion, dislocation and varying focalizations of the narrative are used for both literary and historical effect.[39] Equally important, and equally productive, have been studies that have analysed the wider structures of the work, showing how Thucydides' claims for the simplicity and transparency of his narrative framework (a linear account, divided by summers and winters (2.1.1; 5.26.1)) mask a more complex matrix of narrative units.[40] Important, too, are 'intra-textual' approaches to the work, which draw out the ways in which particular themes or concepts resurface throughout the text: references to or analyses of political failure, for example,[41] or kinship ties,[42] or even the imagery of water and rivers.[43] One such theme, which is explored in several chapters in this book, is the relationship between *logos* and *ergon* – word and deed, or speech and action – which emerges as a key concern both for the historical world that Thucydides describes and for the historical method he uses to describe it.

These studies, and others like them, have (predictably) reached diverse conclusions, but they are united in some core methodological assumptions: that this is a text that repays careful readers; and that such close reading should not be seen as a purely 'literary' undertaking. Rather, better understanding of Thucydides' narrative craft is intrinsic to and inseparable from critical engagement with his historical project.

Reading This Book

As will have become apparent from this Introduction, there is no single reading of Thucydides that will satisfy everyone – which is one important reason why his text is still so compelling. Likewise, there is almost certainly no *Companion* to Thucydides that will satisfy everyone, nor even one that can fully encompass the hugely diverse ways in which his work has been read, used and understood. Accordingly, this volume does not make any claims to be comprehensive. Rather, what it aims to offer is a starting point – or indeed a set of starting points – from which readers can go on to explore

---

[38] Particularly important in setting the agenda for 'literary' readings of Thucydides are Hunter 1973; Stahl 2003 [1966]; de Romilly 2012 [1967].

[39] See especially Hornblower 1994; Rood 1998b.

[40] Especially significant contributions are those of Rawlings 1981 and Dewald 2005, which inform and are developed by the studies of Rusten (Chapter 6) and Munson (Chapter 7) in this volume.

[41] Explored by Kallet 2001: ch. 2.   [42] Fragoulaki 2013.   [43] Vivian 2021.

Thucydides more fully. (To that end, each chapter includes a selection of suggestions for further reading.[44])

As we have seen, Thucydides has been read for many purposes – as a historical source; as a literary artefact; and as a theorist of historiography, politics or international relations. This volume aims to shed light on all of those approaches and to show how they interact with one another.

Part I ('Context and Methods') explores the ways in which Thucydides' text was constructed, how it was intended to be read and how it can be read. We start (in Grethlein's Chapter 2) with an investigation of the literary and intellectual context in which Thucydides created his work, before going on to address some long-standing, and still central, Thucydidean questions: his construction of historical authority (Beasley, Chapter 3); his use of sources (Rhodes, Chapter 4); the question of the speeches (Greenwood, Chapter 5); the organization and articulation of the narrative (explored through a detailed reading of the structure of Book 1 by Rusten in Chapter 6 and in relation to the work as a whole by Munson in Chapter 7); and (in Irwin's Chapter 8) some 'worked examples' of the sort of close, critical reading of specific episodes (in this case: the *Pentecontaetia* and the Athenian plague) that Thucydides' text requires of its readers.

The question asked by Part II ('Themes and Content') could be summed up as: 'what does Thucydides tell us about ...?'. The chapters in this part are structured around the major themes of Thucydides' history: war (Crowley, Chapter 9), empire (Low, Chapter 10), identity (Fragoulaki, Chapter 11), political leaders, structures and ideologies (Ferrario in Chapter 12 and Balot in Chapter 13) and justice (Woodruff, Chapter 14). Each of these chapters aims to illuminate both the themes themselves and Thucydides' particular perspective on them.

Part III ('After Thucydides') concentrates on Thucydides' impact, both within antiquity (Pitcher in Chapter 15 and Kennedy and Kaldellis in Chapter 16) and beyond. Hoekstra (Chapter 17) demonstrates how the story of Thucydides' early-modern reception is not just about Hobbes; Lianeri (Chapter 18) traces Thucydides' complex reception in modern historiography (showing, again, that the von Rankean reading of Thucydides was not the only one possible); and Schlosser (Chapter 19) explores Thucydides' enduring appeal to realist (and other) theoreticians of contemporary politics. Finally, Mynott, one of Thucydides' most recent translators, offers his reflections on the challenges of working with this most demanding and rewarding of texts (Chapter 20).

---

[44] For even further reading, the comprehensive (and thematically arranged) bibliographies in Rusten 2009a: 479–513 offer excellent starting points.

PART I

Context and Method

2

JONAS GRETHLEIN

Establishing a New Genre

Thucydides and Non-historiographic Memory

Seeing Thucydides in the Contemporaneous Field of Memory

Leopold von Ranke, one of the outstanding historians of 19th-century Germany, had no qualms that Thucydides was the 'father of all true history'.[1] Many of his colleagues agreed. Besides exerting a major influence on the development of ancient historiography, Thucydides played a prominent role in the shaping of history as a scholarly discipline. We are thus used to envisaging Thucydides as part of the history of historiography. This is a perfectly legitimate view, and yet it does not yield the full picture. The framework within which we tend to see Thucydides was not yet fixed when he composed his account of the Peloponnesian War. Surely, Herodotus and other authors wrote history before Thucydides or simultaneously with him,[2] but as the absence of a *terminus technicus* for historiography in the 5th century BCE indicates, the generic conventions had not yet fully crystallized. Instead of assessing Thucydides against the backdrop of a genre that was still to emerge and was influenced not least by him, I suggest viewing him in the context of his own time, notably the non-historiographic field of memory in the 5th century BCE. Thucydides, I will try to show, was very concerned with setting his work off against other approaches to the past; the critical engagement with various commemorative media was crucial to his definition of a new genre.

History was by no means discovered by the first historians; they merely developed a new literary genre for reporting the past. While epic and tragedy concentrated mostly, but not exclusively, on the distant past of myth, recent events figured in other poetic genres, especially in elegy. Orators, in diplomatic as well as epideictic speeches, frequently marshalled past *exempla* and emphasized historical traditions. The past was further recorded in inscriptions and evoked in statues and paintings. When Herodotus and Thucydides

---

[1] Ranke 1888: 574.   [2] Cf. Fowler 1996; Porciani 2001.

wrote history, they entered, one could say, a crowded field. Confronted with a wide array of commemorative media and genres, the first historians had to legitimize their new approach. We are inclined to regard historiography as the privileged mode of remembering the past, but I suspect that even after its establishment the views of ancient Greeks on history were shaped more strongly by oral traditions and what they heard in the theatre and assembly. It is, for example, striking that Thucydides' notion of a single war from 431 to 404 BCE seems not to have been the general view in the 4th century BCE. In the orators, we find various other periodizations of the military encounters in the last third of the 5th century BCE.[3]

The background just sketched allows us to reconsider Thucydides' polemics against *logographoi* and poets in the methodological reflections of Book 1.[4] *Logographoi* are usually translated as 'prose-writers', and the thrust of Thucydides' invective, it is widely assumed, is especially directed at Herodotus. This understanding, however, is based on a lexicographical *petitio principii*. In the extant texts from the classical period, *logographos* means 'speech-writer' or 'orator'. Given the prominence of oratory as a commemorative medium, this meaning makes good sense. It also ties in nicely with Thucydides' critique. *Logographoi*, he rants, are enamoured with the *muthodes*; that is, as Flory has argued,[5] patriotic stories. This criticism fully applies to the speakers of *epitaphioi logoi* and other orators who celebrate Athens' glorious past. Herodotus, who seems to have recited parts of his work in oral presentations, may have been included, but the main targets of Thucydides' polemic were orators. In the same vein, the poets against whom Thucydides polemicizes are not confined to Homer, as many scholars believe. The 'New Simonides', a lengthy fragment devoted to the Battle of Plataea, has reinforced Bowie's thesis that elegy was used to narrate historical events.[6] Tragedy is another genre in which Athenians encountered stories that qualify as patriotic as well as a 'competition piece to be heard for the moment' (Thuc. 1.22.4).

It is not only Thucydides' proem that highlights the array of genres against which he pits his own take on the past. The narrative as well reflects his efforts to establish a new genre. Time and again, Thucydides embeds other commemorative media in his account and invites the reader to compare them with his superior form of memory. The *History of the Peloponnesian War* thus features what I suggest labelling 'meta-history'.[7] When Demodocus sings in the *Odyssey*, we speak of meta-poetics: Demodocus' songs mirror

---

[3] Cf. de Ste. Croix 1972: 294–5.
[4] For a more extensive discussion, see Grethlein 2010b: 206–14.   [5] Flory 1990.
[6] Bowie 1986. On the New Simonides, see Boedeker and Sider 2001; Kowerski 2005.

and refract the performance of the Homeric bard. Likewise, historiographic works can comment on their own representations of the past by featuring various acts of memory. Of course, speeches and inscriptions are different from historiography, and yet they represent alternative media for evoking the past. Especially at the beginning of Greek historiography, when the genre was still in need of establishment, meta-history lent itself to complementing explicit methodological reflections.

In this chapter, I would like to discuss three examples of meta-history. As verbal echoes show, Pericles' funeral speech implicitly continues the polemics levelled at oratory in the proem. In the Mytilenean Debate, Thucydides has Cleon voice a compelling critique of Athenian *theatrokrateia*, and yet, just as Cleon is liable to his own critique of oratory, the *History of the Peloponnesian War* features some of the vices it criticizes in other commemorative genres. The digression on the tyrannicide illustrates the havoc that can accrue from faulty memory. Seen against the backdrop of this meta-history, a new facet of Thucydides' claim to usefulness comes to light, as the final section in this chapter will argue.

Pericles' Funeral Speech: A Critique of Epideictic Oratory

Pericles' funeral speech is one of the most famous passages in the *History of the Peloponnesian War*. It is now widely accepted that the speech is not a faithful rendering of Pericles' words but an artfully crafted part of Thucydides' narrative. For my interpretation, it is crucial that funeral speeches provided the semi-official memory of classical Athens. While no *epitaphioi logoi* from the 5th century BCE have been preserved, those from the 4th century BCE feature a more or less fixed catalogue of virtues and past events that were marshalled to praise the war dead of each year.[8] Repeated nearly every year in front of a large audience at the Kerameikos, this catalogue must have had a huge impact on the Athenians' view of their past. Now Thucydides, by embedding an *epitaphios logos* in his *History of the Peloponnesian War*, invites the reader to compare his take on the past with this institution of democratic *memoria*. General similarities and pointed echoes of his own methodological reflections in the proem throw into relief the superiority of the new commemorative genre.

The claims to truth and usefulness as well as the aspiration to furnish eternal memory align the speech with Thucydides' work. Striving for *pistis*,

---

[7] For further analysis of meta-history in ancient historiography, see the contributions to Grethlein and Krebs 2012.

[8] Cf. Loraux 1986a.

presenting evidence (*tekmērion, sēmeion, marturion*) and aiming for exactness (*saphēs*), Pericles is reminiscent of Thucydides. Just as Thucydides concentrates on the most recent war, which he considers more significant than all previous ones, Pericles calls the recent achievements the greatest and touches on earlier history only in a *praeteritio*. More pointedly, Pericles asserts (2.41.4): '... we are not in need of Homer for praise nor of any other who will charm with his verses for the moment [*to autika terpsei*] whose claims the factual truth will destroy'. This recalls Thucydides' rejection of poets mentioned earlier in this chapter and is verbally echoed in the following assertion (1.22.4): 'And the results, by avoiding patriotic storytelling, will perhaps seem the less charming [*aterpesteron*] for listening ... It is composed rather as a possession for all time than a competition piece to be heard for the moment [*es to parachrēma*].'

The reverberations draw our attention to the marked differences between funeral speech and history. While polemicizing against Homer 'and any other who will charm with his verses for the moment', Pericles refers to the *terpsis* (charm) that the honour of the funeral speech generates (2.44.4). Another assertion is even more telling (2.42.2): 'As to the qualities for which I have praised [*humnēsa*] the city, the virtues of these men and men like them have given honour [*ekomēsan*] to them ...' This jars with 1.21.1 where Thucydides juxtaposes his reliable reconstruction of events with the poetic accounts that are corrupted by praising (*humnēkasi*) and adorning with exaggerations (*epi to meizon kosmountes*). Pericles' presentation of his speech as part of an *agon* (2.42.1; 2.45.1) also clashes with Thucydides' refusal to deliver a 'competition piece' (*agōnisma*). While rejecting poetic accounts for their excessive praise, Pericles' speech features the very elements that Thucydides criticizes in poetry and oratory. The verbal echoes of Thucydides' methodological reflections underline the discrepancy between historiography and funeral speeches as commemorative media.

Thucydides has Pericles flag the reason for the shortcomings of the *epitaphioi logoi*. At the beginning of his speech, Pericles remarks (2.35.2): 'To speak in due proportion is difficult where grasp of the truth itself is hardly assured.' Either the listener is familiar with the topic and of good will or he is ignorant and envious. Not the veracity of the account but the listener's knowledge and attitude are crucial to the success of the speech. The necessity to satisfy the expectations of the audience sets the *epitaphioi* apart from the *History of the Peloponnesian War*. Whereas Thucydides claims to stick with the facts, the orators strive to flatter their audience. Trenchantly, the audience's knowledge and attitude, which are the gauges of the *epitaphioi logoi*, are two factors that Thucydides tries to even out in his reconstruction of the past (1.22.3): 'It took much effort to find out the facts, because eye-witnesses did not report the same about the same events, but according to individual favour or ability to remember.'

The fact that it is Pericles who delivers the speech underscores the failings of the institution. Thucydides drives home that, unlike his successors, Pericles did not pander to the *dēmos* (2.65), and yet the conventions of the public funeral force him to 'follow the custom and try to conform with the wishes and opinions of each one of you as far as possible' (2.35.3). The glossy image of Athens in the funeral speech is deconstructed in the account of the plague, which is positioned pointedly immediately after it. Pericles' assertions about Athens' selfless benefactions (2.40.5) are a far cry from the ruthless power politics highlighted by Thucydides. Also the stable constitution and harmonious polis life lauded by Pericles are unmasked as mere rhetorical ornaments when he himself is fined by the *dēmos* (2.65.3).

Pericles' funeral speech implicitly continues the explicit critique of orators in the proem. Seen against the backdrop of the embedded commemorative medium, the virtues of Thucydides' work shine with particular brilliance. Instead of trying to endear himself to his audience, Thucydides claims to strive to capture the truth, unpleasant as it may be. The implied critique of an important democratic institution highlights the anti-democratic thrust that Thucydides shares with many other contemporaneous intellectuals.[9] Plato, one of the most fervent critics of democratic Athens, is equally critical of public oratory. In one of his dialogues, he even expresses his objections in a similar form. The *Menexenos* offers not so much a straightforward funeral speech as a pastiche that exposes the conventions of funeral speeches. Like Thucydides, Plato homes in on the self-aggrandizing view that is ridiculously removed from reality. Their ideological differences notwithstanding, both authors identify the orators' inclination to please their audiences as a key fault of democracy.

Cleon (and Thucydides) on *Agon* and Spectatorship

My second test case features a meta-historical comment that is more complex and shows that the *History of the Peloponnesian War* is infiltrated precisely by what Thucydides criticizes. In 428/7 BCE, Mytilene, the largest polis on Lesbos, defects from the Delian League but is then forced to capitulate by an Athenian army. Goaded by Cleon, the Athenian assembly decides to execute all male citizens of Mytilene. The next day, however, the Athenians regret this decision and call in another assembly. While Cleon

---

[9] Cf. Ober 1998 for a panorama of intellectual critics of the Athenian democracy.

fervently pleads for sticking with the decree, Diodotus, arguing that leniency will serve Athens better, carries the day. Much has been written on the Mytilenean Debate, which is 'as much about how to conduct debate in the ekklesia as about the fate of Mytilene'.[10] For my argument, I would like to concentrate on one aspect in Cleon's critique of the Athenian assembly:

> In such contests [*agōnōn*] as these, the state awards others the prizes yet bears the risks itself. You are the ones responsible; by mismanaging the games [*kakōs agōnothetountes*], you with your habit of approaching words as a spectacle [*theatai men logōn gignesthai*] and action as a recitation, of envisaging [*skopountes*] future activities on the basis of fine speeches about their feasibility and events that have already happened on the basis of splendid words of criticism, instead of using your powers of sight to give greater credibility to what has been done than what has been heard; perfect at being tricked by novelty in speech and at not wishing to make sense of what has been scrutinized, slaves to everything outlandish in turn and detractors of the ordinary; each one wishing above all for speaking ability of his own, but if that fails racing [*antagōnizomenoi*] everyone else to keep from appearing left behind in pursuing the argument, to be ready with instant approval when a point is made, and to be as keen in anticipating what is said as you are slow in foreseeing the consequences; seeking, I would say, something different from the life we lead without enough understanding of actual conditions; in short, overcome by the pleasure of listening, like men seated indulging in watching sophists [*sophistōn theatais eoikotes*] rather than to deliberate for their city. (3.38.3–7)

Thucydides' scorn for Cleon comes to the fore as he introduces him as 'in general the most violent of the citizens and by far the most persuasive among the people at that time' (3.36.6). Cleon's speech is marred by more than one *non sequitur* and by internal contradictions. For example, Cleon's claim that severe punishment of Mytilene will serve as a *paradeigma* for other allies (3.40.7) is undermined by his observation that the Mytileneans were undeterred by the fate of other allies punished for their defection (3.39.3). The passage quoted above brims with rhetorical figures such as antithesis, chiasmus, isocolon and hyperbaton. Cleon indulges in the kind of rhetorical display that he condemns as trickery that dazzles the Athenians. His very invective against flashy performances is itself a rhetorical firework. And yet, while Cleon's arguments undercut themselves, scholars have heard Thucydides' voice in his invective against public oratory and its reception. As Andrewes notes, '... Kleon's comment on Athenian delight in sophistry is prolonged well beyond its immediate tactical usefulness, and I cannot help

---

[10] Gomme, in Gomme et al. 1945–81: vol. II, 315. Cf. also the further discussion of Cleon's speech in Chapter 5 of this volume.

suspecting that Thucydides through these speeches was trying to say something that he himself thought important about the assembly and its leaders'.[11] By having the brutal demagogue Cleon voice his own critique of oratory, Thucydides gives his engagement with other media concerned with memory an additional twist.

The reverberations of Thucydides' own position are strongest in the polemics against the agonistic inclinations of the Athenians. Cleon's rejection of the *agon* as a suitable model for political deliberation evokes the presentation of the *History of the Peloponnesian War* as 'a possession for all time, not a competition piece [*agōnisma*] to be heard for the moment' (1.22.4), a claim that juxtaposes the written form of historiography with an oral presentation. More specifically, Thucydides seems to cast his work in the mould of an inscription in order to underscore its longevity. Thereby he slyly transforms and appropriates the epic notion of 'imperishable fame'. In the echoes of Thucydides' self-fashioning in Cleon's speech, the mention of sophists pinpoints epideictic speeches as the target of the critique, and yet it is worth considering broader resonances. The performances of tragedy were part of an actual *agon*. The reference to drama is supported by Cleon's emphasis on spectatorship. We should not forget that theatre and oratory were aligned with each other in classical Athens: the Theatre of Dionysus in Athens hosted speeches as well as plays, and while orators strived to render their pleas dramatic, tragedy was highly rhetorical. Cleon's invective singles out oratory, but, just like Thucydides' rejection of a 'competition piece heard for the moment', it is levelled generally against a culture of performance that embraces theatre as well as oratory.

As much as Thucydides offsets his own approach by contrasting it with other commemorative modes, the very criticism of the idea of an *agon* bears out the common ground he shares with poets and orators. Thucydides is entangled in a dynamic that is not unlike the self-contradiction of Cleon, who, though himself the biggest bully, decries the antagonistic tendencies of oratory while in the same breath discrediting his opponents as either irresponsible or bribed. Thucydides' proem, which is capped by the juxtaposition of his work with a 'competition piece heard for the moment', has the form of an *auxesis*. In addition to elaborating on the superiority of his work over other takes on the past, Thucydides goes out of his way to demonstrate that the Peloponnesian War surpassed all earlier wars. He thereby slyly elevates himself above Homer and Herodotus, who dealt with less important events. This reveals that Thucydides is far from immune to the lure of the

[11] Andrewes 1962: 75.

agonistic presentation that bedevilled democratic Athens. His rejection of epideictic competition-ship is itself part of an *epideixis* that proves that no war compares to Thucydides' war.

There is another point in Cleon's speech that also lets us grasp the infusion of Thucydides' work with what he criticizes. Cleon blames the assembly for mixing up words with deeds. They would believe what they hear rather than what they see. Drawing on the widespread idea that vision is the most reliable sense, Cleon puts his point pungently as a 'dissonance of senses': the Athenians 'approach words as spectacles', 'envisage future events on the basis of fine speeches' and 'indulge in watching sophists'. While closing their eyes to what is in front of them, they visualize and put much stock in mere words. Cleon's polemics chime in with Thucydides' agenda that neatly keeps words and deeds apart and is opposed to 'adorned' and 'embellished' presentations of the past. More generally, Thucydides is highly aware of the capacity of the visual to deceive. In the proem, for example, he points out that if later generations base their assessment of Sparta on the relics that are visible, they will err and significantly underestimate its power (1.10). Later in the run-up to the Sicilian Expedition, Thucydides narrates how an exhibition of treasures lures the Athenians to believe the claims of the Egestans of having sufficient funding for a war against Syracuse (6.46).

That being said, Thucydides couches the insights he promises in visual imagery. Cleon's reproach that the Athenians 'envisage [*skopountes*] future activities on the basis of fine speeches' strikingly echoes Thucydides' address to those 'who wish to envisage clearly [*to saphes skopein*] both past events and those that at some future time [*tōn mellontōn*], in accordance with human nature, will recur in similar or comparable ways'. The critique of words that make the audience 'envisage future activities' unmitigatedly applies to Thucydides' work as he presents it himself. That vision is more than a metaphor for intellectual activity comes to the fore in Plutarch's praise of Thucydides for his *enargeia* (*de glor. Ath.* 347a): 'Assuredly Thucydides is always striving for this vividness in his writing and it is his desire to make the reader a spectator, as it were ...'. Like the orators attacked by Cleon, Thucydides is a master of graphic narrative, which lets the reader see scenes with their inner eye.[12] The *History of the Peloponnesian War* contains quite a few vivid vignettes such as the fighting at Pylos and the Syracusan harbour scene singled out by Plutarch. Of course, Thucydides would rush to point out that he puts *enargeia* in service of an account that yields the truth, but don't we find similar assertions in the orators?

---

[12] On the vividness of Thucydides' narrative, see Grethlein 2013a: ch. 2; and on the rhetorical foundations of that vividness, see Greenwood (Chapter 5).

As the notions of *agon* and spectatorship illustrate, Thucydides' critique of other forms of memory is ambiguous. On the one hand, Thucydides virtuously uses the explicit and implicit juxtaposition of his work with other genres and media to throw into relief the novelty and superiority of his approach. On the other hand, the critique itself lets on about Thucydides' debt to poetry and oratory. He takes the orators to task for their epideictic *agones* but is himself heavily invested in making his own work outshine others. While criticizing the spectacles of oratory and arguably also drama, Thucydides himself knows how to write graphically. By no means do I deny the discrepancy between Thucydides and other forms of memory. The high methodological standards indeed set his report of the Peloponnesian War apart from other accounts. And yet, the *History of the Peloponnesian War* is imbued with the rhetorical culture from which Thucydides takes such pains to distance himself.

The Tyrannicide: The Price of Faulty Memory

The tyrannicide in 514 BCE loomed large in Athenian memory. The failed attempt of the Peisistratid Hipparchus to seduce the handsome Harmodius, the decision of Harmodius' lover Aristogeiton to take revenge and the assassination of Hipparchus by the couple lent itself to storytelling. The prominence of oral traditions on the tyrannicide can still be gleaned from drinking songs and comedies that refer to it. Take, for example, a scholion transmitted by Athenaeus that illustrates the use of the tyrannicide as a foundation myth for Athenian democracy (896P): 'Fame shall be yours forever throughout the earth,/Dearest Harmodius and Aristogeiton,/ Because you slew the tyrant/And made Athens a place of equality under the law.' The statues of the tyrant slayers, placed prominently on the Agora, as well as monumental and vase painting made sure they were not forgotten. Thucydides adduces the tyrannicide as an example of faulty memory in 1.20.2 and later expatiates on the topic when he narrates the Mysteries scandal and the mutilation of the Herms (6.54–9). In this digression, he showcases the detrimental consequences of faulty memory.

It is often assumed that Thucydides corrects the account of the tyrannicide in Hellanicus and other writers, but such a view once again unjustifiedly privileges historiographical records. In the introduction of his discussion, Thucydides announces that he will 'show that neither the others nor the Athenians themselves say anything accurate about their own tyrants and about what happened' (6.54.1). Authors such as Hellanicus may be implied, but in speaking of 'the Athenians' and their 'hearsay' and commenting on the impact that the faulty tradition of the tyrannicide had on the general political climate in Athens, Thucydides addresses not a specific version but the popular view based on oral tradition. He corrects this view in three respects. First, he points out that not Hipparchus but Hippias was the tyrant of Athens. Moreover, the assassination was less a political act than the culmination of a failed love affair. Finally, it was not the cruelty of the Peisistratid regime that triggered the tyrannicide, but inversely the assassination of his brother made the tyrant Hippias cruel. In Thucydides' description, the Peisistratid reign is reminiscent of the golden age under Pericles when 'what was in name a democracy became in actuality rule by the first man' (2.65.9). By criticizing the traditional view on the tyrannicide, Thucydides targets a popular story that was at the core of Athens' democratic identity. He reduces the heroic deed of two men sacrificing their lives for the fight against a hateful regime to a conspiracy that feeds on personal motives and drives a previously benign ruler into cruelty.

Thucydides elaborates on the tyrannicide not only to set the record straight, but also to show the far-reaching implications of untested assumptions about the past. The digression is embedded in the account of the witch-hunt triggered by the desacralization of the Mysteries and the mutilation of the Herms in 415 BCE. Alcibiades was the most prominent victim of this climate of fear, suspicion and denunciation. Accused of being involved in the scandals, he was called back from the fleet sent out to Sicily and then fled to Sparta, whom he then advised in their fight against his home town. At 6.15, Thucydides goes out of his way to emphasize the harm that the exile of Alcibiades brought Athens. The digression on the tyrannicide is framed by the comment that erroneous beliefs about the tyranny added fuel to the irrational fears and suspicions in 415 BCE. Stahl captures the entanglement of present turmoil and memory of the past:

> It is precisely this false myth which becomes in its turn – a hundred years after the fact! – a concrete political factor, in that it excites the people's fear of tyranny to such a degree that again the domestic peace of the city is destroyed and the very order of Athenian society is threatened ... Thucydides shows historical misconception as a direct cause of action which has jumped the rails of rational control.[13]

Paradoxically, the faulty knowledge of the tyrannicide leads to the very excesses that the Athenians strive to avoid. The persecution of suspects in 415 BCE parallels the measures taken by Hippias against potential conspirers after the assassination of his brother. While the Athenians believe

---

[13] Stahl 2003: 8.

that 'the tyranny of Peisistratus and his sons had become harsh [*chalepēn*] in its last stage' (6.53.3), they 'were at this time harsh [*chalepos*] and suspicious of those who stood accused over the Mysteries, and they had the impression that all had been done for an oligarchic and tyrannical conspiracy' (6.60.1). The verbal echo highlights the range of consequences that a careless engagement with the past can have: efforts to avoid tyranny effect tyrannical behaviour.

The juxtaposition of Thucydides' reconstruction and the oral traditions of the tyrannicide is reinforced by the vocabulary in which the Athenians' enquiry into the scandals of 415 BCE is couched (6.53.2):

> After the fleet sailed, the Athenians in fact had not slackened in their investigation [*zētesin*] of the acts committed regarding both the Mysteries and the herms, and instead of testing [*basanisai*] the informers they found [*heurein*] everything grounds for suspicion, arresting some very upright citizens because of their own trust in scoundrels and putting them in prison, since they felt it more essential to investigate the affair exhaustively and find out than to let anyone accused, however worthy he seemed, escape without proof [*anelegkton*] on account of the informer's vileness.

The passage echoes Thucydides' claim that his work is different from the accounts of poets and orators that are 'without proof' (*anexelegkta*, 1.21.1): 'Such, then, I found [*heuron*] to be ancient history, although it was difficult to trust every piece of evidence. For men accept one another's accounts of past events, even if they are about their own countries, with a uniform lack of examination [*abasanistōs*]' (1.20.1). The overzealous investigations of the Athenians in 415 BCE not only contrast with their sloppy memory of the tyrannicide, they also evoke the foil of the methodological standards on which the *History of the Peloponnesian War* is predicated.

The Usefulness of the *History of the Peloponnesian War*

The detriment caused by the faulty memory of the tyrannicide leads me to my final point. The meta-historical dimension as outlined in this chapter permits us to reconsider the usefulness to which Thucydides lays claim for his work (1.22.4):

> And the results, by avoiding patriotic storytelling, will perhaps seem the less enjoyable for listening. Yet if they are judged useful by any who wish to look at the plain truth about both past events and those that at some future time, in accordance with human nature, will recur in similar or comparable ways, that will suffice. It is a possession for all time, not a competition piece to be heard for the moment, that has been composed.

It is debated whether Thucydides wishes to provide his readers merely with a better understanding of past events or also with the ability to make conjectures about the future. There is also a controversy concerning the character of the insights to be gained: are they purely intellectual or do they have practical relevance?[14]

There is, I think, no reason for confining the usefulness of the *History of the Peloponnesian War* to the comprehension of past events. Thucydides explicitly mentions 'human nature' due to which future events will be 'similar or comparable' to past ones. History does not repeat itself, and yet the notion of an unchanging human nature provides the ground for illuminating comparisons. This is made explicit in the analysis of the Corcyrean stasis (3.82.2): 'And many hardships afflicted the cities during the civil wars, hardships which happen and will always happen as long as men have the same nature, sometimes more and sometimes less strong, varying in their forms as each change of fortune occurs.' In the eyes of Thucydides, the *History of the Peloponnesian War* offers material that facilitates the analysis of the present and meditation on future events. While not a handbook for politicians, Thucydides' work is fashioned as a history lesson with practical relevance.

However, the exemplary analysis of the Peloponnesian War and the penetration of human nature do not exhaust the usefulness that Thucydides ascribes to his work. His engagement with other forms of memory highlights a further point. As presented by Thucydides, the instability and confusion of 415 BCE were partly due to an insufficient grasp of the past. The painstaking analysis in the *History of the Peloponnesian War* yields a fuller understanding of the past and thereby could have reduced the political turmoil. The high methodological standards flaunted by Thucydides are thus endowed with political significance.[15] The orators' eagerness to cater to the tastes of their audiences, which Thucydides contrasts with his orientation towards facts, appears as one of the primary reasons for the downfall of Athens after the death of Pericles. The critical method that Thucydides showcases in his work is a lesson that may be even weightier than the insight into human nature and the analysis of specific events. It is of use for the statesman as well as the historian.

The occurrence of the central terms of Thucydides' methodology in key situations of the Peloponnesian War drives home the political relevance of his approach. Take, for example, the beginning of the Sicilian Expedition (6.8.2): 'The Athenians called an assembly and heard from the Egestans and

---

[14] For a bibliography, see Grethlein 2010b: 210.   [15] Cf. Kallet 2006.

their own envoys much that was attractive and untrue [*epagōga kai ouk alēthē*], in particular, as for the money, that a great amount was available in the temples and treasury. They then voted to send sixty ships to Sicily . . .'. Thucydides fully unmasks the Egestans' plunder only later when the Athenians discover how their envoys had been tricked into believing that the Egestans had great sources of wealth at their hands (6.46). Adopting the perspective of the Athenians, he makes the deceit tangible for his readers. 'Attractive and untrue' (*epagōga kai ouk alēthē*) harks back to Thucydides' meditation on his method. At 1.21.1, he sets himself off against *logographoi* whose accounts are 'more attractive for listening than with regard to truthfulness'. As the echo shows, Thucydides' critical accuracy is highly relevant to politics: applied to the promises of the Egestans, it might have spared the Athenians a big disaster.

Today, only few historians eagerly seek access to the offices of those in power; in general, the academic setting removes historical scholarship from political concerns. Most historians would not hesitate to call the critical method Thucydides' lasting legacy to their discipline. However, viewed in the context of Thucydides' efforts to establish his approach in the field of memory, his critical methodology looks different. What today appears to be the marker of academic scholarship untainted by practical considerations was an important part of Thucydides' claim to the usefulness of his work. Through the meta-history as explored in this chapter, Thucydides highlights his critical accuracy as key to responsible politics. It is not in the least the neglect of the methodological virtues showcased in the *History of the Peloponnesian War* that leads to the downfall of the Athenian Empire. Ironically, Thucydides' close entanglement of historiography with politics proliferated a method that proved crucial in the formation of history as an academic discipline.

Further Reading

On the role of Thucydides in the formation of modern historiography as an academic discipline, see Morley 2014 and Lianeri (Chapter 18). Grethlein 2010b, 2011 situates Thucydides in the contemporaneous field of memory. Moles 1999 has some sharp observations on the semantics of inscriptions as part of Thucydides' self-fashioning. Hornblower 2004 investigates the relationship between Thucydides and Pindar. Cornford 1907 is a seminal study of the impact of tragedy on Thucydides' historiography; Macleod 1983: ch. 13 ('Thucydides and Tragedy') is more cautious and emphasizes the Homeric model. His fine discussion of major speeches (Macleod 1983: chs 9–11) also provides a good starting point for Thucydides and oratory.

While Woodman's reading of Thucydides (1988: ch. 1) is premised on his controversial thesis that ancient historiography closely follows the rules of rhetoric, Yunis 1996 and Ober 1998 explore Thucydides' critical engagement with contemporaneous oratory and democracy. Kallet 2001: ch. 1 and Greenwood 2006: ch. 2 offer different angles on the role of vision in the *History of the Peloponnesian War.*

3

TOM BEASLEY

Thucydidean Self-Presentation

Introduction

Anyone wishing to write about Thucydides' self-presentation must confront a peculiar problem: perhaps the defining feature of his narrative presence is the lack thereof. Unlike his predecessor Herodotus, who frequently obtrudes on his own narrative to guide the audience through competing *logoi*, Thucydides only rarely becomes a tangible presence in the narrative of the Peloponnesian War. To take just one metric, Carolyn Dewald has counted 1,087 first persons in Herodotus' *Histories*;[1] in contrast, David Gribble's list of narrator interventions in Thucydides contains just sixteen such forms.[2] The first person is by no means the only measure of a narrator's presence, but in this case it does provide a vivid illustration of a truth to which most readers of Thucydides would surely assent: Thucydides does not make himself keenly felt, at least as narrator, in his text. And indeed, one does not need to read far in the scholarship on Thucydides to encounter some variation of the formulation that the *History* seems to 'tell itself'.[3]

The suppression of the narrator's presence hardly represents an idle, still less a natural, choice. It is, rather, fundamental to how Thucydides' narrative achieves the aura of authority it has possessed for most readers. Thus it has been observed that 'the most persuasive rhetorical device in Thucydides' armoury of narrative techniques is the direct expression of uncontested and enumerated fact'.[4] In other words, the narrative discourse of Thucydides' history – its 'narrator-less' style of narration – is in no small

---

[1] Dewald 1987: 150, n. 10.

[2] Gribble 1998: 47–9, 64–5. Note, however, that Gribble's list excludes the Archaeology and the second prologue (1.1–23; 5.26). For a fuller accounting of Thucydides' first-person forms, see Lang 2011: 129–38.

[3] Thucydides' claim that the war will show its greatness 'from the events themselves' (*ap' autōn tōn ergōn*) certainly encourages this reaction (1.21.2). The assimilation of history and historiography in Thucydides is insightfully explored in Loraux 1986b.

[4] Goldhill 2002: 42.

part responsible for imbuing it with its authority.[5] Readers trust Thucydides' narrative because it adheres to a cohesive and internally consistent view of the world and because they are willing to grant the honesty, rigour and intelligence of its author. In effect, something about Thucydides' self-construction persuades readers to assume his accuracy and veracity, even, or rather *especially*, when he minimizes his presence as narrator. Why?

This chapter is an attempt to answer this question. In the first section I approach the issue by examining various manifestations of Thucydides' presence in the Peloponnesian War narrative. I proceed in order of increasing explicitness, concluding with the Archaeology – the survey of the Greek past that opens Thucydides' work (1.2–19) – and the passages that bookend it (1.1; 1.20–2). In the second section I look more closely at the Archaeology and surrounding passages, since they represent the most explicit and sustained instances of Thucydidean self-fashioning. After briefly reviewing the Archaeology's reception, I conclude by offering a somewhat heterodox interpretation of its role in Thucydides' programme of self-presentation.

The Thucydidean Narrator, or: Why We Believe Thucydides

In Book 3 Thucydides depicts the fall of Plataea, a *polis* that, though allied to Athens, was destroyed by its long-time enemy, Thebes (acting in concert with Sparta), after Athens had declined to come to Plataea's aid. Thucydides describes the city's destruction:

> The number of Plataeans thus massacred was not less than two hundred, with twenty-five Athenians who had shared in the siege. The women were taken as slaves. The city the Thebans gave for about a year to some political emigrants from Megara, and to the surviving Plataeans of their own party to inhabit, and afterwards razed it to the ground from the very foundations, and built on to the precinct of Hera an inn two hundred feet square, with rooms all round above and below, making use for this purpose of the roofs and doors of the Plataeans: of the rest of the materials in the wall, the brass and the iron, they made couches which they dedicated to Hera, for whom they also built a stone temple of a hundred feet square. The land they confiscated and let out on a ten-years' lease to Theban occupiers. The adverse attitude of the Spartans in the whole Plataean affair was mainly adopted to please the Thebans, who were thought to be useful in the war at that moment raging.
>
> Such was the end of Plataea in the ninety-third year after it became the ally of Athens.[6] (3.68.2–4)

---

[5] So Connor 1985: 5: 'the narrative discourse of Thucydides itself establishes the authority of the writer and persuades us to listen with respect, if not total assent'.

[6] Translations by Richard Crawley, with modifications.

The passage certainly evokes the earlier quoted phrase, 'the direct expression of uncontested and enumerated fact'. Most remarkably, when the killing and enslavement of the Plataeans is recounted, it is with the same apparent dispassion and precision with which the building materials of an inn are listed. The absence of emotionally charged language or traditional pathetic detail (women weeping, old men clutching their groins) in this tragic scene does much to further the impression of objectivity. Moreover, in addition to the author's restraint, the sheer quantity of detail also inspires trust because it suggests meticulousness on Thucydides' part. One is perhaps encouraged to assume that he could adduce this level of detail for almost any event, if he so chose. Finally, note that Thucydides, as narrator, is nowhere to be found. No first-person pronouns or verbs appear in this passage, nor does any alternative version of the events. If Thucydides shapes the narrative (and he most certainly does), he seems to do so invisibly.

Yet a closer look will show that the narrator's presence is not quite so invisible after all. On the contrary, this passage is the product of numerous choices large and small, none self-evident or natural, all of which are calculated to produce certain responses in the reader. To take just one example: at 2.1 Thucydides announced his intention to narrate the events of the Peloponnesian War in chronological order by summers and winters. Here, however, he has departed from that scheme by manipulating the chronology. Strictly speaking, the building of the inn and temple to Hera belong not at this point in the narrative but to the following summer: 'the city the Thebans gave for about a year to some political emigrants from Megara ... and *afterwards* razed it to the ground' (emphasis added). In other words, Thucydides evidently felt the details of the inn and the temple significant enough to warrant deviating from his chronological plan. Why? Perhaps because the construction of an inn from materials that previously belonged to the (permanent) homes of the Plataeans heightens the pathos of the uprooting of their *oikoi* (households). This effect is what Simon Hornblower has called 'tragic *akribeia*' (precision or specificity), and though it is not nearly so overt a play on the reader's sympathies as what one finds in some later historiographers, it communicates the depth of the Plataeans' loss all the same, and *without obviously detracting from the aura of objectivity.*

In this way Thucydides makes his presence as narrator felt, if only subterraneanly, by shaping the narrative in ways that lead readers to certain conclusions, even while inclining them to believe that they have arrived at those conclusions unaided. These are the aspects of Thucydides' narrative technique – the subtlety and seeming invisibility with which he manipulates chronology, juxtaposes events and elucidates motivation[7] – that have been for some the proof of his objectivity and/or literary acumen, and for others evidence that he almost brainwashes his readers.[8] Such is what might be termed the objectivity-effect of Thucydides' narrative; reactions to it will, and have, varied. Yet it is unquestionably one of Thucydides' fundamental strategies not only for shaping the reader's response to his text, but also, paradoxically enough, for communicating his own self-construction. Thucydides' seeming absence from the narrative encourages the reader to regard both the work and its author as authoritative.

It is in this broader context of Thucydides' 'narrator-less' mode of narration that those fairly rare instances in which he foregrounds his presence must be considered. Let us therefore investigate these deviations and examine how they function when embedded within the 'objective' style of discourse that is Thucydides' mainline practice.

One very rare category of narrator intervention is the offering of alternative versions of events. For example, in discussing the Plataean execution of some Theban prisoners, Thucydides leaves unreconciled the opposing accounts of the Plataeans and Thebans (2.5.5–7). The Thebans claim that an oath was sworn to return the prisoners upon their withdrawal; the Plataeans deny it. Thucydides offers no judgement. What is the effect of this unanswered question? As with Herodotus, Thucydides' very refusal to decide the contentious issue demonstrates his objectivity. Unlike Herodotus, however, this technique is not a recurring feature of Thucydides' history. Nestled within a narrative that almost never pauses to problematize itself or its sources, the very infrequency with which Thucydides exercises this kind of caution serves as an implicit guarantee of the reliability of the rest of the work.

Another category of narrator intervention occasionally achieves the same effect: the marking of a superlative.[9] For example, in discussing the losses of the Ambraciots in their fight against the Amphilochians, Thucydides remarks:

> Indeed, this was by far the greatest disaster that befell any one Hellenic city in an equal number of days during this war; and I have not set down the number

---

[7] For more on Thucydidean narrative, see Munson (Chapter 7). See also Hornblower 1994; Rood 1998b.

[8] Hunter 1973: 4, writes of how Thucydides' narrative technique 'influence[s], even brainwash[es] the reader into thinking as he should think, i.e., as Thucydides would have him think'. See Wallace 1964 for a similar judgement. See also Stahl 2003 [1966] and de Romilly 2012 [1956] for classic expositions of the workings of Thucydidean narrative.

[9] Thucydides' fondness for superlatives is discussed in more detail by Grant 1974: 83–7; see also Macleod 1983: 140–1.

of dead, because the amount stated seems so out of proportion to the size of the city as to be incredible. (3.113.6)

Here the narrative ceases to (seem to) tell itself for a moment, as the narrator steps forward to observe from his synoptic perspective that the Ambraciots' losses turned out to be the greatest in the entire war (at least for the interval of time involved). But in stepping forward, the narrator also displays a pointed restraint in refusing to give an exact tally, lest he strain the readers' credulity. If your response is like mine, then you imagine a massacre that is probably larger than Thucydides' 'incredible' number, even as you find yourself more inclined to believe Thucydides' numbers elsewhere by virtue of his self-consciousness here. This is a neat trick, and one that implicitly distinguishes Thucydides from authors who would offer incredible numbers unselfconsciously.

Not all of Thucydides' superlatives have the effect of shoring up his credibility, though. More typically they pause the narrative to observe some peak or nadir, often of suffering and misfortune. For example, Thucydides speaks of the plague at Athens as the greatest and deadliest pestilence in memory (2.47.3); he remarks on the moment when Athens' naval strength was at its height (3.17); he observes that the massacre at Mycalessos was the worst in suddenness and brutality (7.29.5); and, perhaps most famously, he comments that the destruction of Athens' expedition to Sicily was the greatest feat not only in the Peloponnesian War, but also, in Thucydides' opinion, in Greek history (7.87.5). These superlatives do little to bolster Thucydides' authority in any obvious way; indeed, it is likely that his judgement of the Sicilian expedition was rather controversial. (One wonders whether his contemporaries would have readily assented to the idea that this undertaking was greater than the Trojan War.) They do, however, align quite well with Thucydides' explanation for why the Peloponnesian War is 'most worthy of recounting' (1.1.1): it was 'the greatest upheaval' (1.1.2) and 'went on for a very long time and there occurred during it disasters of a kind and number that no other similar period of time could match' (1.23.1). In other words, the occasional superlatives offered *in propria persona* bolster Thucydides' early claims about the size of the Peloponnesian War and the value of recording it. Some later readers have expressed discomfort with the way the objective and rigorously factual narrative of Thucydides coexists with these more subjective, even rhetorical-seeming arguments for the war's greatness,[10] but it is worth noting that Thucydides himself apparently felt no

---

[10] I am thinking especially of the so-called catalogue of *pathemata* (calamities) at 1.23.2–3, which, as Hornblower 1997–2010: *ad loc.*, notes, turn out to be 'rarely, sporadically, and very briefly recorded in his narrative'. Cf. Munson (Chapter 7), who notes the echo between this passage and the account of the plague in Book 2.

such incongruity, at least to judge from the general absence of qualification or apology.

Before turning to the more sustained passages of first-person inquiry, there is a final category of narrator intervention to discuss: Thucydides' characterizations of individuals and events. These include Thucydides' assertion about the real cause of the Peloponnesian War (1.23.6); his favourable evaluation of Pericles and unfavourable evaluation of his successors (1.139.4; 2.65); his judgement of Cleon as 'the most violent' man in Athens (3.36.6); his insistence that the Peloponnesian War truly was a single twenty-seven-year war rather than two separate wars broken up by a shaky peace (5.26); his commentary on Athens' reasons for invading Sicily (6.1); his characterizations of Alcibiades (6.15.2–4) and Antiphon (8.68.1–2); and his judgement about the superiority of the regime of the Five Thousand (8.97.2). At one time these judgements tended to be treated as 'individual outbursts of opinion', to be used essentially as interpretive anchors.[11] It has been increasingly recognized, however, that these narrator interventions are deeply implicated in their narrative contexts and 'were never intended to bear a wider interpretive burden'.[12] To extract a given intervention from its context and treat it as Thucydides' ultimate verdict on a given subject may therefore distort its meaning. For this reason I hesitate to generalize about these passages, except to note the following. Thucydides' commentary displays a general tendency towards praise of those people and constitutional arrangements that manage and even restrain the *dēmos* without violence, while at the same time criticizing demagogues and the fickleness and ignorance of the mob.[13]

I make this observation even at the risk of overgeneralizing because it seems to me that the historian's inclination to criticize the *dēmos*, along with its pieties and its champions, echoes key facets not only of his own self-presentation, but also of his strategies for fashioning it. Consider, for example, Thucydides' lengthy excursus on the victim of the Athenian tyrannicides Harmodius and Aristogeiton (6.54–69). Thucydides employs both inscriptional evidence and first-person argumentation in order to demonstrate that the mass of Athenians is wrong in believing that Hipparchus was tyrant when he was slain, when in fact his brother, Hippias, ruled the city. Thucydides goes on to claim that, in spite of the masses' belief that the tyranny was always harsh and oppressive, it in fact only became so *after* Hipparchus' death, in reaction to the killing. Now, why does Thucydides

[11] Gribble 1998: 41. [12] Connor 1977: 298.
[13] On Thucydides' presentation of democratic governance, see Balot (Chapter 13); and on the role of leaders, see Ferrario (Chapter 12).

halt the Peloponnesian War narrative to argue these points at length? An obvious political motive is suggested by the context in which the excursus appears; namely, the Athenian decision to recall and prosecute Alcibiades amidst the panic surrounding his alleged involvement in what the people imagined to be a tyrannical coup. Yet as much as Thucydides' implicit goal here may be to fault the masses for their hysteria, his explicit reason for including the digression is a bit different: he means to show that the Athenians have no more precise information than anyone else about their own past (6.54.1).[14]

This statement is not just a matter of political dissent[15] – though it is most certainly that – but also a sterling example of the primary technique Thucydides uses to craft his self-presentation. Thucydides defines himself in contradistinction to others; that is to say, he defines himself by identifying the qualities that make him different from and superior to his predecessors and contemporaries. To see this strategy in action, one need only look to 1.20, where Thucydides makes precisely the same argument about the Athenian tyrannicides but at much shorter length. Yet here, as before, he does so for the express purpose of proving that 'most people deal with traditions, even traditions of their own country, by receiving them all alike as they are delivered, without applying any critical test whatever' (1.20.1). The obvious implication is that Thucydides is not like 'most people' in this respect but rather applies the critical scrutiny that others neglect. Thucydides similarly distinguishes himself from Herodotus (1.20.3),[16] the poets and logographers (1.21.1) and also perhaps from his predecessor Hecataeus (1.22.2),[17] always on the grounds that his scrupulous pursuit of the truth sets him apart. No matter to whom Thucydides compares himself, he always insists on his own uniqueness and superiority.[18]

It is this quality of Thucydides' self-presentation that has, I think, invited so many to identify with him/it. When Thucydides writes of how little effort the masses take to excavate the truth and then promises that it will be

---

[14] On the historiographical and meta-historical significance of this passage, see Grethlein (Chapter 2).

[15] Ober 1998: 54–121.

[16] Where Thucydides' correction of the alleged misconception that Spartan kings have two votes each and about the existence of the 'Pitanite lochos' constitutes 'a clear reference' to Herodotus 6.57.5 (so Hornblower 1991–2010, *ad loc.*).

[17] Thucydides' promise not to compose the events of the war 'as they seemed/appeared to me' may echo and criticize Hecataeus' opening statement: 'I write these things as they seem to me to be true' (*BNJ* 1 F1).

[18] As Grethlein (Chapter 2) shows, Thucydides' criticisms are aimed not just at historical writers but also at other modes of commemorating the past (to which he also attempts to represent his work as superior).

enough if 'the few[19] who will wish to see the clear truth of what happened' (1.22.4) judge his work useful, what reader will conclude that they do *not* belong to this elect? In this way Thucydides' self-construction fairly invites the reader to participate in it, and by virtue of this participation to assent to it.[20] From this contract an authority is born. And perhaps no passage better embodies and explains this process than the review of Greek history that opens Thucydides' work, the Archaeology.[21]

The Archaeology, Rationality and *Logos*

One of the Archaeology's most influential interpreters has called it not only 'a rationalist manifesto in every sense of the word',[22] but also a text that 'introduces certain methods on which history today continues to rely'.[23] It is not difficult to see why the Archaeology might inspire such sentiments, given its rigorous and unsentimental handling of the Greek past and its excision of everything pious and legendary. In Thucydides' hands, the Athenians' patriotic myths are pointedly deconstructed, their autochthony now proof of the poverty of their soil rather than their connection to the land (1.2.5). In a similar way, figures like Minos and Agamemnon become strikingly contemporary, as the former is recognized as the architect of the first naval empire (1.4) and the latter is said to have bound his followers to him by power rather than through suitors' oaths (1.9). Traditional accounts are thus scrubbed of the mythological or legendary, as the past is shown to have been animated by the same factors that shaped the events of Thucydides' lifetime: wealth, fleets and imperial power. All of this looks so startlingly modern that it is no wonder that one of Thucydides' 19th-century admirers judged him 'not only the first but the only Greek historian who, avoiding both unquestioning belief in the sagas and unquestioning doubt, knew how to use the secure elements from them for historical ends'.[24] Even before Thucydides explicitly distinguishes himself from his predecessors and contemporaries,

[19] I have taken a liberty with the translation of *hosoi*, which is properly translated as 'as many as'. Given the context of the passage, in which Thucydides contrasts his own readership with those who would prefer the aural pleasure of 'the legendary' (*to muthodēs*), the quantitative relative seems to me to have the effect of limiting the size of Thucydides' expected audience.
[20] Thucydides' construction of his position as someone with privileged access to knowledge and his inclusion of the audience in that construction are explored in more detail by Irwin (Chapter 8).
[21] For further discussion of the Archaeology, with particular attention to its structural function, see Rusten (Chapter 6).
[22] de Romilly 2012 [1956]: 151.   [23] Ibid., 147
[24] Roscher 1842: 139, quoted in Morley 2012: 120.

the Archaeology has been making this argument implicitly by virtue of its thoroughgoing revisionism.

Yet the Archaeology's contribution to Thucydides' self-presentation is more than just implicit. This is because it does not just present the result of Thucydides' deconstruction of the heroic past but actually affords the reader the rare opportunity to witness him in the act of 'us[ing] the secure elements from [myths] for historical ends'. In the Archaeology Thucydides does not simply assert that, for example, the Greeks ventured no grand joint under-taking prior to the Trojan War. Rather, he *proves* it by citing the uninten-tional evidence furnished by Homer, who refers to the Greeks only by *polis*, presumably because he lacked a word for that which did not yet exist: the Hellenes as a whole (1.3.3). Similarly, Thucydides cites evidence for his argument that Carians colonized the islands; namely, the Carian graves discovered on Delos during its purification (1.8.1). Most famously of all, Thucydides openly reckons with the evidence of Mycenae, whose small size poses a special challenge of interpretation. Though one might be tempted to conclude that the city (and thus the expedition launched by its king) was insignificant, Thucydides argues that size alone is an imprecise measure of power. Here he offers a remarkably far-sighted analogy. He posits that someone judging Athens and Sparta's power from their future architectural remains would be likely to significantly overrate the former and underrate the latter (1.10).

What unites these and other passages in the Archaeology is the fact that they all find Thucydides explicitly adducing, evaluating, interpreting and offering conclusions on the basis of evidence. And while it would be mislead-ing to suggest that all or even most of the Archaeology features this degree of evidential self-consciousness, those portions that do have generally seemed so novel and incisive in their critical acumen that they have played an important role in shaping Thucydides' reception. Combine all of this with the Archaeology's remarkable density of first-person forms and other markers of authorial presence[25] and the view that the Archaeology repre-sents a rationalist manifesto by antiquity's most modern historian is not far to seek. Here more than anywhere else in his work, Thucydides seems to be emphatically and personally present, a virtuoso showing off a new and rigorous method of source criticism, all in the service of an iconoclastically clear-eyed view of the past.[26] Such, it has been thought, is the Archaeology's unique contribution to Thucydides' self-presentation.

[25] Lang 2011: 132–3.   [26] Connor 1984b: 28–9.

In what follows, however, I would like to problematize these conclusions a bit. There is one aspect of the Archaeology whose rationalism has, I think, been far more self-evident in the 19th, 20th and perhaps 21st centuries CE than it likely would have been in the 5th or 4th century BCE. I refer here to the Archaeology's techniques of source criticism.

There is a tendency to regard the Archaeology's handling of evidence as an announcement of Thucydides' new critical method and thus a key component of his programme of self-presentation. The Archaeology is taken to be proof of Thucydides' new-found rigour and devotion to truth, insofar as it opens a window onto the kind of evidential analysis that, we assume, must have gone on behind the scenes of the Peloponnesian War narrative, but which its narrator-less mode of narration keeps from view. I believe, however, that this formulation gets the significance of the Archaeology exactly backwards. Its source criticism is not a demonstration of Thucydides' proud new method, but rather an anti-programmatic demonstration of everything that Thucydides will *avoid* in his narrative of the Peloponnesian War. The Archaeology's method is vital to Thucydides' self-presentation, it is true, but only insofar as it defines his work *e contrariis*. It stands as an example of everything that his work *is not*.

This is not an intuitive conclusion. Given how impressive, even virtuosic, the Archaeology's reconstruction of the past is, it may seem perverse to argue that the methods on which it relies were anathema to Thucydides. For this reason, it will be helpful first to denaturalize the Archaeology a bit by examining the history of some of the terms that have attached to it, such as 'rationalizing' and 'scientific'. It will be seen that the application of these words to the Archaeology is by no means as natural or as self-evident as it may seem.

Consider: in the quotation that introduced this section, the Archaeology was said to have pioneered certain methods on which history still relies. And indeed, the author of that quotation, Jacqueline de Romilly, is even more explicit a few pages later: 'in a number of cases his innovations are the source of actual historical methods still in existence today'.[27] It should not detract from de Romilly's unfailingly sensitive analysis of the Archaeology to observe that she evaluates the passage against modern standards of historical research. Nor need one disagree with her favourable appraisal to note that when she describes the Archaeology's methods as being 'of a truly scientific quality',[28] Thucydides can have had no such quality in mind in the

---

[27] de Romilly 2012 [1956]: 149.

[28] Ibid., 151. On the same page at n. 9, de Romilly also suggests that Thucydides' argumentation in the Archaeology was 'laying the foundation of several other modern

5th century BCE. Both the standards of 'scientific history' and the view that Thucydides attained to them are of much later vintage.

Though the best-known exposition of these ideas in English is probably Charles Cochrane's *Thucydides and the Science of History* (1929), they originated in the previous century among the so-called Thucydidean Germans: historians such as Leopold von Ranke, Barthold Georg Niebuhr, Wilhelm Roscher and Eduard Meyer, who were united not only in their admiration for Thucydides, but also in their conviction that, even if he did not reach modern standards of historical criticism, he came as close as any of the ancients had or could.[29] Now, it is surely no coincidence that the first people to regard Thucydides as a (proto-)scientific historian were the very same as those who are credited with having laid the foundations of modern 'scientific' historiography. These historians, especially Niebuhr and von Ranke, sought to remove history from the domain of philosophy by grounding it in 'scientific' principles of research and source criticism.[30] Against this background it is understandable why they might find in Thucydides not only a kindred spirit, but also a forerunner of their own beliefs about how to do history. Just as they sought to reshape historiography as a modern scientific endeavour, so too did Thucydides seek to produce a work that was more rigorous, objective and truthful than what passed for history in his own time. In this way the self-conscious iconoclasm of Thucydides' self-presentation was well suited to the use that these historians would make of him; namely, as an authority for their own model of how to write history.

In short, the reception of Thucydides as a scientific historian *avant la lettre* speaks volumes about those doing the receiving. But how much does it illuminate Thucydides' own aims and motivations? Most today would agree that, however much Thucydides' self-presentation may have resonated with his 19th-century admirers, the standards of 'scientific' historiography were simply alien to the 5th and 4th centuries BCE. A. J. Woodman, for instance, has used the comparative evidence of modern war journalism to argue that

---

sciences, from political geography to sociology'. She does not push this too far, however, noting Thucydides' own awareness of his method's limitations: 'Although rational reflection on these relationships led him to pave the way for these sciences, he was not so imprudent as to apply his conclusions to the establishment of the facts.'

[29] On Thucydides' reception in 19th-century Germany, see (as well as Lianeri, Chapter 18) Murari Pires 2006b; Morley 2012; Süßmann 2012 and Meister 2015.

[30] In foregrounding their devotion to 'scientific' source criticism, this formulation oversimplifies these historians' views on history, particularly vis-à-vis its literary component and philosophical context. So, in the case of von Ranke: Iggers 1962: 17; Vierhaus 1990.

the objectivity-effect of the Peloponnesian War narrative is less likely to derive from its accuracy per se than from the fact that Thucydides has simply suppressed almost all evidence of the difficulties he confronted in assembling that narrative.[31] Thus Woodman suggests that '[Thucydides] has ... misled the majority of modern scholars, who have mistaken an essentially rhetorical procedure for "scientific" historiography at its most successful'.[32] For Woodman, to label Thucydides' work 'scientific' is to court anachronism because, however 'scientific' it may have appeared to modern eyes, ancient historiography was in many ways a rhetorical enterprise.

Significantly, Woodman's point extends to the Archaeology as well. Since the express purpose of the passage is to demonstrate the greatness of Thucydides' subject matter (1.1.2–3), this 'rationalist manifesto' must be acknowledged to exist in the service of an *auxesis*, an instance of standard rhetorical amplification.[33] But it does not stop here. The Archaeology's 'rhetorical' purpose cannot, in fact, be neatly separated from its 'scientific' methods because its very techniques of argumentation and source criticism have been shown to overlap with those found in the forensic oratory, tragic drama and medical writing of his era.[34] And these latter corpora (many of the medical texts included) are clearly more agonistic than 'scientific', more concerned with victory over one's opponent than with objective (still less empirical) ascertainment of truth. To give just one example of how argumentation that is seemingly scientific in one light can look rhetorical in another, consider that the same features of Thucydides that de Romilly has identified as logical and rational – the use of first-person forms, evidential discourse, arguments from probability[35] – are equally to be found in Herodotus, the Hippocratic corpus and forensic oratory. The same applies to many of the Archaeology's techniques of analysis and argumentation. Modus tollens, inference about invisible matters from visible signs and reasoning from analogy are all shared properties among Thucydides and other less scientific, more rhetorical authors.[36] So if the techniques of

[31] Woodman 1988: 23.　　[32] Ibid.　　[33] Ibid., 6–7.
[34] Forensic oratory: Plant 1999. Euripidean drama: Finley 1967: 1–54. Medicine: Rechenauer 1991. On intellectual affinities more generally, see Corcella 2006; Rogkotis 2006; Thomas 2006; Hornblower 2009.
[35] de Romilly 2012 [1956]: 145–6.
[36] Thomas 2000 offers a systematic examination of these features in Herodotus and the Hippocratic corpus, as well as in forensic oratory and among the Presocratics. Throughout she observes the resemblances between them and Thucydides (e.g., at 168–70, 191–2, 199, 210–11 and 219–22). Tellingly, she observes of Thucydides that he 'refers to his own historical methods in [evidential] terms, [but] he actually tends to do so in an austere manner, and leaves to the speeches the more flamboyant claims; this suggests that he thought such claims appropriate to speeches'. See also Lloyd 1979; Lateiner 1986.

analysis, the modes of argumentation and the overall purpose of the Archaeology grow from the same soil as what one finds in Herodotus, Antiphon or *On Ancient Medicine*, what, finally, makes the Archaeology different from, more 'scientific' or less 'rhetorical' than these?

The current *communis opinio* seems to be that, while Thucydides was undoubtedly influenced by his predecessors and contemporaries and employed methods comparable to theirs, he did so more successfully or with a greater, even unique, devotion to truth and accuracy. Thus it has been said that '[b]y the end of the Archaeology we recognize that it is in fact an *epideixis*, a rhetorical display piece, *and not a conventional one, but an exhibition of a new technique of analysis* and a fully appropriate proemium to the rest of the work, emphasizing in good rhetorical fashion the greatness of its subject matter'.[37] Notice that in spite of the many similarities between the Archaeology's methods and those found in court speeches, the Hippocratic corpus and among the Sophists, the Archaeology nonetheless exhibits 'a new technique of analysis'. And in spite of the fact that the Archaeology is acknowledged to be a rhetorical display piece, it is then qualified as 'not a conventional one'. The Archaeology thus manages the remarkable feat of appearing very much in line with the intellectual techniques and trends of its era while also eclipsing them. It manages to share characteristics with texts typically labelled 'rhetorical' while transcending that label. By some alchemy Thucydides has transmuted the base rhetorical material found in other texts into something more rational, more logical, more 'scientific' in the Archaeology.

There is an obvious dilemma here. An anti-programmatic dimension to the Archaeology offers a way out. Suppose that the habits of expression and the techniques of analysis that Thucydides shares with these other authors are not something that he must be made to transcend. Suppose instead that the overlap is very much the point. If the Archaeology is meant to be self-consciously anti-programmatic – an object lesson in the kind of work that Thucydides' narrative of the Peloponnesian War will not be – then there is

---

On the relationship between speeches and Thucydides' self-presentation, see further later in this chapter.

[37] Connor 1984b: 29 (emphasis added). More recently Gregory Crane 1996; 32, has made a similar point: 'the professional rhetorician used an *epideixis*, "show-piece", to demonstrate his methodology. Thucydides' Archaeology serves precisely this function, at the same time introducing Greek history as a whole and Thucydides' historiographic methodology.' Rood 2006: 233–4, quotes Connor, but adds the important qualification (n. 19) that 'in one sense the historical method Thucydides uses in the Archaeology is precisely not the method he uses in his narrative of the (contemporaneous) Peloponnesian War'.

no need to justify Thucydides' use of evidential discourse. By embodying precisely what Thucydides will avoid when narrating the *erga* (events) of the Peloponnesian War, the Archaeology's rejected method implicitly distinguishes the historian from all the (inferior) predecessors and contemporaries who employed it.

To better understand how an anti-programmatic Archaeology contributes to Thucydides' self-presentation, it will be helpful to review the terms in which Thucydides characterizes his history. In the first place, he states that it is 'not as much a *competition piece* for immediate *performance*', but rather a 'possession for all time' (1.22.4, emphasis added). Similarly, he cautions that *the absence of legendary material* may make his work less pleasurable for *performance*, but for those who wish to *see* the clear truth of what happened, it will be sufficient if his work is judged useful (1.22.4). Finally, Thucydides contrasts his work to that of the poets, who falsely enlarged events in their *singing*, and also to that of the logographers, who assembled their accounts more with an eye to *performance* than the truth, as a result of which their tales *won out* into the realm of *the legendary* (1.21.1). Reviewing these characterizations, a clear pattern emerges. Those against whom Thucydides defines himself create works that are aural, ephemeral and agonistic. Thucydides' work, in contrast, is (constructed as) visual, eternal and non-agonistic. Where others sing or assemble pleasing fictions in order to obtain victory in performance, Thucydides has written a work of laborious accuracy with an eye towards its eternal utility rather than transitory success.

Perhaps no image better symbolizes these qualities than the one implicit in Thucydides' famous claim to have crafted a 'possession for all time'. This phrase, in combination with the language that surrounds it, evokes the idea of a monumental inscription.[38] In so doing, it effectively constructs Thucydides' work as a monument not only of the Peloponnesian War, but also of his own written achievement. Like a monument, his work is immortal, not ephemeral. Like a monument, it commemorates a victory achieved, rather than serving as an attempt to secure one. And like a monument, it is more a visual and tangible thing than an aural one. In short, Thucydides' monumental metaphor succinctly captures the qualities that set his work apart from the transitory competition pieces of poets and logographers: it is visual/tangible, long-lasting and non-agonistic.

If one were to reframe this programme using the categories commonly employed by Thucydides himself, one might say that where others produce

[38] Immerwahr 1960; Moles 1999; Bakker 2006.

44

logos (speech – sometimes rational or intellectual speech, but above all speech), Thucydides' work is *ergon* (work or deed).[39] Of course, Thucydides' text is also by definition *logos*, since it is a linguistic production. But Thucydides nonetheless presents it as a *logos*-which-is-not-*logos*, as a monumental *ergon*, in order to convey its categorical difference from and superiority to the temporary, inaccurate and agonistic speech of poets and logographers.

It is here, in the gap between ephemeral, aural *logos* and eternal, physical *ergon*, that the Archaeology's anti-programmatic purpose begins to come into focus. Consider: in spite of the totalizing force of Thucydides' inscriptional metaphor, not all of his work would seem to attain equally to the status of *ergon*. Here I am thinking above all of the speeches (*logoi*), which, in the famous chapter on methodology (1.22), are referred to exclusively with words connoting speech (in contrast to the *written* events (*erga*) of the war)[40] and are also composed to a lower standard of accuracy than the war's events.[41] If the speeches are implicitly excluded (or at least distanced) from the charmed circle of *ergon*, then perhaps there are other portions of the work that likewise bear too close a resemblance to *logos* to be fully embraced by Thucydides' programmatic metaphor. The most obvious candidates are those passages that do not recount the *erga* of the Peloponnesian War (i.e. the several longer excursus and perhaps certain geological and

---

[39] Parry 1981. On *logos* as a broad, pre-disciplinary word that embraces all manner of intellectual endeavour in the late 5th and early 4th centuries BCE, see Schiappa 1999: 66–82.

[40] This observation is less tautological than it may seem. In the first place, it is striking that Thucydides differentiates the speeches from the events in categorical terms: 'as many things as were said in speech [*logōi eipon*] . . . the events of the things that were done [*ta d' erga tōn prachthentōn*]'. The categorical distinction between *logos* and *ergon* is key here; otherwise *logōi* and *ta erga* are simply redundant. Furthermore, the verbs Thucydides employs for the composition of the speeches and events are markedly different both semantically and grammatically. The speeches 'have been spoken' (*eirētai*), while the events are what Thucydides personally 'deemed worthy to write' (*ēxiōsa graphein*). Though one might argue that the passive form *eirētai* is meant to bolster Thucydides' claim to fidelity (i.e. Thucydides did not use the first person because he did not personally compose the speeches), I rather suspect that it is a function of the general derogation of *logos* in these chapters. Because *ergon* has an exalted status, Thucydides takes personal responsibility for narrating the *erga* of the war while distancing himself from the *logoi* in his text.

[41] The bibliography on the two sentences detailing Thucydides' procedure for composing the speeches is voluminous; for a full discussion of the problem and references to further studies, see Greenwood (Chapter 5). Here I will limit myself to observing that the promise to compose the speeches 'just as each [of the speakers] were seeming to me to speak what was necessary concerning the matters at hand' is matched by the opposite promise for the events of the war. In the latter instance, Thucydides affirms that he did not think it proper to write the *erga* of the war 'just as they were seeming/appearing to me'.

scientific digressions as well). But there is one passage that not only belongs quite definitely to the realm of *logos*, but also defines the distance between *logos* and *ergon* in Thucydides. That passage is the Archaeology, and it serves as a paradigmatic example of the kind of *logos* that Thucydides' *ergon* will *not* be.[42]

Why should the Archaeology belong to the category of *logos* rather than *ergon*? Because of all that it shares with other texts that were acknowledged to be *logos* in Thucydides' time. The techniques of analysis, the style of argumentation, the emphatic, sometimes agonistic first-person voice – all of these features find parallels in the *logoi* of orators like Antiphon, doctors like the Hippocratics, playwrights like Euripides and historians like Herodotus.[43] Most of these texts either depict, constitute or participate in contests of words, where victory is won through successful presentation of evidence and forceful first-person argument.[44] The Archaeology finds Thucydides doing likewise. In the Archaeology he not only reconstructs the past but also *argues* for that reconstruction (i.e. presents evidence in the first person), assimilating the Archaeology to that category (*logos*) from which he elsewhere distinguishes his work. It is not a coincidence that the evidential discourse of the Archaeology is never employed for the events, or *erga*, of the Peloponnesian War, though it does appear in speeches and antiquarian digressions.[45] Because evidential discourse had connotations of *logos*, Thucydides only used it in the most *logos*-like portions of his work: the speeches (*logoi*) of historical actors and excursus into the past.[46] He eschewed it entirely for the Peloponnesian War narrative, however, in order

---

[42] Cf. the analysis of Greenwood (Chapter 5), who makes the case for seeing the whole of Thucydides' work as, in some respect, *logos* rather than *ergon*.

[43] See n. 36.

[44] Thomas 2000: 219: 'Yet in the intellectual world of the fifth century, especially, the latter half, outright polemic and explicit criticism and explosion of your opponent's opinions was raised to levels of vitality that makes Thucydides' own restraint seem, rather, to be the element that needs explaining.'

[45] A search of the *Thesaurus Linguae Graecae* (TLG) database shows that, with the exception of 2.50.2, every evidential use of *tekmērion* and *sēmeion* occurs within either a speech or an excursus. I would argue that Thucydides' use of *tekmērion* at 2.50.2, where he offers the refusal of animals to eat human corpses as proof of the exceptional nature of the plague at Athens, is more a medical proof than one intended to support the narrative of the *erga* of the war.

[46] Thomas 2000, 227–8: 'the conclusion seems inescapable that such expressions had strong overtones of rhetorical persuasion, overtones that Thucydides wanted to avoid: part of the language of proof and demonstration in a world which included early scientific (medical) enquiry, Herodotus, epideictic oratory and therefore presumably earlier oratory in general. Given its prominence in oratory, it either had, or rapidly took on, somewhat flashy tones, those of the performance, the epideictic display.'

to avoid tainting the *erga* of the war (and the *ergon* that was the mainline of his work) with the suggestion of *logos*.[47]

So the Archaeology is Thucydides' anti-programmatic demonstration of *logos*. Yet the question remains: why open the work anti-programmatically? Why begin with a demonstration of what it will not be?

In the first place, anti-programmatic statements ease the path to a programme of positive self-definition. It is easier to identify what one *is* by first pointing to what one *is not*. In this sense the Archaeology served as a useful point of departure for Thucydides' figurative programme, since it provided the reader with a tangible example of the kind of aural, ephemeral, agonistic *logos* that Thucydides' *ergon* will reject. In other words, it allowed him to fashion his self-presentation *e contrariis*.

Such a strategy may have been especially imperative for Thucydides due to his decision to suppress most traces of his role as narrator of the Peloponnesian War. At least in comparison to Herodotus, Thucydides' 'narrator-less' style of narration looks innovative (in degree if not in kind), and as such it presumably required situating, contextualizing and justifying. The Archaeology served precisely this function: by couching radical ideas in a familiar style of discourse, it permitted a 5th- or 4th-century BCE audience to dip its toes into Thucydidean waters before taking the real plunge into the 'narrator-less' mode of the Peloponnesian War narrative. And since the Archaeology's style of discourse and techniques of analysis were not only at the cutting edge of intellectual inquiry but also forms of common currency in Thucydides' era, shared across 'disciplines' and characteristic of a broader intellectual culture of competitive debate, the Archaeology offered an additional benefit: it demonstrated Thucydides' mastery of the very techniques of *logos* that he would soon reject, making that rejection all the more authoritative. The message, in effect, is that Thucydides can employ *logos* as effectively as any logographer, but for the Peloponnesian War he has something different and better in mind: *ergon*.

---

[47] It has been remarked to me that Thucydides does, in fact, present evidence in the course of the Peloponnesian War narrative (and indeed this view of Thucydides' use of evidence is presented more fully in Rhodes' Chapter 4), especially in the quoted treaties in Book 5 and 8, which, in the case of the former book, seems meant to support Thucydides' assertion that the Peace of Nicias was a peace in name only. I would argue, however, that Thucydides' avoidance of terms like *tekmērion* and *sēmeion* here proves (admittedly *ex silentio*) that evidential discourse was in some sense tainted for him, at least vis-à-vis the Peloponnesian War narrative, because it carried a whiff of the courtroom, or the assembly, or perhaps competitive display more generally. To offer the treaties as *tekmēria* would violate his programmatic claim to have crafted an *ergon* rather than mere *logos*.

It will be noted that terms like 'rationalizing', 'scientific' and 'rhetorical' were largely absent from the preceding discussion, jettisoned in favour of the categories employed by Thucydides himself: *logos* and *ergon*. The latter categories make it possible to resolve the question of whether the Archaeology's techniques of analysis are rhetorical, rationalizing or somewhere in-between. Once those techniques are recognized as characteristic of *logos*, the dilemma melts away, and at the same time Thucydides' decision to eschew them for the mainline of his work becomes explicable. No matter how impressive Thucydides' handling of evidence may seem today, the terms, techniques and mode of discourse associated with it were redolent of the contests of words that occurred in the assembly, in the courts, on the stage and in debates between intellectuals in the late 5th and early 4th centuries BCE. And as we have seen, Thucydides' work was meant to be something very different: uncontested and uncontesting *ergon*.

There is, perhaps, an irony here. It is not difficult to see why the Archaeology would look rather different to 19th-, 20th- and 21st-century eyes, for which evidence has more positivistic associations, evoking the laboratory, the archive, the excavation, etc. These changed contexts and connotations made Thucydides an authority for those who saw in him a (proto-)scientific historian in their own mould and so claimed (their interpretation of) his self-presentation for their own. Yet Thucydides' own programme of self-presentation took quite the opposite path. He proclaimed his accuracy by repudiating an evidential discourse that evoked for him not devotion to truth but competitive intellectual display. And though I suspect that Thucydides would have been pleased by the general thrust of the Archaeology's reception – above all the idea of its exceptional rigour and intellectual power – I cannot help but think that he would also have been surprised by the route by which those conclusions were reached.

Further Reading

On objectivity and authority in ancient historiography generally, see Marincola 1997. Rood 2006 provides an excellent discussion of Thucydides' historical method and its relationship to his programme of self-presentation. Crane 1996, Bakker 2006 and Edmunds 2009 offer important insights into a vital element of Thucydides' self-construction: his representation of his work as something written. Moles 1993 and Greenwood 2006 are important treatments of the idea of truth in Thucydides. We have seen that the Archaeology is a vital locus of self-presentation in Thucydides. Hunter 1982 and Dewald 2009 both offer insightful comparative readings of Thucydides' and Herodotus' initial narratives. On the culture of competitive intellectual display against which Thucydides defined himself, see above all Thomas 2000. On Thucydides' use of evidence generally, see Hornblower 1987: 73–109; on his use of evidence in the Archaeology specifically, see Reynolds 2009.

4

P. J. RHODES

Thucydides' Use of Evidence and Sources

For Thucydides' use of evidence and sources a fundamental distinction must be made between the history of 435–411(–404) BCE and the earlier history treated in parts of Book 1 and occasionally mentioned elsewhere.[1]

The period from 435 BCE Thucydides lived through as an adult; he says that he started work at the beginning of the war (1.1.1) and that his exile gave him access to people on the anti-Athenian as well as the Athenian side (5.26.5). R. S. Stroud has argued that the amount of detail he offers on Corinth suggests that he spent part of his exile there.[2] His starting point will have been his own direct knowledge, from personal observation and involvement: he suffered from the plague and saw others suffering (2.48.3); in 424/3 BCE he was a general sent to the Thraceward region, and he went to Thasos and returned from there in time to keep Eïon but not Amphipolis out of Spartan hands (4.104.4–106), but he tells us only later that he was exiled on account of that episode. Close to that direct knowledge will be what he learnt from others at the time in conversation and from more formal reports. There will not have been any previous narrative on which he could draw: his job was to shape what he knew and to add to what he knew by discovering further information.

Some further information will have been available in documents: notoriously, documents are directly quoted in Books 4, 5 and 8 (i.e. both in the

---

[1] Cf. Luschnat 1974: 767. Finley 1942: 104–7, in a discussion based on 1.22, concluded that '[i]n the narrative then, if not in the speeches, Thucydides has maintained an ideal of absolute and rigidly tested truth', and he admired the multitude of details that Thucydides managed to discover. Gomme in his introduction gave one paragraph on Thucydides' silence on his sources and the fact that we can rarely check what he tells us (Gomme et al. 1945–81: vol. I, 28–9). Hornblower 1987 has a chapter on 'Use of Evidence' (73–109), which ranges widely, makes several points that are made here, notes the absence of arguments from personal names and etymology and from coinage and discusses the use of technical and non-technical language.

[2] Stroud 1994.

apparently more finished narrative of the last part of the Archidamian War in Books 4 and 5 and in the apparently less finished narratives of the period after the Peace of Nicias and the beginning of the Ionian War in Books 5 and 8). There seems to be a documentary basis for similar material presented elsewhere without direct quotation, such as the treaties paraphrased in 3.114.3 and 4.16.1–2; and we may wonder how far such passages as Pericles' review of Athenian resources in 2.13 depend on Thucydides' memory and/or notes of what Pericles said and how far Thucydides checked the figures in documents. Behind Thucydides' narrative lay a great many public decisions and transfers of money in Athens and elsewhere that are likely to have generated documents: some inscribed on stone or metal, some displayed for a short time on whitewashed boards, many others never published but placed on papyrus in an archive, in which cases we are left to wonder how long they were preserved and how easily an inquirer who wanted to find them could do so.

But, even if we suppose that all the documents that Thucydides wanted to consult were preserved and that his searches for them were always successful, much of the information that he wanted will never have been recorded in a document. For instance, it will have been documented that in 433 BCE the Athenians decided to make a defensive alliance with Corcyra, and it may have been documented that the decision was spread over two days (1.44). But no document will have stated that the balance of opinion changed from the first day to the second, or why the Athenians finally decided as they did. It will have been recorded, though Thucydides does not tell us, who proposed that final decision; though it will not have been recorded what Pericles' position was, unless he was himself the proposer of that final decision. There will have been a record of how many ships were sent, what money was expended and who were the commanders – and indeed an inscription survives that records payment from the treasury of Athena and names the commanders (1.45; cf. OR 148 = *IG* I³ 364.1–12). There may, piecemeal, have been records outside Athens of how many ships from which states formed the Corinthian navy and who were their commanders, though here we may think it highly likely that Thucydides' information did not come from those records (1.46.1–2). There will certainly have been no documents recording the course of events when the navies engaged in battle (1.46.3–50). Athens' decision to send a further squadron will have been documented, again with financial details and the names of the commanders, and again there is a document that survives, which this time on the identity of the commanders disagrees with the transmitted text of Thucydides (1.51; cf. OR 148 = *IG* I³ 364.13–24). Hornblower drew attention to this revelation that there must have been another debate in the Athenian assembly, which

Thucydides reveals only in passing:[3] the narrative was not necessarily organized so as to play down this debate and the resulting decision to commit a larger force to Corcyra, but the fact serves as a reminder that Thucydides did not mechanically compile a chronicle but carefully shaped his narrative. Again, what happened when and after this second Athenian squadron arrived at Corcyra will not have been documented (1.52–5).

Much of Thucydides' material, then, cannot have come from documents, and I think it would be a mistake to suppose that documents were so fundamental to his work that every detail that could have come to him from a document, such as the numbers of ships and the commanders in the two expeditions sent to Corcyra, did come to him from a document.[4] For episodes at which he was not present he will have relied as far as he could on men who were present. For explanations of decisions and events, in addition to his own judgement he will have had access to the opinions of others, including men who were present on the occasions in question, whether they were involved in such a way as to make their explanations authoritative or not, and these opinions could have reached him both through private conversations and through public speeches.[5]

There are some matters for which particular informants have been suggested (cf. earlier in this chapter for Corinth). It has sometimes been thought that Thucydides' knowledge of Spartan activity in the north-east between 424 and 421 BCE was obtained from Brasidas after Thucydides had gone into exile, and Hornblower agrees;[6] but H. D. Westlake noted that the detailed information continues to and beyond Brasidas' death and suggested instead Clearidas, who joined Brasidas in late summer 423 BCE (4.132.3).[7] P. A. Brunt argued that Alcibiades is likely to have been Thucydides' informant on some incidents and possibly on all the affairs in which he was involved (and even on the overthrow of the Pisistratids). That some of Thucydides' information came from him is plausible; there are nevertheless passages in which Thucydides is critical of Alcibiades (such as 6.16.3, 8.48.4, 81), but an attempt by E. Delebecque to distinguish between material from Alcibiades and material from elsewhere was too mechanical.[8] Recently R. J. Lane Fox suggested that when Thucydides quotes documents (cf. earlier in this chapter) this is due not to a change of method but to his good fortune

[3] Hornblower 1991–2008: vol. I, on 50.5.
[4] 'The major ancient Greek historians used oral interviews and personal testimony wherever they could': Lane Fox 2010: 26.
[5] Hornblower 1987: 78–80, suggests that attributed motives are sometimes based on good information but sometimes simply guessed.
[6] Hornblower 1987: 79; cf. earlier, e.g., Grundy 1911: 36–7.
[7] Westlake 1980 (= 1989): 78–83.   [8] Brunt 1952 (= 1993): 17–46; Delebecque 1965.

in obtaining from some Spartans, in particular Lichas, documents of which they had copies (and that documents are not mentioned in his prologue because the documents, like his other material, reached him as a result of his inquiries addressed to individuals): he claims that 'Thucydides never went near a documentary store or deposit'.[9] That is an intriguing possibility, but if Thucydides did become conscious of the value of documents there is no reason why he should not actively have searched for them.

Thucydides' chapter on method, in his prologue, begins with the speeches in his history (1.22.1). These are discussed separately by Emily Greenwood in the next chapter, so here I will simply indicate briefly what I have expressed elsewhere.[10] Thucydides has certainly rewritten speeches in his own manner, and he allows a speech delivered in one context to respond to a speech delivered in another context to a greater extent than can have happened in fact; but his claim to a degree of authenticity is to be taken seriously, and the arguments used are those that he knew had been used or genuinely believed might have been used. The extent to which he allows his speakers to disagree with one another, on matters of fact as well as opinion, makes it clear that none should be seen as mouthpieces for Thucydides himself.

He then proceeds to deeds (§2) and contrasts the element in the speeches of what he judged appropriate (*hōs d' an edokoun emoi ... ta deonta malist' eipein*) with the reliance for the deeds not on chance informants or his own judgement (*hōs emoi edokei*) but on investigating each matter with as much precision as possible (*hoson dunaton akribeiai*); and he adds that this was difficult because differing witnesses gave different accounts (§3; cf. 7.44, 71). Since he was human and had attitudes and beliefs that may have affected his evaluation of evidence, we cannot expect him to have succeeded in establishing the truth on every point, but we should not doubt that he tried hard and intelligently to do that. But his readers are expected to trust him. Normally he reports simply what he believes to be the truth without indicating the basis for his belief or the points at which there were alternative versions that he has rejected. Exceptionally, on the Theban attack on Plataea in 431 BCE he reports Theban and Plataean accounts of one matter without deciding between them (2.5.5–6). But on the death of Themistocles he states what he believes (a natural death) and then notes that some alleged suicide (1.138.4); on the question of whether in 423 BCE Scione defected to Brasidas before or after the truce between Athens and Sparta was agreed he reports the disagreement but states firmly that the defection was after the truce (4.122); and

---

[9] Lane Fox 2010, quoting p. 25.
[10] See my introductions to Rhodes 1988, 1994, 1998, 2014, and to Hammond 2009.

in 411 BCE, when Tissaphernes went to Aspendus but failed to bring Phoenician ships to the Aegean, he first confesses to difficulty over understanding the reason for this but by the end of the chapter he has decided on the reason (8.87). We have a surprising instance in the account of Cylon's attempt to become tyrant of Athens in the 630s or 620s BCE: Delphi had encouraged him to make his attempt at the greatest festival of Zeus, and he tried at the time of the Olympic festival but was unsuccessful; Thucydides, not normally disposed to believe in oracles, wonders if the oracle had meant Athens' festival of Zeus, the Diasia (1.126.4–6).

It was hard to discover how many men fought in the Spartan army at the battle of Mantinea in 418 BCE because of 'the secrecy of the state', but from the structure of the Spartan army he makes a calculation (5.68.2–3), as he calculated from the *Iliad*'s Catalogue of Ships how many men were in the Greek force that attacked Troy (1.10.3–5). In connection with the campaign of Mantinea he admits to uncertainty about the motivation: in the manoeuvres before the actual battle, when Agis led the Spartan army towards the enemy one man shouted out that he was aiming to cure one error with another, and Agis withdrew, 'whether because of the shout or because he had some sudden thought whether different or on the same lines' (5.65.2–3). It is not certain whether the account that was finally accepted of Athens' religious scandals in 415 BCE was correct or not, but the fact that the case was closed was of great benefit to Athens (6.60.2–5). It was even harder to find out what happened in the night-time battle at Syracuse in 413 BCE than to find out what happened in the daytime battles (7.44.1–2).

For the period before 435 BCE Thucydides did not have the same direct and almost-direct knowledge as a starting point; and except in his account of the *Pentecontaetia*, included not as a general account but as a justification of his 'truest reason' for the Peloponnesian War (1.89–118: note the introductory sentence, 89.1, and the opening and closing of a ring in 88, 118.2), he did not provide a narrative but focused on particular points.

The account of Athens during the *Pentecontaetia* in Hellanicus' *Atthis* is the only earlier account that Thucydides mentions explicitly (1.97.2). There are grounds for thinking that what he says of Greek colonization in Sicily (6.2–5; cf. 3.88.2–3) is derived from Antiochus of Syracuse.[11] Herodotus' history was certainly known to Thucydides: 1.20.2 criticizes him on two points, though without naming him, and Hornblower has argued that Thucydides constantly presupposes knowledge of Herodotus in his readers and that in his speeches he regularly relies on Herodotus for allusions to the

[11] See Dover in Gomme et al. 1945–81: vol. IV, 198–205; Hornblower 1991–2008: vol. III, 267, 272–4.

past.[12] On some controversial points Thucydides rejects or accepts a version without making it clear who championed that version: 'the majority of the Athenians'[13] mistakenly think that Hipparchus was Pisistratus' eldest son and was reigning tyrant when he was killed in 514 BCE (1.20.2, 6.54.1 – but here Herodotus agreed with Thucydides); and 'those of the Peloponnesians who have received the clearest account' (rather than 'those who have received the clearest account of Peloponnesian affairs') support the story about Pelops and his descendants that Thucydides tells (1.9.2).

Here as for events from 435 BCE onwards Thucydides is likely to have started from what he thought he knew about the past, and when he needed confirmation or further information he investigated as best he could. To confirm the correctness of his account he cites various considerations in support, and in the Archaeology in the opening chapters of Book 1 he makes frequent use of such terms as *tekmērion* ('indication'; e.g. 1.1.1), *paradeigma* ('instance'; e.g. 2.6), *dēloun* ('demonstrate'; e.g. 5.2), *sēmeion* ('sign'; e.g. 6.2), *marturion* ('witness'; e.g. 8.1) – Hornblower notes that these terms are treated as equivalent, not being distinguished as they were by the later rhetoricians[14] – and also *eikos* ('reasonable likelihood'; e.g. 4.1).

As bases for his arguments we find the common name of the Greeks (1.3), current practice in primitive areas as a pointer to earlier practice in more advanced areas (1.5–6), the manner of burials on Delos as an indication that the people buried there were Carians (1.8.1) and physical remains of cities, which are said to be unreliable as a guide to their power and importance in the past (1.10.1–3). In reporting the evacuation of Attica at the beginning of the Peloponnesian War, Thucydides remarks that this was traumatic because for a long time most of the Athenians had lived in the countryside (2.14). He then digresses on the early history of Athens and the unification attributed to Theseus, and (this time without using any such word as *sēmeion*) he cites the festival of the Synoecia that celebrated that unification. He goes on to say that the original city comprised the acropolis and the area to the south, citing as a *tekmērion* that that is where the oldest sanctuaries were founded (2.15). A rare use of such language in connection with the events of his own time comes in his account of the plague. The disease demonstrated (*dēloun*) that it was different from the customary illnesses: a *tekmērion* is that there was a

---

[12] Hornblower 1991–2008: vol. II, 122–45.
[13] And perhaps Hellanicus: Hornblower 1991–2008: vol. I, 57.
[14] Hornblower 1987: 100–6. For an alternative (and more heterodox) interpretation of the significance of Thucydides' use of the language of proof in the Archaeology, see Beasley (Chapter 3).

total absence of the birds that prey on dead bodies, whereas dogs stayed with their owners and themselves died (2.50).

Poetry is used in what Thucydides considers to be a rational way. The Trojan War was greater than its predecessors but inferior to those of Thucydides' time, 'if again it is right to have some belief in the poetry of Homer here', with allowance for the likelihood that as a poet he would exaggerate (1.10.3; cf. 21.1; other citations 3.2, 5.2, 9.4); and then Thucydides proceeds to take the two crew sizes mentioned in the *Iliad*'s Catalogue of Ships as maximum and minimum and to calculate the number of Greeks who went to Troy (1.10.4–5). 'Homer' is quoted again – this time in fact the *Homeric Hymn to Apollo* – as evidence for the great festival of Apollo held on Delos in the past (3.104.3–6). Hesiod is not similarly used, though there is a passing reference to the place where he was believed to have died (3.96.1). Thucydides remarks polemically that there was no connection between Teres the king of Thrace and Tereus who in the legendary past married the Athenian Procne, daughter of Pandion: the names are different, and it is not likely that Pandion would marry his daughter to a man so far away as Thrace (2.29.3). The connection that Thucydides rejects had perhaps been made in a tragedy, and he observes that poets referred to the nightingale as the Daulian bird (a usage that now survives only in Latin poetry).[15]

Inscriptions are cited when they help Thucydides to make a point: the original and the later text on the Serpent Column (1.132.2–3); dedications of the younger Pisistratus as evidence of his archonship (6.54.6–7: one survives as ML 11 = *IG* I³ 948, but in spite of Thucydides' comment its lettering is not faint); and 'the *stele* about the wrongdoing of the tyrants' on the Athenian acropolis to confirm that Hippias was Pisistratus' eldest son (6.55.1–2). Rather different is the epitaph of Archedice of Lampsacus (6.59.3), which seems to be cited for the remarkable claim that it makes rather than to support a point. And before citing the inscriptions to support what he believes about the tyranny he claims that he can give his version more accurately (than others) *akoēi*, 'from oral sources' (6.55.1).

Different kinds of source lie behind letters allegedly exchanged between Pausanias and Xerxes (1.128.6–9.3), one written by Pausanias to Artabazus but opened by the messenger, who found that it contained instructions that he himself should be killed (1.132.5), and one sent by Themistocles to Artaxerxes (1.137.3–4). Themistocles did become a dependant of Artaxerxes, and it is plausible that he should have sent a letter but less

---

[15] Gomme, in Gomme et al. 1945–81: vol. II, 90 with n. 1, suspecting that Hellanicus had adopted it.

plausible that an authentic text of it should have reached Thucydides. Pausanias' letter to Xerxes looks like an attempt to trump a rumour in Herodotus 5.32, and probably there was in any case not enough time for Pausanias to send a letter and receive a reply during his first spell in Byzantium, to which Thucydides attributes the exchange. The letter opened by the messenger is part of an exciting story in which it is hard to draw the line between original fact and later elaboration. In his whole story of Pausanias (1.94–5, 128–35.1) Thucydides seems certain of his guilt on charges that were never proved, and the likelihood is that he accepted too uncritically stories that were vouched for by high-ranking men in Sparta when Pausanias was dead and could not counter them.

From the standpoint of modern historians, where the facts that Thucydides reports are not directly attested he seeks confirmation in the right kinds of way, even if there are points where we judge that his reasoning has led him astray. If the early inhabitants of Delos were not Carian, that is because the burial practice that he identifies as Carian was not peculiar to the Carians but was followed also by Greeks in the past. He realizes that epic poetry needs to be used with caution as evidence, but he accepts as a Greek of the classical period was bound to do that the legends of early Greece are true in their main outline (though as a 5th-century BCE Athenian he will have seen in tragedy that they could be presented with varying details and emphases[16]), and in his calculation from the Catalogue of Ships he is relying on details that we should say ought not to be relied upon. His kind of rationality insists, however, that Agamemnon commanded the Greeks against Troy because he was the most powerful ruler more than because the suitors of Helen were bound by the oaths of Tyndareus (1.9.1; similarly in 480 BCE the Spartans as the most powerful of the Greeks took the lead against the invading Persians, 18.2), and that the formulaic description of Agamemnon as ruling 'many islands and all Argos' shows that he must have had a navy (9.4).

Thucydides believed that interpreting prose-writers as well as poets needs caution, since they are concerned more with attractiveness than with truth (1.21.1). Nevertheless, he includes some chronological details that probably come from one or more prose texts: the Boeotians arrived in Boeotia in the sixtieth year after the capture of Troy, and the Dorians occupied the Peloponnese in the eightieth year after that capture (1.12.3); and Ameinocles of Corinth built ships for the Samians 300 years before the end of 'this' war, and Corinth fought a naval battle with Corcyra 260 years

---

[16] Hdt. 2.113–20 believed that Helen was kept in Egypt and not taken to Troy, but he still believed that she had been abducted from Sparta.

before (13.3–4). The Greeks were fond of the kind of succession in which *A* was supreme for *x* years, then *B* for *y* years, and so on; and there are signs in 1.8.2, 13–14, of the succession of thalassocrats, foremost naval powers, of which there is a developed version in Diodorus Siculus 7.11.[17]

Today's Thucydides is far removed from the totally dispassionate Thucydides of a century ago. I remarked earlier in this chapter that his own attitudes will inevitably have affected his evaluation of the evidence on which he relied, and it is worth noting some ways in which that may have happened.

Although he did not believe that gods intervene to change the course of human affairs, he did believe in *tuchē* (chance), occurrences that cannot be foreseen and therefore cannot be allowed for in one's planning (cf. the remark attributed to Pericles on the plague, 2.61.3). In the episode at Pylos in 425 BCE (4.3–23, 26–41) the Athenians gained a spectacular success thanks to the policy brought to completion by Cleon, but Thucydides disapproved of Cleon (cf. 3.36.6, 4.21.3), thought sensible men judged him more likely to die in the attempt than to succeed (4.28.4) and probably disapproved of the venture as un-Periclean. Chance plays a very large part in this story as Thucydides tells it; and, while Cleon could not have known that Nicias would push him into a position in which he had to take command (4.27–8), there is reason to think that there was more good planning by Demosthenes and Cleon and less pure chance than Thucydides seems to have believed, and that his disapproval of the man and of the achievement has conditioned his presentation of the story.[18]

The sophists of the late 5th century BCE were fond of such contrasts as that between *phusis* (nature, which cannot be other than it is) and *nomos* (in the sense of convention, what some human beings have decided one way but others in another context might have decided another way).[19] Another contrast that we encounter frequently in Thucydides is that between *logos* (word, what people say) and *ergon* (deed, what is really the case);[20] and Thucydides was clearly proud of his ability to penetrate the words and expose the realities. For a man who thinks on those lines it is easy to suppose that the words are always false and there is always a reality that belies the words; but that may on occasion be too cynical a view. For instance, in writing about the disintegration of the regime of the Four Hundred in Athens in 411 BCE (for which, as an exile, Thucydides was dependent on

[17] See especially Forrest 1969: 95–106, esp. 95–6.   [18] See especially Marshall 1984.
[19] See Woodruff (Chapter 14).
[20] For further discussion of the *logos* versus *ergon* distinction, see Beasley (Chapter 3) and Greenwood (Chapter 5).

informants), he says that the opposition was led by such men as Theramenes and Aristocrates, deeply implicated in the oligarchy, who claimed (*hōs ephasan*, 'so they said') that they were afraid of the Athenians at Samos and Alcibiades and of the harm that might result from the Four Hundred's approach to Sparta, and for that reason called for the genuine involvement of the Five Thousand and a more equal (*isaitera*) regime. However, this was a political smokescreen (*schēma politikon*, Hornblower's translation), and most of them were inclined to this kind of position through individual ambition (8.89.2–3). Andrewes was troubled by the contrast between this and Thucydides' approval of the resulting intermediate regime; Hornblower thinks that for Thucydides 'a good constitution could be the work of bad and hypocritical men'.[21] But in any case I suspect that Thucydides has been led astray by his form of contrast, and that Theramenes and Aristocrates, while they may indeed have been affected by individual ambition, may also have been sincere in their worries about the Athenians at Samos and the negotiations with Sparta and in their desire for a more equal regime.

Thucydides' attitude to religion may have distorted his judgement too. Almost always he seems not to be a believer in gods or in oracles, portents and the like.[22] Gomme was himself uninterested in religion and said little about it; Hornblower saw that as one of the weaknesses in Gomme's commentary and in his own sought to redress the balance.[23] There do seem to be places where Thucydides' attitude to religion has led to an unbalanced treatment of the material available to him. One by now notorious instance is the account of the escape of the men from Plataea in 428/7 BCE (3.22.2): he says that the men had their right foot bare to get a better grip on the mud, but of course from that point of view having both feet bare should have been better still, and this 'monosandalism' had a religious significance, of which Thucydides must have been aware though he fails to mention it.[24]

For a religious organization that should have been relevant to Thucydides' political interests, Hornblower focuses on the Delphic amphictyony. In reporting the Sacred War of the 440s BCE Thucydides refers to the Delphians and Phocians but not to the amphictyony (1.112.5). Sparta's colony of 426 BCE at Heraclea in Trachis, just west of Thermopylae, Thucydides explains in political terms with reference to the neighbouring

---

[21] Andrewes, in Gomme et al. 1945–81: vol. V. 298–300; Hornblower 1991–2008: vol. III, 1010–11.

[22] Cf. Fragoulaki (Chapter 11); but notice his treatment of the oracle upon which Cylon relied when trying to become tyrant of Athens (see 54).

[23] Cf. Hornblower (1991–2008): vol. II, 10–13; Hornblower 1992: 25–53.

[24] See P. Lévêque and P. Vidal-Naquet; and L. Edmunds, cited by Hornblower (1991–2008): vol. I, 406–7.

peoples. Delphi is mentioned only for being consulted about the colony's foundation (as frequently happened), but after 346 BCE Heraclea had one of the two Malian votes in the amphictyony (e.g. *C. Delphes* ii 36 = RO 67. i. 9, ii. 23), and Hornblower suggests that this applied from its foundation and was an additional motive for the foundation; he notes also other possible religious aspects of the foundation about which Thucydides is silent.[25] In the following winter Athens 'purified' Delos: that religious event is one that Thucydides treats at some length (3.104), and he subsequently notes a sequel (5.1, 32.1). The only explanation given by Thucydides is that this was done in response to an oracle; Diodorus (12.58.6) sees it as a reaction to the plague; and among several suggestions by Hornblower are responses to the alignment of Delphi and Olympia with the enemy and to Sparta's foundation of Heraclea (and he wonders whether Thucydides himself was involved in the purification).[26]

Athens' religious scandals of 415 BCE are introduced with a factual statement that could equally well have been made by a believer or by a non-believer (6.27.1). As Thucydides proceeds with the account, he mentions previous damage to images by drunken young men (28.1), and he pays more attention to a possible political dimension (27.3, 28.2, 60.1, 61.1–3) than to the religious dimension, though he does use the verb *asebein* in conjunction with the men recalled from Sicily (53.1).

These are of course examples from one area of the general truth, namely that a historian who aspires to be more than a mechanical chronicler must – and Thucydides undoubtedly did – decide which of the things that he might record are important and which are not, and which of the possible explanations of a course of action are to be taken seriously and which are not. It does appear that Thucydides' attitude to religion frequently led him to attach less importance to religious events and explanations than others might think they deserved.

Political attitudes also could lead to distortion. Thucydides belonged to a prominent Athenian family; until his exile in 424/3 BCE he presumably lived in Athens, and he was himself involved in public affairs at any rate to the extent of being elected general for that year. He will have known how Athenian politics worked in terms both of formal constitutional rules and of informal political practice within the framework of those rules, not from reading or from asking others but from the inside. What we know of how Athenian politics worked, from reading the texts of various kinds that are

---

[25] Hornblower 1991–2008: vol. I, 502; Ibid., 1992: 189–90); cf. Flacelière 1937: 40 n. 2.
[26] Hornblower 1991–2008: vol. I, 517–25; Ibid., 1992: 190–6.

available to us, indicates that, although Pericles might have been exceptionally influential, neither he nor anybody else could control policy to the extent of ensuring that the assembly always voted as he wanted, and that Pericles had to compete against rival politicians just as the politicians of other generations did.[27] If Thucydides had not been influenced by his admiration for Pericles and his view that to work successfully the democracy needed to be firmly controlled by a wise leader, his knowledge of Athens ought not to have allowed him to write that the Athenians 'elected Pericles general again and entrusted all their affairs to him' (shortly after deposing him, a fact that Thucydides does not mention, though he does state that they fined him), and that his leadership amounted to 'democracy in word but in deed rule by the first man', whereas his successors competed in trying to gratify the *dēmos* (2.65.3–10).

For the conduct of the war Thucydides attributes to Pericles a policy of relying on Athens' superior financial resources (1.141.3, 142.1, 143.1, 2.13.2-6) and avoiding defeat and unnecessary risks (1.144.2, 2.13.2, 65.7), and he gives perfunctory accounts of the large-scale naval activity of the first two years of the war (2.17.4, 23.2, 25, 30, 32, 56, 58). However, the evidence available to us shows that in the early years of the war the Athenians were spending their money at an unsustainable rate and addressed that problem only after Pericles' death (OR 160 = *IG* I^3 369), and this evidence suggests that Pericles may in fact have hoped that demonstrations of invincibility would quickly lead the Spartans to acknowledge that their war against Athens could not succeed.[28] What Thucydides attributes to Pericles may have been true of his public pronouncements, but if his vision had not been clouded he ought to have seen that what he has told us was not the whole truth.

The subsequent Greek historian who seems to have come closest to Thucydides in his approach to the task was Polybius in the 2nd century BCE. In the course of his criticism of Timaeus, he wrote, '[e]vents happen in many places at once, and it is not possible for the same man to be in several places at the same time .... What remains is that one should enquire from as many people as possible, believe those who are worthy of belief, and not be a bad judge of reports which come in' (Polyb. 12.4c.4–5). Timaeus lived in Athens and thought mistakenly that access to the memoirs of earlier generations gave him a good basis for writing history (25d.1). Assiduity in the study of memoirs is only one of the three parts of history, and it ranks third

---

[27] Cf. Rhodes 2000: 465–77.   [28] Cf. Ibid., 1988: 210–11.

behind seeing the places and experiencing politics and warfare (25i.2). Reading books is less valuable than interrogating witnesses (27.3–4).

In that spirit Thucydides will have added to his pre-existing knowledge by questioning people and evaluating what they told him. Evidence of other kinds – from inscriptions and documents, from poetry, from earlier histories – could be used where it helped to support what he wanted to say, but it was supplementary, not fundamental. He was thorough (on those terms) and intelligent in his search for the truth, but he was not inhuman, and there are places where to us he seems to have misjudged the material available to him.

Further Reading

On Thucydides and his sources in general, see especially Hornblower 1987: 73–109; also Finley 1942: 104–7; Gomme, in Gomme et al. 1945–81: vol. I, 28–9; Luschnat 1974: 760–4.

On Thucydides and Corinth, see Stroud 1994. On Thucydides and Brasidas, see Grundy 1911: 36–7; Westlake 1980 (= 1989): 78–83; Hornblower 1987: 79. On Thucydides and Alcibiades, see Brunt 1952 (= 1993): 17–46; Delebecque 1965, the latter of whom distinguishes too mechanically between material from Alcibiades and material from elsewhere. For a suggestion about Thucydides and documents, see Lane Fox 2010.

5

EMILY GREENWOOD

Rhetorical History

Speeches in Thucydides

The term 'rhetorical history' was traditionally used to describe a model of history writing in ancient Greece and Rome in which formal, stylized speeches were an integral part of the historian's account and their explanation for why certain decisions were taken.[1] In the wake of postmodern historiography the term 'rhetorical history' has rather different connotations, signalling the inalienable narrativity of every historical account, from the formal fictions that inhere in all writing, to the question of history's emplotment.[2] The study of Thucydides' speeches has been profoundly influenced by this shift.

Concurrently, the classification of what counts as a speech in Thucydides has grown more and more diffuse. In his study of Attic oratory from Gorgias to Lysias, published in 1868, Friedrich Blass listed forty-one speeches in Thucydides, only counting speeches in direct discourse.[3] Writing in 1972, William West counted fifty-two speeches in direct discourse, eighty-five in indirect discourse, three mixed speeches that combine direct and indirect discourse and the Melian Dialogue.[4] According to this inventory, there are a total of 141 speech presentations in the *History*. Recent research has placed greater emphasis on the neglected category of speeches in indirect discourse and has suggested expanding this category further to include 'reports of thoughts, perceptions, feelings, and motives – often presented as if they were utterances'.[5]

---

[1] See Fornara 1983: 142: 'It would be almost impossible to overstate the importance of formal speeches in Greco-Roman historiography, for they present us with the reactions, intentions, and expectations of the movers of events and provide a clarification of the issues driving powers at war or citizens in internal disputes.'

[2] See White 1973, 1987, 1999.   [3] Blass 1868.   [4] West 1973.

[5] Debnar 2013: 271. Debnar draws analogies between indirect discourse and 'indirect thought' – Thucydides' account of what a given character was thinking. At pp. 277–8 she analyses the depiction of Cleon in the assembly debate over Pylos and points to the intertwining of indirect discourse and indirect thought at 4.27.3–4, suggesting that the

Ancient rhetorical and literary criticism recognized that the incorporation of speeches in historical accounts involved questions of selectivity and distribution, from the question of who gets to speak to the choice of words allocated to them. In his critical essays on Thucydides, written in the 1st century BCE, Dionysius of Halicarnassus finds fault with the speeches that Thucydides writes and the speeches that he did not write. A good example is Dionysius' objection to Pericles' funeral oration in the second book of the *History* (2.35–46), which was already renowned in Dionysius' day (he describes it as *periboētos*, 'acclaimed').[6] In Dionysius' opinion, of all the funeral orations delivered in Athens in the course of this war the context for this oration was the least remarkable:

> The Athenian dead in this case are those who fell in the first Peloponnesian invasion; but they were quite few in number, and these few had done nothing distinguished, as Thucydides himself admits. ... Why ever, then, does the historian lay open the public tombs for a few cavalrymen who earned no glory and no power for the city ... Leaving aside all the other land- and sea-battles in which many men died who deserved funeral tributes much more than the ten or fifteen cavalrymen of the Attic militia, what of those Athenians and their allies who died in Sicily with Nicias and Demosthenes in the sea-battles, the land engagements and finally in the lamentable retreat?

In addition to criticizing the criteria for inclusion and omission in the speeches, Dionysius also disputes the plausibility of some of the words that Thucydides puts into the mouths of speakers, pointing to the words of the Athenian representatives in the Melian Dialogue as a particularly egregious example of malign invention. In chapter 41 of *On Thucydides*, Dionysius considers whether '[Thucydides] has composed the dialogue in such a way that it is consistent with the facts and fits the character of the delegates to the meeting', quoting Thucydides' own formula at 1.22.1 that he had composed all speech in the *History* 'adhering as closely as possible to the general sense of what was actually said'. Dionysius finds it completely implausible that the Athenians would ever have voiced the arguments that they express in the Dialogue: 'in the Melian dialogue the wisest of the Greeks adduce the most disgraceful arguments, and invest them with the most disagreeable language.

---

latter often resembles 'internalized speech'. See also Scardino 2012 on indirect speech. Laird 1999 was influential in putting pressure on the received distinction between direct speech and indirect speech in Greek and Roman historiography. See ibid., 148: 'in historiography, the words of personages in direct discourse present no more and less of a dilemma than words presented in indirect discourse'.

[6] Dionysius of Halicarnassus *On Thucydides*, 18 (in Usher 1974). All quotations and citations of this chapter are taken from Usher's edition.

Perhaps it was because the historian bore his city a grudge for the sentence passed on him that he has deluged her with these reproaches, which were calculated to make her universally hated ...'

Dionysius is primarily interested in the speeches as rhetorical compositions, as models for emulation or criticism; in keeping with the self-consciously didactic tone of this treatise, he is keen to set out his aesthetic principles and to rule on which Thucydidean speeches and which parts of which speeches are suitable models for imitation.[7] What is more, for Dionysius the realm of aesthetic criticism encompasses an aesthetics of history – his preferred, edited version of the past.[8] But Dionysius is just one of Thucydides' readers in antiquity, and his polemics hint at a broad spectrum of views on the qualities of Thucydidean speeches; for instance, in chapter 37 of *On Thucydides* he mentions the popularity of the Melian Dialogue among admirers of Thucydides' style.

Notwithstanding the particular context in which Dionysius of Halicarnassus wrote his critique of Thucydides and his particular aesthetic programme, he poses cogent questions about the rationale behind the speeches. Why, indeed, did Thucydides write a funeral oration for Pericles at the end of the first year of the war and not for any other – far more significant – campaigns? Thucydides does not gloss over the fact that there were other public funerals in the war. In the preamble to Pericles' funeral oration he remarks that '[t]hese are their rites of burial, and they observed this practice throughout the whole war, whenever they had occasion' (2.34.7). Another curiosity is that we do not find this funeral oration to be lionized by Pericles' or Thucydides' immediate contemporaries.[9] When Aristotle discusses Pericles' funeral oration in the *Rhetoric*, he cites another funeral oration – the oration that Pericles delivered after the Athenian campaign against Samos.[10] Dionysius' answer as to why Thucydides places this speech here is because he wanted to exploit Pericles' character (*prosōpon*) and, given that Pericles would die in 429 BCE, this was a suitable juncture at which to have him give a speech in praise of Athens before her fortunes began to turn in the war.[11]

In a similar vein, modern critics have explained the place and role of the funeral oration in the narrative as a way of ironically framing its idealized,

---

[7] *On Thucydides*, 42: 'These are the speeches of Thucydides which should be emulated [*zēlōta erga*], and it is from these that I suggest writers of history should select their models for imitation [*mimēmata*].'

[8] See Wiater 2011: 135 and ch. 3 in general.

[9] Pericles' funeral oration in Thucydides is satirized in Plato's *Menexenus*; see Greenwood 2018: 74–5 with bibliography.

[10] Aristotle *Rhetoric* 1365a 29–32 (see also ibid., 1411a1–4).   [11] *On Thucydides*, 18.

exemplary version of Athens within a broader setting that highlights the fragility and contingency of many of its ideals. As one of the architects of the war who will not live to see its end, Pericles is a powerful mouthpiece. But the more substantial difference between Dionysius' critique and the way in which scholars tend to read this speech now is that we consider the presentation of any given speech to be indivisible from the rhetoric for the work as a whole. In addition to the narrative placement of speeches and their role within the structure or *taxis* of the work, modern studies of the speeches have been preoccupied by what James Morrison has called 'speech–narrative interaction' – the way in which the dialogue between speeches and narrative creates structures of meaning, whether through cross-references or through the creation of a 'polyphonic, dialogic narrative' in which his authorial voice co-opts the voices of others in order to stage a critical dialogue about the interpretation of the past.[12]

Dionysius' passing reference to Thucydides exploiting the character or mask (*prosōpon*) of Pericles is pertinent. One of the many functions that the direct speeches play in the *History* is a dramatic one, since the mimesis of live speech adds vividness and immediacy, putting the audience/readers in the same arena as the historical actors. Hence the most dramatic section of the *History* is the Melian Dialogue, in which the speakers alternate with each other in quick succession, with no authorial mediation – the author has become playwright.[13] However, as we will see later in this chapter, the mimetic quality of the speech in direct discourse is only one dimension of the rhetoric of Thucydides' *History*, since they are contained within a work that is, in a larger sense, itself a very long *logos*, on an analogy with deliberative oratory, addressed to an open-ended audience of imagined readers.[14] In this sense, the direct speeches in Thucydides are akin to the words of characters in Greek tragedy who perform actions and articulate words that carry additional layers of meaning for the playwright and his audience.[15] At the same time, in their presentation of the thought, psychology, hopes and expectations of historical characters via speeches,

---

[12] Morrison 2006a. Stahl 2009, first published as Stahl 1973, also analyses the relationship and interaction between speech and narrative. 'Polyphonic, dialogic narrative' is a quotation from Dewald 2005: 21. Tsakmakis 2017: 271, also picks up on this theme, suggesting that the speeches 'broaden the reader's perspective' and are part of a 'dialectic process'.

[13] In chapter 38 of *On Thucydides*, Dionysius describes this as a switch from narration (*diēgēma*) to dramatic dialogue (*dialogon dramatikon*).

[14] Compare Connor 1985: 6: 'Reader and author stand in a different relationship. They are not colleagues, but performer and audience.'

[15] See Vernant and Vidal-Naquet 1990: 114.

Thucydides' narrative places readers in their midst. In this larger *logos* the individual speeches contribute to the 'experiential' and 'participatory' aspect of the *History*.[16]

Speech as Action/in Action

To better understand the role that the speeches play in Thucydides' *History*, it is helpful to distinguish between speeches as a narrative device and speeches as a historical phenomenon. Live speeches, in which politicians and rulers confronted their audiences, were the medium of politics all across the Greek world. Colin Macleod phrased it elegantly: '[w]hy does oratory deserve a place in the work of a good historian like Thucydides? In part because that place corresponds to its place in history.'[17] Although many speakers in Thucydides construct an opposition between words/speech and deeds/action (see, e.g., Pericles at 2.35), speeches manifestly do get things done and have a decisive impact on action. As Andrew Laird has noted, 'most of the speeches in Thucydides' *History of the Peloponnesian War* are also *speech acts*: encouragements, commands, promises, threats'.[18] At the mundane level, the presence of speeches in Thucydides' *History* reflects the fact that deliberation and debate through the contemplation and judgement of competing speeches preceded any significant action in the war. Examples include whether or not to declare war, whether or not to enter into alliance, whether or not to invade a particular territory, the swearing of treaties, appeals for clemency and logistical decisions about how to prosecute a particular campaign. In short, not only are speeches the medium of diplomacy, but in the world in which Thucydides wrote, and for which he wrote, there was no war without speeches and no end to war without speeches.

One of the best examples of the efficacy of speech as action comes from a successful campaign in northern Greece by the Spartan general Brasidas in 424 BCE. Brasidas is campaigning in Thrace with the express aim of persuading Athens' Thraceward subject-allies to switch sides to the Spartans, thus destabilizing the Athenian alliance in a region that was crucial for Athenian imports. Brasidas first tries diplomacy (but with the threat of military coercion in the wings). The first stop is the *polis* of Acanthus, where he gives a brief speech in which he stresses, among other things, the reliability and integrity of the Spartans – 'men whose deeds correspond so closely to their words' (4.87.1), deploying a familiar trope. Thucydides then narrates

---

[16] Quoting Connor 1985: 9–10. More recently and extensively, see Grethlein 2013a: 36–9, on the role of speeches in making the narrative experiential.

[17] Macleod 1983: 69.   [18] Laird 1999: 148 (emphasis in the original).

the impact of the speech on its target audience, who have a debate about whether or not to secede from their alliance with the Athenians and join the Spartans – although Thucydides does not give us their speeches (4.88.1). Thucydides tells us that the Acanthians were taken in by Brasidas' rhetoric, but he notes their double motivation, as they were also influenced by the vulnerability of their grape harvest: '[m]oved both by Brasidas' persuasive words and by their fears for the grape harvest, they decided to secede from Athens'. The adjective translated as 'persuasive' here is *epagōgos* ('seductive'), a word always used to signal deceptive rhetoric in the *History* (e.g. 6.8.2).[19]

Thucydides depicts Brasidas engaged in a slick rhetorical campaign as much as an effective military campaign. At 4.108.2–3 he switches to indirect discourse to better describe the rhetorical phenomenon of Brasidas and to avoid the tedium of relaying similar speeches – modified subtly to reflect the specific audience - in direct discourse: 'Brasidas was presenting himself generally in a moderate way and made it clear at every opportunity in the speeches [*en tois logois*] that he gave that he had been sent out to liberate Greece'.[20] From Acanthus he moves on to Torone, where citizens are 'emboldened by the recent trouncing of the Athenians in Boeotia and *by the seductive but misleading assertions of Brasidas*' (*tou Brasidou epholka kai ou ta onta legontos*, 4.108.5, emphasis added). At Scione he repeats the speech, with local variation, and the Scionians are also excited by his words (4.121.1).

There is a credibility gap, not just because Brasidas' speeches are reinforced by troops, but also because Thucydides' readers can see the rhetorical manipulation at work in Brasidas' supposedly straight-talking speeches, including in his 'rhetoric of anti-rhetoric'.[21] We lack specific information about any of Thucydides' contemporary readers/audiences, but we do know that they were seasoned consumers of rhetoric and alert to all of the tropes of political rhetoric.[22] Part of the intellectual pleasure of Thucydides'

[19] See Greenwood 2006: 70.
[20] Sears 2015 has an astute discussion of Brasidas' speech at Acanthus and his campaign in the Thraceward region in the context of the morality of interstate relations. Sears explains the tensions in Brasidas' diplomacy through an analogy with Rousseau's concept of 'forced freedom' in *The Social Contract* (1762), concluding that Brasidas pursued a policy of coercive liberation and was sincere in his commitment to liberating and then protecting the cities that came over to Sparta. This interpretation is fully compatible with the idea that Brasidas employed rhetorical skill and misrepresentation in convincing the citizens of Acanthus to transfer their allegiance to Sparta.
[21] For the term, see Hesk 2000: ch. 4.
[22] It is safe to assume that, in choosing to begin his *Hellenica* (*Greek History*) at the point where Thucydides' narrative breaks off, Thucydides' younger contemporary Xenophon

History for his ancient Greek readers was precisely the leisurely appraisal of speeches as a remote audience, and he would have assumed a high degree of rhetorical sophistication and a facility for judging speeches. So when, in the preamble to Brasidas' speech to the Acanthians, Thucydides remarks that Brasidas 'was in fact not a bad speaker for a Spartan' (4.84.2), he both alludes to stereotypes about laconic and unshowy Spartans while at the same time expecting his audience to look beyond this stereotype and analyse Brasidas' successful rhetorical performance.

In case this sounds too academic, we should recall that, when they turned from their leisure reading of Thucydides, his 4th-century BCE readers would themselves have had to make decisions of comparable weight and moment, whether as political advisers giving speeches to the assembly, as generals in the field encouraging their troops, as ambassadors on a diplomatic mission or as themselves part of an audience voting on a critical issue. As Elton Barker has argued, in the critical presentation of so many speeches in his *History*, Thucydides reproduces the drama and the uncertainty of decision-making familiar to his readers.[23]

This idea of rhetorical debate as theatrical/dramatic spectacle in front of an audience is the gist of the most explicit criticism of speech-making anywhere in the *History*. In a famous passage in Book 3, in the course of an assembly debate to reconsider Athenian policy vis-à-vis the citizens of Mytilene, the Athenian politician Cleon harangues his audience with a caricature of their participation in deliberation in the assembly – one of the main organs of Athens's direct, participatory democracy – as being 'more like an audience of spectators at a performance of sophists than men deliberating about matters of state' (3.38.7). Previously he has referred to them as 'spectators of speeches' and 'listeners of deeds' (3.38.4). And just to ramp up the criticism even more, Cleon claims that the pleasure that the Athenians derive from speeches (*hēdonē logōn*) is incompatible with possessing an empire (3.40.2). In short, Cleon heaps suspicion on rhetorical competence and the specious properties of rhetoric while giving his own consummate

---

was one of Thucydides' readers. Although we have sources for the 4th-century BCE reception of Thucydides (see Hornblower 1995), we do not have any explicit testimony about the response to the *History* in Thucydides' lifetime, if indeed parts of it were circulated or performed.

[23] Barker 2009: 206–7: 'On the one hand, Thucydides structures debate as an agon in such a way as to empower the reader to look into arguments of the kind that dominated the political decision-making arena and that compelled its listeners to adopt certain courses of action.' Compare Goldhill 2009: 36, on Sophocles' use of on-stage audiences in his plays to engage 'the audience in the theatre in the process of moral choice and debate'.

rhetorical performance.[24] It takes his opponent, Diodotus, to point out the paradox in Cleon's argument, namely that there is no deliberating about the future without words: '[a]s for words [*logoi*], anyone who argues seriously that they should not guide our actions is either stupid or has some personal interest at stake: stupid, if he thinks there is any other way to explore the future [*to mellon*] in all its uncertainty ...' (3.42.2). This statement encompasses both the reality of Athenian government, which the 4th-century BCE politician Demosthenes would describe as a 'form of government based on speeches' (*en logois hē politeia*),[25] and *logos* as the medium for Thucydides' historical judgement and historical narrative.

Messengers

Another felicitous blending of rhetoric in history with rhetoric in composition is the role that messengers and heralds play in Thucydides' *History*. In the period in which Thucydides was writing, messengers and heralds criss-crossed the Greek world and adjacent lands as carriers and mediators of *logos*.[26] Their importance is evident in the fact that Thucydides denotes the formal beginning of the Atheno-Peloponnesian War as the point at which communication was confined to heralds (2.1). The movements of these messengers between battlefields and cities, travelling in space and time, creates a vivid impression of the circulation of *logos* during the war and the knowledge gap between those in the field and those at home. In the very first battle of the war, the time delay involved in messengers travelling between Plataea and Athens means that the Athenians deliberate about and send instructions about a state of affairs that no longer holds (2.6.2–3):

> [The Athenians] sent a messenger to Plataea with orders to tell them not to initiate any action over the Theban men they were holding until the Athenians themselves had had some discussion about them. They had not been told the news of their death, since the first messenger had gone out at the same time as the Thebans were entering the city, and the second left immediately after their defeat and capture; so the Athenians knew nothing of what happened subsequently.

[24] For further exploration of this paradox in the context of Thucydides' views of the connection between rhetoric and historiography, see Grethlein (Chapter 2).

[25] Demosthenes 19.184.

[26] For the distinction between messengers and heralds and the status and role of heralds, see Lewis 1996: 50–6, 63–8. Letters also play a role in diplomacy, but a much smaller one than speeches delivered by heralds or messengers. Typological studies of the speeches in Thucydides tend to treat letters as a category of indirect speech (see West 1973).

These messengers and heralds, who conveyed *logoi* backwards and forwards in the war, serve a narratological function in revealing the disappointment of expectation (and, less frequently, positive reversals of expectation) as audiences who anticipate one piece of news receive another. In places they are also reminiscent of the messenger in tragedy, like the soldiers who reached Athens from Sicily bearing news of Athenian defeat, and who were disbelieved (8.1.1).[27] At 3.113.5–6, Thucydides conveys the scale of the disaster (*pathos*) that befell the Ambraciots with the detail that, when the Ambraciot herald, who had been sent out to request the recovery of the bodies of the Ambraciot dead from an earlier skirmish, learns that in the interim a relief party sent out by the Ambraciots has also been wiped out, he cries out and is so confounded by the news that he goes away without delivering his message (*apraktos*). The detail of the messenger overwhelmed by unfolding events is both a scene from history and a hypertragic narrative conceit.

The Soundscape of War

When ancient literary critics praised Thucydides' style, one of the qualities that they highlighted was the *enargeia* of his writing (Plutarch *Life of Nicias*, 1.1). This effect is primarily associated with visual clarity, but in the literary sphere any visual effects are produced by the written word and through manipulation of diction, so this vividness is a product of rhetoric.[28] When we consider speech in Thucydides, we should also consider the noise of war, since this, too, like the speeches, had a palpable psychological impact on the characters in Thucydides' *History* and constituted its own argument.

Examples of the noise of war include the shouting (*kraugē*) and screaming (*ololugē*) of the women and domestic slaves that confront the Thebans as they struggle to press home their surprise night-time invasion of Plataea (2.4.2); the Spartans trapped on the island of Sphacteria, hemmed in by the Athenians, and 'deaf to the word of command on their own side because of the louder shouts of the enemy' (4.34.3); Brasidas in the attack on the city of Torone '[raising] his army to shout in unison and spread panic throughout the city' (4.112.1); or the confused soundscape of the night battle at Epipolae, where sound becomes the crucial sense: Syracusans cheering each other on and yelling, the Athenians demanding their password from each other and revealing it to the enemy in the process and then falling into

---

[27] See Greenwood 2006: 88–9.

[28] At *Poetics* 1455a22–4 Aristotle recommends that the tragic playwright should visualize his subject matter 'before his eyes', so that he can see it as clearly (*energestata*) as if he himself had actually been present at the events.

further confusion because they cannot distinguish the singing of the Paean by their side from the Syracusans singing the Paean (7.44.4–6).

Whose Words?

We have seen how Dionysius raised concerns about Thucydides' criteria for selecting speeches for treatment in his *History*. Modern scholars have noted passages in which Thucydides records that other speeches were given – typically in the context of assembly debates – while only giving us an account of one or two speeches, or sometimes simply noting the occurrence of a debate with a cursory summary and no account of individual speeches. Famous examples include Pericles' speech to the Athenian assembly at 1.140–4 on the eve of war. In the preamble to this speech, Thucydides states (1.139.4):

> The Athenians then called an assembly and proposed a general debate, resolving to consider the whole question and give their answer once and for all. Many people came forward to speak, representing the views of both sides, some arguing that they should go to war, and some that the decree should not stand in the way of peace but should be rescinded. Then Pericles came forward, the leading man in Athens at the time, supremely capable both at speaking and in action, and he advised them as follows.

Similarly, in his discussion of the Athenian assembly debate over the fate of Mytilene, Thucydides tells us that there was an initial debate, in which the Athenians voted for a motion (proposed by Cleon, 3.36.6) to put the entire adult male population of Mytilene to death and to enslave the women and children (3.36.2–3). However, he does not record any of the speeches in this initial debate but instead gives us an account of the debate at the assembly meeting that met to reconsider the motion (3.36.6–49.1).[29] Again, we are told that 'various opinions were expressed' (3.36.6), but the only speeches given are the paired speeches of Cleon and Diodotus, who represent the opposite poles of argument *pro* and *contra* putting the Mytilaeneans to death.

The Athenian assembly debates about the Sicilian expedition (6.8-26.1) follow a similar pattern. Thucydides gives us a brief outline, in indirect speech, of an initial meeting in which the Athenians voted to send sixty ships to Sicily in response to an appeal from the Egestans (6.82), but he then gives us an account of the speeches made at a subsequent assembly meeting, with speeches from Nicias (in direct speech at 6.9–14 and 20-3 and in indirect

[29] Dionysus of Halicarnassus criticizes this omission in chapter 17 of *On Thucydides*.

speech at 6.25.2) and Alcibiades (in direct speech at 6.16.18), and an intervention by an unnamed Athenian (in indirect speech, 6.25.1). In the transition between Nicias' first speech and the speech of Alcibiades, Thucydides remarks that 'most of the Athenians who came forward spoke in favour of the expedition and against rescinding the previous vote, through there were also some who argued the contrary' (6.15.1). When the scene shifts to Syracuse, again we are told that an assembly was held and various speeches were made: 'some by those who gave no credence to reports of the Athenian expedition and some by those taking the opposite view' (6.32.3), but we are only given speeches by Hermocrates (6.33.1–34.9), Athenagoras (6.35.2–40.2) and an unnamed general (6.41.2–4).

These 'suppressed speeches' are nonetheless instances of speech presentation, since they register the existence of debate and dissent, and they also remind us of the author's role in presenting selected speeches as part of an overarching argument. In terms of trying to reconstruct the diversity of opinion in different political communities and the dynamics of assembly debates, we might wish that Thucydides had chosen not to suppress these speeches (assuming that he had sufficiently detailed notes to reconstruct them), but narratologically it is our gain. The piling up of multiple speeches for every debate would clog up the narrative and upset the balance between authorial account (*logos*) and the speeches (*logoi*) of the historical actors. This is not, however, to endorse the opinion of Cratippus, recorded by Dionysius of Halicarnassus, that the speeches 'not only impede the action but also cause annoyance to the audience' (*On Thucydides*, 16). The question of the selection of speeches in the *History* pits aesthetics against history and exposes the tension between reading Thucydides' *History* as a highly original, idiosyncratic and complex work of literature and political thought versus reading the *History* as a source for Greek history.

Thucydides' *Logos* on *Logos*

The last word here will go to Thucydides' own explicit statement about how he treated the challenges of speech presentation in the writing of his *History* (1.22.1):

> As to what was said in speeches by the various parties either before they went to war or during the conflict itself, it was difficult for me to recall the precise details in the case of those I heard myself, just as it was for those who reported back to me on cases everywhere. What I have set down is how I think each of them would have expressed what was most appropriate in the particular circumstances, while staying as close as possible to the intention of what was actually said.

This explanation of Thucydides' procedure in the case of the speeches is contrasted with his approach to *erga* (actions, events) in the next section at 1.22.2. These words have been the focus of intense and painstaking debate, as readers have tried to reconcile (1) Thucydides' apparent interest in reporting the precise details (*tēn akribiean*) of the speeches as an ideal standard, even if it proved impossible to achieve in practice, with (2) the criterion of words that were appropriate (*ta deonta*) for the occasion, and at the same time with (3), a commitment to staying as close as possible to 'the intention of what was actually said' (*tēs xumpasēs gnōmēs tōn alethōs lechthentōn*).[30] These tensions are important, but the focus on elucidating them and the effort to resolve them has led to a reductive depiction of the domain of *logos* and speech in Thucydides' *History*. Thucydides' argument and the language that he uses in this chapter follows on closely from the preceding discussion of the shortcomings of popular memory and the scant regard for truth in other genres that deal with the representation of the past (1.20.3–21.2). Having just criticized poets and writers of prose accounts (*logographoi*), the former for 'exaggerating for artistic purposes' (*kosmountes*) and the latter for privileging the persuasive manipulation of their audiences over telling the truth, Thucydides is concerned to contrast his own approach to narrative and to emphasize his respect for accuracy wherever feasible. This is a statement that is at once specific to topical debates about the appropriate truth criteria for *logos* while at the same time establishing a contract with his audience/readers.

This contract resembles that between speaker and audience in Attic oratory, and it is highly likely that the pragmatic, political conception of knowledge that we find in extant deliberative oratory influenced Thucydides' case for his *History*.[31] At 1.22.4, he claims that his work will suffice if it is judged useful by those who want a clear insight into past events and events that are likely to happen in much the same way in the future. Readers have noted an allusion to the formulae for the public scrutiny of inscribed decrees in democratic Athens in the phrase '*hosoi boulēsontai skopein*', but the stress on the likely course of future events also recalls the preoccupation with the future in assembly debates both in Thucydides' *History* and in deliberative oratory from the 4th century BCE. The claim to

---

[30] Hornblower 1994: 45–7, has an excellent discussion of the interpretation of this passage and its tensions and contradictions.

[31] For further discussion of the 'deliberative' texture of Thucydides' *History*, see Greenwood 2016: 87–91; and for more exploration of the ways in which Thucydides engages with and responds to contemporary rhetoric, see Grethlein (Chapter 2).

be advising the Athenian *dēmos* in its best interests for the future is a staple of deliberative rhetoric.[32]

The strong association between prospective knowledge about the future and sumbouleutic rhetoric in contemporary Greek thought is clearer still in Aristotle's *Rhetoric*. One of the ways in which Aristotle distinguishes between the different species/types (*eidē*) of rhetoric – in addition to different categories of audience – is in respect of their orientation to past, present and future time (*chronos*):[33]

> Each of these has its own 'time': for the deliberative speaker, the future [*ho mellōn*] (for whether exhorting or dissuading he advises about future events), for the speaker in court, the past [*ho genomenos*] (for he always prosecutes or defends concerning what he has done); in epideictic the present [*ho parōn*] is the most important; for all speakers praise or blame in regard to existing qualities … (*Rhetoric* 1358b13–18, trans. Kennedy 1991)

In staking out the temporal span of his *History* as offering a clear picture of both past events and future events, Thucydides likens the content of his work to two major sources of contemporary political knowledge, namely deliberative and judicial rhetoric. At the same time, Thucydides' reader/listener is cast in the role of a judge through the use of the vocabulary of *krisis* (*krinein*, 1.22.4).[34] The implicit charge to the reader is to read/listen to this work and then deliberate about its usefulness for developing a clear, accurate understanding of the past and as a reliable guide to events as they unfold and to probable future events.

Further Reading

A good starting point is the volume of essays edited by Stadter 1973, which offers several different approaches to the speeches and, as its last chapter, includes a bibliography of scholarship on speeches in Thucydides from 1873 to 1970. Macleod 1983: ch. 9 – first published in 1975 – remains a cogent study of the intersection of rhetoric and history in Thucydides, using the Athenian assembly debate in Book 6 of the *History* as a case study. This should be read in conjunction with Stahl's discussion of the relationship between the speeches and the course of events in Books 6 and 7 of the *History* (Stahl 2003: 173–88; also published as Stahl 2009), in which Stahl

---

[32] Demosthenes' *Olynthiac* orations begin and end with this *topos* (1.1 and 3.1), but perhaps the most explicit use of the future-orientated audience-interest theme occurs at Demosthenes *Philippic* 1.51.

[33] *Rhetoric* 1358a36. [34] Listener – cf. the verb *akouein* at 1.22.4.

analyses the ways in which the differing perspectives of the speeches and the surrounding narrative produce the ironic gap between planning and outcome that is central to historical insight in Thucydides.

For readers who have German, Scardino 2007 is a comprehensive study of the speeches in Books 7–9 of Herodotus and Books 6 and 7 of Thucydides in their respective narrative contexts and in comparison with each other. Laird 1999 is an important, theoretically informed study on speech presentation in Latin literature and includes much of interest for the study of speech presentation in Thucydides, including a section on Thucydides 1.22.1–2 (pp. 144–8). Good studies of rhetoric and the culture of speech-making in Athens include Yunis 1996 and Hesk 2000.

Accessible general discussions of the speeches include Hornblower 1994: 45–72, Greenwood 2006: 57–82, and Pelling 2009 – initially published as Pelling 2000: 112–22.

6

JEFFREY S. RUSTEN

Prolegomena to the Peloponnesian War

Thucydides Book 1

Thucydides' War Structure Compared to Herodotus'

One might claim that since Herodotus devotes only Books 7–9 to Xerxes' actual campaign against Greece (during which he uses campaigning seasons in years like Thucydides), this fact might be thought to mark Books 1–6 as his Prolegomena. But he has a larger overall organizational structure, following the barbarian kings who seek to rule the Greeks; first Croesus, and then the Persians who defeated him down to Xerxes. He takes up this king-based structure at 1.5–6, just a few pages into his work, and it suffices to encompass (admittedly with many digressions) everything from that point on until the end of his work.

By contrast, Thucydides' organizational plan by years of the war, subdivided into summers and winters, is announced only at the beginning of Book 2. Scholars have generally deemed this organization to be brilliantly executed in Books 2.1–5.24 and 5.85–8.1, where speeches, military actions and other narratives and analyses are integrated into the year-by-year story of the war's progress.[1]

But this year-by-year organization does not extend back to the substantial amount of Thucydides' writing that precedes the war's start, which is packed with a variety of different material:

1.1: The decision to write this war and its magnitude.

1.2–19: An analysis of the evidence for the magnitude of earlier Greek warfare.

Since this chapter was completed, it has become clear that Thucydidean usage requires that the phrase τὴν ἐκβολὴν τοῦ λόγου ἐποιησάμην in 1.97 means not 'I wrote a digression in my narrative' but 'I have abandoned my plan' (presumably the plan announced in 1.23 of going back only as far as Corcyra). For details, see Rusten (2020).

[1] Regarding the success of 5.25–83 and 8.2–109 scholars are in ongoing debate; see Rusten 2015.

1.20–3: The current war – magnitude, methods, reception, sufferings and organization of the upcoming pre-war narrative.

1.24–65: The path to Athenian intervention on behalf of Corcyra against Corinth (including speeches and a battle narrative) and its siege of the Corinthians at Potidaea (435–431 BCE).

1.66–87: Quartet of advice-speeches on war against Athens addressed to the Spartans.

1.88–118.2: Athens' expansion after the Persian War until the peace treaty of 440 BCE.

118.3–46: Final negotiations until the dissolution of the peace (speech by the Corinthians at Sparta, negotiations (evoking the stories of Cylon, Pausanias and Themistocles) and speech by Pericles at Athens).

It is not immediately obvious what overall structure this book really has. As one might expect, Thucydides discusses his choice of topic and methodology and embarks on a pre-war narrative; but instead of proceeding chronologically, he leaps from the moment of publication (chapter 1) back to the distant Greek past (chapters 2–19), before describing his methods (chapters 20–23), then gives a narrative from the years just before the war (chapters 24–87), then moves back again to the interval after the war with Persia (chapters 88–119) and finally forwards again to the eve of hostilities (chapters 119–146), within which we are directed back again to the post-Persian war careers of Pausanias and Themistocles.

In the late 19th and early 20th centuries, scholars generally agreed on the reasons for these disjunctions: the author had died with his work unfinished, and it was either published in the incompletely revised state in which Thucydides had left it or put together from scraps by a posthumous editor. But these same scholars had no agreement about the details, and today this 'analyst' approach to Thucydides is almost completely rejected;[2] for Book 1 in particular we will see later in this chapter that there are passages that show that, whatever we may think of its organization's success, it must be admitted that Thucydides came up with it himself. Thus Dionysius of Halicarnassus in the 1st century BCE was right to observe that Thucydides himself had deliberately chosen in Book 1 to disturb the chronological sequence of events, and he faulted him for two such

---

[2] Rusten 2015. But since this was written, a vigorous defence of analytic criticism for Book 1 in particular has been made in Liberman 2017, discussed in the introduction to Rusten (in preparation).

disruptions; another ancient critic quoted by the scholia noted another disruption, but this time he singled it out for praise.

Let us start by examining the ancient critics' reactions, then how Thucydides himself presents each disruption to the reader and what he seems to gain from it; then let us look at the prevalence of other kinds of disjunctions – especially in style and modes of historical writing – throughout Book I and finally question whether this tendency is not to be found in the later, chronologically based narrative as well.

Three Chronological Interruptions in Thucydides Book I

A Demonstration of Method (1.2–19, the 'Archaeology')

The first chronological interruption comes after the initial three sentences of the work and is forcefully attacked by Dionysius (*On Thucydides* ch. 20, trans. Usher 1974):

> One can see even better the unevenness of the historian's treatment if one considers that, while omitting many important events, he nevertheless makes his introduction some five hundred lines long as he attempts to prove that prior to this war the Greeks achieved little, and nothing worthy to be compared with it . . .. Again, the introduction contains so many elaborate arguments to prove his proposition, that it has become a sort of history on its own. The writers of the rhetorical handbooks prescribe that the introduction should adumbrate the arguments that are to be used by providing actual summaries of what is to be revealed later. Thucydides has actually done this at the close of his introduction, dealing with it in fewer than fifty lines before he begins his narrative.[3] And this makes it unnecessary for him to drag in that lengthy disparagement of the greatness of Greece . . . what occasion did he have to introduce these events and others like them before the narrative proper?
>
> If I may be allowed to state my opinion without giving offence to gods or men, I think that the introduction would have been most effective if he had made the concluding section follow directly upon the introductory section, omitting the whole of the middle section (followed by a quotation of 1.1 followed immediately by 1.21ff, omitting everything in between).

Dionysius' point is that, if 1.1–23 constitutes the preface to the work, the argument for the inferiority of previous wars is completely disproportionate to the rest of its contents. We might add that it directs attention away from his announced subject and employs a form of argumentation that will be almost entirely absent from later narrative.

---

[3] Referring to the enumeration of the many sufferings in the Peloponnesian War (1.23.1–3).

Yet the digression is not introduced by Thucydides as a diversion from his opening but as an explanation of it.[4] He starts by saying:

> Thucydides of Athens composed the war the Peloponnesians and Athenians fought against each other. He started to work as soon as it broke out, since he foresaw it would be important, and most noteworthy of all before it. This deduction was based on the peak of every aspect of preparedness reached by both entrants, and the observation that the remaining Greek peoples were joining one side or the other, either from its outbreak or planning it later.
>
> For [gar] this was in fact the largest mobilization by Greeks as well as a component of non-Greeks, extending over more or less the entire population. For [gar] preceding ones, including those of the more distant past, although impossible to determine clearly after so much time, were nonetheless important neither in wars nor for other ends.
>
> This belief is based on my study as far back as possible, and the deductions I concluded were convincing. For [gar] long ago, what is now called Greece probably did not have a stable population ...

Dionysius claims, in effect, that Thucydides should have assumed readers would accept his conclusion on his war's magnitude and moved on. Why does he argue it at length? Most scholars treat it as rhetorical *auxēsis*, the 'build-up' of his topic.[5] Yet while doggedly restating this negative thesis in 2–19, Thucydides also characterizes the sources for earlier history and offers his own categories of analysis and innovative methods for assessing it. Of the four main preoccupations of this section (proving his initial thesis, denigrating the sources, new methodologies and new categories of analysis), the first two prove to be much less in evidence than the last two.

What seems to be a *digression* that postpones his statements on method in 1.20–3, is in fact a *demonstration* of historical method as applied to previous periods. That he is focused on method and interpretation is shown by the exact repetition of framing words at the beginning (1.3) and the end (1.20.1) of this section, relating to conclusions (*heurein, hēuron*) about the past (*ta gar pro autōn kai ta eti palaitera, palaia*) based on inferences from evidence (*tekmēriōn ... pisteusai xsumbainei, tekmēriōi pisteusai*). This 'ring composition' is how Thucydides indicates the contents – as it were, the titles – of this entire section, which is mistakenly called the 'Archaeology' and should more rightly be called the *tekmēria*, the 'deductions from evidence'.

---

[4] A simple *gar* is used to introduce a long digression here as it will be again at 89.1 (*Pentecontaeteia*), 6.1.2 (the 'Sicilian archaeology'), 6.54.1 (the tyrannicides) and 7.57.1 (the catalogue of allies at the last battle in Syracuse).
[5] Nicolai 2001: 203.

As has often been noted, many of the economic, geographical and military themes of the following narrative are prefigured in these *tekmēria*;[6] that is not to say that the method of the *tekmēria* will be the method of his main narrative (see especially Beasley's Chapter 3), since that will deal with events of his own lifetime where he has much better evidence at his disposal (and rarely discusses his truth-seeking process). But it is crucial to him to present to his readers not only his own war, but also a comprehensive interpretation of evidence for the entire history of Greek military action since its earliest attestations.

The Truest Cause: Portraying Athenian Hyper-Aggression in 479–438 BCE (1.88–188)

The second chronological interruption in Book I is announced in advance by the author himself at the end of his preface (1.23.4–6):

> Its [the war's] beginning was the dissolution by Athenians and Peloponnesians of the thirty years' truce which they had made after the capture of Euboea. *The accusations and disputes that led to its dissolution I wrote in my pre-war narrative first*, so that no one need ever investigate what led to the start of such a great war among Greeks. *The reason that was truest, but most invisible in speech, I consider to be that Athens' growth, and the fear of it by the Spartans, compelled them to war*; but the publicly alleged charges that preceded the dissolution of the truce and the start of the war were as follows. (Emphasis added)

As Dionysius realized (chs. 10 and 11), the words 'I wrote in my pre-war narrative first' (*prougrapsa ... prōton*) are not redundant but indicate that the narrative behind the charges and countercharges of 435–431 BCE (especially over Corcyra and Potidaea) will come first (1.24–65); thereafter Thucydides will move backwards to chronicle Athens' dramatic rise to power after the Persian War in 479–439 BCE (1.88–118). He reminds us of this announcement by repeating the relevant words 'the Spartans were afraid' at the point (1.88.1) when his flashback starts.

Dionysius has several good reasons for objecting to this arrangement (*On Thucydides* ch. 11, trans. Usher 1974):

> But he ought to have stated at the beginning of his enquiry into the true causes of the war the cause which he considered to be the true one: for not only was it a natural requirement that prior events should have precedence over later ones, and true causes be stated before false ones, but the start of his narrative would have been far more powerful if he had adopted this arrangement. It would not even be possible for anyone wishing to defend his methods to argue that these events were minor and insignificant, or that they were well-known and had

---

[6] Kallet-Marx 1993a: 21–36; Ober 2009; Foster 2010: 8–43, among many others.

become hackneyed by previous reference, so that it was unnecessary to start with them. He himself considered that it was because this period had been neglected by earlier writers that it merited historical enquiry; and he says so in an actual passage (followed by a quotation of 1.97.2)

What, then, does Thucydides hope to gain by beginning instead with Epidamnus and Corcyra at 1.24?

First of all, he is able to contrive an imposing end to his preface, followed by a dramatic opening mention of Epidamnus in asyndeton, one that recalls the way Herodotus begins his own story with Croesus (as discussed earlier in this chapter). Second, with this sequencing he can follow the detailed narrative of back-and-forth allegations and grievances built up at 1.24–87 – right at the point of the Spartan vote that will mean war – with a reminder of the 'truest reason'" (1.88.1) that leads eventually to a concentrated record of Athens' ceaseless military aggression over the preceding fifty years to show what *really* underlies the Corinthians' outraged speech at 1.68–71. Thucydides himself at 1.97.2 calls this flashback a serious disruption when he says, 'I have discarded my plan' (*tēn ekbolēn tou logou epoiēsamēn*),[7] a blunt authorial acknowledgement of how ill-fitting it is in this place.

The Lion Smiles (Excursus[8] on Cylon, Pausanias and Themistocles)

The third chronological interruption in Book 1 comes in the linked stories of the coup attempt of Cylon in Archaic Athens and the ends of the careers of Pausanias and Themistocles after the Persian War.[9] Yet Thucydides himself does not designate these as interruptions to his narrative, nor does Dionysius criticize them as such. Evidently this is because these three flashback stories are not claimed as his own by the author (there are no first-person authorial statements) but seemingly generated by his characters, the representatives of Athens and Sparta in the final phase of negotiations before the treaty is abandoned.[10] Thus they have the air of remaining in the present.[11] The stories are also integrated into the larger section 1.119–46 and serve as a

---

[7] See the note on this passage in Rusten 2020.

[8] I follow Hornblower 2004: 308, in preferring this term to 'digression' for a change in topic that is organic to its context.

[9] Although I hope that my discussion below shows the improbability of their proposal, it would be out of place here to argue explicitly against the suggestion of Westlake 1989, Parker 2005 and Blösel 2012 that this section's style and contents cannot go back to Thucydides himself and are taken from the poorly attested writer Charon of Lampsacus.

[10] The Themistocles narrative is actually generated by characters within the Pausanias story – what von Wilamowitz-Moellendorff 1902 called a 'digression within a digression'.

[11] It thus has something in common with Herodotean 'story-telling speeches', as noted by Hornblower 2004: 308–16.

bridge that takes us from the speech of advice by the Corinthians on the upcoming war, delivered at Sparta (1.120–4), to the speech of advice by Pericles to the Athenians that concludes the book (1.139–46).

Rather than ancient critique, this excursus was, according to two scholia on Thucydides 1.126, singled out for praise:

> In admiration for the clarity of the narrative relating to Cylon, some have said 'here the lion smiled', meaning Thucydides.
>
> The rhetorician [Aelius Theon] admires greatly the narrative relating to Cylon, and advises youths to learn it diligently so that they can imitate it.[12]

Clearly this source is not judging the passage chronologically in the context of Book 1 as a whole but as a free-standing composition;[13] and even though the praise is technically limited to the first story, it applies to all three, which are in the same limpid style (more on that later in this chapter) and form an interlocking unit. Hornblower has described well its sequence of connections:

> The organization of this whole final section of Book I is extremely skilful; the transitions are all natural, but all different. Pre-war diplomacy introduces Kylon; a curse involving breaches of the rights of suppliants links Kylon and Pausanias ... evidence of treachery links Pausanias and Themistokles, whose outstanding qualities link him to Pericles, who shares the taint of the Kylonian killing, and who will ... close the phase of pre-war diplomacy in favour of the active fighting which begins Book II.[14]

The focus of these stories is also different, and unique within Book 1: individual leaders have been little on display in this book, and the *Pentecontaeteia* dispenses with them entirely; but now the focus is on the individual and comes close to biography (more on that later in this chapter).

As Hornblower notes, the point of the three stories seems to lie in their conclusion, and the entire excursus culminates in an effusive (and syntactically difficult; cf. Dionysius of Halicarnassus *On Thucydides* 16) eulogy of Themistocles. Ending with this figure might point, as Hornblower suggests, to a parallel with the later eulogy of Pericles at 2.65.6–13, although the two passages have only superlatives in common – their political talents are different. But we should note Themistocles has been selected and his story

---

[12] Kleinlogel 2019: 455 lines 89–91.

[13] Von Wilamowitz-Moellendorff might have had the second scholion in mind when he chose to include the three stories alone (and no other passages of Herodotus or Thucydides) in his *Griechisches Lesebuch* for schools (von Wilamowitz-Moellendorff 1902).

[14] Hornblower 1991–2008: vol. I, 203; cf. Ibid., 2004: 311–13.

has been told in a way that offers a complete contrast to the two previous ones: Cylon misinterprets an oracle (something the Herodotean Themistocles would not have done) and never achieves anything; Pausanias is granted power but is undone by it into savagery and folly and at the crucial moment is tricked by his slave. Themistocles, after a brilliant career, loses power[15] but eludes death by cleverly navigating three crucial encounters (in parallel episodes showing his talent for one-on-one persuasion). He lives on in honoured exile in Persia (by implicit contrast not only with Cylon and Pausanias, but also with Herodotus' Demaratus and Hippias who are quasi-parasites).

And Themistocles does not appear for the first time in Thucydides here: the historian has contrived to make him into Book 1's most frequently recurring character. He plays a major role in all three interruptions: the *tekmēria* (1.14.3 on Athens' navy), the *Pentecontaeteia* (1.90–3 on Athens' walls, with a vigorous speech announcing Athens' emergence as a Greek power) and here at 1.135–8 (his escape from Greece). He is even named by the Athenians in Sparta (1.74.1) as Athens' greatest contribution to the war.

The extravagance of Themistocles' culminating obituary is thus not based solely on his contrast to Cylon and Pausanias but his entire role in Book 1: advocate of naval power, greatest Athenian strategist, master trickster of walls against Spartans and far-thinking planner of the Piraeus walls. The ultimate narrative goal of this excursus seems clear.[16]

Six Modes of Historical Writing

We have seen that, although they all involve an interruption of chronology, these three sections are utterly different from each other in overall style or mode of writing. But the chronologically continuous sections are also quite different from each other stylistically: 'versatility' is not a trait conventionally applied to Thucydides' writing,[17] yet the longer individual sections of Book 1 appear to prefigure no less than six separate historiographic genres:

[15] In contrast to Pausanias, Themistocles seems to be presented by Thucydides as falsely accused; another contrast is in the parallel exchanges of letters with Xerxes where Themistocles is a master, Pausanias a fool. Many scholars have posed the unanswerable question of what sources Thucydides might have had for such a negative portrait of Pausanias and such a positive one of Themistocles; it is more worth noting that his source choices all have the effect of heightening the contrast between them.

[16] So also Foster 2010; Moles 2010.

[17] Dionysius of Halicarnassus conceded that Thucydides showed it 'in two or three places' (*On Thucydides* ch. 3; Hornblower 2004: 308), none of them in Book 1.

(1) The *tekmēria* (1.2–19) represent analytical speculation based on evidence filled with first-person statements using terms of deduction and subjective judgement, exemplifying a wide variety of methods, which, together with the Hippocratic *On Ancient Medicine*, demonstrate 'an established tradition of speculation into the origins of culture'.[18]

(2) The path to Athenian intervention in Corcyra (1.24–55) is in itself a unity with a (strikingly asyndetic) beginning, a middle and an end. It escalates from Epidamnus to Corcyra and then to Corinth (the major aggrieved party in Book 1), and then (after a textbook antilogy) to Athens, culminating in two battles that form a conclusion without a resolution: Athens now dominates the Ionian Sea, but an additional escalation is to be expected. The tension between its completeness as a narrative and its subordination to a bigger story prefigures works like Sallust's *Jugurtha*.[19]

(3) Four viewpoints on Athens versus the Peloponnese (1.66–87). Very differently from Antiphon or the other speeches in Book 1, this is not a paired tetralogy but resembles more an operatic quarrelling quartet – no two agree with each other, but they do not respond to each other either. Each stands alone, and they are delivered on three different occasions to three different audiences. Such a collection of intensely characterized and disengaged positions recalls the speeches of Euripides' *Iphigenia at Aulis* or *Orestes*.[20]

(4) The *Pentecontaeteia* (1.100–17) is a chronicle, listing events in order of sequence without authorial comment and minimizing the role of individuals. This was perhaps the style of the Atthidographers Hellanicus or Philochorus.[21]

(5) The excursus on Cylon, Pausanias and Themistocles (1.125–38) is contrariwise completely biography based and a sort of romance, with vivid detail, fateful miscalculations and hair's-breadth escapes, very much in the style of the short stories in Herodotus sometimes called 'novellas'.[22]

(6) The speeches of the Corinthians (1.120–4) and Pericles (1.140–4) on each side of the excursus are all on the same theme (predications about the war) and contradict or support each other on many topics, even though neither of the speakers has been heard by the other.

---

[18] Schiefsky 2005: 159.
[19] Discussed as a deliberate 'historical fragment' by Levene 1992.
[20] Mastronarde 2010: 234–45.   [21] Harding 2007.
[22] Trenkner 1958; Aly 1969. For Herodotean aspects of this excursus, see esp. Munson 2012: 250–6.

These styles do not so much complement each other as offer a sampler of different modes of historical writing. But instead of conceiving it through the analysts' metaphor of Book 1 as an editor's pasteboard of unconnected fragments, one could imagine Thucydides is either adapting models now lost or is himself creating these forms; does Thucydides, to use a discredited but once seductive theory linking human foetal development to the evolution of the species,[23] intend the ontogeny of his war to recapitulate a phylogeny of the modes of historical writing?

But that would be to assume that he leaves these modes behind when he starts his war proper, which (with the possible exception of the *Pentecontaeteia*)[24] is not really the case. They will be on display (some only briefly) at times deemed appropriate in the following year-by-year war books: when he analyses the evidence for the tradition on the tyrannicides (6.55) or the myth of Tereus (2.29.3); when he expands the story of the mini-war against Sicily (6–7); when he presents a cacophony of divergent pre-war attitudes in an inconclusive debate at Syracuse (6.32.3–41); when he retells with breathless detail the failure of Harmodius' and Aristogeiton's plan (6.56–8);[25] and finally when he uses contrasting pre-battle speeches to set forth the key issues in an upcoming conflict.[26]

The Uses of Disjunction

Carolyn Dewald's study of the structure of Thucydides' war narrative naturally omits a detailed discussion of Book 1, but she notes that '[m]uch meaning in Book 1 ... arises out of juxtapositions that ask us as readers to supply the narrative connections ourselves'.[27] This insight can guide us to a final observation in the analysis of Book 1 that, beyond the three major chronological flashbacks and the divergent styles in individual sections, there are numerous disjunctions *within* the sections of Book 1 defined earlier in this chapter:

(1) The *tekmēria* are divided by framing repetitions (or a 'ring composition') into nine distinct subsections on different topics, some with further subdivisions.[28]

---

[23] Gould 1977. Ziegler 1929 imagined that the 'Archaeology', *Pentecontaeteia* and Pausanias–Themistocles were historiographical experiments of Thucydides' youth.

[24] But even this style might be considered to recur when he chronicles the successive waves of migration into Sicily (6.2.1–6.5).

[25] Other excurses: Hornblower 2004: 308–16   [26] Luschnat 1942; Leimbach 1985.

[27] Dewald 2005: 161.   [28] For these, see the commentary in Rusten (in preparation).

(2) The chapters on method are subdivided (the transitions are effected by antithesis) into sections on the war's general magnitude, the composition of its speeches, its actions, its expected reception, the length and number of sufferings it brought about and the presentation of its causes.

(3) The four speeches at Sparta are given on three different occasions with different audiences.

(4) Within the flashback in 1.88–118 there are two distinct sections.[29]

If in fact we take all of these into account, Book 1 is not made up of five or even seven sections but is additionally broken up either by rings/frames or by topic or style dozens of times. Indeed, the only section that seems organic and has any length is the story of Corcyra, as we saw earlier in this chapter. For Thucydides, disjunction on the small level as well as the large is not a necessary evil, but delimitations that separate adjacent sections from each other are a preferred technique, which is the opposite of transition.

In the subsequent narrative that is ordered strictly chronologically, shifts of time will be much more subtle,[30] but Thucydides' penchant for disjunctions in topic and style that is on display in Book 1 will continue to serve him well in the later books, as Dewald notes – just think of Book 2 where the raid on Plataea is followed by the first invasion of Attica by Archidamus, then the funeral oration, then the plague, then Pericles' last speech and obituary. These are juxtapositions and antitheses for which Thucydides is not criticized but is famous.

How then can Book 2 and what follows be deemed – as noted at the start of this chapter and so differently from Book 1 – a brilliant deployment of diverse elements within the constraints of narrative? Probably because from this point on disjunctions between events and their corresponding shifts in style are not perceived to be occurring at the whim of the historian but as belonging to the nature of war itself.

Further Reading

The problems of the overall organization of Thucydides Book 1 are discussed by Hammond 1952; Rood 1998b: 205–48; Moles 2010, among many others. For the history and a defence of the 'analyst' view of Book 1, see Liberman 2017. For studies of the three 'interruptions', see de Romilly

---

[29] 88–96 and 97–118 are chronologically continuous but stylistically totally different; see Rusten 2020.

[30] For the whole topic, see Rood 2007.

2012: 144–79 on the 'Archaeology'; Stadter 1993 on the *Pentecontaeteia*; and Moles 2010 on the Cylon–Pausanias–Themistocles excursus. More detail on all of the subjects discussed in this chapter is to be found in the introduction and my commentary on Book 1 for *Cambridge Greek and Latin Classics* (Rusten in preparation).

7

ROSARIA VIGNOLO MUNSON

Time and Foresight in Thucydides

How would Thucydides have ended his work? Like him, we all know the outcome of the war he sets out to describe. We also know that after the humiliation of losing empire, ships, walls and constitutional government Athens was given the opportunity to reinvent itself as best as it could, and it did so fairly well. Thucydides, however, often gives no clear idea, or even gives a misleading idea, of the endgame. This feature of his work is most likely not exclusively due to a literary preference for experiential narrative.[1]

In a much-discussed passage, Thucydides presents his history as a *ktēma es aiei*, a 'possession forever', capable of communicating to his readers a useful lesson for the future not through outright prescriptions, but by merely describing the way in which humans behave in circumstances that may well repeat themselves. Well, what is the lesson?[2] Like a journalist writing on current events, he respects specific facts and their contexts. These in turn point to what the historian regards as general truths, applicable to the human actions and historical circumstances of many other different times and places. But when we come to the (interrupted or lost) end of his work, we are left without answers to some fundamental questions specifically about *Thucydides'* time and place, questions that appeared to be a part of the raison d'être of his didactic project. Is hegemony a desirable goal? If so, what constitutes a wise imperial policy? What is the best system of government? To what extent can a state balance the demands of interest versus justice? *What is best for Athens after 404 BCE?*

---

[1] 'Experiential' is Grethlein's felicitous term for a narrative that enables the reader to experience the past as if it were present. This feature of Thucydides' prose is related to the *enargeia* (vividness) his ancient readers admired (see Plutarch, *De glor. Ath.* 347a, and Greenwood, Chapter 5), but also depends on the practice of focalizing events mostly from the point of view of the historical agents who, unlike the narrator, are ignorant of subsequent outcomes (Grethlein 2013b; see also Grethlein 2010a).

[2] See Gomme et al. 1945–81: vol. I, 149–50; de Romilly 1958; Farrar 1988: 131–3; Kallet 2006; among many others (including Grethlein, Chapter 2).

In the 19th and 20th centuries scholars reacted to the provisional features of the *History* with feverish attempts to determine which sections were written earlier and which later.[3] That project has failed and has long been out of fashion, although it has yielded some useful analyses. We are now perhaps excessively attached to the idea that a great work of historiography has to be completely unified rather than processual. With the support of narratology, however, several scholars have helped us to explore the internal coherence of the text while also mapping its extraordinary diversity.[4]

This diversity, as Dewald (2005) has demonstrated, begins at the formal and structural levels. Book 1 represents a sort of proem that contextualizes the antecedents and causes of the Peloponnesian War largely by means of analeptic *logoi* written in different styles, including scenes with speeches and debates.[5]

The war narrative starts for real at the beginning of Book 2. From this point on to the end of the so-called Archidamian War (431–421 BCE, corresponding to Books 2–5.24), Thucydides announces that he will follow a chronological format by campaign seasons (2.1–2). Each summer and winter are further subdivided into 'units', usually set off by formulaic markers of time: 'that summer', 'the same summer', 'somewhat later', 'during these events', etc. The individual units within each cluster vary greatly in length, structure and complexity, with the simplest merely consisting of a minimally narrated sentence of the type: 'At a certain time, in a certain place, x and y happened' (e.g. 3.99). More frequently this core is expanded to varying degrees and in different ways, taking forms already present in Book 1.

Thucydides never renounces the arrangement by summer and winters that he employs in the Archidamian part of his work. In the so-called second introduction at 5.26.1, in fact, he renews that programme for the rest of his project. But in Book 5.25–116, which treats the period of the Peace of Nicias

[3] For an example of the excesses brought about by the 'Thucydidean Question', see Canfora 2006, which restates this scholar's long-held position and discusses earlier views.
[4] See especially Carolyn Dewald, Timothy Rood and Simon Hornblower. My debt to these scholars far exceeds the extent to which I will be able to cite them in this chapter, even though they may not always agree with my approach.
[5] An analepsis is a flashback, which goes back to a time previous to the ongoing narrative. A 'scene' is a section of text in which the length of time occupied by the action in the 'story' almost comes to coincide with the length of the narrative. Almost at the opposite end of a scene is a 'summary' (e.g. 'two assemblies were held', 1.44.1; 'the Athenians captured Eion', 1.94.1); see de Jong 2014: 79–87, 93–4, 171. For further analysis of the style and structure of Book 1, see Rusten (Chapter 6).

(from 421 to 416 BCE), the subdivision between units is less clear-cut. Very short units multiply but become more dense and unclear, somewhat 'like notes taken for a fuller, more developed account not yet written'.[6] Direct discourse disappears, even in the most developed units.

In Books 6 and 7 the paratactic presentation changes more radically to a hypotactic one, in a well-rounded and unified monograph with 'a clear dramatic shape that prepares the reader for the tragic conclusion at the end of Book 7, the destruction of the Athenian fleet in the harbour of Syracuse'.[7] Finally the last book is characterized by the peculiar compression typical of the Peace of Nicias section, but it also presents analeptic jumps and parallel narratives (e.g. at 8.45.1, 63.3) that suggest 'in becoming' the hypotactic structure actualized in Books 6 and 7.[8]

These variations in narrative structure are combined with internal instabilities of interpretation. It is almost impossible even now to read the *History* straight through without wondering whether its author knew that a certain extratextual event *y* had already happened at the time when he was writing about *x*, or whether later event *y* has any bearing on his (or our) judgement of *x*. In historiographical writing, Grethlein has introduced the term *telos* to designate 'the point in the light of which the events narrated are envisaged', while Greenwood theoretically distinguishes an 'unreal future', which is future to the actors in the narrative but not to the narrator, from a 'real future' for the narrator himself.[9] This chapter examines statements that predict or foreshadow the future (prolepses), displaying an awareness or opinion about 'what will be' with respect to the point in the text where the statement appears. Reviewing this material suggests that Thucydides' *telos* (or *telê*) and his unreal future constitute variable entities. In the case of Herodotus, in spite of the presumably protracted composition and publication of his work and its seemingly provisional conclusion, modern scholarship in the last fifty years has been able to show fairly well where the historian stood politically and morally at the far end of his own time.[10] By contrast, Thucydides leaves us shockingly in the dark about the ultimate meaning and consequences of the war he has described.

---

[6] Dewald 2005: 123.   [7] Ibid., 144.   [8] Ibid., 151–4.

[9] Grethlein 2016: 60; Greenwood 2016: 91. In the same collection edited by Lianeri 2016a on the future or 'futures' in Greek historiography, see also esp., for Thucydides, the chapters by Lianeri and Bassi.

[10] The most conservative date for the publication of Herodotus' *Histories* is 430–425 BCE; Raaflaub 1987; Stadter 1992; Moles 1996. Some scholars, however, place it considerably later, c. 415 BCE (Fornara 1971a, 1971b, 1981) or even after 404 BCE (Irwin 2018).

Prolepses in Book 1

Book 1 will provide a first sample for surveying various types of possible prolepses. Proleptic statements are formulated either by the narrator or by their speaking or thinking actors.[11] Both can be referential, when they predict that something will happen in the world (e.g., 'it is going to rain'), or self-referential, when they announce what will be said and why (e.g., 'I am going to tell you the truth'). In Thucydides, self-referential actorial prolepses are an almost obligatory rhetorical feature of the speeches that the historian reports, and they contribute to the exploration of the historical role of reasoning and persuasion in relation to action (e.g. 1.32.1). Self-referential prolepses voiced by the narrator are those in which Thucydides talks about his own text: what he is going to cover, how he will organize the material or what he wants to achieve, as when he promises that his work will constitute a possession for all times.[12]

The Narrator's Predictions

The reason that his *History* will be useful, Thucydides says, is that the future will more or less resemble the past because 'the human condition' (*to anthrōpinon*) always remains the same (1.22.4). The expression of this idea, frequently repeated in the course of the work,[13] brings us to glosses at the referential level (i.e. statements that, proleptic or not, interpret the real-world content of the *logos* rather than talking about the *logos* itself).[14] The generalization that the human condition always stays the same is also an example of how gnomic statements in the present tense can have proleptic import, reaching far into the future (into a 'real future', in Greenwood's terminology). A potentially unlimited future is also invoked by different non-gnomic interpretive comments, such as speculations about how

---

[11] Genette 1980: 33–85, esp. 67–78.

[12] See also other programmatic statements announcing the work as a whole or sections within it: 1.1, 23.5, 97.2.

[13] E.g. at 3.82.2, 84.2; 4.108.4 and many other times in speeches. This does not mean, of course, that Thucydides has a cyclical view of history; see Momigliano 1966: 11–12.

[14] See, e.g., the non-proleptic interpretive gloss: 'Being based on the mainland Agamemnon would not have held power over any islands except local offshore ones (which would not have been "many", unless he possessed a significant navy)' (1.9.4, translated by Mynott 2013a, as are all other quoted passages below). Here the hypothetical syntax clearly signals that this statement is the narrator's interpretation of a historical fact. Glosses of this sort are often in turn identified by self-referential markers of the type 'in my view' (e.g. 1.9.1, *moi dokei*). On what I call 'referential' interventions by the narrator, see Gribble 1998.

posterity will interpret the past.[15] Also undetermined but at a shorter range are references to the present of narration (i.e. the time when Thucydides was writing) with no further specification of what that time is.[16]

Aside from these vague references to the future, all of the prolepses in Book 1 are internal (i.e. they do not reach beyond the chronological limit of the main narrative of the work as we have it) and tend to cover a limited extent of time within the Archidamian War. Thucydides, for example, expresses his judgement that the political dynamics between Athens and Sparta made a military conflict an all but necessary outcome (1.23.5).[17] He also anticipates some of its features: already at its inception, he says, he had predicted that it would be the greatest of wars (1.1.1: a 'backward prolepsis'; i.e. an analepsis containing a prolepsis). The passage that lists the countless sufferings and unparalleled natural disasters of the period (1.23.1–3) culminates in the only specific reference to a singular future event, *the* plague, which broke out in Athens in the second year of the war (429 BCE; 2.47.3), left the Athenians exhausted in the fourth year (3.3.1, 3.13.3) and flared up again in the fifth year (3.87). The nearby mention of the evils of *stasis* (1.23.2) finds immediate correspondence in the pre-war affair of Epidamnus (1.24–7), but if it foreshadows the horrendous outcomes in Corcyra, it similarly reaches as far as 427 BCE.[18]

Actorial Predictions

But Thucydides' *History* is a polyphonic text, reflecting the speech or thoughts of multiple actors.[19] Even the alleged voice of the divine received through omens and oracles is one among many and always filtered through more or less reliable human reporting and interpretations.[20] Predictions

---

[15] E.g. 1.10.2: on the basis of the material remains of Sparta and Athens, people will misjudge their respective power.

[16] Especially those of the 'even in my time' type (e.g. 1.5.3) and reports to what people say 'now' (e.g. 1.20.1), both familiar Herodotean features. See 106–7.

[17] For recent scholarly objections to translating *anagkasai es to polemein* as 'made the war inevitable', see Lateiner 2017.

[18] The *stasis* in Corcyra in turn represents a historical model for the rest of Greece later on (*husteron*, 3.82.2; see 105–7 on the *stasis* in Athens). According to Thucydides it ended in 425 BCE 'at least as far as *this war* is concerned' (4.48.5, emphasis added). On the basis of Diod. Sic. 13.48, 'this war' here refers to the Archidamian War of 431–421 BCE. See Gomme et al. 1945–81: vol. III, 497; vol. V, 412.

[19] Hornblower 1994: 134–5; Dewald 1999, 2005: 18–20; Lianeri 2016b: 13–16.

[20] E.g. Delphi's promise of victory for the Spartans and help from the god is a matter of report (1.118.3, 54.4); the Pythian prediction of disaster if the Pelasgian ground is occupied is open to different interpretations (2.17.1–2); the prophecy that war would

made by characters have no special authority unless they appear to be confirmed by the narrative of facts or by the opinion of the narrator himself. These actorial prolepses occur most often in the context of deliberations, and they are an important part of Thucydides' focalization of the historical agents' motives for actions or policies. In the *History* the ability to predict is a basic qualification for leaders and planners. Thus a remarkable interpretive gloss praises Themistocles' talent (*xunesei*) for foreseeing (*proeōra*) what would happen and what was better or worse even in the distant and hidden future (1.138.3). The subsequent narrative makes clear that what Themistocles correctly predicted was that Athens would grow to become the leader of Greece and that such primacy would depend on the cultivation of naval power. In Thucydides' time, an outgrowth of Themistocles' hegemonic position is the estimate that Athens can or should do nothing to avoid war with the Peloponnesians, an opinion that is voiced on the Athenian side of the conflict by Corcyreans, the Athenian assembly and especially Pericles, who is Themistocles' obvious heir.[21] That view echoes the judgement of the narrator (1.23.5) and represents the basis for the Athenians' decision not to attempt to preserve the peace by negotiating with the Spartans.

The various speakers' descriptions of what the course of the war will be like depend on what side they are on or on whether they favour undertaking it in the first place. Both the Spartan king Archidamus and Pericles agree that the Peloponnesians will have trouble acquiring money and ships (1.80.2–81.4; 141.2–143.2), but only the dovish Archidamus (and not the supporters of war on either side: the Corinthians, Sthenelaidas and Pericles) expresses the idea that this will/would be a 'great' and difficult war (1.80.2).

Actorial generalizations that unexpected obstacles arise in any war, sometimes with the added reference to the role of chance (*tuchē*), are frequent in Book 1 and elsewhere and have different rhetorical purposes: to warn the opponent or one's own side; as self-encouragement in the face of unfavourable odds; or as a justification for the failure of previous calculations.[22] In Pericles' first speech, however, that commonplace is embedded in another generalization that introduces one of the unifying themes of the *History*: that of the instability of the decisions of the *dēmos*. Often people are persuaded to go to war only to lose their determination when *tuchē* intervenes to disrupt

come with a plague (*loimos*) may have mentioned a famine (*limos*) instead (2.54.2–3). For a divine prediction unambiguously verified by facts, see 99.
[21] 1.33.3, 44.2, 144.3. *Contra* Corinthians, 1.42.2.
[22] E.g. 1.78.1, 84.3; 2.64.1; 4.20.2; 7.61.3.

even the best-laid plans (1.140.1). This actorial gnomic prediction comes true when the assembly turns against Pericles after the outbreak of the plague (2.60.1, *moi prosdechomenōi*, 'I expected this!').[23]

How Far in the Future?

The narrator of any part of Book 1 knows more than his characters about subsequent outcomes. The question is: how much more? How long will the war last? Archidamus' statement that it might be inherited by the next generation (1.81.6) raises the issue of implicit or 'ironical' prolepses, when speakers seem to be unwittingly alluding to future outcomes they could not have known about.[24] By the same token, does Archidamus' apologetic plan to acquire support from either Hellenes or barbarians (1.82.1) communicate the author's awareness of subsequent Greek embassies to Persia, or even of the role that Persia will ultimately play in favour of Sparta?[25] Is the speculation by the Athenian envoys that if the Spartans were to inherit the hegemony they would be even more unpopular than the Athenians are 'now' merely based on past Spartan performance in 478 BCE (1.77.6), or is it designed to make the reader think, beyond the confines of the text, of the harshness of their rule after the defeat of Athens in 404 BCE?

Thematically, of course, not only actorial predictions but whole episodes and scenes can be regarded as 'programmatic' to the extent that they implicitly seem to anticipate much later ones.[26] Whether they are also modelled on them, it is impossible to know for sure. What is certain is that in Book 1 the reference to the latest and most specific event (the plague of 429–427 BCE) only occurs in the isolated introductory prolepsis that emphasizes the sufferings that will come with the war (1.23.3). Aside from that passage, the theme of the human cost for all sides, and most especially the Athenians, will only start to become prominent with the account of the plague in Book 2.[27] Other prolepses in Book 1 mainly discuss future strategy and material resources; they do so, moreover, in a context that suggests that the Athenians had the advantage in these respects, so that their decision not to try to avoid the conflict was the right one.[28]

---

[23] E.g. 2.21.3; 3.37.3; 7.14.4, 8.1. For *hoper/hoion philei homilos poeien* ('as is the way of the multitude'), see 2.65.4; 4.28.3; 8.1.4. Cf. 6.63.2.

[24] For narratorial prolepses about the ultimate outcome, see 98 on 2.65.12 and 98–9 on 5.26.1.

[25] Cf. 2.7.1. Actual embassies to Persia: 2.67; 4.50.2. Persian role after 413 BCE: 2.65.12, and see 8.5–6 and *passim*.

[26] See esp. Rawlings 1981.   [27] See Lateiner 1977b; Gribble 1998: 51.

[28] Cf. Connor 1984b: 41 on what he calls 'the recurring paradox of the first book', *contra* Rood 1998b: 22–3.

Prolepses in the Narrative of the Archidamian War and the Peace of Nicias

Unpredictable Sufferings

Starting in Book 2, speakers mix generalizations about the uncertainty of war with predictions of what is going to happen as the basis for their specific war plans. As the character Diodotus emphasizes, deliberation is mostly about the future.[29] Many of these actorial predictions turn out to be misguided, however, especially when they have to do with the actions of the enemy.[30] One of these misguided actorial predictions is proleptically reported by the narrator in his narrative of the actions of Brasidas in Chalcidice (424 BCE): the belief that all Spartans matched Brasidas in excellence would influence pro-Spartan sentiment among the disaffected Athenian allies after the Sicilian expedition of 415–413 BCE.[31] At the shorter term, several other outcomes defy previous expectations: if the plague is a blow for Athens, things are reversed in the Pylos affair, when chance occurrences, unlikely contingencies and uncharacteristic behaviours contribute to producing an *anelpiston pathos* ('unexpected loss') for the Peloponnesians (4.55.1).[32]

The narrator, for his part, is now more tentative in the face of unexpected events. The new paratactic shape arguably signals that he is not always as ready to detect results as he was in Book 1. Many of the simplest units are merely designed to carry the story forwards by keeping up with developments in particular settings; others amount to decontextualized entries recording something that happened apparently just because it did without specifying its importance.[33] The plague is certainly important, but its causes

---

[29] 3.44.3, 46.4, 48.2. Diodotus' talk about talk, coupled with Cleon's preamble in the Mytilenean Debate (3.37–9, esp. 39.1) is one of the most spectacular cases of self-referential actorial prolepsis in the *History*.

[30] E.g. 2.11.3, 7, 20.3 (Archidamus predicts that the Athenians will meet the Peloponnesian army in a land battle); 21.1 (the Athenians hope the Peloponnesian army will not advance farther than Eleusis); 4.76.3 (the Athenians expect that the capture of Delium will enable them to control Boeotia); 77.1 (Demosthenes expects to seize Siphae; cf. 4.89.2, 101.3). For the discrepancy between planning and success due to human miscalculation or accidental events, see especially Stahl [1966] 2003: 75–99; on *elpis* (hope, expectation), most frequently of favourable outcomes that remain unrealized, see Stahl [1966] 2003 *passim*; Schlosser 2013; Lateiner 2018.

[31] 4.81.2–3, implicitly contradicted by the narrative of Spartan actions in Book 8; see also the evaluation of Thucydides-narrator at 8.96.5.

[32] 4.1–23, 26–41, with 55.1. Rood 1998b: 24–57.

[33] Most strikingly, natural phenomena with no apparent consequence, e.g. 2.28 (solar eclipse), 3.87.4 (earthquakes), 3.116 (eruption of Aetna), 4.52.1 (solar eclipse and earthquake); see Munson 2015.

are impossible to assess (2.48.3), unlike the causes of the war Thucydides has so clearly diagnosed at the beginning of his work.

The painful experience of the plague as an irrational event dominates Book 2. Its description (2.47.3–54) is immediately preceded by the Funeral Oration unit (2.34–47.1), which falls in the correct chronological place at the end of the previous winter, but whose inclusion is entirely optional from the point of view of the course and strategy of the war. Already before this scene, Thucydides slips a mention of the future epidemic in a referential gloss that emphasizes Athenian might in the first year of the war:

> [The expedition against Megara] was the greatest Athenian force assembled together, since the city was at peak strength and *had not yet been struck by the plague*. (2.31.2, emphasis added)

This prolepsis amounts to a reading direction for the *Epitaphios* sequence, which is allowed to communicate its own inspiring message but is also designed to work in thematic opposition to the subsequent narrative: the brilliant democratic experiment is vulnerable to external catastrophes. Even the loftiest civic values or, indeed, the most basic of civilized customs will crumble in the face of unbearable hardships. The description of the plague represents the paradigmatic episode for the contemplation of inexplicable *pathos/pathemata* that Thucydides has announced at 1.23.1.[34]

On the Athenian side, the plague is the first major fulfilment of the speakers' generalizations in Book 1 about the predictable occurrence of unpredictable things.[35] In this moment of despair for Athens, Pericles reaffirms his faith in the value of reasoned foresight (*pronoia*, 2.62.5), but he must also acknowledge that the unexpected interfered with planning (2.64.1). While he wants the Athenians to keep focusing with energy on the present war, therefore, he also encourages them to consider their accomplishments *sub specie aeternitatis*, as it were: their glory will endure 'even if we do now have to accept some eventual loss' (2.64.3). Whether Pericles' words ironically look forward to the Athenian defeat of 404 BCE or whether they simply express another theoretical commonplace about an indeterminate future ('all things must come to an end', *panta gar pephuke kai elassousthai*), they lead directly to the most important metanarrative passage in the *History*, where Thucydides for the first time explicitly mentions the final outcome of the war.

---

[34] These words are used in reference to the plague at 2.54.1 and 65.2. Cf. 6.12.1, 26.2.
[35] See 94–5.

The First External Prolepsis: Retrospective Confirmation

At 2.65, the retrospective on Pericles' career includes praise of his foresight (*pronoia*), which, according to Thucydides, became even clearer after he died. What we have here is an analepsis including a mixed actorial/narratorial prolepsis: at the time of the outbreak of the war Pericles 'was a far-sighted judge of the city's strength' (*prognous tēn dunamin*) and predicted its success (*ephē periesesthai*), if only the Athenians 'held back, looked after their navy, did not try to extend their empire during the war and did not expose the city to risks' (2.65.5–7). Thucydides confirms the correctness of this view: in spite of the fact that the Athenians, guided by the self-serving or ineffectual post-Periclean leaders, did the opposite, he says, their resources were so great that they repeatedly recovered from all sorts of blunders, especially the Sicilian disaster. Even after this they were able to stand up to a broad coalition of states, including eventually Persia, and only succumbed in the end on account of internal dissension (2.65.12).

Thucydides' evaluation of Pericles (the analeptic part), combined with the anticipation of developments Thucydides does not or has not yet covered, creates an implicit self-referential bridge between the earlier and the later parts of the work. Given the overall tone of the pre-plague narrative, the identification of the narrator with his character is here very strong:[36] both were right *on the basis of what each of them knew at the time*, when Pericles was in charge and Thucydides had begun writing about the war.

The Second External Prolepsis: Revision

Chapter 2.65 takes for granted the idea that the Peloponnesian War lasted from 431 to 404 BCE. By contrast, the next explicit statement that alludes to a date so far in the future (5.26) is devoted to arguing the point.

In Book 5, the stipulation of the Peace of Nicias marks the end of the ten-year war that Thucydides now calls *ho protos polemos* ('the first war') because, as it turns out, there will be other phases.[37] The narrator of this part of the *History* is 'the same Thucydides' (*ho autos Thoukudidēs Athēnaios*, 5.26.1) as at 1.1.1, but he now speaks in terms of a twenty-seven-year war, which included the peace period (since this peace was far from peaceful; cf. 5.25) and ended when 'the Spartans and their allies put an end to Athenian rule, and captured the Long Walls and the Piraeus' (5.26.1).

---

[36] *Contra* Foster 2010: 217, who argues that in this passage 'Thucydides displays both Pericles' talents and his limitations'.

[37] 5.24.2 Previously simply 'this war'; see n. 18.

To his polemic against a potential opponent to this view (*tis*, 'someone', 5.26.2: perhaps his former self),[38] Thucydides appends the report of early prophecies that the war would last for precisely twenty-seven years, adding that he remembers them as being public knowledge from the very beginning (5.26.4):

> And this is actually the only reliable fact that those who put their trust in oracles have got right. *I always remembered* that *from the very start of the war* up to its end there were many who prophesied that it would last 'thrice nine years'. (5.26.3–4, emphasis added)

'*Now*, you tell us!' the reader will say.

Thucydides' tendency to delay material until it becomes most relevant may explain the omission of the astonishing twenty-seven-year response until this point in his narrative. Other oracles concerning outcomes of the war point to the outbreak of the conflict, the evacuation of Attica with consequent crowding into the city and the advent of the plague.[39] These may have been more influential in guiding thought and action at the beginning of the conflict and therefore more worth recording in the first two books of the *History*. Nevertheless, in the context of various speculations back then about the likely length of the future war (see especially Archidamus, 1.81.6), the fact that Thucydides does not mention what he now, in Book 5, says were generally known, specific predictions on the subject is hard to explain, except for in terms of his scepticism towards such prophecies at a time when he was reporting the preliminaries and beginning stages of the war with no real knowledge about how many years the war would really last. This analepsis, therefore, is a sign of the revisionist nature of the so-called second introduction at 5.26 and of the provisional knowledge displayed in Book 1.

True Predictions and False Expectations

The issue of the length of the war is in Thucydides related to the theme of Athenian power and endurance, but that theme soon becomes ambiguous: are the Athenians justifiably self-confident or reckless? In Books 1–2.46 they have ships, naval skill, walls, subject cities, money and imperial organization as well as unstoppable energy (see the Corinthian portrayal of the Athenian character at 1.70). After the outbreak of the plague, when they are discouraged and somewhat diminished, Pericles reminds them that their naval supremacy still makes them the actual or potential masters of the entire

[38] Or, possibly, Hellanicus; see Jacoby *FGrHist* (1923–58) IIIb suppl. vol. 2: 16, n. 147.
[39] 2.8.2–3, 17.1–2, 54.4.

world (2.62). Correspondingly, one of the most important points of 2.65 is that of Athenian resilience in spite of their own policy errors and external impediments. Athens' enemies are frequently disappointed because, as we learn only retrospectively (in analepses *cum* prolepses), at the beginning of the war they thought that the Athenians would yield quickly (4.85.2, 7.28.3).

The idea that the Athenians often defy their enemies' false hopes also appears in an interpretive gloss in the narrative of the eighth year of the war, when the successful rebellion of Amphipolis causes great consternation at Athens and commensurate optimism among other Chalcidian allies, who underestimate Athenian power and now plan to secede:

> They preferred to make their judgments on the basis of wishful thinking rather than prudent foresight [*pronoia asphalei*], as men often do when they indulge in uncritical hope [*elpidi*] for what they want but use their sovereign powers of reason to reject what they prefer to avoid. (4.108.4)

These are scathing words, which no doubt reflect Athenian rage at the loss of Amphipolis (in which Thucydides was personally involved, 4.106) and may express a measure of schadenfreude at the imminent fate of the Chalcidian cities: some of them will be re-subjected at the time of the Peace of Nicias, others will suffer severe punishment.[40] The message to all and sundry not to underestimate Athenian power reinforces the foresight (*pronoia*) of Pericles at 2.65. But there is another side to this picture. The generalization on the subject of irrational hope (*elpis*) requires a broader application. As the narrator has already observed at the time of Pylos, Athenians too can be misguided, especially in unexpected success:[41]

> For such was their current run of good fortune that the Athenians felt the right to expect that nothing would go wrong for them, but that they could accomplish the possible and the impracticable alike . . . .. The reason for this attitude was the success of most of their undertakings, which defied rational analysis [*para logon*] and so added to the strength of their hopes. (4.65.4)

That this comment is appended to the narrative about the Athenians' disappointment at the failure by their generals to subdue Sicily in 424 BCE prepares us for the account of the great expedition of 415–413 BCE in Books 6 and 7. But the ambiguity attached to the notion of the relentless activism of the Athenians also emerges from the Melian Dialogue at the end of Book 5.

---

[40] Mende, 4.130; Torone, 5.3.2–4; Scione, 5.32.1.
[41] 4.21.2, 41.4; cf. 17.4. Stahl [1966] 2003: 150. For *elpis*, see n. 30.

Prolepsis in the 'Peace' Years

The narrative that covers the (actually warlike) peace years is fast-paced, crowded with moves and, after the second introduction at 5.26, remarkably free of narratorial prolepses. On the actorial side, the calculations of individuals and cities are particularly petty and volatile. A tangle of mostly inconclusive diplomatic activities is interspersed with military operations. The clauses in the inserted treaties (a new feature) will remain largely unfulfilled. The absence of direct speeches confirms the general message that none of the numerous debates of this period was particularly worth reporting in detail and leaves little scope for interesting predictions.[42] The most expanded unit in this section is devoted to the strategy and logistics of the Battle of Mantinea, whose outcome re-establishes Spartan control in the Peloponnese and calms the diplomatic turmoil (5.65–82).

But something unexpected happens at this point, narratively speaking. Thucydides' notice of the Athenian expedition against Melos in the summer of 416 BCE (5.84) blooms into a scene as developed and absorbing as the debates in the first books of the *History*, only now in a different, dialogic form (5.85–114). This expanded episode reopens the topics of foresight and Athenian power. The hope of the Melians, who think that Sparta and the gods will save them, seems even more irrational than the optimism of the Chalcidian cities at 4.108, while the Athenians' expectation that they will conquer Melos is fulfilled easily enough this time.[43] But Thucydides' David-obliterated-by-Goliath staging of the Melian Dialogue signals a moralistic intent such as we had not seen in his earlier accounts of the strategic operations by which Athens kept control of the sea. Here the Melian leaders are irresponsible but also somewhat heroic, and the Melian people are victimized. Athenian rhetoric blends rigorous logic with an almost fanatical appeal to cosmic laws.[44] The Athenians acknowledge the possibility of the end of their empire (already voiced by Pericles) only to shrug it off.[45] With no help from narratorial interventions, the Melian Dialogue presents as the flipside of Athenian activism an unprecedented self-confidence, unchallenged for the moment, but not boding well in the long term.

---

[42] Cf. Rood 1998b: 89–93.

[43] The Melians were not so helpless, nor the Athenians so determined back in 426 BCE (3.91.1–3). Dewald 2005: 137–43.

[44] 5.105.1–3. Ostwald 1986: 305–12.   [45] 5.91; cf. 2.64.3, p. 97.

Prolepses in the Narrative of the Sicilian Expedition

According to Xenophon (*Hell.* 2.2.3), Athenian public opinion recognized the moment of reckoning for Athenian actions against Melos and other cities in 404/3 BCE. In Thucydides' text, implicitly at least, that same self-awareness on the part of the historian, at least, comes much earlier. 'In the same winter' in which the Athenians conquer little Melos (416/15 BCE), they also resolve to make an expedition against the huge island of Sicily, with the intention to conquer it, 'most of them ... unfamiliar with the size of the island and of the large number of inhabitants there (both Greek and barbarian), and ... unaware that they were taking on a war on almost the same scale as that against the Peloponnesians' (6.1.1). The Melos–Sicily chronological and thematic continuity resembles somewhat that which obtains in the case of the Funeral Oration and the plague, with the first unit, historically less important, foreshadowing the other.[46] Both the Melian and the Sicilian campaigns are initiated at the time when the Peace of Nicias was still formally in force; both appear weakly motivated, vaguely pre-emptive and optional – very different from the 'necessary' war of 431 BCE (1.23.6).

As much as it looks backward (and forward), the account of the Sicilian expedition in Books 6 and 7 represents a semi-autonomous monograph, characterized by a special ideological thrust. Thucydides' brilliance and specificity on the subject of military operations, deliberations or internal and inter-city politics are here integrated in the old-fashioned model of the *koros* (entitlement)–*hubris* (insolence)–*ate* (recklessness) sequence that self-consciously duplicates Herodotus' interpretation of the Persian Wars, complete with the theme of violation of boundaries (6.13.1). Here Athens plays the role of Persia and Syracuse that of Athens.[47]

The narrative (unlike the equally polished Book 1) is shaped like a tragedy because Thucydides anticipates its disastrous ending from the very beginning and never lets us forget it. It is, one might say, a largely implicit proleptic narrative, which knows from the start where it is going. Almost everyone on either side agrees at the outset that the Athenians want to conquer Sicily while they are *de facto* still at war with the Peloponnesians.[48] In contrast

---

[46] See 97.

[47] Connor 1984b: 175–6; Rood 1999: 154–64. The semi-autonomous nature of the Sicilian monograph is detectable, for example, from the introduction of Alcibiades (6.15), who has already been introduced at 5.43.2 (Hornblower 1991–2008: vol. III, 337).

[48] Cf. 6.1.1 (narrator); 6.8.4, 10.1, 11 (Nicias); 6.17.6–8, 18.4, 90.2–3 (Alcibiades); 6.33.2, 76.2 (Hermocrates); 6.88.1 (Camarinans); 7.66.2 (Gylippus). The only exception is the dishonest Euphemus (6.86.3). Cf. already in 427 BCE, 3.86.4. Thucydides considers it a violation of Periclean policy (2.65.7).

with Alcibiades' optimistic expectations, Nicias' early prediction that 'we shall find it hard to conquer the enemy and come through safely ourselves' (6.23.1) is reinforced by the ominous mutilation of the Herms (6.27.3) and by people's fear – even in the midst of triumphant preparations and extravagant hopes – that they might never get to see their friends again (6.30.2). Once the campaign gets under way, Athenian successes are presented as temporary, followed by inactivity or disappointments.[49] The narrative amounts to a catalogue of Athenian mistakes or arbitrary reversals.[50] While the second expedition is already sailing, the reader wishes it would never arrive, understanding that even the fallback goal of Demosthenes to save the Athenian army (7.42.5) will not be realized. Reports of loss of morale abound, with Syracusan self-confidence growing to a ferocious pitch, along with Athenian *aporia* and grief.[51]

The tightness of the Sicilian narrative is largely due to the insistence with which it looks forward to its own conclusion. Two passages reach out to a continuation of the story beyond its end. As the narrator first anticipates, Alcibiades' ambitious lifestyle 'was largely responsible later for the destruction of Athens' (6.15.3), and the suspicions it caused among the *dēmos* 'in no time at all [*ou dia makrou*] brought about the downfall of the city' (6.15.4). This is the third and last explicit far-reaching prolepsis in the work (with 2.65 and 5.26), but, unlike the other two, it shrinks the interval between the failure in Sicily and the ultimate defeat of Athens in 404 BCE and almost conflates them.[52] Secondly, the Athenian violation of the Peace of Nicias (6.105) leads to a Peloponnesian invasion of Attica and the occupation of Decelea, whose ruinous consequences the Athenians had to endure 'summer and winter', evidently for several years in the future (7.27.3–28.4). Here, in a breathless paragraph, Thucydides describes the distress and unbelievable fighting spirit (*philonikian*) of the Athenians and the surprise of a generalized observer (*tis*), who looks back to the beginning of the war when the Greeks thought that the Athenians would hold out for a maximum of three years

[49] 6.71.1, 74, 79.3; 7.5–6, 24, 43.7.

[50] Among others: 6.46 (Athenians duped by Egesta and disappointed by Rhegium); 70.3, 71.2 (no cavalry); 49–50.2 (Lamachus' plan ignored); 53, 88.4–92 (Alcibiades recalled ends up in Sparta); 101.6 (Lamachus dies); 7.4.6 and 24.3 (Nicias settles at Plemmyrium, which is eventually captured; both passages with narrator's commentary); 7.6.4 (Athenians fail to blockade Syracuse); 48–9 (withdrawal delayed).

[51] Syracusan confidence: 7.2.2, 25.9, 46, 56, 59, 66–8, 71.5. Athenian discouragement and fear: 7.11–15, 24.3, 27.3–28, 50.3, 55.1, 71.6–7, 72, 75–6, 79.3, 80.3.

[52] Gribble 1999: 182–3, points out that the verb *esphēlan* at 6.15.4 echoes *esphalēsan* at 2.65.12 and argues that 6.15 refers both to the deposition of Alcibiades in 415 BCE, which led to the failure of the Sicilian expedition, and to that in 406 BCE, which ultimately led to the defeat of Athens in the war. See also Hornblower 1991–2008: vol. III, 340–1.

(backward prolepsis; i.e. prolepsis within an analepsis). But the Athenians have so much defied others' expectations (*ton paralogon tosouton poiēsai*) that seventeen years later they have attacked Syracuse and even now, with the Peloponnesians in Attica, would not withdraw (7.28.3).

The idea that the Athenians were now oppressed by two wars at once recalls Thucydides' initial judgement that with the Sicilian expedition 'they were taking on a war on almost the same scale as that against the Peloponnesians' (6.1.1). But the suggestion of recklessness is here recombined with that of endurance, as in the prolepsis on the Sicilian campaign within the praise of Pericles' *pronoia* at 2.65. The difference is that Books 6 and 7, while detailing the strategic blunders of execution, also make clear that, in Thucydides' opinion, the expedition should not have happened in the first place. At 2.65.11, by contrast, besides ignoring its moral implications, Thucydides minimizes the doomed aspect of the enterprise and limits himself to criticizing its mismanagement: 'it was *not so much* a mistake in judgment about the enemy they were attacking *as* a failure on the part of those sending the men abroad to follow up this decision with further support for them' (emphasis added). More importantly, this same passage stresses the recovery *after* Sicily, when, in spite of such a serious defeat, the Athenians were able nevertheless (*homōs*, 2.65.12) to mount a successful resistance against a coalition of enemies old and new.

Prolepses in Book 8

After Sicily

The idea of recovery is reintroduced in Book 8 shortly after Athens' choral grief that rounds up the tragic ending of Book 7. The Athenians' consternation, recriminations and fear are (again: 'nevertheless', *homōs*)[53] soon replaced by their will to resist with all the resources they can still muster (8.1.3). On the other side, neutral cities, Peloponnesians, Persian satraps and subject-allies of Athens all make plans or take action, expecting that neither Athens nor the war will last long (8.1–2, 8.4). The Chians revolt and are caught by surprise when Athens reacts by attacking them: like many others, 'they had believed in the speedy collapse of Athenian power'. Thucydides praises the Chians poignantly for always managing their city well (8.24.4) and attributes their misfortunes to the fact that 'they were caught out here by one of those unaccountable contingencies [*paralogois*] of human life' (8.24.5). The tone is here far more sympathetic than in the gloss condemning

---

[53] Connor 1984b: 212–13; Gribble 1998: 60–1; Rood 1998b: 254 n. 16.

the Chalcidian rebels for their lack of foresight (4.108.4). Circumstances are of course different in 413 BCE. The Chians provide the first illustration of the unexpected hardships of the eastern Greeks stemming from Athenian resilience and Spartan inadequacies: they are destined either to remain subjects of Athens or to be enslaved to the Persians by the very Spartans who had promised to liberate them from Athens. This new reality is emphasized proleptically by Thucydides' verbatim report of the three treaties between the Peloponnesians and the Great King.[54]

The Provisional Logos

The narrative in Book 8 is complicated because it has to move around between the naval war in various locations of the Ionian Sea and the Hellespont, the political *stasis* in Athens and the alternative assembly established by the Athenian navy at Samos – all interacting with one another.[55] As in Book 5, there are treaties but no direct discourse. The allocation of speech is here more sorely missed since the numerous indirect debates and potential speeches raise important strategical issues and propose major political changes we would like to know more about.[56]

There are almost no proleptic statements, but we find, on the other hand, a high proportion of non-proleptic narratorial glosses. At the self-referential level, Thucydides expresses an unprecedented uncertainty about his *logos*, identifying some of the information he conveys as the product of hearsay or his own opinion.[57] Referentially, the narrator intervenes more often than usual to evaluate people or interpret events (as in the passage about Chios cited above), and it is mainly upon these judgements that we must rely in our attempt to infer Thucydides' views about his city's future.

Thucydides' evaluations in this section of the work are, however, hard to contextualize or reconcile. Alcibiades restrains the Athenians at Samos from sailing off to fight the oligarchs in the city at 8.82, and when he later does the same thing, he is credited with doing the state a great service 'for the first time' (8.86.4).[58] When Phrynichus refuses to fight at Miletus, Thucydides

---

[54] 8.18, 37 and 58, discussed by Munson 2012: 262–4. For the hardships of the Chians, see also 8.38.3, 40.1, 60.2.

[55] Dewald 2005: 144–54.

[56] See e.g. the indirect speeches of Phrynichus at 8.27.1–4 (with Hornblower 1991–2008: vol. III, 826) and 48.4; of Pisander and others at Athens (53); the assemblies in Athens and at Colonus at the time of the oligarchic coup (66–7); the Athenian assemblies at Samos (76, 81, 86, 88); and the council and assembly in the Theatre of Dionysus (93–4).

[57] 8.46.5, 50.3, 56.3, 64.5, 87–8. Lateiner 1976; Munson 2012: 269–72.

[58] If *proton* ('first') of the Vatican MS is correct; Hornblower 1991–2008: vol. III, 1001.

praises him as 'a man not without intelligence [*ouk axunetos*] – not only now or in this matter, *but just as much later* in whatever he was involved in' (8.27.5, emphasis added).[59]

Phrynichus is one of the leaders Thucydides mentions by name as especially active in the oligarchic coup at Athens, which was carried out by 'many intelligent men' (*ap' andrōn pollōn kai xunetōn*, 8.68.4).[60] Thucydides also praises Theramenes as 'able in council and debate' (8.68.4), and especially Antiphon as 'second to none among the Athenians of his day in excellence [*aretē*] and his powers of thought and expression'.[61] Thucydides' expressed admiration for the oligarchs distinguishes the narrative of the Athenian *stasis* of 411 BCE from its paradigmatic antecedent of 427 BCE, Corcyra, or even the affair of the Herms in 415 BCE.[62]

The oligarchic horrors in Athens, according to the narrator, were not as horrible as the democrat Chaereas reported (8.74.3). This ambivalence is surprising in the light both of previous evaluations in the *History* and of what we know about subsequent events not included in it. At 2.65.11, Thucydides identifies the struggle among post-Periclean leaders as the ultimate cause of the Athenian defeat in 404/3 BCE. In Book 8, by contrast, the vivid pages he devotes to the *stasis* (8.65–70) nowhere anticipate its consequences in the long term or allude to the second oligarchical challenge in 404 that eventually brought the city to surrender. Is the narrator historicizing himself by expressing his hopes in 411 BCE for the emergence of a new leadership?

The celebration of Antiphon as the mastermind of the revolution in 411 BCE is amplified by a proleptic notice of his prosecution and death after the fall of the Four Hundred, when 'he mounted what was undoubtedly the best defence against a capital charge that was ever heard to my time' (*mechri emou*, 8.68.2). One would like to know what *mechri emou* means, exactly, but it is at least certain that Antiphon was executed in 410 BCE, when the

---

[59] This is at least a little odd in light of this man's collusion with the Spartan admiral Astyochus (8.50–1), although treasonable behaviour arguably does not negate intelligence.

[60] Thucydides elsewhere only attributes *xunesis* (intelligence) to Themistocles (1.138.3), Theseus (2.15), Pericles (2.34.6; cf. 1.140.1) and Brasidas (4.81.2).

[61] 8.68.1: ἀνὴρ Ἀθηναίων τῶν καθ' ἑαυτὸν ἀρετῇ τε οὐδενὸς ὕστερος καὶ κράτιστος ἐνθυμηθῆναι γενόμενος καὶ ἃ γνοίη εἰπεῖν. The τε ... καὶ ... καὶ construction makes it difficult not to give to the word *aretē* a moral sense suggesting integrity, distinct from Antiphon's intellectual abilities. *Contra* e.g. Ostwald 1986: 360.

[62] Corcyra: 3.80–5; 4.46–8. Herms: 6.27–8, 53, 60–1. The killings of the demagogue Androcles and other 'unsuitable individuals' at Athens, much less the execution of the rascally Hyperbolus at Samos (8.73.3), do not seem to be from the point of view of the text entirely negative measures (although *anepitēdeious* at 8.65.2 may reflect the discourse of the oligarchs; on deviant focalization, see Hornblower 1994: 135).

Four Hundred were replaced by the government of the Five Thousand.[63] Thucydides' narrative of this change of regime begins with the split between moderate oligarchs and the extremists, with Antiphon unambiguously a member of the second group: he endorses the treasonable fortifications at Eetionea and participates in the embassy negotiating peace with Sparta on highly unfavourable terms.[64] Thus Thucydides implicitly counts him among those who, in words remarkably close to his judgement of leaders at 2.65.7, 'were driven by private ambition' (8.89.3). Once the Five Thousand are voted into power, that moderate democratic regime, which executed Antiphon, receives in turn Thucydides' special praise:

> And *for the first time in my life at any rate* the Athenians appear to have enjoyed good government, with a moderating balance between the few and the many, and this was the thing that first began to lift the city out of its sorry state. (8.97.2, emphasis added)

Here we do not know, once again, in what period 'for the first time in my life' locates the narrator. The comparison with other forms of government may involve not only the radical democracy and the oligarchy of the Four Hundred, but also the full democracy that was restored outside of the chronological range of Thucydides' text as we have it, first just a few months after the Five Thousand were established and then again after the fall of the Thirty in 403 BCE.

The most important point, however, comes at the end of the passage: the constitutional change 'first began to lift the city from its sorry state'. Thucydides' very last words about the internal state of affairs in Athens are about restored confidence.

Things Are Looking Up

Also on the military side, as on the topic of Athenian party politics, Book 8 pursues the theme of Athenian recovery without providing explicit anticipation of events after 410 BCE. Although everything that happens is initially precipitated by the Athenian defeat in Sicily, soon that disaster is mostly recalled only by the enemies of Athens or through Thucydides' mentions of the various western contingents that have now joined the Peloponnesian offensive.[65] Two analeptic references in Thucydides' voice (8.96.1 and

---

[63] [Plut.] *X orat.* 833e–f; Ostwald 1986: 402. Neither the notice of the death of Lichas 'afterwards' (8.84.5) nor that of the exile of Hermocrates (8.85.3) has a longer proleptic reach. See Gomme et al. 1945–81: vol. IV, 67 and vol. V, 281–5; Hornblower 1991–2008: vol. III, 995 and 998. On 'in my time' prolepses, see 93, n. 16.

[64] 8–90; cf. 89.2, 91.1–3.   [65] 8.26.1, 29, 35.1, 45.3, 61.2, 84–5, 91.2, 104–6.

8.96.5) play down its impact. In the first of these he represents the revolt of Euboea as causing in Athens 'a sense of shock … greater than ever before. *Neither the disaster in Sicily, great as it seemed at the time, nor any other event had ever scared them as much*' (8.96.1, emphasis added). Sicily is here reduced to a *xumphora* that has been overcome; one of many, somewhat on the scale of the Egyptian disaster during the *Pentecontaetia*, which Thucydides has chosen to report in a miniature version of the Sicilian narrative (1.104 and 1.109–10).

At the time of the revolt of Euboea, the Athenians' greatest terror – that the enemy would sail against Piraeus – did not materialize:

> Instead … the Spartans proved themselves to be the best possible opponents for the Athenians …. They were completely different from the Athenians in temperament – the latter quick and the former slow, the latter enterprising and the former cautious – and this benefited the Athenians a great deal, especially as a naval power. *The Syracusans prove the point.* They were most like the Athenians in character, and also their most successful opponent. (8.96.5, emphasis added)

In other words: the failure in Sicily was a special case, now over and done with. In the present war, the odds are weighted in Athens' favour.

So, even the consequences of the loss of Euboea are temporary, and the Athenians are able to react. A first small naval victory at the Hellespont again enhances their morale:

> Before this they had come to fear the Peloponnesian fleet, as a consequence of their succession of smaller failures and the catastrophe of Sicily; but now they were released from their self-reproaches and no longer felt the same respect for the enemy's prowess at sea …
>
> When … the Athenians heard the news of their good fortune – coming especially as it did following the recent disaster at Euboea and their internal conflicts – their spirits revived and they came to believe that if they tried hard to regain the initiative things could still go their way and bring them success. (8.106.2–5)

Nothing that happens in the little that is left of Thucydides' narrative contradicts this expectation or reverses the positive direction of the pattern 'they had formerly expected negative *x*, but now they expected positive *y*'. The Athenians take Cyzicus (8.107), and Alcibiades has been recalled and is active as a general. His successes at the Hellespont, not covered by Thucydides, are shortly forthcoming. From the Athenian viewpoint, the interrupted *History* ends on a high note.

Conclusion

The external prolepses at 2.65, 5.26 and 6.15.3–4 make clear that, in the strict sense, the war Thucydides promises to describe (1.1) ends with the defeat of Athens in 404/3 BCE. But considering the attention that the historian has devoted to antecedents, causes and preliminaries, his topic may also have allowed for a description of an aftermath. What is sure is that Book 8 as we have it does not look forward to a tragic ending. It rather resembles those Archidamian War sections where human fortunes appear too unstable to allow for predictions about ultimate results, and it seems also to echo Book 1, which emphasizes Athenian power.

Thus the historian's explicit range of vision changes: it sometimes seems to fall short of 404/3 BCE, and sometimes it may extend beyond it to yet another Athenian recovery. It is somewhat disappointing that Thucydides does not give us the means to look into the future, in particular for issues like the fully restored democracy, the facts after Aegospotami, the government of the Thirty, the second restoration of democracy after that and perhaps the foundation of the new naval league. The work as a whole, at any rate, is not the equivalent of a teleological narrative (like Books 6 and 7) that just happens to be interrupted before a predictable ending. History as a whole is a journey through events, some of which have just occurred or are still unfolding under the historian's eyes or are being re-evaluated in the light of subsequent experiences. It goes on and on, and we often cannot tell *where* it is going or where we definitively stand in relation to it. It may seem like a paradox, but an important part of the lesson we derive from a work designed not 'for the moment' but 'for all time' is this: that all historiography is provisional.

Further Reading

Generally on the application of narratological theory to ancient texts, see de Jong 2014. Hornblower 1994 gives a compact but wide-ranging account of narrative and narratological techniques in Thucydides; Rood 1998b shows how this method of reading can be applied to the text as a whole. Dewald's 2005 analysis of the structure of the *History* is another fundamental contribution. Less explicitly theoretical but still closely engaged with the interaction between Thucydides' historical narrative and his wider purpose(s) are de Romilly 1956 (who finds an underlying argument for human rationality in Thucydides' account) and Stahl 2003 (who argues for a recurring theme of human error).

8

ELIZABETH IRWIN

Labouring for Truth in Thucydides

Introduction: Exerting Oneself

As he concludes the monumental proem to his *History*, Thucydides reveals to his readers an unpleasant truth about truth (1.20.3): 'So little trouble [*atalaipōros*, lit. 'without labour'] do people [*pollois*, lit. 'the many'] take to search out the truth [*hē zētesis tēs alētheias*], and so readily do they accept what first comes to hand [*ta hetoima*].' Labour, it seems, is a prerequisite for getting at the truth, and – quite frankly – the majority of people simply will not bother; any old version will do. Readers disquieted by this truth, however, need not despair. Two chapters later Thucydides reassures them that, though the many may be work-shy, he himself has spared no effort to investigate the events of his war (1.22.2–3):

> As to the events of the war themselves, however, I resolved not to rely in my writing on what I learned from chance sources or even on my own impressions, but both in the cases where I was present myself and in those where I depended on others I investigated every detail with the utmost concern for accuracy. This was a laborious process of research, because eyewitnesses at the various events reported the same things differently, depending on which side they favoured and on their powers of memory.[1]

Accurate accounts of the past are not easy to come by, to be sure, but readers are told they are in the good hands of a narrator who not only knows what it takes to get at the truth, but expressly intends to share with them the fruits of his labour (1.23.5): 'To explain why they broke the treaty I first set out the reasons they gave and the matters of dispute between them so that no one in future ever need enquire [*tou mē tina zētēsai*, lit. 'search', 'conduct a *zētēsis*'] how it came about that so great a war arose among the Greeks.' Simply put, he's worked hard so they don't have to, and yet generous as this offer may

---

[1] Translations of Thucydides are those of Mynott 2013a, at times lightly altered.

seem, if accepted, it creates an uncomfortable paradox for truth-seekers: Thucydides has invited his readers to eschew the need to conduct their own *zētēsis* for the causes and events and instead to rely on the purported accuracy and truth of what he has made available to them; but in doing so they risk becoming the 'many' whom he has implicitly disparaged just moments earlier. A privileged group of readers is implied – those few who have chosen to pick up the text; but these people, enticed by the display of the proem, are nevertheless implicitly assured that the very thing that would distinguish them from those many unprepared to labour has been rendered unnecessary ('so that no one in future ever need enquire'). Certainly Thucydides' invitation to toil less has been gratefully received by many (however difficult they may find the actual reading of his text to be): his is the version not only reached for (*ta hetoima*) but deemed the authority on the causes and differences of the Atheno-Peloponnesian War; relatively few look elsewhere, and almost all other sources, if consulted, are held in disdain.

This chapter will show that this paradox, standing at the forefront of Thucydides' account, has been designed to stand as an implicit *caveat* to readers that the account he provides of the war will render truth only if they handle it not as the work-shy many, but with their own truth-seeking labour. The term he uses for the former group, the 'many' (*polloi*), implies its contrast, the 'few' (*oligoi*), and both terms, of course, are laden with class and political associations for a late 5th-century BCE Athenian context. And here an uncomfortable inference begins to suggest itself: if one wants to get at the truth about this war, one cannot read with the focalization of 'the many', of the side whose democratic constitution privileges the judgement of the *polloi*; that is, one must not read as Athenians would.[2]

Through the combination of his authoritative rhetorical stance and his confidence that his version will be definitive, Thucydides' text successfully became the version of the war that is 'to hand'. But if readers convinced of his authority or seeking what is convenient accept the results of his laborious *zētēsis* in place of their own, how will they too not become the *polloi* when they reach for it? In what follows, I address the questions of what Thucydides' text requires of readers intending to avoid its trap and what labouring in the *zētēsis* for the truth entails. Section I demonstrates the labour needed to search outside Thucydides to find those events that he has omitted but are crucial to understanding the mounting dissatisfaction with the ethics and policies of Athenian *archē* so responsible for the outbreak

---

[2] As for those prepared to labour, among these would be – above all – the Peloponnesians: Thuc. 1.123.1; Ael. *VH* 13.38; Xen. *Mem.* 2.1.21–34; with Irwin 2013b: 284–5.

of the war. Section II performs a *zētēsis* for the truth found buried in Thucydides' text itself, analysing a famous episode in Thucydides' account of the war – his 'Plague' narrative – to demonstrate how a truer account has been embedded in his text for those prepared to labour for it. In the conclusion, I discuss his motives in presenting events as he has done, as well as the ethics of making the *zētēsis* for the truth about Athenian *archē* and its major proponent require so very much labour.

Section I The Missing Truth: Athenian 'Growth'

Searching for the truth means, first of all, looking for what is not 'to hand'; that is, going outside Thucydides to find out what else there is to know about the history he purports to narrate. The omissions one finds in Thucydides' so-called *Pentecontaetia* (the 'Fifty Years' between the Persian and Atheno-Peloponnesian wars, 1.97–117) should have compromised his credibility forever. Although there he promises an *apodeixis* of the *archē* ('an account of the empire'), 'how it grew', and even criticizes a colleague's version of events (Hellanicus', on which, see Dion. Hal. *Thuc.* 10), his own text is hardly without fault. He never tells readers of the removal of the Delian funds to Athens in 454 BCE. He makes no reference to the Periclean Citizenship Law of 451 BCE ([Arist.] *Ath. Pol.* 26.4 with Irwin 2015b), a law that excluded from citizenship the issue of relations between Athenian citizens and non-Athenians, even members of the Delian League, which had as its ideological basis shared Ionian kinship. Those of mixed descent, their status now that of 'bastards' (*nothoi*), would therefore never be in a position to vote on policies that might govern the disposal of the monies of their common fund located as it now was in Athens. Moreover, Thucydides also never tells readers of a cessation of hostilities with Persia, the so-called Peace of Callias (c. 449 BCE), when technically speaking 'tribute-payment' ought to have also ceased since there was no longer an enemy (Meiggs 1972: ch. 8 and appendix 8). His omission has allowed some to deny that such a peace was made – wrongly, since it both lurks in Herodotus' account of Callias, whose presence in Persia around this time 'for other reasons' is noted (Hdt. 7.151–2) and is entirely consonant with Thucydides' failure to mention a later peace with Darius II (c. 423 BCE), a silence that occurs brazenly in a context in which he is imputing medism to Sparta (Thuc. 4.50 with Rhodes 1998: 242, 'the most serious of his omissions'). Movement of the Delian funds, the Citizenship Law, and peace with Persia, as well as other un-dateable events, such as the requirement that capital offences be tried in Athens, a major complaint of the allies (Thuc. 1.77, [Xen.] *Ath. Pol.* 1.16 with Rhodes 2007: 27; Marr and Rhodes 2008: 90–1; Raaflaub 2009:

106–7) – an accurate account of Athenian 'growth' would require these events to have been recorded.

Some apologists for Thucydides would argue that he simply could not include everything, indeed just as all his omissions could not be included here (on his omissions in the *Pentecontaetia*, see Gomme et al. 1945–81: vol. I, 361–413). That defence might just have worked had there been no pattern visible regarding which side benefitted from his omissions. But it also does not work from a simple comparison of Thucydides with Ephorus on one of the rare occasions in which they present nearly identical material. I speak of Pericles' 'resources speech' at the beginning of the Atheno-Peloponnesian War (Thuc. 2.13.2–9 and Ephorus, *apud* Diod. Sic. 12.39–40). Both authors claim to present *the* speech that Pericles gave to assure the Athenians that their economic superiority over the Peloponnese would guarantee their victory in war. But while both versions of the speech fastidiously list the funds available to Athens in very similar terms, two differences are critical. First, Ephorus specifies what Thucydides does not: that these were the funds that had been transferred to Athens from Delos. Second, there is the timing of the speech in relation to the outbreak of the war: Ephorus places the resource speech *before* the Peloponnesians declare war, whereas Thucydides' account renders the delivery's occurrence as *after* this time. As Thucydides presents it, the Athenians are going to use their own resources to defend their city, having been compelled to do so by a warmongering Peloponnese. By contrast, Ephorus' sequence presents Pericles as persuading the Athenians that they did not need to back down from their policy towards Megara, considered to be a violation of the Thirty Years' Peace, because victory was guaranteed them by the surplus of funds acquired from the Delian League treasury. In this case, only one author can be right about when the speech was first given – and it is far from clear why Ephorus should always have to be the one who is wrong.[3]

Section II The Hidden Truth: Athens' 'Plague'

My main focuses in this chapter are, however, the truth that Thucydides embeds in his text and the kind of labour that his text requires from those readers who seek to find it. I take as a case study the 'Plague'. The truth of this event will have as its background the Athenians' behaviour vis-à-vis the Delian treasury, despite Thucydides' silence regarding it. Historicity – and

---

[3] Thucydides seems to address those who might remember things otherwise (or have sources that do): Thuc. 1.144.1–2 looks forward to the resources speech, while Thuc. 2.13.2–9 implies that its content had been aired frequently before.

indeed epidemiology – aside, the occurrence of a plague is certainly important already in Thucydides' proem as the basis for his assessment of his war's superlative 'greatness' (1.23.3). The Plague was quite simply the most calamitous of those marvellous events that occurred during his war and was on the scale of those things that, when handed down by tradition, are scarcely believable. Thucydides repeats this verdict in the opening of his Plague narrative proper (2.47.3–48.3). When it comes to causes, however, his account becomes rather more complicated. He tells us its origin, or rather a series of things 'said' about it (2.48.1–2):

> It first came, so it is said [*hōs legetai*], out of Ethiopia beyond Egypt, and then spread into Egypt and Libya and into most of the territory of the Persian King. When it got to Athens it struck the city suddenly, taking hold first in the Peiraeus, so that it was even suggested by the people there that the Peloponnesians had put poison in the rain-water tanks (there being no wells yet in the Peiraeus). Later on it reached the upper city too and then the mortality became much greater. I leave it to others – whether physicians or lay people – to speak from their own knowledge about it and say what its likely origins were and what factors could be powerful enough to generate such disruptive effects. For my part I will say what it was like as it happened and will describe the facts that would enable anyone investigating any future outbreak to have some prior knowledge and recognise it. I speak as someone who had the disease myself and witnessed others suffering from it.

Ethiopia 'is said' (*legetai*) to have been where it started, and 'it was said' (*elechthē*) by those in the Piraeus that the Peloponnesians had poisoned their cisterns. Neither claim inspires great confidence, and consequently Thucydides' choice to forgo speculation on origins and causes seems, as he presents it, both sensible (at least if one accepts that they were in fact unknowable) and even admirable, since with it Thucydides seems also to reject unverified calumny about the enemy and chooses instead to provide what he implies will be useful to his readers: a description of the course of the Plague so that it might be recognized should it occur again (2.48.3).

A reader prepared to labour with his text will find, however, that this admiration has been deceptively won. Later in Thucydides' account, it emerges that little practical assistance can be had from his description: if, as he makes explicit (2.51.2–3), no treatment could help, little of any practical good could arise from recognizing the Plague. His lurid description certainly makes for (as he well knew it would) a gripping read, but the utility it purports to offer – that of possible future recognition – has had in practice limited medical value, since diagnosing the Plague from his account has defied consensus among modern readers. The sheer amount of scholarship on the subject demonstrates how highly effective Thucydides' misdirection of readers' labour here (*legatō*: 'let him (i.e. someone else) say') has been.

Thucydides' refusal to go into causes has both a rhetorical function and an agenda. Coming hard upon his reporting the belief of some that the Peloponnesians had poisoned the cisterns, the refusal grants his account the air of objectivity: he seems to dismiss unverified reports of Peloponnesian foul play. 'Seems to dismiss', I say, because in fact he never actually rules out this possibility, and instead has recorded for all time that the Peloponnesians could be thought by some capable of doing such a thing. More importantly, however, such a dismissal also allows him to throw out the search for causes with the poisoned bath (cistern) water, allowing him to evade the task of ascribing responsibility for the Plague without creating the impression that this evasion was intentional. Instead of an account of its cause, he supplies a purple passage, a *logos*, whose engrossing (and at times gross) details distract readers from certain basic questions about how contemporaries explained the outbreak of plague-like conditions in Athens. Religious causes were readily available, such as the choice to break the Thirty Years' Peace and abandon the countryside, Mother Earth (already so conceptualized in Solon 36.4 W), to the ravages of the enemy; so too was a rationalistic one: the overcrowding of the city, particularly the Piraeus, where sources of fresh running water (*krēnai*) did not yet exist – as Thucydides seems to admit, albeit unemphatically. And there was a single person responsible for these situations: Pericles.

Thucydides has already sidestepped the issue of causes just thirty chapters earlier, in chapter 17, when he first alludes to the overcrowding of the city that led to the homeless occupying even sacred precincts, including one under the Acropolis, the so-called Pelargikon:

> When they arrived in Athens only a few of them had homes or places they could take refuge in with friends or relatives. Most settled in uninhabited parts of the city and occupied the sanctuaries and the shrines of heroes, except for the Acropolis and the Eleusinium and anywhere else that was securely closed off. Occupation of the area called the Pelargikon under the Acropolis was actually forbidden by a curse and there was even the tail-end of a Pythian oracle to the same effect, which said: 'better the Pelargikon unused'. Nevertheless, under the pressure of the moment it too was fully occupied. *And it seems to me that the oracle was in fact fulfilled in the opposite way to what they expected. It was not because of the unlawful occupation that troubles were visited on the city, but the necessity of occupation was because of the war,* although that was not mentioned when the oracle foretold that no good would ever come from its occupation. (2.17.1–2, emphasis added)

According to Thucydides, the religious folk have got cause and effect inverted – they *believe* that occupying the Pelargikon *caused* the bad to happen, but it is rather the case that the necessity of occupying sacred land was a *result* of a bad situation such as the war was (Longrigg 2000: 57). No less deft at manipulating oracles than Themistocles, Thucydides sidesteps precisely the questions of whether a war policy should have been adopted that would lead to such overcrowding as would require occupation of sacred land and whether the war should have been allowed to break out at all.

He likewise deploys his evasive strategy in the Plague narrative itself. There Thucydides will finally admit, in chapter 52, that the overcrowding in the city had some part to play in the epidemic. This admission, however, occurs at some great distance from the Plague's origin, both in terms of narrative (some four gripping chapters later) and in terms of geography (Ethiopia, at least as 'it is said'). But other authors reflect causes closer to home. Libanius is likely to be reflecting classical sources when he adduces Pericles as a well-known example of how whole communities suffer for the wrongdoing of a single man (*Orat. ad Antioch.* (16) 50–1). He places the Athenian general among *mythical* examples in a passage where plague is prominent, and he groups Pericles with the likes of Oedipus and Agamemnon:

> Who does not know how the army of the Achaeans was seized by Plague through the wrong doing of Agamemnon, how at sea they suffered on account of the crime of Ajax. Did not the Athenians pay the penalty as a collective for the hybris of Pericles towards Megara, and the Thebans suffered plague when Oedipus killed Laios and did so although Oedipus was ignorant of whom he killed?

Divine anger as a source of disease was a traditional belief, and as such would certainly have suggested itself to contemporaries, whether owing to their own religious conviction or in order to discredit Pericles, or a mixture of both. Moreover, to audiences weaned on the *Iliad*, Apollo would have seemed the obvious god to be responsible for such a disease. Thucydides records that Delphic Apollo supported the rightness of the Peloponnesian cause (2.54.4), and himself encourages readers to adopt the literary focalization of the *Iliad*'s plague (see e.g. Woodman 1988: ch. 1): the rough dismissal of the Spartan herald owing to the motion initiated in the assembly by Pericles is evocative of Agamemnon's treatment of Chryses, leading, in Thucydides' narrative at least, to the herald's Iliadic allusion to this day becoming 'the beginning of evils' (Thuc. 2.12.3; *Il.* 5.63, 11.604, 22.16). And then plague fell. But this literary precedent for Apollo's anger may distract readers from a search for historical reasons for the god's wrath – that is, those religious reasons voiced by contemporaries at the time. Diodorus, likely relying on Ephorus, reveals that the Athenians attempted to appease *Delian* Apollo to counter the Plague. It had 'seemed', he says, that Delos had become tainted by burials, and so they purified the island by removing the corpses and reinstated the festival of the Delia, which had ceased to be observed for some time (Diod. Sic. 12.58). Thucydides of course mentions the purification – the consequence, he says, of 'some oracle' – but he provides no further clarification (3.104.1–2). Rather, he chooses instead to furnish so elaborate and diverting a Homeric digression as to distract philologists – ironically the *oligoi* among readers – from the question of causes and to facilitate the erroneous assumption that the interruption in the celebration of the Delia occurred in the remote past, much closer to Homeric times than 425 BCE. But without a doubt neglect of the Delia belonged to recent times: more precisely, sometime after 454 BCE when the tribute of the Delian League ceased to be brought there annually. The interruption of the festival for this reason, however, is a fact that Thucydides no doubt wanted to hide from readers since he has already hidden from them the removal of the funds from Delos in the first place.

Both Diodorus' account and Thucydides, however, admit to ambiguity regarding the cause that they state for Apollo's anger and the Athenians' response. Diodorus says, 'as it seems [*dokousan*]' (12.58.6), it was owing to the defilement of burials in Delos, and Thucydides claims that most of the Delia had been discontinued 'through misfortunes [*hupo xumphorōn*]', 'as is likely [*hōs eikos*]', but this is a rather disingenuous way to speak when the likely misfortunes were those he knew very well to have been caused by the Athenians. In fact, the supposition that a god was angry, whether at the violation of the Thirty Years' Peace (the *hubris* of Pericles towards Megara, as Libanius puts it) or the appropriation of Delian funds to adorn the Athenian acropolis and then to wage war against other Greeks, or both, seems to be what was historically likely to have been a common view; moreover, it is a view that can be detected in Thucydides' own account – for those prepared to roll up their sleeves and do a little work with the text, as we will now do.

First of all, this is a view that Thucydides will eventually admit. After the lurid and lengthy Plague narrative, readers will learn that among the Athenians there were those who found an explanation in religion, in an oracle that seemed to predict the Plague (2.54.2):

And in their distress they not surprisingly remembered the following verse, which the old men claimed had been recited long ago, 'A Dorian war shall come and with it plague [*loimos*].' There was some disagreement among them as to whether the word used by the men of old was not 'plague' [*loimos*] but 'famine' [*limos*], but in the present circumstances the view naturally prevailed that it was 'plague', as people matched their memories to their sufferings. I fancy at any rate that if another Dorian war should visit them after this one and if that were accompanied by a famine they would probably recite the verse that way. There were those who also recalled an oracle given to the Spartans when the Spartans asked the god whether they should go to war and he answered that victory would be theirs if they fought with all their might and promised that he would himself take their side. They therefore supposed that what then happened was the fulfilment of the oracle, and indeed the plague did begin straight after the invasion of the Peloponnesians; and although it did not get into the Peloponnese to any significant extent, it invaded Athens in particular and after that other densely populated areas elsewhere.

By pointing out the possibility that the *loimos* of the oracle will no doubt at some point be construed as *limos* in the future, should the situation arise,[4] Thucydides seems to dismiss the validity of religious interpretations of the cause of the Plague. His evoking as a truism the capacity of people to alter their memories to suit the occasion serves to undermine the possibility that their current interpretation may be correct.

I say 'seems to dismiss' any religious interpretation – an interpretation that has to do with a foretold Dorian war – because Thucydides would have expected privileged readers to appreciate two allusions lurking in this passage that in turn point to who and what should be held accountable for the plague. One allusion is literary. In Hesiod's *Works and Days* (240–3), the poet tells how 'one bad man' can be responsible for the collective ills of his city:

> Often even a whole city suffers for a bad man [*kakou andros*] who sins and devises presumptuous deeds, and the son of Cronos lays great trouble upon the people, famine and plague together [*limon homou kai loimon*], so that the people perish away … (trans. Evelyn-White 1914)

The difference between *loimos* and *limos* here becomes immaterial; what matters is the one bad man who is responsible, and in the case of Athens that man could only be Pericles – at least such was thought by Libanius' sources, and likely was implied in Sophocles' *Oedipus Tyrannos*.[5] The second allusion is historical and belongs to an event that Thucydides has not narrated, though it was one that he clearly knew (e.g. 2.65.12, 5.26.1): namely, the end of the war. There would be a (second) Dorian war, and it would be the consequence of a renewal of the Athenians' disastrous expansionist policies originally formulated by that same man. And this time, the Dorian war

---

[4] Furley 2006: 419.   [5] Knox 1956, 1957; most recently Mitchell-Boyask 2008: 56–66.

brought *limos* ('starvation') in 405/404 BCE through a blockade of the Piraeus (Xen. *Hell.* 2.2.10–11; cf. Diod. Sic. 13.107.4):

> Now the Athenians, being thus besieged by land and by sea, knew not what to do, since they had neither ships nor allies nor provisions; and they thought that there was no way out, save only to suffer the pains which they had themselves inflicted, not in retaliation, but in wantonness and unjustly upon the people of small states, for no other single reason than because they were in alliance with the Lacedaemonians. On this account they restored to the disfranchised their political rights and held out steadfastly, refusing to make overtures for peace even though many were dying in the city from starvation [*limos*].

In dismissing the religious from his narrative, Thucydides may have sought to garner the approval of rationalist readers of his day and the future, but this dismissal had another purpose: for it is a way to dismiss moral evaluations from his narrative without this seeming to have been his intention, since what he seems to be dismissing – rationally to us – is a religious explanation. But leaving aside the concomitant dismissal of a moral viewpoint implied in the religious, this dismissal is problematic in terms of his own project. For even if he did not subscribe to the truth of the religious beliefs expressed at the time, the removal of religious arguments against Pericles when their existence was a historical phenomenon must be recognized as a falsification of the historical record. It belonged to a true account of the war, but thanks to the occluding power of Thucydides' *logos*, so ready to hand, it can be found only through some considerable effort.

Moreover, Thucydides hedges his bets on what the future will know. His use of allusion here – literary to Hesiod and historical to the end of the war – is designed precisely to convey to the privileged few the truth that he both knows and worries they too might know and expect from him given the pretentions of his proem, while allowing him simultaneously to tell an entirely different story to the *polloi* for whom the *zētēsis* of the truth is too difficult an affair. While many of those privileged few will admire the subtlety of his embedded critique, it remains possible for the *oligoi* among them to realize that, although Thucydides hasn't exactly lied, he may be found morally culpable for making the truth – and indeed a moral truth – require such exertion. Moreover, although the first level of intelligent readers may be satisfied with the truth they find in this critique, it falls far short of what Pericles deserves. There is, however, insufficient space here to go deeply into Thucydides' portrayal of that figure,[6] for there is one further step to this

---

[6] On this, see Samons 2007; Vogt 2009; and more recently Azoulay 2014; Samons 2016.

demonstration of the labour required to garner truth from Thucydides' Plague narrative.

Thucydides' 'Summer of Plague' continues: during that same summer, when the Peloponnesians were ravaging the countryside and plague was killing the Athenians, Pericles mounted the largest expedition of the Ten Years' War, an armament in fact equal in size to that sent to Sicily. He led a hundred Athenian ships and fifty of the allies' with the purpose of ravaging the coast of the Peloponnese and of drawing the Spartans away from Attica – and no doubt also to escape the Plague in the city. Despite its scale, the campaign had absolutely no effect.[7] The Spartans' second invasion was the longest of the war – forty days – and accomplished little. Although at one point it is claimed that the Athenians expected to take Epidaurus, in the end they captured only tiny Prasiae. Thucydides' *logos*, however, neither acknowledges explicitly the mediocrity of the *erga* nor explains this failure. Plutarch, however, provides a more explicit assessment and an explanation (*Per.* 35, emphasis added):

> On sailing forth, Pericles seems to have accomplished nothing worthy of his preparations, but after laying siege to *sacred* Epidaurus [*tēn hieran Epidauron*], which awakened a hope that it might be captured, he had no such good fortune, because of the plague. Its fierce onset destroyed not only the Athenians themselves, but also those who, in any manner so ever, had dealings with their forces.

Plutarch's application of the label 'sacred' to Epidaurus makes readers aware of the choice to assail Epidaurus of all places when one's city is afflicted by plague. Since it is likely that the Athenians were being denied access to the healing sanctuary during the war, the choice to storm the city of the healing god does not seem to have been random, and the contradictory notions of piety it suggests point to desperation. Indeed, the fact that, hard upon the Peace of Nicias, the Athenians introduced Asclepius into the city suggests the desire not to find themselves ever in such a vulnerable position again.[8]

Plutarch's account otherwise challenges Thucydides' version of events. For while both authors report of plague breaking out in the fleet, Plutarch says this happened at Epidaurus, while Thucydides places the occurrence of the epidemic later at Potidaea. There is nothing inherently implausible in either's claim that plague broke out among the fleet, since it was unlikely not to have been latent among some within such a huge force. But where did the disease break out? Traditionally, we follow Thucydides, the contemporary, and dismiss Plutarch, who either himself conflated the besieging of 'sacred'

[7] Westlake 1969: ch. 5.   [8] Garland 1992: 118; Parker 1996: 180.

Epidaurus with an outbreak of plague or preferred a source that did: such an opportunity to recount instantaneous divine punishment was too good to be resisted, and yet also, we feel certain, too poetic to be true. That dismissal may, however, be too convenient: given Thucydides' own preferences – an author ever averse to allowing religion into his text[9] – it is just as possible that he is the one who has intentionally altered events, moving the plague away from the inauspicious besieging of 'sacred Epidaurus' where it could be construed as punishment of his one and only, Pericles. We would seem to be stuck in *aporia*, and in such cases Thucydides' account always prevails.

In this case, that he should win out is remarkable, since a closer examination of his own account (2.55.2–58) makes explicit (albeit unemphatically) that the *erga* were as Plutarch describes. And yet it is understandable. Most readers 'switch off' when they encounter the seemingly rhetoric-free style and the mind-numbing detail of this tedious passage (quoted in whole below to demonstrate the point, and with emphasis added):

> *Pericles, however, who was general*, still held to the same opinion he had had at the time of the earlier invasion: namely, that the Athenians should not go out to oppose them. Nonetheless, *while the Peloponnesians were still in the plain and before they reached the coast, Pericles began preparing a naval force* of a hundred ships to attack the Peloponnese and when they were ready he put to sea. He took on board these ships 4,000 Athenian hoplites and 300 cavalry on horse-transports that were newly constructed from old vessels; and with them went a further force of fifty ships from Chios and Lesbos. *When the Athenian force set sail they had left the Peloponnesians occupying the coastal district of Attica. On reaching Epidaurus in the Peloponnese they despoiled most of the land there and then attacked the city. They had some hopes of taking it but did not succeed.* Putting to sea again from Epidaurus they despoiled the land at the Troezen, Halieis and Hermione, all of them coastal areas of the Peloponnese. They then set off from there and came to Prasiae, a coastal town in Laconia, where they wasted the land, captured the town itself and destroyed it. *After these operations they returned home, where they found that the Peloponnesians were no longer in Attica but had also withdrawn. All the time the Peloponnesians were in Athenian territory and the Athenians were away on naval ventures the plague was taking its toll both of the Athenians in the armed forces and those in the city.* Indeed it was even said that the Spartans were making haste to leave the territory through their fear of the plague, since they learned from those deserting the city that it was present there and they could at the same time see people burying their dead. But *in this invasion they did in fact stay longer than ever before and despoiled all the land, remaining in Attica for about forty days.*

---

[9] Hornblower 1992.

During *the same summer Hagnon* son of Nicias and Cleopompus son of Cleinias, who were fellow generals with Pericles, *took over the army he had employed and went straight on to attack the Chalcidians in Thrace and Potidaea* (which was still under siege). On their arrival they brought siege-engines to bear on Potidaea and did all they could to take it. *But they made no progress either in capturing the city or in achieving any other objective commensurate with their efforts; for the plague had attacked them here too and was a terrible affliction for the Athenians, wreaking destruction on their army as even soldiers who had previously been healthy now caught the disease from those in Hagnon's army.* (Phormio, and his 1,600 men, however, were no longer in the Chalcidice.) *Hagnon therefore returned to Attica with his ships, having in the space of about forty days lost to the plague 1,050 hoplites from a total of 4,000, while the original force of soldiers stayed in the area and went on besieging Potidaea.*

According to Thucydides, Pericles sets out while the Peloponnesians are in the Paralia, and he returns with his fleet after they have left for the Peloponnese. At that point, his fleet, now under Hagnon, sails to Potidaea where, far from Epidaurus, plague prevents them from accomplishing anything 'worthy of their preparations' (*oute talla tēs paraskeuēs axiōs*), a phrase similar to that used by Plutarch, albeit of Epidaurus (*out' allo ti dokei tēs paraskeuēs axion drasai*). Difficult to see as it is tucked safely away in the middle of a welter of detail is the text's explicit confession that the Plague had broken out in the army under Pericles in the campaign that included the siege of Epidaurus: 'all the time the Peloponnesians were in Athenian territory and the Athenians were away on naval ventures the plague was taking its toll both of the Athenians in the armed forces and those in the city'. Thucydides seems to cover his tracks by then having Pericles' fleet go directly (*euthus*) to Potidaea, where he can then be explicit about the Plague breaking out in Pericles' force, or rather what *had been* Pericles' force, without evoking any religious associations that would make it seem like the healing god had punished the army who dared to besiege 'sacred Epidaurus'. And here the name of Pericles' replacement, Hagnon ('Undefiled'), is rather conveniently auspicious given that he has 'cleansed' Pericles' campaign of any suggestion of impiety that an outbreak of plague during it might lead one to infer.[10] Moreover, that Hagnon's campaign is said to have been, like that of the Peloponnesians, also forty days is designed to lull an inattentive

---

[10] On 'speaking names' in Thucydides, see Hornblower 2000. Hagnon's plague-ridden Potidaean campaign is also recounted by Diodorus (12.46), who, however, places it in the subsequent archon year. Thucydides' dating is always preferred, and yet, given the difficulties his account presents (e.g. the awkwardness of the reference to Phormio (which Gomme et al. 1945–81: vol. II, 165 call 'a remarkable piece of careless writing by

reader into thinking that these are the *same* forty days, but of course they were not.

Conclusion

I conclude with the obvious question raised by our labour: why would Thucydides have gone to the added labour of making his readers have to conduct their own should they want the truth? A generous reading might understand Thucydides as having deemed this the most powerful way to demonstrate an important, yet implicit, lesson that he felt compelled to impart, albeit to his more thoughtful readers. But the point might have been felt so important as to warrant a less arduous didactic method, one less prone to many of his readers' misconstrual – or perhaps better said 'half-construal'. For when readers find, as they have, opposing views of Athens and Pericles and then claim one or the other as the 'real' view of their historian, they fail to recognize that the double-sidedness of his *logos* has been intentionally designed to render them responsible for their understanding of the war and the actions of its proponents, whether (as the majority) they accept Thucydides' account more or less at face value or (as many within the privileged few) they accept the sincerity of the critique that they understand to be articulated in their more sophisticated reading. One might say that the text manufactures a kind of complicity, whether with Athens or with Thucydides.

On this understanding, the complexity of Thucydides' account – its dual argument – has to do with the portrayal of Pericles and *archē* that Thucydides wishes to present to his contemporary Athenian readers and to the future. In the case of the former, his account courts them with a sophistically wrought vision of how they might – after all that they had done – still become a source of 'wonder' for the future: he will hand down a version of the war with which Athenians can be content, one in which Periclean policy and *archē* were not flawed from their inception but derailed owing to his premature death during Athens' epidemic and the inferior leadership of those who followed (Thuc. 2.65).

In terms of our case study of Section II, the rhetorical 'achievement' of Thucydides' account is to present a 'Plague' at Athens without it carrying its customary religious – that is, ethical – interpretation: it has to be a 'Plague' so that it is unforeseeable, 'greater than *elpis*', as Pericles claims (2.64.1), and as such therefore capable of exculpating Pericles from the charge of flawed

---

Thucydides') and to the 'earlier soldiers'), the possibility that he has moved the event forward cannot be ruled out.

calculations, thereby preserving the reputation of his superlative *sunesia* ('intelligence'), and also capable of elevating the war to Homeric proportions. Moreover, it renders the Athenian defeat (which goes unnarrated by Thucydides) less of a victory for Sparta – for who would have won, readers are led to ask, had there not been a plague? 'Certainly not the Peloponnesians', readers might obediently conclude, although we might understand from what we've been told that had there been no plague the Peloponnesian forces would have stayed much longer than the forty days that they did (the longest campaign in the war) and brought the war to an end that summer.

The truth may be rather more simple, after conducting some labour required from us by the text: Pericles was responsible for the 'Plague', creating as he did conditions ripe for disease(s) of epidemic proportions; and the Athenians shared the responsibility because they continued to follow him. But Thucydides is responsible for future readers' focalization of these conditions as 'Plague' – his *logos* has distorted the *erga*. What afflicted Athens need not have been one exceptional illness, as Thucydides so aggressively asserts, nor 'from Ethiopia' as hearsay said, but instead more mundane, common illnesses taken to superlative heights because of overcrowding. Perhaps one was predominant: typhus and smallpox have been thought of as the forerunners, but now DNA analysis has begun – not without controversy – to suggest typhoid as the likely culprit (Papagrigorakis et al. 2006a, 2006b), a disease historically often concomitant with typhus. One can best see the effects of Thucydides' account – the misdirection of labour – in the modern 'at-hand' source, Wikipedia, where, for example, typhoid is ruled out: 'as the disease is most commonly transmitted through poor hygiene habits and public sanitation conditions, it is an unlikely cause of a widespread plague, emerging in Africa and moving into the Greek city states, as reported by Thucydides'. Thus goes the version of the *polloi* who have been encouraged to make a medical diagnosis rather than a moral one.

Thucydides followed the textbook rhetorical practices of his day: the way to deceive successfully – as Socrates makes clear was well known – is to make a 'likeness' of the truth and distort it by increments, making small departures (*Phaedr.* 261e–2b, 273d), for then the similarity of this new version to what people think they know will induce them to accept it – so readily to hand – as the truth. For to do otherwise would seem too much like work. Of course, readers can be held responsible for how they respond to the text, whether and how they choose to labour in their reading and indeed just how they choose to react to what their labour yields, should they uncover the critique of Pericles and his Athens that Thucydides has prepared for only the few to find. Will they refrain from passing judgement, as they are entitled to do, on an author who has chosen to make it so laborious for all but the few to see a truth that had been clear at the time even to some among the Athenian *polloi*? And how will they react if they recognize that such truth might constitute a reading of the text that is, admittedly, more sophisticated, but also dangerously complicit?

Further Reading

A solid treatment of Thucydides' account of the *Pentecontaetia* ('Fifty Years'), including a catalogue of his omissions, can be found in Gomme et al. 1945–81: vol. I, 361–413. For the transformation of Athens' leadership of the Delian League to possession of an *archē* ('empire') of subjects, see Meiggs 1943, 1972, as well as Rhodes 1993b, 2007. The collection of ancient sources by Hose 2006 renders the search for the truth about the Atheno-Peloponnesian War marginally less arduous, and Plutarch's *Life of Pericles* (with the useful companion of Podlecki 1987) is indispensable for its diverse collection of 5th-century BCE sources. Flower 2009 is a good place to start on the subject of religion during the Atheno-Peloponnesian War, and Furley 2006 discusses Thucydides' handling of it.

For modern discussions of Thucydides that challenge his (self-)portrayal as the objective historian, see Woodman 1988: ch. 1; Green 2004; Loraux 2011 [1980]. Connor 1985 (with the response of Robinson 1985) provides a good short analysis of the means whereby Thucydides manufactures the authority and status that his work has come to enjoy, which is further elaborated upon by Rood 2006; on this, see also Beasley (Chapter 3). The dual nature of Thucydides' portrayal of Pericles is manifest in scholarship on the subject: Vogt 2009, for example, embodies the more traditional positive reading, while the potential to read a (subtle) critique was seminally discussed by Connor 1984b. For the multiple readings Thucydides expected of his readers, see Rawlings 2016.

Further reading on the Athenian 'Plague' is endless and multifaceted, dealing as it does with the literary, cultural and epidemiological aspects of Thucydides' account. The most rewarding recent treatments are those of Demont 2013, Kallet 2013b and Bruzzone 2017, who cite the expected bibliography on the subject, while Marshall 1990 deserves much more attention than it has hitherto garnered.

PART II

Themes and Content

9

JASON CROWLEY

Thucydides and War

It is a privilege to have Thucydides' account of the Peloponnesian War. Even unfinished, his text is invaluable, not just because of its author's impressive intellect,[1] but because Thucydides, unlike his predecessor, Herodotus, or the later tacticians, like Asclepiodotus, married those impressive intellectual qualities to the authority he brought to his subject not just as a mere participant,[2] but as a participant with senior command experience.[3]

As he himself explains, he was elected as one of Athens' ten *stratēgoi* for 424 BCE[4] when he was in his mid-thirties.[5] Autobiography, however, was not Thucydides' aim, and this appointment is merely the visible apex of a military career that is impossible to reconstruct. Nevertheless, given the propensity of the Athenian *dēmos* to elect and re-elect commanders with extensive experience and proven competency, it seems likely that, at the time of his appointment, Thucydides satisfied both criteria.[6] His elevated socio-economic status[7] suggests he may have served aboard ship as *trierarchos* or on horseback in Athens' semi-professionalized cavalry corps.[8] Hoplite service, however, was attractive to the Athenian elite,[9] and given the ideological

---

[1] Hornblower 1994b: 136–90, 191–250; Hunt 2006: 385–413; see also n. 17.

[2] For the military limitations of Herodotus, see Lazenby 1993: 68–70; Hornblower 1994b: 198–204; Vela Tejada 2004: 136–7; Hunt 2006: 389; and for those of Asclepiodotus, see Hornblower 1994b: 191–250; Oldfather 1923: 229–43.

[3] For Thucydides as soldier, see Hornblower 1994b: 73–109, 191–205; Hunt 2006: 385–413.

[4] Thuc. 4.104.4; cf. Cawkwell 1987: 1–19.

[5] Thuc. 5.26.5; Hansen 1980: 167–9, 1999: 88–90, 227–8.

[6] Hamel 1998: 14–23, with Arist. *Ath. Pol.* 22.2, 61.1–2, 64.4; Plato *Gorgias* 455b–c; [Xen.] *Ath. Pol.* 1.3; Xen. *Ap.* 20, *Oec.* 20.6–9, *Mem.* 1.7.3; cf. Plato *Laws* 6.755b–756b; Thuc. 6.72.1–2; Xen. *Mem.* 2.1.28.

[7] Thuc. 4.105.1; Hornblower 1994b: 1–6.

[8] For this division of labour, see, e.g., Arist. *Ath. Pol.* 7.3–4 (on the connection between wealth and cavalry service); Lys. 21.5–10 (on trierarchies).

[9] Lys. 14.4–10, 16.13; Crowley 2012: 23–4, 124.

and military primacy of the phalanx,[10] it seems unlikely that the *dēmos* would elect Thucydides to the *strategeia* if he had never served in the ranks as a hoplite or a subordinate commander.[11]

Certainly, to be an effective *stratēgos*, Thucydides had to be able to command on both land and sea,[12] and at the high point of his military career, when he was assigned to an area of operations around Amphipolis,[13] he was doing just that.[14] The apex of Thucydides' career, of course, was also its conclusion,[15] but his subsequent exile not only allowed him to devote himself fully to his account of the war; it also allowed him to interrogate the Spartans and their allies, and therefore offer a view of the conflict from both 'sides of the hill'.[16]

The Autonomy of War

Thucydides' view of the war, then, was inclusive, but it was not impartial. By carefully selecting the events he presents, their emphasis, order, content, context and collocation, and by manipulating his reader's emotional engagement with his text, Thucydides attempts to guide his reader's interpretation, and ensure that interpretation is sympathetic to his main aim, which is to provide a timeless understanding of human conflict.[17] In doing so, Thucydides envisions a war that is not merely a bellicose state that exists in opposition to peace, but one that functions like an autonomous third force that imposes upon its human creators its own dark dynamic in which chance

[10] Karavites 1984: 185–9; Connor 1988: 21–9; Hanson 1996: 289–312, 2005: 198; Cartledge 1998b: 62–3; Pritchard 1998: 44–52; Runciman 1998: 733; Strauss 2000: 292–7; Roisman 2002: 136–41, 2005: 106–7, 109, 111; Crowley 2012: 100–4.

[11] Crowley 2012: 35, 117, 123–4, with progression through the ranks envisaged and contravened in Xen. *Mem.* 3.4.1; cf. Xen. *Eq. Mag.* 2.1–7.

[12] Since commands and the forces allocated to them were mission-orientated (Thuc. 3.91.1–2, 4.2.1–4, 27.5–28.3, 90.1, 5.2.1, 6.8.1–26.2, 7.16.1–17.1, with Hamel 1998: 14–23), combined operations were common (Thuc. 4.3.1–40.2, 89.1–101.4, 6.25.1–26.2, 31.1–32.2, 43.1–44.1, 94.4, 98.1–4, 7.33.3–6, 42.1–2), as was coordination with naval assets (Thuc. 4.3.1–40.2, 6.25.1–26.1, 36.1–41.4). See also Lazenby 2004: 1–15; Hunt 2006: 385–413; Wheeler 2007: 186–223.

[13] Thuc. 4.105.1. It seems likely that Thucydides' connections in this area made him particularly suitable for this assignment. For further discussion, see Sears 2013: 74–89, and for other evidence of Thucydides' particular interest in and knowledge of Thrace, see Fragoulaki (Chapter 11).

[14] Thuc. 4.104.1–7.3.   [15] Thuc. 5.26.5; Ellis 1978: 28–35.

[16] Thuc. 4.104.1–107.2, 5.26.5; Westlake 1980: 333–9; cf. Liddell Hart 1948, which demonstrates the problems entailed by such access.

[17] Thuc. 1.22.1–4, 3.82.2; Hunter 1973: 177–84; Connor 1984b: 3–19, 231–50; Hornblower 1994a: 59–99, 1994c: 34–44; Rood 1998b: 3–23, 285–93; Dewald 2005: 1–22, 155–63; Raaflaub 2013: 3–21.

reigns supreme.[18] In this unpredictable environment, men cannot control their own destinies, and, subject to capriciously changing circumstances, they suffer reversals of fortune and undeserved denouement.[19]

Thucydides' war is also the realm of both continuity and change: war itself remains a constant force, but because the environment it creates is morally and culturally corrosive, those who operate under its influence become progressively brutalized.[20] This is not, however, to say that, for Thucydides, war was without a certain glory, or that, subject to its dark dictates, men were entirely impotent.[21] By the time Thucydides was writing, the art of war was highly advanced, and in the furtherance of their operational aims, commanders could rely on a range of military specialisms, as well as the combined arms tactics required for their coordination.[22]

The Art of War

As Thucydides reveals, such military forces were task-dependent, and although their strength and composition reflected the aims for which they were mobilized, they were normally formed around a core of hoplites[23] whose primary role was to engage the enemy in close-quarters combat.[24] Unfortunately, whilst the role of hoplites is understood, how exactly they discharged it remains the subject of an ongoing debate for which Thucydides is partially to blame.

He wrote for a militarily informed audience who did not require a description of interpersonal combat, and so he left this aspect of warfare undescribed.[25] Consequently, whilst it is clear that hoplites offset their lack of tactical mobility by adopting a rank-and-file formation called a phalanx,

---

[18] Thuc. 1.78.1, 122.1, 140.1, 2.11.4, 3.30.4, 4.17.4–5, 18.1–5, 55.1–4, 62.3–4, 5.14.3–4, 7.61.1–3; Hornblower 1994b: 155–90.

[19] Consider, for instance, the Thebans at Plataea in 431 BCE, who were killed when their relief force was delayed by unexpected rain (Thuc. 2.2.1–5.7; cf. 5.26.5, 7.86.1–5). See also Adkins 1975: 379–92; Roisman 1993: 11–22; Golfin 2011: 213–39.

[20] Thuc. 3.82.2; Lateiner 1977a; Connor 1984b: 79–107; Pritchett 1991: 218–19; Hornblower 1994b: 155–90; Luce 1997: 86–98; Kallet 2001; Hanson 2005: 65–121, 163–99, 271–314; Hunt 2006: 402–3; Strauss 2007: 240–7; Nevin 2008: 99–120.

[21] Consider Thucydides' portrayals of Brasidas, Demosthenes and Themistocles (see ns. 96 and 112).

[22] See n. 12.

[23] Thuc. 2.13.6–9, 31.1–3, 54.1–4, 4.89.1–101.4, 5.61.1–5, 66.1–74.3; Lazenby 1985: 16–17; Hunt 2007: 108–46; Crowley 2012: 22–6.

[24] Hanson 1991: 63–84; Lazenby 1991: 87–109; Schwartz 2009: 79–95.

[25] Grundy 1911: 240–2; Gomme et al. 1945–81: vol. I, 10–24; Hunt 2006: 385–13; Whitby 2007: 54–81; Rhodes 2008: 83–8; Crowley 2012: 40–1.

it is not clear how this formation operated whilst in contact with the enemy.[26]

Naturally, this problem has attracted significant scholarship, yet interpretation is so underdetermined by evidence that two mutually exclusive models of hoplite combat currently coexist. Orthodox scholars argue that the phalanx was a close-order formation in which all ranks pushed forward whilst the front rank engaged the enemy in weaponized combat,[27] whereas others envisage a less rigid system in which the front rank engaged their opponents in relatively open-order combat whilst those to their rear replaced casualties and provided protective depth and moral support.[28]

Thankfully, despite this ambiguity, the reason why composite forces were formed around a core of hoplites remains obvious: in main force encounters, the outcome of battle is decided by opposing phalanxes.[29] Such engagements thus formed the *schwerpunkt* of battle, and since this encouraged concentration of force, Greek armies usually fought without the benefit of a tactical reserve.[30] The amateur nature of most Greek hoplites also encouraged tactical simplicity,[31] and during Thucydides' time there were only three main approaches to battle: the professionals of Sparta preferred flanking manoeuvres,[32] the Thebans favoured the deepened column[33] and the Athenians, and presumably the rest of the Greeks, were limited to linear battle, in which phalanx met phalanx in a brutal trial of strength.[34] Each approach, whilst distinct, relies on the same foundation, which Thucydides and other Greek authors call *eutaxia*.

---

[26] Consider Kagan and Viggiano 2013: xi–xxi.

[27] See Grundy 1911: 267–73; Hanson 1991: 63–84, 2000: 171–84; Luginbill 1994: 51–61; Schwartz 2009: 187–94; Crowley 2012: 57–66.

[28] See van Wees 2004: 172–91, with similar views in Cawkwell 1978: 150–3, 1989: 375–89; Krentz 1985: 50–61; Goldsworthy 1997: 5–25; Rawlings 2000: 233–59; Matthew 2009: 395–415.

[29] Consider the battles of Delium, 424 BCE (Thuc. 4.89.1–101.4), Mantinea, 418 BCE (5.66.1–74.3), and Syracuse, 415 BCE (6.67.1–70.4).

[30] For an exception, see Thuc. 6.67.1–70.4 (Syracuse, 415 BCE).

[31] Hence the need for professional units like the Theban Sacred Band (Plut. *Pel.* 17–19; Xen. *Hell.* 7.1.19) and the one thousand men the Argives maintained at state expense (Thuc. 5.67.2). For Spartan professionalism, see Arist. *Pol.* 8.1338b; Plato *Laches* 182e–183a; Thuc. 2.39.1–4; Xen. *Lac. Pol.* 7.1–6, 11.1–8. For military training generally, see Pritchett 1974: 208–31; Tritle 1989: 54–9; Hunt 2007: 108–46; van Wees 2007: 273–99; Crowley 2012: 2–3, 25–6, 34, 50, 64, 70, 81, 117, 123–4.

[32] Consider the battles of 1st Mantinea, 418 BCE (Thuc. 5.66.1–74.3) and Nemea, 394 BCE (Xen. *Hell.* 4.2.13–23).

[33] Consider the battles of Delium, 424 BCE (Thuc. 4.89.1–101.1), and Leuctra, 371 BCE (Xen. *Hell.* 6.4.8–15).

[34] Consider the Battle of Syracuse, 415 BCE (Thuc. 6.67.1–70.4).

Sadly, beyond a sense of 'good order', the precise meaning of this term is not clear. However, since the root of the word relates to arrangement, and since the phalanx is an arrangement of men by rank and file, the term most likely describes a formation whose constituent hoplites are successfully maintaining their assigned positions, which was vital for three reasons.[35] Firstly, the lateral deployment of files, and the serried ranks this produces, results in a deep formation naturally resistant to penetration. Secondly, the first rank, by presenting a wall of shields and spear points facing the enemy, provides the phalanx with its capacity for both attack and defence. Thirdly, casualties sustained in this front rank can be replaced by surviving members of each damaged file, who move forward to take the place of the fallen, thereby maintaining the continuity of the shield wall and the phalanx's concomitant capacity for combat.[36]

Eutaxia, then, is the difference between an army and an armed mob. As such, it functions in Thucydidean battle narratives as a precondition, if not an actual guarantee, of victory, whereas the loss of *eutaxia*, and the progressive descent into its antonymic condition, *ataxia*, is the precursor of inevitable defeat.[37] For Thucydides, therefore, battles were won by well-ordered hoplites, but they are not the only type of warrior to appear in his narrative.

Cavalry, of course, also had an important part to play, albeit one limited by the underdeveloped nature of Greek equestrianism. This restricted Greek horsemen to the role of light cavalry, in which the horse acted as a mobile weapons platform from which the rider discharged a missile, usually a javelin, at an oblique angle as he moved past his target.[38] In addition, Thucydides describes another type of cavalryman, armed with a bow, although it is not clear from his narrative whether the horse archer possessed the requisite skills to engage his enemy on the move or whether he did so merely at the halt or after dismounting.[39]

Light infantry, who rely primarily on missiles in combat, also appear in Thucydides' narrative. Beyond the baggage carriers, who merely threw

---

[35] Crowley 2012: 49–53, see also Pritchett 1985: 44–93; Wheeler 2007: 186–223.

[36] Crowley 2012: 53.

[37] Consider how Thucydides depicts the Battle of Syracuse, 415 BCE (6.67.1–70.4), as a clash between Athenian *eutaxia* and Syracusan *ataxia*, with the contrast determining the course and the outcome of the battle (Crowley 2012: 49–52). For this concept generally, see Thuc. 2.11.9, 84.2, 3.108.1, 4.126.5, 8.25.3; and for naval applications, see 2.84.2, 91.4, 92.1, 3.77.2–3, 7.40.3, 68.1, 8.105.2; see also n. 64.

[38] Xen. *Anab.* 3.2.18, *Eq. Mag.* 1.21, *Eq.* 12.11–13; Spence 1993: 34–163; Worley 1994: 59–122; Hyland 2013a: 493–511, 2013b: 512–26.

[39] Thuc. 2.13.8, 5.84.1, 6.94.4; Xen. *Mem.* 3.3.1; cf. Aristophanes *Birds* 1178–85, also Spence 1993: 56–60; Worley 1994: 32, 70, 81.

stones,⁴⁰ and the rarely mentioned *hamhippoi*, lightly equipped warriors who coordinated closely with cavalry,⁴¹ Thucydides' narrative features three main types of light infantry. The first two, namely archers and slingers, whilst effective against light infantry and cavalry, were otherwise of limited value against hoplites in formation.⁴² However, the weapon deployed by the third, namely the javelin, was deadly, especially when deployed by the javelin thrower *par excellence*: the peltast, whose skirmishing skills made him the most lethal light infantryman on the Greek battlefield.⁴³

Naturally, given their mobility, both cavalry and light infantry could operate autonomously. In 426 BCE, for instance, Aetolian light infantry ambushed a small force of Athenian marines and their allies in broken terrain near Aegitium, and having fixed them in place and dispersed their protective screen of archers, they wore them down with javelins until the survivors broke ranks and fled.⁴⁴ Similarly, during the Archidamian War, the Athenian cavalry conducted a mobile defence of Attica to restrict the activities of enemy ravagers and limit their impact on Athenian territory.⁴⁵

In main force encounters, however, this autonomy did not extend to forcing a decision on the enemy.⁴⁶ Consequently, both cavalry and light infantry were militarily subordinate to the hoplite phalanx and were relegated to auxiliary roles focusing primarily on force protection. Accordingly, they appear in Thucydides' narrative protecting hoplites as they deploy,⁴⁷ defending them from the hostile attentions of enemy light infantry,⁴⁸ guarding their flanks⁴⁹ and covering them as they retire.⁵⁰ However, if sufficient forces were available, cavalry and light infantry could also be used offensively. Cavalry was often deployed against the flanks of enemy formations;⁵¹ light infantry, when protected by hoplites, could wear down

⁴⁰ Pritchett 1991: 65–7; van Wees 2004: 61–5, 68–71.
⁴¹ Thuc. 5.57.2; cf. Arist. *Ath. Pol.* 49.1; Xen. *Hell.* 7.5.23, with Spence 1993: 58–60; Lazenby 2004: 114.
⁴² Thuc. 2.81.8, 100.1–5; cf. Xen. *Anab.* 3.4.1–6, with McLeod 1965: 1–14, 1972: 78–82; Pritchett 1991: 1–65; Trundle 2010: 139–60.
⁴³ See Thuc. 3.94.1–98.5 (Aetolia, 426 BCE), 4.3.1–6.2, 8.1–23.2, 26.1–40.2 (Sphacteria, 425 BCE) and Xen. *Hell.* 4.5.7–8, 11–17 (Lechaeum, 390 BCE), with Best 1969; Trundle 2010 139–60.
⁴⁴ Thuc. 3.94.1–98.5.
⁴⁵ Ibid., 4.95.1–3, also 2.19.2, 22.2–3, 3.1.1–2, 7.27.5, 8.71.2; Hanson 2005: 35–64, 201–23; Spence 2010: 111–38.
⁴⁶ Grundy 1911: 274–81; Gomme et al. 1945–81: vol. I, 10–24; Hanson 2001: 201–32; Hunt 2007: 108–46, with n. 29 in this chapter.
⁴⁷ Thuc. 6.67.1–70.4 (Syracuse, 415 BCE). ⁴⁸ Thuc. 3.94.1–98.5 (Aetolia, 426 BCE).
⁴⁹ Thuc. 4.89.1–101.1 (Delium, 424 BCE) and 5.66.1–74.3 (1st Mantinea, 418 BCE).
⁵⁰ Thuc. 6.67.1–70.4 (Syracuse, 415 BCE) and 5.66.1–74.3 (1st Mantinea, 418 BCE).
⁵¹ Thuc. 4.89.1–101.1 (Delium, 424 BCE).

opposing troops[52] or ambush them from cover;[53] and the mobility offered by both of these auxiliary arms made them ideal for the pursuit of routed troops.[54]

This utility, however, did not camouflage the subordination of cavalry and light infantry, and their marginalization was reinforced further by prevailing norms and values.[55] As sociologists recognize, in belligerent geopolitical environments, masculinity tends to be defined militarily,[56] and in classical Greece, a man's claim to manhood largely depended on the extent to which he took and passed the test of combat.[57] This disadvantaged both light infantry and cavalry, who relied on missiles and mobility and sought to avoid direct engagement with their enemies,[58] since their style of fighting did not seem, to the Greeks, to provide a test as severe as that faced by the hoplite.[59] The hoplite engaged his enemy directly in close-quarters combat, and since this offered the most demanding test a man could face, the hoplite not only fully earned his status as a man, but was also accorded a level of prestige that eclipsed that of his auxiliaries, whose claim to masculinity was much less secure.[60]

This prejudice was, for light infantrymen, further reinforced by snobbery. They, of course, were too poor to afford the expense of mounted warfare or hoplite service,[61] and consequently their military and ideological subordination was compounded by the fact that they were the social inferiors of those members of the socio-political elite, like Thucydides, who produced the historical accounts of the battles they helped fight.[62]

---

[52] Thuc. 4.3.1–6.2, 8.1–23.2, 26.1–40.2 (Sphacteria, 425 BCE).

[53] Thuc. 3.105.1–109.1 (Olpae, 426/5 BCE); cf. Xen. *Hell.* 5.1.10–13.

[54] Thuc. 2.79.6 (Spartolus, 429 BCE), 3.98.1–5 (Aetolia, 426 BCE), 5.10.9–10 (Amphipolis, 422 BCE). See also Xen. *Anab.* 3.1.2.

[55] Adkins 1960: 73, 249; Hunt 1998: 1–3; Roisman 2002: 128, 2005: 1–2, 84–101, 105; Christ 2006: 88–142; Crowley 2012: 86–8.

[56] Adkins 1960: 73; Andreski 1968: 20–74; Hunt 1998: 1–3; Berent 2000: 258; Roisman 2005: 1–2, 105; cf. Bransby 1992: 232–3.

[57] Thuc. 4.126.1–5; Crowley 2012: 88–96.

[58] Thuc. 2.13.8, 4.3.1–6.2, 5.84.1, 6.94.4, 8.1–23.2, 26.1–40.2, 126.1–5; Xen. *Anab.* 3.2.18, *Eq. Mag.* 1.21, *Eq.* 12.11–13.

[59] Anderson 1991: 15–37; Lazenby 1991: 87–109; Hanson 2000: 55–88, 135–93; Crowley 2012: 103–4.

[60] Garlan 1975: 78–133; Connor 1988: 21–9; Runciman 1998: 733; Hanson 1996: 289–312; Pritchard 1998: 52; Strauss 2000: 292–7; Roisman 2002: 130, 2005: 106–7; Crowley 2012: 103–4.

[61] See n. 8.

[62] For Thucydides' status, see 4.105.1–2; Hornblower 1994b: 1–6; Dewald 2005: 13; and for his affinity for hoplites, see Dover 1973: 37–8; Hornblower 1994b: 160–8; Hanson 2005: 123–61; Rhodes 2011: 21–2.

It is unsurprising, therefore, that Thucydides' battle narratives focus on hoplites, whose actions consequently overshadow those of their auxiliaries. In his description of the Battle of Syracuse (415 BCE), for instance, Thucydides acknowledges the presence of slingers, javelin throwers, stone throwers and archers, as well as a squadron of Syracusan cavalry. Despite this, he not only dismisses the light infantry engagement that preceded the clash of hoplites as typically indecisive, but also ignores the Syracusan cavalry until the battle is decided, after which they suddenly appear in order to prevent pursuit of the beaten Syracusan hoplites.[63] Similar patterns are observable in Thucydides' accounts of naval engagements, which are often narrated with terms and concepts derived from hoplite combat, in which sailors – typically men of low status who met their enemies indirectly – were occluded by the glamorous triremes they crewed.[64]

Such vessels were so familiar to Thucydides' readers that he did not feel the need to describe their operational characteristics,[65] but, whilst he clearly considered the trireme a Panhellenic constant, his narrative reveals three divergent approaches to naval combat, each requiring differently configured ships.[66] The first, admired by Thucydides, involved stripped-down ships engaging in elegant manoeuvres designed to enable an attacking vessel to strike its opponent in the rear quarter with its ram.[67] The second, which Thucydides considered old-fashioned, involved sturdy ships packed with infantry who grappled and then boarded their adversaries – a tactic that, to Thucydides, made naval engagements resemble battles on land.[68] The third involved the redesigning of the trireme's prow to provide the frontal strength required for head-to-head ramming, a technique most suited to enclosed waters that precluded manoeuvre.[69]

This naval sophistication, together with the complex character of terrestrial warfare, demonstrates that the Greek art of war was, in most respects,

---

[63] Thuc. 6.67.1–70.4. For the occlusion of other arms, see Gomme et al. 1945–81: vol. I, 10–24; Pritchett 1985: 44–93; Hunt 2006: 385–413; Hornblower 2007: 22–53; Trundle 2010: 139–60; Brice 2013: 623–41; Rawlings 2013: 46–73.

[64] Cartledge 1998b: 63–4; Pritchard 1998: 44–9; Roisman 2002: 128–31, 136–41, 2005: 109, 111; Strauss 2007: 223–36, with Miller 2010: 304–38.

[65] Morrison and Williams 1968: 244–325; Casson 1971: 77–96; Wallinga 1992: 130–64; Morrison et al. 2000: 35–46; Strauss 2007: 223–36; de Souza 2013: 369–94.

[66] Morrison and Williams 1968: 313–25; Hirshfield 1996: 608–13; Hanson 2005: 235–69; Strauss 2007: 223–36; de Souza 2013: 369–94.

[67] Thuc. 2.83.1–84.5, 86.1–92.7, 89.1–11 (Naupactus, 429/8 BCE); Lazenby 1987: 169–77; Whitehead 1987: 178–85.

[68] Thuc. 1.45.1–55.2 (Sybota, 433 BCE).

[69] Thuc. 7.34.1–8 (Naupactus, 413 BCE), 36.1–38.2, 39.1–41.5, 52.1–54.4 (Syracuse, 413 BCE).

highly advanced, and yet, as Thucydides reveals, siege warfare remained stubbornly underdeveloped. The Greeks deployed citizen warriors, so they were unwilling to accept the casualties entailed by storming enemy defences, and without torsion-based artillery they were unable to reduce those defences from a distance.[70] Technological innovation, of course, was not entirely absent. Thucydides was fascinated by the primitive flamethrower the Boeotians deployed against the Athenian fortifications at Delium in 424 BCE,[71] as well as by the range of measures and countermeasures, such as battering rams and the gravity-powered engines used to destroy them, at Plataea in 429 BCE.[72] His fascination, however, reflects the novelty of such techniques,[73] and it is telling that Plataea fell to neither breach nor storm, but instead to the most basic method of all: circumvallation.[74] This denied the targeted community both reinforcement and resupply and led, if terms were not negotiated, to the failure of the defence through the physical incapacity of the defenders.[75] Circumvallation, therefore, was reliable, but it was also slow and expensive, and if it was used against a coastal community it had to be augmented by naval blockade.[76]

Opposing Forces

Thucydides, then, envisages a Panhellenic art of war, and he situates in the differing capacities each of the protagonists possessed in its three major aspects – namely land, sea and siege warfare – an explanation for the dreadful nature of the Peloponnesian War. Athens, naturally, could not use her fleet against Sparta, which was located many miles from the sea, and her army was incapable of taking that peculiar *polis*, even though it was famously unfortified, because it would have to defeat the Spartans in open combat first.[77]

---

[70] On siege warfare in the Peloponnesian War, see esp. Seaman 2013: 642–56. Other useful studies of aspects of siege warfare in the classical period are Grundy 1911: 245–6, 261–2, 282–91; Marsden 1969: 5–173; Lawrence 1979: 39–66; Lazenby 2004: 31–48; Hanson 2005: 163–99; Strauss 2007: 237–47; Chaniotis 2013: 438–56.

[71] Thuc. 4.100.1–5; cf. 4.110.1–116.3.   [72] Thuc. 2.71.1–78.4, 3.20.1–24.3, 52.1–68.5.

[73] Grundy 1911: 282–91; Hanson 2005: 163.   [74] Thuc. 2.78.1, 3.52.1.

[75] Thuc. 1.115.2–117.1 (Samos, 440 BCE), 1.63.1–67.1, 2.58.1–3, 68.1–9, 70.1–4, 3.17.2–3 (Potidaea 432–430 BCE), 2.69.1–2, 3.52.1 (Plataea, 429–427 BCE), 3.2.1–6.2, 8.1–18.5, 25.1–30.4, 35.1–50.3, 4.52.1–3 (Mytilene, 428–427 BCE), 5.84.1–115.4, 116.2–4 (Melos, 415 BCE).

[76] Consider the sieges of Samos, 440 BCE (8.38.2–4, 40.1–3, 55.2–56.1, 60.2–3, 61.1–3, 63.1–2), and Syracuse, 415–13 BCE (6.75.1–7.16.2, 21.1–26.3, 31.1–33.6, 35.1–72.4).

[77] Hence Pericles' 'island strategy' (Thuc. 1.143.3–5, 2.13.1–9, 22.1–24.1, 55.2, 60.1–65.13; see also ns. 67, 81). For the capabilities of the Athenian and Spartan armies, see Lazenby 1985; Crowley 2012.

This was not a realistic proposition for amateur Athenian troops, who, despite their impressive levels of experience and veterancy, were no match for the professionals of Sparta. Spartan hoplites enjoyed the twin advantages entailed by the exploitation of the helots, namely a militarized system of education and the ability to live, essentially, as a parasitical military elite, free to practise and develop the tactical skills learnt in their youth.[78] This ensured that Spartan hoplites were more psychologically resilient and tactically aware than those fielded by other Greek *poleis*, and their unmatched ability to maintain their *eutaxia* under pressure and manoeuvre whilst in contact with the enemy allowed them to approach battle in a way that was simply beyond their Athenian counterparts.[79]

The Athenians, following the advice of Pericles, refused to engage the Spartan army and instead retired behind their fortifications, which the Spartans could not breach and would not storm. Moreover, because Athens was connected to the Piraeus by the Long Walls, the Athenians were able to receive seaborne supplies funded by imperial revenue and could therefore withstand siege indefinitely.[80] To defeat Athens, then, Sparta had to control the sea, yet this would require her underfunded and amateur navy to meet an imperially funded and professional Athenian war fleet whose ability to engage in the most sophisticated style of naval combat, in which manoeuvre preceded ramming, ensured such a contest was unwinnable.[81] Neither side could, therefore, defeat the other. Athens could not win until she produced an army superior to that of Sparta, and Sparta could not win until she produced a fleet superior to that of Athens.[82] Naturally, such a momentous transition was unattractive to both parties, and other, more traditional, ways were sought to break the stalemate that ensued.

Sparta and her allies regularly ravaged the territory of Attica.[83] In 424 BCE, they dispatched a small force of helots and mercenaries under the command of Brasidas to attack Athenian interests in the Thraceward region.[84] The Spartans even established a fort at Decelea in 413 BCE, after

---

[78] For helotage, see Hodkinson 2000: 113–49 (with further references), and for the *agōgē*, see Xen. *Lac. Pol.* 2.1–4.7; Hodkinson 1983: 245–51; Kennell 1995; Ducat 2006.

[79] See n. 31.

[80] Thuc. 2.13.2–14.2, 2.16.2–17.3; Cawkwell 1987: 40–55; Pritchard 2010: 1–62.

[81] For the contrast Thucydides draws between 'naval' Athens and 'hoplite' Sparta, see 1.73.1–86.5, 93.3–8, 120.2, 121.2–5, 141.2–4, 2.10.1–3, 11.1–9, 13.2–14.2, 16.2–17.3, 63.2–5, 85.1–3, 86.1–92.7, 4.12.3, 14.3, 40.1–2, 5.72.2–4, 75.3, 6.11.6, 83.1, 7.21.1–5, 34.7, 66.1–3, 8.96.1–5; Hanson 2005: 3–34; Pritchard 2010: 1–62.

[82] Kagan 1974: 17–42, 1987: 413–26; Lazenby 2004: 1–15, 31–48, 251–7; Hanson 2005: 35–64, 88–121.

[83] Thuc. 2.11.6, 19.2, 22.1–24.31, 47.2, 71.1, 3.1.1–3, 26.1–4, 4.2.1, 5.14.3.

[84] Thuc. 4.78.1, 80.1–5, 103.1–106.4, 5.6.2–11.3.

which the Athenians were denied access to Attica for the rest of the war.[85] The Athenians were more proactive. They launched amphibious raids around the Peloponnesian coast,[86] which succeeded in the defeat and capture of the Spartan garrison stationed on Sphacteria in 425 BCE,[87] and they conducted punitive operations against Megara,[88] which culminated in the near capture of that city in 424 BCE.[89] In the same year, their overly ambitious attempt to knock Thebes out of the war ended in decisive failure at the Battle of Delium,[90] and six years later, their even more ambitious plan to build an anti-Spartan coalition in the Peloponnese ended in decisive failure at the Battle of Mantinea.[91] As if incapable of learning from their mistakes, the Athenians then compounded these two famous failures in 415 BCE when they launched a huge expedition against Syracuse, which not only failed spectacularly in 413 BCE, but also resulted in the loss of the entire expeditionary force.[92]

The Cost of Conflict

These operations, and others like them, did not break the deadlock, but, as Thucydides reveals, they did produce an abundance of human suffering.[93] This, for the Greeks, was a recognized consequence of conflict, albeit one overshadowed by the prestige of war,[94] reflected in Thucydides' own choice of subject.[95] It is striking, then, that although his narrative contains examples of heroism,[96] the glory of combat burns brightest in Pericles'

[85] Thuc. 6.91.6–93.3, 7.19.1–20.1, 27.2–28.4, 8.69.1–3; Xen. *Hell.* 1.1.35.

[86] Thuc. 2.23.1–3, 25.1–26.2, 30.1–2, 54.1–6, 3.7.1–6, 16.1–4, 91.1, 94.1–3, 4.42.1–44.6, 53.1–54.4, 56.1–57.4, 101.3–4, 6.105.1–3, 7.26.1–3. For amphibious operations, see Lazenby 2004: 31–48; Strauss 2007: 223–36; de Souza 2013: 369–94.

[87] Thuc. 4.3.1–6.2, 8.1–23.2, 26.1–40.2.

[88] Thuc. 2.31.1–3, 3.51.1–4, 4.66.1–74.4, 109.1.   [89] Thuc. 4.66.1–74.4, 109.1.

[90] Thuc. 4.89.1–101.1.   [91] Thuc. 5.44.1–47.12, 66.1–74.3   [92] See n. 37.

[93] Thuc. 1.23.1–3; Gomme 1937: 116–24; Connor 1984b: 231–50; Hanson 2005: xxiii–xviii, 65–88, 289–314.

[94] Thuc. 1.76.1–4, 120.3, 2.41.4, 61.1, 63.1–3, 64.2–6, 4.59.2, 62.2; Plato *Laws* 1.641a–b, 3.690b, *Resp.* 1.338c; Xen. *Eq. Mag.* 8.7, *Mem.* 2.1.28; Hunt 1998: 153–4; Low 2007: 161–73; Crowley 2012: 89–92; Rawlings 2013: 46–73.

[95] Thuc. 1.1.1–3; Garlan 1975: 15–51; Hornblower 1994b: 191–205; Vela Tejada 2004: 138–9.

[96] Consider his portrayal of Brasidas at Methone, 431 BCE (Thuc. 2.23.1–3, 25.1–3), Pylos, 425 BCE (4.11.1–12.2), Lyncus, 423 BCE (4.124.1–128.5), and Amphipolis, 422 BCE (5.6.2–11.3), with Westlake 1980: 333–9; Connor 1984b: 108–40; Hornblower 1994b: 155–68; Hunt 2006: 385–413. For analogous admiration of Demosthenes and Themistocles, see Connor 1984b: 191; Hornblower 1991–2008 vol. II, 38–61, 1994b: 155–68; Hunt 2006: 385–413; Rhodes 2011: 20.

funeral oration for the dead, whereas, for the living, the experience of war is portrayed as a grim and fearful ordeal.[97]

He depicts the Battle of Delium in 424 BCE as a claustrophobic crush of struggling men in which the Athenian left is driven back by the Theban deepened column, whilst on the right the Thespians are enveloped and almost annihilated by the encircling Athenians, who become so confused that they start to kill each other.[98] Similarly chaotic scenes dominate his description of the Athenian night assault on Epipolae in 413 BCE, in which isolated groups of attackers are simultaneously fighting the enemy, killing each other, fleeing and falling from cliffs, whilst others march blindly into the unfolding disaster.[99]

Such narratives are undeniably brutal, but they are not unrepresentative, and others are even more appalling. His description of the defeat of a small force of Athenian marines and their allies in Aetolia in 426 BCE is particularly grim: they were surrounded by Aetolian light infantry who deluged their opponents with javelins until their nerve broke, and when the Athenians and their allies turned and tried to flee, they were subjected to a running massacre in which most of the exhausted, lost and confused men who survived the initial rout blundered into an exitless woodland that the Aetolians simply burned around them.[100] Thucydides' account of the Spartan disaster on Sphacteria in 425 BCE is equally evocative. This describes how an isolated unit of Spartan hoplites was overwhelmed by a much larger Athenian assault force, yet, despite their hopeless situation, the dust, their thirst and their mounting losses, they fought desperately until their acting commander, whose original predecessor had been killed, and whose replacement had been so badly wounded that he lay amongst the collected corpses, finally surrendered to stop the pointless slaughter of his exhausted men.[101]

Luckily, the surviving Spartans were too valuable to mistreat, but others were not so fortunate. After the Battle of Sybota in 433 BCE, the Corinthians were so keen to slaughter enemy sailors struggling in the water that they rowed repeatedly amongst the wreckage, not realizing that some of the helpless men they were killing with javelins and archery were actually their allies.[102] The Thebans were also victims of vengeance. In 431 BCE, after the troops they had sent to seize Plataea had been defeated and the survivors

---

[97] Thuc. 2.42.3, also 1.80.1–2, 2.8.1, 11.1, 20.2, 21.2, 6.24.3; Gomme 1937: 116–24; Lazenby 1991: 87–109; Hornblower 1994b: 110–35; Yoshitake 2010: 359–77; Crowley 2012: 86–8.

[98] Thuc. 4.89.1–101.2.   [99] Thuc. 7.43.2–45.2.   [100] Thuc. 3.94.1–98.5.

[101] Thuc. 4.3.1–6.2, 8.1–23.2, 26.1–40.2.   [102] Thuc. 1.45.1–55.2.

captured, the refusal of those men to round up leading Plataeans was rewarded by their swift execution at the hands of very people this act of clemency had been intended to impress.[103] This brutality was then repaid in 427 BCE, when the defenders of Plataea were captured and executed by the Spartans to please their Theban allies.[104] Not even the Athenians were immune. After their expeditionary force was defeated on Sicily in 413 BCE, those who survived the retreat to and massacre at the Assinarus were herded into an abandoned quarry by the Syracusans, where many died of thirst, hunger, exposure and disease.[105]

Thucydides also emphasizes the human cost of the war by revealing its effect on the living. In his account of Athenian-led operations in Amphilochia in 426/5 BCE, he describes the confusion of the Ambraciot herald who, while attempting to negotiate the return of the bodies of those Ambraciots killed after the Battle of Olpae, was instead presented with the arms and armour stripped from over a thousand corpses, and when he belatedly realized that this signified the massacre of the Ambraciot relief force at Idomene, he was so overcome by grief that he left the enemy camp having forgotten his original mission.[106] An analogous reaction amongst the surviving Athenians also highlights the tragic nature of the retreat from Syracuse in 413 BCE, during which the abandoned sick and the wounded crawled pitifully after the able-bodied, who wept as they left their helpless comrades to the tender mercies of the vengeful Syracusans.[107]

Communities, of course, did not just suffer casualties in combat: many *poleis*, like Melos in 415 BCE, experienced the horrors of andrapodization after succumbing to siege;[108] others, like Corcyra, descended into murderous *stasis*;[109] the coastal settlements of the Peloponnese were terrorized by Athenian amphibious raids that had no military purpose beyond the misery they caused; and Mycalessus was destroyed in 413 BCE by Athenian-led Thracian mercenaries in an attack that, judging by the emphasis placed on the unnecessary nature of the assault, the helplessness of the town and the gratuitous slaughter of its inhabitants, seems to have particularly disgusted Thucydides.[110]

---

[103] Thuc. 2.2.1–5.7.   [104] Thuc. 3.52.1–68.5.   [105] Thuc. 7.77.5–87.6.
[106] Thuc. 3.105.1–113.6; cf. 7.71.1–7.   [107] Thuc. 7.75.2–5.
[108] The process of turning people into *andrapoda* (literally, 'man-footed things'), a term used by the Greeks to denote slaves. Notable instances of andrapodization include Torone, 422 BCE (Thuc. 5.3.2), Scione, 421 BCE (5.32.1), and Melos, 415 BCE (5.116.4). For further discussion, see Gaca 2010: 117–61.
[109] Thuc. 3.69.1–85.3, 4.44.1–48.6.
[110] Thuc. 7.27.1–30.3; Dover 1973: 41; Connor 1984b: 7; Hanson 2005: 3–34, 77; Hornblower 2007: 27.

The fate of individuals also lends pathos to Thucydides' melancholy narrative.[111] Each is different: Pericles is wise; Brasidas is brave; Cleon is corrupt; Lamachus is steady; Demosthenes is reckless; Nicias is pious. Yet, despite their differences, they all share the same fate: they are unable to control the war that rages around them, and in the end they are consumed by that omnivorous conflict, which devours the good and the bad with equal enthusiasm.[112]

Thankfully, the Peloponnesian War, like all wars, eventually came to an end – ironically, when conservative Sparta seized control of the sea and starved ostensibly innovative Athens into submission. By this time, however, the war had spread death and misery across the Hellenic world for twenty-seven years.[113] Naturally, Thucydides was not unmoved by this, and while he may manipulate his readers' emotions for his own authorial purposes,[114] by charting the impact of the Peloponnesian War on the lives of those who lived through it, he offers, in addition to a political, strategic and tactical analysis of that conflict, an invaluable insight into the human experience of war.

Further Reading

The best introduction to the nature of war in the Greek world is van Wees 2004; Sabin et al. 2007 contains more detailed discussions of many aspects of Greek warfare (including its representation in contemporary historiography). On the 'experience' of hoplite battle, the work of Hanson (esp. 1991, 2000) remains fundamental, even though (as we have seen) his conclusions are not universally accepted.

[111] Adkins 1975: 379–92; Hanson 2005: 65–88.
[112] Pericles (Thuc. 1.111.1–3, 114.1–117.3, 139.4–145.1, 2.12.1–14.2, 34.1–46.2, 55.2–56.6, 59.1–65.13); Cleon (3.36.1–50.3, 4.3.1–6.2, 8.1–23.2, 26.1–40.2, 5.2.1–3.6, 6.1–12.2); Lamachus (4.75.1–2, 5.19.1–2, 24.1–2, 6.8.2); Nicias (3.51.1–4, 4.27.1–28.5, 42.1–4, 53.1–54.4, 117.1–119.3, 129.1–131.3, 5.15.1–19.2, 23.1–24.1, 46.1–5, 6.8.1–26.2, 44.1–7.87.6); Demosthenes (3.94.1–98.5, 102.3–7, 105.1–114.4, 4.3.1–6.2, 8.1–23.2, 26.1–40.2, 66.1–74.4, 5.80.1, 7.16.1–17.1, 26.1–3, 31.1–5, 33.1–6, 35.1–2, 42.1–86.3, with n. 96).
[113] Thuc. 1.6.1–6, 1.10.1–3, 1.69.1–71.7, 2.37.1–46.2, 5.107.1, 8.96.1–5; Connor 1984b: 108–40, 174; Kagan 1987: 413–26; Hanson 2005: 271–87.
[114] See n. 17.

10

POLLY A. LOW

Thucydides on Empire and Imperialism

Thucydides did not claim to be writing an account of the Athenian Empire, nor a study of Athenian imperialism; his work (or so he tells us in his opening statement) is a history of a war, of a struggle that was 'more momentous than any previous conflict' (1.1.3). But the rise and fall of the Athenian Empire was central to the story of that war (or at least the story of the war as Thucydides told it), not just because war and empire overlap in time, space and protagonists, but also because (again, in Thucydides' eyes at least) those two stories are inextricably connected at a more fundamental level: the Athenian Empire – or more precisely the fear that its power provoked – was the underlying cause of the Peloponnesian War (1.23.6); the Peloponnesian War, in turn, precipitated the collapse of the Athenian Empire.

It is, therefore, not surprising that Thucydides' text has become central to modern analyses of the Athenian Empire. It is an exceptionally important (though, as we shall see, neither infallible nor comprehensive) source of data about the organization; indeed, for much of the Athenian Empire's history it is our only contemporary narrative of its activities. It has also been seen to offer much more than this: not just an account of the facts of empire, but an exploration of the structures, dynamics and morals (or absence of morals) of Athenian imperial power – or perhaps even imperial power *tout court*. However, the fact that Thucydides does not explicitly articulate these questions – still less his answers to them – adds an extra interpretive challenge: readers of Thucydides need first to decide exactly what problems Thucydides was trying to explore and then to establish what (if any) solutions he might be proposing. But a challenge is also an opportunity; one reason why Thucydides continues to be probed as both a historian of and a thinker about empire is precisely because his text is open to multiple approaches and to multiple interpretations.

This discussion does not, therefore, hope to offer a definitive account of Thucydidean thinking on the Athenian Empire. But it does aim to outline some of possibilities of using his work as a source for the history and ideology of empire in the Greek world – and, perhaps, beyond.

Delian League and Athenian Empire

What was the 'Athenian Empire'? The label is, of course, a modern invention, as is its alternative – and apparently more neutral – name, 'Delian League'. Thucydides, like other ancient authors, uses various terms to describe the organization, of which the least ideologically loaded is *archē* ('rule')[1] – although even this label carries certain implications about the nature of the organization, and in particular about the hierarchies of power within it. The reason that this matters is because the nature of the organization – and the nature of Athens' control of it – is generally thought to have changed quite dramatically in the course of its history; the names that historians (ancient and modern) choose to apply to it are, therefore, not simply objective labels, but often reveal specific beliefs about the nature of Athens' power at a given moment.

It is therefore preferable – though still not entirely straightforward – to start not with labels but with descriptions. In 478/7 BCE, in the aftermath of the Persian withdrawal from mainland Greece, the Athenians invited Greek states to participate in a multilateral alliance, of which the Athenians were to be the leaders (*hegemones*). The original terms and objectives of the alliance are, however, quite uncertain: Thucydides' claim (1.96.1) that it was a strictly delimited alliance, with an explicit goal of seeking revenge on the Persians, is not implausible. It is clear, though, that other versions of the League's mission statement were in circulation, notably that recorded in the Aristotelian *Athenaion Politeia* (23.5), which suggests an open-ended, potentially eternal alliance based on the wide-ranging principle of 'having the same friends and enemies' (that is, on the principle of mutual defensive and offensive obligations).[2]

Uncertainty also surrounds the exact size and membership of the League, particularly in its early years. Thucydides gives the impression that the League's membership was more or less identical to the alliance of Greek states that had fought against Persia (he notes only the withdrawal of the Spartans from the alliance: 1.95.2; that other Peloponnesian forces followed Sparta is hinted at, at 1.95.4, but not stated explicitly). Other sources suggest

---

[1] Other terms for imperial rule are discussed later in this chapter.

[2] On this, see Rhodes 1993a, *ad loc.* (noting that the *Ath. Pol.* 'goes far beyond what other texts tell us of the objectives of the League'). For further discussion, see Brunt 1953: 149–52; Hammond 1967.

that the membership of the alliance was more extensively reshaped at this point (the *Ath. Pol.*, for example, talks of an alliance of 'Ionians': 23.5); it is clear, too, that the 'Hellenic' alliance against Persia had itself expanded considerably in the final phase of the Persian Wars (Thuc. 1.89.2; Hdt. 9.106), even if the details of exactly which states joined and on what terms remain murky.[3] The original membership of the Delian League might, then, have been as high as approximately 140 states,[4] but what is undeniable is that the League grew rapidly and dramatically. By the time that the Peloponnesian War broke out, its membership was around 190 cities and communities,[5] and expansion continued in the early phase of the war, probably reaching an acme in the 420s BCE.[6]

The growth in scale of the Empire seems to have been accompanied by a change in its ethos, although both the timing and the extent of that change remain subjects of considerable debate. What is undisputed is that the voluntary nature of the alliance disappeared: members who attempted to leave were forcibly reintegrated (Thucydides says that Naxos was the first state to suffer this fate: 1.98.4), and states were also added to the alliance by force (as was the case for Carystos in Euboea; Thuc. 1.98.3). Rather harder to pin down (though it is clear that they must have happened) are changes in the alliance's organization and administration. By the 420s BCE, the Athenians had developed a complex set of processes for extracting financial contributions (*phoros*, 'tribute') from their allies; there is also good (albeit incomplete) evidence for Athens' use of a range of other political, judicial and military forms of control.[7] What all of this adds up to, in the eyes of both ancient commentators and modern scholars, is a fundamental shift in the nature of the organization. In Greek terms, what had started as *hegemonia* (voluntary alliance) had become *archē* (rule), or even *tyrannia*

---

[3] On the history and scope of this alliance, see Brunt 1953.

[4] The estimate of Merrit et al. 1939–53: vol. III, 194–224 (though their methodology, which starts from the maximum possible membership and excludes states whose early participation cannot be proven, is likely to generate higher numbers than one that seeks positive proof of participation).

[5] Meiggs 1972: 527, based on the tribute quota list of 433 BCE.

[6] The tribute assessment decree of 425/4 BCE (OR 153) names approximately 380 cities, but this is certainly an 'optimistic' (OR, *ad loc.*) catalogue. The list includes twice as many cities as are known to have paid in any one year, and it names cities (notably Melos) that were certainly not part of the Empire at this point.

[7] Summarized in Meiggs 1972: chs 11 and 12. For more detail on administrative and financial structures, see Samons 2000; Constantakopoulou 2013: esp. 34–8. On judicial interference, see de Ste. Croix 1961a, 1961b; Low 2013. On officials, see Balcer 1976. On garrisons, see Nease 1949.

(tyranny);[8] in modern (Anglophone) terminology, the 'Delian League' had become the 'Athenian Empire'.

Much modern debate has centred on the problem (or perceived problem) of locating that change at a particular point in time and thus finding an explanation for it: was the League always fated to turn into an empire, or was it propelled in that direction by the pressures of war, failures of leadership or some other contingent historical factor?[9] Those debates are certainly valuable (both for our understanding of the nature of empire and for our analysis of 5th-century BCE Athenian history), but what is more important in this context is to note how little help – or how little explicit help, at least – Thucydides gives in reconstructing this shift from voluntary alliance to coercive empire. That a change happened is something that Thucydides makes clear: 'the Athenians', he notes at 1.99.2, 'were not the old popular rulers they had been at first'.[10] But the chronology of this development is, in Thucydides' account, conspicuously vague; and he also gives notably little information about the growth in the machinery of empire (mentioned earlier in this chapter), as well as what seem from other sources to have been some critical moments in its development (two notorious omissions are the Peace of Callias, an agreement that ended the conflict with Persia and was, in Thucydides' version, the Delian League's *raison d'etre*; and the transfer of the League's treasury from Delos to Athens).[11]

This is not to say that Thucydides has no value at all as a source for the development of the Athenian Empire, nor that the picture of the Empire that he gives is entirely static: the organization that Thucydides describes at 1.97 is quite clearly not the same – in operation or in ethos – as the one that we find in his narrative of the 420s and 410s BCE. But because Thucydides gives us only selected snapshots of the activities and ideology of Athenian imperialism in this period, he leaves his readers with the task – or the opportunity – of providing the larger frame for those disconnected vignettes. In constructing that frame, we can turn to sources other than Thucydides (other historians, comedy and tragedy, epigraphic and material evidence),

---

[8] *Ath. Pol.* 24.2–3; the transition from hegemony to empire is explored at greater length in Isocrates' mid-4th-century BCE pamphlet *On the Peace* (esp. §§82–95). For Thucydides' account of the transition, see later in this chapter.

[9] A sample of views: Kallet 2013a (arguing that the seeds of empire are visible from the early 5th century BCE, if not earlier); Meiggs 1943 (who sees the 450s BCE as the critical period); Mattingly 1963 (who sees the Empire as a development that begins in the 440s BCE, but comes to full fruition in the 420s BCE).

[10] Except where stated otherwise, translations in this chapter are those of Crawley 1874, sometimes lightly adapted.

[11] On these omissions, see Irwin (Chapter 8).

which can help to supplement or correct Thucydides' historical narrative.[12] But it is also possible to dig deeper into the things that Thucydides does say about empire and to attempt to extrapolate from these observations some wider theories about the history and nature of Athenian power in the 5th century BCE. The rest of this chapter seeks to explore what (some of) those extrapolations could look like.

Empire, Obligation and Reward

What gives one state the right to rule over others? Thucydides' text explores various possible answers to that question, some offered in the historian's own voice and others presented by various speakers in the *History*. (The latter set of arguments, of course, cannot necessarily be taken to be ones that Thucydides himself endorsed.)

One justification for empire that can be found in the work might be familiar from the imperial rhetoric of other times and places: empire is not a privilege but a duty, and one that is exercised for the good of those ruled. The benefits that the imperial power reaps from its position can, in turn, be represented as a legitimate reward for the burden that they have taken on. In the context of Athenian imperialism, this line of argument typically has a specific point of reference: the Persian Wars. As we have seen, the alleged persistence of the Persian threat even after 478 BCE seems to have been used to justify the League's existence. But as well as this, Athenian actions during and immediately after the Persian invasions of Greece are used to legitimize the city's position of leadership. These arguments for legitimation take two broad forms. First: that Athens was the only Greek state that was willing to take on the role of leader; more specifically, the only other plausible candidate for the role – Sparta – was actively unwilling to take on this responsibility (a claim that appears both in Thucydides' narrative at 1.95 and in a speech he gives to the Athenian ambassadors at 1.75).[13] Athens therefore (or so the Athenians say) did not actively seek their position of leadership; rather, it was thrust upon them. Second: that the Athenian contribution to the Persian Wars entitles them to retain and enjoy the fruits of their dominant role. They have done the Greeks a great service by fighting 'alone' at

[12] For a useful overview of these sources and the challenges in using them, see Osborne 2000: 5–8.
[13] We should note that the reasons given for Sparta's reluctance to take over leadership of the Greeks foreshadow themes that will (for Thucydides) also be relevant to their initial failure in the war: timidity, slowness to act and lack of initiative (cf. esp. Thuc. 8.96.5). For further discussion of Thucydides' construction (and occasional blurring) of the polarity between Spartan and Athenian national characters, see Fragoulaki (Chapter 11).

Marathon (a falsehood, but apparently a pervasive one) and by making the greatest contribution to the anti-Persian forces in 480–478 BCE;[14] the Greeks now owe them something in return.

Versions of these arguments can be found in several sources from classical Greece,[15] and it seems likely that their presence in Thucydides' account reflects the fact that this was a widespread – perhaps even dominant – mode of explaining and justifying Athens' imperial power. But are these arguments with which Thucydides himself agreed? Certainly, he seems to accept the immediate causal connection between the Persian Wars and the creation of the Delian League (indeed, as noted earlier in this chapter, his narrative makes more of this connection than some other ancient accounts). But all readers of Thucydides should know that immediate causes might not necessarily be the most important causes; this alone should prompt us to look more closely at this apparently straightforward model of imperial origins. Once we do so, it is not hard to find signs of ambivalence. Some of those hints appear in Thucydides' narrative. How loaded, for example, is his decision (at 1.96.1) to describe the alliance's anti-Persian objective as a *proschēma*? Should we translate this word as 'justification' or 'excuse'?[16] The suspicion that Thucydides might have the second meaning in mind is supported by the structure of the narrative that follows. The progression from the foundation of the (professedly) anti-Persian organization (at 1.96.1) to the 'enslavement' of Naxos and other Greek states (at 1.98), a process that in historical time spanned around twenty years, is covered in Thucydides' narrative in a little over two paragraphs. Is this extreme compression of the narrative merely pragmatic (the history of the Empire was, as we have already noted, not Thucydides' main subject) or is it intended as another hint that the 'Delian League' was never more than a respectable cover story for Athenian imperialism – and a cover story that rapidly crumbled at that?

The use of the Persian Wars as justification for empire is more straightforwardly undermined in several speeches given by both Athenians and non-Athenians. In justifying their desire to secede from the Athenian Empire, the

---

[14] Thuc. 1.73.4 (Marathon), 6.83.1 (Persian Wars as a whole). For the regular deployment in Athenian discourse of the claim to have 'fought alone at Marathon', see Walters 1981.

[15] The question is explored at great length in Isocrates' *Panegyricus* (but see esp. §§92–100 for the argument that Athenian imperialism can be justified by the city's contribution to the Persian Wars); compare also the emphasis on the Persian Wars (and Athens' role in it) in Lysias' *Epitaphios* §§27–43. The (non-Athenian) historian Theopompus takes a more sceptical view, claiming (at F153) that the Athenians use the history of the Persian Wars to 'mislead the Greeks'.

[16] Rawlings 1975: ch. 4, 1977.

Mytileneans are adamant that they no longer believe Athens' claims to be fighting Persia and protecting the Greeks: 'we did not become allies of the Athenians for the subjugation of the Greeks, but allies of the Greeks for their liberation from Persia; and as long as the Athenians led us fairly we followed them loyally; but when we saw them relax their hostility to Persia, and tending towards the enslavement of their allies, then our fears began' (3.10.3–4). Hermocrates of Syracuse is, if anything, even blunter. Athenian imperialism was, he claims, never about freeing the Greeks: 'in the struggle against the Persians, the Athenians did not fight for the freedom of the Greeks, or the Greeks for their own freedom, but the former to make the Greeks their slaves instead of Persia's, the latter to change one master for another, cleverer indeed than the first, but cleverer for evil' (6.76.4).

In speeches given by the Athenians themselves, the scepticism is less absolute, but it is still detectable. The first full-length Athenian speech in the work does include the conventional justification of empire (the Athenians provided the greatest resources to the fight against Persia, made the greatest sacrifices and so on: 1.74), but it introduces it in a way that draws attention to its hackneyed nature ('we are rather tired of continually bringing this subject forward': 1.73.2); moreover, as we will see later in this chapter, their arguments for the legitimacy of Athens' empire are based not on the past or current threat from Persia, but on much wider claims about human nature and the motivations of states. The Athenian ambassador Euphemus (responding to the speech of Hermocrates mentioned above) is blunter. The Athenians, he asserts, 'deserve to rule because we placed the largest fleet and an unflinching patriotism at the service of Greece' (6.83.1); but having made that claim, he then seems immediately to reject it in favour of a more pragmatic argument: 'we make no fancy claims to having a right to our empire because we overthrew the barbarian single-handed, or because we put ourselves at risk for the freedom of our allies, rather than for a general freedom (including our own) ...'.

Thucydides might not, therefore, explicitly tell us that he believed that the Athenian assertion that their Empire was deserved reward for saving Greece from Persia was nonsense. But he certainly provides numerous invitations to his readers to scrutinize, and perhaps reject, such arguments. That, however, raises another question: if the Persian Wars are not the real root of Athenian imperialism, then what is?

Explaining Empire: Fear, Honour and Profit

What, then, does Thucydides offer as the 'truest cause' of the existence of empire? To find the clearest indication of this, we can return to the speech of the Athenian ambassadors in Book 1. Here, as we have seen, the Athenians do pay rather weary lip service to the conventional, Persian War-based justification of empire. But they then proceed to offer an alternative explanation based not on contingent historical developments but on what (they argue) are persistent truths of human and interstate behaviour:

> It follows that it was not a very wonderful action, or contrary to the common practice of mankind [*apo tou anthrōpeiou tropou*], if we did accept an empire that was offered to us, and refused to give it up under the pressure of three of the strongest motives: fear, honour, and profit [*hupo <triōn> tōn megistōn nikēthentes, timēs kai deous kai ōphelias*]. And it was not we who set the example, for it has always been the law that the weaker should be subject to the stronger. (1.76.2)

This is a justifiably famous claim,[17] and one that is often pointed to as summing up the distinctively Thucydidean view of empire. We should, of course, note that this is presented as an Athenian argument, not Thucydides' own; nevertheless, the way in which the ideas are formulated – particularly the appeal to unchanging human nature – does seem consonant with views that the historian himself endorses elsewhere in the work.[18] And the three key factors to which the Athenians appeal – fear, honour and profit – are also themes that recur in the *History* and deserve further scrutiny.

The claim that Athenian behaviour is driven by honour (*timē*) is probably the most conventional part of the ambassadors' formulation. The idea that the quest for honour was a driving force for both individuals and states is visible in a whole range of Greek texts, from Homeric epic to inscribed decrees. The connection between ruling and honour is also well-established,[19] and the specific connection between Athens' position of imperial rule and the city's status in the Greek world is also something that appears in other sources (e.g. Demosthenes 9.74, with a touch of nostalgia for lost glories). That Athenian imperial policy is shaped by the quest for honour is an idea that surfaces elsewhere in Thucydides' text too – although we should note that this desire for honour is not (in Thucydides' account) necessarily unproblematic: he makes his Pericles warn the Athenians against getting carried away with their quest for honour (2.63.1); later, he suggests that the unrestrained pursuit of personal honour was a key factor in causing Athens' downfall (2.65.7).

---

[17] For its importance in contemporary analyses of international relations, see Schlosser (Chapter 19).

[18] For 'human nature' as part of Thucydides' own world view, see especially 1.22.4.

[19] In Homer, see Cairns 1993: 95–103; in inscribed decrees, see Lambert 2011. More generally on the concept, see Cairns 2019: 75–9.

The singling out of *ōphelia* ('benefit' or 'profit') as a driving factor in Athens' imperial behaviour is more novel. Its appearance here draws attention to a distinctive feature of the Athenian Empire, and a prominent theme of Thucydides' work: namely, the connection between power and wealth. That the Empire caused massive amounts of wealth to flow into Athens is undeniable; and although the modern debate about what exactly the Athenians did with that wealth is ongoing, what is absolutely clear is that many ancient commentators saw a clear connection between Athens' enrichment (particularly through the collection of tribute) and its oppression of its subject-allies.[20]

Thucydides, however, has a particular interest in the relationship between power, empire and profit.[21] This is a theme whose importance has already been flagged in the 'Archaeology'. The story of the first empire in the Greek world is (for Thucydides) a story of the annexation of resources, and of the deployment of those resources to attain more power (1.4, on Minos' 'thalassocracy'). When he comes to describe the foundation of the Delian League, one of the very few pieces of administrative information that he provides relates to the introduction and organization of the system of tribute payment (1.96.2). The centrality of tribute to the maintenance of empire recurs at critical points of the narrative: in Pericles' catalogue of Athens' accumulated wealth, reported just after the outbreak of war (2.13); and in the description of the Athenians' decision to abolish tribute in the midst of the looming disaster of the Sicilian Expedition. (This description – not coincidentally – is juxtaposed with the appalling account of the massacre at Mycalessus, carried out by mercenaries who had been left unpaid as a result of Athens' financial mismanagement (7.29–30).) Athens' empire brings wealth; and as their wealth drains away, so too does the city's grip on power.

In Thucydides' world, therefore, wealth both sustains and is sustained by imperial power. But there is an important complication: wealth – and the desire for wealth – is also a destructive force. This, too, is foreshadowed at an early stage of Thucydides' history: Pericles, in his final speech, warns the Athenians against excessive acquisitiveness (2.62.3); and in his 'obituary' for Pericles, Thucydides argues that it is his successors' quest for personal *ōphelia* (as well as *timē*) that dooms Athens to failure (2.65.7–8). The destructive consequences of this drive for wealth are exposed particularly

---

[20] The connection is most arrestingly presented in Plutarch's *Pericles* 12, but it is visible in contemporary sources too: e.g. Aristophanes *Wasps* 655–63 (for the claim that allied *phoros* funded pay for Athenian jurors); Isoc. 8.82 (for the spectacle of display of *phoros* at the Great Dionysia). For further discussion, see Kallet-Marx 1994.

[21] Explored in detail in Kallet-Marx 1993a; Kallet 2001.

sharply in the Sicilian Expedition: the Athenian *dēmos* (according to Thucydides) was motivated by the belief that this enterprise would allow them to 'earn wages at the moment, and make conquests that would supply a never-ending fund of pay for the future' (6.24.3). The quest for profit that drives imperial expansion, if allowed to get out of control, can also destroy it.

The third element of the Athenian ambassadors' formula – fear – is perhaps the most interesting of all. At first sight, the inclusion of this element might seem paradoxical: why should the most powerful city in Greece be afraid? But what Thucydides' text proceeds to explore is the proposition that it is not power itself that makes the Athenians afraid, but rather the fear of the consequences of losing it. Pericles warns the Athenians of this in his final speech:

> You cannot decline the burdens of empire and still expect to share its honours. You should remember also that what you are fighting against is not merely slavery as an exchange for independence, but also loss of empire and danger from the animosities incurred in its exercise. Besides, to step back is no longer possible, if indeed any of you in the alarm of the moment has become enamoured of the honesty of such an unambitious part. For what you hold is, to speak somewhat plainly, a tyranny; to take it perhaps was wrong, but to let it go is unsafe. (2.63.1–2)

For Pericles, the proper goal of the Athenians should therefore be to keep tight hold of their existing empire. Post-Periclean leaders take a more expansionist approach to imperial security, but Thucydides suggests that they (or at least some of them) are driven by the same underlying motivation.[22] According to (Thucydides') Euphemus, justifying – or at least explaining – the Athenian invasion of Sicily: 'fear makes us hold our empire in Greece, and fear makes us now come, with the help of our friends, to arrange affairs safely in Sicily ...' (6.83.4).

Fear, honour and profit are, then, not just guiding forces for the Athenian ambassadors in Book 1, but also factors that seem to shape Thucydides' analysis of the Athenian Empire over the course of its history. It is worth noting that none of these three factors are uniquely applicable to imperial powers. Honour, as we have seen, is pervasive in Greek culture. Profit is less talked about but (in Thucydides' world at least) is certainly not an objective only of imperial states (compare, for example, the Corinthians' warning to

---

[22] A partial exception to this pattern is visible in the Melian Dialogue, where the Athenian ambassadors boast of their freedom from fear (e.g. at 5.91); though even here there is still a concession that future defections by smaller states might be a cause of anxiety.

smaller states, outside the Athenian Empire, who risk seeing their profits being squeezed by Athens' growth: 1.120.2). And fear, in particular, is a powerful force in Thucydides' explanations of the foreign politics of all states, not just in this period (it is central to his explanation of the causes of the Peloponnesian War at 1.23: Athenian power caused Spartan fear), but across Greek history (he claims that it was fear that drove the Greeks to join Agamemnon's expedition to Troy: 1.9.4). These factors are not, therefore, sufficient conditions for the creation of an empire; they might provide the motive, but any causal model still needs to find room for the opportunity, and in particular the opportunity for these three factors to work together to produce their (allegedly) inevitable outcome. Contingent factors – the Persian Wars and the nature of Athenian politics (and perhaps Athenian character) – therefore need to retain some role in explaining why empire fell into Athenian hands.

A picture of imperial origins that emphasizes abstract, impersonal forces might seem much more rational, even 'scientific', than one based on revenge and glory. But it is not, of course, unbiased. Indeed, its very claim to universality masks an important element of subjectivity. If we accept Thucydides' (or Thucydides' Athenians') claim that there is nothing 'unusual, or contrary to human nature' in what they have done, it might follow that the Athenians should become less liable to censure for the excesses of their Empire. The Athenian Empire is (according to this model) called into being by factors that are not only predictable, but even inescapable.[23] We could note, in fact, that the Athenian ambassadors are made to talk of having been 'conquered' (*nikēthentes*: 1.76.2) by these three forces – fear, honour, profit – as if all Athenian agency in the formation of their Empire had been entirely surrendered. This stripping away of historical agency and historical contingency is one of the things that has made this model for explaining the growth of empire so appealing to post-ancient theorists of imperialism, but it also risks limiting – or at least distorting – our understanding of how this empire was understood in Thucydides' own time.

The End of Empire

Thucydides therefore offers us more than one way to explain why and how the Athenian Empire came into being and what drove it to behave in the way

---

[23] For further discussion of the (alleged) inevitably of empire and the moral or ethical ramifications of this, see Woodruff (Chapter 14).

that it did. And he also has important – if sometimes tantalizingly elusive – ideas about the reasons why their rule failed to persist.

One reason why these ideas are elusive is because Thucydides' narrative does not cover the final collapse of the Empire. His comments on the last years of the war (and, by extension, of the Empire) are therefore found only in proleptic digressions, most famously those in the 'obituary' of Pericles at 2.65. Here, Thucydides seems to suggest that defeat could have been avoided if the Athenians had been better led after Pericles' death and (as a consequence, in Thucydides' logic) had made better decisions about the management of the war. The connection between the outcome of the war and the fate of the Empire is not made absolutely explicit in this passage, but the dots are there for those readers who wish to join them: Pericles' policy, as Thucydides presents it at 2.65, was one that would have enabled Athens both to maintain their Empire and to win the war; in fact, maintaining the Empire is portrayed as being critical to avoiding defeat ('they would win through if they kept patient, looked to the maintenance of their navy, and did not try to extend their Empire in the war': 2.65.7, trans. Hammond 2009). The beginning of the tale of the end of the Empire, as recounted by Thucydides in Book 8, is certainly consistent with the view that the fate of the Empire and the outcome of the war are inextricably connected. The disastrous failure of Athens' misguided attempt to expand into Sicily sparks a wave of defections from the Empire, which further weakens Athens' position in the war. However, as Thucydides makes clear (8.1), this in itself was not enough to finish off either the war or the Empire; and already in Book 2 he has suggested that other factors (political unrest within Athens and interference from Persia: 2.65.12) will also be relevant to explaining these final phases. But exactly how Thucydides would have weighted these various factors remains unclear.

That being so, it is no surprise that it is also not at all easy to reconstruct Thucydides' view of the specific cause (or causes) of the collapse of the Athenian Empire. Again, we might usefully deploy Thucydides' own distinction between superficial and underlying explanations. The superficial cause is plain enough: the Athenians lost their Empire because they lost the Peloponnesian War (as Xenophon reports, dismantling of the alliance was a condition of the peace agreement that ended the war: *Hellenica* 2.2.20). But did Thucydides believe that there were deeper forces that drove the Empire to destruction?

One possible answer to this question might lie in an idea that appears not in Thucydides' own voice, but in words that he attributes to a number of speakers: that is, the image of the Empire as tyrant. The comparison is made first, as a warning to other Greeks, by Corinthians at 1.124.3, and then by three Athenian speakers: Pericles (2.63.2), Cleon (3.37.1) and – slightly more obliquely – Euphemus (6.85.1).[24] The comparison is intended to say something about the nature of the Athenian Empire: tyrannical power is illegitimate, acquired and maintained by trickery or force, or both; the tyrant is driven by greed and self-interest; and he disregards established laws and conventions. All of these charges could be made (*mutatis mutandis*) against the Athenian Empire. But the comparison with tyranny might also help us understand why Athenian power does not survive. Another characteristic of tyrannical rule, as the Greeks understood it, was that it was inherently unstable: tyranny would never persist for long, precisely because of its illegitimacy, cruelty and lack of self-control.[25] To liken an empire to a tyranny, therefore, is also to suggest a particular view of its chances of survival (and of the reasons why it will not survive).

Is this the conclusion that Thucydides intended his readers to draw about the Athenian Empire? Caution is necessary, for more than one reason. First of all, we need again to remember that these comparisons with tyranny are made by Thucydides' speakers, not in the historian's own voice. The fact that multiple speakers (including characters as different as Pericles and Cleon) make the same point does show that this was a comparison that Thucydides wanted to represent as being an established part of political discourse – and even if we can say no more than this, this is still something worth noticing. Can we go further? Thucydides' narrative undoubtedly contains numerous episodes in which the Athenians behave in ways that could be labelled 'tyrannical' (according to the definitions outlined above),[26] and it is certainly not an impossible leap to conclude that he also viewed the Empire as a tyranny. But the leap is still needed.

One reason why the 'unstable tyranny' model of imperial collapse is appealing, however, is because it seems broadly consistent with another – albeit once more largely implicit – line of analysis that we might detect in Thucydides' account. Let us return to the tricolon of imperial motivators discussed in the previous section: honour, fear and profit. As we have seen, these are factors that can be depicted as driving a state towards empire, but

---

[24] The concept of 'imperial tyranny' is thoroughly analysed by Tuplin 1985.

[25] See, briefly, Andrewes 1974: 21–3; Thucydides' comments on the Athenian tyrants (at 6.54) suggest that he was aware of but did not entirely endorse the popular view that tyranny was necessarily a corrupt and corrupting form of government (see Grethlein (Chapter 2) for further discussion of this section of Thucydides' text and Balot (Chapter 15) for Thucydides' views on tyranny more generally).

[26] For example: population displacement at Histiaea (1.114.3); mass executions and property confiscations at Mytilene (3.50), Melos (5.116) and Scione (5.32); and the problematic relationship with wealth, discussed earlier in this chapter.

they are also potentially destructive if they are pursued with too little moderation or with distorted purposes (e.g. with an eye to what benefits individuals rather than the state as a whole). Honour, fear and profit, in other words, not only compel a state to acquire an empire; they also encourage behaviours that can lead to an empire's destruction.

From that initial observation, we could develop two possible theories of imperial collapse. The first of these would not look wholly out of place in some contemporary theoretical contexts. The Athenians (one might see Thucydides as arguing) get trapped in a version of the 'security dilemma': their anxieties about the security and prosperity of their rule lead them to overreact to perceived external (e.g. from Sparta) and internal (i.e. from their subject-allies) threats by, in the former case, aggressive military action and, in the latter, repressive strategies of control and resource extraction; but those actions in fact lead to countermeasures from the other parties (war with Sparta; more resistance from subject allies). In the end, the perceived threats turn into real ones, and measures that were intended to ensure the well-being of the Empire end up leading to its downfall.[27]

An alternative theoretical model would return Thucydides to a more conventional (for classical Greece) context. One might argue that this explanation for imperial downfall – that uncontrolled ambition (of various sorts) leads to disaster – is, essentially, a moral one: excessive greed, whether for money or for honour or for power, is ultimately self-destructive; those who fail to exercise self-control (*sophrosynē*) will inevitably be punished for this failing. This model very clearly influences Herodotus' presentation of the failure of the Persian Empire (a story that is almost certainly intended to carry some sort of lesson for the 5th-century BCE Athenians).[28] And it is an argument that is much more explicitly applied to the Athenian Empire in Isocrates' *On the Peace* (a text from the middle years of the 4th century BCE):

> And so far did they [i.e. the Athenians of the 5th century BCE] outdo all mankind in recklessness that whereas misfortunes chasten others and render them more prudent our fathers learned no lessons even from this discipline. And yet they were involved in more and greater disasters in the time of the Empire than have ever befallen Athens in all the rest of her history. (8.85–6)

There is, to be sure, nothing quite so blunt in Thucydides, but it is possible to see how one could start from Thucydides' text and arrive at Isocrates' conclusions without having to perform any violent conceptual U-turns along

---

[27] For a brief exploration of the problem, see Low 2015: 64–5.
[28] See especially the final section of the *Histories* (9.120–2), with Irwin 2018.

the way. An important difference (not least in its influence on the reception of Thucydides' presentation of this model) lies in the level of explicit moralizing that Isocrates provides and that Thucydides, for the most part, does not. This might bring us back to a characteristic of the Thucydidean picture of empire that we have already noticed: that is, its tendency to strip away from it the possibility of human agency and therefore of human control. For Isocrates, the Athenians are very clearly to blame for their actions; the same is less obviously or straightforwardly true for Thucydides.

This, then, leads to a second question about the collapse of the Athenian Empire. Is this pattern of imperial rise and fall – however it is conceptualized or theorized – inescapable? Was the Empire doomed to fail, or might it have survived if only the Athenians had acted differently or made different decisions? Yet again, this is a question to which there is more than one plausible answer. Both of the models outlined earlier in this chapter encourage the conclusion that the cycle of imperial boom and bust was impossible to break, being driven by either the inevitable forces of interstate politics or the failings of human nature. Thucydides' narrative of the very early stages of the Delian League (and Athenian Empire) can be read as being consistent with that conclusion, in that it seems to show that Athens' slide into tyrannical behaviour started early and progressed quickly: the League is founded at 1.96; by 1.98.4 the Athenians are 'enslaving' the Naxians, in contravention of 'established practice'.[29] As we have already seen, Thucydides' narrative is dramatically compressed at this point, but that compression is not accidental. Is Thucydides encouraging us to conclude that the fate of the Empire was set as soon as (or even before) the terms of the Delian League were settled?

For an alternative interpretation, we need to turn once more to 2.65, and to Thucydides' analysis of the reasons for Athens' defeat. On this point, Thucydides is quite clear: the failure can be attributed to Pericles' untimely death and to the fact that post-Periclean leaders abandoned his policy of moderation (a policy that may itself be largely a Thucydidean construction – but that is not critical in this context, since we are dealing here with Thucydidean theories, not with historical reality). A possible conclusion to draw from 2.65 might be that Athens' tumble into excess could have been avoided given better leadership. In other words: Athens might, by the start of the Peloponnesian War, already be on the upper reaches of the slippery slope

---

[29] The Greek term used here (*to kathestēkos*) is slightly ambiguous: a literal translation would be 'the established thing'; this might be a reference to a specific agreement or treaty (e.g. the terms of the Delian League) or a more general allusion to accepted practices of behaviour between states. In practice, as Gomme notes (Gomme et al. 1945–81: vol. I, 282), the outcome is the same: the Athenians are contravening expected standards of behaviour.

to disaster– the Empire is, in Pericles' final speech, already 'like a tyranny' – but the plummet into the abyss might still have been arrested. After Pericles' death, though, the slide begins again; by the time of Cleon's speech, the Empire *is* a tyranny, and its fate is sealed.

If that is a possible reading of Thucydides' text – and the 'if' needs to be emphasized – then it raises still further questions. Above all, we are left wondering what, exactly, the critical variable is. Should our conclusion be that Athens was unusually unlucky in that it had only one politician (Pericles) who was skilled enough to withstand the corrupting forces of imperial power, and that a well-managed polity would more easily have been able to withstand the pressures – systemic or moral – that the Empire created? Or should we see Pericles as the anomaly: the one man who might have been able to avert the inevitable? To put it another way: is imperial collapse (in Thucydides' eyes) the exception or the rule?

Conclusion

The fact that this chapter ends with an unanswered question is not coincidental. Thucydides does not give us a neat answer to the problem of the Athenian Empire – nor, indeed, does he clearly delineate what (he thought) the fundamental problems were. Did the Athenian Empire fail because it represented an inherently illegitimate form of power? Or was its collapse due to more historically or politically contingent reasons? As I have tried to show in this discussion, Thucydides explores (or allows his characters to explore) both of these possibilities, but he does not give us a clear-cut solution.

These questions lead us to a second area of uncertainty. Is Thucydides offering us an exploration of the mechanics of this particular instance of hierarchical interstate control (the thing we have come to call the 'Athenian Empire') or is he providing a model of power – of empire – that can legitimately be applied to other places and periods? As we have seen, there are certainly elements of his discussion that invite us to extrapolate universal lessons from this specific case. But there are also elements – including some things that Thucydides presents as universal – that are quite closely rooted in the particular context of 5th-century BCE Greece.

That final point deserves emphasis. There is a tendency to treat Thucydides as a writer who is unusually detached from his own time and place, and this is a reading that Thucydides himself encourages. But our understanding of Thucydides' picture of the Athenian Empire becomes much richer when we are alert to the ways in which he is responding to contemporary analyses of this remarkable institution, whether in order to undermine widely held beliefs (e.g. that the Persian Wars explained and justified Athenian imperialism) or to complicate – but perhaps ultimately reinforce – deeply held concerns about the corrupting effect of excessive power.

Further Reading

The clearest brief survey of the history of the Athenian Empire is Rhodes 1993b, while Meiggs 1972 remains the authoritative English-language study of the subject, covering key themes as well as offering a narrative account of the Empire's rise and fall. Non-Thucydidean sources, both literary and epigraphic, are collected in Osborne 2000 (which also includes very helpful contextualizing notes and other guidance). A long-standing controversy, not explored in this chapter, is the question of the 'popularity' of the Athenian Empire (i.e. was the Empire, as Thucydides' account seems to suggest, perceived by its subjects as an exploitative tyranny or did it in fact bring benefits to both rulers and ruled?). This debate played out especially in three important articles of the mid-20th century: de Ste. Croix 1954; Bradeen 1960; de Romilly 1966. Finley 1978 takes a more explicitly economic approach to the question of cost and benefit, but also has important things to say about the nature of imperial power in this period, as, too, do de Romilly 1963 and (for a useful perspective from a theorist of contemporary politics) Doyle 1986: 54–81.

11

MARIA FRAGOULAKI

Ethnicity in Thucydides

Introduction

When thinking of ancient Greek ethnicity and the notion of the Other it is Herodotus rather than Thucydides who first springs to mind. Herodotus' rich ethnographic material and his fondness for unlocking the mysteries of foreign cultures have rightly been viewed as a rediscovery and redefinition of the Greeks' ethnic sense of belonging.[1] His pages also contain valuable material on Greek ethnic characteristics: it is against a backdrop of constant tension between fragmentation and unity among the Greeks that we find the memorable definition of Greekness (put into the mouths of Athenians addressing Spartans), which dominates all discussions of ancient Greek ethnicity: '[We] are all Greeks – one race [*homaimon*], speaking one language [*homoglōsson*], with temples to the gods and religious rites in common, and with a common way of life [*ēthea homotropa*]' (8.144.2).[2]

Yet it is Thucydides who concentrates on what might be called 'internal ethnic Otherness'; that is, the character and interrelations of the ethnic subgroups of the Greeks and different communities within the Greek world (the *Hellenikon*, a term found in our sources, including Thucydides, to denote the Greeks (*Hellenes*) as a whole).[3] This is not surprising, since the war he aimed to describe and explain was one among Greeks. In addition to the conflicts and convergences within the *Hellenikon*, Thucydides was also occupied with the role of the 'foreign factor' – what the Greeks called 'barbarians' – in Greek affairs. This discussion of ethnicity in Thucydides aims to address the following interrelated questions: what is Thucydides' contribution to our understanding of ancient Greek ethnicity? What is the

---

[1] E.g. Hartog 1988; Munson 2001, 2014; Gruen 2011; Skinner 2012; Thomas 2013.
[2] Translations used: for Herodotus: R. Waterfield (Oxford World's Classics, 1998); for Thucydides: M. Hammond (Oxford World's Classics, 2009), with minor changes of mine.
[3] On the *Hellenikon* and the idea of panhellenism, see Konstan 2001; Price 2001 ('internal war'); Hall 2002; Mitchell 2007; Hornblower 2008.

role of descent and cultural factors in constructions of ethnicity in Thucydides and in 5th-century BCE Greece more broadly? What is the role of ethnicity in his description and analysis of an ethnic conflict? In this enquiry, Herodotus will be a constant point of reference.

'Ethnicity' is a modern term, related to nationality and other modern concepts, and it derives from the Greek word *ethnos*, which was used by the ancient Greeks to designate a social – and often political – entity with distinct and shared characteristics.[4] These characteristics are primarily cultural and may be expressed through language, customs, values, beliefs, mythical and historical narratives of descent, memories and emotions, material culture and so on. The theoretical landscape of ethnicity is extremely rich. Among the most influential theories in discussions of ancient ethnicity and ethnogenesis are those represented by the work of Benedict Anderson (*Imagined Communities*) and by the ethnosymbolist school, whose pivotal figure is Anthony Smith.[5] Ethnicity is inherently dynamic and negotiable, since the sense of ethnic belonging is a matter of individual and collective (self-)perceptions and therefore relative to time and place and prone to change, like all social phenomena. This is in opposition to the concept of racism, which assumes fixed, essentialist hierarchies based on genetically determined biological types.[6]

Ancestors, blood ties and descent do play a role in ancient Greek ethnicity and in the construction of individual and communal identities. The notion of descent at the interstate level reflects human family models and hierarchies, as the idiomatic use of the word *sungeneia* ('kinship') shows. *Sungeneia* (*xungeneia* in Thucydides) primarily applies to biological kinship between individuals. When transferred to the intercommunal level, *sungeneia* encompasses ties between communities, such as the relationship between a *metropolis* and its foundations (*apoikiai*), or the ties between the *apoikiai* of the same mother-city and their own foundations or the ties between members of the same ethnic group (Ionians, Dorians, etc.) more broadly. Nevertheless, the concept and practice of intercommunal kinship are flexible and go well beyond *sungeneia* in the strict sense (i.e. ties based on some form of collective

---

[4] On archaic and classical Greek contexts of *ethnos* (and *genos*), see Jones 1996; McInerney 2001; Morgan 2001, 2003. Cf. 165–6.

[5] Smith identifies six defining factors of an ethnic group (*ethnie*): a collective name; a common myth of descent; a shared history; a distinctive shared culture; an association with a specific territory; and a sense of solidarity (Smith 1986: 21–31). On ancient Greek ethnicity, see Hall 2002; Luraghi 2008: 9–10; Derks and Roymans 2009; Luraghi 2014; McInerney 2014.

[6] Ashcroft et al. 2013: 96. On forms of racism in the Greco-Roman world ('proto-racism'), see Isaac 2004; McCoskey 2012; Jesse 2014 (primordialism versus constructivism).

descent) to encompass a range of social and political mechanisms that create interstate connections. Political systems and power relations are also closely associated with constructions of ethnicity, and Thucydides provides many excellent insights into these interrelations.[7]

Greeks and Others

Thucydides opens the Sicilian books (6 and 7) with a digression on the 'barbarians' of Sicily (6.2.6); that is, the populations of the island before the arrival of the Greek settlers, whom he calls Sikeliots (*Sikeliōtai*). The ethnic name is also found in Old Comedy (Eupolis K-A fr. 303, vol. 5, 474), so it is not necessarily Thucydides' invention. Of the 'barbarians' of Sicily, the people of Egesta (Segesta, an Elymian city) are arguably the most significant non-Greeks in Thucydides, and certainly in the Sicilian books, who managed – with fervent pleas, little financial and military help and many false promises – to lure the Athenians into the disastrous Sicilian Expedition of 415–413 BCE. Their appearance and disappearance in the narrative is an excellent example of strong authorial agency.

Thucydides says that the Egestaeans were of Trojan descent and came to Sicily after the fall of Troy (6.2.3). In authorial and rhetorical passages, time and again these people are tagged as 'barbarians' (*barbaroi* or *allophuloi*, another term indicating ethnic Otherness) (6.2.6; 9.1; 11.7; 7.57.5) and as being in close interaction with the Athenians. They appear as the most secure non-Greek allies and friends of the Athenians in Sicily (6.6.2; 10.5; 18.1). Yet despite their explicit characterization as 'barbarians', there are indications in the text that point to a certain familiarity with Greek manners: they seem to be familiar with Greek social and religious rituals, such as supplication (6.19.1) and the entertainment of guests (*xenisis*, 6.46.3). The temple of Aphrodite Erykina (6.46.3) and intermarriages between them and people from the Greek (and Dorian) city of Selinous (a colony of Hyblaia Megara; 6.4.2), about sixty kilometres to the south, further attest to the Greek element in their culture. Aphrodite's temple on Mount Eryx itself was a symbol of the mixed culture of the area (including native Sicilian, Italic, Greek and Phoenician elements) and was linked with the myth of the Trojan Aeneas' coming to the west after the fall of Troy together with Greek heroes such as the Homeric Odysseus. Sources outside Thucydides and archaeological evidence testify to a cultural fusion and to the Greek (and especially

---

[7] Jones 1999; Low 2007; Patterson 2010 (on myth's role in constructions of kinship); Fragoulaki 2013.

Dorian) element in the ethnic profile of the Egestaeans, which is underplayed in Thucydides.[8]

The theme of Trojan Otherness first emerges in the opening section of Thucydides' *History*, known as the 'Archaeology'. The Trojan War is presented as the first common undertaking of the Greeks against ethnic Others, occurring at an early time and representing a decisive moment in the gradual construction of a panhellenic sense of ethnic belonging (1.3.1–2). Thucydides stresses the role of ethnic names in this process, using Homer as evidence. He says that nowhere does Homer use the term 'barbarians' to refer to the Trojans, apparently because he does not use the term 'Greeks' (*Hellēnes*) either (1.3.3). The idea of ethnic self-definition by opposition to the Other might be detected in Thucydides' statement. But as in the case of the Egestaeans, Trojan Otherness was not only opposed, but also very proximate to Greekness, and in the course of the *History* we find the general category 'barbarians' acquiring different degrees and sorts of Otherness.[9]

In the history of 5th-century BCE Greece, the Persians appear to be the more prominent category of 'barbarians', comprehensively called 'the barbarian' (*ho barbaros*, 1.18.2; cf. Hdt. 7.163.1). Yet Thucydides, who wishes to underscore the magnitude and complexity of 'his own' war, tends to keep the Persians in the background of his account, some exceptions aside.[10] Already in the opening of the 'Archaeology' the 'previous conflicts' (1.1.1) are deemed less noteworthy than the war between the Peloponnesians and the Athenians. This is a first implicit reference to both the Trojan and the Persian wars, which, in the 'Archaeology', feature as the pivotal events of Greek history from early times until the Peloponnesian War (1.3; 1.9.4; 1.12.1; 1.14.2; 1.18.2; 1.23.1). 'Who saved Greece from the Persians' is one of the big questions of the 5th century BCE, found in both Thucydides and Herodotus (Hdt. 7.139). Thucydides' answer suggests a contrast between the 'unity' of the past (or rather the ideology and rhetoric of it) and the divisions of the present: he says that the victory over 'the barbarian' was Athens' and Sparta's common accomplishment and the result of their 'common front in battle' (*homaichmia*; 1.18.2–3). This latter term is loaded with emotional overtones, especially in the light of the famous definition of Greekness found in Herodotus, which contains a number of *homo*-starting words (*homaimon, homoglōsson, homotropa ēthea*; see earlier in this

[8] Fragoulaki 2013: 304–5. Cf. Vlassopoulos 2013: 105–13.
[9] On Greeks and Trojans, see Erskine 2001; cf. below on the Molossians (Epirus, north-western Greece); on Greeks and Others more generally, see Harrison 2001; Rosen and Sluiter 2010.
[10] Munson 2012, with bibliography.

chapter), underscoring the things shared by the Greeks. That said, it is Herodotus too who, alongside constructing the idea of unity, exposes the conflicts within the Greek alliance in the Persian Wars.[11] Thucydides shows that it is this idea of unity that the Peloponnesian War came to demolish for good, bringing to the fore the tensions, grievances and differences among the Greek communities.

As with the Trojans, there were not only conflicts but also contacts between the Greeks and the Persians, which can be traced in Thucydides. Already in the 'Archaeology' we hear of the Asian origins of mythical ancestors of the Peloponnese (1.9);[12] and in the context of Thucydides' uneven reporting of Greco-Persian diplomacy, it is Sparta rather than Athens that occupies his attention. The episode of the intercepted letter of King Artaxerxes I to the Spartans shortly before his death (424 BCE) is a well-known incident (4.50). Another is the excursus on Pausanias the Regent, which, together with its narrative pair – the excursus on the Athenian Themistocles (see later in this chapter) – poses questions of ethnic characteristics in connection with distinguished individuals.[13] Letter exchange takes place in the Pausanias excursus as well, this time between Pausanias and the Persian king Xerxes. Pausanias expresses the wish to marry the king's daughter in exchange for the freedom of Greece (1.128.7). His pro-Persian inclinations (note the term 'medism', 1.135.2) are also reflected in a number of cultural criteria, such as his eating and dressing habits and the general demeanour of an Oriental archon. As for Pausanias' violent manners, the stereotype of Spartan harshness intersects with the tyrannical harshness of Oriental despots, so well depicted in Herodotus.[14]

The Thracians receive an impressive amount of attention in Thucydides. The geographical and ethnographic tour de force on Thrace (2.96–8) is probably not unrelated to Thucydides' own ties with the region or to Herodotus' interest in it.[15] Thucydides describes a vast territory occupied by several barbarian tribal communities and uses a number of cultural criteria to describe Thracian Otherness: the role of gold and silver and gift exchange (also drawing a comparison with the Persians, 2.97.4; cf. 1.129.3);

---

[11] Baragwanath 2008: 171–8.   [12] Cf. Gruen 2011: 229.
[13] On Pausanias' portrait in Herodotus (4.81.3; 5.32) and interaction with Thucydides, see Hornblower 2013: 133; cf. Herodotus 9.78–82, with Flower and Marincola 2002: 11–15.
[14] On the violent character of Spartan generals, see Hornblower 2011a: 250–74. For the comparison of Pausanias' generalship to a tyranny, see 1.95.3. On Sparta and Persia, see Lewis 1977; on Athens and Persia, see Miller 1997.
[15] Zahrnt 2006; Graninger 2015.

the modes of warfare of different tribes of the region; and political organiza-tion and proneness to plundering (2.98). Interaction between non-Greek and Greek elements was intense, especially in the coastal area of Thrace, which was studded with Greek settlements of Ionian stock (the Chalcidic cities of the north). Athens had vital and long-standing interests in the area and a number of settlements on the Thracian Chersonese and westwards, among them Amphipolis on the river Strymon (4.102; 5.11; see also later in this chapter). Thucydides also refers to the Thracian Sadokos, the son of the Odrysian king, and his admission to the Athenian citizen population (an institution of civic inclusion known as 'naturalization') (2.29.5; 2.67). The language by which Sadokos' naturalization is described ('becoming an Athenian', *ton gegenēmenon Athēnaion*, 2.67.2) reflects the transformative power of political and cultural institutions (on Sadokos' participation in the Apatouria, see Ar. *Ach.* 145–6).[16] Such ethnic transformations destabilize the fixed boundaries of descent groups and the validity of rigid and obsolete models of kinship based solely on biology, which have been superseded by post-1970s anthropological discourses.[17] There were also moments when interactions between the Greek and the barbarian elements could have disastrous results, as in the havoc wreaked by the dagger-carriers of the Thracian tribe of the Dii under the leadership of the Athenian general Diitrephes in the small Greek (Boeotian) community of Mycalessus in main-land Greece. Thucydides' explanation of the barbarism of these Thracians has an essentialist flavour: 'For the Thracian race [*genos*], when they are feeling confident, are extremely bloody, equal to any of the barbarians' (7.29.4). A good part of these Thracians die by drowning as they try to escape (7.30.2). Death by drowning due to an inability to swim is viewed in Greek and Roman sources as a barbaric way of dying.[18]

The geographical closeness and at the same time cultural alienness reported of certain groups of mainland Greece, such as the Ozolian Lokrians, the Aetolians and the Akarnanians, neighbouring *ethnē* in central and western Greece, reflect another challenge in the study of Greek ethnicity. Nominally they seem to belong to the Greek world, but their ethnographic characteristics (and indeed their positioning *vis-à-vis* the Hellenic Genealogy, as defined by Hellen and his descendants) are barbaric.[19]

---

[16] In this connection, Pericles' citizenship law (451/50 BCE) (Arist. *Ath. Pol.* 26.3), not mentioned in Thucydides, might be viewed as a mechanism of collective transformation and ennoblement of the citizen body; Blok and Lambert 2009.

[17] Strathern 1992; Carsten 2000.

[18] On swimming in Greek, Roman and later European nationalistic discourse, see Hall 2006: 155–87. On Thucydides, the Thracians and Mycalessus, see Kallet 1999; Sears 2013; Fragoulaki 2020a.

The desperate choice of the citizens of the Greek city of Ambrakia in Akarnania (a Corinthian *apoikia*, 2.80.3) between two potential ways of death, both by enemy hands, illustrates the role of the barbarian Other in a setting of a disrupted unity within the Greek *ethnos*. The Dorian Ambrakiots, Thucydides says, preferred to be slaughtered by the Greek (and Ionian) Athenians, if need be, rather than by the neighbouring Akarnanians and Amphilochians, both of whom were viewed by the Ambrakiots as different sorts of 'hateful Others' (*echthistōn Amphilochōn*, 'most hateful Amphilochians', 3.112.7). The Akarnanians were thought of as barbarians, while the Amphilochians were a community of Akarnania, 'linguistically hellenised' (*hellēnisthēsan tēn glōssan*, 2.68.5) by the Ambrakiots themselves; this latter case was the sort of 'hateful Other' that was at times very close to one's ethnic self.

In the 'Archaeology', the Aetolians are referred to as part of Greece, but their way of life and military defence in Thucydides' time are represented as backward and reminiscent of barbarian groups (1.5.3). In addition to fitting the 'quasi-evolutionary account of Greek warfare after Troy'[20] in the 'Archaeology', this passage is further evidence of Thucydides' interaction with Homer, and the Homeric Catalogue of Ships in particular, where the Aetolian *ethnos* is mentioned (*Il.* 2.638–44). The Iliadic and other poetic catalogues of the archaic period, such as the Hesiodic Catalogue of Women (*Ehoiai*), where the Aetolians are also mentioned, are important sources of mythistorical material on Greek ethnicity.[21] Thucydides supplements his Aetolian ethnography, in the context of the Athenian campaign in the region, by providing us with a section (3.94–8) comparable to that on Thrace. He looks at their warfare, political organization, language and eating habits. As has been pointed out, these two passages on the Aetolians are the earliest references to the political organization of *ethnē*, and they have fuelled negative assumptions of primitivism in relation to *ethnē*:[22]

> The Aetolian *ethnos* was a large and warlike group who however lived in unwalled villages ... and used only light arms ... The Eurytanians, the largest tribe of the Aetolians, spoke a dialect more unintelligible than any of their neighbours and are believed to eat raw meat. (3.94.4–5)

---

[19] Hall 1997: 47; Dougherty and Kurke 2003: 30.   [20] Morgan 2003: 8.

[21] E.g. Hall 1997: 42–4; McInerney 1999: 120–7; Fowler 2013: 122–30. On the Aetolian *ethnos* in Thucydides, see Bommeljé 1988; on Thucydides' use of poetry, see Rhodes (Chapter 4); on the Mycalessus episode as Homeric interaction, see Fragoulaki 2020a.

[22] Morgan 2003: 7–10.

Gender provides an interesting angle from which ethnicity might be viewed. Women as individuals are generally absent from Thucydides. More often than not, they feature anonymously, together with children, as groups affected by the war.[23] They may also appear implicitly and anonymously in references to intermarriages between ethnically mixed communities, as in the case of 'barbarian' Egesta and 'Greek' Selinous (6.6.2), or royal houses. In the latter case, Stratonike, a politically important Macedonian princess and sister of King Perdikkas (2.101.5), gets a mention by name (2.101.6).[24] Another named royal woman is the Thracian queen Brauro, who killed her husband (and whose very name suggests *barbarism*) (4.107.3). There is also the anonymous queen of the 'barbarian' Molossians in Epirus, whose piety is the opposite of that of Brauro: she hosts the Athenian Themistocles and saves his life by teaching him the Molossian ritual of supplication and its persuasive power (1.136.3). The representation of Molossia and its queen in the episode as a civilized refuge of suppliants, a miniature Athens of the fringes, may be connected with Athens' increasing interest in the area in the 420s BCE. The queen's cultural closeness to the Greek world, and indeed Athens, might be one reason why she remains 'respectfully' unnamed.[25]

Greek Ethnicity: Tribal and Civic Identity

The 'Archaeology' provides ample evidence of Thucydides' attention to key factors of Greek ethnic identity: genealogies, colonization, ethnic names and shared history and culture. Hellen, the son of Deucalion, makes his appearance in this section as the eponymous ancestor of the Greeks (Hellenes) (1.3.2). He and his sons provided the charter myth of the main tribal divisions of the Greeks in the historical period: Aeolians, Dorians, Ionians and Achaeans. Terms denoting 'race', 'tribe' or 'ethnic group' (*phulon*, in the compound *allophulos*, 'belonging to a different ethnic group', 1.2.4; *ethnos* (1.3.2); and *genos*, in the compound *xungenes*, 1.6.4) are introduced in the

---

[23] The naming of Chryseis, the priestess of Argos, is exceptional in that she is part of a sequence of chronological markers (2.2.1).

[24] Cf. Carney 2010: 413. Regarding Macedonian ethnicity, Thucydides seems to refer to Macedonian troops as a separate category, being neither Greek nor barbarian (4.124.1; cf. 4.125.1); on the other hand, he decisively endorses the narrative of Argive (Temenid) descent of the Macedonian kings (2.99.3; 5.80.2), being part of the *communis opinio* of the classical period regarding the Greekness of the Macedonians (cf. Hdt. 5.22); Hatzopoulos 2011; cf. Hall 2001; Zahrnt 2006.

[25] On Athens and Molossia, see Fragoulaki 2013: 270–6. Key passage: 2.45.2; cf. Schaps 1977; Cartledge 1993; Hornblower 1991–2008: vol. II, 339 on 'women as agents in non-Greek areas'; Kallet-Marx 1993b; Crane 1996: 75–92.

'Archaeology', together with ethnographic and cultural criteria. It is here that Thucydides uses for the first time the recurrent phrase 'in virtue of kinship' (*kata to xungenes*, 1.6.4) to explain the similarity of dress and hairstyle between the early Athenians and their kinsmen, the Ionians. He is consistently attentive to similarity of practices (*to homoiotropon*) either in the cultural (1.6.6) or in the political sense (7.55.2), and he meticulously reports on customs (*nomima*) and language (*phōnē* or *glōssa*) in colonial or military contexts (e.g. 3.112.4; 6.5.1; 7.44.6; 7.57.2).

Intercommunal kinship (*xungeneia*) is an overarching theme in the *History*.[26] Thucydides' factoring of the so-called *Kerkyraika* (1.24–55) (a quarrel between an old and proud mother-city of Greece, Corinth, and its *apoikia*, Corcyra, over a third kin settlement of the same line of colonial descent, Epidamnus) into his complex explanation of the war in a provocatively pronounced manner leaves no doubt about the role of 'soft' factors (narratives of hatred and friendship, ethical codes and hierarchies) in war and politics – and a violent civil war at that, as the Peloponnesian War was, where perceptions of identity play a key role in constructing irreconcilable cleavages.[27] It is in this context that we are provided with the first catalogues of allies (1.27.2; 1.46.1). But the most impressive catalogue of allies in Thucydides is that before the battle in the Great Harbour of Syracuse (413 BCE; 7.57–8), which powerfully illustrates how narratives of ethnic belonging 'that normally determine alliances fail to hold':[28]

> These were the nations who fought at Syracuse on either side, coming against Sicily or on behalf of Sicily, choosing sides not so much on grounds of moral principle or kinship, but either as contingent factors, or interest or necessity determined it. (7.57.1)

After this opening phrase, in the rest of the catalogue Thucydides provides a number of examples of cities fighting against their colonial and/or tribal kinsmen. He comments on the incongruity of Aeolians fighting against Aeolians (and more precisely those from their mother-locality, the Boeotians) (7.57.5) and on the Dorian Argives fighting on the side of the Ionian Athenians, thus going against fellow Dorians (7.57.9). On the other hand, despite the acknowledged coercive character of the alliance between the Athenians and their tributary allies, such as the Eretrians and Chalcidians of Euboea or the Keians and Andrians of the Cyclades, he

---

[26] Fragoulaki 2013.
[27] See Kalyvas 2006 for a comparative political perspective, concentrating on the Greek Civil War of 1943–9, with appreciation of Thucydides' pioneering contribution to the understanding of the phenomenon.
[28] Connor 1984b: 196.

168

presents this alliance as a more 'natural' one on account of the common Ionian – and indeed colonial – descent between Athens and these communities (7.57.4).

The significance of Thucydides' evaluations can only be felt if this catalogue is read in the light of the excursus on the Greek colonization of Sicily at the opening of the Sicilian narrative, an authorial tour de force on early Sicilian history of catalogic tenor (6.2–5). It is also an expanded list of the kinship relations between Greek *metropoleis* and their settlements in Sicily and concurrently a codified map of ethnic claims, which enables us to read and assess the impacts of reversals of kinship relations set out in the Syracusan catalogue of allies.

Thucydides' nuanced and complex map of Greek ethnicity coexists with a vein of bipolarity and stereotyping, which is mainly related to schemas such as 'Athens versus Sparta', 'Ionians versus Dorians' or 'east versus west'.[29] Ethnic stereotyping is based on essentialist views of innate and immutable characteristics and differences between social groups, as reflected in phrases such as 'enemies by nature' (*phusei polemioi*, 6.79.2) or 'kinsmen by nature' (*phusei xungeneis*, 6.79.2). In the representation of the two major enemies, Athens and Sparta, ethnic stereotypes are constructed on the junction of ethnic and civic characteristics: that is, the features of each city's Ionian or Dorian identity together with its particular constitution and structures of civic organization and cultural characteristics (*tropoi*, *nomima*). Speeches provide crucial evidence for the sketching of the Athenian and Spartan characters, and the question of focalization is central here: how are the Athenians or Spartans represented through their own voices or the voices of others, including the authorial voice? Does the rhetoric of ethnicity mutate in the course of the war and its narration?[30]

The Corinthian speech to the Spartan assembly in approximately 432 BCE (1.68–71) is the key locus for looking at the Athenian and Spartan national characters in Thucydides. In an effort to mobilize their Dorian kinsmen to pursue the war against the Athenians, the Corinthians juxtapose Athenian daring, quick reactions, mobility, self-confidence and constant desire for more achievements and possessions with Spartan quietness (*hēsuchia*, 1.69.4), good sense (*sōphrosunē*, 1.68.1), dilatoriness, reluctance to leave home, slowness, old-fashioned way of life (*archaiotropa epitēdeumata*) and

---

[29] On Dorians and Ionians, see Alty 1982; Pelling 1997; Luginbill 1999 (a psychological explanation of the war based on a rigid opposition of Athens' and Sparta's national characters); Price 2001: esp. 147–61.

[30] Debnar 2001: 3; Scardino 2007: 681–2; Strasburger 2009; more generally on speeches in Thucydides, see Stadter 1973; Porciani 2007; Pelling 2009; Greenwood (Chapter 5).

religious over-scrupulousness (1.71.2; cf. 1.118.3; 5.54.2; 7.18.2). This general opposition between the two national characters emerges in several rhetorical and authorial passages in the *History*, at times to be confirmed, blurred or even reversed.

Another key locus for Athenian identity, through a nationalistic lens, is Pericles' Funeral Oration (2.35–46). It is an 'emic' (an insider's) description of what is presented as an active and extrovert society of distinct character (2.39.1) that is open to different sorts of imports (goods, 2.38; friends, 2.40.4–5). This openness is found cheek by jowl with the ideology of Athenian autochthony (2.36.1), based on the myth of the Athenians' provenance from the Attic soil, and praise of the democratic constitution (2.37, 41). The Athenians' 'relaxed life-style' (*aneimenōs diaitōmenoi*, 2.39.1) evokes the 'relaxed life-style' (*aneimenē diaita*, 1.6.3) of their kinsmen, the Ionians, in an earlier authorial passage.

Nicias' indirect and much shorter speech to the Athenian troops, characterized by Thucydides as 'old-fashioned speaking' (*archaiologein*), just before the crucial battle in Syracuse (413 BCE; 7.69.2) is another 'emic' description of Athenian character. Nicias, the wholly un-Athenian, conservative and laconizing Athenian general as presented by Thucydides, delivers a more traditional depiction of his own city, referring to ancestral pride, gods and familial and tribal values. At the other end of the spectrum, Alcibiades' rhetoric employs the ideology of helping those in need and being open to strangers as the moral underpinning of the expedition to Sicily (415 BCE) and Athenian imperialism more generally (6.18.2).

A hegemonic twist of the kinship argument is found in the address of Euphemus, the Athenian representative in the Camarina debate. Euphemus defends the Athenian leadership of the Ionians by contrasting Athenian courage and resistance in the Persian Wars with the servility of the Ionian *ethnos* as a whole (6.82), as part of a wider stereotypical contrast between east and west in the classical period.[31] Athenian military excellence was also confirmed from an outsider's ('etic') perspective in the Spartan general Brasidas' hesitation to engage high-quality Athenian troops in Amphipolis, who were 'pure Athenian citizens' (*Athēnaiōn katharon*, 5.8.2).[32]

---

[31] Pelling 1997; Mac Sweeney 2013. In the same debate, the Syracusan Hermocrates uses the Dorian versus Ionian stereotype (6.77.1; 80.3) against Athenian imperialism and in favour of Dorian unity and resistance. For the interlocking of 'soft' and 'hard' factors in the justification of Athenian imperialism, including emotions and national character, see Low (Chapter 10).

[32] On Athenian identity, see Ober 1989; Loraux 1993; Connor 1994; Hornblower 2011b: 132–5 (myths).

In Spartan speeches, good sense (*sōphrosunē*) and a certain lack of conventional rhetorical polish (cf. Sthenelaidas' blunt 'I don't understand all this Athenian talking', 1.86.1) emerge as distinctive features of the Spartan ethnic character. On the other hand, the authorial comment about Brasidas being 'not a bad speaker, for a Spartan' (4.84.2) indicates one of the un-Spartan qualities of this exceptional Spartan. Also, a number of authorial passages refer to the distinctiveness of the Spartan constitution and manners. Among these, the comment about the secrecy of the Spartan *politeia* stands out in sharp contrast to Athenian openness (5.68).[33]

More generally, as in the case of Athenian democracy, the Spartan constitution is central to the construction of Sparta's ethnic self.[34] Among its distinctive features are: the antiquity of the dual kingship in close relationship to its foundation rituals (5.16.3); the relationship between ephors and kings (1.131.2); the 'archaic' system of decision-making by shouting rather than by voting (1.87.2; cf. the Corinthian reference to the Spartans' old-fashioned way of life, 1.71.2); the idea that Sparta has always been free from tyranny (1.18.1); and its *eunomia* (1.18.1), a concept referring not so much to the city enjoying 'good laws', but mainly to the city being where the laws are respected.[35]

If each of the two cities is cast in a distinct and unique light, there are also moments when these characteristics are destabilized and the boundaries of ethnic character are blurred. Spartan religiosity is seriously compromised, for example, by their impious treatment of Plataea, a panhellenic symbol in the period after the Persian Wars (3.68). A compromised morality also emerges from the Athenian 'etic' description of the Spartans in the Melian Dialogue as people who blatantly equate 'comfort with honour, and expediency with justice' (5.105.4); the outcome of the Melian episode, as presented by Thucydides, corroborates this statement. And although the Ionian Athenians have their own claim to manly courage, it is the Dorians who are traditionally (self-)identified with manliness and freedom (cf. 5.9.1, Brasidas addressing Peloponnesian troops).

---

[33] Cf. Hdt. 9.34–5 (Teisamenos of Elis, the diviner, and his brother Hagias being the only outsiders ever to be admitted to Spartan citizenship). For Spartans in Thucydides, see Cartledge and Debnar 2006; more generally, see Powell and Hodkinson 1994. On suspicion as another Spartan feature, see, for example: 1.102.3–4, in their relationships with tribal outsiders, such as the Athenians; 1.132.2; 5.16.1; 34.2, between themselves; 4.80.3–4, towards the Helots.

[34] Derks and Roymans 2009: 1, on the relationship between ethnic identities and political systems.

[35] '[W]hat Sparta had was not so much law as *order*. And Thucydides knew that when he praised her,' Powell 2001: 242 (emphasis in original).

The stereotype is pronouncedly destabilized in the context of a battle outside Miletus in Ionia in 412 BCE. Thucydides comments on the somewhat unexpected outcome of the battle on ethnic grounds: 'A particular circumstance of this battle was that the Ionians on both sides had the better of the Dorians' (8.25.5). The Chians, though Ionians, are remarkably 'Spartan' ('Dorian Ionians')[36] in their possession of 'good sense' (sōphrosunē, 8.24.4) and a large number of slaves (8.40.2). The good order of their state (kosmos, 8.24.4) and the 'quietness' of their ruling officials (hēsuchian, 8.24.6) are further attributes alluding to Spartan–Dorian ethnicity.[37] The Dorian (and Corinthian) Syracusans, on the other hand, are islanders and a democracy (of sorts), and their growing confidence and adaptability to the challenges of the war put them in a clearly Athenian light (7.55.2; 8.96.5).

The fluid and dynamic character of ethnic characteristics can often be felt in the undermining and reaffirmation of stereotypes: there are moments of 'untypically Spartan' confidence and energetic pursuit of the war (7.18.2–4) and, conversely, moments of 'untypically Athenian' irrational fear (panic), loss of hope and despondency. Yet 'untypically Spartan' confidence and activity are set against an overarching and basic feeling that 'the gods are watching us', constitutive of Spartan morality (7.18.3; cf. 1.118.2–3). By the same token, 'untypically Athenian' despondency is succeeded by 'typically Athenian' determination and action. The authorial iterative presentation of the Athenians' evaluation of major setbacks and losses as being the worst possible reflects the cycle of despair and recovery of a basically optimistic nation. The sea and the navy are the standard recourses of the Athenians and the sources of their reborn determination each time. Their defeat in the Sicilian expedition – 'the most unfortunate event for those who were defeated' (7.87.5) – causes fear and utter despair (8.1.2), followed by an astonishing resilience (8.1.3). The same psychological cycle of dismay (greater than that caused by the Sicilian defeat) and rejuvenated determination is reported in connection with the loss of Euboea (8.96.1; 8.97.1).[38]

Shifts of identity, too, provide chances to observe the fluid boundaries of ethnicity. In the run-up to the Peloponnesian War, the Corcyraeans seem to have exploited the Phaeacian and Homeric aspect of their ethnic make-up in

---

[36] Hornblower 2011b: 39.
[37] Cf. Hdt. 1.65.4; Hornblower 1991–2008: vol. III, 819; Cartledge 1998a: 1–12.
[38] Cf. Pelling 1997: 65: 'By the end of the work Athens is still new-fangled and enterprising, Sparta is still an ideal enemy to fight with because she is still so stick-in-the-mud (Thuc. 8.96.5); but the categories have been heavily qualified too, with all those unspartan Spartans, and Sparta even becoming a sea-power. There as here the categories are simultaneously challenged and asserted, by a process of continual redefinition and renuancing.'

an attempt to detach themselves from the influence of their Dorian mother-city Corinth (cf. 3.70.4; the hero-cult of the Homeric king Alcinoos).[39] Naturalization is another mechanism of ethnic transformation, which has already been mentioned in relation to the Thracian 'Athenian' Sadokos. Naturalization could also apply to whole communities. The collective granting of Athenian citizenship to Plataea, an Aeolian city allegedly founded by Thebes (3.61.2), is a representative example (3.55.3; 63.2). Plataea's exceptional closeness to Athens replicated the loyalty of an *apoikia* to its mother-city and is described by the Thebans, the slighted mother-city, as 'atticism' (3.62.2).[40] But the most striking and rewarding description of the transformative power of ritual for the ethnic identity of a whole community in Thucydides is the refoundation of Amphipolis, an Athenian 5th-century BCE *apoikia* in Thrace (4.102.3), by the Spartan Brasidas in 424 BCE.[41] Brasidas, himself an un-Spartan Spartan, as we saw, posthumously assumes the role of the city's new founder. Thucydides provides valuable insight into the religious dimension of the colonial phenomenon and the malleable character of intercommunal kinship by describing in some detail what might be viewed as a collective ritual of adoption on the civic level.[42]

Conclusion: Ethnicity, Historical Explanation and Authorial Agency

The role of ethnicity in Thucydides can be viewed in the light of two interrelated questions: the first regarding the author's analysis of the Peloponnesian War and of the war as a more general phenomenon; and the second regarding the literary dimension of his work and relationship with tradition. Both are closely bound up with Thucydides' Athenian identity and with the ethnic identity and historical consciousness of his 5th-century BCE audience.[43] The shared historical and cultural contexts upon which this audience drew in order to perceive and 'fill in the gaps' in Thucydides' narrative were different from those of later and modern audiences, who might also be exposed to theories of ethnicity and concepts such as 'nationalism' or 'racism'.

Foundation traditions and the stories of the Greeks about their origins were part of these shared cultural contexts, whose immediacy and

---

[39] Cf. Rusten 2011 (on the Homeric and mythological background); Fragoulaki 2013: 78–9 (also on the Athenian western expert Phaiax, 5.4).

[40] Cf. Hdt. 6.108.1.   [41] For further analysis of this episode, see Ferrario (Chapter 12).

[42] Cf. 4.42.2: the Dorian Corinthians of Thucydides' time were previously Aeolians; Hdt. 8.73.3, on the 'Doricization' (*ekdedōrieuntai*) of the Cynourians, originally autochthonous Ionians of the Peloponnese, by the Argives.

[43] Marincola 1997; Baragwanath 2008 (on Herodotus' audience); Grethlein 2010b.

experience might escape that of a modern reader. For example, the reason behind what might seem an incomprehensible relief operation of the Peloponnesian fleet on their way to Sicily in support of the Euesperitans in northern Africa (7.50) can be explained if we are aware of the colonial ties between four generations of cities, Sparta – Thera – Cyrene – Euesperides, and their Herodotean and Pindaric intertexts (Hdt. 4.147–58; 5.42; Pi. *Pythians* 4 and 5). The brief mention of the Euesperitan episode in Thucydides seems to be the only textual vestige of this rich material.[44]

The tracing of ethnic information in Thucydides enables us to perceive the complexity of the war, the interrelations between major and minor centres and historical actors and the multiplicity of factors affecting interstate relations in moments of crisis, decision-making and military action. Alongside the two main protagonists of the war, Athens and Sparta, and other mainland centres of power, as well as other major allies of those cities (such as Corinth) or neutral parties (such as Argos), Thucydides' focus is also turned to communities that might be perceived as peripheral – either in terms of their locality or in terms of their size, power and fortunes in relation to the main thrust of the war. For example, Epidamnus on the Illyrian coast, quite off the beaten track, occupies much attention in the *Kerkyraika* and is presented as perhaps the most decisive factor that precipitated the outbreak of the Peloponnesian War (what Thucydides calls 'apparent causes', 1.23.6; with p. 168 in this chapter). Similarly, the account of 'family' problems between the two Aeolian cities in Boeotia, Plataea and its mother-city Thebes initiates the main narrative of the Peloponnesian War; the 'Plataean drama' occupies a big part of Books 2 and 3, together with its kin-city in the north-eastern Aegean, Mytilene. And there is also Dorian Melos, whose fame is owed to an author hard at work: building on ethnic stereotypes, in the 'Melian Dialogue' Thucydides constructs a philosophical debate on imperialist ideology and the interaction between considerations of power and ethical and affective factors, such as justice, the gods and stead-fastness to kinship (*xungeneia*).

The episode of Mycalessus (7.29–30) is another instance when local history comes into Thucydides' focus and becomes relevant to the narrative of the war at large. On this occasion, the ethnic factor and the stereotype of the 'barbarian bloodthirstiness' of the Thracians (7.29.4) is called upon to explain the massacre of a small Greek community of Boeotia, otherwise untouched by the war. More generally, an explanatory *topos* in Thucydides is the success or failure of military undertakings as a result of

---

[44] See Hornblower 2004: 114, 246–7. On Spartan colonial activity in Thucydides, see Fragoulaki 2020b.

the ethnic cohesion of troops (or the lack thereof). The pattern is applicable not only to the dichotomy 'Greeks versus barbarians', but also to the differences of fighting cultures within the *Hellenikon* (cf. the frightening effect of the harsh Dorian singing of the *paean* (a war song) on the Ionian Athenians in the general confusion of the night battle of Epipolae, 7.44.6).

National characteristics and stereotypes run deep in Thucydides' explanation of the war and its outcome. Thucydides points out that due to their different temperaments and political constitutions Athens and Sparta were the ideal enemies for each other (8.96.5). On the other hand, the Syracusans, being 'of similar character' (*homoiotropoi*, 8.96.5; cf. 6.20.3; 7.55.2) to the Athenians, were the worst possible enemies. What is the point of this broad brushing of ethnic features, which is anyway toned down or overturned at other moments? It might be suggested that this is Thucydides' reasonable means of explaining the inexplicable – his interpretation of the unexpected and disastrous outcome of the Sicilian Expedition and of the irrationality (*ho paralogos*, 7.55.1) of the war itself.[45]

Closely related to his explanatory mode and his engagement with the war as a complex phenomenon, where foresight (*pronoia*) and unpredictability coexist, is his interaction with prose and poetic genres of memory. This is particularly evident in the Sicilian books, which provide some of the most polished and dramatic pages of Thucydides. His representation of the Athenians' utter defeat in Sicily has been viewed as part of his systematic interaction with the Homeric text and the fall-of-Troy theme.[46] The Athenian expedition to Sicily in 415–413 BCE is represented as an act of collective madness, isolated from Athens' long-standing interest and previous initiatives in the west. The handling of Egesta's ethnic identity is arguably part of this programme. As we saw, Thucydides effaces the Greek (and Dorian) aspect from the city's mixed ethnic character and presents the Egestaeans as barbarians who managed to drag the Athenians into an absurd and disastrous undertaking. By doing so, Thucydides underscores the irrationality of the Athenian decision to sail to Sicily, a dangerous and largely unknown island to the Athenians, as presented in his work.

Last but not least, there is the question of Thucydides' intertextual relationship with Herodotus. This relationship can be studied from different perspectives, one of which is the modelling of the Peloponnesian War, and

---

[45] On *ho paralogos* in Thucydides' narrative of the war, see Munson (Chapter 7).

[46] Hornblower 1991–2008: vol. III, 745, on Thucydides' mediated interaction with Homer via Herodotus (2.120.2) in the use of the same word (*panōlethria*, 'utter destruction', 7.87.6) for the Athenian defeat in Sicily. Strasburger 1972 is fundamental on the topic; a more recent discussion, also containing further bibliography, is Rutherford 2012.

especially the Sicilian Expedition, on Herodotus' account of the Persian Wars, with the Trojan War and its own literary representations as a third intermediary.[47] Another is a close comparative reading of the colonial and ethnic information in the two authors. Melos, for example, is nearly absent from Herodotus, whereas information about the foundations of Thera and Cyrene is extremely rich. Conversely, in Thucydides, Thera and Cyrene are almost absent (see earlier in this chapter about Euesperides), whereas Melos owes to the 'Melian Dialogue' its everlasting fame. In general, Thucydides tends to provide ethnic or colonial information where Herodotus does not do so and vice versa; and when both authors demonstrate an interest in a locality, the material provided in each case presents striking differences.[48]

The study of ethnicity in Thucydides enables us to perceive different levels and notions of ethnic selfhood and Otherness outside and within the Greek world. Narratives of ethnic origins, solidarity or enmity, stereotypes and their destabilization are part of his representation of ethnic identities as culturally constructed and thus dynamic and fluid. Thucydides' analysis acknowledges the role of collective beliefs, ideologies, emotions and ethics in ethnic conflicts such as the Peloponnesian War. These cultural and emotive parameters interact with power, security, expansionism and other 'hard' factors. Thucydides pays due attention to the interaction of 'hard' and 'soft' factors and to the rational and irrational motives of communities and individuals, especially in ethnic conflicts. Ethnicity plays a key role in his explanatory schema, underscoring the complexities and multiple factors at work and revealing his dialogue not only with his own past and present, but also with the future.

Further Reading

For a fuller exploration of many of the issues raised in this chapter, see Fragoulaki 2013; more generally on ideas of ethnicity and identity in the Greek world, see Hall 1997, 2002. Two very relevant studies of Thucydides' presentation of the war – not solely concerned with ethnic identity, but exploring issues very pertinent to this theme – are Price 2001, who probes the way in which Thucydides represents the 'community' of Greek states (and its divisions) in his narrative of the war, and Hornblower 1992, whose exploration of Thucydides' suppression of religious aspects of the war includes important observations on his representation of Ionian and Dorian ethnicity. Finally, Rengakos and Tsakmakis 2006 bring together several useful studies of Thucydides' presentation of Greek and non-Greek communities (Sparta, Argos, Sicily, Thrace and Persia).

---

[47] Rood 1998a; Harrison 2000; Kallet 2001: 97–120.   [48] Fragoulaki 2013: appendix ii.

12

SARAH BROWN FERRARIO

Thucydides and Leadership

Introduction: Leadership in Classical Athens – and in Thucydides

Under the radical Athenian democracy of the later 5th century, nearly all
governmental offices were evenly divided amongst the ten political divisions
of the citizenry (the tribes) and determined by random draw.[1] Thus, the
presider over the Assembly changed daily; the *prytaneis* (leadership commit-
tee) of the *boulē*, the Assembly's executive council, rotated roughly every
month; and juries were selected by an allocation machine that dropped
marbles next to name tickets.[2]

How was 'leadership' defined in this environment? While leadership in
classical Greece might be ascribed to a cultural group or an entire city-state
(e.g. Athens in the Persian Wars, as Hdt. 7.139.1–6), in Greek thought in
general – and in Thucydides – states were still composed of people, who
imbued their *poleis* (cities) with complex character, engaged in collective
decision-making and invoked distinct identities as 'Athenians', 'Syracusans'
or 'Spartans'.[3] Within these states, qualifications for individual leadership
were socially determined. An aspiring leader in classical Athens, for
example, generally needed aristocratic birth, elite education, personal
wealth, talent in public speaking, experience in practical affairs and the

I remain very grateful to the editor, Polly A. Low, to my research assistant for this project,
Andrew Hagstrom, and to the anonymous readers who furnished helpful suggestions and
additional references. All dates are BCE, all unlabelled citations are to the text of Thucydides
and all translations are mine. Much (though not all) of the first section's material on the
Periclean model and its relationship to the Athenian *stratēgoi* is derived from Ferrario 2014;
thanks are due to Cambridge University Press for standing permission to present similar
versions of these ideas in other contexts.

[1] For an introduction to the Athenian 'radical' democracy, see, e.g., Stockton 1990.
[2] For such a *klēroterion* from the 3rd century (e.g. Agora I 3967), see Thompson and
Wycherley 1972: 53, pl. 39b. On sortition in Athenian politics, see Kosmetatou 2013.
[3] In Thucydides, see, e.g., Athenian and Spartan temperaments (1.70.1–71.3, 1.84.1–85.1);
Athenian identity in the Funeral Oration (2.35.1–46.2); the disposition of the Syracusans
(6.38.2–40.1); Nicias fearing the Athenian *dēmos* (7.14.4–15.2).

respect of both peers and subordinates to succeed.[4] Under the radical democracy such a man could potentially exercise great power without holding formal office. In practice, however, he might serve in one of the few remaining elected positions: the generalship.[5] Ten *stratēgoi* (generals) were chosen every year, one from each tribe, and they not only held military commands, but also acted as chief counsellors to the *dēmos*, the Athenian citizenry.

Because political and military affairs were central to the Greek view of history,[6] the Athenian *stratēgoi* naturally attract significant attention from Thucydides. But he is not so much concerned with their character as he is with their relationships with the Athenian *dēmos*. For Thucydides, the association between leader and led is an essential determinant of the direction taken by a state.[7] Pericles, in particular, has a special ability to guide the *dēmos* of Athens at critical moments while still letting it believe (or pretend) that it remains in control (see 2.65.9), often using his *logoi*, 'words', to elicit or depict what the Athenians are invited to claim as their own *erga*, 'deeds'.[8] This careful conversion of individual thought and rhetoric into action by a citizen group is re-examined in Thucydides' treatments of Cleon, Nicias and Alcibiades, whose occasionally problematic interactions with the *dēmos* lack certain facets of Pericles' skill.

But Thucydides also shows Pericles' guidance being perceived as centrally important by combatants *on both sides* of the Peloponnesian War.[9] This in turn invites consideration of the applicability of the Periclean 'model' to other *poleis*. Are any of Pericles' distinctive qualities perceptible in other exchanges and collaborations between leaders and led? Does Thucydides employ the same techniques in his coverage of non-Athenian leaders that he uses in his treatment of Pericles? More broadly, can a sketch of effective Thucydidean leadership be created across the boundaries of cities and

---

[4] Waterfield forthcoming.

[5] On the elections and authority of generals and archons, see, e.g., Badian 1971; Develin 1979; Hamel 1998: esp. 79–83.

[6] E.g. Starr 1968: 91–4; Momigliano 1972: 283–4, 290.

[7] Ferrario 2014: 106–44; see also Tsakmakis 2006.

[8] On the connotations of the terms *logos* and *ergon* and their associated concepts, see Parry 1981: 11. The *logos/ergon* distinction has been related to many aspects of Thucydides' work: for its relevance to understanding Thucydidean speeches, see the discussion of Greenwood (Chapter 5); and for arguments exploring its centrality to Thucydides' conceptualization and representation of his historiographic project, see Beasley (Chapter 3).

[9] Athenians: e.g. 2.65.6–7; Spartans: e.g. 1.127.1–2.

constitutions?[10] In this chapter, after a brief review of key Athenian leader–*dēmos* relationships, closer readings of Thucydides' treatments of Hermocrates, Archidamus and Brasidas, with particular attention to selected examples of their speeches, reveal thoughtful interaction with the Periclean model far afield from Athens. It is naturally impossible to know with certainty Thucydides' personal opinion of Pericles the human being. But as other figures in Thucydides redeploy the leadership methods and rhetorical strategies of Pericles the character, the historian's ideas about leadership in general are revealed in greater depth. Pericles is both more than a *stratēgos* and more than a mere template: rather, in the manner of a theme, he embodies certain characteristics and behaviours upon which other leaders present elaborate variations.

Pericles and His Athenian Echoes

In the history of Thucydidean studies, Pericles has been variously interpreted as Athens' greatest hope, as a creature of singular ambition and even as a proxy for the prescriptive voice of Thucydides himself.[11] But he may also represent a way of thinking about other Thucydidean leaders. We begin at his end, with his obituary and its introduction (2.65.1–13). In this section, Pericles is credited with moderation, forethought, immunity to bribery and a superior ability to direct the *dēmos* (2.65.5–8). Various superlatives both here and earlier,[12] along with the famous claim that Athens' democracy was really the 'sovereignty of its leading citizen' (2.65.9), emphasize Pericles' unique abilities. Finally, at 2.65.10–12, Thucydides characterizes the next generation of political leadership as self-aggrandizing and demagogic by contrast, a dangerous combination at a time when (in Thucydides' eyes) the *dēmos* was in dire need of guidance.[13]

---

[10] The emphasis here is upon the leadership of persons, mainly named individuals. Leadership in Thucydides is also productively analysed from a very different perspective by scholars of international relations; see, e.g., Bagby 1994.

[11] Indispensable to Athens: e.g. Kagan 2009: 75–97; Azoulay 2014: 127–36; ambition: e.g. Bloedow 2000; Thucydidean stand-in: e.g. the bibliography collected by Foster 2010: 1 n. 1. Will 2003, in the title of his book, calls Pericles Thucydides' 'hero'.

[12] E.g. esp. Athens under Pericles called *megistē*, 'greatest, most powerful' (2.65.5), and Pericles described as *pleistou axion*, 'most worthy' (2.65.4); *adōrotatos*, 'least subject to bribes' (2.65.8); and *dunatōtatos*, 'most influential' (1.127.3, 1.139.4). All of these instances are focalized upon the Athenian *dēmos* or upon the voice of the historical narrator: cf. Ferrario 2013: 184–5.

[13] This passage is widely acknowledged as implicating Alcibiades, but it also contains criticisms applicable to other leaders: e.g. Gomme, in Gomme et al. 1945–81: vol. II, 194–9; Connor 1984b: 75–6 esp. n. 58.

SARAH BROWN FERRARIO

Connecting 2.65 more deeply with other Thucydidean passages and with other contemporary evidence complicates some of these assertions,[14] but it does not undermine Pericles' ability, established in Thucydides' text mainly through his speeches and their impact, to lead the *dēmos* without appearing to arrogate final authority to himself. Pericles' three major successors, however, are all depicted as deficient in some aspect of this crucial skill. Cleon may be *pithanōtatos*, 'most persuasive', but he is also *biaiōtatos*, 'most ferocious', and *dēmagōgos*, 'a demagogue'.[15] Alcibiades rouses the Assembly for the Sicilian expedition (6.19.1) – by depicting his own personal qualities and behaviours as assets to the city (6.16.1–3) and himself as an individual agent of political and military action (6.16.6–17.1).[16] Nicias is explicitly wary of the *dēmos* when he requests reinforcements for Sicily (7.14.4) and openly attempts to shift blame for the expedition's fate away from himself and onto the Assembly (7.14.3, 7.15.1–2).

Periclean leadership is further recollected through echoes of vocabulary, phraseology and ideas from Books 1 and 2 in Thucydides' later coverage of Cleon, Nicias and Alcibiades. Cleon, twice introduced at strategic moments with wording that reverses the meaning of important passages about his predecessor,[17] often emerges as an 'anti-Pericles',[18] although the contrasts may sometimes come in style rather than in substance. Cleon accuses the *dēmos* of incompetent leadership during the Mytilenean Debate[19] – but his citation of its 'tyrannical' behaviour towards its allies echoes Pericles' same reservations on the subject (3.37.2, with 2.63.2).[20] Despite his bullying swagger (4.21.3–22.3), Cleon is mocked when he is forced to take over Nicias' command at Pylos (4.27.3–28.5) – but he nevertheless manages a successful campaign (4.39.3). Nicias shares many of Pericles' civic values but lacks his verbal skill and political acumen.[21] His failed rhetorical gamble to halt the Sicilian Expedition by exaggerating the resources required

[14] E.g. Connor 1984b: 60–3; Rood 1998b: 133–58; Kagan 2009: 75–97; Azoulay 2014: 127–36.
[15] 3.36.6 (introduction into the narrative) and 4.21.3 (arguing against peace).
[16] Macleod 1983: 71–2.
[17] E.g. Rood 1998b: 147 on 3.36.6 with 1.139.4, also citing Connor 1984b: 79 n. 1; Ferrario 2014: 121–2, comparing 3.36.6 and 4.21.3 (Cleon) with 1.127.3 and 1.139.4 (Pericles).
[18] E.g. Connor 1971: 87–136; Cairns 1982; Yunis 1991; Rood 1998b: 146–9; Will 2003: 68–88; Bearzot 2004; Ferrario 2014: 121–3; cf. also Lang 1972 (providing the phrase 'anti-Pericles' in the title); Wohl 2002: 74–5.
[19] Rood 1998b: 146–8, citing esp. 3.37.1, 3.38.4–7.
[20] I am grateful to an anonymous reader for this point and for the more complex reading of Cleon that it is supporting.
[21] E.g. Lateiner 1985: 209–13.

demonstrates his inability to manipulate the *dēmos* (6.19.2–26.1), and Thucydides does not even pretend to quote his trite exhortation speech before the battle in the Great Harbour of Syracuse.[22] Alcibiades is uniquely charming, but he is wanting in Pericles' efficacy and completely willing to abandon the *polis* for personal ends.[23] These three commanders are therefore individually deficient in various elements of Pericles' leadership qualities,[24] but they *all* lack Pericles' careful way of leading the *dēmos* to adopt his own designs. In other words, they cannot convert their speech into productive, collaborative civic action.

An important key to Periclean leadership may therefore be found in the successful manipulation of the relationship between *logos* and *ergon*.[25] Thucydides does not dwell significantly upon Pericles as a military commander – that is, as a doer of deeds; rather, he shows Pericles using his words to empower the *dēmos* as the agent of the city's actions.[26] The process is established in Pericles' first speech, advocating war and laying out his strategy (1.140.1–144.4). Pericles' forethought (cf. 2.65.5–6) emerges in the close connections between this speech and that of the Corinthians at 1.120.1–124.3, a link that makes him appear almost omniscient.[27] His task, however, is not to assert his own abilities, but rather to guide the *dēmos* into believing as he believes. One of his signature tools for this, visible even in the opening of this speech, is what we might call 'incorporative rhetoric', where Pericles moves gradually from using the first-person singular to employing the first-person plural as if agreement is a foregone conclusion (e.g. 1.140.1, contrasted with 1.140.2–3), ascribes real or anticipated action to the *dēmos* or to the plural 'you' rather than to himself (e.g. 1.140.5, 1.144.1–2) or elides his own identity into an extended discussion of 'the Athenians' as a whole (e.g. 1.142.2–143.5, 1.144.1–3). While Pericles himself is never fully absent from the argumentation (e.g. the first-person interjections at 1.141.1 and 1.143.5), his individual perspective is gradually minimized until the speech concludes with a rousing, unifying remembrance of the deeds wrought by the generation that fought in the Persian Wars (1.144.4). Pericles' speech has therefore created a bridge between the *collective* accomplishments of the Athenians' ancestors and the new war that they, acting as democratic agents, now take as their own.

---

[22] Ibid., esp. 201–8. [23] Bloedow 1991; see also Ferrario 2014: 135–43.

[24] This is a widely shared observation: e.g. Connor 1984b: 75–6; Rood 1998b: 158.

[25] Parry 1981: esp. 150–85.

[26] Ibid., 153, calling Pericles' war policy in his first speech 'a creation not of *ergon*, but of *logos*'.

[27] E.g. Connor 1984b: 49.

The more abstract Funeral Oration (2.35.1–46.2) also employs incorporative rhetoric and emphasizes the relationship between *logos* and *ergon*. Indeed, its very prologue uses both techniques when Pericles expresses the traditional speaker's despair of matching his words to his subjects' accomplishments (2.35.1–3)[28] and worries that listeners may have trouble imagining themselves as agents of similar deeds (2.35.2). While the speech does acknowledge some unresolved social tensions when read in its cultural context,[29] its rhetorical strategy clearly takes on the prologue's challenges as it subsumes the identity of the individual citizen (including the speaker) into the larger body of the *polis*.[30] The Funeral Oration is not designed to motivate immediate action; rather, it aims to realign its audience's attitude towards civic accomplishment by characterizing who and what 'the Athenians' really are. The city therefore becomes the collective agent of Athenian *erga* past, present and future.

All of this, however – the image of Athens itself as eternal agent, the meaningful conversion of the leader's words into the *dēmos*' deeds – is called into question during the plague, which follows the Funeral Oration at a distance of little more than sixty words.[31] Now, human actions in the form of *technē* ('skill'), *therapeia* ('medical treatment') and even religious observance have no effect upon the pestilence (2.47.4, 51.2–4, 52.3, 53.4). The Funeral Oration's civic vision dissolves not only in the horrifying images of improvised burials and hijacked funeral pyres (2.52.4), but also in the breakdown of moral behaviour and the abandonment of the very words once used to describe it (2.52.3 and especially 2.53.1–4). Language, an Athenian leader's most powerful tool, can be of little use when the meaning of the fundamental word *kalos* ('good, noble') is undermined and reverence and irreverence are construed as leading to the same place (2.53.3 and 2.53.4, respectively). The challenge for Pericles' final speech is abundantly set.

In his 'second speech' (2.60.1–64.6), we see Pericles under pressure from the *dēmos* when (in Pericles' reading) personal suffering from the plague threatens to fragment the body politic and hamper its efficacy (2.60.2–4, 61.2–4, 62.3, 63.3; cf. 64.6). As the speech begins, the ambassadors sent to explore a truce are unsuccessful, and the *dēmos* does not know what to do (2.59.2). Ironically, although the *dēmos* is angry at itself for having acted on Pericles' previous recommendations, it nevertheless seems unable to

[28] On this trope, see, e.g., Kennedy 1963: 48–51, 154–66.
[29] Ferrario 2014: 42–4, 174–6.   [30] Loraux 1986a: esp. 132–71, 233–8.
[31] For further analysis of the structure of this section of Book 2 and its implications, see Munson (Chapter 7).

accomplish anything new without his guidance. His remedy comes in the form of *logoi*. Pericles begins by acknowledging the current distance between himself and the *dēmos*, and he offers logical defences of his own qualities and refutations of the arguments against him (2.60.1–7). He deliberately criticizes the *dēmos*' change of heart (2.61.2–3) rather than its essential nature,[32] and he then moves quickly to discuss the shared interests and shared dangers represented by Athens' empire (2.62.1–63.3), both of which emphasize the collective nature of the *polis*. And he again invokes the past as an inspiration for the present (2.62.2–3, 63.1, 64.6). His closing section echoes many of the sentiments from the Funeral Oration (2.64.2–4), offering implicit support for his assertion that he has remained consistent even as the *dēmos* has wavered (2.61.2) and continuing to espouse communal outlook and action. These *logoi* are quickly converted into *erga* as Pericles succeeds in stopping the useless embassies and arousing emotional commitment to the war effort (2.65.1). The individual personal grudges against him result in a fine (2.65.3), and the *dēmos*' disposition is realigned towards both the common good and Pericles' guidance (2.65.4–5).

In the face of the plague, all of this might seem almost too good to be true, but Thucydides has guided the interpretation by suppressing an important detail. As Rhodes points out (Chapter 4), Pericles was indeed 'elected general' at this time (2.65.4) – but he had also previously been *removed* from that position at the time he was fined.[33] Thucydides has quietly permitted the reader to assume a continuity of Pericles' leadership across the extraordinarily difficult episode of the plague, with the dramatic presentation of Pericles' second speech serving as a reassertion of the tools of effective rhetorical leadership. The extent to which those tools may be shared by some of Thucydides' other leaders now occupies the remainder of this discussion.

The Syracusan: Hermocrates

Hermocrates is a favoured comparison with Pericles in Thucydidean scholarship,[34] given both his substantial role in the text[35] and his roughly analogous political position. Like Pericles, Hermocrates offers counsel to a

---

[32] Contrast, e.g., Cleon during the Mytilenean Debate: Rood 1998b: 146–9.

[33] See Azoulay 2014: 148, interpreting the judicial actions behind the removal described by Diod. Sic. 12.45.4 and Plu. *Per.* 35.4.

[34] E.g. the bibliography collected by Grissom 2012: 104 n. 22; and Hinrichs 1981: 47 n. 7.

[35] Hermocrates is the third most voluminous speaker in Thucydides, after Pericles and Nicias: Hinrichs 1981: 47; cf. West 1973: 7–15.

democratic populace by virtue of his wisdom and experience.[36] He seems to share many of the leadership qualities that Thucydides attributes to Pericles,[37] and he also, like Pericles, has some of his characteristics high-lighted by contrasting figures (most notably, Athenagoras shares features with Cleon and Alcibiades, 6.36.1–40.2).[38] A closer reading of Hermocrates' relationship with his audiences, however, particularly regarding the conversion of speech into productive action, also demonstrates that Pericles' more specific rhetorical methods are discernible in Hermocrates' presentation, and that within the world of the text, these methods are still efficacious, even in a non-Athenian context.

Hermocrates' introduction into Thucydides' narrative comes as he addresses a congress of dissenting Sicilian states at Gela (4.59.1–64.5). His argument that the *poleis* of Sicily should set aside their differences will ultimately prevail (4.65.1–2; cf. 4.58.1), and his speech redeploys some of Pericles' techniques for empowering audiences' collective ownership of civic action. These include the prioritization of general interests over the separate concerns of states and individuals (e.g. 4.59.1, 4; 60.1, 2; 61.1, 2, 3; 62.2, 3; 63.1; 64.4, 5); the subsumption of the persona of the speaker into a shared vision of corporate purpose, often articulated in the first-person plural (e.g. 4.59.4; 61.1, 3, 6; but cf. 64.1–3); and the self-conscious employment of *logoi* to link external action, both past and present, to current need, thereby inviting and inspiring *erga* (e.g. especially 4.59.4 and 4.62.2). In Pericles' case, the motivating externals tend to be either *exempla* from the past, generally from the Persian Wars, or prescient articulations of the resources and motivations of the enemy. Here in Hermocrates' Gela speech, the externals focus upon the Athenians, often specifically upon their designs on Sicily (e.g. 4.60.1, 61.7, 63.1, 64.5), constructing a sense of collective purpose through a perception of shared danger. These potent *logoi* easily motivate the *ergon* that Hermocrates seeks: the Sicilians call an end to their infighting and attempt to make an agreement with Athens (4.65.1–2).

Hermocrates' second speech (6.33.1–34.9) is also given before a factional-ized audience, this time of Syracusans puzzled and alarmed by reports of the

---

[36] On the democratic government in Syracuse before and during the Peloponnesian War, see Robinson 2000 and Rutter 2000, the former advocating for somewhat stronger Athenian parallels than the latter. While there is evidence for political structures and behaviours in Syracuse that share important features with those of Athens, and while the rhetoric of Thucydides in particular invites comparisons between them, this does not mean that their constitutions mirrored one another.

[37] Westlake 1958–9: 266 n. 1, citing Bender 1938: 82–103.   [38] Bloedow 1996.

approaching Athenian expedition.[39] Like Pericles, Hermocrates believes himself possessed of a good understanding of the situation (6.32.3, 33.1; cf. Pericles' *pronoia*). But the resemblance soon fades. Hermocrates claims to be an individual defender of his *polis* (6.33.1) and positions himself in an adversarial position to the Syracusan *dēmos*: 'even as you marvel, the Athenians are hastening against you' (6.33.2); 'do not be left unguarded because you look down on [them] or ignore the entire situation because you do not believe it' (6.33.3); 'I think this would be most advantageous, but you because of your accustomed quietude would least likely be persuaded of it right away' (6.34.4). And his former powerful advocacy of Sicilian unity has here been replaced with the far less ambitious aspiration that at least some Sicilians ('the Sicilians … all together, or if not, as many of us as possible') might be willing to sail with the Syracusans to Tarentum (6.34.4).

This speech, lacking in the inclusive rhetorical techniques both of Pericles and of Hermocrates himself at Gela, provokes disparate responses ranging from credence to derision (6.35.1) and arouses no immediate action. A comparand for Hermocrates here may be Nicias, whose own recent advocacy also fell short (6.15.1; cf. also 19.2, 24.1–4). Nicias was immediately followed in his speech by a demagogic opponent, Alcibiades (6.16.1–18.7). Here, the next speaker after Hermocrates is Athenagoras, introduced in terms almost identical to those once used of Cleon (*pithanōtatos tois pollois*, 'most persuasive of the multitude', 6.35.2). The rhetorical surprise, however, is the speech of the unnamed Syracusan *stratēgos* who closes the debate (6.41.1–3). He dismisses the preceding war of words (*diabolas*, 'slanderous speech', 6.41.2) in favour of a pragmatic middle argument, namely that Syracuse will suffer nothing by standing ready for war. The *logoi* of Hermocrates and of Athenagoras have therefore been redefined as damaging talk rather than as counsel that enables action, and no civic *ergon* follows: instead of taking action in assembly, the Syracusans depart without a vote, leaving the generals to continue their preparations (6.41.3).

The next opportunity to observe Hermocrates' relationship with his *dēmos* comes after the Syracusans' loss in their first battle against the Athenians (6.70.3–4). Thucydides here provides a new, more extensive introduction that resonates with the description of Pericles at 2.65.8–9:

> Hermocrates the son of Hermon came forward, a man in other respects inferior to no one in his wisdom, and in this war both capable through experience and

---

[39] See Westlake 1958–9: 239–40, 242, 249 on the fractious nature of the Syracusan *dēmos* and of the Sicilians in general.

notable for his resolve. He emboldened [the Syracusans] and did not allow [them] to surrender to the present situation. (6.72.2)

The brief indirect speech that follows (6.72.3–5) returns to some of the positive rhetorical techniques of Pericles. Hermocrates respects the nature of the Syracusan people, criticizing their disorder in the battle rather than their cultural tendencies (6.72.3) and promising that training will magnify their positive qualities (6.72.4). He provides a cogent analysis of the damage done by lack of practice and presents a viable remedy: the appointment of experienced generals who can train the army properly (ibid.). The generals, he suggests, should be authorized to make independent decisions, but in a crucial rhetorical turn he acknowledges that this charge must come from the *dēmos*: 'they [sc. the Syracusans] should swear an oath to [the generals] to let them lead in the manner in which they were expert' (6.72.5). In other words, the generals are to derive their authority by mandate from the *dēmos*, the *dēmos* is to enhance its military abilities through the training offered by the generals and the cause of the *polis* is to advance through the productive collaboration of leaders and led. Here, as with Pericles and the Athenians, the Syracusans respond to this *logos* with *erga*, and Hermocrates is selected as one of the generals (6.73.1).

Hermocrates' final speech in Thucydides is a brief, indirect exhortation urging the Syracusans to engage the Athenians in a decisive naval battle despite their inexperience (7.21.3–5). It shares its general context and rhetorical features with 6.72.3–5 (discussed immediately above), the speech of encouragement after the loss of the first battle. Here in Book 7, Hermocrates again carefully differentiates between a people's essential nature and their circumstances. In the earlier speech, the people in question were the Syracusans, but here they are the Athenians, whose naval prowess is characterized as having been acquired under Persian duress rather than being inborn (7.21.3). Hermocrates further suggests that the Syracusans, too, could demonstrate to their enemies the kind of courage that the Athenians habitually use to frighten others (ibid.). Whether this courage is intended to be understood as a native Syracusan quality or a plausible 'acting job' is not entirely clear from Hermocrates' syntax. The Athenians, for example, are characterized in this passage with an adjective as *being* 'bold', *tolmērous*, as opposed to their enemies, who *act* boldly with a participle, *antitolmōntas*; and the Syracusans are said to have the potential to 'furnish' (*hupechein*) courageous behaviour. But the slippage seems to be a syntactical reflection of the substance of Hermocrates' argument, as he holds that the Syracusans will make a very real, damaging impact upon the Athenians simply by daring to attack. In other words, the Syracusans are being invited to stage a rhetorical performance of strength and courage that Hermocrates suggests will end with real results: their *logos*, in his view, will become an *ergon*. The speech has almost immediate effect: assisted by other sympathetic speakers (including the Spartan Gylippus), Hermocrates rouses the Syracusans for the conflict, and their passions run high (*hōrmēnto*, 7.21.5, connoting emotional impulse rather than rational calculation).

The conversion of false *logos* into real *ergon* is at the core of Hermocrates' final major appearance in Thucydides.[40] Hoping to cut off a potential Athenian overland retreat after the battle in the Great Harbour, Hermocrates advocates blockading the escape routes. When his fellow leaders are not optimistic that the exhausted army will participate, Hermocrates instead dispatches false deserters who recommend that the Athenians postpone their march out for a night to avoid the Syracusan guards – guards that Hermocrates has actually not been able to station (7.73.1–4). The deception works, the Athenians delay for *two* nights, and the Syracusans have time to establish their traps (7.74.1–2). Hermocrates has therefore managed to circumvent obstructions to collaborate with his *dēmos* and turn the situation to collective advantage. This independent trickery deployed at a critical moment seems to recall not Pericles, but rather another prominent Athenian leader who used similarly deceptive tactics: Themistocles.[41]

The Spartans: Archidamus and Brasidas

It is generally appreciated that Thucydides' Archidamus is also constructed as a foil to Pericles. The two leaders' speeches in Book 1 rehearsing their attitudes towards the impending conflict are in responsion with one another (1.80.1–85.2, with 1.140.1–144.4),[42] and their personal relationship as *xenoi* helps to motivate Pericles' pre-emptive surrender of his estates to his *polis* lest Archidamus spare them out of either friendship or malice (2.13.1). For Pericles, then, as likely for Archidamus, the aristocratic bond of *xenia* is a manipulable political tool that can affect a leader's relationship with his people. Pericles' renunciation of his property aligns well with his general political methods: although the act is tied to both Athenian and Spartan perceptions of his individual authority (ibid.), it is an ostensibly

---

[40] His last mention comes at 8.26.1.

[41] On the trick before Salamis, see Hdt. 8.75.1–80.2; on the trick of the Themistoclean Wall, see Thuc. 1.90.1–93.2.

[42] E.g. Gomme, in Gomme et al. 1945–81: vol. I, 247–51, 463–4; de Romilly 1963: 30–2; Edmunds 1975: 91, 94–7; Bloedow 1981: 130–5; Hornblower 1991–2008: vol. I, 226.

democratizing gesture that acknowledges the sovereignty of the *dēmos*. But Pericles' interpretation of Archidamus' potential motivations also recommends broader investigation of the Spartan king's relationship with his own *polis*. To what extent might Archidamus share other rhetorical and leadership strategies with Pericles?

During his introduction and speech at the war congress in Sparta, Archidamus is said to be recognized as *xunetos*, 'intelligent', and *sōphrōn*, 'wise' (1.79.2); he further characterizes himself as *empeiros*, 'experienced', in armed conflict, which he claims affects his desire (and that of men like him) for more war (1.80.1). The words for these various political virtues do not precisely duplicate those used elsewhere of Pericles or Hermocrates, but they nevertheless overlap in sentiment,[43] emphasizing the application of past knowledge to the formulation of sound judgements about the future. Archidamus' speech in turn strongly suggests that this characterization is accurate, as it recalls not only Thucydides' presentation of the king, but even the historian's own preface (e.g. 1.80.2 with 1.1.1).

Archidamus' speech also deploys some of the same incorporative rhetorical techniques as do the speeches of Pericles and Hermocrates. Archidamus begins by introducing his own past wartime experience, but then ascribes the same opinion to others of his age group, noting that his contemporaries also understand that war is not inherently desirable (1.80.1). He then shifts into the first-person plural, staging deliberative questions to encourage his audience to reconsider their stance (1.80.3–81.6). This section of his speech does close with a return to his own sentiment, but via a dramatic personal verb, *dedoika*: 'I am afraid instead', he says, 'that we are going to leave this war behind even for our children' (1.81.6).

Having attempted to draw the Spartans into his thought processes, Archidamus next provides prescriptions for action and speculations about its potential consequences (1.82.1–5). He does take ownership of his recommendations (e.g. *keleuō*, 'I urge', 1.82.1), but the mixture of verb and pronoun forms in the remainder of the section keeps the focus balanced towards 'we' and 'us' rather than towards any anticipation of opposition. This passage closes with a gnomic observation that anticipates sentiments later expressed by Pericles: individual interests can be destructive of corporate action (1.82.6).

As Pericles and Hermocrates will also do later in the narrative, Archidamus next defends his people's nature, here against the criticisms of the Corinthians (1.68.1–71.7, especially 70.1–4). The Spartan tendency to

---

[43] See Parry 1981 (n. 8 in this chapter) regarding the broader correlation of concepts across a range of Greek vocabulary.

be 'slow' and 'hesitant', Archidamus argues, is really 'wise prudence', because it limits their response to emotional appeals (1.84.1–3). The anticipation of other areas of Thucydides' text continues with an ironic nod to the first section of Cleon's demagogic speech during the Mytilenean Debate (3.37.3–4), as Archidamus notes that the Spartans are not sufficiently learned to be suspicious of their own *nomoi* ('laws', or 'customs') and are so strict with themselves as not to transgress those *nomoi* (1.84.3). In a thinly veiled criticism of the Athenians, he then emphasizes the Spartan focus upon *ergon* over *logos* (1.84.3–4). The Spartan ways, Archidamus concludes, have been handed down from their ancestors, and 'we', he states, 'benefit by retaining them' (1.85.1). He closes with a series of measured prescriptions, including the dispatch of messengers to the Athenians, but he concludes with the admonition, 'at the same time, ready yourselves for war' (1.85.2), arguing that the preparation itself will be frightening to the enemy.

The ephor Sthenelaidas counters by advocating an immediate vote for war. His opposition may be partly ascribed to the political tensions inherent between kings and ephors,[44] but Sthenelaidas is also interacting with two other leadership paradigms represented elsewhere in Thucydides. Firstly, Sthenelaidas plays the demagogue, concentrating upon emotional arousals to vengeance (1.86.1–5).[45] He converts *logos* directly into *ergon* as he demands a physical reflection of the voice vote (1.87.1–3), a demonstration that will eventually lead to the ultimate *ergon*, the declaration of war. But in falsely (according to Thucydides) claiming that he cannot tell which side dominated in the call of acclamation (1.87.2), Sthenelaidas also becomes a trickster figure along the lines of Themistocles and Hermocrates. The brevity of Sthenelaidas' speech, his emphasis upon passion over reason and his use of deception as a rhetorical tool all contrast starkly with Pericles' behaviours and therefore with Archidamus' redeployment of that model just moments before. But Archidamus had not advocated quietude for its own sake: he simply did not support an immediate rush to war and preferred negotiation alongside precautionary preparations. And neither Archidamus nor Sthenelaidas can be taken as advocating positions that are opposed to Spartan values: as Debnar points out, they simply define those values differently.[46] The question of why Sthenelaidas' less developed argument prevails has therefore been much debated.[47]

---

[44] On the Spartan state and its governmental system generally, see, e.g., Cartledge 2001b.

[45] Cf. Rood 1998b on Cleon (with ns. 17–19 in this chapter).   [46] Debnar 2001: 73.

[47] On the speech of Sthenelaidas and its impact, see, e.g., Bloedow 1981, 1987; Allison 1984; Debnar 2001: 69–76. It is true that Sthenelaidas is the one who advocates bluntly for Sparta's allies, but the implications of both leaders' speeches extend beyond that point (Pelling 1991: esp. 123–5).

Bloedow connects the emotional state of the Spartan assembly here with that of the Athenians on the verge of the Sicilian Expedition.[48] Some insight may therefore come from another important reference to the Athenian disaster in Sicily: at 2.65.11, during the reflection upon Pericles. Even a power such as Athens, Thucydides says here, could operate on anti-Periclean principles, most notably when Athenian leadership gave over too much control to the *dēmos* (2.65.10). During the debate at Sparta, Sthenelaidas' request for a physical division of the vote requires the attendees to assume visible, individual ownership of their opinions, shifting responsibility away from the speaker and onto the populace. The populace is therefore essentially compelled to take immediate control, which may help to explain in part why Archidamus' call for moderation fails. Sthenelaidas, in his emotional demand for popular action, stages a visible, collective rejection of the leadership principles that both Pericles and Archidamus have deployed.

Archidamus' next speech (2.11.1–9), delivered to the Peloponnesians at the Isthmus before their first invasion of Attica, echoes his previous one in its acknowledgement of experience in warfare (2.11.1). It also anticipates some of the traditional language that will soon appear in Pericles' Funeral Oration, including calls to live up to the past and look to future reputation (e.g. 2.11.2, 9).[49] It further emphasizes the corporate identity of the Peloponnesians and implicitly invokes their common ancestry (2.11.1–2). Like Hermocrates' final speech, too, this one reflects that a theoretically dominant enemy may be thrown off balance by surprising action (2.11.4). The key difference here is that the necessary daring is to be accompanied by a healthy degree of Spartan apprehension that will foster true readiness (2.11.5). The closing invocation calls for obedience and a united front from the combatants (2.11.9). This speech admittedly has no action hazarded upon its efficacy (the *ergon* of the invasion will proceed regardless, 2.12.1–5), but it nevertheless shows a Spartan voice participating in paradigms of discourse also observable in other Thucydidean *poleis*.[50]

Archidamus' last detailed treatment in the narrative comes during his investment of Plataea (2.71.–78.4), where his initial demands for support, then his elaborate offer of occupation-in-trust (2.72.1, 72.3), are outweighed by the emotionally direct promises of the Athenians (2.73.3–74.1). His

---

[48] Bloedow 1981: 143.

[49] On the connections between Thucydides' pre-battle speeches and the Funeral Oration, see Zoido 2007: 147–9.

[50] On the paradigmatic nature of Thucydidean pre-battle speeches, see Luschnat 1942; Leimbach 1985.

advances spurned, Archidamus prepares to besiege Plataea, but he prefaces his attack with a prayer (2.74.2–3).[51] In the world of the narrative, his invocation of 'the gods and heroes that occupy Plataea' may not actually reach Plataean ears, since their final rejection of the Spartan terms is made *apo tou teichous*, 'from the fortifications', but it is almost certainly audible to the Spartans.[52] It may even be scripted for Archidamus' Spartan audience, especially because it employs a recurring Spartan theme: that the Spartans are compelled to act because they have been wronged (the Plataeans have broken their oath: see 3.68.1–2). The recollection of the Persian Wars adds an ironic note (the Battle of Plataea had been Sparta's greatest triumph in that conflict: see Hdt. 9.1.1–89.4 and cf. Thuc. 3.54.3–4, 56.5, 57.2–3, 58.4–5, 59.2), and the request for divine support subtly acknowledges the role of the Spartan king as high priest.[53] This is, then, a prayer intended to build common cultural cause with a Spartan audience, and it precedes a terrifying siege, as the determined Spartans turn immediately from *logos* to *ergon* and destroy Plataea.[54]

Particularly in the earlier portions of Thucydides' narrative, the Spartans are often characterized both by others and by themselves as a cautious people,[55] despite the emphasis upon *ergon* in their leaders' speeches. This disconnect is significantly resolved, however, in Brasidas, a man of action gifted with sufficient rhetorical skill to assume leadership even of peoples who are not his own.[56] His early rescue of Methone (2.25.2) wins him the approbation of the Spartan community and foreshadows his largely self-determined agency throughout the rest of his career.[57] His activities against Phormio and against the Piraeus (2.85.1–94.4); at Pylos, where he is

---

[51] This is especially notable in Thucydides, whose discussion of religion is very limited: e.g. Hornblower 1992.

[52] Also observed by Debnar 2001: 100, although for slightly different interpretive reasons.

[53] On the priesthood of the Spartan kings, see Cartledge 2001a: 63.

[54] After breaking off at 2.78.4, the tale of the city's capture concludes at 3.52.1–58.5.

[55] The Spartans are often said to adapt during Thucydides' narrative towards ways of thinking and acting that are more like those of the Athenians; on speech, see Debnar 2001, citing on action (3 n. 6) Wassermann 1964: 292 (add 290, 296); Edmunds 1975: 139–42.

[56] Brasidas' 'un-Spartan' qualities are widely appreciated: e.g. Westlake 1968: 148–9; Hornblower 1991–2008: vol. II, 38–61; Debnar 2001: 173; Sears 2020 (though noting that Brasidas does still have much in common with other Spartan leaders), all with references.

[57] Hornblower 1991–2008: vol. I, 281, citing Westlake 1968: 149 n. 1. Spartan – indeed, any ancient Greek – field commanders were to an extent empowered to act in the moment, although they might be charged with specific goals, recalled or reprimanded: e.g. Cartledge 2001a: 61 on Spartan kings; Debnar 2001: 175 n. 10, citing Hodkinson 1983: 265–73 on other Spartan commanders.

wounded in heroic fashion during an attempted solo landing (4.11.4–12.1); and before Megara (4.70.1–73.4) all contribute to this general picture of 'daring and independence'[58] as Thucydides prepares his account of Brasidas' Thracian campaign. In the north, where Brasidas will be seen delivering *logoi* along with *erga*, one of his greatest strengths will be his successful cultivation of the crucial leader–populace relationship beyond his own *polis*.[59]

As the Thracian operations begin, Thucydides relates that Brasidas aspired to this command, and that he is respected at Sparta as being *drastērios*, 'active, effective', literally 'a doer' (4.81.1). His campaign, which involves abundant negotiation alongside warfare, renders him 'of much worth' (*pleistou axion*) to the Spartans (ibid.) as he conducts himself as a 'just and moderate man' (*dikaion kai metrion*, 4.81.2). His *aretē kai xunesis* ('excellence and intelligence', ibid.) win over the Athenian allies to revolt to the Peloponnesians, since 'he was the first [*prōtos*] [of the Spartans] who went out and seemed to be good in every regard' (4.81.3). This passage resonates in several ways with the treatment of Pericles and Athens at 2.65.4–13. As Connor has noted, the phrase *pleistou axion* is also used of Pericles at 2.65.4, and both discussions differentiate between earlier and later time periods in the experiences of their respective *poleis*.[60] Both passages highlight Sicily as a turning point (4.81.2, with 2.65.11–12), and both leaders are described as being *prōtos*, 'first'. Pericles may be the 'first citizen' inside his *polis* (2.65.9), but Brasidas is here perceived as being first in a variety of ways *outside* of his *polis*, and he further manages to make others believe that he is characteristic of his people (4.81.3). Brasidas' notional public, then, is no longer the Spartans, but his immediate local audiences.

As Brasidas approaches Acanthus, its *dēmos* and their opponents are at odds over whether to side with Sparta (4.84.1–2). Given a hearing alone before the Acanthians, Brasidas is distinguished from his origins by Thucydides, who notes that he was not *adunatos* (not 'incapable') in public speaking, despite being a Spartan (4.84.2).[61] The situation now calls for an accomplished speech designed to reconcile competing interests and ingratiate a prospective leader with his new audience.

Brasidas opens with a key Spartan theme that he will use repeatedly: the freedom of Greece and of its individual *poleis* (4.85.1, 6; 86.1, 4; 87.3–6).[62]

---

[58] Debnar 2001: 174–7 (quote at 175), analysing these passages.

[59] Westlake 1968: 148.   [60] Connor 1984b: 130 n. 52.

[61] On the Spartans' 'laconic' speech, see, e.g., Debnar 2001: 6–9, with references.

[62] This was already a well-trodden topic in Greek discourse: see Raaflaub 2004: esp. 118–202.

He then suggests that the Spartans had already considered the Acanthians to be inclined towards their friendship (4.85.4). But his incorporative rhetoric quickly vanishes as he recalls the opposition that he has met, and he submits that the Acanthians will obstruct their own freedom and everyone else's if they discard his offer of alliance (4.85.5). Such a rejection might imply that others should be unwilling to join the Spartan coalition, either because of Brasidas' inefficacy or the 'unjust' nature of the freedom they would gain (4.85.6).

Brasidas now pulls back and introduces a different argumentative tactic, first characterizing himself as a liberator (4.86.1), but then smoothing over the distinction between himself and his audience by promising that he does not intend to create political *stasis* ('strife' or 'division', 4.86.3–4), which would be a source of blame for 'the Spartans' (sc. not merely for himself, 4.86.5). This section of the speech closes with a gnomic statement and a promise of Spartan protection that emphasizes openness and action as opposed to secrecy and rhetoric (4.86.6–87.1). The best guarantee, Brasidas holds, comes from men whose *erga* align with their *logoi*, their deeds arising exactly as their words promise (4.87.1).

In the final section of his speech, Brasidas' content seems to recollect the prayer of Archidamus before the first invasion of Attica (4.87.2), promising to call the 'local gods and heroes' to witness both the justice of his case and the destruction that he will wreak upon Acanthian territory if he receives a negative reply (4.87.2–3). His closing, however, sounds more like a pre-battle exhortation in its calls to 'be the initiators of freedom for the Greeks', 'establish eternal glory' and 'place the most beautiful epithet upon the entire *polis*' (4.87.6).[63] After significant debate, Brasidas' speech ultimately carries the day for revolt from Athens (4.88.1) – and his words will do so in other cities, too.[64]

Many of the rhetorical techniques and themes in this speech are familiar from Thucydides' other leaders, particularly from Pericles: the emphasis upon shared future experience; the use of incorporative rhetoric; the deliberate minimization of the persona of the speaker; the connection between *logos* and *ergon*; and the summons to aspire to glory and adorn the *polis*. But Wylie points out another essential quality of Brasidas' efficacy as a negotiator: his 'always recognizing the need to allow the coerced to save face'.[65]

---

[63] On themes in ancient pre-battle speeches in general, see Zoido 2007; on Thucydidean ones, see Luschnat 1942; Leimbach 1985.

[64] See Wylie 1992: 81, citing 4.114[.3, Torone] and 4.120[.3, Scione], where Thucydides says that Brasidas delivered essentially the same exhortation.

[65] Wylie 1992: 92.

Just as Pericles was able to lead the Athenians while allowing them to believe (or pretend) that the *dēmos* was actually in control, Brasidas offers his new subjects the chance to tell themselves that they are determining their own destiny.

Brasidas' rhetorical and behavioural formula is redeployed at Torone, where he again acts with moderation, giving the Athenians extra time to collect their fallen comrades despite their refusal of his initial offer of safe departure (4.114.2). He further emphasizes to the Toroneans that those who had worked to admit the Spartans were directing their efforts 'not towards servitude or because of money [sc. bribes], but towards the good and freedom of the *polis*' (4.114.3). Here, Brasidas is ascribing motivations to his faction of Toronean supporters that match the rhetoric that he generally employs when trying to win over other cities. Indeed, Thucydides notes that this was 'very similar' to his speech at Acanthus (4.114.3). The same thing happens at Scione, where Brasidas again 'said what he said at Acanthus and Torone' (4.120.3). But the Scionaean response is extraordinary: they give Brasidas the signal public honour of a golden crown, and 'individually' (i.e. without public sanction) they decorate him with *tainia*, ceremonial head-bands, and honour him 'like an athlete', in a manner that recalls the behaviours characteristic of a hero cult.[66] Brasidas' *logoi* have therefore created a new way for his audience to think about his position and his value.

Thucydides presents the final confrontation between Cleon and Brasidas at Amphipolis (5.6.1–10.12) as a recapitulation both of Brasidas' leadership qualities and of the image that Brasidas has created for himself. Brasidas' foresight emerges as he predicts Cleon's decisions at 5.6.3 and 5.7.1; his *empeiria* and *tolma* ('experience' and 'boldness') are praised by the Athenians who chafe at Cleon's delays (5.7.2). Brasidas assesses his forces and chooses a daring stratagem with a small detachment to be personally led by him (5.8.1–5), then offers a pre-battle speech to encourage his troops (5.9.1–10). The speech features a compact introduction appealing to the standard subjects of heritage, freedom and temperament (5.9.1) before Brasidas previews his strategy. This includes perceptive speculation about the mindset of the Athenian enemy (5.9.3,6) and closes with a direct admonition to Clearidas (who will be commanding the bulk of the troops) to act like a true Spartiate, and to the allies to follow with willingness, take care for their reputation and show obedience, all qualities that Brasidas says make for good warfare (5.9.9). He closes, finally, with another exhortation to

---

[66] Ferrario 2014: 202, 207–10, 231–2.

freedom (ibid.) and with a promise that his actions will not fall short of his words (5.9.10).

When the battle begins, Brasidas' perceptive reading of the Athenians' uncertain body language beckons him to a rapid attack (5.10.5–6). He is wounded and rescued (5.10.8), but he dies shortly after hearing of his victory (5.10.11). The acknowledgements of his death by the Peloponnesian allies and especially by the Amphipolitans outstrip even the heroic treatment that he received at Scione. Not only does he receive a funeral at public expense (*dēmosiai*, 5.11.1), but he is named the new *ktistēs*, or colonial founder, of Amphipolis and buried in its *agora* (public square), where his grave receives the attentions of a cult. Amphipolis' true founder, Hagnon, is expelled from his former status (ibid.), completing the conversion of what was originally an Athenian colony into a Spartan ally,[67] and what was originally a Spartan commander into a hero.

Brasidas does indeed display some of the qualities of a Homeric warrior,[68] but he also participates strongly in now-established models of Thucydidean leadership. The collaboration between leader and *polis* in Thucydides is investigated in greatest detail through the relationship between Athens and Pericles, but the diversity and scale of Brasidas' experience with *poleis* beyond his own both emphasizes the significance of this relationship and explores other facets of it. The example of Brasidas also powerfully demonstrates the performative aspects of leadership,[69] showing that *logoi* that seem to be or even promise to be supported by *erga* can prove nearly as potent as the *erga* themselves.[70]

Conclusion: 'Good' Leadership in Thucydides

Despite his pervasive emphasis upon leadership and its potential to create effective action, Thucydides is not generally interested in whether his leaders are 'good' people in a philosophical or (less still) a psychological sense.[71] Although these individuals can certainly display moral qualities, they may share those same qualities with entire cities, or they may deploy them only

[67] On the meaning of this extraordinary gesture, see Ferrario 2014: 230–3; cf. also Fragoulaki (Chapter 11) for the ethnic dimension of this event.

[68] Hornblower 1991–2008: vol. II, 32–61; Howie 2005.

[69] He therefore helps to explain the popular reception of Alcibiades: see Debnar 2001: 172, who calls 'Alcibiades, like Brasidas . . . a master of images crafted with words'; and cf. Bloedow 1973.

[70] See Parry 1981: 69.

[71] A case could be made that Nicias is the very limited exception: see his 'obituary' at 7.86.5.

for utilitarian purposes.[72] Thucydides' investigation of leadership tends to be more specific: how did leaders construct and maintain their authority, both in appearance and in reality? How did they try to use that authority to advance the aims of their states?

Whether or not Thucydides saw himself as preparing a leadership study, his treatment of that topic certainly influenced his best-known continuator, Xenophon (c. 430/25–355/4?). Xenophon was profoundly interested in leadership in all the ways that Thucydides was not: ethics, character, biographical experience.[73] And yet, Xenophon's *Hellenica* picks up the narrative of Greek history at almost precisely the point where Thucydides' text concludes. In the earlier section of Xenophon's *Hellenica*, in particular, one finds not only particularly vivid coverage of Alcibiades and his reception by the Athenian people, but also depictions of the failures of the Athenian *dēmos* to make sound decisions without effective guidance.[74] In other words, Thucydides' priorities continue to play an important role in Xenophon's thinking,[75] even as an individual's personal qualities become of increasing significance to Xenophon's intellectual consideration of leadership.[76]

Some of this, to be sure, is topical: the most specific literary allusions to Thucydides and to his leaders are most easily observed when the subject matter of later historians is still inhabiting his world, or at least his era.[77] But the discussions of Thucydidean reception in Part III of this volume point towards the rich variety of ways that Thucydides' leaders, assisted rather than hindered by their paradigmatic qualities, lent themselves to interpretation as *exempla* in later ages. Even today, Thucydides continues to be required reading at military academies,[78] not only for what he has to say about fighting a war, but also for what people still feel that he has to teach about leading one.

[72] See Woodruff (Chapter 14) – although Woodruff interprets Thucydides' interests in individual human virtue differently than I do.
[73] E.g., amongst the vast bibliography, Buxton 2016 and especially Gray 2011.
[74] Most notably the Arginusae affair, Xen. *Hell.* 1.6.24–7.35.
[75] A good demonstration of this is Rood 2004.
[76] This is an important theme for Xenophon generally: e.g. Sandridge 2012; Tamiolaki 2012, 2016.
[77] Soulis 1972 treats the textual resonances of Thucydides in Xenophon's *Hellenica*; Fromentin and Gotteland 2015 (a chapter in a volume on the rapidly developing topic of Thucydidean reception) and Hornblower 1995 show how the use of Thucydides by other ancient writers changes over time as his work begins to be employed for more abstract purposes. See also Pitcher (Chapter 15).
[78] See, e.g., Cook 2006; Murray 2013.

Further Reading

I confine my remarks here to items dealing specifically with Thucydides, and mainly those available in English. For those beginning with this broad subject, Balot et al. 2017 and Rengakos and Tsakmakis 2006 both present abundant topical discussions. Westlake 1968, despite the title, is significantly directed towards arguing for evolution in Thucydides' working and writing style. A start-to-finish study of Thucydides' text, replete with insights about individual figures and much else, is Connor 1984b; Connor 1971 also provides valuable treatments of post-Periclean leaders and leadership.

On more specific subjects, Azoulay 2014 on Pericles shows how multiple types of evidence can contribute to the portrait of a leader; Foster 2010 offers a more specifically targeted approach to the same individual. Debnar 2001 presents close readings of the Thucydidean political (though not the military) speeches given and heard by Spartans. Works that are especially prominent in the history of Thucydidean scholarship include Bender 1938, Luschnat 1942, de Romilly 1956, 1963 and Parry 1981. Loraux 1986a, despite dealing with a topic that extends beyond Thucydidean studies, is also extremely important for understanding the cultural context of late 5th-century Athens.

13

RYAN K. BALOT

Thucydides on Democracy and Other Regimes

Thucydides presents warfare as the most illuminating framework within which to understand and evaluate human activities, above all politics. War proves to be the ultimate testing ground of our resolve to transcend the exigencies of our embodied lives – a 'violent teacher', as he said, which forces its students, willing or not, to focus on basic needs and desires, especially of the body (3.82). As a result, war also puts to the test the regimes (*politeiai*) that we construct to address those exigencies, whether of the body or the soul. Through diverse forms of social organization, we protect ourselves, we struggle with our fears, we pursue standing with others and we satisfy materialistic wants. The key is to understand the speeches and deeds of diverse regimes at war – particularly, as we will see, of democracies at war. For, even if Thucydides found the lower classes contemptible, he expressed admiration for the attainments of democracies based at their core on demotic liberation and power. In Thucydides' vision, democracies make possible the most complete political education for observers because they conceive the greatest ambitions – not only heroic accomplishment but also freedom and flourishing – and yet they typically fall prey to the fault lines inherent in their own systems. The tragedy of democracy, for Thucydides, is mitigated only by the stubborn resolve of the *dēmos* to keep going together.

This comparatively sympathetic presentation of Thucydidean democracy differs from both standard and minority interpretations. From Hobbes onward, most have read Thucydides as an unequivocal critic of democratic self-governance and as particularly contemptuous of the *dēmos*' claims to prudence or justice.[1] Conversely, others allege that Thucydides favours Sparta over other regimes because of its stability, moderation and even piety.[2] Still others find in Thucydides a basic contrast between absolutism

The author would like to thank Seth Jaffe for helpful comments on the penultimate version of this chapter.

[1] Cf. Ober 1998, 113–20.   [2] Strauss 1964; Orwin 1994, with Balot 2015.

and independence rather than a firm commitment to either oligarchy or democracy.[3] Or they see in Thucydides' text an invitation to readers to think openly, to revise continually and to exercise critical judgement for themselves – activities that can aptly be associated with democracy.[4] While each of these approaches has its merits, my own view is that Thucydides' text is both more general and more specific, disclosing for its readers instead a vantage point from which to size up the limits and opportunities of diverse regimes, which must be judged within the context of the strict particularity of events unfolding with and against one another. It was through the particularities of speech and deed that Thucydides intended to construct a timeless monument of political understanding. More precisely, Thucydides begins by presenting his key themes – freedom and flourishing, violence and peace, speech and deed – through the prism of particular regime types. Then he enables his readers to step back from particular cities – Athens or Sparta, Corinth or Thebes – in order to take a new perspective on regime types, understood in categorical terms – democracy, oligarchy, monarchy and so on. In the process he reveals not only what is peculiar to Athens or Syracuse, for example, but also what is distinctive of and peculiar to these regime types, construed as models of social organization.

Among the diverse regime types that Thucydides puts on display, democracy is the most gripping or memorable (1.10, 2.41), even the most paradigmatic. The Thucydidean democracies represent the cardinal emblem of the historian's own moderately pessimistic vision of human limits and possibilities.[5] To discern this point adequately, it is essential to see what scholars have too often neglected: that Thucydides stages the unfolding drama of not one, but two, outstanding democracies in the *History*. Two democracies are most prominent – Athens and Syracuse – and they compete internationally and ideologically with Sparta (an oligarchic 'mixed' regime), Persia (a monarchy), historical tyrannies and a variety of other regimes that undergo continuous evolution over the course of the *History*.[6] Through comparing and contrasting Athens and Syracuse we learn a great deal about what these democracies' distinctive features might be, the limits they typically show and the opportunities they reveal. In comparing and contrasting these regimes, both in themselves and against the background of non-democratic regimes, Thucydides worked within the spirit of Athens' own intellectual horizons.[7] So far from rejecting his native city's innovative and self-conscious culture, the historian carried to the limit his own exploration of democracy's political ambitions and tragic limitations.

---

[3] Pope 1988.   [4] Mara 2008.   [5] Cf. Cogan 1981 for a more extreme view.
[6] Cf. Raaflaub 2006: esp. 195–212; Jaffe 2017a: 394–401.   [7] Cf. Nichols 2015: 169–84.

Athenian Democracy at First Sight

In their speech at Sparta just before the war, certain Corinthian envoys describe the Athenians as daring, innovative, resilient and unusually patriotic (1.70) – in short, as a 'modern' power capable of approaching a changed world with adaptive strategies (1.71). It was essential to their projects, the Corinthians argue, that the Athenians disregard the bodily consequences of their actions; they refuse to allow warfare, in particular, to confine their vision to basic needs. They steadfastly keep their eyes on a distant horizon. By contrast, the Spartans are slow, traditional and fearful (1.70). Admittedly, the Corinthians offer this characterization before the long and wasting war could have its full impact on Thucydides' chief protagonists. But their speech was convincing enough to persuade the Spartans, after a nudge by the ephor Sthenelaidas, to declare war on Athens for its aggressions against other Greeks, above all their own allies (1.86–7). Interestingly, Thucydides says, the Spartans were motivated by fear of Athens more than by their allies' speeches, which focused on Athenian injustice and their need for Sparta to defend them (1.88, 1.118). The initial contrast between Greece's leading democracy and its leading non-democratic power could hardly be sharper.[8]

The actions of the war described by Thucydides typically illustrate the truth of these assessments, beginning with the Pentecontaetia and lasting throughout the work.[9] Consider two examples among many. First, towards the end of Book 2, Thucydides describes the actions of the Athenian general Phormio, who was guarding the straits near Naupactus with twenty Athenian ships. The Spartans and their allies were trying to transport soldiers to a theatre of war in western Greece, where they had hoped to detach the Acarnanians from the Athenian alliance. In the first movement, Phormio forced the Peloponnesian ships to fall into disorder, sank an admiral's ship and captured twelve others (2.84). After the battle, the Spartan authorities reinforced their fleet heavily, in ignorance of the Athenians' nautical skill and willingness to try unexpected strategies in order to defeat their slower-witted foes (2.85). In the ensuing battle, several of Phormio's ships were captured in a narrow strait; but, through a series of daring and unexpected actions (2.91), the Athenians recovered their strength, recaptured their own ships and defeated the larger Spartan flotilla (2.92). It was Phormio's more sophisticated understanding of the situation and his crews' daring and

[8] Cf. Edmunds 1975: 89–93, Connor 1984b: 36–47; and recently Jaffe 2017c: 62–76, 198–9.
[9] Rawlings 1981: 80–5; Connor 1984b: 36–47.

experience at sea that gave Athens this unlikely early victory at a significant strategic location. As the opposing generals' speeches make clear, the Athenians had developed a novel form of courage at sea and a willingness to innovate and change plans on the spot, all of which made their unlikely success possible (2.87, 2.89).[10] Their activities complement Thucydides' earlier notice that the Spartans grew fearful even of Athenian assistance in 464 BCE, during the revolt of their helots, because of the Athenians' 'unorthodoxy', which was illustrated tangibly by the Athenians' pre-eminence in novel strategies of siege warfare (1.102).

If Phormio's victories off the headlands of Rhium illustrate the aggressive and active side of democratic innovation, then the plague at Athens discloses another, more responsive dimension of the Athenian character. In Thucydides' description, the plague was an experience of unimaginable suffering, both physical and mental. Adults lost control of their bodily functions, as painful coughing, uncontrollable retching and an intolerable burning sensation attacked them over the course of days or weeks (2.49.3–5). Suffering from memory loss, they failed to recognize friends and even to know themselves (2.49.8). Thucydides offers these sharp reminders that, despite their audacity and precocity, the Athenians were just as vulnerable as other human beings to suffering from unexpected setbacks or failures over which they had no control. Perhaps they were even more vulnerable than others, in that their untraditional strategies, such as densely packing citizens into the city from outlying areas, meant that disease could spread more easily and destructively throughout the entire city (2.52). The body has limits that even democrats will be forced to acknowledge (cf. 2.41 with 2.52.3 and Orwin 2016). Under the pressure of the failures of their individual bodies, Thucydides emphasizes the Athenians' increasing shame-lessness and lawlessness as social creatures (2.52–3): they stole funeral pyres, indulged in transitory pleasures and abandoned traditional worship of the gods.

What is most striking about Thucydides' account is that this civic convul-sion, which he renders so memorably and dramatically, caused very little serious damage to this city. Phormio's notable successes were won shortly after the plague narrative; and, despite the need for Pericles to fortify the Athenians' lagging spirits (2.59, 2.65), the war effort was far from crippled.[11] Scholars have often observed the juxtaposition of this set piece with the Periclean Funeral Oration and made much of the possibility that the plague undercuts the optimistic representation of Athens given by its most

[10] Cf. Ober 2010; Balot 2014.   [11] Cf. Balot 2016.

distinguished leader.[12] What is really notable, however, is that Athens did not quickly descend into civil war – not even close. The contrast between Athens and another naval democracy, Corcyra, could hardly be clearer, especially since Thucydides took special pains to create verbal echoes between his account of the Corcyraean civil war (3.82–3) and the Athenian plague.[13] Considering the twenty-seven years of the war as a whole, in fact, the plague was quickly forgotten and hardly mentioned again after the winter of 427/6 BCE (3.87, though cf. 6.12). Thucydides' point, I think, was not only to suggest Athens's undeniable vulnerability, but also to draw attention to the city's resilience. Resilience is a character-istic that the Corinthians had stressed (1.70), although the Athenians' response to failure has frequently been neglected by comparison with their restless acquisitiveness. Even if the plague caused despair or hopelessness among its victims (2.51, 2.59), the Athenians were disposed to confront setbacks resolutely and confidently (cf. 1.70).[14] That is why, for example, just after the plague's first onslaught, and after losing over 25 per cent of their soldiers at Potidaea, the Athenians brought their siege of the city to a successful completion (2.70). The home authorities even proceeded to blame the generals at Potidaea for failing to push their undoubted success to the limit.

In relating these episodes, Thucydides is typically more interested in defining the national ethos or character of democracies than in tarrying with their institutional structures or laws. His presentation strongly suggests that the key to understanding democracies at war – his ostensible subject – is to join up their cultural ethos with their habits of making war and taking decisions. It is essential now to follow his reflections on democracy at its peak on through his striking comparative analysis of democracies towards the end of the war as Athens confronts its democratic 'other', Syracuse. Along the way, we observe that Thucydides' own forte – to link interpret-ation with action or to connect speech (logos) with deed (ergon) – also turns out to be the great strength of democracies as such.[15] Even if Thucydides went into exile from Athens after his defeat at Amphipolis (5.26), the historian's own daring experiments in historical and philosophical thought

---

[12] Connor 1984b: 63–75; Raaflaub 2006: 191–3, 197, 199; cf. also the discussions of Munson (Chapter 7) and Ferrario (Chapter 12).

[13] Noted by, for example, Macleod 1979; Connor 1984b: 99–102.

[14] Fisher and Hoekstra 2017: 379–81.

[15] On logos versus ergon as a key theme in Thucydides' representation of his historical project, see Beasley (Chapter 3), and on its importance to his understanding of political leadership, see Ferrario (Chapter 12).

were developments of the daring experimentalism, whether militarily, politically or intellectually, of the democracies that he describes.[16]

Democracy at Its Height

The clearest bridge between Thucydides' intellectual activities and democratic thinking can be found in Pericles' Funeral Oration. Although the
historicity of Thucydides' speeches is contested, Thucydides concerned himself with their veracity (at 1.22; cf. Hornblower 1991–2008: vol. I, 59), and
it is likely that Thucydides presented Pericles' own underlying arguments.[17]
Pericles' deservedly famous speech is central to the Thucydidean presentation of democracy because it reveals – and even enacts – the critical point
that democracies strive not only to attain freedom and the power to rule, but
also to acquire self-understanding. By contrast with Sparta, which did not
observe the ritualized funeral oration, the Athenians led an examined life in
which they explained their behaviours to themselves – and even explained
why their democratic regime supplied the best possible context for human
well-being and the realization of human potential. By contrast with other
known orators in the epitaphic genre, Pericles does not dilate on the subject
of Athens' history; instead, his purpose is to explicate the customs
(*epitēdeusis*), regime (*politeia*) and way of life (*tropoi*, 'character') that
accounted for Athens' success (2.36).[18] What follows is an illuminating
analysis of the Athenian democracy as a cultural framework that
Athenians were to be proud of and embrace, that was superior in every
respect to that of its rivals and that enabled citizens to realize their potential
for intellectual, political and ethical development.[19] Pericles' stirring aspir-
ations for the city, however, competed with the Athenians' desire to rule
others and to achieve heroic recognition through pursuing imperial power.

Pericles' emphasis, like that of Thucydides, is on the Athenian democracy as
a particular cultural (as opposed to institutional) formation. What matters to
him is the equality and freedom that Athenians enjoy, and in particular their
ease with one another in their everyday lives (2.37). These characteristics were
unusual for a *polis*; they were distinctively democratic. The Athenians live
beautiful lives and develop themselves intellectually without diminishing their
firmness and without losing sight of the significance of their civic functions

---

[16] Cf. Nichols 2015: 169–84, with Strauss 1964.

[17] Cf. Ziolkowski 1981: 188–95; Yunis 1996: 61–6; Balot 2014: 14–15. The problem of
interpreting Thucydides' statement on speeches at 1.22 is explored further by Greenwood
(Chapter 5).

[18] Cf. Ziolkowski 1981; Loraux 1986a; Balot 2014: 25–46.

[19] Balot 2014: 25–46, 2017.

(2.40). In fact, the Athenians are paradigmatic Greeks, living in a city that is the 'school of Hellas', precisely in the sense that their regime enables them to develop the human excellences – of intellect, of deliberation, of courageous action, of friendship and generosity towards others and of leadership in the Greek world – to an unrivalled extent – indeed, to the limits of human potentiality. According to Pericles, each Athenian citizen is fully self-governing and endowed 'with exceptional grace and exceptional versatility' (2.41, trans. Warner 1954). Pericles' chief point is that, because of its democracy, Athens encourages its citizens to flourish as human beings to the highest degree through the cultivation of their civic and personal virtues.[20]

Intriguingly, Pericles sets these inspirational remarks against the backdrop of the Athenians' acknowledged need to maintain freedom through courageous military action: 'Make up your minds that happiness depends on being free, and freedom depends on being courageous' (2.43, trans. Warner 1954). On the one hand, Pericles strove to redefine courage as a less blind or pugnacious and more deliberative and democratic ideal (2.40.2–3; Balot 2014). In doing so, he furthered the project of envisioning Athenian democracy as the paradigmatic realization of the highest human excellences. On the other hand, Pericles points out that the city's achievement of beauty and excellence, construed as elements of the most ambitious human vocation, depends on continuing warfare and imperialism – and, indeed, on a conception of the city's freedom that involves the enslavement, or at least oppression, of other Greeks.[21] As commentators have observed, Pericles' Funeral Oration does not praise the Athenians' justice; and, in fact, in his final speech in the *History*, Pericles notoriously likened the Athenian Empire to a tyranny, which the Athenians had to maintain on pain of their own enslavement (2.63; cf. 3.37).[22] Hence, Pericles' aspirational vision of the city, while real and stirring, was also penetrated by deep ambiguities that threaten its obvious appeal just beneath the surface.[23]

Readers are left with a double vision – a blurred vision – of the utopian Athens evoked by Pericles. The city's eudaimonistic goals – its desire to create a free and open political life in which citizens can cultivate their talents to the highest degree – explain vividly why the Athenians should 'love' the city and its power and why they should, at the limit, be willing to die for the city (2.43). Yet this virtue-based approach is already in competition with the Athenians' desire to attain to the freedom of mastery over others and to leave memorials, as Pericles said, of both the good things and the bad things that

---

[20] Balot 2017.   [21] Raaflaub 2004: 166–80.
[22] Connor 1984b: 73–5, 89–91; Orwin 1994; Ober 1998: 89–91; Balot 2001: 172–8.
[23] Balot 2014: 109–28.

Athens has done (2.41.4). Athens, Pericles says, needs no Homer to recount its glories (2.41.4), but that very statement illustrates the extent to which even Periclean Athens was in thrall to traditional standards of heroic, militaristic glory. If Pericles' speech helps to explain how 'Athens at first sight' could succeed at Rhium and prove resilient during the plague, then Thucydides' narrative reveals, over time, how the pressures of war strained even this most stubborn regime to its psychological, political and military limits, precisely because of the fault lines revealed in Pericles' speeches themselves.

Democracy under Pressure

Thucydides narrated the plague episode shortly after he presented Pericles' Funeral Oration, a juxtaposition clearly designed to make visible Athens' vulnerability just at the pinnacle of its (apparent) attainment of rational control over the city's affairs. More important was the vulnerability intrinsic in Athens' hegemonic position with respect to other Greek cities and the fractures within the deliberative process that Pericles had so exalted. Already in 428 BCE, and even earlier (3.2), Mytilene, a prized ally, was preparing to revolt from Athens' empire and to seek Spartan help in doing so. In their approach to the Spartans, the Mytilenean ambassadors present a far different picture of Athens. Instead of acting as leaders with a generous spirit, they declare, the Athenians calculatingly manoeuvred so as to gain maximal power over their allies, especially the strongest ones (3.10–11). Intent on enslaving the other Greeks, in fact, Athens maintained its empire through fear rather than friendship (3.12). Rationalizing their own self-interests carefully, the Spartans agreed to help the rebels, although in the event their support proved to be unhelpful and even non-existent. Ultimately, after serious disputes between the Mytilenean leaders and *dēmos*, the city submitted to the Athenian general Paches and his troops, who had been laying siege.

What to do with the captured Mytileneans? The Athenians reacted angrily at first and decided to execute the entire male population, not only the chief instigators. But after a day's interval they underwent a change of attitude, on the grounds that the initial punishment seemed excessive (3.36). What follows is a debate in which Thucydides reveals not only the democracy's capacity to reconsider key issues of justice and prudence, but also the difficulties and ambiguities of the deliberative process exalted by Pericles.[24] Whereas the hawkish Cleon berates his fellow citizens for softness and ineffective imperial governance, the otherwise unknown Diodotus (whose name means 'gift of the god') convinces the Athenians to impose a more

---

[24] Macleod 1978; Saxonhouse 1996; Ober 1998: 94–104; Saxonhouse 2006: 151–63.

lenient punishment. On the one hand, the Athenians agree with Diodotus that prudent self-interest tells against condemning all those swept along, willy-nilly, in the act of rebellion, and against believing that harsh punishments are likely to prevent 'hope and desire' from motivating political actors to seek independence (3.45). On the other hand, Diodotus argues successfully that the Athenians would be wrong to kill those, such as the lower-class Mytileneans, who had helped them as soon as they were armed (3.47). Prudence and justice would seem to cooperate in Diodotus' speech, and yet he himself insists that it is impossible to combine the two, at least in this particular case (3.47). What, then, are we to make of Diodotus' speech? In what way does it illuminate the workings of the democratic regime?

Diodotus brings about an outcome that is both prudent and just precisely by arguing that prudence and justice cannot be combined in this case.[25] His deception of the *dēmos* paradoxically furthers the Periclean goal of making the democratic Athenians the just and generous leaders that they sought to be. Strikingly, the democracy becomes adequately virtuous only through the corruption of its deliberative practices, which Pericles himself had identified as central to the city's political functioning. Diodotus states bluntly, in fact, that successful democratic oratory requires deception (3.43). Speakers must lie in order to be convincing, he says, because the *dēmos* will always be suspicious of their leaders' graspingness, even when orators seek the common good. Formally or informally, democracies continually put their leaders on trial for the advice they give and the influence they exert.[26] The *dēmos* is confident and even jealous of its power. In spite of Diodotus' critique, the *dēmos*' attitude is understandable: as Thucydides himself points out, democratic leaders necessarily vie with one another for pre-eminence, they strive to satisfy the *dēmos*' frequently imprudent desires and they let their private ambitions and greed take precedence over the city's welfare (2.65). To that extent, the people's suspicion is essential to the regime's health. On the other hand, Thucydides offers a number of examples in which the *dēmos* unfairly blames its leaders for decisions taken by the assembled Athenian citizens themselves, starting with the decision to go to war altogether at Pericles' suggestion – which led the *dēmos* to fine their greatest leader and only eventually to reinstate him (2.65; cf. 5.26, 7.14–15, 7.48). If the democracy functions successfully only through oratorical deception and if the *dēmos* fails to accept responsibility for its decisions, then certainly the Athenian democracy cannot live up to the admirable ideals of virtuous character and open deliberation evoked by Pericles.

[25] Cf. Orwin 1994: 142–62; Saxonhouse 2006: 151–63.
[26] Finley 1962; Zumbrunnen 2008.

These points are sharpened as Thucydides' narrative proceeds, above all when the Athenians attacked the strategically insignificant island of Melos in 416 BCE. According to the Athenian ambassadors, the islanders' unwillingness to join the Athenian Empire made Athens look weak (5.95, 5.97). Their speech illustrates that, under the pressures of war, Pericles' ideal vision of the democracy has become bankrupt. To the Melians' concerns about their own enslavement (5.92, 5.100) the Athenians respond without respect or generosity, rejecting the standards of nobility to which the Melians appeal on the grounds that honour deserves no respect in contexts of unequal power (5.89, 5.101, 5.111). In the place of nobility, they offer only the cold laws of power politics – to rule wherever possible – to which they subscribe (5.105). The freedom celebrated by Pericles has undergone two significant alterations. First, the Athenians have come to regard freedom as the capacity to project power over others rather than to realize ideals of leadership or virtue.[27] Second, their freedom to project power has in fact become a constraint on their political and military activity, in that they find themselves compelled to devastate the would-be neutral Melos, for symbolic reasons if nothing else.[28] The Mytilenean and Melian episodes have brought the Periclean consensus to a virtual crumbling point (2.65; cf. Balot 2014).

Thucydides reinforces these points in his presentation of the Athenians' Sicilian Expedition and its aftermath. But his critique of democratic Athens is qualified by his acknowledgement of the city's persistent strength – its capacity to field an impressive armada supported by the utter dedication of Athens' citizens. On Thucydides' showing, the citizens fully embrace the city and its power, as Pericles had urged them to do (2.43). Cooperating with and extending this dedication to the city, the Athenians prove to be highly resilient. Even if Thucydides criticizes them for their hubris in the midst of success (e.g. after Pylos, 4.65), their response to crisis or failure is even more significant. They will not yield to pressure; they pull themselves together. Democracy is stubborn.

Syracuse and Athens during the 'Sicilian Books' (Books 6 and 7)

Although prior to 415 BCE democracies had generally supported democracies and oligarchies had supported oligarchies, Thucydides' sixth and seventh books at last enable readers to witness the comparative strength and self-justifications of two democracies at different stages in their evolution as ambitious, imperialistic powers. When they reach Books 6 and 7, readers

---

[27] Cf. Raaflaub 2004: 166–80.   [28] Wohl 2002.

will already be familiar with Athens' self-interested dealings in Sicily. Indeed, the great expedition of 415 BCE was the more fully committed extension of earlier, more tentative forays. In 427 BCE, taking advantage of their supposed kinship with Leontini, the Athenians had sent a force under Laches to explore the possibility of attacking Sicily; the Syracusans and their Sicilian allies were at least nominally at war with Athens (3.86, 3.88, 3.90, with Raaflaub 2006: 202–3). These Athenian generals left the scene only when Camarina, Gela and Syracuse had negotiated a fragile peace among the Sicilian Greeks, but the Athenians continued their military activities in Sicily through 425 BCE, despite their ongoing operations in various other theatres of war, including the western part of mainland Greece and the Peloponnese. Even in 422 BCE, in fact, they sent out Phaeax to take advantage of political struggles at Leontini and to stir up war against Syracuse, because of its desire for power over others (5.4). The implication is that, after Pericles' death, the Athenians largely ignored their great leader's advice to avoid expanding the scope of their imperialism during the war with Sparta. Readers come to understand democracy through analysing the city's deeds in the light of its politicians' speeches.

Already in these early efforts in Sicily, the Athenians were not only carrying on their own traditions of imperialism, but also showing that they had inherited the Persian inclination to dominate smaller, generally disorganized Greek cities to their west.[29] This interpretive lens emerges prominently in the speech attributed to the Syracusan Hermocrates, who in 424 BCE convinced the people of Camarina and Gela, and the Sicilian Greeks in general, to reach an armistice (4.58–65). It is in this speech in particular that readers begin to discern the democratically based similarities between Athens and Syracuse.[30] Like Themistocles during the period of the Persian Wars (cf. 1.137–8), Hermocrates calmly explains why the Sicilians should fear the future and fear Athens, thereby encouraging them to forge a peace that would enable Sicily to defend itself and to live in freedom (4.61–3). He invokes the Dorian ethnicity of the Sicilian Greeks and interprets their fate, as Sicilians, as a shared and unified one vis-à-vis the 'external' world of mainland Greece (4.64). Although Hermocrates expatiates on the benefits of peace (4.62), he says explicitly that he expects the Sicilian Greeks to go to war with one another again, after the Athenians have withdrawn (4.64). More chillingly, he admits that Syracuse is generally disposed to act

---

[29] Cf. Rood 1999.

[30] Cf. Rutter 2002; the comparison between Athens and Syracuse is further explored, with particular reference to Thucydides' portrayal of their respective political leaders, by Ferrario (Chapter 12).

aggressively towards its neighbours (4.64), while declining to blame those who pursue imperialism, on the grounds of the natural human desire to rule wherever possible (4.61). For the other Greeks of Sicily, these statements should strike an ominous note, considering Syracuse's general pattern of dominating them and of establishing an intricate network of alliances in the region – a proto-imperialist strategy (e.g. 3.86, 3.88, 3.103, 3.115, 4.24–5, 5.4–5). Hermocrates' arguments can be understood in their proper light only if they are viewed as establishing the incipient groundwork for projects of imperialism similar to those of Athens (cf. 6.78, 6.85, with Orwin 1994: 163–71).

Already in 424 BCE, we are meant to imagine the rise of Syracuse as an imperial democracy, from its early efforts to dominate the Sicilian Greeks until its own 'Salamis' experience in its victory over the invading Athenians in the Great Harbour. Syracuse is another Athens, following the imperial democratic prototype roughly one half-century later (cf. 7.56–9). If Athens is the 'first democracy', then Syracuse is the 'second democracy'. In its speeches and its deeds, this 'second Athens' resembles Thucydides' paradigmatic democracy: it is innovative, it shows qualities of leadership, it abandons traditions that prove no longer useful and it exhibits great daring and resolve. Like Athens, Syracuse was a restless power, a city always in motion, as Thucydides' 'second Archaeology' of Sicily amply reveals (6.2–5). It has not yet, however, 'graduated' to the level of idealistic self-consciousness or self-knowledge attained by Athens at its peak, in the Periclean Funeral Oration. Rather, Syracuse is a more pragmatic and ruthless imperial power, as it must be in its early stages; it is led by an exceptionally intelligent and courageous man, Hermocrates, who resembles the outstandingly intelligent, innovative and energetic Themistocles (compare 6.72 with 1.138; cf. e.g. 7.73); Hermocrates' speech at Gela is shot through not with references to nobility and leadership, but instead with a tolerance of and even admiration for powerful cities that display the ambition to rule (4.61, 4.64; cf. Hermocrates at Camarina, 6.78). By contrast, Athens remains Thucydides' exemplary city, in the sense that its course of growth and development reveal much more about human possibilities, limits and experience altogether than Syracuse's comparatively undeveloped political life could yet do.

Athens' paradigmatic qualities explain why, in describing the Sicilian Expedition, Thucydides emphasizes the Athenian perspective.[31] The historian takes the Athenians as his quasi-tragic protagonists, beginning with the infamous 'Sicilian Debate' between Nicias and Alcibiades, proceeding with

---

[31] Greenwood 2017.

the celebratory launching of the great armada and working through the Athenians' tactical operations and victories and losses, before culminating in the 'total destruction' (*panōlethria*) of the entire force. In order to explain the Athenians' decision to send their vast army to Sicily in 415 BCE, Thucydides staged a debate between Nicias and Alcibiades, leaders of sharply contrasting character. The 'Sicilian Debate' is highly revealing of a diverse range of democratic characteristics; the foundation of these characteristics is that while the democracy permits a variety of human types to address the Assembly, the *dēmos* itself must judge among them. The *dēmos* habitually distorts the democratic process by conflating its own partisan *eros* for advantage, status and materialistic wealth with an appropriate, Periclean *eros* for the city's welfare and the prospect of a peaceful political existence. The democracy proves to be unstable and imprudent before it needs to display its admirably stubborn resolve.

Nicias is moderate and perceptive about the Athenians' genuine interests. In a quasi-Periclean spirit, he advises the Athenians – quite sensibly – to avoid opening another front in their war before they can be confident of their position on the Greek mainland (6.10; cf. 7.18). Like Diodotus, he wants the Athenians to reverse a previous decision on a matter of great importance (6.14), but the Assembly chooses the other option this time, under the influence of his selfish, erotic and glamorous rival Alcibiades. While Nicias repeatedly rejects the passions of his rival's youthful followers, and while he champions the prerogative of citizens opposed to their increasingly fervid militarism (6.12–13), Alcibiades convinces his fellow citizens that they face a choice between freedom and expansion on the one hand, and an idleness that is tantamount to slavery on the other (6.18). In the event, Alcibiades succeeds in convincing his fellow citizens that their imperialistic character is their necessary fate (6.19) – in effect, that their imperialistic 'freedom' has established for them the ultimate constraint. In the face of these arguments, Nicias' attempts to resist the charges of cowardice and defective patriotism were merely futile (6.13, 6.24). His efforts to reopen the debate, to frighten the Athenians into desisting through magnifying the expense of the expedition (6.19) and to lie in Diodotean fashion in order to bring about a superior outcome only intensified the Athenians' *eros* and made the eventual failure even more devastating. The Sicilian Debate provides a theoretical 'clinic' on how the *dēmos*' judgement can move from misguided to abysmal through a process of distinctively democratic prejudices, dysfunctions and distortions.[32]

---

[32] Ober 1993; though cf. Canevaro 2019: esp. 371–81.

Presumably, the decision-making process in a healthier democracy would be free of such distortions. While the Athenians were celebrating the magnificence of their armada (6.32), the Syracusans held a debate that contrasted with the Athenians' debate in several important respects. No doubt Thucydides intended his readers to compare and contrast these juxtaposed democratic assemblies.[33] Hermocrates perceived the Athenian threat well in advance and exhorted his fellow citizens to take bold steps in order to confront the danger: not only to form alliances with other Sicilians and Italian Greeks, but also to meet the Athenians aggressively at Tarentum in order to frighten them with their unanticipated daring (6.33–4). In the ensuing debate, Hermocrates was personally attacked on the charge of trying to seize power for himself and his partisans (6.38). In laying this charge, Hermocrates' rival Athenagoras argued that '*dēmos*' meant the entirety of the citizen-body, not simply the wealthy or elite, and that the ordinary citizens could judge for themselves how to address the rumours of Athens' invasion (6.39–40). For Athenagoras, even Hermocrates' apparently reasonable suggestions seem a threat to democratic – and to his own – power. What is striking is that a Syracusan general shuts down the debate, criticizes Athenagoras' personal attacks on Hermocrates and his supporters, and he decides to prepare for war and investigate the possibilities of alliances all on his own (6.41). Syracuse was saved through less debate, not more – constraints on discussion, not the free play of popular judgement. Thucydides presents the Syracusan democracy in a favourable light only because the citizens adhered patriotically to the city's decisions when taken by exceptionally intelligent generals and statesmen. Genuinely open debate was less effective. Readers will recall that Athens at its height was also governed by its leading citizen (2.65). Such is, in any case, Thucydides' didactic reconstruction; not all students of democracy's epistemic potential would agree.[34]

Much of the rest of Books 6 and 7 covers the action of Athenian fighting in Sicily, where Syracuse managed to forge numerous alliances and to win the support of the Peloponnesians under the Spartan general Gylippus. Before he turns to this narrative, however, Thucydides offers a brief but telling account of the Athenian 'tyrannicides', who were popularly credited with overthrowing the Peisistratid tyranny and establishing democracy (6.53–9). The details of the story are less important than Thucydides' emphasis on the tyrants' intelligence (6.54) and on the Athenians' ignorance of their own past (6.53–4), which led them to distrust their leaders in 415–413 BCE (6.60),

---

[33] Balot 2001: 159–72. [34] Landemore 2012.

especially Alcibiades (6.53; cf. 6.15). Contrary to the idealistic Periclean Funeral Oration, the Athenians do not know themselves, their history or the reasons for their own success. Their success resulted from particular combinations of intelligent (but unchallenged) leadership, the energy and commitment of ordinary citizens and the innovativeness characteristic of their way of life. Athenians were resolute, but they were not particularly cultivated in either judgement or character.

Hence, when they met another energetic democracy, Syracuse, they were confounded: they confronted another, equally daring city; they could not destabilize Syracuse's democratic government, which was itself resolute; nor could they discover material advantages, since Syracuse was also a large and wealthy democracy (7.55; cf. 6.69, 8.96). Inspired and guided by their own intelligent leaders, such as Hermocrates, the Syracusans led the other Greeks (including the Spartans) into danger and showed themselves to be energetic, courageous and, in the event, victorious (7.56, 7.73). Notably, on the advice of Hermocrates, the Syracusans held back from pitched battles with the Athenians – an imitation of the novel 'island strategy' recommended by Pericles during the Archidamian War (6.99; cf. 1.143). The Syracusan victory in the Great Harbour (7.59–71) was the second Salamis for this 'second democracy', which was striving, like democracies in general, to break free of its subordinate position and to become pre-eminent (7.56, 7.66–7). By contrast, Athens suffered a total destruction, Thucydides says (7.87), chiefly because of the traditionalism and piety of its leading general in Sicily, Nicias (7.50, 7.86). Things might have gone differently if Nicias had been able to trust the home authorities enough to tell them directly that retreat was the best option, while it was still realistic, but, as we have seen, ordinary democratic citizens cannot be trusted to own their own decisions (7.48; cf. 7.14–15, 8.1).

Conclusion: Democracy Again and the Thucydidean Alternatives

Does Thucydides provide serious alternatives to democracy, whether first or second? The most obvious contender is Sparta, an unusual 'mixed' regime that typically supported oligarchies; Sparta tends to defy ordinary constitutional taxonomies. Of Sparta one can say on the positive side that it won the war eventually (2.65, 5.26); that it genuinely subscribed to traditional piety (7.18), which aided its social cohesion (cf. Orwin 1994); and that it was a stable and internally strong regime (1.18). But Sparta is not a serious candidate for admiration for several reasons. First, the city's traditionalism was a great obstacle to its capacity to address the changing realities of 5th-century BCE warfare and politics (1.69–71, 2.93–4). The Spartans' policies were driven by fear either of Athens (1.88, 1.90; cf. 5.109) or of their own helots, who were a constant source of civil tension (1.101–3, 1.128, 4.41, 4.80). They were irresolute, especially in the face of failure (4.55–6). The Spartans were proud of their ignorance and despised *logos* (1.86, 4.84). Despite their military strength, the Spartans were not genuine leaders, did not assume the mantle of true *hēgemonia* after the Persian Wars (1.95) and were sluggish in pursuing even their own interests (4.108, 8.96). Finally, and most importantly, the Spartans were dishonest and unjust, arranging their own and their allies' affairs simply in accordance with their own self-interests (2.67, 3.68, 5.105, 7.18).[35]

With respect to other contenders, Thucydides' evaluation is equally complex. Thucydides is emphatic that tyranny is unlikely to be successful for very long because of the tyrant's habitual pursuit of his family's interests as opposed to the common good (1.17). As we observed when examining the Peisistratid tyranny, however, Thucydides reflects positively on the tyrants' intelligence and their openness to policies that benefitted the entire city (6.54). They respected the rule of law and took care to observe traditional religious practices, while also adorning the city. In these ways, they avoided the characteristic pitfall of tyranny (i.e. the creation of too sharp a dichotomy between one's own narrowly construed self-interests and the interests of one's city as a whole). Thucydides does not offer a conclusive evaluation of these tyrants – or of the Athenian king Theseus, a monarch whose political intelligence he similarly praises (2.15). However, Thucydides' praise of the tyrants and his presentation of democratic leaders in general, such as Themistocles, Pericles and Hermocrates, may provide the key to understanding his famous statement from late in the work that the best regime in his time was a prudent mixture of the few as leaders and the many as stakeholders, which satisfied the interests of both few and many (8.97).

Throughout the work, Thucydides had spoken admiringly of Athens' ambitions and achievements (even during the Sicilian Expedition: 7.28), while also criticizing the city's instability and excesses. Although the democracy was capable of significant achievements, Thucydides revealed that Pericles' vision of the city was unrealistic or utopian, especially when Athens was exposed to the pressures of a long, wearing war. All the same, Thucydides showed that Athens could endure suffering – first in the plague, then after the Sicilian disaster and even during the plague of its own civil war in 411 BCE, the subject of Book 8. Concussed by their defeat in Syracuse, the Athenians refused to concede defeat; to the contrary, they took measures to

---

[35] Cf. Orwin 1994: 75–86; Balot 2015.

institute political and economic reform, even to the extent of appointing a small group of older men to counsel the city (8.1, 8.4). The stubborn, resilient, energetic *dēmos* finally showed good judgement when the city reached the breaking point; the city made sound decisions and the people acted effectively (8.15). Shortly thereafter, they endured the rule of a brutal oligarchy of 400 men (8.45–97), who proposed to govern 'moderately' (8.53). This regime revealed in practice what Thucydides regarded as the central failing of oligarchies that succeed democracies: infighting rooted in personal ambition and arrogance (8.89).

In describing the broader-based regime that succeeded the Four Hundred, Thucydides says that the 'blending of the few and the many was harmonious [*metria*]'. He approved of this constitutional mixture apparently because it held out the promise of genuinely institutionalizing moderation. He says precious little about its internal structure. Scholars have frequently debated its blend of oligarchy and democracy, in reference both to the distribution of decision-making power and to the question of whose interests were served by the regime.[36] However those questions may stand, if we compare this regime to the prudent democracy that prevailed just after the Sicilian reversal, then it seems fair to say that Thucydides held that political 'mixture' could achieve success by incorporating the virtuous stubbornness of the ordinary citizens while also elevating a corps of intelligent leaders whose power would not be subject to the vagaries of democratic decision-making. Such is an interesting idea for the best regime, one that provided the foundations for Plato's philosophical mixture of monarchy and democracy in the *Laws* (693d).

Further Reading

Of central importance for the interpretation of Thucydides on the various types of regime is Connor 1984b. A helpful contextual discussion of Thucydides on Athenian democracy can be found in Ober 1998. A fuller account of my interpretation of democratic virtues and deliberation in Thucydides and elsewhere can be found in Balot 2014. On the Mytilenean Debate and on the democratic virtue of 'revisability', see Orwin 1994 and Saxonhouse 1996. For an illuminating study of the case that Thucydides makes for Athens and for Sparta and of Thucydides' relationship to Plato and Aristotle, see Strauss 1964.

---

[36] Cf. Gomme et al. 1945–81: vol. V, 331–9; Connor 1984b: 227–30; Pope 1988: 288–9; Jaffe 2017a: 404–5.

14

PAUL WOODRUFF

Justice and Morality in Thucydides

Thucydides has traditional ideas about what justice is, but he has a novel approach to the place of justice in human life: justice matters more in speeches than in motivation. This does not mean that justice does not matter in human life. Injustice is a symptom of a breakdown in society, and it carries a cost – further breakdowns and disruption. Human events follow patterns for the most part, and one of these patterns is the cycle that leads from such breakdowns as civil war to an erosion of morality and a spiral of violence. In a related pattern, overreaching by one city, though it may seem safe for a time, frightens other cities into armed opposition. Tyranny is not safe, for entirely human reasons. Here Thucydides breaks with tradition. The gods are not active guardians of morality; in fact, they play no direct role in human affairs – at least none for which Thucydides' story provides evidence. Human action is sufficient to ensure that injustice does not, in the long run, pay.

A persistent theme in this history is the value that the cities placed on their freedom, a value Thucydides appears to share (Nichols 2015). Athens flourished in large part because of its democratic freedoms (Connor 2017–18), but even Pericles, the architect of some of those freedoms, saw the Athenian Empire as a tyranny maintained by force (2.63.2).[1] Thucydides emphasizes the anger many people held against the Empire, especially that of would-be oligarchs. But he is almost completely silent about the democratic freedoms Athens helped bring to its allies, which evidently led to some popularity of the Empire with common people everywhere. Diodotus tells the Athenians – plausibly – that 'the *dēmos* in all the cities are our friends' (3.47).[2]

---

[1] On empire as tyranny, see 225, and Low (Chapter 10).

[2] Scholars have debated the extent to which the rebellion of Mytilene was supported by the common people. Diodotus' speech suggests that their support was grudging at best (3.47), but they must have been willing to work hard for the oligarchs on the city's defences against Athens (Cawkwell 1997: 97). Of course, they would have had every reason to fear the consequences of defeat by Athens once the rebellion began, whether or not they initially

The Elusive Author

Thucydides lets us know what his characters think about justice and other moral concepts, but he is silent for the most part about his own views. In a few places the mask slips and he speaks on moral issues in his own persona – most notably in his account of civil war on Corcyra (3.82–3)[3] and in his assessments of a few characters. Otherwise we depend on his arrangement of episodes and the content he gives to his speakers.

Thucydides arranges his story in a way that illustrates the danger of overreaching. For example, he mentions three towns where the Athenians enslaved and/or killed the citizens: Scione, Torone and Melos. But only in the latter case does he present us with details and a debate over the morality of the action. Immediately after the debate, he begins his account of the disastrous Sicilian Expedition. This arrangement is unlikely to have been an accident – first he tells of the suffering that Athenian imperial expansion brings to other people, then of the enormous loss that comes home to Athens, apparently as a result of imperial overreach (along with military errors) in Sicily.[4]

The Funeral Oration of Pericles is followed directly by a vivid account of the plague.[5] Pericles' glowing words might make us all 'lovers of Athens', but there is little to love when the plague strips away the veneer of decency, and we may well suspect that Thucydides is showing us that the Athenians are at least partly self-deceived about their glory.

All these things happened, of course, but Thucydides does not report in detail everything that happens. There were other funeral orations and other massacres, but he tells us little about them. And there were surely many reportable events between Melos and Syracuse, but these he passes over, probably so that nothing comes between Athenian self-glorification and harsh reality. The structure Thucydides contrives is akin to that of some tragic plays.[6]

---

supported the rebellion. de Ste. Croix may be right that they tended to be loyal to Athens (1954: 4), but Hornblower holds that all Greeks wanted freedom for their cities, regardless of the form of government (1991–2008: *ad loc.* 1.99.1, 2.8.5, 3.3.4, 3.27.3 and 3.47.1).

[3] 'It is almost certain that Thucydides was personally committed to all the values he describes as having been upset by the Corcyraean revolt' (Ostwald 1988: 60).

[4] Thucydides applauds Pericles' advice not to expand the Empire (2.65.7), which his successors ignored, but places most blame for later debacles on bad decisions at home (2.65.11).

[5] On the significance of this structural patterning, see further the discussions of Munson (Chapter 7) and Ferrario (Chapter 12).

[6] That the kinship is distant is stressed by recent scholars such as Hornblower (1987: 175). Tragic readings of Thucydides were fuelled by Cornford's influential book, which concludes: '. . . as the long agony wore on, as crime led to crime and madness to ruin, it was

Much of what we read about justice and morality in Thucydides is in speeches he has composed (or perhaps remembered). We shall see that his speakers generally agree on what a virtue such as justice consists in. Their differences are mostly over the extent to which justice should be – or even could be – a factor in their decisions. In a few cases (as in the trial of the Plataeans: 3.52–68), speakers differ over whether a set of actions is, on balance, just or unjust. Different speakers present different views on morality or the constraints of motivation, and these positions should be distinguished from each other and from the positions Thucydides takes directly.

The content he gives to his speakers varies from speaker to speaker. We cannot be sure how closely the speeches adhered to what the speakers said, or even to the kinds of things they would have said on such occasions. But in some cases we have reason to think that Thucydides is working from his own ideas about human motivation. The dialogue at Melos, for example, was held in private, without witnesses. The position taken by the Athenian generals probably represents what Thucydides believed they were thinking – to which they may or may not have given utterance. It seems unlikely that, in a rhetorical situation, the generals would be honest enough to say that they did not care about justice. After all, they would have had a case to make: Athenians had made the Aegean region safe from Persians and pirates, and they could reasonably ask every island to pay its share.[7]

The Athenian speech at Sparta also seems closer to what the speakers would have thought than to what they would have said (1.73–9). Again, in such a rhetorical situation, with the status of the Empire in question, we would expect an argument from justice. But instead Thucydides has them give a speech about powerful forces in human motivation. Here, too, Thucydides seems to be showing us how he believed the Athenians understood their own actions – as necessitated by fear, ambition and greed.[8]

---

only from a distance that the artist who was no longer an actor could discern the large outlines shaping all that misery and suffering into the thing of beauty and awe which we call Tragedy' (Cornford 1907: 250). Cornford does not believe, however, that in taking the gods out of the picture Thucydides is putting myth behind him; to the contrary, Cornford says, Thucydides has penetrated to a mythic element more primitive than is found in Aeschylus (Cornford 1907: 242).

[7] Hawthorn argues that the Athenians had 'no substantive interest' in the island of Melos. Their action on Melos 'reads as an act of rage and *hubris*, intended to salve the pain of [the defeat at] Mantinea, humiliate the Spartans, and impress citizens, one suspects, in Athens itself' (Hawthorn 2014: 163).

[8] Most scholars agree that Thucydides did not report the actual words of his speakers, as the style of all the speeches seems to be his own (Rhodes 2014: 8). As to the content, scholars disagree, but the consensus is that Thucydides reports what he thinks the speakers should have said, in view of his theory of motivation and his study of rhetorical structures. On the latter, see de Romilly 2012 [1956]. On content, 'we may suspect that the amount of

Scholars are divided over whether Thucydides shared that understanding. Ostwald thinks Thucydides does hold, with the Athenians, that '*ananke* will always ride roughshod over human judgments of right and wrong' (1988: 61), while Raubitschek has argued that the Athenian speech reveals 'that they exercise their rule moderately and justly in spirit' (1973: 46), and Finley has written that 'the element of compulsion in events was not, to his mind, such that it could not be controlled or directed' (1942: 308).

Some scholars have held that Thucydides followed the Athenians in holding that might makes right.[9] This is wrong in two ways: first, the Athenians do not make the normative claim that might makes right, a claim that would redefine justice along the lines of Plato's Thrasymachus. Instead, the Athenians claim that might trumps justice as a matter of fact.[10] Thucydides' story does not fully support the factual claim, since the Athenians do choose justice on some occasions, as in their second decision over Mytilene. Also, as many scholars point out, the author of the passage on the civil war on Corcyra was not a moral revolutionary.[11]

Virtues

As a translation for *dikē*, the English word 'justice' is too limited. *Dikē* and its cognates cover most cases of what we would call right and wrong and therefore the greater part of morality. A related concept, *to hosion*, overlaps with justice but is used in different contexts; I shall translate it as 'reverence'. Other moral terms important in Thucydides include courage (with its opposite, cowardice), a sense of shame (*aidōs*), good judgement (*euboulia*) and self-control (*sophrosunē*). The ability to honour these moral concepts is

---

attention devoted to the nature of Athenian power in Thucydides' speeches reflects his own obsession with the subject ...' (Rhodes 2014: 8). For a judicious review of the issues, see Pelling 2009, who rightly emphasizes the larger context of the speeches; cf. also Greenwood (Chapter 5).

[9] Murray, for example, 1986: 195, cited in Hornblower 1987: 189 n. 105.

[10] Price gives voice to a common error: 'Cleon's equation of expediency and justice [in his speech about Mytilene] is precisely repeated by the ... Athenian interlocutors in the Melian dialogue' (Price 2001: 100). This is wrong on both counts. Cleon points out in passing that the just action will be expedient, but he does not equate justice with expedience. He does, however, dismiss *epieikeia* (equity) in the name of justice; *epieikeia* calls for setting aside the law in favour of what we think the lawgiver would say about a special case. In the Melian Dialogue, far from equating justice and expedience, the Athenians explicitly set justice aside in favour of their interests.

[11] 'It is astonishing ... that his position could ever have been mistaken, by any reader of the *euethes* passage [on the civil war], ... for that of the immoralists of his generation ...' (Hornblower 1987: 189).

constrained by *ananke* (necessity or compulsion), which sometimes stands for the motivating trio of fear, greed and ambition.

Virtues such as justice and self-control apply equally and with the same meanings to cities and individuals alike. No one in Thucydides urges a distinction between the morality of states and that of individuals.[12] Some modern scholars have distinguished between moral virtues and competitive ones;[13] Thucydides does not recognize such a distinction. Although the Greek word for virtue can refer to non-moral excellence, Thucydides generally uses it in contexts of what we would call moral virtue. When he writes of the effectiveness he admires in certain leaders, he uses language that makes this clear.[14] We must keep in mind, however, that Thucydides thought Pericles' effectiveness was due in large part to his moral qualities.

Human virtue survives best in a stable, peaceful community; it is challenged by war (especially civil war) and by calamities such as plague. The civil war at Corcyra brought on a spate of vicious behaviour that the perpetrators covered with the language of virtue: 'They reversed the customary value of words in their judgement towards actions' (3.84.4).[15] They did not, like Plato's Thrasymachus, reverse the value of justice; that is, they did not, like him, say that justice is 'noble simplemindedness' (Pl. *Rp.* 1.348c12). Nor, like Callicles, did they explicitly introduce a new concept of justice based on nature (Pl. *Grg.* 483d). They simply called bad things by good names, with no attention to the meanings of words.[16] Virtues in Thucydides are what they always were; Thucydides' innovation is to show how false are most people's claims to virtue.

Some virtue words take on different colours in different situations, however. Good judgement from the Spartan point of view is connected to moral virtue (1.84). From the Athenian point of view it is purely practical; Diodotus explicitly sets justice aside in favour of good judgement in the case of the Mytileneans (although he is arguing for a just decision, 3.42.1), while Cleon, arguing for an expedient decision, appeals to justice (3.40.4).[17] Self-

---

[12] Hornblower 1987: 179, 184, disagreeing with de Ste. Croix 1972: 25–8.

[13] Adkins 1960 introduced the distinction; he has been severely criticized by Williams 1993.

[14] So Pericles is 'most effective [*dunatōtos*] at speaking and in action' (1.139.4) and Brasidas is 'a man of action' (*drastērios*, 4.81.1).

[15] All translations are my own, mostly from Woodruff 2021, modified in some cases.

[16] Most scholars agree that this change does not represent a sophistic revolution in the meanings of words, but rather a reversal in the evaluations of actions (Ostwald 1988: 61; Hornblower 1991: 477–9, 483). An exception is Price 2001, who writes extensively of a 'transvaluation of words'.

[17] The exchange supports Diodotus' claim that, in Athens, 'a man who has rather good things to say must tell lies in order to be believed' (3.43.2) – that is, he must appeal to values contrary to his own, as both speakers do in this contest.

control (*sophrosunē*), understood as moderation, is plainly a virtue, but it is understood in some contexts as a code word praising conservative constitutions.[18]

On one virtue Thucydides is especially clear – simplicity (*to euēthes*). Of the moral crisis that arose from civil war, he writes: 'Simplicity, which is the chief cause of a noble spirit [*to gennaion*], was laughed down and disappeared.'[19] This, Hornblower writes, 'is a clear authorial rejection of the "relativistic" teaching of certain of the sophists' (1991–2008: vol. I, 487). This closely follows Thucydides' rejection of the idea that a sense of shame is a guide to virtue: 'Many evildoers are called skilful sooner than the ignorant are called good, and people are ashamed to be called ignorant but take pride in being thought skilful' (3.82.7). Shame is not merely irrational, but, according to Thucydides, it can cause people to lose what virtue they have, just as honour and the desire for honour can lead to overreaching and injustice.[20] We shall see that Lacedaemonians set a higher value on avoiding shame than Athenians do.

Justice

At the centre of the conception of justice are three beliefs, which are held by all parties to Thucydides' debates: first, justice forbids people to take what is not theirs; second, justice calls for punishing the guilty and not the innocent; and, third, justice requires people to keep their promises, especially to abide by treaties they have sworn to keep.[21] When making treaties, the Greeks called the gods to witness and so brought this element of justice under reverence as well. No one in Thucydides' history directly challenges those beliefs,[22] but few people put them consistently into action.

---

[18] Hornblower 1987: 162.

[19] 'Simplicity, which is the chief cause of a noble spirit' (3.83.1): literally, 'simplicity, of which a noble spirit most takes part'. This probably means that simplicity (or openness) is what best explains noble spirit (or generosity). See Nussbaum 1986: 405, 508 n. 24; Hornblower 1991–2008: vol. I, 487.

[20] In the classical period, Greek thinkers were ambivalent about the value of honour (*timē*). Although most people think it worth pursuing, the Athenian speakers list honour (*timē*) along with fear and greed as compelling them to commit the injustices of empire (1.76.2); see Low (Chapter 10) for further discussion.

[21] Punishing the guilty: Cleon against the people of Mytilene (3.39.5). Not punishing the innocent: Diodotus (3.47.3). Keeping agreements: Plataeans' argument that justice required them to keep their agreement with Athens (3.56.3); note also that the Thebans condemn the Plataeans for the injustice of breaking a promise (3.66.3).

[22] The inverted evaluations that arise in civil war do not depend on redefining moral terms (3.82; see 218, n. 11 and 219, n. 16).

Plato's Callicles would reject all three in favour of what he calls 'natural justice', which employs the power of the stronger to subdue the weaker (*Grg.* 483cd, 488b) and to satisfy appetite at any cost (491e–492a). If a Callicles were present at one of Thucydides' debates, he would attempt to justify a power grab on that basis. But Thucydides brings no one remotely like Callicles on stage.[23] The Athenians make no attempt to justify their threat against Melos; instead, they repeat the refrain that justice in this case is irrelevant (5.89). Even Pericles refuses to justify holding on to the Empire; all he says is that it would be 'unsafe to surrender'.[24] The debates are not about what justice requires but about whether to pay attention to justice in a given situation. Even Diodotus, in defending the lives of the innocent people of Mytilene, leaves Cleon's claim to justice unchallenged: of the innocents, he says, 'even if they were guilty, we should pretend that they were not', since he claims that justice and Athenian interest do not coincide in this case (3.47.5).

Justice is essential to the stability of a community and prevents civil war. Plato tells us that Protagoras asserted this (*Prt.* 322c), and he has Socrates develop a similar view in Book 1 of the *Republic* (e.g. at 352c4). Thucydides seems to share this view, and so do some of his speakers. *Pleonexia* (greed or overreaching) is inherently unjust. In the case of Athenian expansion, it frightens the Peloponnesians into war. And the cause of civil war in Corcyra was 'desire for power out of greed and ambition' (3.82.8).

Ambassadors from Mytilene recognize the importance of justice to an alliance in their speech to the Lacedaemonians at Olympia, where they request an alliance against Athens. They have been allied with Athens against the Persian Empire for half a century now, but they are now in open rebellion against Athens. They begin their speech with the claim that alliances depend on justice and virtue:

> First, about justice and virtue, especially since we are composing this speech as a request for an alliance: we know that neither friendship among individuals nor common cause among cities has any chance of lasting unless it comes to be among those who have similar customs and believe in each other's virtue. (3.10.1)

Justice will play no part, however, in their larger argument, which mainly appeals to the advantages the people of Mytilene can give to Sparta, while excusing their betrayal of Athens on the grounds that only fear can hold an

---

[23] Brasidas comes closest to 'might makes right' in speaking of justification by strength (4.86.6), but the justification he gives later is in traditional moral terms.

[24] 2.63, misinterpreted by writers such as Finley, who says that Pericles 'justifies it by the eternal necessity of ruling or being ruled' (1942: 58). No Athenian speaker ever implies that might makes right.

alliance together (3.11.2). They have contradicted themselves: if only fear holds an alliance together, why stress at the outset the importance of justice and virtue to an alliance?[25] They have explained their actions while doing nothing to justify them. In effect, while appealing to justice, they concede that their betrayal of Athens was unjust.[26]

Reverence

Justice and reverence (to hosion and to dikaion) overlap, and sometimes the two words seem to have one meaning (as in hendiadys) embracing the whole of moral virtue in human interactions. Both are applied to the keeping of oaths and treaties. But the use of to hosion by itself focuses on morality as overseen by the gods, and this points to a further difference between justice and reverence in classical Greek culture: the gods matter most when human justice is most likely to fail – when suppliants are involved, for example. Suppliants are weak and depend totally on the reverence of the strong (3.58.3, 59.2, 66.2). When equals are at odds, they can fight it out or go to court and thereby (if they are lucky) achieve justice. The Athenians at Melos are not wrong to set justice aside in dealing with the weak (5.89), but the larger narrative that Thucydides planned would have shown that they are wrong to dispense with reverence in this case, which is the virtue that is supposed to prevent the strong from abusing the weak. Athens, too, will be pleading for mercy when the Spartans win the war. At the end of Sophocles' *Philoctetes*, produced in 409 BCE as Athens was stumbling towards defeat, Heracles warns the Greeks to show reverence when they vanquish Troy (1440–4). Sophocles might well have been fearing for the future of Athens. Later, after the loss of the Athenian navy at Aegospotomi, the Athenians realized that they were likely to suffer what they had done to the Melians, and Thucydides might well have planned to write an Athenian Dialogue matching the Melian Dialogue.[27]

Closely related to *to hosion* is *eusebeia*, which I also translate as 'reverence'; Plato uses the terms interchangeably in the *Euthyphro* as having the same meaning. In summing up the moral catastrophe of civil war on Corcyra, Thucydides says, 'so neither side thought much of *eusebeia*' (3.82.8). Hornblower translates this as 'religion', which is misleading for

---

[25] See Orwin 1994: 64–70.

[26] See Macleod's brilliant analysis of this speech: the Mytileneans are entangled in their own arguments because, like Cleon in his later speech on Mytilene, 'they try to maintain that their action is both just and expedient' (1978: 66).

[27] Rawlings 1981: 246–7, citing the debate over the post-war fate of Athens alluded to at Xenophon *Hellenica* 2.2.20.

modern readers.[28] The concept here is primarily ethical. Thucydides' narrative does not support the traditional belief that the gods punish people for failures of reverence or reward them for exercising virtue.[29] On other religious issues, such as the treatment of sacred places and respect for oracles, Thucydides does not take a clear position. His general attitude towards religion is controversial and would require a discussion too extensive for this chapter.[30]

Thucydides on Character

Thucydides' general view of character is revealed in his comment on the civil war in Corcyra:

> Civil war brought many hardships to the cities, such as happen and will always happen as long as the nature of human beings is the same, although these hardships may be more or less violent or take different forms, as imposed by particular changes in the circumstances. In peace and prosperity, cities and private individuals alike have better intelligence because they are not plunged into the necessity of doing anything against their will; but war is a violent teacher: When it takes away the easy supply of what they need for daily life, war gives to people's passions the quality of their present situation. (3.82.2)

The moral character of a city or of an individual is vulnerable to circumstance. Athenians and Lacedaemonians are able to exhibit different character traits because they operate in different circumstances. The Athenians are defending an empire and so they appear grasping and unjust; the Lacedaemonians could not afford an empire and so they appear as liberators and champions of justice. But neither side is reliably of that character. This is Thucydides' most disturbing thought about morality.

Thucydides admired tyrants who ruled effectively – Archelaus (2.100.2) and Pisisitratus (6.54.5) – and he commended the oligarch Antiphon for his brilliance in speaking (8.68.1). I do not think we can infer anything about Thucydides' moral views from such admiration. He does not assess these men's characters or explain their effectiveness with reference to virtues (as he does in the case of Pericles).

Brasidas, the Lacedaemonian general, has an easier time exhibiting virtue as he parades through northern Greece promising justice and liberation. He

---

[28] Hornblower 1991–2008, *ad loc.*

[29] See, for example, Nicias' claim to reverence at 7.77.2 with the grisly fate his unit actually suffered (7.84); virtue did not earn a reward in his case.

[30] See Hornblower 1991–2008: vol. I, 486, with references, and the important but controversial monograph by Marinatos 1981.

has a reputation for efficiency and intelligence, which earned him his command. On his campaign to win over Athenian allies, he displays justice and moderation to them, with the result that a number of them willingly come over to the Peloponnesian side (4.81.2). But his display of virtue is strategic, and Thucydides makes clear that it is temporary, for the moment (*to te gar parautika*). Brasidas is telling the truth when he states that his objective is not to build an empire on the Athenian model. He is, however, not entirely straightforward when he says that he is acting only to liberate the Greeks from Athens (4.86.1; cf. 4.108.2). After all, his real objective is to weaken Athens. The Lacedaemonians could not afford to police an empire, as they had their hands full at home keeping the helots in check. We do not know whether Brasidas was involved in slaughtering the two thousand high-performing helots after they had been promised their freedom, but Thucydides tells the story immediately before he brings Brasidas on stage (4.80.2–3), and the episode shows clearly what a Lacedaemonian promise is worth: if a pledge is not to their advantage, they will break it. Far from being a moral exemplar, Brasidas illustrates the Thucydidean view that when people display virtue, they usually do so for ulterior ends. In this case, the display was a brilliant success.[31]

As for Pericles, Thucydides' praise is surprising. Pericles is the architect of the two features of Athens to which Thucydides seems most strongly opposed: imperialism and rampant democracy. Besides, the strategic plan for which he praises Pericles is based on a faulty premise: that the war would be short. Pericles has a plan that might succeed in a war of two or three year.[32] Thucydides knows better; he makes Archidamus, who is Pericles' Lacedaemonian foil, rightly predict that if they go to war, they will bequeath the war to their children (1.81). If the Athenians leave the land to be wasted by the Lacedaemonians and put all their effort into sea power, neither side will win until one decides to attack the other's strength. In fact, Athenians will win the first phase of the war on land and Lacedaemonians will win the second at sea. Thucydides' history shows that Pericles was wrong about what the future held.

Yet his admiration for Pericles is undeniable. He tells us that Pericles was moderate and incorruptible; by contrast with those who came after, Thucydides implies that Pericles never sacrificed the true interests of the people to their pleasure. Because he was admired and trusted for his virtues, as well as for his strategic intelligence, he was able to rule as a king in all but name. In a word, Pericles accomplished by virtue what others later achieved

---

[31] Orwin appears to miss this point (1994: 79).
[32] Kagan 2009: 77–81; cf. Cawkwell 1997: 45.

by pandering to voters (2.65.5–10) or what a tyrant might have done by force. Brasidas cultivated a reputation for virtue in order to exploit it; Pericles (if we are to believe Thucydides) is the exceptional character who simply was a man of virtue – and would have been so even if no good had come to Athens or to him from the reputation he earned by his integrity.

Pericles is no unqualified supporter of justice, however. He, too, holds the Athenian view that power trumps justice. The Athenians hold an empire that is like a tyranny and therefore cannot be considered just.[33] In his last speech he makes the point explicit:

> You are in no position to walk away from your empire, though some people might propose to do so from fear of the current situation, and act the part of virtue[34] because they do not want to be involved in public affairs. You see, your empire is really like a tyranny – though it may have been thought unjust to seize, it is now unsafe to surrender. (2.63)

To be sure, Pericles does not speak up for injustice, but he clearly sets justice to one side in view of the danger that would arise if the Empire fell apart. Brasidas, not having an empire to maintain, can afford to act the part of virtue.

Nicias receives high praise in Thucydides' own voice at the end of his life. After his defeat outside Syracuse, Nicias was taken prisoner and immediately executed, either so that he would not reveal the names of his contacts in the city or for fear that he would be able to bribe his way to freedom. On telling this, Thucydides adds, without irony: 'Of all the Greeks of my time, he was the least deserving of such misfortune, because his entire way of life had been governed by aiming at virtue' (7.86.5) – echoing a claim Nicias has made about himself (7.77.2).[35] Indeed, Nicias showed moderation on many occasions and exercised true courage outside Syracuse more than once, rising from his sickbed to defend the oval camp (6.102.2) and leading his division

---

[33] Cleon, who is usually contrasted with Pericles, makes the stronger claim that the Empire actually is a tyranny that can be held only by force (3.37.2), although he appeals to justice for this use of force. The Corinthians speak of Athens as 'the tyrant city' at 1.122.3. Thucydides says most people supported the Lacedaemonians because of their proposal to liberate Greece from the Athenian Empire (2.8.4–5).

[34] Act the part of virtue: *andragathizetai* (echoed by Cleon at 3.30.4) – a challenge to the translator. It is unclear whether Pericles thinks such an action would be truly good or merely apparently so. Hornblower: 'playing at being noble'. Rhodes: 'propose this as a virtuous course'. Either way, Pericles' tone mocks the people who would propose to let the Empire go, and he explains their proposal as due mainly to fear. His answer is not moral: letting go brings greater danger.

[35] Citing Adkins, Hornblower says that Nicias was 'praised for competitive, social excellence' (1987: 169), but Thucydides makes no distinction between moral and competitive virtue.

in good order after their defeat, by contrast with Demosthenes' division (7.80.4).

Like most of Thucydides' characters, however, Nicias is in a situation that limits his capacity for virtue. Courageous he may be in the face of the enemy abroad, but he gives in to fear of the enemy at home – the citizens of the unbridled democracy in Athens. After the defeat at the Great Harbour, Nicias should have agreed with his co-commander Demosthenes to withdraw immediately, but he held back out of fear. As he told the troops:

> For his part he knew too much about the nature of the Athenians to want to be killed unjustly by them on a dishonourable charge. If he had to die, he'd prefer to do so at the hands of the enemy – a risk he'd be taking on his personal initiative. (7.48.4)

This otherwise brave general was more afraid of his fellow citizens than of the enemy. Although Thucydides does not make the point explicit, his telling the story in this way is a terrible indictment of Athens. Human virtue crumbles in bad situations, such as war or plague or the democracy that punishes commanders unjustly for their failures. Nicias deserved censure, however: the failure of the expedition was largely due to his reluctance to engage with force early on, and its disastrous end was due to his cowardice in refusing to extricate ships and men when it was necessary, before it became impossible to do so. Thucydides' unreserved praise for Nicias, therefore, is surprising.[36]

The View from Sparta

In speaking to oppose starting war with Athens, Archidamus states a view about virtues that seems representative of the Lacedaemonian ethos (1.84):

> This slowness of ours is really nothing but clear-headed self-control. It is this that gives us our unique ability to restrain our arrogance in success, and to yield less than other people to misfortune. When people try to excite us with praise into doing something dangerous, we do not let the pleasure of it overcome our better judgment; and if someone tries to spur us on with harsh criticism, we do not let ourselves be swayed by our anger. Our discipline makes us warlike soldiers and gives us good judgment.[37] We are warlike soldiers

---

[36] Scholarly opinion on Nicias is reviewed in a chapter by Rood; he sees in Nicias' life 'a tragic pattern' (1998b: 183–201). Smith argues that Thucydides' statement is not his own verdict but merely reports common opinion (1903: 382–3). Bury writes that, for 'the positive sum of mischief [Nicias] has caused, no measure of punishment would be too great'. He goes on to blame Athens for assigning command to 'this hero of conscientious indecision' (1966: 483).

[37] Discipline: *eukosmon*, or good order. The context shows that Archimadus holds this good order to be the result of their severe *paideia*.

because our *sophrosunē* [sound-mindedness or self-control] is the chief cause of our *aidōs* [sense of shame], and *aischunē* [shame] is the chief cause of *eupsychia* [here, courage];[38] while we have good judgment because our education leaves us too ignorant to look down on our laws,[39] and our *sophrosunē* is too strict for disobeying them ... And we should not think there is much difference between one man and another, except that the winner will be the one whose education [*paideia*] was the most severe. (1.84.2–4)

Virtue begins with severe education, which, unlike education in Athens, puts more emphasis on action than on speech[40] and results in the discipline or good order that yields warlikeness and good judgement. Good judgement to Athenians is the ability to calculate what is to one's own best advantage. But in Sparta, good judgement appears to be a moral virtue, the result of not being corrupted by the study of words, while being restrained by *sophrosunē* – itself the product of severe education. As for courage, it too arises from *sophrosunē*, which is the chief virtue associated with Sparta. *Sophrosunē* explains the Lacedaemonian sense of shame. Shame leads to courage because men who have a sense of shame will not want to be seen doing anything cowardly. Soldiers with these virtues (Spartans believe) will prevail over those who lack them.

The genealogy of Spartan victory, then, is this in a nutshell: severe education leads to discipline, which produces self-control, from which good judgement and courage both derive (the latter by way of a sense of shame). *Aidōs*, which I have translated as 'a sense of shame', may also mean respect or reverence, but in this context plainly has most to do with shame. The capacity to feel shame was an important virtue to the ancient Greeks, but especially so to Lacedaemonians. 'Three things you must do to make war well: be willing, feel shame, and obey your commanders', says Brasidas to his troops before the victory at Amphipolis that will cost him his life (5.9.9). Like Archidamus, he believes that shame holds soldiers back from breaking good order. Indeed, in many of the battles on which Thucydides reports, the

---

[38] Word for word, this translates as: 'a sense of shame takes the biggest part in self-control, and courage takes the biggest part in shame'. When *x* takes part in *y*, it is *y* that explains *x*. For the interpretation of this difficult passage, see Nussbaum 1986: 508 n. 24, and compare 3.83. Rhodes 2014 offers a direct translation: 'because respect is the greatest component of good sense'.

[39] Sophists were forbidden to bring the new learning to the Lacedaemonians. See Plato, *Hippias Major* 283.

[40] On the antithesis of action to speech, see Parry 1981; cf. also the discussions of *logos* and *ergon* by Beasley (Chapter 3) and (especially in the context of political action) Ferrario (Chapter 12).

losing side lost because it broke ranks in disorder. Before tangling with
Illyrians, whom Brasidas regards as barbarians, he encourages his soldiers
by telling them: 'because they [the Illyrians] do not fight in good order [*taxin
echontes*], they are not ashamed to abandon ground under pressure, and give
praise equally to retreat and attack' (4.126.5).

Justice plays no part in Archidamus' speech against war , which, on the
whole, is a pragmatic exercise in good judgement. At the very end, however,
he acknowledges concern about injustice, while pointing out that it would be
unlawful to start a war against a city that is calling for arbitration (1.85.2).
Much later, his compatriots thought there was justice in their defeat at Pylos
because they had refused to go to arbitration (as the treaty required) before
starting the war in the first place (7.18.2–3). Other Lacedaemonians make
much of justice both before and during the war. For example, when Brasidas
threatens to take Acanthus by force, he argues that he is acting in the cause
of justice, in that he is acting to liberate Greece from Athenian domination
(4.87). This is in striking contrast to the argument Athenians will make as
they make a similar threat at Melos.

The Lacedaemonians voted for war with Athens because, they said, they
had 'decided the Athenians were guilty of injustice' (1.87; cf. 1.78). An
ephor, Sthenelaidas, had acted as prosecutor in the case, rightly pointing
out that the Athenians had made no defence against the charge. At the very
end of his short speech, however, he adverts to the growing strength of
Athens: 'Be worthy of Sparta and don't let Athens grow any stronger!'
(1.86). This, Thucydides says, was the real cause for the Lacedaemonian
vote for war: not injustice, but fear of the growth of Athenian power (1.88).

Justice is the theme of the Theban argument that the male survivors at
Plataea should be killed and the women enslaved:

> People deserve to be pitied if they ought not have suffered as they have; if, on
> the other hand, justice requires that they suffer (as with these men), then their
> suffering ought to be a source of delight. (3.67)

The Lacedaemonians did as the Thebans asked, executing the survivors of
the siege at Plataea, but not (says Thucydides) entirely for reasons of justice.
'Virtually everything the Lacedaemonians did against Plataea they did for
the sake of the Thebans, whom they thought would be beneficial to them in
the war' (3.68.4).[41]

---

[41] The justice of the trial staged by Sparta seems a mockery. The question that the judges
have chosen to ask determines the verdict, making evidence and judgement irrelevant
(Orwin 1994: 77). On the debate, see Macleod 1977. On the Spartan willingness to
sacrifice justice to expediency, see Rawlings 1981: 201.

In the dialogue at Melos, the Athenians say that the virtue Lacedaemonians exercise among themselves is not to be trusted in their dealings with outsiders: 'of all the people we know, they are the ones who make it most obvious that they hold whatever pleases them to be honourable, and whatever profits them to be just' (5.105.4; cf. 1.76.1). Thucydides partly agreed with this Athenian verdict. In his pages, Lacedaemonians, more often than Athenians, appeal to justice in announcing a decision they are making in their interests (1.86, with 1.88, 4.87.3). But Thucydides probably holds that this is a common human failing, not one that is specific to Lacedaemonians.

In the dialogue at Melos, Sparta's allies on Melos appeal to justice, while Athenians argue that justice is irrelevant in such a case. Reading closely and in context, we can speculatively conclude that Thucydides is critical of both sides. The Athenians will not be able to maintain their contempt for justice when they are at the mercy of their enemies, as the leaders of Melos point out (5.90) – though Thucydides did not live to write about the ultimate defeat of Athens in the war. On the other side, the leaders of Melos were, like most people who appeal to justice in Thucydides, hypocrites. They refused to allow the Athenian generals to take their case to the common people of Melos (5.84.3), probably for fear that they would give in to Athens and sacrifice their leaders. We learn that there were Athenian sympathizers in Melos from the story of the people's surrender ('there was some treachery', 5.116.3). The 'officials and leading citizens' would have been the losers had the people gone over to the Athenian side. In the dialogue, these leaders ignore warning after warning to look after the safety of their people (5.87, 91, 101, 107, 111); instead, they seem to be bent on preserving their own power under the pretext of justice. The Athenians, after all, have made a fair proposal: 'we would like to rule over you for our mutual advantage' (5.91.2), and, indeed, life under Athenian hegemony was not without advantages.

The View from Athens

Athenians tend to say such things as these:

(1) The strong always rule over the weak (1.76.2, 5.89, 5.105.2).
(2) Justice is irrelevant to the business of empire (2.63.2–3, 3.47.5, 5.89).
(3) We were compelled (verb based on *ananke*) to hold and expand our empire by fear, honour and advantage, and especially by fear (1.75.3, 1.76.2).
(4) Anyone else would have done the same (1.76.1, 5.105.2)

We may wonder whether the Athenians would say such disturbing things outright in public. In real life, speakers on such matters usually try to seize the high ground of justice. Thucydides here probably reveals what he thought the Athenians were thinking rather than what they said, but we cannot be sure, and the matter is controversial. In any event, the Athenians do not hold these views consistently. For example, they argue that they are worthy of their empire (1.76.2), which implies that their claim to empire is just. They also say they have shown more justice and moderation than was necessary in administering the empire (1.76.3–4, 1.77.1), and they demand credit for making good choices. This weakens their claim to be acting under necessity.

More importantly: does Thucydides himself accept the Athenian view that they have been compelled to act as they have? He shows the Athenians making choices after debates that are not determined by *ananke*. History, as he tells it, is not deterministic (Ostwald 1988: 42). In pleading necessity, the Athenians are not in good faith. No doubt they feel a subjective necessity, but they are not objectively compelled to act as they do. Thucydides does not entirely accept the Athenian view of their actions. On the other hand, he appears to agree that fear, greed and ambition are powerful motivators.[42] Justice is real and good, but the people who claim they are moved by it are often lying to themselves and others.

Further Reading

For a quick survey of issues, see Dover 1973. The best work on Thucydides' moral thinking in my view is ch. 7 of Hornblower 1987, a good corrective to views that draw too much on the speeches. Ostwald 1988 is also valuable. Macleod's essays (collected in Macleod 1983) are essential reading for those who know Greek. Orwin 1994 is a detailed study of texts that bear on this topic. Price 2001 represents a well-developed but outlying view.

---

[42] Fear: the case of Sparta (1.88); greed and ambition: the civil war on Corcyra (3.82.8). For further discussion and examples, see Low (Chapter 10).

PART III

After Thucydides

15

LUKE V. PITCHER

Thucydides in Greek and Roman Historiography

But assuredly Chance is the master in all things: it brings all matters to celebrity or plunges them into obscurity with an eye to its own enjoyment rather than to the truth. The achievements of the Athenians, as I see it, were tolerably splendid and significant, but considerably less important than they are held to be by popular repute. However, because writers of great talent cropped up there, the deeds of the Athenians are celebrated as of the greatest importance throughout the world. Thus, the valour of men of achievement is held to be great to the extent that distinguished intellects have been able to laud it in words. (Sallust, *Bellum Catilinae* 8.1–4)

In the passage above, the 1st-century BCE Roman historian Sallust is discoursing upon the uneasy relationship between valour and its publicists. Sallust does not name the writers to whose good offices he attributes the enduring fame of Athens. It is hard not to suspect, however, that Thucydides is one of their number. Already in antiquity, there was a strong disposition to juxtapose Thucydides and Sallust: Quintilian speaks disparagingly of those who try to outdo 'Sallust and Thucydides' in their staccato periods (Quintilian, *Institutio Oratoria* 10.2.17). Velleius Paterculus characterizes Sallust as 'emulous of Thucydides'.[1]

One does not have to look far afield in Sallust's work to discover that Quintilian and Velleius are correct. A little earlier in the *Bellum Catilinae*, he notes as one potential difficulty of writing about displays of conspicuous virtue and glory the consideration that people are resentfully disinclined to believe accounts of achievements that fall outside their own individual capacities.[2] His diction evokes Pericles' claim, in the Funeral Oration for the Athenian war dead that Thucydides allots to him, that 'men can endure to hear others praised only so long as they can severally persuade themselves of their own ability to equal the actions recounted: when this point is passed,

---

[1] V. P. 2.36.2, with Grethlein 2006: 299 n. 2.   [2] Sall. *Cat.* 3.2.

envy comes in and with it incredulity'.[3] There is ample corroborative evidence elsewhere in Sallust's oeuvre for his propensity to appropriate and adapt Thucydidean scenes and passages.[4]

This is not to say that the list of talented writers whom Sallust has in mind in his passage on the achievements of the Athenians begins and ends with Thucydides. Other obvious candidates for inclusion would be Herodotus, Isocrates and the authors of the various other extant Funeral Orations.[5] Even Pindar cannot be ruled out.[6] On the other hand, the fact that this passage about the publicists of Athenian *facta* and *res gestae* (deeds and achievements) comes so soon after a discussion about the difficulties for the historian of writing about the deeds and achievements of others – a discussion couched in terms lifted from Pericles' Funeral Oration – suggests strongly that Thucydides holds an important position, for Sallust, amongst their number. It is tempting to suppose that Sallust's insistence on the fact that the deeds of the Athenians are now celebrated 'throughout the world' (*per terrarum orbem*) recapitulates the globalizing turn of Pericles' Funeral Oration in Thucydides,[7] even if that is not necessarily the only predecessor text that Sallust has in mind.[8]

On one level, Sallust seems to be making a straightforward point in this passage about the dependence of fame, however merited by personal deserts, upon the presence of an obliging panegyrist. Horace, too, notes that brave men lived before Agamemnon.[9] In the context of Sallust's greater work, however, the point becomes significantly less straightforward. Sallust has earlier proclaimed that the significant spheres of human behaviour are all subject to virtue, to *virtus*.[10] In this passage, we discover that the reception of such *virtus* is subject to the prowess of the individual who records it. The earlier assertion of virtue's power is now subsumed in a demonstration of the

---

[3] Thuc. 2.35.2.

[4] Scanlon 1980, with a survey of earlier scholarly responses to Sallust's use of Thucydides at 11–17.

[5] McGushin 1977: *ad loc.*

[6] Consider, for example, Pind. *Pyth.* 7.9–10. Grethlein 2010b: 19 discusses epinician poetry as a possible locus of historical memory. However, the '*ibi*' ('there') of the passage, while its vagueness does not preclude the possibility that some of these celebrants were not themselves Athenians, is not easily applied to Pindar.

[7] As, for example, at Thuc. 2.41.4 ('everywhere, whether for evil or for good, [we] have left imperishable monuments behind us'), and esp. 2.43.3 ('for heroes have the whole earth for their tomb').

[8] Feeney 1994: 144 also argues for allusion in this passage to Thuc. 1.10.2 (on Sparta's buildings as no true index to the report of its greatness) and Thuc. 1.11.3 (on Homer as an unreliable witness to the size of the Trojan expedition).

[9] Hor. *Carm.* 4.9.25–8.   [10] Sall. *Cat.* 2.7.

(potentially) capricious power of the historian.[11] There is a further irony inherent in Sallust's presentation of this argument: the *writers* – the arbiters of fame in this passage – are so well known themselves that the narrator does not need to spell out who they are. The passage is in itself an exemplification of another claim from earlier in the *Bellum Catilinae*: 'both those who have done things and those who have written the deeds of others are, in many cases, praised'.[12]

Sallust is unusual amongst the historians of antiquity in the extent to which his text engages with that of Thucydides. Nonetheless, the passage above exemplifies, albeit in a condensed and heightened form, several features that commonly appear in the responses of later Greek and Roman historiographers to their Athenian predecessor. These are, in short: anonymity; change, redeployment and adaptation of the Thucydidean original; and the importance allotted to Thucydides' Athenian context. It is under these headings that I propose to examine the reception of Thucydides in later Greek and Roman historiography.

Anonymity: Thucydides as Absent Presence

We have already seen that, important as Thucydides is in some respects for Sallust, his name does not appear in the passages that we have already examined. Indeed, the fact that Thucydides is not named is part of the effect of the passage about the good fortune that Athens experienced in its celebrants. This pattern is continued throughout Sallust's works. Velleius' 'aemulum Thucydidis' never, at any point in his extant oeuvre, refers to his predecessor by name.

Such behaviour on the part of the narrator is par for the course in ancient historiography. Classical historians, notoriously, mention their predecessors by name to indicate dissatisfaction or dissent, not indebtedness or emulation. Sallust, for example, may not mention Thucydides, but he does mention Cornelius Sisenna – only to indicate that Sisenna's account of Sulla (by way of implicit contrast to Sallust's own) is in some respects wanting.[13] There are exceptions to this general rule. Velleius, as we have already seen, mentions Sallust's relationship to Thucydides, in a move that is of a piece with his wider inclination to expatiate more freely and in more detail on literary

---

[11] Feeney 1994: 142–5 explores 'the ego of the historian' (145) as it appears in Sallust's *Bellum Catilinae*.

[12] Sall. *Cat.* 3.1. The publicists of Athens thus join the splendid anonymity of the Romans who had to be punished for excessive military zeal in the early days of the Republic, whom the narrator does not bother to name either (Sall. *Cat.* 9.4).

[13] Sall. *Iug.* 95.2 (= *FRHist* 26 T11).

matters than most classical historians are inclined to do.[14] Polybius notes that his history starts at a point that coincides with the end of the memoirs of Aratus of Sicyon.[15] But such exceptions are few and far between.

This reticence is, of course, especially annoying to the modern political or military historian of the ancient world, as it potentially leads to fiddly exercises in *Quellenforschung*. However, it also has an impact upon the dynamics of allusion and intertextuality as they operate between the works of the ancient historiographers, which sets them apart, in certain key respects, from some of the other genres of ancient literature. The ancient historians do not announce their favoured generic predecessors with the flamboyant verve of a Propertius invoking the shades of Callimachus and the observances of Coan Philetas,[16] a Lucretius lauding (albeit with some caveats) Ennius and Empedocles[17] or even, with a little more circumspection, a Vergil declaring that he sings the song of Ascra (the birthplace of Hesiod) through the townships of Rome.[18] This is a simple point, but one worth bearing in mind, since it is relevant to the issue, which we shall address later in this chapter, of whether we can meaningfully speak of a Thucydidean 'school' or 'tradition' of historians in antiquity.

Of course, allusion does not require explicit naming of the text to which one alludes. The majority of allusions in ancient texts do not do so, and (as we have already seen) it is entirely possible for a text to build up quite substantial trains of reference to Thucydides without ever mentioning his name. All the same, the general indisposition of the classical world to state in clear terms the relationship between a historiographical text and its key predecessor(s) has obvious consequences for the study of Thucydidean receptions. At the most pragmatic level, it is not always easy or possible to determine whether Thucydides is a relevant intertext at all.[19] This consideration causes particular difficulties if one engages in the exercise of seeking

---

[14] Pitcher 2011: 236 with n. 22.   [15] See 238.   [16] Propertius 3.1.1.
[17] Lucretius 1.117–26 (Ennius); 1.716–33 (Empedocles).
[18] Verg. G. 2.176. Note, by way of contrast to the *Georgics*, that Vergil's narrator never comes so close to naming key predecessors in the martial epic of the *Aeneid* – the issue is predominantly one of genre rather than of temperament.
[19] Cf. Hornblower 1991–2008: vol. II, 21: 'The problem [sc. 'of Polybius' knowledge of Thucydides] is, however, similar in some ways to Thucydides' silence about Herodotus. There can be no strict proof of influence, polemic, or use without an explicit mention by name, and Thucydides' text contains no such mention.' 'Strict' is an important qualifier, of course, since, as I have already indicated, substantial verbal allusion, even without a name, can make a case for influence all but certain, unless there is a chance that the verbal detail in question is actually the result of a third text that both of the others are using (for a probable case of this, involving the use of Homer by both Herodotus and Thucydides, see Hornblower 1991–2008: vol. II, 124).

significance in the occasions when a text does *not* allude to an 'obvious' predecessor. Modern work on reception can potentially make much use of the notion of predecessor texts as an 'absent presence' – that failure to allude to an important forerunner at a certain juncture can be as pointed as readiness to do so. But sometimes an 'absent presence' is really just an absent absence.

The doubtful chronology of some historiographical works in the ancient world, particularly the earlier and more fragmentary ones, is also pertinent to this sort of problem. There are several passages in Thucydides' history, for example, where a case can be made that he is pointedly (if anonymously) correcting Herodotus. The narrator's tetchy outburst about the Pitanate *lochos* and the votes of the Spartan kings at Thuc. 1.20.3, for example, has often been read as a response to Herodotus' treatment of the same themes.[20] Possible examples may be multiplied.[21] However, in light of the very uncertain 'publication dates' of both Thucydides and Herodotus, and, of course, of the fact that a model of allusion based on final 'publication dates' may not be helpful in handling the interrelations of two authors who may have been contemporaries, it is not altogether surprising that a case can also be made for joint interaction with a lost predecessor, joint aping of a particular generic style or even Herodotus responding to Thucydides rather than the other way around.[22]

Even where such uncertainties about priority or influence are not an issue, the way in which a text positions itself with regard to Thucydides is not necessarily straightforward. Nowhere is this more apparent than in the work by another writer that has the strongest claim to possessing an organic link to the text of Thucydides: the *Hellenica* of Xenophon. The *Hellenica* presents itself as a continuation. Its opening words, 'and after these things . . .',[23] are not immediately comprehensible unless one realizes that the phrase 'these things' refers to the events described in the closing chapters of Thucydides Book 8. A clued-up reader would realize quickly from what happens next that the context is a war between the Athenians and the Spartans.[24]

---

[20] Hdt. 6.57.5 and 9.53.2. On this issue, see Kelly 1981; Hornblower 1991–2008: vol. I, 58.
[21] Hornblower 1991–2008: vol. II, 137–45 conveniently gathers various 'parallel passages' that earlier scholarship had posited.
[22] Hornblower 2011c explores the possibility that Herodotus is reacting to Thucydides' accounts of Potidaea (280–2) and Corcyra (282–3), though confessedly as a thought experiment. Hornblower himself believes that the traffic goes the other way (278) and makes the point that an interest on the part of two authors in similar subjects is not necessarily the result of 'literary indebtedness' (285). Irwin 2013a argues that Hdt. 9.73, on Decelea, is best read as a response to Thucydides.
[23] Xen. *Hell.* 1.1.1.   [24] Earl 1972: 844.

However, the point in that war at which the *Hellenica* begins and the reason why that apparently rather arbitrary point has been selected only make sense if the *Hellenica* is read as the continuation of the Thucydidean text that the narrator has not even bothered explicitly to identify.[25]

One should not undersell the boldness of this move. It is true that there are many examples amongst the works of later historians of texts that are, in a sense, continuations of histories by earlier authors. The Elder Pliny, for example, wrote a work to which his nephew refers as *A Fine Aufidi Bassi*, 'From the End of Aufidius Bassus'.[26] The list of other historiographical works that might be considered (with, it is fair to add, varying degrees of plausibility) to be continuations of others is a considerable one.[27] What is very hard to parallel is the sheer abruptness of the linkage that the *Hellenica* effects between itself and its predecessor. The first sentence of the *Hellenica* could easily pass as the next sentence of Thucydides Book 8 after the latter's untimely termination. Xenophon proffers no preface in which the new author lays out his wares, no expression of authorial intent, not even (as we have already seen) a hint as to *which* text supplies the referent of 'these things'. Contrast Polybius, who, while he explicitly announces that he is making the beginning of his text 'continuous' with the ending of Aratus' memoirs,[28] puts in a preface about the utility of history and those who have argued the case for it beforehand.[29] The lack of any prefatory material to disguise the join between the beginning of the *Hellenica* and the end of Thucydides has even led to the implausible conjecture that Xenophon's original preface has dropped out.[30]

The *Hellenica* is, then, almost unique in the thoroughness with which it seeks to join itself to its predecessor text. Yet closer inspection shows that its relationship to that text is not a simple one. The *Hellenica* may initially seem to read like a seamless continuation of Thucydides. It is, in reality, far from being so. On a factual level, the modern historian can determine that more elapses between the end of Thucydides Book 8 and the beginning of *Hellenica* Book 1 than the simple 'after these things' indicates.[31] The narrative stance, too, is somewhat inconsistent. Most of the important characters

---

[25] Marincola 1997: 238 n. 110.   [26] Plin. *Epist.* 3.5.6 (= *FRHist* 80 T1).
[27] Marincola 1997: 289–92. One should share Marincola's caution in the handling of this issue, however. Quite apart from the fact that the nature of the linkage with the predecessor text varies in individual cases (see earlier in this chapter), the actual evidence that some of the more fragmentary texts *are* in fact continuations is sometimes nugatory. An example of this would be Menodotus of Perinthus, whom Jacoby 1923–58 conjectured to be a continuator of Psaon. Contrast *BNJ* 82 T1 and Biographical Essay.
[28] Polyb. 1.3.3.   [29] Polyb. 1.1.1.   [30] Engel 1910: 45.
[31] Underhill 1900: xvi–xvii.

who will be familiar to the reader of Thucydides do not receive fresh introductions from Xenophon. Pharnabazus and Alcibiades, for example, pop up in the opening pages without any attempt on the part of Xenophon's narrator to explain who they are.[32] On the other hand, Thrasyllos, who makes his first appearance towards the end of Thucydides' narrative, receives the gloss on his introduction in the *Hellenica* that he is 'one of the generals', which the reader primed with Thucydides knows already.

In some respects, the opening of the *Hellenica* does exhibit coherence if one attempts to read it as Thucydides Book 9. One can observe the continuation of themes across the two texts. The ongoing psychological impact upon the Athenians of the Sicilian Expedition is a very palpable presence in the last book of Thucydides. It manifests in both the Athenian response to the revolt of Euboea[33] and the narrator's disquisition upon the similarity of outlook that made the Syracusans more successful in opposing the Athenians than the Spartans generally were.[34] When one turns to the *Hellenica*, one observes that little time elapses before the reader finds Hermocrates and other Syracusan leaders recalling their earlier successes[35] and an aside by the narrator concerning the expedition of the Carthaginians into Sicily under Hannibal.[36]

This latter example, however, arguably shows that the relationship between the *Hellenica* and Thucydides is as much about differentiation as it is about continuance. Hannibal's Sicilian expedition, in Xenophon's rendering of it, is both successful and startlingly abrupt. It takes three months – and one sentence – for him to reduce Selinous and Himera, in marked contrast to the deserts of time and text that Thucydides' Athenians traversed on the same island. The contrast is all the more striking because this event is the one with which Xenophon chooses to end his account of the year 411/10 BCE – the year that began at Thuc. 8.61.1. It is very Thucydidean to note, as Xenophon does in this passage, that a year is ending. But this is also the first occasion on which the reader sees that Xenophon has the very un-Thucydidean narrative tic of tacking a significant event onto his announcement that another year is done. Contrast the typical Thucydidean variations on the theme of 'And the winter ended, and the

---

[32] Xen. *Hell.* 1.1.5 (first appearance of Alcibiades) and 1.1.6 (first appearance of Pharnabazus). By contrast, Alcibiades' lesser-known kinsman of the same name, who will not be familiar to the reader of Thucydides, is introduced with the phrase 'Alcibiades the Athenian, a kinsman of Alcibiades and a fellow exile' (Xen. *Hell.* 1.2.13).

[33] Thuc. 8.96.2: 'Neither the disaster in Sicily, great as it seemed at the time, nor any other had ever so much alarmed them.'

[34] Thuc. 8.96.5.   [35] Xen. *Hell.* 1.1.28.   [36] Xen. *Hell.* 1.1.37.

*x*th year of this war of which Thucydides wrote the history'[37] with the Xenophontic 'And the year ended, in which the Carthaginians under Hannibal made an expedition into Sicily.' The mode of narration at this point exemplifies both continuity and contrast. The war (for the moment) is the same; the game is different. It is also worth observing, perhaps, that this is the point in the *Hellenica* at which Sicily all but disappears from the narrative for several books, with only very occasional exceptions.[38] The opening of Xenophon's history acknowledges Thucydidean emphases but then shelves them.[39]

This story of continuity and contrast with a text that is crucial but never explicitly acknowledged is, of course, much more obvious in the case of Xenophon, who is telling the story of the same war as Thucydides, than it is in the case of most other ancient historiographers. The lesson of the *Hellenica* is, however, worth bearing in mind when we think about Xenophon's successors. The anonymous presence of Thucydides in a text need not equal simple homage or simple repudiation. It is more likely to indicate a position somewhere in between.

Amplification: Thucydides and Athens

The second thing that we noted about Sallust's disquisition upon the encomiasts of Athens is its underlying assumptions about the nature of historical significance and the role that a writer can play in skewing its assessment. The genius of certain writers is responsible for making one Greek city look more important than it actually was. Athens is taken as the paradigmatic example of a case where historiographical coverage has distorted the truth of historical significance.

Significance, of course, is a theme with which Thucydides himself is ostentatiously concerned. Indeed, Thucydides demonstrates an opening preoccupation with the superlative,[40] as opposed to the merely significant, which Herodotus does not: the Herodotean narrator notes an initial interest

---

[37] Thuc. 2.70.4, and many subsequent instances. As noted earlier in this chapter, there is a little variation in wording. The instance at 2.70.4, for example, runs 'these things happened in the winter, and the second year ended of this war of which Thucydides wrote the history'.

[38] These exceptions include one reference to Hermocrates at 1.3.13, a rumour that Polyxenus is leading ships from Syracuse at 5.1.26 and another year-end notice announcing the beginning of Dionysius' tyranny at 2.2.24.

[39] For much more on the relationship between Xenophon and Thucydides in the *Hellenica*, see Rood 2004.

[40] On Thucydides' taste for the superlative, see, in particular, Grant 1974: 84–5.

in deeds that are 'great and wonderful',[41] but Thucydides wastes no time in asserting that the war between the Athenians and the Spartans was the 'greatest disturbance'.[42] This is not to say that superlatives do not attract Herodotus' attention *later* in his narrative – the fate of Panionios of Chios, who suffered the worst punishment that anyone ever underwent, is an obvious counterexample.[43] But Thucydides is the one who puts the (allegedly) unique political significance of his theme on the table from the very beginning of his narrative.

This decision inaugurates a recurring preoccupation in subsequent historiography with the greatness of one's subject matter and, occasionally, with the less impressive gravity of someone else's. Like Thucydides, subsequent historians tend to leave unstated a corollary of this argument, which is that an impressive theme makes for an impressive book – the exact converse, in other words, of Tacitus' brilliantly perverse characterization of his own subject matter with the words 'our work lies in a narrow compass, and yields no glory' (*nobis in arto et inglorius labor*).[44] As well as inaugurating this tradition, Thucydides establishes a benchmark for such overwhelming significance in the shape of the Peloponnesian War. This helps to explain why so many appropriations of Thucydides in subsequent historiography centre around the status of cities, the status of conflicts and so the status of the historians who describe them.

Consider, for example, the case of Appian. Appian's theme is the greatness of Rome, which he explores from the foundation to his own times in the 2nd century CE. Part of the preface to this history is devoted to a comparison between the Roman Empire and those that preceded it. One of these predecessors Appian describes as 'the hegemony of the Greeks', subsuming the pre-eminences of the Athenians, the Spartans and the Thebans, and it comes in for the following criticism from the narrator: 'their wars were not for conquest abroad but rather for pre-eminence among themselves, and they were most distinguished for the defence of their freedom against foreign invaders. Those of them who invaded Sicily with the hope of extending their dominion failed and whenever they marched into Asia they accomplished small results and speedily returned.'[45]

In the grand scheme of history, the reference to Sicily here would seem a trifle bizarre. There is, to be sure, a certain justification in that Sicily is an area that will prove important for Appian's own subsequent narrative. It was, after all, the principal theatre of operations in the First Punic War (of which more later in this chapter), which Appian covered in his (now mostly

[41] Hdt. *praef.*   [42] Thuc. 1.1.2.   [43] Hdt. 8.104–6.   [44] Tac. *Ann.* 4.32.2.
[45] App. *Praef.* 8.

lost) *Sikelika*. This was the fifth book of his history and so one of the first occasions (except for the *Keltika*, which immediately preceded it) on which he depicted his protagonists testing their own mettle beyond the confines of the Italian mainland. One can just about, then, see this passage of the *Proem* as setting up a flattering contrast between the success of Appian's Romans and the comparative failure of Greeks. All the same, the sudden appearance of the western island at this point in the *Proem* might well seem jarring and abrupt.

In fact, the explanation for the presence of Sicily here is simple. The contest of historical subjects is also a contest of historians, and Sicily is a subject that Appian feels compelled to address because it is an arena that loomed so large in the text of Thucydides. In doing so, he shows himself to be a shrewd reader of the earlier historian. Note how, in Appian's summary of the fortunes that befell the Greeks in Sicily, he stresses the hopes that impelled their enterprise: 'Those of them who invaded Sicily with the *hope* of extending their dominion failed ...'. This emphasis recalls Thucydides' account of the Sicilian Expedition, where hope is a notable leitmotif.[46] Appian evokes, then, not just the Sicilian Expedition, but also Thucydides' version of it. The evocation in this context hints at the superiority of not just the Romans over the Greeks, but also of Appian's theme over that of Thucydides. (By contrast, the emphasis in the following sentence of the *Proem*, which stresses the failure of Greek incursions into Asia, aims its sights squarely at Xenophon: one thinks of Agesilaus in the *Hellenica* and all of the *Anabasis*.)

It is instructive to set this moment of one-upmanship with regard to Thucydides in Appian's *Proem* beside a rather more subtle instance in the first book of Polybius, the Megalopolitan historian who wrote a forty-book history covering Rome's rise to domination over the known world in the 2nd century BCE. Although a writer unusually prone, by the standards of extant historiography, to polemic against named predecessors (most notably against Timaeus, whom an audience might perceive to be a rival to his own status as the pre-eminent Greek historian of Rome), Polybius does not typically suffer from obvious status anxiety with regard to Thucydides; his attachment to the idea that the highest form of history is universal history, which Polybius sees as not being viable for events before 220 BCE,[47] contributes to this serenity, and Polybius names Thucydides (in striking contrast to

---

[46] As, for example, in Nicias' speech at 6.68.2. For the significance of hope in Thucydides' account of the Sicilian Expedition, see Avery 1973: 1–6; Rood 1998b: 17. For more on Appian and Thucydides, Strebel 1935, though jejune, is the standard treatment.

[47] Polyb. 1.3.3.

how he treats Timaeus) only once.[48] However, we may discern a telling choice of terms in his characterization of the First Punic War, the description of which Polybius regards as a necessary preliminary to the Hannibalic conflict that will be his main theme. Polybius is at pains to stress that the First Punic War deserves narration because 'it is not easy to find a war that lasted longer than this one, nor one with more thoroughgoing preparations or more uninterrupted activities . . . on either side'.[49] The key combination of terms here is 'longer' and 'with more uninterrupted activities'. The First Punic War (264–241 BCE) lasted for twenty-three years. Polybius' insistence that its engagements were *continuous* during that period looks very much as though it is aimed at thwarting the particular counterexample of the Peloponnesian War – twenty-seven years in length, as Thucydides reckons it, but vulnerable to the objection that it was not one continuous conflict, as Thucydides' defensiveness on that topic makes very clear.[50] Moreover, the Peloponnesian War has already been suggested to the minds of Polybius' readers, even this early in his narrative, by his decision to date the growth of Roman territorial ambition as beginning in 'the nineteenth year after the battle of Aegospotami', the naval disaster that immediately preceded the fall of Athens.[51] The word that I have rendered as 'preparations' above is *paraskeuai* in the Greek. It is common in Polybius, so one should not, perhaps, make too much of its appearance in this passage, but we may note that it is a word that Thucydides also uses when he is making large claims for the resources available to Athens and Sparta in the conflict that is his theme.[52] Once again, Thucydidean vocabulary is deployed in a later historian's understated statement of superiority over the Thucydidean original. It is also striking (to anticipate, for a moment, the topic of the next section) that, while Polybius is unusual amongst later classical historians in the extent to which he shares Thucydides' overt interest in different levels of historical causation and even, like Thucydides, uses the terms *aitia* and *prophasis* to distinguish between two of them, in Polybius it is *aitia* that denotes a deeper level of causation than *prophasis*,[53] whereas in Thucydides it is typically the other way around.[54] There is more going on here than a simple inversion of terms, since Polybius figures the relationship between long-term and short-term causation rather differently from his predecessor, but it is hard not to

---

[48] Polyb. 8.11.3. See also Walbank 1972 :40–1.   [49] Polyb. 1.13.11.
[50] Thuc. 5.26.1–2.   [51] Polyb. 1.6.1.   [52] Thuc. 1.1.1.
[53] Polybius gives a worked example of his (actually threefold) classification of historical causality at Polyb. 3.6.14, following sarcasm about those unable to tell the difference between an *aitia* and a *prophasis* at 3.6.6.
[54] Thuc. 1.23.6.

see the decision to flip the relevant vocabulary as a somewhat pointed statement of methodological independence.

Ancient responses to literature in general thrived on the conflation of the man (or the woman) and the work. This is one of the factors that make ancient biographies of literary figures so unreliable.[55] In the case of historians, however, conflation can carry a special charge: there is an indissoluble link between the stature of the historian and the stature of his subject. Thus, where ancient historians (as keenly agonistic as other authors in antiquity, though not always as straightforward in announcing this) match themselves against Thucydides, a meditation on the greatness (or otherwise) of his Athens is rarely absent. What is particularly interesting about Sallust's spin on the notion is his insistence that a writer on a potentially inadequate topic can impart to that topic a certain lustre through the writer's own intrinsic greatness – rather than revealing his own lack of stature through making a bad choice of subject. Polybius, by contrast, is vocal about the deficiencies of historians who make that kind of selection error.[56] As often in Sallust, what looks like the rehearsal of an old historiographical platitude proves, on inspection, to have a twist.

Adaptation: Thucydides Recast

Thus far, the operations upon the text of Thucydides that we have detected in the subsequent historiographical traditions have not, on the whole, been especially subtle ones. We have looked at one text (Xenophon's *Hellenica*) that fashions itself as a continuation of Thucydides (albeit, as we have also noted, one that quickly begins to advertise its own narrative distinctiveness). We have looked at another (Appian's *Proem*) that engages in a fairly obvious *agon* with Thucydides over the magnitude of the two historians' respective themes.

Many appropriations of Thucydides in the later historians work on a more complex level. Once again, Sallust's *Bellum Catilinae* is illuminating. We have already noted that Sallust includes his own version of the Thucydidean line about how men are unwilling to accept accounts of actions that they know to be beyond their own capacities. It is worth stressing, however, the impact that the change in narrative context has upon the ramifications of this remark. In its original Thucydidean usage, the

---

[55] So, famously, Lefkowitz 1981.

[56] Compare, for example, Polyb. 8.13, on Theopompus' folly in abandoning his history of Greece just at a point (the Battle of Leuctra) where it became particularly memorable in order to write an account of Philip II of Macedon.

observation does not appear, as it does in Sallust, in the course of a disquisition on the hazards that face a historian. Rather, Thucydides' Pericles is explaining the perils that attend upon delivering a speech of praise. Sallust has assimilated the occupational hazards of the encomiast to the occupational hazards of the historian, so pointing up, along with his Thucydidean interest in the possible shortcomings of the general public, his distinctly un-Thucydidean interest in using the historian's narrative voice as a vehicle for praise and blame. Thucydides' narrator, to be sure, is perfectly capable of acknowledging the merits of the agents within his text – one thinks of Archidamus (1.79.2), or of Nicias (7.86.5), or, indeed, of Pericles himself (2.65.5–13) – but there is nothing in this vein to equal the grand comparison of the virtues displayed by Julius Caesar and the younger Cato that Sallust includes after the debate on the fates of the Catilinarian conspirators (Sall. *Cat.* 53).

Sallust was not the only subsequent historian to replay the Thucydidean line about men's unwillingness to believe in acts impossible to them in a pointedly different way. For Cassius Dio, the Greek senator who wrote an eighty-book history of Rome from its foundation to his own consulship in the 3rd century CE, Thucydides is an admired predecessor, to be evoked by name as a reassuring paradigm for the virtues of literary activity in exile.[57] Dio's moments of detailed engagement with Thucydides' work, however, sometimes seem aimed to unsettle rather than to reassure. Pericles' opening spiel from the Funeral Oration about the difficulties of making people believe in the great deeds of the honoured dead becomes, in Dio, the introductory patter in a speech by Augustus in 27 BCE, professing a desire to lay aside his control of the Roman state.[58] Again, the play with the Thucydidean original is subtle. Augustus certainly has affinities with Thucydides' Pericles – competence and complete domination of his polity being the obvious ones[59] – but the differences in how this rhetoric applies to the particular situation are designedly glaring. Augustus, with characteristic self-absorption, is talking about the believability of his *own* behaviour rather than that of the honoured dead, and, crucially, the reader already knows that this instance of that behaviour is 'incredible' for all the wrong reasons: Augustus, in fact, has no intention of laying aside his power, and the narrator has already stated that the point of this speech is to have the people urge him to retain it of their own (more or less) free will.[60] The Thucydidean original of an effectively monarchic leader in a system where the people are nominally having their way is recast in a distinctly darker and more cynical form, as befits Dio's characteristically jaded view of political behaviour.

---

[57] C. D. 38.28.1–2.   [58] C. D. 53.3.1.   [59] Cf. Thuc. 2.65.8–9.   [60] C. D. 53.2.6.

Appropriations of Thucydides in other subsequent historiography are often of this ilk. Thucydidean phraseology may well serve to point up a putative concinnity of practice with the elder historian. But it may equally advertise variation or difference. This tends to be especially true where Thucydides is pressed into service for a passage on historical methodology. Some aspects of Thucydidean reflection on methodology do not strike much in the way of obvious chords with his successors. An obvious example of such a reflection would be his notoriously cryptic animadversions on the difficulty of representing speeches in historiography at 1.22.1, an issue that almost (but not quite) all of the later historians ignore.[61] Other passages, by contrast, fare rather better, and the adaptations to which these passages are subjected are often instructive as to the self-presentation of the adapting historian.

We may illustrate these dynamics of appropriation by looking at the preface of Herodian. Herodian was a historian active in the 3rd century CE, who chronicled the Roman Empire from the death of Marcus Aurelius to the accession of Gordian III. His account is saturated with Thucydidean allusion. While at some points it may legitimately be doubted whether the characteristic vocabulary of Thucydides is being deployed with a particular goal in view,[62] it is hard not to think that its tendency to cluster around his moments of methodological reflection has deliberation behind it. This is nowhere more obvious than in his preface, of which this is a representative sentence:

> If one were to compare the whole period from the time of Augustus, when the Roman regime became a monarchy, one would not find in a span of about two hundred years up to the time of Marcus Aurelius such similar succession of reigns, varied fortunes in civil and foreign wars, disturbances of populations and sacks of cities both in Roman territory and amongst many barbarians, earthquakes and plagues and surprising lives of tyrants and emperors, never or seldom recorded before. (Herodian 1.1.4)

This sentence, justifying the selection of the period covered by Herodian's history, owes an obvious debt to Thucydides' claims for the magnitude of his own subject matter. One notes the stress on disturbances (*kinēseis*), so evoking the *megistē kinēsis* ('greatest disturbance') that the narrator claims the Peloponnesian War to be at Thucydides 1.1.2, where there is also an equivalent emphasis that the perturbation extended to the barbarian world as well. Also ultimately Thucydidean are the allusions to the sacks of cities (Thucydides 1.23.2, though in this case the topic is sufficiently popular in

---

[61] For the very rare exceptions, see Pitcher 2009: 106.   [62] Whittaker 1969: lvi.

classical historiography to arouse the suspicion that this emphasis is purely conventional)[63] and to earthquakes (Thucydides 1.23.3).

To a certain extent, then, Herodian does seem to be borrowing Thucydidean glamour in the celebration of his theme. Yet the differences are as significant as the similarities. The climax of Herodian's sentence, the element that he presents as crowning his narrative's claim to significance, concerns the surprising careers of kings and tyrants, which is not a Thucydidean emphasis at all. Herodian is true to this apparent distribution of interest in his subsequent narrative. He does have an account of plague[64] and of one not particularly impressive earthquake,[65] but he has little to compare with the Great Plague of Athens[66] or with the seismic events that punctuate Thucydides.[67] Herodian is all about the imperial personalities that lend structure to his history: the plague and earthquake in Book 1 of his history are presented not so much for their intrinsic interest as for their effect upon the behaviour and, ultimately, upon the public perception of the emperor Commodus: the plague, besides its general toll on the populace and livestock, provokes the emperor's retreat to Laurentum,[68] while the earthquake is one in a list of portents explaining why 'the Roman people no longer looked upon Commodus with approval'.[69] The veer away from Thucydidean themes towards the personalities of potentates in the programmatic sentence above anticipates a similar slide in Herodian's later text, where natural catastrophes feed into the overriding interest in the careers and fortunes of the powerful.

Herodian, to be sure, is unusual in the lengths to which he goes to advertise his redeployment of Thucydides.[70] All the same, his example should warn us not to assume too readily that an eruption of Thucydidean vocabulary indicates self-branding as an adherent of some notional 'school' of Thucydides, and still less that it indicates a wholesale acceptance of Thucydidean methodology and emphases. The invocation of Thucydides

---

[63] Compare, for example, Polybius' strictures on Phylarchus' excessively emotive account of a sacked city (Polyb. 2.56.8–10) and Tacitus' lament that his chosen subject offers no choice examples of such occurrences (Tac. Ann. 4.32.1).

[64] Herodian 1.12.1. Herodian's restraint in his plague narrative sets him apart from the Thucydidean imitators whom Lucian derides in his treatise How History Ought to Be Written 15.

[65] Herodian 1.14.2.   [66] Thuc. 2.47.3–54.5.

[67] Thuc. 3.87.4, 3.89, 4.56.2, 5.45.4, 5.50.5, 6.95.1, 8.6.5 and 8.41.2 (this list is taken from Hornblower's note on 1.23.2–3; Hornblower 1991–2008).

[68] Herodian 1.12.2.   [69] Herodian 1.14.7.

[70] For a full-scale summary of Herodian's borrowings from Thucydides, see Stein 1957: 219–21.

can be performed in the interests of differentiation from his model just as easily as to advertise allegiance to it.[71]

Conclusion

Thucydides leaves his traces all over the classical historiography that followed him. There are factors that can make detecting these traces and determining their significance far from simple. Historiography's resistance to including overt and named allusions to important predecessors is part of the story here, but not the whole of it. At many points, the Greek and Roman historians demonstrably allude to Thucydides not (or not just) to borrow the lustre of his achievement, but to help themselves explore how their own enterprises and methodologies differ from his. Sometimes the point at issue is subject matter: how significant really was Thucydides' Athens in the grand scheme of things? Sometimes, by contrast, the contest with Thucydides is more subtle. By adapting and redeploying the Thucydidean original, later historians bring into focus the character of their own several concerns.

Further Reading

Hornblower 1995 is an important study of the early reception of Thucydides. Rood 2004 discusses Xenophon's and Diodorus' responses to the historian's work and methods; Scanlon 1980 does the same (in exhaustive detail) for Sallust. Thucydides' impact on later Greek and Roman writers of course extended beyond historiography: Fox 2001 explores reactions to his writing by the satirical author Lucian and the literary critic Dionysius of Halicarnassus (whose *On Thucydides* is one of the most important ancient attempts to analyse and criticize Thucydides' historical and rhetorical methods); Nicolai 2009 likewise analyses the wider impact of Thucydides' text on ancient writers. Fromentin et al. 2010, while uneven in its coverage, gathers studies of the reception of Thucydides across a range of ancient and modern authors.

---

[71] For some much-needed scepticism about the viability of Momigliano's model of competing 'Herodotean' and 'Thucydidean' schools of historiography in the Hellenistic period and beyond, see Schepens 2010.

16

SCOTT KENNEDY AND ANTHONY KALDELLIS

Thucydides in Byzantium

The text of Thucydides' *History* survives because it was copied by hand, first in antiquity itself and then in Byzantium. Other than fragments on papyrus,[1] the Byzantine period represents a bottleneck in the transmission of the text. No translations into other languages were made before the late 14th century, and the Greek text survived only in the territories of the empire of New Rome. This Byzantine reception and sole possession of Thucydides, which interests us here, lasted for over a thousand years after the foundation of Constantinople in 330 CE and witnessed great transformations in the technologies and ideologies that propelled the transmission of classical learning. This chapter will survey the mechanisms of Thucydides' transmission, the reasons why the Byzantines were interested in him, the scholarly apparatus that they developed for his study and the creative uses that some Byzantine authors made of him in their own original works.[2]

While the Byzantines spoke Greek and cultivated classical literature as part of their elite education, in terms of identity they were Christian Romans, not Greeks. They traced their own national-imperial history to Rome and not the city-states of Greece, so they did not preserve Thucydides out of any interest in the Peloponnesian War or democratic politics. However, this began to change in the 14th–15th centuries when the loss of Asia Minor to the Turks forced Byzantines to build up cultural centres in Greece such as Mystra near ancient Sparta. At the same time, some Byzantine intellectuals experimented with notions of Greek identity and descent in response to pressure from Latin colonialism. Before that, most Byzantines had other reasons for preserving Thucydides and studying him intently, despite the acknowledged difficulties of his prose. After all, spoken Greek in Byzantium increasingly diverged from the Attic standard of classical prose, becoming

---

[1] Cavallo 1986.
[2] Previous studies include Vasilikopoulou 1992; Reinsch 2006; Iglesias-Zoido 2011: 121–33; Kennedy 2018a, 2018b.

like modern Greek. Thucydides was an exemplar of 'hard' Attic prose and therefore a model for rhetorical imitation. A database search in the *Thesaurus Linguae Graecae* for his name in Greek texts written after the 4th century CE illustrates this strikingly: a majority of hits occurs in the Byzantine lexica and rhetorical manuals. Thucydides was mined as a lexical resource and used for training in rhetoric.[3]

We must begin by surveying the evolution of the book in Byzantium and the manuscript tradition of Thucydides specifically. The papyrus roll, which was used in classical antiquity, was gradually replaced during late antiquity with the codex (our 'book'); then, starting in c. 800 CE, the ancient Greek script, which consisted until then only of capital letters, was complemented with a minuscule font and a more consistent way of rendering accents, breathing marks and spaces between words. By the end of this process, therefore, the physical aspects of any text of Thucydides were utterly transformed. The Byzantines effectively invented the basic format of the modern Greek book, excepting only the printing press. But this process of transliteration – as the copying into new minuscule is called – was also a bottleneck: texts that did not accord with cultural priorities after the 9th century were simply not copied, and so were lost.[4] In addition, the margins of codices were suited to hosting scholarly comments on ancient authors, like footnotes but all around the text. Ancient commentaries were gradually broken up and converted into such marginalia.[5]

The earliest surviving manuscripts of the *History* suggest that this lengthy text was usually the only work included in a codex.[6] However, over the course of centuries, readers increasingly supplemented Thucydides with other texts, which can tell us something about how they read him. Consider the following epigram from the *Greek Anthology*, which was widely diffused and often appended to the text of Thucydides. It is attributed

---

[3] For his use in rhetorical training, see Kennedy 2018b.   [4] Kaldellis 2012.

[5] On the process of creating scholia, see Wilson 1983b. Kleinlogel 2019 partially replaces the older Thucydides scholia edition of Hude 1927. However, Kleinlogel's update is imperfect and omits a number of ancient scholia because they are preserved only in later manuscripts. For example, the scholia preserved by Basel, Universitätsbibliothek E.III.4 (J), include fragments of ancient material, such as a comparison of Brasidas and the Byzantine general Belisarios: Scholia to Thucydides 4.83, ed. Hude 1927. Scholia 4.92 (the speech of Pagondas) includes a comment on Thucydides' use of the rhetorical heading 'Necessity' (*to anagkaion*), which was used between the 2nd century BCE and the 2nd century CE in deliberative rhetoric. It is important evidence for how Thucydides was used in ancient rhetoric. However, J's scholia are not included in Kleinlogel 2019. To access them, Hude 1927 and the corrections of Powell 1936 are essential.

[6] For the manuscript tradition of Thucydides, see Hemmerdinger 1955; Kleinlogel 1965; Alberti 1972–2000: vol. I, ix–cxcvi (esp. ix–xxviii for a list of manuscripts).

there to Leon the Mathematician, a 9th-century Byzantine philosopher and scholar, but some modern scholars think it may be older.

> Friend, if you are wise, take me in hand. But if you are completely
> ignorant of the Muses, throw away what you do not understand.
> For I am not accessible to everyone, as only a few have admired
> Thucydides, son of Olorus, of the race of Cecrops.[7]

When a Byzantine reader opened up Thucydides, this poem would greet him with an invitation to distinguish himself from the uneducated and appreciate Thucydides' difficult wisdom, which the epigrammatist pointedly says only a few have admired. The fact that later hands would often add this epigram to earlier manuscripts, such as to two of our earliest witnesses (Laur. Plut. 69.2 [F] of the 10th century and Brit. add. 11727 [M] of the 11th century), suggests that Byzantines considered this invitation to esotericism to be an integral part of their reading experience. From the 14th century on, they also paired Thucydides with larger, supplemental texts, which fall into three major types (parentheses indicate what percentage they represent of manuscripts down to the end of the 15th century):

(1) Thucydides paired with Dionysios of Halikarnassos' *On the Peculiarities of Thucydides' Style* and usually with one or both of his lives (23 per cent);
(2) Thucydides paired with one (or both) of his lives (22 per cent);[8]
(3) Thucydides paired with Xenophon's *Hellenica* (9 per cent).

Representing a collective 54 per cent of the surviving manuscripts, these patterns reveal the intellectual context in which Thucydides was meaningful to Byzantine readers. Types 1 and 2 reveal their stylistic and pedagogic concerns, while type 3, although small, is suggestive of an increasing interest in Hellenic history that Byzantines developed in their later period. We can sometimes match patterns to specific intellectuals and writers. For example, Ioannes Tzetzes, whose comments on Thucydides we will discuss later in this chapter, read a type 2, as did Kritoboulos (d. ca. 1470), who imitated Thucydides in his history of the Ottoman sultan Mehmet II (we discuss this work later in this chapter).[9] The Italian antiquarian Kyriacus of Ancona (1391–c. 1455) used a type 1 for his study of Greek in the east, while the

---

[7] *Greek Anthology* 9.583. For the debate over attribution, see Hemmerdinger 1955: 35–7; Westerink 1986.
[8] Palatinus gr. (Heidelberg) 252 (M) of the late 10th or early 11th century is of this type, suggesting that this pairing was popular before the 14th century.
[9] Tzetzes was reading the Palatinus (cited in the previous note); see Reinsch 1983: 68*–9*; Luzzato 1999.

scholar and copyist Michael Apostoles (d. c. 1486) and his scriptorium on Crete produced numerous exemplars of type 1, in part for the Venetian market after the fall of Constantinople in 1453.[10] The scholar-cardinal Bessarion (c. 1400–72) owned a modified version of a type 3 combining Herodotus, Thucydides and Xenophon, which he copied in 1436. This volume reflects Bessarion's desire to have everything under one cover,[11] but it also suggests that he was thinking of Greek history as a historical continuum rather than just taking each author in isolation. These trends are indicative of growing interest among late Byzantines in the history of classical Greece.

The biographies with which the *History* was often paired are interesting in themselves. Most classicists do not realize that our main sources for the author's life are basically Byzantine creations or adaptations based on ancient sources. The main texts include an anonymous life, the biography by Markellinos (6th century) and the entry in the *Suda* (later 10th century); the latter may (or may not) have been based on the *Onomatologos* (alphabetical entries) of ancient writers composed by Hesychius of Miletus in the early 6th century.[12] These biographies reflect the rhetorical, educational and historical perspectives from which ancient and Byzantine readers approached the text.[13] For example, from Markellinos we know that early Byzantine students would read Thucydides after Demosthenes in the course of their rhetorical training, as they moved away from deliberative and judicial oratory into 'strategic advice and panegyric themes'.[14] Indeed, Markellinos celebrated Thucydides as an innovator in the field of rhetoric, crediting him with the invention of the first public speeches subject to rhetorical theory.[15] Thucydides' style and its idiosyncrasies were consequently also major concerns, and Markellinos' *Life of Thucydides* even responds to some of the criticisms of Thucydides expressed by Dionysius of Halicarnassus. The *Suda* also notes that Thucydides switches words from the feminine gender into the neuter, which was an important concern for Byzantine lexicographers. Likewise, in his sympathetic and at times apologetic account of Thucydides, Markellinos praises Thucydides' serious and

---

[10] Powell 1938; Wittek 1953; Barbour 1954–56.   [11] Mione 1968: 76.

[12] The anonymous life and Markellinos still preface many modern editions of Thucydides. For a translation and study of the latter, see Burns 2010; a detailed commentary is available in Piccirilli 1985. The *Suda* is being translated into English online at www.stoa .org. For Hesychius' *Onomatologos*, see Kaldellis 2005.

[13] Carawan 1996; Maitland 1996.

[14] Markellinos, *Life of Thucydides* 1; for Thucydides in the curriculum, see Wilson 1983a: 18–19, 24.

[15] Kennedy 2018a: 45.

lofty style, arguing that it is deliberately inaccessible so that only the wise can sample its mysteries like initiates into a mystery cult. This foreshadows or echoes the themes of the epigram quoted earlier in this chapter.

As a biographer proper, Markellinos shares the general approbation of Thucydides and even contends that Thucydides never let his feelings shape his portrayal of events.[16] In contrast, the anonymous biography was less taken with him as a historian, accusing him of maliciously never missing an opportunity to excoriate the Athenians for their greed and tyranny and noting that he deliberately exalts in Spartan victories and accentuates Athenian defeats.[17] Common to Markellinos and the *Suda* is a curious anecdote about Thucydides breaking into tears while listening to Herodotus recite his *Histories*. In the story, Herodotus then praises the young historian-to-be for his natural scholastic aptitude.[18] Lamentably, the story, which probably derives from ancient scholia on Thucydides, does not tell us why Thucydides cried in the first place, but it became closely associated with these two historians in the Byzantine imagination, making its way, for example, into Photios' *Bibliotheke* and Ioannes Tzetzes (for whom see later in this chapter).[19]

Thucydides was a standard author in the rhetorical curriculum already by late antiquity (or early Byzantium). The 4th-century philosopher, orator and senator Themistios refers to the authors who were being copied at a scriptorium in Constantinople established by the emperor Constantius II (337–61) and lists Plato, Aristotle, Demosthenes and Thucydides.[20] Significantly for the ways in which he was used in Byzantium, which we discuss later in this chapter, Thucydides is often mentioned in the context of rhetoricians and schools of rhetoric. Libanios, the great orator and professor of 4th-century Antioch, claims that he had a compact copy that he would carry around in person, not even giving it to his slave. One day it was stolen and later resurfaced during lessons, as a student had unwittingly purchased it.[21] Thucydides was also among the most quoted authors by Chorikios of Gaza, a teacher and writer of rhetoric in the early 6th century.[22] In one of his orations, Chorikios refers to Thucydides as 'a fount of rhetoric that irrigated Demosthenes by his praise of Pericles'.[23] Indeed, an epigram of one Thomas the scholastikos (6th century?) says, 'I love the three stars of rhetoric because

[16] Markellinos, *Life of Thucydides* 26–7.   [17] Anonymous Life of Thucydides 4–5.
[18] Markellinos, *Life of Thucydides* 54; *Suda* Θ 414.   [19] Piccirilli 1985: xv–xvi, 158–61.
[20] Themistios, *Oration* 4.59d–60b; eds. Schenkl and Downey 1965: 85.
[21] Libanios, *Oration* 1.148–50 (*Autobiography*), trans. Norman 1992: 217.
[22] Listas 1980: 64.   [23] Chorikios, *Opus* 32.1; eds. Foerster and Richtsteig 1929.

they are the best of all rhetoricians. I love your labours, Demosthenes, but I am a huge fan of Aristides and Thucydides.'[24]

In middle Byzantium, Thucydides' role in rhetorical teaching began to shift, as Byzantine rhetors increasingly found him unhelpful. While ancient students would have read Thucydides in class with a teacher like Libanios, Byzantine teachers of rhetoric, particularly between the 7th and 14th centuries, appear not to have continued this practice. Tenth- and 11th-century rhetoricians directed their 'more industrious' students to read Thucydides only if they wanted. Thucydides remained important to individuals who wanted to be erudite, but he was generally overlooked in favour of later writers such as the Church Father Gregory of Nazianzos or Thucydides' imitator, Prokopios of Kaisareia (whom we discuss later in this chapter).[25]

In the later Byzantine period, Thucydides made something of a comeback as a rhetorical text used in classrooms. During the 14th century, the Roman state collapsed into an entity no larger than an ancient city-state, as the Turks seized Asia Minor and then the Balkans. Thus, stories of Greek city-states such as Athens and Sparta and how they had repelled large barbarian armies with limited resources were of greater interest to late Byzantine intellectuals. For example, the 14th-century polymath and historian Nikephoros Gregoras wrote a practice speech remaking the Plataean address to the Spartans (2.72.2–4).[26] Complete with rhetorical analysis in the margins, the text was clearly used to teach rhetoric. However, Gregoras allusively has the Plataeans warn the Spartans against civil war for fear that it will allow the barbarians to settle in Europe. Thucydides thus helped Gregoras express his fear of the rising power of the Turks, who later expanded into Europe while the Byzantine ruling elite waged civil war against one another.[27]

This period also witnessed the first early modern commentary to Thucydides by the Cretan scholar Michael Lygizos. For the benefit of one of his Italian students, Lygizos rearranged Thucydides' prose, paraphrased and explicated Book 1.1–81. The work generally does not include much commentary on Thucydides, as it is largely a simplified version of his work, but it does demonstrate how a Byzantine teacher made the text accessible to second-language learners.[28]

[24] *Greek Anthology* 16.315.   [25] Kennedy 2018a.   [26] Ed. Leone 1970: 751–66.
[27] For analysis of the speech, see Kennedy 2018b: 91–6.
[28] The manuscript (Dublin, Trinity College 231, pp. 37–70) is described by Smyly 1933. Kennedy intends to edit a selection of the text for the revised and expanded version of Kennedy 2018b.

Today, most think of Thucydides as a historian and not a quarry of rhetorical paradigms and eloquence. Most Byzantines, however, took little interest in him as a historical source because they were not much interested in the actual events that he recounts. Chroniclers such as Ioannes Malalas (6th century) and Georgios the Monk (9th century) produced bare-bones accounts of what we call classical Greek history, prosopographically listing important figures such as Thucydides and Socrates as having flourished under this or that Persian king.[29] Monarchical sequences were more compatible with Byzantine ways of organizing history, and so the Persian kings served this function for the classical Greek period. The 12th-century *Epitome of Histories* of Ioannes Zonaras, which was popular until the end of Byzantium, basically omitted most Hellenic history altogether. Notable exceptions to this trend were Eusebios (d. 339) and Georgios Synkellos (d. c. 810), who incorporated Eusebios' *Historical Tables* into his own *Selection of Chronography*. They laconically described key events from Thucydides such as the beginning of the Peloponnesian War, the plague, the Peace of Nicias, the Sicilian disaster and the oligarchical coup of Book 8. However, Synkellos was not indiscriminately repeating Eusebios verbatim. In contrast to Thucydides' analysis of the conflict as a result of Spartan fear of the growing power of Athens, Synkellos, using other ancient sources such as possibly Julius Africanus, saw a woman behind it. He alleges that its cause was Pericles' refusal to revoke the Megarian Decree because the Megarians offended his consort Aspasia by injuring two of her prostitutes.[30] Whereas Thucydides did not convince Synkellos, he did largely persuade the scholar-emperor Konstantinos VII Porphyrogennetos (913–59), who, in a synopsis of Peloponnesian history in his survey of his empire's geography, envisioned the history of Greece from the Persian Wars to the rise of Macedonia as a contest for primacy between Sparta and Athens.[31]

Thucydides was caught up in a more ambitious project set into motion by that same emperor. As both a reader of history and an emperor, Konstantinos VII took more than just an antiquarian interest in history and sought to use it, just as Thucydides did in his plague narrative, as a tool for 'prognosis and remedy', on the assumption that similar patterns of events

---

[29] Jeffreys 1979: 217, 232.
[30] Eusebios, *Historical Tables (Canons)* 114–17 (ed. Helm 1956); Georgios Synkellos, *Chronography* 304, 309–10 (trans. Adler and Tuffin 2002; and see their note at 374 n. 2); cf. Aristophanes, *Acharnians* 519–27; Plutarch, *Pericles* 30–1.
[31] Konstantinos VII Porphyrogennetos, *On the Themes* 2.6; ed. Pertusi 1952: 91.

would recur in the future.[32] He initiated an ambitious project known as the *Excerpta* (or *Constantinian Excerpta*). This massive, fifty-three-volume work consisted of excerpts from ancient historical texts rearranged into thematic units (e.g. on plots, embassies and the like). It would preserve and make available a vast selection of all surviving historical literature that had literary quality and practical use, including Thucydides. Rather than just recopy these historians, the editors of the project culled passages and arranged them in collections according to theme, so that a reader could study a theme multilinearly and discover patterns within it.[33] The project was not successful, as only four of the fifty-three thematic compilations have survived, but the selections from Thucydides in 'On Vices' and 'On Embassies' remain important witnesses to the lost exemplar of Thucydides in the imperial library in the 10th century, from which an important branch of the subsequent manuscript tradition is believed to descend.[34] Within the *Excerpta*, the editors selected a wide range of passages from throughout the *History* and included also material on Thucydides himself from Markellinos' *Life*, such as Thucydides' alleged patriotism when he sacrificed his wealth on behalf of the Athenians.[35]

Among the three major works of middle Byzantine classical compilation, the *Excerpta* failed to endure. By contrast, the *Suda* is still regularly used by classical scholars, as is the *Bibliotheke* of Photios (9th century). This was a series of hundreds of reviews or summaries of ancient texts that the learned patriarch began to write before he took up ecclesiastical office. Many of the works that he included have since been lost, making the *Bibliotheke* an invaluable source. Although Thucydides does not receive a separate entry, it is certain that Photios had read him, probably along with Markellinos' *Life*. Photios holds Thucydides up as a model of Attic style in his entry on Herodotus and reasons that Theopompus of Chios' boast to have surpassed all writers before him could not possibly refer to his literary superiors Herodotus and Thucydides.[36] Thus it is likely that Photios did not include an entry on Thucydides because he considered him a standard author who was already familiar to his readers and who thereby required no introduction. Even so, Photios appears to have disliked the obscurity of his style, praising some of his imitators such as Cassius Dio and Dexippus as clearer

[32] Konstantinos VII Porphyrogennetos, *De administrando imperio* 46.166–9 (ed. and trans. Moravcsik and Jenkins 1967); cf. Thuc. 2.48.3, which the editors confuse with Thuc. 1.22.2.
[33] Németh 2018.   [34] Pérez Martín 2002: 137.
[35] This is in the volume *On Virtues and Vices*: eds. Büttner-Wobst and Roos 1906–10: 30–1.
[36] Photios, *Bibliotheke* codd. 60, 176; ed. and trans. Henry 1959–77.

writers than their model.[37] Nor does the Peloponnesian War as a period seem to have interested him, though he was otherwise a well-versed reader of history. He preferred the history of the Near East and Rome over that of the Greek city-states.[38] His entry on Ctesias' *Persian History* notes the many points on which it diverges from Herodotus and Xenophon regarding Persia, but when he turns to historians such as Diodorus who covered the Peloponnesian War, he shows no interest in comparing them to Thucydides.[39]

Byzantine interest in classical literature took a more scholarly turn in the 12th century, which witnessed the renewed production of commentaries, such as Eustathios of Thessalonike's massive studies of Homer. To be sure, these were based on ancient scholarship, but they included much original material as well.[40] One of the key players in this scene was Ioannes Tzetzes, who wrote scholia and commentaries on ancient poets. Among Byzantine readers of Thucydides, he had perhaps the most vitriolic reaction. Tzetzes' scholia (in Byzantine verse) populate the margins of Palatinus (Heidelberg) graecus 252 (E). He was an acerbic schoolteacher unafraid to speak his mind about Thucydides and the physical form in which he found him. As Tzetzes unhappily trudged through this manuscript's 10th-century minuscule, he corrected its orthography and Attic style until giving up in frustration at a jumbled, unseparated cluster of words at Thuc. 5.16.2, with the complaint that 'the copyist's shit stinks the worst here'.[41] As for Thucydides himself, Tzetzes had little love for the convolution of his thought, snidely remarking, for example, regarding the disputed authorship of Book 8 that the style was too obscure for this to be anyone but Thucydides.[42] However, his most caustic and incisive remarks were reserved for his noted 'farewell' to Thucydides at the end of the manuscript, which attacks Thucydides' canonical status as a historian.[43] In this epigram, Tzetzes first goes after Thucydides the man, wishing that the Athenians had cast him and his book into a pit rather than ostracizing him. He then turns to Thucydides the historian, challenging his premise in Book 1.22 to provide a 'possession for eternity' for those who wish to understand clearly. Tzetzes feels that Thucydides' dark and wooden (*xulōdei*) style has completely befuddled his recollection of events, which previously he thought he understood well based on other authors. Tzetzes is the first author to call Thucydides wooden.[44] Indeed, he even describes himself as a reader as 'struck from above and

---

[37] Photios, *Bibliotheke* codd. 71, 213.   [38] Kaldellis 2012: 79.

[39] Photios, *Bibliotheke* codd. 70 and 244 (Diodorus), 68 (Kephalion), 69 (Hesychius), 82 (Dexippus); cf. Schamp 1996: 22.

[40] Kaldellis 2009.   [41] Luzzato 1999: 27.   [42] Luzzato 1999: 130–2.

[43] English translation in Stanford 1941.   [44] Baldwin 1982: 315.

totally stunned', snubbing the divine status accorded to the work by Markellinos and many ancient rhetors.[45] History, he instructs the reader, should be clear with dignity, persuasive and sweet, like that of Herodotus. In this, he contradicts Thucydides' disavowal of the entertainment value of his work at 1.22.

Thucydides' style was understood to be hard but, perhaps all the more for that reason, was upheld as a model. Byzantines were trained above all in rhetoric, in the modes and orders of what today we would call prose composition. Part of their training required them to write descriptions (ekphraseis) of events and objects, which aimed to make them vivid in the mind of the reader. They were also trained to assume the persona of a person from myth or history and write a speech that they would make under a particular set of circumstances. Side by side with contemporary textbooks full of model exercises, students would use Thucydides as a repository of such ekphraseis and speeches.[46] We saw earlier how embedded he was in the schools of rhetoric. The result was twofold: first, rhetorical education in the later Empire imparted some knowledge of key historical texts, even though history as such was not among its goals; and second, prospective historians already had, from their rhetorical training, all the templates with which to write a 'generic' account of a siege, battle, plague and speech, and needed only to adapt them to the particulars of history – or play allusive games with them.[47]

Many Byzantine historians famously imitated Thucydides in the early and late Byzantine periods following the principals of the rhetorical practice of imitation (mimesis in Greek, imitatio in Latin). This has been a thorny topic since the 19th century. Taking their cue from Lucian's attacks on imitators of Thucydides, including one who allegedly lifted all but the walls of Athens from Thucydides' account of the Athenian plague (How to Write History 15), 19th-century scholars accused late Roman historians writing in Greek (such as Priskos, Prokopios and Agathias) of not only producing slavish, unoriginal knock-offs of Thucydides, but also distorting history in the process: sieges, battles, plagues and speeches in the 5th and 6th centuries CE played out in the same style, vocabulary, thought patterns and even facts as their models in Thucydides.[48] It was later discovered that Byzantine authors in the later centuries had done the same, such as the former emperor

<hr/>

[45] Luzzato 1999: 135; cf. Markellinos, *Life of Thucydides* 28.
[46] On the use of history in rhetoric, see Gibson 2004.
[47] On Thucydides in ancient and Byzantine schools, see Kennedy 2018a, 2018b.
[48] Braun 1885: 61; Thompson 1945: 92–4; Evans 1976: 355.

Ioannes VI Kantakouzenos (r. 1347–54) and the historians of the early Ottomans Laonikos Chalkokondyles and Kritoboulos.

Since then, most Byzantinists have rejected this negative image of imitation. Subsequent research has claimed that imitation rarely entailed factual distortion. Despite the use of an ancient idiom and classical templates, subtle differences highlighted the distinctiveness of contemporary events.[49] Nonetheless, this now conventional wisdom requires revision. When we can compare imitators of Thucydides in the Graeco-Roman tradition to their sources, distortions and the invention of facts are evident. Rhetoric allowed rhetors and historians to invent facts that made their narratives more realistic, such as plague symptoms, and to believe that they had added nothing to the facts. As a template for how to describe events, Thucydides was admired for how plausibly and persuasively he described events, so potential imitators could take words and facts from him to make a narrative more convincing. How much a historian distorted events largely depended on how much personal knowledge they had of them. Eyewitnesses tended to resort to the least invention, while historians of the distant past more frequently deployed invention to create a more plausible and persuasive account of the past.[50]

Just as classicists today increasingly see intertextual relationships as a source of innovative and complex messaging, even subversion, so many Byzantine scholars have rejected seeing imitation as slavish and have begun appreciating how late Roman historians creatively engaged with their classical models and sought to surpass them. Many imported useful images, evaluations and narrative structures from their models, and some even perhaps expected their readers to catch allusions and ponder the significance of strategic alterations. In his account of the Justinianic plague of the 6th century, which is heavily modelled after Thucydides, Prokopios emulates Thucydides, seeking to surpass Thucydides' renowned precision. For example, Prokopios makes Thucydides' language more precise. Thucydides' description of the appearance of blisters on plague victims is taken over word for word in Prokopios' description of the buboes of bubonic plague, but Prokopios adds details on the black colour and size of the buboes.[51] Indeed, he even corrects Thucydides' comment that plague victims threw themselves into wells because of unbearable thirst, suggesting that it was actually madness-induced thirst.[52]

---

[49] The classic statement was by Hunger 1969–70.   [50] Kennedy 2018a: 98–150.
[51] Prokopios, *Wars* 2.22.2; cf. Thuc. 2.49.5.
[52] Prokopios, *Wars* 2.22.25; cf. Thuc. 2.49.6. For this reading of Prokopios' subtle use of Thucydides, see Kennedy 2018b: 143–8.

Despite his use of Thucydides' plague narrative, Prokopios' account of the Justinianic plague also makes a unique intervention in the moral debates of the 6th century.[53] Moreover, allusion was a subtle way of saying certain things indirectly to readers with a classical education while keeping them invisible from readers who lacked it, or at any rate keeping them discreet. In his privately circulated *Secret History*, a vicious attack on Justinian, Prokopios levels the charge of 'innovation' against the emperor; that is, of disrupting ancient practices for no good reason. In his public work, the *Wars*, he ostensibly praises Justinian by saying that 'he was sharp at formulating plans and resolute in implementing his decisions'. But this line is lifted from the speech of the Corinthians about the Athenians at Sparta, only here Prokopios has pointedly omitted the capstone accusation that the Athenians were revolutionary 'innovators'.[54] This quiet omission is in fact a hidden door to the secret work, pointing to what Prokopios would have liked to say openly and accomplished cleverly by means of a classical allusion.[55] There is much more to be discovered here in terms of literary originality.

No Byzantine historian seems to have imitated Thucydides extensively between the 7th and 14th centuries.[56] In explaining his decision to write a loose memoir, the polymath Michael Psellos of the 11th century even draws attention to the fact that he has not dated everything precisely by season as did 'the Historian'.[57] He certainly knew his work, for he explained a phrase about the Trinity in Orthodox theology by citing Thucydidean grammar![58] However, most Byzantine historians preferred later, Roman models such as Prokopios, Josephus, Plutarch or Polybius.[59] The second phase of 'imitation' of Thucydides, in late Byzantium, has been studied less than the late antique phase. Two of its most important authors, Laonikos and Kritoboulos, wrote soon after the fall of Constantinople to the Turks in 1453. Laonikos did something quite interesting: he basically wrote a new Herodotus, replete with ethnographic digressions, only his narrative axis was formed not by the Persians who fail to conquer Greece but by the Turks who now succeed. In his style of writing, however, and in his austerity and avoidance of anecdotes, Laonikos strictly followed Thucydides. His *Histories* are therefore a fascinating literary experiment from the historiographical point of view. As this aspect of his work is studied in a separate monograph, we need not discuss it in detail here.[60]

---

[53] Kaldellis 2007.
[54] Prokopios, *Wars* 3.9.25; cf. Thuc. 1.70.2; for this and more, see Kaldellis 2004: 49.
[55] Similarly Pazdernik 2000.   [56] Reinsch 2006: 758; Kennedy 2018a: 618–27.
[57] Psellos, *Chronographia* 6.73; ed. Reinsch 2014.   [58] Ed. Gautier 1989: 79 (opus 20).
[59] Kennedy 2018a: 619–27.   [60] Kaldellis 2014.

Thucydides also inspired Laonikos' contemporary, Kritoboulos (d. ca. 1470), who wrote a history of the years 1450–67 from the perspective of the Turks; in fact, the work appears to be an encomium of Mehmet II (1451–81), the sultan who conquered Constantinople in 1453. Its title (*Xyngraphē historiōn*) announces its debt to Thucydides. Like Thucydides, Kritoboulos uses seasons as temporal markers, though for clarity's sake he ends his books not with the year of a war but the Byzantine year since creation.[61] Kritoboulos has been seen as a member of a group of Byzantine intellectuals surrounding Georgios Amiroutzes who sought to come to terms with Turkish rule. Explicitly, Kritoboulos seems to write with seeming admiration for his new ruler, deploying Thucydides to glorify the sultan. Diether Reinsch has highlighted how he channels Brasidas' speech at Amphipolis to dignify the sultan's address before the final assault on Constantinople.[62] Also, at the beginning of the work he has Mehmet deliver a lengthy speech explaining how the Turks have risen from humble origins and now stand poised to take the city. Combining echoes of Pericles' Funeral Oration and of the Athenian and Corinthian speeches at Sparta, Mehmet and the Athenians stress how recent their peoples' accomplishments are and that they are known directly by the audience, especially the oldest among them.[63] Like Pericles, Mehmet sees a world full of 'signs' of how his people acquired empire through their labours, virtue and blood.[64]

But like Prokopios, whom he read and imitated, Kritoboulos creates a layered text that combines explicit praise with subversive classical allusions that question the justice of the Turks and their rule.[65] Although he and his circle are usually read as Turkophiles who collaborated with the Turks, a more nuanced perspective is needed. Amiroutzes, Kritoboulos' friend and an occasional companion of the sultan, initially wrote panegyrics for the sultan, but later he quite openly attacked the oppressiveness of Turkish rule. In the first years after the Turkish conquest of Byzantium, many elites, well aware of their history, hoped that the Turks, like the Romans before them, could be induced to embrace Greek culture and that captured Greece would once more capture its savage conqueror, as Horace had said of Rome (2.1 ll. 156–7). However, Amiroutzes expresses his recognition that the Turks were no Romans in a report of his conversations on religion with the sultan, writing: 'The first conquerors of Greece [the ancient Romans]

---

[61] Reinsch 1983: 49*. [62] Reinsch 2006: 765–6.
[63] Kritoboulos, *History* 1.14.1 ed. Reinsch 1983; cf. Thuc. 1.73.2.
[64] 1.14.2 (also 1.14.10); cf. Thuc. 2.41.4.
[65] Kritoboulos' knowledge of Prokopios is evident from the apparatus criticus of Reinsch 1983: 205–6.

imposed only a nominal servitude, even if it appeared heavy and intolerable to the Greeks ... The Romans, however, were so conquered by the cultural ornaments, which they observed among the Greeks, that they themselves became Greeks and abandoned dominion of the world to their Greek successors. But now the difference of religion, compounded by our enemy's natural hatred for us, has brought us to a most severe servitude.'[66] Like his friend, Kritoboulos initially seems to have begun a panegyrical history of Mehmet, hoping that the sultan could be won over by panegyric, like imperial-era Greek sophists once enchanted Roman emperors. However, he gradually became disillusioned with the regime and used Thucydides to tactfully voice the deep-seated disaffection of the new empire's Orthodox community. For example, Mchmet's long, programmatic speech at the beginning of the *History* celebrates the fact that his ancestors conquered through deceit and opportunistic raids against farmers and civilians.[67] Pericles, by contrast, states that the Athenians do not use superior preparations or tricks to win but advance against opponents equally matched.[68] Unlike the Athenians, the Turks allegedly had no honour and attacked the weak.

We may also detect criticism in Kritoboulos' plague narrative, the final scene of his history. Previous scholarship has noted its textual debt to the account in Thucydides and superficially suggested that Kritoboulos included it because he wanted to end his history with a rhetorical flourish.[69] We posit that Kritoboulos assimilates not only Thucydides' words for this scene but also his use of the plague to dismember the ideology of his subject. With the fall of Constantinople in Book 1, Kritoboulos distinctively marks off the Byzantine past from the Ottoman city to follow by speaking of the 'death' of the city in the fires of the Turkish attack.[70] With the city dead, Kritoboulos makes Mehmet's concern to revive the city and adorn it with monuments a central theme of the *History*. On twelve occasions, Kritoboulos reports the forethought (*promētheia*) and providence (*pronoia*) that Mehmet showed when rebuilding the city.[71] And then the plague strikes in Book 5: Kritoboulos closes his history on a much darker and chaotic note than the more optimistic picture of the sultan presented earlier, especially in the Periclean speech at the beginning.

[66] Argyriou and Lagarrigue 1987: 64. [67] 1.14.4–6.
[68] Thuc. 2.39.1–2; Tomadakes 1952: 66–7. [69] Villard 1992; Reinsch 2006: 777–8.
[70] 1.72.3.
[71] 1.73.4–8; 2.1; 2.10; 2.22; 3.9.1–2; 3.11.1–3; 3.11.7; 3.17.4; 4.9.4; 4.14.4; 5.2.4; 5.9; 5.10.3.

To this end, Book 5 presents a subtle change in the author's tone as the world begins to go awry. Admittedly, Mehmet continues to march off against his enemies and promotes the settlement of Constantinople up to a few sections before the plague outbreak. However, the sultan's 'boundless energy' and the cares of his position begin to weigh heavily upon him, his soldiers and his court, so they postpone a campaign out of sheer exhaustion.[72] Kritoboulos intersperses the failed military projects of that year with signs and omens of a dire future. Before the fall of Constantinople, the world had conformed to reason, and experts were able to interpret these omens as signifying divine assent to Mehmet's rise,[73] but Kritoboulos now admits that he cannot explain a column of fire that appeared in the sky; he struggles with naturalistic explanations and then concludes that, at any rate, it presaged mass death.[74] The sheer irrationality of the subsequent events is shown when the plague bursts onto the stage like a 'drunken reveller'. Kritoboulos denies that it was propelled by *logos*: he cannot adequately describe it, nor can the reader adequately understand it.[75]

Despite Mehmet's repeated efforts to resettle Constantinople, the plague shatters the bonds of the emerging Ottoman city. As the plague murders its inhabitants, people flee the city without turning back, burial rituals collapse and civic life evaporates as people barricade themselves in their houses to die. 'The city was emptied of its inhabitants, whether residents or non-residents, and it practically seemed like a desert.'[76] The care and concern of Mehmet for the city are also subversively undone when Kritoboulos reports: 'Expectation of providence completely disappeared and everything was thought to proceed according to probability and chance, as there was no one superintending events.'[77]

In Thucydides, the plague narrative follows directly upon the idealistic, programmatic speech of Pericles and shatters some of its fundamental assumptions. Pericles hopes that the Athenians will fall in love with a beautiful image of Athens and choose to sacrifice themselves for it; he does not talk about what will happen to their bodies if they do so. The plague, however, makes the city look ugly, deformed, sick and unlovable, and Athenians begin to behave in highly selfish ways. Thucydides focuses relentlessly on the disfiguration of their physical bodies. We propose that Kritoboulos grasped this jarring contrast and adapted it to his own purposes. His plague does not come immediately after the sultan's rousing speech. Rather, the two Thucydidean passages come at the start and the end of the narrative, respectively; they serve as bookends for the *History*.

---

[72] 5.10.1; energy: 1.5.2.   [73] E.g. 1.4.4.   [74] 5.14.1.   [75] 5.17.2.   [76] 5.17.2–4.
[77] 5.17.4.

The speech of Mehmet establishes the glory of the Ottomans and inaugurates the new world that they have boldly created. The plague narrative effectively buries that dream in the most grotesque way the classical tradition had to offer.

Further Reading

Maurer 1995 discusses Thucydides' manuscript tradition. The website *Pinakes* (https://pinakes.irht.cnrs.fr/) is an invaluable if occasionally deficient starting point for research into the manuscripts. The scholia to Thucydides have recently been edited by Kleinlogel 2019. However, Kleinlogel omits the ancient scholia from Manuscript J. Maitland 1996 is a good starting point for the Byzantine biographical tradition on Thucydides. Kennedy 2018a and 2018b discuss the place of Thucydides in the rhetorical tradition and his imitators in Byzantium; for the latter, see also Reinsch 2006. For Byzantine scholarship on ancient authors, see Wilson 1983a and Dickey 2007. For how Byzantine thinking about history shaped the reception, survival and formation of the classical canon, see Kaldellis 2012.

17

KINCH HOEKSTRA

Thucydides in the Renaissance and Reformation

Thucydides arrived late to the Renaissance. Once there, he principally spoke to fellow elites about urgent matters of politics and war. Only able to communicate through foreign interpreters, he was understood variously and even contradictorily. We will thus encounter a Reformation Thucydides who counselled avoidance of war and cultivation of moral virtue and rhetorical ability; a reason-of-state Thucydides, who sounded the trumpet of war; and Thomas Hobbes' Thucydides who was critical of both rhetorical politics and military aggression, and illustrates how interpreters were in turn misinterpreted. Of necessity, more figures are excluded than included and accounts are simplified. For example, the Reformation interpretation of the Peloponnesian War as the punishment of vice is not mere moralism but a lesson for prudential politics; and those who used Thucydides as a reason-of-state author typically did so in the name of an overarching political morality. The aim is to provide an introduction to a few significant lines of interpretation, concentrating on distinct views of how to approach or understand the text, on what Thucydides is taken to say about some substantive matters, and on the relation between interpretive approach and substantive meaning.

At the approach of the Renaissance, knowledge of ancient Greek was scant in the west of Europe. A scattered few with good scholarly Greek were to be found for a time in, for example, Otranto in Lecce, Robert Grosseteste's Lincolnshire, William of Moerbeke's Viterbo and papal Avignon. So, too, in northern Italy in the 14th century, where a more or less itinerant Hellenist might provide Greek lessons or manuscript translations. Petrarch, Boccaccio and others undertook a humanist project of

Thanks to Mark Fisher and Derin McLeod for excellent comments on an early draft. Alison McQueen and David Plunkett organized a discussion at Stanford University where I benefitted from questions and comments from them, Daniela Cammack, Desmond Jagmohan, Josh Ober and Lucas Stanczyk.

classical recovery of growing proportions, and this involved beginning to learn Greek and promoting its understanding. Petrarch's view of Thucydides was nonetheless through a dark glass, and he could make out little more than an impression of esteem in his Latin sources. Accordingly, in the catalogue of classical greats in his *Trionfo della Fama*, Petrarch writes briefly if elegantly:

> Thucydides I saw, who well discerns
> the times and places and gallant deeds,
> and on whose blood which field feeds.[1]

At the end of the 14th century, Manuel Chrysoloras arrived from Constantinople and set up in Florence as a teacher of Greek. Influential statesmen and scholars gathered around him to learn, including those who went on to read Thucydides, such as Pier Paolo Vergerio the Elder and Leonardo Bruni, who draws on Thucydides especially as a literary model.[2] Bruni (c. 1370–1444) resisted pressure to translate Thucydides but held him in especially high regard. Bruni's expression of admiration for Thucydides, whom he was able to apprehend thanks to Chrysoloras, illustrates how intertwined could be Renaissance dependence on and contempt for Byzantine learning. Although Procopius tried to imitate Thucydides' speeches, writes Bruni, he is 'as far from the majesty of Thucydides as Thersites is distant from the beauty and power of Achilles'.[3]

A translation of Thucydides into the common language of European letters was finally accomplished by Lorenzo Valla (c. 1407–57) for Pope Nicholas V in 1452. In his preface to the pope, Valla wrote that in undertaking the translation into Latin he was like a soldier who had been sent to

---

[1]
> *Tuchidide vid'io, che ben distingue*
> *i tempi e' luoghi e l'opere leggiadre*
> *e di che sangue qual campo s'impingue.* (Petrarca 1996: 450)

All translations are my own, except I follow that by Rolfe for Gentili's *De iure belli* (Gentili 1933) unless otherwise noted. Passages from Thucydides are translated from the respective Renaissance translations in an attempt to approximate the inherent interpretations. I begin with Petrarch (1304–74) as a matter of convention, though one may question or complicate the idea that he is the founder or father of Renaissance humanism. See, e.g., Witt 2000: esp. 230–91.

[2] See Klee 1990: 23–58; Daub 1996.

[3] Letter of 1443 to Francesco Barbaro, in Griggio 1986: 49–50. It is difficult to understand how his enthusiasm for Thucydides, already expressed in a letter to Pietro Emiliani (or Miani) of late 1407 (dated to October or November of 1407 in Luiso 1980: 38), is consistent with his dismissive attitude towards translating Thucydides in a letter of 17 December of that year, when he writes to Niccolò Niccoli that such effort should instead be directed to more morally improving ends (ibid.: 42). Perhaps his pious refusal was fortified by a reluctance to undertake an enormous task for which he was underprepared.

conquer the most forbidding province of the Greek world for the Roman Empire.[4] Thucydides' history remained daunting in Valla's Latin, but the translation garnered readers from across Europe. Valla's glorious presentation manuscript to the pope seems to have been intended primarily for an audience of one, but his translation eventually had a wide impact. A couple of dozen extant manuscript copies reveal that many were made for other patrons and potentates, and a version was eventually printed in around 1483 and many times thereafter.

Translations into other languages were made from the Latin.[5] So it was that Claude de Seyssel (c. 1450–1520) produced the first complete vernacular version of Thucydides, which he presented to King Louis XII in a lavish illuminated manuscript sometime between 1512 and 1514. This, too, was intended primarily for a readership of the one person at the top of the relevant hierarchy. The exclusivity of the manuscript was a way to protect the work's sensitive military and political counsel, and yet ensured a keen interest in copying it.[6] Seyssel tells the French king that he is providing this history so that the king may 'better understand how you might conduct the regime and government of your realm . . . as well in times of peace as in times of war', and he makes clear that the king can apprehend this teaching 'not so much from the narration of this history . . . as from the profundity and excellence of the orations and harangues . . . which contain universal teaching of all great matters, and the whole art and effectiveness of eloquence'.[7] Seyssel urged his royal reader to focus on the speeches to glean essential precepts and to learn the art of persuasion.

A few years later, Philipp Melanchthon (1497–1560), who was to become Martin Luther's right-hand man and heir of the Lutheran movement, arrived in Wittenberg to take up the professorship of Greek. It is little known – and perhaps surprising – that the devout Melanchthon initiated the most substantial school of Thucydides interpretation in the Renaissance. Melanchthon lectured on Thucydides and may have been responsible for a 1520 publication of the Greek text of the speech of Diodotus (3.42–58).[8] He published a Latin translation of the Corcyrean stasis (3.81.4–84.2) in 1542, which was frequently reprinted thereafter. Melanchthon, the most influential teacher of rhetoric in the first half of the 16th century, provided rough translations of thirty-four of the speeches from Thucydides for use by his students, along with the encomium of Themistocles from 1.138.3 and another version of the Corcyrean stasis; these were published together in

---

[4] See the codex reproduced in Chambers 2008: 1–2.   [5] For a catalogue, see Pade 2003.
[6] Paris, BnF MS fr. 17211. On Seyssel's Thucydides, see esp. Boone 2007: 85–105.
[7] Paris, BnF MS fr. 17211, fol. 3ʳ, 4ᵛ.   [8] Klee 1990: 134–5.

1562 by Melanchthon's son-in-law, Caspar Peucer. In his dedicatory epistle, Peucer notes that the wise read Thucydides not so much for the contest of arms as for the contest of wisdom and justice versus sophistry and injustice.[9]

This reflects Melanchthon's own consistent mode of reading, which combines rhetorical and moral lessons and divides the figures of the Peloponnesian War into the ranks of the bad and the good. Cleon, Alcibiades, Sthenelaidas and others are ranked among the ambitious, turbulent, fickle, seditious and sycophantic. Diodotus and Nicias are put forward for praise as just, moderate defenders of public tranquillity and opponents of unnecessary war. Significantly, Melanchthon places Pericles in the former camp: along with Alcibiades, he is the consummate example of *polupragmosunē* (understood as meddlesomeness, activism, interventionism), that 'great and pernicious vice that displeases God and multiplies the troubles of human life' and induced them to destroy Greece.[10]

Melanchthon was the main force of Lutheran irenicism during his life, working to minimize the roiling confessional strife within Lutheranism and between Lutherans and Catholics, Calvinists, Zwinglians and others. His moralized reading of Thucydides is bolstered by his interpretation of the entire war between the Athenians and Peloponnesians as a civil war. 'As Thucydides says, in sedition are all forms of evil things ... this can be seen in the civil war of the Greeks, which is called the Peloponnesian, and which was full of the saddest examples [*exempla*]. Many cities were utterly obliterated, many citizens killed, and with natural affection extinguished, relatives carried out savagery against each other. With such horrible punishments did God manifest his wrath against Idols and lusts.'[11] Melanchthon finds in Thucydides a narrative that parallels contemporary conflict in Germany and that confirms the retributive power of a just God.

Of the several other important Lutheran figures who interpreted Thucydides similarly, I will mention just one. David Chytraeus (1531–1600) went to study with Melanchthon in 1544. Chytraeus moved to Rostock in 1551, where he became a pillar of the Lutheran church and worked to reorganize the university there on the model of Wittenberg. A series of successively augmented editions of his lectures on Thucydides appeared from 1562 to 1594. These manifest a particular concern with an integrated chronology as part of a religious account of human history that synchronized the classical with the biblical. The actions, principles and

---

[9] Peucer in Melanchthon 1562, sig. *2ʳ.
[10] Letter of January 1545, no addressee specified (Melanchthon 1642, col. 193). See Melanchthon 1550: 98 and 1582: 485–7.
[11] Melanchthon 1559: 181. See also, e.g., Melanchthon 1564: 209.

characters of classical Greeks are subject to the true scriptural standards. Following in Melanchthon's footsteps, he takes the side of Diodotus against Cleon, the Melians against the Athenians, and Nicias against Alcibiades. Chytraeus also presents Pericles as an example of vicious obstinacy and Alcibiades as a vainglorious fool, excoriating them for leading their commonwealth to disaster by indulging in unnecessary war.[12]

Chytraeus applies such moral interpretation and direction to both individual and political comportment. So he writes in the *Chronologia* of 1563 that Thucydides provides 'many counsels about life and about actions done prudently or rightly, which this part of Philosophy, which is called Moral or Ethical or Political, delivers; he illustrates it not only with orations and the most serious maxims [*sententiae*], but also with remarkable counsels and the Examples of consequences, which much more effectively than bare precepts move and compel the minds of men. For a HISTORY written wisely, is truly a possession for all time, as Thucydides names it, a lasting thesaurus of examples.'[13] Chytraeus argues that Thucydides effectively describes the contemporary tumults in Germany and that his illustration of 'how to govern a Republic or Empire wisely' is still applicable.[14]

'The whole history of this war is an extraordinary assembly, both of the wrath of God and the punishments of the unjust desires and the horrors of the wicked', Chytraeus writes, 'and of many counsels and Rules for living life rightly and properly. Civil war, which the Greek commonwealths waged among themselves, entirely overturned not only Athens but the power and virtue of all Greece.'[15] He blames the pride and obstinacy of Pericles for the war and its attendant disasters, and like other Lutherans focuses on the war being unnecessary and thus unjustified. He goes on to say that 'Alcibiades from blind and juvenile ambition and shallowness [*levitas*] later brings the war to Sicily and restarts it in Greece'.[16] Chytraeus concludes that 'these examples admonish us about the causes of horrible wars, and to avoid calamities, and not to initiate wars, at least about any non-necessary matters'. He here invokes as a general rule a precept of Melanchthon's: not to do something unless there is something necessary to do; and he says that this and similar precepts, and indeed the wisest rules of life, are to be found in the speeches of Thucydides – where they are more vigorous and

---

[12] See Chytraeus 1567: 9, 356–70, 379–82.

[13] Chytraeus 1563, sigs. K8ᵛ–L1ʳ. Despite my translation here, '*exempla*' are not mere examples, but edifying cases or anecdotes of exemplary behaviours. Collections of *exempla* constituted a popular medieval genre (see Tubach 1969 and the *Thesaurus Exemplorum Medii Aevi*).

[14] Chytraeus 1563, sig. K8ᵛ.   [15] Chytraeus 1563, sig. L1ᵛ.

[16] Chytraeus 1563, sig. L2ʳ.

numerous than in the many arguments of the philosophers.[17] The Lutheran Thucydideans emphasize the imprudence of aggression and expansion, coupled with a moral and a religious lesson against avarice and prideful ambition. This is a message that can be found in maxims that may be extracted from Thucydides, but the moral is also to be found in the story itself and how those who lived in accordance with wicked maxims were cast down. As Chytraeus argues, Thucydides does not provide his political wisdom only in orations and precepts, but by illustrating the *euentus*, the outcomes or consequences of actions and counsels.[18]

The Lutherans' reformed rivals showed that they, too, could find high-minded principles in Thucydides, though with varying degrees of punctiliousness in relating the proffered precepts to the arc of the history. The Calvinist Innocent Gentillet (c. 1532–88) is a good example. In his *Anti-Machiavel*, he denounces what he calls the tyranny besetting France – not of the king, but of the Italian and Italianizing courtiers, advisors and officials.[19] It is difficult to determine whether Gentillet is an absolutist as he claims and truly repudiates the monarchomachs' argument for a right of resistance,[20] or someone of essentially monarchomach ideas who is trying a more subtle strategy, or above all a moderate Calvinist concerned to work out a solution with the *politiques* such that Calvinists and moderate Catholics can control the situation and live together.[21] His approach is to extract what he presents as Machiavelli's political maxims, which pretend to be of general applicability, and to show that the Florentine's recommendations have in fact led to disaster. History, as for the Lutherans, reliably demonstrates the fall of the wicked.

Gentillet tries to show that action in accordance with Machiavellian maxims brings about failure, even on a proper reading of Machiavelli's favourite, Livy. He puts two Greek historians, Thucydides and Xenophon, in the category of those who can also be relied upon to test Machiavelli's teachings.[22] A salient deployment of Thucydides comes in refuting the

---

[17] Chytraeus 1563, sig. L2ʳ.   [18] Chytraeus 1563, sig. L1ʳ.

[19] Gentillet 1576 (*Discours, svr les moyens de bien govverner et maintenir en bonne paix vn Royaume ou autre Principauté ... Contre Nicolas Machiauel Florentin*).

[20] So d'Andrea 1970.

[21] Presumably under the leadership of François, duc d'Alençon, to whom the work is dedicated. D'Andrea (1970: 411 n. 33) notes: 'Gentillet obtained permission from the Genevan authorities to publish the *Discours* on October 21, 1575, after the book had been examined by Beza.'

[22] They are on the short list of those '*qui sont tous bien authentiques & approuuez, & qui par vne prescription de temps immemorial, ont gagné la reputation d'estre bons tesmoins & sans reproche*' (Gentillet 1576: 12–13). Machiavelli himself seems to have had only a cursory or mediated acquaintance with Thucydides.

maxim that the Prince should not observe faith when it would be disadvantageous.[23] Gentillet provides an extended reading from Book 1 of Thucydides, arguing that the disastrous Peloponnesian War was due to the Corcyreans and the Athenians interpreting a treaty inequitably and unreasonably, despite the equitable and reasonable interpretation offered by the Corinthians and Lacedaemonians. The Corcyreans were thereby destroyed and the Athenians defeated.[24] So it is that 'perfidy brings ruin on the perfidious'.[25] Gentillet's readers cannot take solace in a corollary that their enemies will destroy themselves, however, for they threaten to destroy France before then with civil war and all manner of wickedness. He first calls his readers to better reading: Machiavelli does draw on some authoritative historians (though rarely on Thucydides), but he distorts their sense, failing to treat them fully or apply them correctly.[26] Read properly, the exemplary ancient historians are supposed to demonstrate the falsity of wicked principles. On the basis of these historical claims Gentillet calls his readers to action, saying that if they do not drive Machiavellian government out of France, they will be guilty before God of many murders and massacres and convicted and attainted of impiety, atheism and tyranny.[27]

This call to resist tyranny in order not to be guilty of it is echoed in the most famous of the monarchomach texts, the 1579 *Vindiciae, contra tyrannos*. The author (or authors) also invokes the righteous authority of the Corinthians from Book 1 as they call for help. 'Hence Thucydides says: "Tyrants are not only those who reduce others into servitude; much more so are those who are able to keep such violence in check but do not do it …" And he is right.'[28] More activist than their Lutheran counterparts, such authors maintain that those who do not intervene are at least complicit in tyranny.

These Calvinist authors are themselves guilty of a strongly motivated reading that depends on extracting what suits them and ignoring what does not. Gentillet denounces Machiavelli's misreadings but distorts both

---

[23] Gentillet 1576: 437 (Maxim 21).   [24] Gentillet 1576: 463–5.
[25] Gentillet 1576: 453.   [26] Gentillet 1576: 6–7.   [27] Gentillet 1576: 10.
[28] 'Brutus' 1579: 232–3, referring to Thucydides 1.69.1. Compare Hobbes' more accurate 'For not he that bringeth into slauery, but he that being able to hinder it, neglects the same, is most truely said to doe it' (Hobbes 1629: 36). Importing the idea of tyranny into this passage fits the purposes of the *Vindiciae* well but may be based on more than rhetorical convenience or the tight conceptual connection between tyrannizing and enslaving: it may be influenced by the Corinthians' characterization in their second speech at Sparta (1.122.3 and 1.124.3) and did have precedents, as in the translation by Francesco di Soldo Strozzi [1545]: 33, relied on, e.g., by Nannini 1557: 8. The language of 'violence' is interpolated, bringing out the character of tyranny and the stakes of resistance against it.

Machiavelli and the ancient sources that are supposed to confute him, including Thucydides.[29] Some Calvinists are keen to peddle maxims of state of their own and are as cavalier as anyone in plundering the ancient texts for opinions conformable to their own outlook. Julius Wilhelm Zincgref, for instance, who quotes the same passage from the Corinthians' speech as the author of the *Vindiciae*,[30] repeatedly extracts moralistic one-liners from Thucydides, with scant attention to how they were embedded in the text. None of these can be called subtle interpretations, but the prize surely goes to his use of Thucydides 5.104, where the Melians reply to the Athenians that, as far as fortune goes, they trust that the gods will not favour them less, since they resist as innocent men invaded by the unjust.[31] This is Zincgref's authority for the dictum that God gives victory not to the stronger but to the better. Notoriously, the Athenians overwhelmed the Melians, killing all of the adult males, enslaving the women and children and then populating the place with their own colonists. So much for judging a maxim by its outcome.

Zincgref frequently borrowed from another retailer of Thucydidean maxims, Justus Lipsius (1547–1606).[32] Lipsius (who by turns professed to be Catholic, Lutheran and Calvinist) treats Thucydides as an outstanding authority on subjects political, diplomatic and military. It is generally accepted that Lipsius' favoured historian and political authority is Tacitus, so it is noteworthy that he puts Thucydides at the head of the historians who wrote in Greek and then places Tacitus in a parallel position for those who wrote in Latin.[33] Although he has a taste for excerpting rather prosaic

[29] For example, see the strained use of Thucydides in the rebuttal of Maxim 23 at Gentillet 1576: 502.

[30] Zincgref 1619, sig. Bb1^r, the call for intervention becoming legible in the immediate context of its citation. In 1618, the nobles of Bohemia rebelled against the new Catholic king, Ferdinand, a conflict generally understood as the beginning of the Thirty Years' War. In the following year, the Calvinist Frederick V, head of the Protestant Union and of the Palatinate (the Electoral Palatinate of the Rhine, a territory of the Holy Roman Empire), accepted their offer of the throne of Bohemia. The Holy Roman Empire, the Catholic League and above all Spain responded by seizing control of the Palatinate during the next few years. As we will see addressed by Bacon and Hobbes later in this chapter, this led many in Protestant countries to push for military intervention against Spain and her allies to liberate the Palatinate and contain the Imperial–Spanish threat. His fate dependent on that of the Protestant Palatinate, Zincgref encourages intervention against encroaching tyranny while also criticizing expansionism, e.g., in Zincgref 2011 [1626]: 51 (Apophthegm 112).

[31] Zincgref 1619, sig. [F4]^r.   [32] In the following, I draw on Hoekstra 2012.

[33] Lipsius 2004: 732–4 (in the 'notes', printed with the *Politica* from 1590). The two Greeks Lipsius here singles out as superior are Thucydides and Polybius; his Latin list is topped by Tacitus, Sallust and Livy. He says that Sallust would have been first of the Latin writers had his work survived entire, and he refrains from saying more on the basis that his praise

sayings, Lipsius does not read Thucydides so crudely as do some of his predecessors. For example, rather than routinely cutting a phrase from one of the speakers and telling us that it has the authority of 'Thucydides', he generally distinguishes the speaker – though evidently to mark off those worthy to be authorities (mostly Archidamus, Brasidas and above all Pericles, 'most prudent Athenian') from those unworthy.[34] So Lipsius says that Cleon is 'lying' when he asserts that 'most dangerous to ruling [*Imperio*] are compassion, flattery, and lenity', recommending instead 'calm power' and forgiveness of the afflicted.[35] And he denounces as wicked Euphemus' doctrine that 'for a ruling man or city nothing is unjust that is advantageous', preferring the view of Xenophon and Cicero that the true riches for a prince are virtue and justice.[36]

When Lipsius does quote 'Thucydides', however, this is not always because the historian has spoken in his own voice. So he simply gives Thucydides – rather than Cleon – as the source of the observation that those who are duller generally administer the commonwealth better than those who are sharper.[37] That he does not credit Cleon with this maxim may suggest that Lipsius wishes to detach a thought of which he approves from a character of whom he disapproves. He does the same elsewhere, however, with a quotation from Diodotus.[38] It seems he is in each case elevating what he regards as an underlying truth about politics, identifying both political teachings as 'arcana' (secrets or hidden doctrines).[39] These 'arcana' are hardly mysterious or enigmatic, though they may count as paradoxical in the Renaissance sense of being unconventional. Lipsius seems to have something deeper in mind, however, when he says that Thucydides is 'everywhere secretly [*occulte*] instructing, and guiding one's life and actions'.[40] Thucydides instructs everywhere, so the teaching is to be found throughout,

for Sallust is the same that he has supplied for Thucydides. (As the works of Tacitus and Livy are also extant only in part, Sallust seems disqualified from primacy because not *enough* of his work survives.)

[34] The reference to Pericles ('*prudentissimus Atheniensium*') is in Lipsius 2004: 556.

[35] Lipsius 2004: 330 (re. Thucydides 3.40.3).

[36] Lipsius 2004: 320, referring to the pronouncement in Thucydides 6.85.1 as '*Malitioso*'. As usual, Lipsius gives the Greek, his '*iniustum*' here translating *alogon*.

[37] Lipsius 2004: 356, from Cleon in Thucydides 3.37.3. Others who cite this popular passage include Montaigne, Botero, Gentili and Hobbes.

[38] Cf. Lipsius 2004: 368, citing Thucydides 3.42.6.

[39] Jan Waszink (in Lipsius 2004: esp. 88, 201) argues that Lipsius was a reason-of-state theorist invested in *arcana imperii* who nonetheless eschewed such language to elude its Machiavellian associations. Yet Lipsius does explicitly identify *arcana* of government, though intriguingly solely from Thucydides (cf. also Lipsius 2004: 360, re. Tacitus *about* such *arcana*).

[40] Lipsius 2004: 732 ('*occulte ubique instruens, actiones vitamque dirigens*').

not only in the precepts, speeches or authorial pronouncements; and he instructs secretly, thus his instruction is not even reducible to what is stated in the text.

Lipsius ultimately allows for the legitimacy of 'reason-of-state' policies, including some kinds of deception, territorial expansion and preventative attack, but when he draws on Thucydides it is generally for moderate moral counsel. Alberico Gentili (1552–1608) specifically commends Lipsius for authorizing preventative military attack, but unlike Lipsius, he associates this position with Thucydides. (Gentili was publishing *De iure belli* in instalments while Lipsius brought out subsequent editions of his *Politica*; the *De iure belli* was published in complete form in 1598.) The special authority Gentili accords to Thucydides is readily seen in the unfolding of his discussion of prevention, where he considers Cicero's argument that to accept the principle that one may attack another for fear of attack would lead to the unacceptable result that everyone will always be in danger of attack. To overcome Cicero's authoritative endorsement of this moderate position, Gentili appeals to the especially valuable opinion of Thucydides, 'an eminent and wise man'.[41] 'Yet the reply of the Mytilenians to the Athenians was right', he writes, quoting Thucydides:

> If we seem to any one unjust, because we revolted first, without waiting until we knew clearly whether they would do us any harm, such a man does not consider well; ... since they always have the opportunity of doing harm, we ought to have the privilege of anticipating our defense.[42]

It may be that all are in greater danger if they understand that anticipation or prevention is legitimate, but it remains the case that if a commonwealth is likely to be harmed and it is safer to anticipate than to delay, then they may legitimately anticipate. This is sanctioned by the fundamental right of self-preservation. 'Defense is in accordance with the law of nature and of God, has the consent of all nations, is born with the world, and is destined to endure so long as the world lasts; and this no civil nor canon law can annul.'[43] Already in 1587, Gentili had cited the passage from Thucydides where the Plataeans argue that in attacking the Thebans they were justly avenging an injury, and that 'by the Law of all Nations it is lawfull to repell

---

[41] Gentili 1933: 2:63/1:100–1.

[42] Gentili 1933: 2:63/1:101, quoting Thucydides 3.12.2–3 (substituting 'right' for 'reasonable' in the translation of Gentili's judgement ('*rectè*')).

[43] Gentili 1933: 2:312/1:507. Gentili illustrates this with Pericles' position that in the name of self-defence it would even be licit to melt the gold from the statue of the goddess for the war effort (Thucydides 2.13.5).

an assailing enemy'.[44] Gentili does not reflect on Thucydides' presentation of the initial assault as having come about because 'the *Thebans* foreseeing the Warre, desired to praeoccupate *Plataea*, (which was alwayes at variance with them) whilest there was yet Peace, and the Warre not openly on foot'.[45] Yet when he maintains that what this 'common law of all' sanctions is not only a right of defence but a right of conquest, he appears to provide a justification for the Theban aggression that had justified the Plataean attack.[46]

Like Lipsius, Gentili cites Thucydides dozens of times on a range of topics. In Thucydides' text he finds a distinction of war from brigandage, examples of religious motives for war, evidence of the Greek prohibition of killing suppliants and a delineation of different kinds of alliance; he also appeals to Thucydides when discussing the status of refugees, punishment for seizure of property, the legitimacy of a prince's defence of the subjects of another prince, illegitimate construals of the terms of an agreement, rights over hostages, burial of the enemy, claims to conquered territory, what is due to captives, whether the adjacent sea is included in a dominion and more. In many cases, Thucydides is brought in to provide authoritative backup for a stated position. But authorities can disagree, and it is notable that his encomium of Thucydides as an especially weighty authority comes when he uses him as a trump in his argument in favour of anticipatory attack.

By contrast, even in the cold-eyed *De iure praedae* of 1608, Hugo Grotius (1583–1645) cites Thucydides for the traditional just war position that war is only legitimate in response to an injury.[47] He also appeals to Thucydides to uphold constraints on just war, in particular the condition that one party may proceed only if the other refuses to reach a judicial settlement of the dispute.[48] In the *De iure belli ac pacis*, too, Grotius works from the position – now ascribed to Augustine – that 'a just cause for undertaking a war can be nothing other than injury'.[49] Whereas in the *De iure praedae* Grotius had relied on Cleon to argue for the *necessity* of punishing the one who has committed injustice, however, by the time of the 1631 edition of the *De iure belli ac pacis* he takes seriously Diodotus' response that punishment should not be meted out even to a guilty party unless some good will result.[50]

[44] Gentili 1587: 29, quoting Thucydides 3.56.2 (English here from Hobbes 1629: 174).
[45] Hobbes 1629: 82 (Thucydides 2.2.3).   [46] Gentili 1587: 29.
[47] Leiden, UL, BPL 917, fol. 54ʳ (ch. 9), where Grotius quotes Thucydides 1.120. I refer to this manuscript as from 1608, as the date by which it was likely complete, but it was largely drafted years earlier; for details, see van Ittersum 2009.
[48] Leiden, UL, BPL 917, fol. 44ᵛ (ch. 8), quoting Thucydides 1.85.2.
[49] Grotius 1625: 123.
[50] Compare Leiden, UL, BPL 917, fols 146ʳ and 149ᵛ (and Grotius 1625: 399) with Grotius 1631: 289.

Like most who argue from the requirement of precedent injury, Grotius expands the category or extends beyond it in specific ways. Grotius commends Thucydides for the view that some actions are necessitated by our nature and thus not to be punished, and he stands close to Gentili and others when he emphasizes that the natural principle of self-preservation may entail the legitimacy of attack even when it is not a response to an aggressor's injustice.[51]

Having let his argument run beyond the opening position that war can only be justified as punishment of injury, Grotius enlists Thucydides to rein it back in. For the prevention of injury to be a just cause, 'imminent, and nearly immediate, danger is required'; I may not anticipate another simply because he arms himself, but may do so if he arms himself with a manifest intention to kill me and I am unable to rely on an authority to protect me.[52] In support, he lifts the quotation from Cicero that Gentili had used in weighing the question of anticipation.[53] But instead of appealing to Thucydides to outrank and countermand Cicero, Grotius enlists Thucydides alongside him as a *critic* of an overly permissive right of anticipation based on fear. Rather than invoking the speech of the Mytilenians in the third book, he offers a passage from Book 1 against acting on the basis of uncertain future threats, and then he joins Thucydides in condemning those caught up in the Corcyrean civil war who pre-empted the future misdeeds of others by doing evil themselves.[54]

Grotius explicitly targets Gentili's argument justifying prevention. He objects that 'some propound what is intolerable: that according to the law of nations it is right to take up arms to reduce a growing power which expanding too much could harm us'.[55] Grotius concedes that such a measure may be expedient but denies that this expediency justifies. 'Defence against uncertain fear is to be sought from divine providence and from harmless precautions, not from force.'[56] The Spartans failed to meet this criterion of just war: 'Thucydides holds that the true cause of the Peloponnesian war was the Athenians' growing power and the Lacedaemonians' mistrust.'[57] Such 'fear of a neighbouring power is not a sufficient cause', however: 'for to be just, defence must be necessary, which it is not unless it is known that the other has not only sufficient power, but also the intention' to attack; and this conviction must amount to a 'moral certainty'.[58] Although he argues for the

---

[51] Grotius 1625: 420.   [52] Grotius 1625: 125.   [53] Grotius 1625: 126.
[54] Grotius 1625: 126, rendering Thucydides 1.42.2 and 3.82.5.
[55] Grotius 1625: 136, where the marginal annotation is 'Alb Gent. lib. I.c.14'.
[56] Grotius 1625: 136.   [57] Grotius 1625: 467, referring to Thucydides 1.23.6.
[58] Grotius 1625: 468.

legitimacy of some aggressive actions abroad, Grotius demonstrates that the text of Thucydides could be used to articulate and insist on limits to such aggression within the framework of the law of nations, and not only of biblically based natural law. In Grotius we can see the civil lawyer adjudicating between the Reformation Thucydides and the reason-of-state Thucydides. This deliberate attempt at balance was unusual, however, and the latter Thucydides came to dominate the discussion.

In 1624, while Grotius was finishing the *De iure belli ac pacis*, Francis Bacon addressed a manuscript essay to Prince Charles (who became King Charles I in the following March) in which he argued that just apprehensions *are* a legitimate ground of war even if one has not suffered an injury. He focuses on the criterion of *'iust Feare of the Subuersion of our Ciuill Estate'* and argues that it has far-reaching implications for his country's foreign policy.[59] The validity of this justification means that war must be waged with Spain 'not for the *Palatinate* onely, but for *England*, *Scotland*, *Ireland*, our *King*, our *Prince*, our *Nation*, all that we haue'. To show that a war on foreign soil is tantamount to self-defence, Bacon says that he must prove 'that a *iust Feare*, (without an Actuall Inuasion or Offence,) is a sufficient Ground of a *War*, and in the Nature of a true *Defensiue*'.[60] Integral to that proof is an appeal to the authority of Thucydides.

> [I]t is good to heare what time saith. *Thucydides*, in his *Inducement* to his Story of the great *Warre* of *Peloponnesus*, sets downe in plaine termes, that the true Cause of that *Warre* was; *The ouergrowing Greatnesse of the Athenians, and the feare that the Lacedemonians stood in thereby*; And doth not doubt to call it, *A necessity imposed vpon the Lacedemonians of a Warre*: Which are the Words of a meere *Defensiue*: Adding, that the other Causes were but specious and Popular.[61]

Bacon then quotes at some length from Book 1. Thucydides gives us 'what time saith', and although time speaks to both Bacon and Grotius via the same text, the message is antithetical. Bacon takes Thucydides to authorize alignment with the position Gentili had taken and repudiation of traditional positions that still served as important premises for Grotius.

The basic logic of the necessity of prevention, later elaborated in Hobbes' discussion of the state of nature, is a logic that is also forcefully conveyed in

---

[59] Bacon 1629: 13, 4.

[60] Bacon 1629: 12. Bacon takes himself to be quoting the criterion *'iustus metus qui cadit in constantem virum'* from Roman private law (ultimately from Digest 4.2.6 (Gaius)), extending it from individuals to commonwealths, as civil lawyers had frequently done. For context about the Palatinate and the perceived threat of Spain, see n. 30.

[61] Bacon 1629: 13, referring to Thucydides 1.23.6.

popular print. John Reynolds, also in 1624, takes the Athenian rather than the Lacedemonian example as warrant for war, urging Parliament to tell old King James 'that old *Pericles* made the greatnesse of his generositie and courage, to reuiue and flourish on his Tombe, when hee caused the *Athenians* to warre vpon the *Pelloponessians* ... Tell him that to transport Warre into *Spaine*, is to auoide and preuent it in *England*.'[62] As is especially common among those who cite snippets from the text or are taken with an impression of Athenian glory, the conclusion is a call to arms: 'Wars, Wars, then ye, (with cheerefull hearts and ioyfull soules) let vs prepare our selues for Warrs.'[63]

When Hobbes was immersed in producing his translation of Thucydides in the mid-1620s, the dominant outlook of the early modern Thucydideans was that of the war party. Given Hobbes' bellicose reputation, we might expect that he shared the view of Bacon, who was also his employer around this time. In interpretive approach, however, Hobbes sounds more like the Lutheran Thucydideans when he writes in his prefatory note 'To the Readers' that 'the History it selfe' instructs not by 'discourses inserted' but by 'the contexture of the Narration'.[64] Hobbes finds Thucydides' instruction less in the claims made in the speeches or in authorial statements – the nearly exclusive sources for bellicose Thucydideans such as Bacon – but in Thucydides' account of what *happens* in the course of the history. Thucydides' teaching, according to Hobbes, is to be found in what is 'meerely narratiue'.[65] Hobbes emphasizes that Thucydides' history has a unity as a whole and should be considered as a single body.[66] Doing so shows that Thucydides criticizes the Athenians 'by the necessity of the narration, not by any sought digression. So that no word of his, but their own actions do sometimes reproach them ... So cohaerent, perspicuous and perswasiue is the whole Narration.'[67] Hobbes quotes Lipsius' commenda-tion of Thucydides for 'euery where secretly instructing, and directing a mans life and actions'.[68] Hobbes' own judgement – which also recalls the Lutheran view that the wisdom of Thucydides is revealed in the *euentus* or outcomes – is similar: 'open conueyances of Precepts (which is the Philosophers part) he neuer vseth, as hauing so cleerely set before mens eyes, the wayes and euents, of good and euill counsels, that the Narration it selfe doth secretly instruct the Reader, and more effectually then possibly can be

---

[62] [Reynolds] 1624, sig. B[1]ᵛ.   [63] Ibid., sig. B2ʳ.

[64] Hobbes 1629, sig. A3ʳ. As we saw, the Melanchthonians also looked to Thucydides for authoritative maxims, so in this sense Hobbes goes further in prioritizing the narrative. For a more complete version of what follows, see Hoekstra 2016.

[65] Hobbes 1629, sig. A3ʳ.   [66] Ibid., sig. a4ʳ.   [67] Ibid., sigs. a2ᵛ–a3ʳ.

[68] Ibid., sig. b1ʳ. Cf. n. 40.

done by Precept'.[69] What, then, is the secret instruction that Thucydides reveals in his narration of events?

Hobbes argues that 'men profit more by looking on aduerse euents, then on prosperity. Therefore by how much mens miseries doe better instruct, then their good successe, by so much was *Thucydides* more happy in taking his Argument, then *Herodotus* was wise in chusing his.'[70] The kernel of Thucydides' instruction is what his readers can learn from the 'euents, of good and euill counsels' and the Athenian actions that result in failure and misery.

Hobbes criticizes the Athenian leaders who flattered the people's pride in their commonwealth and thereby drove the Athenians 'headlong into those actions that were to ruine them'.[71] This sets up a parallel between the Athenians' disastrous expedition to Sicily and the proposals by Bacon and other members of the war party to venture against Spain, thus breaking with the more conservative policy of James I in favour of the aggressive adventuring promoted by his son Charles. Pericles tells the Athenians early in the war that they may prevail so long as 'you doe not ... striue to enlarge your dominion, and vndergoe other voluntary dangers'; Hobbes comments that '*Thucydides* hath his mind here, upon the Defeat in *Sicily*, which fell out many yeares after the death of *Pericles*'.[72] Hobbes' Thucydides teaches that the Athenians would have been saved had they continued to follow the more cautious policy of the leader whom Hobbes characterized as a wise monarch (a Pericles markedly different from both the proud, imprudent and bellicose figure condemned by the Melanchthonians and from the Pericles praised by the likes of Reynolds, who procures safety, glory and greatness by taking Athens to war). The Athenians instead followed the counsel of Pericles' glory-seeking ward, Alcibiades, and embarked on a devastating expedition abroad. So it is that Thucydides presents Hobbes' readers with the instructive 'euents, of good and euill counsels'.

Gentili and Bacon used Thucydides to justify preventative attack. In his later works, Hobbes proposed an abstract version of this justification in his argument about the state of nature, a condition of war between free individuals or sovereign states. But this abstract argument was the starting point of his philosophy of peace and the preservation of the people. And his edition of Thucydides should be seen as consistent with this end, issuing a vivid warning to and about those who threatened the peace.

---

[69] Ibid., sig. a3ʳ; see sigs. A3ᵛ and a4ᵛ.
[70] Hobbes 1629, sig. a3ᵛ (responding to Dionysius of Halicarnassus).   [71] Ibid., sig. a1ᵛ.
[72] Ibid.: 78 (Thucydides 1.144.1).

Hobbes sees in Thucydides a cautionary history fitted to the politics of his own times, as well as a model for his own actions. Hobbes' position in the 1620s is a precarious one, reflected in his description of those who disagreed when the party for expanding the war had grown powerful in Athens: 'the good men either durst not oppose, or if they did, vndid themselues'.[73] He immediately goes on to tell us that Thucydides' own way out of this dilemma was to avoid the usual political arena and focus on the writing of his history.[74] 'It is therefore no maruell, if he meddled as little as he could, in the businesse of the Common-wealth, but gaue himselfe rather to the obseruation and recording of what was done by those that had the mannaging thereof.'[75] Hobbes, too, focuses on that history while much of the public and many of the powerful, including his patrons, are spoiling for a fight that could lead to England's ruin, and on his understanding of how Thucydides was able to influence the influential without undoing himself.

Reflecting on the demagogues who drove Athens into intervening abroad and apparently also on the warmongering politics of the parliaments of the early 1620s, Hobbes writes: 'such men onely swayed the Assemblies, and were esteemed wise and good Common-wealths men, as did put them vpon the most dangerous and desperate enterprizes'.[76] Reflecting, it seems, on the plight of those like Hobbes himself as well as Thucydides, he observes the risks faced by those who instead gave 'temperate, and discreet aduice'.[77] In Thucydides, Hobbes found a model of prudent political action through writing. What Hobbes offers to his patrons and proposes to publish is a translation of a work by someone else, about other times, with a helpful apparatus and plenty of encouragement to read the work through and consider the arc of the narrative and what it reveals about the policies that led to the Athenians' miseries and defeat. Hobbes reckons that the way to intervene most effectively in contemporary politics is to let Thucydides speak for himself.

Thucydides was salient in the Renaissance for his moral, prudential, political and military counsel, though he also figured in assessments of how to write history, in catalogues of rhetorical modes and materials and in many other discussions. Because of his reputation for a rare truthfulness and discernment, Thucydides spoke with great authority to those at the head of state, though such counsels turned out to be as varied as those of a

---

[73] Hobbes 1629, sig. a1ᵛ.

[74] Ibid.: Thucydides 'forbore to come into the Assemblies, and propounded to himselfe, a priuate life ...'. Hobbes immediately goes on to discuss Thucydides' views about 'the gouernment of the State', so he does not take a focus on writing in the context of a private life to preclude writing about public or political matters.

[75] Ibid., sig. a2ʳ.　　[76] Ibid., sig. a1ᵛ.　　[77] Ibid.

fractious assembly. The amplitude of Thucydides' text, disparate approaches to reading it and divergent assumptions about what in it constituted exemplary wisdom or action all combined to ensure that an inexhaustible work inspired a variety of resourceful interpretations.

Further Reading

Pade 2003 is a meticulous inventory of the editions, translations and commentaries up to the beginning of the 17th century. Accounts of Thucydides in this period are in Cambiano 2000, Pade 2006, Pires 2007, and Iglesias-Zoido 2011; a number of chapters relevant to the period may also be found in Fromentin et al. 2010 and Lee and Morley 2015. Single-author approaches to the broader reception are Meister 2013 and Morley 2014. On the Renaissance use of Thucydides to promote military intervention, see Hoekstra 2012. On the Lutheran Thucydides, see Richards 2013. On Hobbes' Thucydides, see especially Iori 2015, Warren 2015: ch. 5, and Hoekstra 2016.

18

ALEXANDRA LIANERI

Narratives of Thucydides and the 19th-Century Discipline of (Ancient) History

> We cannot simply see time pass: it passes *by (means of) us*. The past traverses us and comes to haunt the present in such a way that no present, no moment, no epoch, can be homogeneous. This jeopardizes the possibility of opposing the past to a present that would now be *our own*.
>
> Sylviane Agacinski, *Time Passing: Modernity and Nostalgia*, 2003
> (emphasis in original)

The Paradox of Thucydides' Historiographical Modernity

'What I think is typically Greek is the critical attitude towards the recording of events, that is, the development of critical methods enabling us to distinguish between facts and fancies.'[1] With this statement, Arnaldo Momigliano, in his seminal essay 'The Herodotean and the Thucydidean Tradition', questioned historiographical genealogies that set the beginning of the critical historical method in the 19th century. His argument was that the critical component of the modern discipline was to be identified in antiquity's passing into modern historical thought, and particularly what he called the Thucydidean tradition. At the same time, Momigliano was painstakingly suspicious of fictions of origin and strived to unmask their role in authorizing present concepts of history: there was a 'nineteenth-century cult for Thucydides', he wrote, which 'we have inherited'.[2]

This reflexive perspective – at once attentive to antiquity's modern presences and critical of the foundational discourses of Western historical consciousness – foregrounds Thucydides' 19th-century reception as a key

I am grateful to Richard Armstrong, Polly Low and Antonios Rengakos for their critical comments on previous versions of this chapter.

[1] Momigliano 1990: 30.   [2] Momigliano 1990: 50. See also Momigliano 1984, 2012.

moment for modern historical thought. The institutionalization of history as a university discipline involved the consideration of Thucydides as a predecessor of historical science by historians ranging from Barthold Georg Niebuhr, Leopold von Ranke and Wilhelm Roscher to George Grote, Thomas Arnold, Eduard Meyer and J. B. Bury, among others.[3] But what made it possible for such canonical figures of the modern discipline to hail Thucydides as 'the father of all true history', a 'jewel of historiography' and a 'modern',[4] at the very moment they set out to formulate their new critical methods and theory of historical study? How can we account for Thucydides' powerful modern presence from a perspective that has also dispelled foundational narratives of history-writing that presume a developmental link between ancient historiography and modern European historical consciousness?

My concern is with approaching Thucydides' reception in the light of what seems to be a fundamental paradox of the 19th-century discipline of history, to which we are still heirs: that Greek and Roman historiographical classics maintained a vital – even though conceptually ambiguous – modern presence, even, or particularly, when their key concepts, methods and perspectives on history and historical time were identified as bygone and obsolete. What are we to make of this transtemporal time-passing? If past time, as Sylviane Agacinski writes, passes to the present by means of us, and through this move jeopardizes the economy of what we recognize as 'our own' history and historical worldview, the paradox of Thucydides' time-passing invites us to interrupt the boundaries and limits through which the 19th-century disciplinization of historical practice has allowed us to understand professional history-writing.

In this chapter I examine the interruptive force of Thucydides' modern presence by focusing on moments when this form of time-passing presents itself unevenly and incoherently. I study the constitution of the 19th-century turn to Thucydides as a fundamental but also ambivalent intellectual basis for the self-positing of the historical discipline as science. My point of departure is how Thucydides' history operated 'as a kind of midwife of modern historical science', as Ulrich Muhlack phrases it, prompting historians to test and clarify their own concepts.[5] It needs to be noted, however, that the outcome of this engagement was not a methodologically coherent paradigm but a fuzzy network of contested concepts, to use W. B. Gallie's term,[6] highlighting tensions and antinomies in modern historical thinking. In the following pages,

---

[3] Murari Pires 2006a; Muhlack 2011; Morley 2012. See also Süßmann 2012; Lianeri 2015.
[4] Murari Pires 2006a; Muhlack 2011; Morley 2012, 2014.   [5] Muhlack 2011: 180.
[6] Gallie 1956.

I focus on a specific manifestation of these antinomies. I study the role of Thucydides in the 19th-century delimitation of modern historiography as 'science' through a twofold conceptual and narrative gesture: first, the construal of Thucydides' 'critical' history as a founding moment of the modern discipline and its particular claim to an objective understanding of the past; and second, the positioning of Thucydides against the background of a dual narrative of ancient and modern historiography and historical time, on the basis of which the discipline sought to establish its methodological objectivity. In the end, my interest is in nodes of tension and contestation created by the interweaving of these narratives and the ways they both affirmed and challenged history's claims to autonomization and disciplinary boundaries.

In order to explore this multilayered narrative structure, I draw on Allan Megill's configuration of distinct narrative types, which underpinned the self-positing of the modern discipline of history and its claims to an authoritative, objective understanding of past time. The historical accounts in question may thus be divided into: (1) *master narratives*, which claim to offer an account of some particular segment of history, as was, for instance, the history of Greek and Roman historiography; (2) *grand narratives*, which claim to offer an authoritative account of history generally – what we may designate as 'History' – in which master narratives are inscribed; and (3) *metanarratives*, most commonly belief in God or in a rationality somehow immanent in the world, which serve to justify the grand narrative.[7] According to Megill, professional scientific historiography has presupposed the existence but not necessarily the telling of a single and coherent grand narrative of History and historical time, towards which its particular understanding of the past would converge. The Enlightenment tradition of universal history, shaping Kant's essay 'Idea for a Universal History from a Cosmopolitan Point of View' (1784) and sustained by Schiller's and Hegel's philosophies of history, was grounded in the assumption that 'there is a single History and we already know what it is'. That is to say, there is a metanarrative principle – such as reason – that will render the itinerary of History legible when used for the understanding of the events of the past. But such a conviction, Megill argues, deprived historical practice of its rationale, for it involved only research as to whether a philosophical principle could be demonstrated, not an enquiry into what the past was about. Formulated against this attitude, 19th-century historical science upheld the idea that even though there is a single 'History', its telling needs to be deferred until further critical research has been done; some even recognized that we may never be

---

[7] Megill 1995: 152–3.

able to tell it in its final form.[8] Hence, for example, the philosophical school in Berlin centred around Hegel held that reason determines the ends and laws of history. By contrast, the historical school centred around Schleiermacher – including Savigny, Eichhorn, Niebuhr and subsequently Ranke – argued that reason had no such *a priori* determined power;[9] but members of this school nonetheless retained faith that a universal outline of historical time could be discovered.

Significantly, the deferral of a conclusive grand narrative of History required a commitment of historians to an idea of method, which served itself to justify the discipline's autonomy. Thucydides was then called upon to represent the foundations of this commitment. On the basis of appeals to his method and objective recording of events, Thucydides 'was read increasingly ... as the founder of critical historiography (in contrast with the credulity of Herodotus) and even ... as the inventor of history as science'.[10] In Niebuhr's words: 'the first real and true historian, according to our notion, was Thucydides: as he is the most perfect historian among all that have ever written, so he is at the same time the first: he is the Homer of historians'.[11] At the same time, appeals to historical totality and the unity of a single History were not erased. They were formulated as the functions of a reconfigured historical perspective that negotiated the modern temporality of the explosive and profoundly transforming present with the attempt to impose an overall coherence upon historical time through the construction of a single History. Reinhart Koselleck traced both temporalities in late 18th-century European, and especially German, thought: on the one hand, there was an understanding of modernity through the notion of new and unrepeatable time; and on the other, there was the configuration of a concept of history as a 'collective singular', a totalizing narrative implying that the plural 'context of action was incorporated into the knowledge' of the story of the past – that is to say, implying the convergence of *res gestae* (that is, things done) and *historia rerum gestarum* (the history of things done). This notion stood in contrast with previous conceptions of history in the plural as *Geschichten* (histories).[12] Appeals to singular History remained central to the self-understanding of historical science until the beginning of the 20th century, manifesting as belief in a grand narrative or partial attempts to construct it; this in turn allowed historians to legitimate their conviction that their understanding of the past is an objective representation connected to the standpoint of History itself.[13]

---

[8] Megill 1995: 158–9; see also Iggers 2011; Zammito 2015.
[9] Beiser 2011a: 258–9, 2011b; Iggers 2011.   [10] Harloe and Morley 2012a: 9.
[11] Niebuhr 1852a: vol. I, 169.
[12] Koselleck 2002: 112–13. See also Călinescu 1987; Osborne 1995.
[13] Krieger 1989; Megill 1995.

Where does Thucydides stand in narratives seeking at once to identify his methodological commitment to unrepeatable events of the past and to configure a story of ancient historiography and historical time? Such a question is important not only for the understanding of the past of (our) professional historical practice, but also because it still bears upon the larger question of the significance of historical scholarship in the larger intellectual map of human and social sciences. Thucydides' role in the genealogical discourses and narratives of the discipline was ambiguous. On the one hand, the configuration of a master narrative of ancient and modern Western historiography affirmed his position as the first scientific historian. On the other hand, the need to sustain this story by relating it to a grand narrative of History – a narrative claiming to demonstrate the processual temporal connections and parallels between antiquity and European modernity – remained in conflict not only with Thucydides' temporal perspective, but also with the modern methodological commitment to historical critique, as well as the sense of the estrangement of the past and the division of historical time. By studying these conflicts, I seek to explore Thucydides' role in 19th-century debates about historical science and the specificity of the discipline of (ancient) history, while simultaneously foregrounding pathways firstly between historiography and philosophy of history; secondly between historical science's narrative, literary and rhetorical components; and thirdly between history-writing and politics.

Narratives of Thucydides and Western Historiography; or Where Does the Time of the 'Historical' Begin?

The conceptual limits and institutional borders of professional historiography began to be set in the first decades of the 19th century by the configuration of history as science – a label that was meant to unify a set of methodological principles and a theory of history justifying the autonomy of the discipline: its emancipation from the authority of ancient historians and the paradigm of *historia magistra vitae* (history as the guide to life); its dissociation from rhetoric, theology and jurisprudence; and its distinction from the fields of philosophy of history, ethnography and anthropology.[14] The critical evaluation of sources, as a method advanced by archival research, comparison and contestation of the truth of documentary evidence, was central to this process of disciplinization. The scientific approach to history was formulated in association with Ranke, but also with reference to

---

[14] Koselleck 2004: 26–42; Wang and Fillafer 2007; Beiser 2011a: 70–1.

his predecessor and historian of antiquity, Niebuhr, the first professor of history at the new University of Berlin in 1810, whose critical examination of Roman history was reconfigured by Ranke for the modern period.[15] This approach was understood as historiography based on the strict reconstruction of the 'facts' of the past as they emerged through a critical examination of evidence (the sources), avoiding at once the moral judgements, the rhetorical repertoire of *historia magistra vita* and recourse to theory: that is to say, a commitment to strict 'objectivity', in the sense of holding to the facts of history, along the lines of which Ranke's famous dictum *'wie es eigentlich gewesen'* ('how it really was') was perceived.[16]

Historians of classical reception have noted how this famous phrase already echoes Thucydides' reflections about historiographical accuracy in 1.22 and 2.48.3, with some arguing that Ranke drew directly on the statement of the latter passage ('I shall tell it as it happened'), which he translated.[17] As translation, however, inevitably involves interpretation of meaning, such an observation can only reaffirm the inscription of Thucydides in the self-positing of modern historical science. It cannot answer the question of what his legacy meant to modern historians. At the most immediate level, answers to this question are to be sought in Thucydides' legitimating authority in academic institutions still dominated by the status of classical studies. Aviezer Tucker is therefore not wrong in arguing that Thucydides' name was evoked by modern theorists of historical science 'rhetorically, to convince': Ranke characterized him as 'the ultimate master historian', with the intention of making his own radically novel ideas fit with established models.[18] On the other hand, we may note how Thucydides' 19th-century apotheosis, to use Francisco Murari Pires' term,[19] offered no immediate basis of self-legitimation, as it involved a conflict with the established canon of classical historiography. Thucydides had been largely marginalized by the Enlightenment and the 1789 generation in favour of Plutarch and Polybius,[20] and he was ultimately 'rescued ... in the eleventh hour' by Herodotus' admirers: 'it was not until the second part of the eighteenth century ... that the general climate of opinion began to change to the definite advantage of [Thucydides]'.[21] Even though the precise moment of this shift is contested, the distance between, say, Voltaire's and Fustel de Coulanges' lack of attention to Thucydides and the primary role

[15] Iggers 2011.
[16] On the different meanings of the postulate of objectivity, see Megill 1994.
[17] Grafton 1997: 69; Meister 2015: 203.   [18] Tucker 2016: 363.
[19] Murari Pires 2015.   [20] Vidal-Naquet 1990: 230, 2000: 15; Grell 1993; Urbinati 2012.
[21] Momigliano 1990: 50, 49.

attributed to him by Niebuhr and Ranke[22] suggests a turn that cannot be reduced to a merely rhetorical appeal to classical authority. Moreover, as we shall see, it is not merely the appeal to Thucydides but the narrative articulation of the historian's place that was of importance to the modern historical discipline.

Rather than separating appeals to Thucydides' critique from self-defining debates about historical science, I suggest setting them in the centre of such debates. In doing so, I do not seek to affirm Thucydides as Ranke's predecessor but to follow Momigliano's legacy of unmasking historiographical presuppositions of the modern discipline not merely by engagement with its subject matter – historical data – but also by juxtaposing conflicting historical accounts, and especially conflicts over the beginning of historiography. In Chris Lorenz's terms, drawing on Paul Feyerabend: historiographical prejudices are found by contrast, not by analysis.[23] And no contrast has been so prominent and consequential in the modern historical discipline than that underpinning the presence of Thucydides in the genealogies of Western historical thought.

Ranke, who wrote his (now lost) dissertation on Thucydides, claimed the novelty of his endeavour in the very statement that recognized Thucydides as a modern. 'No one', he wrote, 'can have a pretension to be a greater historian than Thucydides. On the other hand, I have the pretension to attempt to achieve something different from the historical writing of the ancients.'[24] Niebuhr's admiration for Thucydides went hand in hand with his call for disengagement from ancient historians, expressed paradigmatically in scrutinizing every word of Livy on the early Roman period and his new account of the subject based on source criticism. In 1903, Bury, successor to Lord Acton as Regius Professor of Modern History at Cambridge and key theorist of historical science in Britain, gave his inaugural lecture on 'The Science of History'. This work emphatically acknowledged Niebuhr and Ranke as the key theorists of scientific method whose event-focused practice Bury contrasted with Thucydides' and Polybius' notion of *historia magistra vitae*, which jeopardizes the discipline by making it 'no more than the handmaid of social science'.[25] Five years later, Bury's lectures at Harvard on *The Greek Historians* hailed Thucydides for configuring 'a new conception of history writing', for setting up 'a new standard of truth or accurate reproduction of facts, and a new ideal of historical research', but also as 'the founder of "political" history in the special sense in which *we* are accustomed to use the term'.[26]

[22] Payen 2015.   [23] Lorenz 2013.   [24] Ranke 1981: 164.   [25] Bury 1903: 16.
[26] Bury 1958: 78, emphasis added.

This paradoxical presence of the Greek historian never quite dissolved into a mere rhetorical gesture but delimited a *contested node* in the field of modern historiography, a realm of tension that accentuates the ambiguities and prejudices underpinning the discipline's intellectual framing. At the roots of this contestation lies a tradition that was fundamental to Niebuhr's and Ranke's distinct form of historicism: that of German philological criticism, configured by classicists such as Friedrich August Wolf and Gottfried Hermann. Building on Wolf's examination of the Homeric poems in the late 18th century, classical philology of the period insisted that the study of antiquity must rest on *Quellenkritik*, the critical examination of the sources. As this postulate was increasingly deployed to set the terms for a new holistic science of antiquity (*Altertumswissenschaft*), philology came to be characterized by a fundamental conflict: between the methodological principle of source-critical investigation and the inclusion of a wide variety of source materials (beyond classical texts) on the one side and the quest for a coherent and totalizing narrative of antiquity on the other. The notion of *Altertumswissenschaft* as unified field of research was then predicated at once on critical method and on supposing the historical unity of its object – in other words, the narrative configuration of antiquity's temporal coherence and geographical totality, which meant that the boundaries of philological science would exclude both the broad field of 'prehistory' and the 'Orient'.[27] In the phrasing of the 'Postclassicisms Collective', the autonomy of *Altertumswissenschaft* was guaranteed by the uneasy conjunction of the idealization of the ancient world as a temporal unity and its methodological reconstruction as 'a heap of fragmentary remains'.[28]

The multifarious impact of late 18th-century classical philology upon the modern discipline of history is a story that has still to be told.[29] Niebuhr, who lectured in Berlin alongside Wolf, in 1827 described Wolf's *Prolegomena to Homer* as 'those wonderworthy investigations in which the higher branch of criticism reached its perfection'.[30] The historian of Rome not only applied the critical methods of the *Prolegomena* to his study of Roman history, but also drew on the particular historical worldview underpinning the philological science of antiquity: the idea that the classical past was no longer transparent to the present but consisted of textual and material remains, out of which the unity of antiquity's story had to be

---

[27] Grafton 1985; Harloe 2013.   [28] Postclassicisms Collective 2020: 34.

[29] On philology's reconfiguration as science of antiquity, see the important work of Harloe 2013, as well as reflections on the topic in Goldhill 2011; Turner 2014.

[30] Niebuhr (1827), 'Die Sikeler in der Odyssee', *Rheinisches Museum* 1: 257; quoted in Grafton 1985: 28.

extracted. In addition to Niebuhr, Ranke learned much from the critical methods and theory of philology from Hermann;[31] while in Britain, Bury identified Wolf's book as the single source of historical science, which 'gave historians the idea of a systematic and minute method of analysing their sources'.[32] In the next section, I approach the paradox of Thucydides' historiographical modernity through the philological tension between the methodological appeal to source criticism and the deployment of an *a priori* principle of totality and narrative coherence through which the *Altertumswissenschaft* reconstructed the story of antiquity. Accounts of Thucydides were uneasily entangled between disciplinary genealogies of critical method and reconstructions of a unified story of historiography. These were apparently centred on the relics of the past, but ultimately posited a totality of History that was greater than its constitutive parts, in that it evoked a metanarrative of time that served to justify the distinct relationship between classical antiquity and European modernity.

Thucydides as Historiographical Paradigm and Historical Relic

Configuring Thucydides as the founder of historical science entailed tracing in his work the critical postulates that affirmed the discipline's methodological boundaries. So Niebuhr praised the ancient historian for using a precise dating system, for recording events with caution and after careful critical examination, for scrutinizing information as regards its authenticity and for adding nothing to the historical records, considering it 'unnecessary to do more than to make [these] known'.[33] According to this assessment, also shared by the leading practitioners of the new discipline,[34] Thucydides may have occasionally erred, but 'it is inconceivable that he should anywhere have taken up and published mere fancies'.[35] Ranke and Roscher in Germany, but also Thomas Arnold, Grote and Bury in Britain, viewed Thucydides through the lens of contemporary debates on method, emphasizing his critical enquiry while explaining away aspects of the *History* that were not compatible with modern historical method.[36]

Niebuhr praised Thucydides for his focus on the evidentiary realm and for presenting the truth of events beyond the rhetorical or paradigmatic uses of history. Yet, when he engaged with the main thematic of Thucydides' narrative, the Peloponnesian War, the commanding role of events collapsed under the voice of the historian narrating them. As Niebuhr wrote, 'The

---

[31] Iggers 2011: xvii.   [32] Bury 1903: 10–11.   [33] Niebuhr 1852a: vol. I, 169.
[34] Muhlack 2011; Morley 2012; Meister 2015.   [35] Niebuhr 1852a: vol. I, 169.
[36] Muhlack 2011; Morley 2012.

Peloponnesian War ... is the most immortal of all wars, because it is described by the greatest of all historians that ever lived.'[37] This is an eloquent if ambivalent apprehension of the primacy of the historian's voice over the past: in Koselleck's terms, an inscription of the plural context of *res gestae* into historical narrative. Phrasing his appraisal in a sonorous appeal to Thucydides' diachronic value, Niebuhr indicated that the *History* retains its grandeur as a historiographical endeavour. But this declaration constituted something of a rupture in the modern paradigm of historical science. Setting the debate on method within an immortal timeline of historiography inaugurated by Thucydides, the phrase foregrounds the Peloponnesian War as an event that was uniquely important not in its own right, but because it attracted the greatest ever historian, the one at the origin of history-writing. Significantly, Hegel, writing from the viewpoint of philosophy of history, made an analogous contention. 'In the Peloponnesian War', he wrote, 'the struggle was essentially between Athens and Sparta. Thucydides has left us the history of the greater part of it, and his immortal work is the absolute gain which humanity has derived from the contest.'[38] Both writers weave Thucydides' achievement into a history of historical consciousness that, as we shall see, becomes part of a larger narrative of History as such. By contrast, Thucydides himself, while never effacing the importance of his gaze and storyline, nonetheless justified his choice of subject matter by appealing to a different order of significance: it was the Peloponnesian War's supreme greatness in comparison with previous wars, he wrote, rather than his authority that made his endeavour worth undertaking.[39]

There is then an irresolvable tension in Niebuhr's shift from the methodological identification of the events of history to a master narrative of historiography going back to Thucydides. At the outset of this narrative Niebuhr set Thucydides' distinctive gaze on the events, which was made to rule over the time of *res gestae*. Thucydides, he wrote, participated in the construction of this gaze with regard to contemporary events of the war, from the assessment of Pericles and the Athenians to the Sicilian Expedition. On the other hand, with regard to early Greek history, the ancient historian did not move beyond appearance, as he had no way of scrutinizing legendary tales and disclosing the events behind their stories – a task that Niebuhr himself felt competent to assume with regard to Livy. Thucydides could only claim historical certainty for a restricted period of his past: 'as far back as the

---

[37] Niebuhr 1852a: vol. II, 34.   [38] Hegel 1861: 277.
[39] Thuc. 1.1.1–3. On the importance of this claim to the magnitude of the subject in earlier phases of Thucydidean reception, see Pitcher (Chapter 15).

beginning of the Olympiads, Thucydides speaks with confidence; but of the earliest times and of all that precedes the Trojan period, he evidently speaks with uncertainty'.[40] On the events of earlier history, however, and particularly 'in regard to the Trojan period, he follows Homer alone, and uses the expression φαίνεται [*phainetai*, "it seems"]'. Consequently, 'his judgment was biased and influenced by the prevailing opinion, or he did not venture publicly to propound his own views respecting the reality of that event'.[41]

Niebuhr's acknowledgement of this rupture echoes Wolf's use of critical philology in the attempt to identify the historicity of Homeric poetry in opposition to assumptions about continuity and the paradigmatic value of classical literature.[42] But it is also indicative of a broader reconfiguration of the idea of history and historical time in the decades after the French Revolution, when the preoccupation of Western thought with lines of division and discontinuity shaped the modern historical worldview. According to Peter Fritzsche, awareness of temporal rupture and the inability to repossess the past manifested as a feeling of loss that turned the past into a problem of knowledge and a great source of disquiet – the past as the 'nagging, unmasterable presence of absence'.[43] One of the most striking implications of this notion of rupture was the attempt to restore life to the darkness of the past through the study of its remains. In this respect, modern historical science, for Niebuhr, involves a component that distinguishes it from Thucydides' history: the standpoint of the enquirer who confronts a strange past, the stories of which are no longer integral elements in the languages of the present; as a result, the available remains of that past need to be reconstructed.

The modern historian approaches these stories through a methodological shift that Stephen Bann placed at around 1800, 'from "specimen" to "relic"', a shift that 'alerts us to a radical change in conceiving' the objects of philology and their relationship to past time insofar as specimens have an exemplary and monumental value, while relics are to be understood as parts of a story of the past.[44] The modern historian is thus one who, 'after gazing for years ... sees the history of mistaken, misrepresented, and forgotten events *rise out of mists and darkness*, and assume substance and shape, ... when by unwearied and conscientious examination he is continually gaining a clearer insight into the *connexion* of all ... parts, and discerns that immediate expression of reality which emanates from life'.[45] This gaze no longer addresses documents and evidence but relics transforming into a

---

[40] Niebuhr 1852a: vol. I, 170.   [41] Niebuhr 1852a: vol. I, 170.
[42] Grafton et al. 1985.   [43] Fritzsche 2001.   [44] Bann 1984: 85–6.
[45] Niebuhr 1831: vol. II, 14, emphasis added.

storyline. The historian mediates the emergence of all *connected* parts, which take form as 'the nymph in the Slavonic tale takes the body of an earthly maiden beneath the yearning gaze of love'.[46] There are certain qualities attributed to this gaze that cannot be derived from the critical engagement with ruins but are predicated on the ability to unveil the unity of past in the form of narrative coherence. As Richard Armstrong observes, Niebuhr's 'objective gazing' deploys the rhetoric of romance alongside the label of *Wissenschaft*. It thus presupposes a whole gnostic quality of the mind that ultimately manifests itself not only as historical critique, but rather as '*critique and divination*'.[47] It is the premise of both qualities that allows Niebuhr to lay claim to an authoritative historical consciousness by identifying the coherence of historical narrative with the metaphoric unity of the body of History: 'This I may say without arrogance, that he who refuses respect to my *History* deserves none himself.'[48]

Thucydides was made to participate in the modern genealogy of critical historical method but not in this distinctive authority of the historian's gaze over the darkness of the past. Narratives of ancient historiography considered him as a paradigm for the procedural component of historical science but also stressed his distance from the holistic modern narrative of ancient history, which considered Thucydides and his time part of the disordered relics of antiquity. The tension between these lines of reception is of major significance not only for illustrating the diversity of the historian's modern presences, but also as an index of the self-positing of historical science. Who is said to begin a story and the terms in which this beginning is configured, as Edward Said writes, is central to the production of difference from pre-existing traditions, while also authorizing subsequent texts as part of a unified legacy.[49] Of what meaning and value was Thucydides' position in these conflicting stories? What were the traditions from which he was separated and what kind of limits did his *History* set for the modern discipline?

Grand Narratives of Thucydides' *History* and Ancient Historical Time

The moment marked by Thucydides' *History* was formulated as a multi-leveled rupture establishing at once disciplinary, epistemological and political boundaries. As Tim Rood has argued, during the 19th century, Thucydides' work was opposed to Herodotus as a point of transition from ethnography to history, but also as a break with the Herodotean broad cultural canvas of the past, which Thucydides narrowed down to political

---

[46] Ibid.   [47] Armstrong 2005: 174, emphasis in original.
[48] Niebuhr 1852b: 330, emphasis added.   [49] Said 1975: 3.

history.[50] By the same token, Thucydides was made to represent history's dissociation from a rhetorical and literary tradition. According to Niebuhr, Thucydides was to be separated from Herodotus on the basis of a distinction between poetry and prose, setting the elements of form and myth beyond the concerns of the discipline. Herodotus became a transitional figure still expressing a poetic, divine and mythical sense of time: 'his work, therefore, is not an ancient Greek history', Niebuhr contended, 'but has an epic character'.[51] With the exception of 'a few isolated remarks on the origin of nations and tribes', Herodotus passed over several events of early Greece 'in silence', 'has no chronology, which in fact he entirely neglects', and 'received all his traditions about the Greeks from the λόγιοι [logioi]', the logographers whom we must understand 'in the true sense of the term, [as] collectors of traditions of the past. These traditions, however, were not history, but popular and *poetical* stories.'[52]

The narrative of transition from poetry to prose was linked to a narrative of rupture in the ancient world, exploring Thucydides' age as experiencing new temporal structures, through which Niebuhr gathered together in a *single* epochal frame the stories of ancient historiography and historical time. Niebuhr considered the absence of historical consciousness in early Greece as the product of an age in which 'people lived onward, without looking backwards', and those who engaged with the past only did so 'through the medium of traditional and poetical tales'. What divided the poetical from the historical age was the movement towards the critique of traditional stories, but also towards the creation of narrative links between past, present and future. In the age of poetry, Niebuhr noted, men are 'contemplating only in the regions of fantasy and imagination', centred on acts of distinction and 'great exploits of heroism' celebrated in song.[53] In the age of history, 'reflection and thought become prominent', so certain individuals approach the 'two sources from which the sentiments of preceding generations may be discovered, viz. chronological records and traditions'.[54]

This temporality was expanded beyond Greek history by means of an analogy between the ancient and modern European historical consciousness and experience of time. Niebuhr identified the age of Thucydides in fundamentally modern terms, as an epoch of 'progress', 'movement', 'acceleration' and 'development'.[55] As he wrote: 'Even towards the time of the Persian

[50] Rood 2020.   [51] Niebuhr 1852a: vol. I, 168.
[52] Niebuhr 1852a: vol. I, 168, emphasis added.   [53] Niebuhr 1852a: vol. I, 182.
[54] Niebuhr 1852a: vol. I, 182.
[55] Koselleck 2002, 2004 explores the articulation of modernity in the period between 1750 and 1850 as 'new' and accelerated time, involving a sense of disconnection from the past and a sense of an explosive and transformative present giving way to the future.

wars, an increasing acceleration in the movements of life was perceptible; and from that time until the end of the Peloponnesian war, during a period of eighty years, the movement is such that the nation, with incredible rapidity, passes through all stages in literature and in the manifestations of life.'[56] Thucydides' achievement both reflected and grasped this condition of movement and change: 'As the actual life offered so much to relate that could not be related in verse poetical narrative was soon followed by historical narrative, which more easily satisfied the general desire to remember the things that were happening.'[57] Thucydides was linked to the moderns because his historical method reflected the new temporal structures and experience of time that were taking place around him. Niebuhr argued for a similar development of Roman history, which he divided into poetical, transitional and historical periods, and he defended this scheme also by analogy, identifying it as a universal phenomenon across several traditions.[58] In this account there is a significant parallel between the temporality of ancient Greek and modern European histories: the rapidity of Greek historical time, he writes, 'is of the same kind as that which we see in modern history', as, for instance, in Germany 'from 1740, until the end of the last century'.[59]

Still, Niebuhr's argument was not confined to an analogy that would have ultimately set Thucydides within in a cross-continental, cross-disciplinary and cross-cultural, ethnographic context. The relationship between Thucydides' critical method and the temporality of acceleration was rather construed in the light of the disciplinary field of 'ancient history', configured itself by the unifying gaze of a grand narrative of historical time. Even though Niebuhr's delimitation of this field evoked the principle of critical method, it was the historical worldview of classical philology that provided the key concept for its borders. With regard to this field, Niebuhr wrote, we must set aside the 'synchronistic history of nations' for two reasons. The first is lack of reliable evidence: 'we confine ourselves to describing the actions, the life, and sufferings of man, as *man in history*'.[60] So, with regard to Egyptian history, Niebuhr notes that 'I have made the remark, that we have no traces of the Egyptians having ever had a history of their own. They had indeed a chronology, but true history they had not.'[61] The second and more emphatically formulated reason is the need for narrative coherence, which is provided by a metanarrative of ancient and modern history, and structured by the opposition between Graeco-Roman antiquity and European

---

[56] Niebuhr 1852a: vol. I, 301.   [57] Niebuhr 1852a: vol. I, 303.   [58] Momigliano 1957.
[59] Niebuhr 1852a: vol. I, 301.   [60] Niebuhr 1852a: vol. I, 2, emphasis added.
[61] Niebuhr 1852a: vol. I, 63 n. 4.

modernity. So, according to Niebuhr, while 'the history of nations like the unchangeable Chinese ... admits of no division at all', and Islamism forms an epoch for the Eastern nations, in 'the history of European nations ... an epoch presents itself at the time when the modern nations begin to form themselves, and our political system commences its development', and so 'history naturally divides itself into ancient and non-ancient'.[62] The boundaries of this division, Niebuhr explains, are not chronological. Rather, 'the relation of ancient history to the conditions of our own time constitutes the ground of this division'.[63] If the division between 'ancient' and 'modern' history was to be made in chronological terms, Niebuhr explains, and 'we were to say, for example, that ancient history extends down to the fifth century of our era, a portion of Chinese history would belong to antiquity'. But Chinese history falls outside of the field of ancient history: 'there is no connexion whatever between that nation [the Chinese] and any portion of ancient history'.[64]

The principle behind the subject matter of ancient history is what Niebuhr identifies as a 'philological standard' entailing that 'the nations whose literature is termed classical, are placed in the foreground; while the others retire into the background and become subordinate to the former'.[65] As a consequence, the story of the ancient world needs to exclude synchronic temporal structures that would have implied that 'the affairs of many nations' (in other words, 'China, Japan and the Negro tribes') 'ought ... to have a place in ancient history'.[66] But the events and stories that occurred in these nations and the knowledge that may arise out of their study form 'no part of our plan, the kernel of which is the history of Greece and Rome'.[67]

Niebuhr's delimitation of his research objectives meant that the new disciplines of philology and ancient history could formulate an interconnected story of antiquity and European modernity as the paradigmatic grand narrative of history as such. So even though his theory of Greek poetics and prose was criticized, not least by those who wished to defend the historiographical value of Herodotus' and Livy's 'literary' writing, his account of Thucydides had a vital significance for ancient history and historical science. Niebuhr placed Thucydides at the beginning of a story that distinguished (Western) historical consciousness from its poetical origin, but also from cross-cultural interaction and the passing on of knowledge about the past. By the same token he estranged Thucydides' story as a relic that was to be understood within the limits of ancient history and the story of

---

[62] Niebuhr 1852a: vol. I, 2–3.   [63] Niebuhr 1852a: vol. I, 3.
[64] Niebuhr 1852a: vol. I, 3.   [65] Niebuhr 1852a: vol. I, 5.
[66] Niebuhr 1852a: vol. I, 4.   [67] Niebuhr 1852a: vol. I, 5.

historiography and historical time. This dual contention allowed him to set the geographical boundaries of 'ancient history' as Graeco-European and the field's disciplinary boundaries as formulated in opposition to literature and rhetoric on the one hand and anthropology and ethnography on the other. But a consequence of this was that Niebuhr's Thucydides accentuated the interplay between the grand narrative of ancient and modern history and the methodological focus on evidence that the ancient historian was called upon to support.

Niebuhr's use of Thucydides to separate Greek historiography from its 'origin' was repeated in Ranke's argument that 'among the Greeks, history developed out of poetry and then emancipated itself from poetry'.[68] In Britain, Thomas Arnold also construed Thucydides in terms of movement from the age of poetry to the age of history, stressing the founding role of the break between them: 'it is impossible that there should have existed, along with the poetical version of the early Greek history, another version of a simpler and truer character'.[69] In the mid-19th century, George Grote spelled out the disciplinary and political implications of this rupture for Britain and, indeed, the whole of Europe: the autonomization of historiography from its poetic origin and of Graeco-European history from its synchronic affiliations. The distance between Homer and Thucydides, Grote argued,[70] manifests a multifarious break attesting to a future-orientated time: 'the introduction of prose writing' in Greece involved 'the commencement of a *separate branch of literature for the intellect,* apart from the imagination and emotions wherein the old legends had their exclusive root';[71] but also a wider advance that was manifested 'socially, ethically and intellectually': 'Philosophy and history were constituted, prose writing and chronological records became familiar; a canon of belief more or less critical came to be recognized.'[72] Building on Niebuhr's non-synchronic vision of ancient history, Grote associated Thucydides with a temporality that crossed no boundaries but was self-engendered and self-accomplished: 'The transition of the Greek mind from its poetical to its comparatively positive state was self-operated, accomplished by its own inherent and expansive force – aided, indeed, but by no means either impressed or provoked from without.'[73] The power of this beginning is so violent that it provided the figure of Thucydides with its vital metaphor: 'From the poetry of Homer, to the history of Thucydides ... was a prodigious step, but it was the native growth of the Hellenic youth into an Hellenic man.'[74] The story of

---

[68] Ranke 1973: 34.   [69] Arnold 1835: vol. III, x.   [70] Grote 1843: 160–1.
[71] Grote 1880: 365, emphasis added.   [72] Grote 1880: 451.   [73] Grote 1880: 463.
[74] Grote 1880: 463.

Greek history was then made to articulate a metanarrative of Greek and European historical consciousness, progressive mind and rationality – 'the progressive spirit of Greece, serving as herald and stimulus to the like spirit of Europe'.[75] Thucydides, alongside Greek philosophers, it is argued, made possible a transition from a primordial time of creation and imagination to a time of reflection focused on the contemporary world. He delimited the beginning of historiography, but also the beginning of a narrative appealing to the temporality of Greek and European historical process, in opposition to 'the stationary mind of Asia, occasionally roused by some splendid individual, but never appropriating to itself new social ideas or powers, either for war or for peace'.[76]

Conclusion: Time Passing and Criss-Crossing Boundaries

From Niebuhr to Grote, the reception of Thucydides was marked by the tension between the procedural focus on the critical historical method and a narrative of ancient historiography that negotiated an Enlightenment notion of a single History of ancient and modern historical time. The notion of Thucydides' break from poetry signalled at once the invention of historical critique and an *a priori* route, one mapping the limits of European space onto the course of a single, unified and coherent historical time. As such, it involved a movement beyond method and evidence, a movement through which this concreteness, as Ranajit Guha puts it in relation to Hegel's history, was made to yield to a foundational metanarrative and a mathesis of comparison that matched 'the coordinates of intercontinental space by those of universal time – geography by history'.[77]

These languages were at once epistemological, institutional and political. That the figure of Thucydides came to mark the beginning of historiography and the limits of ancient history had crucial implications for the new discipline and its distinct claim to the past. But it also had clear implications for the Western temporality of primitive others, which was to dominate anthropology and ethnography up until the early 20th century,[78] and to provide the logic of colonialism. Already in Niebuhr, the delimitation of the discipline of ancient history involved a forceful political component. 'There is no doubt', he wrote, 'that Egypt must become the possession of a civilized European power; it must sooner or later become the connecting link between England and the East Indies. ... When that shall have been accomplished new treasures will be brought to light and Egyptian antiquity will be laid open

---

[75] Grote 1857: 241.   [76] Grote 1857: 241.   [77] Guha 2002: 3.   [78] Fabian 2014.

before our eyes: *we stand at the very threshold of a new era in the history of antiquity.*'[79]

Still, what is remarkable about Thucydides' 19th-century reception is that it also played an unsettling role as an intellectual past whose 19th-century time-passing also jeopardized the boundaries of the modern discipline of history. On the one hand, Thucydides stood out as a paradigm of critical method that set aside narratives of historical movement and transformation, and established the objectivity of the historian's gaze. On the other, Thucydides' history had to be situated in a precarious historical totality, wherein foundational narratives were undermined by the modern concepts of disjuncture and discontinuity between past and present. This dual affiliation raised the question of history's open-ended pathways towards literature, rhetoric, ethnography and philosophy of history; that is, the fields that scientific historians, from Niebuhr and Ranke to Bury, theorized as a threat to the autonomy of historical practice.[80] The precariousness of Thucydides' position in these narratives requires us to confront the ambiguity of the limits and boundaries that underpinned the discipline of history. By the same token we are able to identify the politics of the ancient historian's disciplinary reception: the role of the figure of Thucydides in the Eurocentric and colonial deployment of a 'practical past', to use Hayden White's concept, but also the articulation of this past as an unsettling field in which grand narratives of Western rationality and historical consciousness were undermined.

Since my story of this dual process of the establishment and provocation of disciplinary boundaries has been told with the intention of remaining attentive to the present, it seems appropriate to conclude it with a series of questions about the normative implications of our study of Thucydides' 19th-century time-passing. How can historians combine the suspicious critique of evidence, which was formulated by way of encountering Thucydides, with the rejection of the idea of a single History and an expansive reconfiguration of historical languages of methods? How can the disciplinary boundaries of (ancient) history be drawn in a way that allows them to be fluid and precarious through their confrontation with ethnographic, anthropological, literary and cross-cultural perspectives on the past? In what terms can we engage with the modern reception of Thucydides beyond the binary oppositions of cyclical versus linear time, or between *historia*

---

[79] Niebuhr 1852a: vol. I, 63, emphasis added. On classics and colonialism, see Vasunia 2013.

[80] As Ranke wrote about Hegel, he would 'first list the abstract definitions of the nature of the spirit and then mention the means which spirit uses to realize its idea', proceeding 'at once to prove their abstract principle by reference to the concrete': Ranke 1973: 49. See also: Beiser 2011a: 258, 2011b; Iggers 2011.

magistra vitae and the modern postulates of critical and objective historical representation?[81] How might Thucydides' history and its post-classical time-passing inform, for instance, reflection on a temporality of crisis and a history that is intertwined with memory? In an age that privileges disjunction and rupture over the idea of a single narrative of History, how can we rethink Thucydides with a view to reflecting on the epistemology and politics of our notions of history and historical time?

Further Reading

Arnaldo Momigliano's essays in *The Classical Foundations of Modern Historiography* (1990) are a vital starting point for the study of Thucydides' reception. Greenwood 2006 and Morley 2014 are seminal in the discussion of Thucydides' criss-crossing passages into modern Western historical theory and practice. For an overview of Thucydides' reception, see Meineke 2003, Harloe and Morley 2012b, Meister 2013 and Lee and Morley 2015, including a focus on national traditions of reception. Essays in Lianeri 2011 examine Thucydides' reception in the intellectual frames and temporal structures through which modern Western historiography linked itself to Greek and Roman antiquities. Tsakmakis and Rengakos 2006 and Balot et al. 2017 contain important discussions of reception. Earley 2020 discusses the transition from the 19th-century turn to Thucydides as the father of historiography to a 20th-century vision of the father of international relations. Finally, essays in Harrison and Skinner 2020 provide important insights into the reception of Thucydides in relation to Herodotus' modern itineraries.

---

[81] Lianeri 2018.

19

JOEL ALDEN SCHLOSSER

'What Really Happened'

Varieties of Realism in Thucydides' *History*

I

The year 2017, in the words of one commentator, was the 'summer of misreading Thucydides'.[1] United States Senators quizzed the Secretary of Defense on the historian; Graham Allison, a Harvard professor of government, briefed the national security adviser and his staff at the White House on the 'Thucydides Trap'; op-eds protested misreadings while also accusing the Trump Administration of acting like the Athenians.[2]

The theory that conflict likely occurs when a rising power threatens to displace a ruling power – the so-called Thucydides Trap – appears to have been the most proximate cause of the most recent flurry of citation and attribution, but invoking Thucydides in the political sphere has never required a defence. As Seth Jaffe comments in a review of Allison's argument: 'for a man so long dead, Thucydides is rarely out of the news'.[3] Thucydides has long been an authority to which political leaders pay obeisance – even if often wrongly. His so-called realistic portrayal of human nature and the bellicose situation human beings find themselves in stands at the core of his continuing political influence.

The 'realism' that Thucydides has been long adduced to support stems from a particular reception of Thucydides predominant since the middle of the 20th century: that of international relations and its 'realism' school of

I note my thanks to Mark Fisher and Polly A. Low for perceptive readings of an earlier version of this chapter. Many thanks also to students at Carleton College and Deep Springs College with whom I thought through Thucydides. And special thanks to gifted teachers who introduced me to Thucydides: Laurence Cooper, Peter Burian and Peter Euben.

[1] Schake 2017.
[2] The precipitating cause of this upswell of Thucydides was the publication of Graham Allison's *Destined for War* (2017), which expanded on his September 2015 essay entitled 'The Thucydides Trap: are the U.S. and China headed for war?'.
[3] Jaffe 2017b.

thinking.[4] In this 'conventional reception of Thucydides', as Laurie Johnson describes it,[5] scholars rely on Thucydides to explain why states behave as they do and, in particular, why they go to war. Thucydides provides the origins of theories of the balance of power, with culture and ideology being subordinated to military might as the most significant factor. The forces inherent to the international system compel state action, born of the imperative to survive at any cost.[6]

In this chapter, I want to contextualize two principal varieties of realism that have been attributed to Thucydides, reading these as different receptions that depend upon what Neville Morley has called the 'foreknowledge' of a disciplinary perspective.[7] One variety of realism – the conventional realist reception – reads Thucydides as a structural analyst of classic power politics; the other – a new political realism – takes up Thucydides as a student of political complexity where history, moral psychology and misjudgements of political actions create a tragic political universe. I will show in what follows how these receptions presume a particular meaning for the elusive promise Thucydides makes of his work, namely that it will be a 'possession for all time'. The varieties of realism I describe take Thucydides' text as useful for their particular questions; this in turn leads them to interpretations that define this use – what makes the text a possession for all time – in particular ways. Both approaches balance fidelity to the text with fidelity to their own assumptions, reading Thucydides as telling his readers 'what really happened',[8] delivering stark truths that remain unsettling for contemporary audiences as well as ancient ones.[9]

In the final section of this chapter, I suggest that the frame of 'what really happened' need not contain all receptions of the realism of Thucydides' History. Indeed, the assertion of realism as a first principle often displaces contestation about what is realistic in the first place. The interpretation and appropriation of Thucydides by democratic activists associated with the political organizing coalition Industrial Areas Foundation (IAF) intimate

---

[4] Here I should note that Allison's particular usage shifts from the typical realist paradigm by emphasizing cultural factors. Jaffe 2017b provides an illustration of this approach to Thucydides.

[5] Johnson 2014: 391.

[6] Here I focus on recent political receptions of Thucydides, leaving aside others (e.g. ancient historiography or more literary receptions) that are part of the broader and ongoing reception.

[7] Morley 2016.

[8] I mean this in a general sense, not as a specific allusion to Ranke's scientific history and *wie es eigentlich gewesen* (on which, see the discussion of Lianeri, Chapter 18).

[9] Lee 2016 advances an argument similar to mine here, one that I only discovered after having drafted my own.

another reception, one that insists on what Margaret Leslie calls 'the usefulness of anachronism' as opposed to the usefulness of lessons on reality. In
this reception, organizers and activists take the *History* from its context to
draw lessons for insurgent political practice, and Thucydides is enlisted in a
political project he could hardly have imagined.

II

Hans Morgenthau may hold responsibility as the originator of the dominant
realist reception of Thucydides that began in the 20th century. In his influential *Politics among Nations*, first published in 1948, Morgenthau associated
Thucydides with the claim that 'international politics is of necessity a power
politics'.[10] Morgenthau emphasized that international politics consisted in
certain patterns and repetitions; an understanding of human nature shapes
and animates these forms. The Athenian envoys' statement that 'fear,
honour, and interest' compelled them to advance their empire (1.75) stands
as the starting point for articulating a realist account of state behaviour.[11]

The classical realism of Morgenthau has a sibling in structural realism.
Kenneth Waltz's *Theory of International Politics*, published in 1979,
focused on the structure of international politics, emphasizing that without
an overarching power to control states, the status quo was anarchy. Within
this anarchic system, Waltz proposed, states acted rationally to preserve
themselves and pursue their interests. Thucydides' text provides a snapshot
of such anarchy, where norms are subordinated to the imperatives of
strength and self-preservation.

The cynosure of the realist reception of Thucydides comes in the narrator's description of the 'truest cause' (*alēthestatēn prophasin*) of the conflict
between Athens and Sparta at 1.23.6. As Richard Crawley translates this
passage:

> The real cause, however, I consider to be the one which was formally most kept
> out of sight. The growth of the power of Athens, and the alarm which this
> inspired in Sparta, made war inevitable.[12]

[10] Morgenthau 1993: 38, quoted in Johnson 2014: 392.
[11] Tompkins n.d. details the rhetorical context of the Athenians' assertions, which he argues
has much to do with provoking a particular Spartan response. Realists generally ignore
these contexts.
[12] Crawley translation, revised by Strassler in Strassler 1996. 'Inevitable' here is a contested
reading of *anagkasai*; the English 'forcing' may be more appropriate. Cf. also Low
(Chapter 10). All quotations of Thucydides come from this edition unless otherwise
indicated. All Greek citations come from the Oxford Classical Text: Jones and Powell
1942.

Realists tend to focus on the first two sentences of this passage: the true cause and the logic of Athens' growing power and Sparta's resulting alarm. Here is the basis of the realists' reality: growing power and the fear it incites in others.

What is this power? Thucydides' account does not precisely say – he describes the Athenians as becoming *megalous*, which is not actually one of the usual words for power. (Adam Parry, for example, cites *dunamis, dunatos, biazomenoi, ekratesan* and *kreissonon*.[13]) Realists point to the military preparations Thucydides emphasizes from the beginning of his narrative. The war's greatness stems from each side's reaching an acme of such preparations (1.1); Thucydides' greatness, for these readers, stems from his seeing such preparations as the necessary consequences of the structure of world politics.

For conventional realist receptions of Thucydides, all states pursue power, and this pursuit especially shapes the Athenians. Realists often link this explanation of the true cause with the Athenians' later statement to the Melians about how power acts:

> Of the gods we believe and of men we know, that by a necessary law of their nature they rule wherever they can. And it is not as if we were first to make this law, or to act upon it when made: we found it existing before us, and shall leave it to exist forever after us; all we do is to make use of it, knowing that you and everybody else, having the same power [*dunamis*] as we have, would do the same as we do. (5.105.1–2)

The Athenians' claim that the powerful rule wherever they can under-scores the realists' insistence on the basic anarchy of the international system: rules depend upon the powerful to enforce them; no moral consider-ations obtain. The Athenian thesis here, moreover, amplifies an earlier statement by the Athenian envoys at Sparta that 'it has always been the law that the weaker should be subject to the stronger' and that human nature would not lead one to 'refuse dominion' (1.76). For conventional realist receptions this names a 'basic mechanism' in human nature, describing how human beings, in Robert Gilpin's words, 'always seek to increase their wealth and power until other humans ... try to stop them'.[14]

You might wonder: are the realists right about Thucydides? The Athenian thesis is complicated by the Athenians envoys' acknowledgement that the Spartans' retreat prompted their rise to power; the Spartans thus seem to disprove the Athenian thesis that human nature would not lead one to refuse

---

[13] Parry 1972: 52.　　[14] Gilpin 1988: 593, quoted in Welch 2003: 304.

dominion.[15] Realists also tend to ignore the differences between statements in the narrator's voice and those attributed to particular speakers. 'Identifying realist "misreadings" of Thucydides', David Welch points out, 'has become something of a cottage industry.'[16] Whether or not the readings interpret Thucydides well, they have proven long-lived. Much of the cottage industry of correction misses, however, the lack of concern international relations scholars evince for well-grounded, hermeneutically sound interpretations of Thucydides. International relations scholars have little truck with the literary: Thucydides does not offer romances for a day; he instead has crafted 'a possession for all time'. International relations scholars maintain that Thucydides simply recognizes what has always been the case – making him the first of a line of thinkers eventuating in their own discipline. It is much less important what Thucydides meant than what he put in motion, namely a powerful analytic for understanding world politics.[17]

Although the historical circumstances informing its reception are varied and complex, Thucydides' description of the *History* as a possession for all time illuminates one possible explanation for the successful uptake of Thucydides the realist. The entire passage reads as follows:

> The absence of romance in my history will, I fear, detract somewhat from its interest; but if it be judged useful by those inquirers who desire an exact knowledge of the past as an aid to the understanding of the future, which in the course of human things must resemble if it does not reflect it, I shall be content. In fine, I have written my work, not as an essay which is to win the applause of the moment, but as a possession for all time. (1.22.4)

I find this last sentence especially illuminating: Thucydides contrasts his work's purpose as a possession for all time with one that would 'win the applause of the moment'. It will not attract readers as romance might; instead, it promises usefulness for rarer readers seeking exact knowledge of the past. Thucydides seems to indicate a kind of strangeness in his text, a lack of fit with contemporary tastes and standards, as proof of its durable value.[18]

This lack of concern for applause of the moment informs the conventional realist reception of Thucydides as well. As Robert Keohane notes in his account of the origins of realism, the arbitration movement, Woodrow Wilson's speeches during World War I and the Kellogg–Briand Pact of

---

[15] Thank you to Mark Fisher for offering me this example.   [16] Welch 2003: 307.

[17] The Athenian thesis needs consideration in terms of the whole of the text. That is, the realist reception is not so much a misreading as a failure to consider the broader context.

[18] I might add that, like Socrates' *atopia*, Thucydides' strangeness eschews immediate gratification for the sake of a deeper or more searching education.

1927 to 'outlaw war' exemplified an approach to international relations that realism sought to challenge.[19] E. H. Carr's classic *The Twenty Years' Crisis, 1919–1939* was an 'attack' on these views. When World War II and its aftermath elevated the realist perspective, Thucydides' *History* rose with the flowing tide. Realism became the 'new orthodoxy' and Thucydides its authoritative founder.

This story suggests, however, how Thucydides the realist may not still serve the same function he once did. The status of orthodoxy does not fit a writer who insisted on thinking against the grain. The conventional realist reception of Thucydides now seems ready to win applause of the moment. The countermovement within international relations theory to receive Thucydides as not a realist but a constructivist suggests a shift towards reasserting a different Thucydides to disrupt his settled reception. Constructivists have insisted that ideas and ideals matter as much as material interests, countering the typical realist claim that the desire for power motivates all states. Anarchy, in Alexander Wendt's classic phrase, is what states make of it.[20] Moreover, Thucydides' attention to the characteristics of different states and how human nature plays out through different political dispositions and choices suggests an alternative founding narrative. For these readers, Thucydides is not a realist but a constructivist.

Although they counter the realist reception of Thucydides, the claims of the constructivists still rest on assertions about 'what really happened'. As one of the leading advocates of the constructivist interpretation, Richard Ned Lebow, writes, Thucydides' *History* 'suggests that interest and justice are inextricably connected and mutually constitutive'.[21] The Melian Dialogue does articulate the Athenian belief that the powerful make the rules; it also reveals, in Daniel Garst's reading, how the Athenians destroyed the rhetorical culture that had supported their successful expansion.[22] Constructivist readings do not assert that Thucydides concerns himself with phenomena irrelevant to international relations theory today, but rather that realist thinkers have missed crucial phenomena that Thucydides presents. In other words, 'Thucydides is both a realist and a constructivist'.[23] Both involve claims about a fundamental reality. Both believe Thucydides tells his readers what really happened. They simply disagree about what reality Thucydides described.

---

[19] Keohane 1986: 8.   [20] Wendt 1992.   [21] Lebow 2001: 559.   [22] Garst 1989.
[23] Lebow 2001: 559.

III

The conventional realist reception of international relations does not have the only claim to a realist interpretation of Thucydides. In recent years, a new form of realism has arisen in political theory. Related to the classic realist tradition by virtue of their common ancestor in Thucydides, this 'new political realism', as it is most frequently called, promises, in Raymond Geuss's words, to 'start from and be concerned in the first instance ... with the way social, economic, political, etc., institutions actually operate in some society at some given time, and what really does move people to act in given institutions'.[24] Similar to the conventional realist receptions, this new realism begins from a critique of idealism. Rejecting the focus on theoretical accounts of politics as they *ought* to be, the new political realists insist, in Mark Philp's words, on being action-focused, on politics' being seen as historically located, and that political action 'should be understood more like a craft or art rather than a process of applying theory'.[25]

New political realists turn to Nietzsche to guide their reception of Thucydides. Nietzsche read Thucydides as a realist who exemplified what he called a 'courage in the face of reality':

> *Courage* in the face of reality ultimately distinguishes such natures as Thucydides and Plato: Plato is a coward in the face of reality – consequently he flees into the ideal; Thucydides has *himself* under control – consequently he retains control over things.[26]

Thucydides' realism, according to Nietzsche, not only consists in a clear-eyed vision of 'what really happened', but also possesses a strength of character that could withstand and endure whatever he saw. By implication, reality does not simply lie 'out there' to be found; we also must develop our courage to see what's there despite our desires to look away.

The new political realist reception of Thucydides stems from what Karuna Mantena has called a 'moderating realism' that focuses less on the enduring structure of world politics than on criticizing how 'absolutist ethics, ideological certitude, and utopian schemes can threaten political order and lead to unrestrained uses of power'.[27] While the conventional realist reception remains predominant, the new realism questions how this power might best be used. Thucydides offers a realist response to this question through his

---

[24] Geuss 2008: 9.

[25] Philp 2012: 630. My account of new political realism here draws on Schlosser 2014.

[26] Nietzsche 1990: 118 (emphasis in original). I would contest Nietzsche's reading of Plato. Unfortunately, Geuss repeats this tendentious reading in much of his writing.

[27] Mantena 2012: 456.

form of historical enquiry. For the new political realists, historical enquiry stands as a counterpoint to the Kantian strand in political theory, exemplified in the work of John Rawls, which in its strongest sense posits that politics is not merely infused with value (a view that few would contest), but rather that you must begin from an ideal theory of ethics to start thinking about the human social world. This approach takes ethics as an object of research separable from politics, as understandable apart from particular historical contexts and as the necessary preliminary subject of study prior to any evaluation of political realities. Only after attaining an ideal theory of how you should act can you apply such a theory to the action of political agents; only then do the empirical details of any given historical situation enter consideration.

The contrast with Nietzsche's critique of idealism and invocation of Thucydides is obvious. Inspired by Nietzsche, the new political realists seek to reframe enquiry into politics around the constitutive elements of politics itself: the moral psychology of political actors; political conflict understood in terms of both values and interests; the institutions that mediate these conflicts; and the distinctiveness of the political sphere. As Geuss puts it, one should ask with Lenin: 'who whom?'.[28] That is, *who* does what to *whom*? Political theory must concern itself with particular people doing concrete things to other particular people. Ideal theory cannot begin to answer these questions; indeed, idealism shrinks from the terrifying realities that enquiry into such questions will discover. In contrast, new political realism proffers a political theory where enquiry is located in the world of contemporary politics and grounded in historical reality. Ideal theory seeks to identify an account of justice or the good abstracted from the motivations and situations of particular political actors, but realism asks simply 'what could make what work': the causal conditions, the motivations and the contextual bases for assessing success.[29]

Historical enquiry functions to contextualize political actors' motives, beliefs and desires; any understanding of political reality depends on *locating* political actors in historical space and time. An account of an engaged realist history thus begins with Thucydides, who functions as the exemplar of precisely this mode of enquiry. Bernard Williams identifies in Thucydides a commitment to the kind of truthful history necessary to combat modern delusions; Geuss describes Williams' project as inspired by the ideal of a 'Thucydides who philosophizes'.[30] Geuss's account of what Thucydides teaches resonates with his own manifesto of realism today: Thucydides

---

[28] Geuss 2008: 23.   [29] Philp 2012: 7.   [30] Geuss 2005: 233.

offers 'unprejudiced theoretical sympathy' for a 'wider spectrum of possible human motives'; Thucydides also rejects the dominant attitude of optimistic history, favouring not pessimism but a realistic approach to a world whose historical development is not, in Williams' words, 'intrinsically shaped to human interests'.[31] Finally, Thucydides' history is action-focused, aiming to instruct political actors about the true nature of their interests. Thucydides, in other words, anticipates the new political realist project of today: refusing to see history through the lens of ideology; facing the same complex reality faced by political actors; and engaging his own time rather than fleeing into the sunlit space of 'pure theory'.

Geuss explains Nietzsche's preference for Thucydides in two ways that illuminate this particular reading of Thucydides. First, writes Geuss, Nietzsche held that Thucydides saw much more capaciously than Plato. 'Thucydides had an unprejudiced theoretical sympathy for, and hence understanding of, a much wider spectrum of possible human motivations.'[32] Whereas the conventional realist reception appreciates Thucydides' parsimonious explanations that rest on the unchanging structure of world politics, the new political realists read Thucydides as a thinker of change and contingency. Thucydides' historical enquiry embraces the whole political world and educes a welter of dynamic complexity.

Nietzsche also admired Thucydides for his pessimism. Nietzsche diagnosed the philosophical tradition as deeply optimistic in ways that occluded a clear confrontation with human suffering, hopelessness and lack of progress. Thucydides is 'immune' to 'forms of wishful thinking' and thus rejects the 'shallow optimism' to which many forms of thinking are prone.[33] Even those affiliated with the conventional realist reception, I might add, have this proclivity: although they may criticize international institutions that promise an end to war, they nonetheless envision grand strategies capable of forestalling conflict. For the new political realists, in contrast, conflict stands at the heart of political life and cannot be eliminated. There are no laws of history that might inform a solution to the political problem; understanding human motivation, particular regime types and institutions can serve practical judgements about how best to cope with conflict, but this understanding cannot save human beings from it.

This second contrast with the conventional realist reception points to an assumption underlying the new political realist reception. The conventional

[31] Williams 1993: 163.
[32] Geuss 2005: 220. Although Plato and Thucydides see the world differently, I would dissent from Geuss's assertion that Thucydides sees more.
[33] Geuss 2005: 224.

realist reception tends to read Thucydides as a social scientist millennia ahead of his time. New political realists interpret him instead as a tragic political thinker. 'Thucydides should be seen to stand with Sophocles', writes Geuss.[34] The insights garnered from Thucydides serve 'how we might bear up'; that is, how to endure and cope with the ineluctable challenges of being human and living in political communities.

Such a tragic reading of Thucydides has no single lodestar in a particular passage from the *History*, but rather in broader claims about the scope and sweep of the narrative as a whole. The description of the plague puts this reading of the *History* in relief. Striking without forewarning, the plague throws Athens into chaos. Even the narrator of the *History* confesses power-lessness against it:

> All speculation as to its origin and its causes, if causes can be found adequate to produce so great a disturbance, I leave to other writers, whether lay or professional; for myself, I shall simply set down its nature, and explain the symptoms by which perhaps it may be recognized by the student, if it should ever break out again. (2.48)

The *History* will 'set down its nature', but it makes no promises about an antidote. Readers must confront the fact that little helped against the plague; one could only pity those suffering the disease's horrific effects. Both science and religion are impotent. W. R. Connor comments: 'the possibility of predicting and controlling the future ... erodes'.[35]

Thucydides does not promise solutions. Here the new realist reception resists arguments about the Thucydides Trap and the hopes Allison pins to learning from Thucydides' diagnosis. Thucydides offers a means of predicting but not controlling the future. At a more radical level, the text's motif of what Connor calls 'the subversion of *logos*' calls into question the very idea that language could conduce to learning – that it could bridge historical and circumstantial differences and provide a way of avoiding the mistakes of the past. Thucydides' *History* does not offer many examples of good judgement informed by a clear-eyed assessment such as what it offers. When 'words lose their meaning',[36] language and history begin to contribute to the destructive-ness of war.[37]

The new political realists can point to the critique of hope and the poor judgments that inform such hopes – phenomena that span the *History*. In the Melian Dialogue, the Athenian envoys characterize hope as 'danger's com-forter'. The envoys tell the Melians:

---

[34] Geuss 2005: 225.   [35] Connor 1984b: 244.
[36] To quote White 1984 on Thucydides 3.82.   [37] Connor 1984b: 244–5.

Hope, danger's comforter, may be indulged in by those who have abundant resources, if not without loss at all events without ruin; but its nature is to be extravagant, and those who go so far as to put their all upon the venture see it in its true colours only when they are ruined. (5.103)

Although there is ambiguity in *elpis kindunōi paramuthion*,[38] the Greek here translated as 'hope, danger's comforter', the new political realist reading would emphasize how hope deludes both the powerful and the powerless.[39] Thucydides narrates how this delusion befalls the Athenians' subject-states in the eighth year of the war, when the tides of the conflict have begun to shift. Other cities subject to Athens, hearing of the capture and of the generous terms given to Amphipolis, feel encouraged to change their condition and revolt. Here the narrator comments:

Indeed, there seemed to be no danger in so doing; their mistake in their estimate of the Athenian power was as great as that power afterwards turned out to be, and their judgment was based more upon blind wishing than upon any sound prediction; for it is a habit of mankind to entrust to careless hope what they long for, and to use sovereign reason to thrust aside what they do not want. (4.108)

Here the subject-allies of Athens fall prey to hope's deceptions, stoked by their longing for freedom: wanting to escape subjection to the Athenians, desire deludes these cities into believing that they could resist, if not defeat the Athenians. Hans-Peter Stahl writes: 'even in the face of his own destruction, man refuses to recognize the reality of the situation ... instead he flees into unreality, or better: into a world of fantasy produced by his own wishes'.[40] The subsequent massacre of the Melians shows just how deadly such fantasies – the lethal wages of hope – can be.

Yet the Melian Dialogue also marks a turning point for the Athenians as well. In their speech at Sparta in Book 1, the Corinthians characterize the Athenians as always achieving what they hoped for, but Thucydides' narrative reveals how the Athenians' success now prompts confusion between what is possible on the basis of their strengths and what is impracticable and exceeds their means. Hope becomes the basis for all future calculations and bears bitter fruit in the Sicilian Expedition.

[38] Schlosser 2013 elaborates this ambiguity and its implications for *elpis* in Thucydides and politics more generally.

[39] The new political realist reading here approaches the tragic reading of Thucydides offered by Lebow 2003, among others.

[40] Stahl 2003 [1966]: 166.

Indeed the expedition became not less famous for its wonderful boldness and for the splendour of its appearance, than for its overwhelming strength as compared with the peoples against whom it was directed, and for the fact that this was the longest passage from home hitherto attempted, and the most ambitious in its objectives considering the resources of those who undertook it [*epi megistēi elpidi tōn mellontōn pros ta huparchonta epecheirēthē*]. (6.31)

Hobbes's translation highlights the logic of hope in this final phrase: 'for that it was undertaken with so vast future hopes in respect of their present power'.[41] These 'vast hopes' (*megistēi elpidi*) assure the Athenians of their success despite the magnitude of the undertaking or their ignorance of Sicily; inflated to grand proportions by erotic desire, their hopes exceed the Athenians' resources. Adam Parry comments that this passage emphasizes 'the divergence between perception and reality' characterizing Athenian policy after Pericles.[42]

'Plato could not have written such a characteristically clear-sighted, analytically rigorous, and uncompromising Thucydidean text as the Melian dialogue', asserts Raymond Geuss.[43] This observation illuminates the broader context of the reception of Thucydides by the new political realists: although a reading of Thucydides stands at the foundation, these are thinkers concerned above all with the ongoing legacies of idealism, in particular how an idealist approach to ethics and politics leads not just to errors and delusions, but to bad politics. Thucydides' *History* proves its usefulness by exemplifying the courage to face reality while also depicting this disturbing reality to its readers. New political realists view this reality as more dynamic than the structural view adverted by the conventional realist reception; power plays an elemental, electrifying role.

IV

As I have suggested already, these two receptions of Thucydides' realism not only share their nomenclature but also advance homologous claims that Thucydides instructs his readers about 'what really happened'. The conventional realist reception reads Thucydides as teaching that a certain structure holds in world politics; the new political realists advance the interpretation that Thucydides illuminates the manifold nature of the historical forces shaping all aspects of reality. Yet neither reception of Thucydides takes

[41] Hobbes 1975.
[42] Parry 1981: 18. I should note that the failure of the Sicilian Expedition is not explained solely by the Athenians' misjudgement; the causes of the disaster are complex.
[43] Geuss 2005: 220.

cognizance of the other. Although they focus on somewhat different domains – conventional realist receptions on the international sphere and the new political realists on more localized ethical and political issues – they presume particular ontologies that are not entirely reconcilable. The inexhaustible complexity of historical reality asserted by the new political realists contrasts with the simpler world of states motivated by fear, honour and interest developed by the classical realists.

In a critique of the new political realism, Bonnie Honig and Marc Stears point out how realists of all stripes have placed their views of reality in larger stories about the way the world works. Treating Williams and Geuss (as well as James Tully) in particular, Honig and Stears detail how each focuses on some facts to the exclusion of others, telling their particular stories in partial and thus contestable ways.[44] Not allowing for any dissonance to emerge from their accounts, each thinker effectively silences what does not fit the narrative arc. For Williams and Geuss's historical pessimism, this means leaving out moments of optimism and collective change. Although Honig and Stears do not discuss more conventional classical realist receptions of Thucydides, the critique can easily extend to their assumptions about the immutable structures of world politics. For Honig and Stears, an unreflective historical narrative occludes events that do not fit the realists' paradigms and robs them of the kind of nuanced and complex understanding of political reality that might best educate judgement.

By not pausing to consider the stories that hold their beliefs about what is real (and their readings of Thucydides), realists both classic and new political also displace a broader politics of reception. As Elizabeth Wingrove has argued, any given reception configures 'a universe of political meaning', meaning that the relationship with the past developed by a particular interpretation stands on unarticulated political positions in the present. Wingrove shows how this insight transforms classical reception studies from a space of academic policing to a site of political displacement. 'Something critical to politics … is being displaced, on and through the classical encounter.'[45] Understanding this can lead contemporary interpreters to recognize that 'political theory happens at the "point" of reception: through an interrogation of what has happened there, but also what can or should'.[46] The two realist receptions of Thucydides surveyed thus far both set aside the arguments about what really happened and instead proceed on the assumption that reality is clear. It is what Thucydides says it is. This papers over the moments of 'reality' they choose as their focus. It closes down the political

---

[44] Honig and Stears 2012: 198.   [45] Wingrove 2016: 119.   [46] Ibid.

space prior to reception, a space where contests over what really matters for thinking about politics should be sustained. Into this political space of reception I would like to offer a third variety of realism – a radical democratic one. Here I take inspiration from Bonnie Honig's 'interruption' of the received Antigone, an argument she pursues in *Antigone Interrupted*, 'to find another Antigone who may have a different impact on democratic theory and may offer a different prod to our political imagination'.[47] As Honig and Stears help illuminate, the regnant realisms both displace the contestable claims about political change on which they rest: the conventional realist reception views the international system of anarchy within which states operate as immutable; the new political realists place their account of historical complexity within a tragic story of unceasing political struggle. What might a different plotting of Thucydides yield for political practice today? How might an alternative narrative illuminate other varieties of reality?

The IAF offers one possible plot that diverges from the conventional realist reception as well as its new political realist cousin. The IAF is a national community-organizing network established by Saul Alinsky and others in 1940. First called 'The Back of the Yards Neighborhood Council' for the area in Chicago, IL, where it undertook its earliest work, the IAF seeks to engage ordinary people by organizing them to articulate and express their collective voice about decisions affecting their lives. Now an interfaith and multiracial network of community organizers, the IAF offers training services and professional organizers under contract to local organizations. Rather than directing staff from a national level, organizations are grouped into semi-autonomous regions, with regional staff directed by a supervisor. Yet the national organization exists in part to facilitate training and develop leaders who can then train local organizers in each region. These training sessions focus less on technical issues than on teaching the IAF's organizing principles and broader philosophy of politics. The IAF training sessions offer a chance for organizers and community leaders to reflect on the broader stories they tell and to develop more flexible approaches to seemingly intractable problems. Here is where Thucydides arises, as Mark Warren describes:

> The first session asks participants to role play the Athenian conquest of the Melians as chronicled in Thucydides' *History of the Peloponnesian War*. The IAF believes that many people who get involved in social justice politics are too righteous and fail to understand that politics is about practical power. In the story, the Melians heroically defend their liberty, refuse to give into the

Athenians, and are eventually slaughtered. The point of the exercise is to show that negotiation and compromise over interests, not the assertion of principles, constitute the essence of politics, and consequently the basis for IAF political activity.[48]

They're Melians! They have to be more flexible! Organizer Ernesto Cortes tells Jeffrey Stout to warn against Stout's encouraging leaders in an action in Los Angeles to act according to principle.[49] Don't be the Melians, the IAF training emphasizes. Learn to compromise. Or, as the IAF dictum attributed to Alinsky frames it, 'no permanent enemies, no permanent allies'.[50]

Whether or not a careful reading of the *History* permits the interpretation that the IAF trainers suggest, I want to highlight how this approach to the text offers a democratic alternative to the other two principle varieties of realism. According to the IAF reading of Thucydides, 'what really happens' (notice the present tense) depends on what people do. Reality is not limited to the power of states, nor to the power of historical forces. Instead, reality is what people make of it – ordinary people like those trained as organizers.[51]

This interpretation of Thucydides rests on a story about popular power and political change. Although the *History* may prove at best ambivalent about the Athenian democracy it describes, recent interpretations of the *History* might provide one textual starting point in the text's construction of a particular kind of participatory reader. Thucydides presents characters in the *History* who advance claims and predictions that events then contravene.[52] Summarizing this work, Christine Lee describes how 'the reader must engage in the arduous task of threading together speeches and deeds, patiently unstitching and re-stitching, in the hopes of weaving a meaningful pattern out of the disparate and untidy phenomena of politics. ... Thucydides demands active participation in a way that democracy must as well if it is to flourish.'[53]

Pivoting from the silent, unaccountable Athenian *dēmos* to the vociferous organizers of the IAF may strike some as anachronistic, but this new perspective proves useful for contesting the political displacement enacted by classical and new political realists.[54] Both place their receptions of Thucydides in depoliticized contexts characterized by limited agency and (in the case of the conventional realist reception) leadership restricted to

---

[48] Warren 2001: 223.
[49] Stout 2010: 179. See Bosworth 1993 for a similar argument from a historical perspective.
[50] Quoted in Stout 2010: 122.
[51] New political realism is concerned with individual agency but not collective agency. For this democratic reception, power consists in what Hannah Arendt 1970: 44, calls 'action in concert'.
[52] Euben 2010.   [53] Lee 2014: 348. Cf. also Irwin (Chapter 8).   [54] Leslie 1970.

elites. The IAF reception shows one way in which Thucydides' *History* can circulate much more promiscuously – and the unruly mob he disdained can make of his text what it will.

Further Reading

What Welch 2003 calls the 'cottage industry' of corrections to conventional realist receptions of Thucydides persists. The essays collected in Lee and Morley 2015 provide a useful summation of the field. The new political realism has its most political statement in Geuss 2008 and the clearest linkage to Thucydides in Geuss 2005. Stout 2010 provides a stirring overview of IAF work as well as a narrative of their reception of Thucydides' Melian Dialogue. Euben 2010 provides a riposte to the previous political appropriation of Thucydides in the conventional realist vein.

20

JEREMY MYNOTT

Translating Thucydides

In *Alice through the Looking Glass*, the Red Queen poses a translation problem:

> 'Do you know languages? What's the French for fiddle-de-dee?'
>
> 'Fiddle-de-dee's not English', Alice replied gravely.
>
> 'Whoever said it was?', said the Red Queen.
>
> Alice thought she saw a way out of the difficulty, this time. 'If you'll tell me what language "fiddle-de-dee" is, I'll tell you the French for it!', she exclaimed triumphantly.
>
> But the Red Queen drew herself up rather stiffly and said, 'Queens never make bargains'.[1]

The Red Queen refused to negotiate, but translation is often described as a form of negotiation, in this case between the language and assumptions of the original text and those of its intended readers in the target language.[2] The hopes and needs of these later readers are often expressed in terms of 'relevance'. What does this text have to say to us, now? I offer here some reflections on Thucydides as a voice with contemporary 'relevance' and on the ways in which a translation can and should affect our sense of this. I take as my principal example the experience of completing a new translation of Thucydides for the series 'Cambridge Texts in the History of Political Thought'.[3]

It was very striking to me when starting this project to see how little other recent translators of Thucydides had to say about the problems involved in their endeavours. After all, it takes years of quite hard work to translate a

---

This chapter is a revised and expanded version of Mynott 2013b: 49–62.

[1] 'Queen Alice', Carroll 1871: ch. 9.

[2] See, for example, the title of Eco 2003 (*Mouse or Rat: Translation as Negotiation*). In the same spirit, Eco also insists that translation is to be thought of as from 'text to text' not from 'language to language'.

[3] Mynott 2013b.

text like Thucydides, in the course of which one is continually confronting not only particular difficulties in the text but also general questions about what in *principle* it might be like to produce a good translation of Thucydides. This is one's daily uncertainty and anxiety. Yet the most translators usually do in the short prefaces they are conventionally allowed is to give a brave smile and a wave and say that it has all been really rather difficult but very worthwhile in the end; they then tend to make just one methodological statement, which is almost formulaic in its recurrence and brevity – to the effect that they have sought to produce a version that is both 'accessible to the modern reader and faithful to the original'. But there are few hints that there might be any real tension between these objectives or any larger issues raised by them.

I suppose the motivation for this reticence is largely an admirable professional modesty about the role of the translator compared to that of the author who originated the work and the scholar whose task it is to explain and interpret it. But this does risk encouraging a level of naivety in the readership about what it is for something to *be* a translation, particularly in a relatively unsophisticated (or monoglot) student or general readership; and this apparent modesty may in the end imply a certain unconscious presumption, or even arrogance, about the role of the translator as the privileged intermediary in the process and the authentic voice of the author.

The American critic Susan Sontag describes her experience as a young woman brought up in the American south-west voraciously reading her way through the world's literature. She proceeds from American classics to British ones and then, in an almost imperceptible transition, and still reading in English, to the classics of European literature and in particular Russian literature. She knew of course that she was then reading foreign authors, but she says:

> Had I recognized an awkward sentence in a novel I was reading by Mann or Balzac or Tolstoy, it would not have occurred to me to wonder if the sentence read as awkwardly in the original German or French or Russian, or to suspect that the sentence might have been 'badly' translated. To my young, beginning reader's mind, there was no such thing as a bad translation. There were only translations – which decoded books to which I would otherwise not have had access, and put them into my hands and heart. As far as I was concerned, the original text and the translation were as one. Question: who is the greatest Russian author of the 19th century? Answer: Constance Garnett.[4]

[4] Sontag 2007.

And that was just the criticism made by the Russian/American author Joseph Brodsky, who complained that English-speaking readers could barely tell the difference between Tolstoy and Dostoevsky because they weren't reading the prose of either one. They were reading Constance Garnett.

I want to suggest by contrast that all translators of Thucydides are unavoidably also *interpreters*, as Hobbes himself recognized in so describing his translation on his original title page. I will say something about the special difficulties posed by this text and some of the solutions I chose to adopt. But this will be far from a self-serving comparative exercise. Anyone who has completed a translation of Thucydides will have a lively sympathy with all their predecessors, who constitute a very small guild in need of some solidarity, if not an actual support group.[5] And in any case I want to say that just as our understanding of Thucydides' text should be sensitive to *its* historical context and the circumstances of *its* composition, so too different translations of Thucydides have characteristics defined partly by *their* circumstances of publication – the times at which they are written, of course, but also the imprints and series in which they appear and their different intended readerships and purposes.

My own translation appears in a series of texts in the history of political thought, intended principally for students in the social sciences and humanities, who will be studying the texts in English. A key objective of this series is to present each author and text in their proper cultural and historical context and to avoid importing into our understanding of them anachronistic concepts and categories derived from later developments and theories. But anachronism in all its forms, both explicit and more subtle, threatens the translator at every level, and I start with the most general.

The title of this Cambridge series refers deliberately to 'political thought', not 'political theory'. Thucydides is a foundational author who stands at the very start of reflective thinking about politics in the Western tradition. That gives his voice a great freshness and originality, but it also presents us with an immediate problem of classification, since the sort of distinctions we now make between political science, political theory, political history and the study of international relations did not exist in his day, though he has on occasion been claimed as the ancestor of each of these modern 'subjects'. But it is surely evident that such a work, through the issues it embodies and the

---

[5] In my case sympathetic support was available from a surprising source. I discovered that Martin Hammond was concurrently working on a translation of Thucydides for Oxford University Press in their 'World's Classics' series (Hammond 2009) and that we were living only five miles apart in rural Suffolk, each unknown to the other until late on in our projects.

reflections it prompts, can be important *in* or *for* political theory, even if it is not formally one *of* political theory. Hobbes makes that point very nicely in the Preface to his own translation of Thucydides, where he describes him as 'the most politic historiographer that ever writ', though (as he goes on to say) one who generally achieves his effects not through commentary on his own narrative but through the narrative itself, whereby 'he maketh his auditor a spectator'. Hobbes is borrowing this analogy from Plutarch, whose comment is worth quoting in full:

> Simonides calls painting 'silent poetry' and poetry 'talking pictures'. For the actions that painters portray while they are still going on, literature describes and records after they have taken place. And although artists use colour and form and writers use words and phrases to represent the same things, it is only in their medium and mode of imitation that they differ, and both have one and the same end; so the most effective historian is the one who makes a painting of his narrative through the emotions and characters he portrays. Certainly, Thucydides is always striving for these visual effects in his work, avid to make the reader a spectator, as it were, and to engender in readers the same emotions of consternation and disturbance felt by those who actually witnessed the events.[6]

Plutarch anticipates in this last sentence an objective often recommended in works of translation theory – that the translator should seek to reproduce in the modern reader the effects the text would have had on its original audience.[7] And those effects include ones that might be suggested by the literary genre the work is assigned to and the title under which it appears.

In modern terms, Thucydides' work is in fact most often described as a 'history', though it was conceived in a 5th-century BCE milieu of still emergent literary forms in drama, rhetoric, logic, science and philosophy as well as in history, and at a time when literacy was rare; and his work draws on most of these other genres (as well as on the earlier model of Homer's oral epic). Thucydides himself does not actually call his work a *historia*, though almost everyone, except Hobbes, translates the very first sentence of the work as if Thucydides had written *sunegrapse tēn historian* rather than the more direct *sunegrapse ton polemon*. The key word to emphasize here is surely *sunegrapse*. Thucydides himself is quite likely to have dictated his work to one or more amanuenses; and parts of it may well have been read out to audiences – in particular, one imagines, the speeches and the more dramatic narrative sections. But it was clearly a crucial fact for

---

[6] Plutarch, 'The Fame of the Athenians', *Moralia* 346f–347a.
[7] See, for example, *passim* in the following works: Radice and Reynolds 1987; Eco 2003; Walton 2006; Bellos 2011.

Thucydides, and part of the originality he claimed, that he *wrote it down* and so made a permanent record that could be studied, discussed and returned to as a trusted reference.

I follow Hobbes in translating this opening sentence, 'he wrote the war'. Indeed, I go somewhat further. The series objectives I described imply a strong intellectual and pedagogic agenda of reading the authors in context, and I tried to take this seriously in various ways. First, and no doubt controversially, I do not call the text by its traditional title, 'The Peloponnesian War', which is not a title we have any evidence Thucydides himself used and which was seen to be one-sided even in his own time.[8] The first reference to the traditional title I can find is in the work of Diodorus Siculus, some 350 years later than Thucydides.[9] I therefore adopt a title suggested by the opening sentence, *The War of the Peloponnesians and the Athenians*, taking that in effect to be his title page.

Secondly, in structuring the work I give precedence typographically to the internal divisions by years and campaigning seasons that Thucydides himself used (and saw as his particular innovation in chronology[10]) rather than to the conventional division into 'Books', which was again a later editorial intervention.[11] These two tactics are intended to help prevent us projecting false assumptions on to the work even before we start reading it.

Coming to the text itself, some of the recurring difficulties are very familiar. Thucydides has been famous since antiquity for his extraordinary style. Dionysius memorably remarked, 'the number of people who can understand the whole of Thucydides can be easily counted, and there are parts of it not even these can manage without a grammatical commentary',[12] and most translators would be happy to adopt that as their epigraph. The text is often articulated in very long and complex periodic structures, consisting of a succession of unmarked coordinate clauses, which it is difficult to render in intelligible contemporary English. Crawley in his original 1874 edition did feel able to match these, in length at least, for a Victorian readership brought up on the prose of Johnson, Gibbon and Macaulay; but for the Landmark textbook edition of his translation (published in 1999) one notices that many of these sentences have been reduced in length and simplified. Lattimore, in his 1998 Hackett translation, with his greater

---

[8] See 5.28 and 31, where from the standpoint of the Peloponnesians it is called 'the Attic War', that is the 'Athenian war'.

[9] Diodorus Siculus, 12.37.2.

[10] See further the notes of Mynott 2013a on the text at 2.1 and 5.20.2–3.

[11] On this, see Kennedy and Kaldellis (Chapter 16).

[12] *On Thucydides*, 51. I cite Dionysius on Thucydides at length in appendix 2 of Mynott 2013a: 594–9.

emphasis on 'fidelity to the text', does still try valiantly to preserve the original structures, but most modern translators break them up.[13]

Thucydides is also wilfully obscure in his *style*. He experiments a good deal with vocabulary and word order and indulges in harsh forms of rhetorical *variatio*, with many special effects and distortions that were evidently regarded as 'difficult' even in his own day. Now, does the translator have an obligation to reproduce difficult Greek in difficult English to convey the same effects and produce the same reactions? This is a serious issue and a pervasive one (but not one much, if at all, discussed). It is very hard for translators to stop themselves trying to smooth all this out in the interests of producing an 'accessible' text, even if it is not then a 'accurate' one in every sense, and even if this exposes a conflict between the translators' professional modesty and their evident (but always unstated) belief that they can actually *improve on* Thucydides. There is a strong temptation to slip into paraphrase in decoding some of Thucydides' more complex sentences and ideas in order to provide a smoothness and immediate readability that is all too often lacking in the original. Crawley (1874), followed by Jowett (1881) and Warner (1954) – both of whom leant very heavily on Crawley – are all perhaps sometimes seduced by their own sense of style and (more ironically) by their intuitions about 'what it would have been appropriate for Thucydides to say in the circumstances'. A particular example is the rendering of the famous passage in the Melian Dialogue at 5.89 where Crawley produced the memorable translation 'the strong do what they can and the weak suffer what they must'. This has a fine ring to it, is much quoted and has found its way into many textbooks of political theory and international relations, but (as various people have pointed out) it is not what the Greek actually says. The clauses are not balanced so neatly in the original and the words 'what they must' in the second clause of this English version are pure invention. Hornblower, in his monumental commentary, translates as 'the powerful exact what they can, and the weak have to comply'. I place more stress on the introductory word *dunata* and translate as 'the possibilities are defined by what the strong do and the weak accept'.[14]

In general, Hobbes has probably succeeded better than anyone else in finding an appropriate 'voice' for Thucydides. His translation may now be thought inaccurate in some particular respects, in the light of later advances in textual and linguistic scholarship, but where it especially succeeds is in

[13] See further the comments in Mynott 2013a: xxxi–xxxiv, and the notes to the text on 1.9.2, 21.1, 36.1; 2.42.4; 4.55.1–3; 6.13.1, 101.1.
[14] See also Hornblower 1991–2008: vol. III, 233–4; Beard 2010.

catching something of the rugged strength, rhythms and confidence of Thucydides' prose, as well as his intellectual sophistication.

Thucydides wrote at an early stage in the development of Greek prose and was undoubtedly trying to forge an original style for what he rightly regarded as a new form of enquiry. The meaning is sometimes highly compressed and, as with poetry, resists decompression. At its best, his prose is very powerful and arresting, but often he seems to be straining too hard for his effects with artificial contrasts, asymmetries and abstractions. In addition, there are the purely practical uncertainties of knowing which parts of the text Thucydides himself regarded as finished and which were only drafts. In the case of some obscure passages, therefore, one can never be quite sure whether one is dealing with clumsy expression, unrevised draft, unreliable textual transmission, overwrought stylistic innovation or deliberate ambiguity. The translator has to make choices, and the reader in English should be made aware of these where possible.

The text is internally complex in other ways too, in that it contains within it a range of different 'voices' and kinds of text: long narrative accounts of campaigns; vivid reportage of key events such as the great plague and the various battle scenes; dialogue and debate; texts of letters and of treaties; occasional authorial asides; longer political analyses, such as the famous account of civil conflict at Corcyra; a few biographical sketches and 'obituaries'; and of course the speeches by participants that are both part of the action and commentaries upon it and that themselves vary a good deal as between free-standing speeches, debates, battlefield addresses, proclamations and conversational exchanges. Thucydides does have a very distinctive and recognizable overall style, but I would suggest there are more variations within this than have always been recognized.

Then there is the large issue of *cultural distance*. Unsurprisingly, many of Thucydides' concepts and assumptions do not map neatly on to our own. There is no precise English equivalent of *polis*, *dēmos*, *stasis*, *aretē*, *logos* and so on; and, in reverse, even such apparently universal concepts as 'conscience', 'fairness', 'morality' and 'human rights' have a history of their own and rarely, if ever, have exact equivalents in the language of this period. Words and phrases like 'political party', 'revolution', 'counter-revolution' and 'civil war' come to a translator's mind all too readily in the wish to make the text of Thucydides familiar to us and lend a superficial relevance to the passages in question. These expressions may have their uses, but it is easy to import with them associations that are misleading. And I would suggest in fact that one more often finds a deeper sense of relevance precisely in *reflecting* on such differences than in drawing easy parallels, just as studying a foreign language can make one more self-conscious about one's own.

One solution to this sort of difficulty that is sometimes adopted is to represent such terms in transliteration to remind us of their foreignness and resist any contamination of meaning from the target language; but this soon comes to seem a counsel of despair as the page becomes increasingly furred with these italic substitutes, which remain as opaque in English letters as they were in Greek and so defeat the very project of translation.

Moreover, this difficulty arises not only with the sort of moral and political concepts that naturally attract most interest and attention, but also with more humdrum terms for distances, seasons, times, names and places. It might be thought that here at least one could just translate 'word for word', but consider the following: a 'stade' in Greece was a measurement of about two hundred yards, so there are between eight and nine stades to the mile. But if you translate 'about ten stades' as 'about one and a quarter miles' you get an unacceptable combination of precision and approximation. And is it better to render a place like *Enneahodoi* (1.100) as 'Enneahodoi' or as 'Nine Ways'? What then about *Amphipolis*, the later name of the same place, whose etymology and relationship to *Enneahodoi* are explained at 4.102? The place names in such cases originally signified something significant about their geographical or political situation whose connotations might need to be either preserved or avoided. Would we, for example, want to see *Cambridge* translated as 'Pont-du-Cam' in a French work? If inclined to answer 'yes', you might consider the further cases of Oxford, Aberystwyth, Chipping Norton ... It gets even worse with coinage, and some translators have made rash attempts to translate *drachmai* into modern currencies and values (though not yet, as far as I know, into euros).

All of this underlines the continual need to be aware of context and authorial intention. The classic expression of the possible snares and delusions is set out by Collingwood in his *Autobiography* (1939), where he is taking to task the Oxford 'realists' of his generation for foisting their own moral vocabulary on to the Greeks and then criticizing them for their use of it:

> It was like having a nightmare about a man who had got it into his head that *trieres* was the Greek for 'steamer', and when it was pointed out to him that descriptions of triremes in Greek writers were at any rate not very good descriptions of steamers, replied triumphantly, 'That is just what I say. These Greek philosophers ... were terribly muddle-headed and their theory of steamers is all wrong.'[15]

Collingwood's nightmare is actually realized in some modern Bible translations from the Greek New Testament. For example, the passage in Matthew

---

[15] Collingwood 1939: 64.

V 41, which in the *Authorised Version* is translated 'And whosoever shall compel thee to go a mile, go with him twain', is in the *Good News Bible* very bravely rendered as 'And if one of the occupation troops forces you to carry his pack one kilometre, carry it two kilometres'.

The distinction that is often made between literal and free translation begs or avoids the main issue, since it does not correspond to the difference between an accurate and an inaccurate translation. You can be inaccurate and untrue to an author's voice precisely by being *too* literal in translating their words and structures into another language that has its own and quite different forms of expression. But if you free yourself from the original too far, you then risk importing larger assumptions and ideas that are anachronistic in a deeper sense and therefore also 'inaccurate'. How then can one translate the words, the idioms and the sentences in a way that stays true to the sense, the style and the intentions?

We struggle to find good metaphors for this process of interpretation. The distinction between form and content, which has been given new currency in the electronic age, is naïve in this context, as if the essence of Thucydides' meaning could be fully extracted and then re-expressed without alteration, addition or subtraction of sense in any number of other forms. The medium does indeed affect the message. Nor can we think of different languages just as alternative vehicles, each conveying passengers to the same destination with the same experience of the journey travelled. A more attractive metaphor may be that used by the Chinese sage Mencius (372–289 BCE), whose advice to the reader of the ancient Chinese *Odes*, already difficult to understand in his own day, was to 'let his thought go to meet the intention as he would a guest'.

There is no final theoretical answer to this conundrum. If translation is a form of negotiation, as I suggested at the beginning of this chapter, then it is no surprise if it involves compromises. And all translators do in the end make a series of pragmatic decisions based on the different kinds of readers they and their publishers have in mind and their different objectives. Nonetheless, you can't make Thucydides into a contemporary just by misrepresenting him. The issue of 'relevance' has to be addressed at a quite different level. Hobbes again gives us the key:

> But Thucydides is one, who, though he never digress to read a lecture, moral or political, upon his own text, nor enter into men's hearts further than the acts themselves evidently guide him: is yet accounted the most politic historiographer that ever writ.[16]

---

[16] Hobbes 1629: Preface.

That is, Thucydides achieves his effects and purposes through a very detailed, 'thick' description of the war he has taken as his subject. He does have occasional authorial asides and, more especially, he does have the key participants explain in their speeches their view of the overall situation and their motivation for their own actions (indeed their speeches are very significant 'actions' in themselves); but for the most part he lets the narrative speak for itself. That is, he tends to address the universal through the particular. And that is a characteristic not only of history but also of epic and drama, which were the most familiar literary forms of his day, and of the novel, which is one of the most familiar forms of ours. Perhaps we should think of these literary forms as a kind of continuum, which might have at one end of it philosophy, dealing with the most general considerations and expressed in a largely abstract way, and at the other end literature and history, with their emphasis on particular, lived experience. Works of political theory, as we now usually understand it, would on this model cluster close to philosophy at one end of the continuum; but works at the other end, whether fiction or non-fiction, may still be important *in* or *for* political theory through the issues they embody and the reflections they prompt. Would not Sophocles' *Antigone*, Shakespeare's *Julius Caesar*, Tolstoy's *War and Peace* and Gibbons' *Decline and Fall* all qualify, in their different ways, under this larger rubric? And does this not enrich as well as enlarge our conception of the subject? My suggestion at any rate is that we take seriously the form in which Thucydides chose to write and that we find his political thought more in the densely textured detail of his work than in the more explicit generalizing comments embedded within it.

If we read his work this way, we can see that Thucydides does indeed contribute in important and distinctive ways to many of the central issues of political theory as we now conceive it. Among the themes explored in his history are:

- The nature of *political judgements* – the circumstances in which they are conceived, the kinds of calculations that underlie them and the assessments we should make of them from different standpoints in the later course of events. For example, Thucydides gives us a fascinating picture in his first two books of the crucial judgements made by the key participants on each side as they contemplate the possibility of war and decide whether to commit to it. Pericles is a central character here, as revealed through his own speeches and decisions and the reactions to these of others, on both sides; it has indeed been suggested that the whole of the rest of the work is effectively a vindication of Pericles' initial 'foresight' (*pronoia*). And in later books the expressed political judgements of other major figures like

Cleon, Brasidas, Nicias, Hermocrates and Alcibiades are also partly constitutive of the broader action of the war as Thucydides portrays it and equally in need of complex interpretation.

- Closely connected are the different kinds of *persuasion and influence* available to such agents in advocating their chosen policies. These include the role of rhetoric and argument, which may take on a different kind of importance in a predominantly oral culture; the forms of public pressure and support that can be exerted through established institutions in the different kinds of polity; and the relative importance of individuals, social classes, ruling groups and international relationships in reaching decisions.

- We are thereby led to reflect on the characteristic decision-making *processes* in each case and on the comparative strengths and weaknesses of the different political *constitutions*, especially in Athens and Sparta. The principal characters offer some explicit thoughts on this: Cleon, for example, roundly declares that a democracy is incapable of running an empire (3.37); and the Corinthians criticize the Spartans for being so constitutionally rigid and inward-looking as to be incapable of external initiatives (1.68–71); while Thucydides himself compares and contrasts the national characteristics of Syracuse, Sparta and Athens (8.96.5).

- There are dramatic illustrations too of what happens when such established political procedures and conventions break down, as in the kinds of *internal conflict* within states that Thucydides describes as *stasis*. We are shown how one kind of breakdown can lead to or be mirrored in another, most famously in the case of Corcyra at 3.82–4, as the political disintegration is matched by a social, psychological and even linguistic disintegration. There is also a brilliant vignette of 'the rule of terror' in Athens at 8.66, which shows how insecurity can breed civic distrust and confusion.

- The speeches and debates provide many examples of the explicit *justifications* the different participants offer for their political choices, including what we would think of as 'moral' justifications, which compare the competing claims of self-interest and such other-regarding virtues as justice, respect and compassion; or, more interestingly perhaps, which represent these as ultimately conflicts between different forms of self-interest. The dramatic debates over Mytilene (3.37–48) and Melos (5.85–113) are especially good sources for these kinds of arguments, but such conflicts are in fact pervasive throughout the text and serve to connect it with the larger philosophical discussions going on in Greek society at that time. They raise important questions too about how far the moral and political concepts of this culture can be mapped on to those of our own.

- More generally, we are given very rich material for reflection – though in the form, I am suggesting, of specific historical illustration, not formal argument or general theory – on the confused but dynamic interplay of *reasons, causes and motives* in the explanation of behaviour, both of individuals and of states; and we are continually reminded of the extent to which the actual outcomes are also the product of what Thucydides portrays as the inexorable forces of 'chance and necessity'.

Reflecting on Thucydides' treatment of such themes surely leads to a deeper sense of his foundational importance for the Western tradition of political thought than does the process of just extracting neat 'opinions' from him in lazy support of one's favourite causes and arguments. This is not at all to suggest that he is not 'relevant' to our current preoccupations and to our attempts to understand them in the context of whatever larger historical dynamics or more universal human values may underlie them. It was his own hope, after all, that his work would be of permanent value in just these ways. It is rather to respect the form in which he chose to write and the context in which his work was created. There is more than one way to contribute to such political reflection, and my suggestion is that differences in culture and context can be as suggestive as similarities when they are properly distinguished and understood. If we acknowledge in advance the gaps in our knowledge and our cultural distance, we are more likely to resist the temptation to simplify or over-interpret Thucydides and thus to mis-translate him.

Keats famously spoke of Shakespeare and other great writers as having what he called 'negative capability', the capacity to 'be in uncertainty' and therefore to resist neat categorization. And Isaiah Berlin identifies Turgenev as one such when he praises his habit 'of holding everything in solution – of remaining outside the situation, in a state of watchful and ironic detachment, uncommitted, evenly balanced ... For him reality escapes all ideological nets, all rigid, dogmatic assumptions, defies all attempts at codification.'[17]

Thucydides surely shares something of this quality too. His most enduring virtue may lie more in his intellectual temper than his quotable conclusions. We get the strong impression of an intense, penetrating gaze: quite unflinching and unsentimental but with a deep sense of the tragedies and ironies of the human condition; very knowing about its hopes, fears and vanities; fascinated by the political interactions of individuals and groups; aware of the role of chance and circumstance in interacting with human purposes to create the outcomes we call 'events'; and curious about details and their

[17] Berlin 1978: 148.

significance, serious about facts and about how the world works. That is surely quite sufficient by way of 'relevance'.

Further Reading

As noted in this chapter, the challenges of translating Thucydides have received notably little scholarly attention. An exception, and an excellent overview of both the theory and practice(s) of Thucydidean translation, is Greenwood 2015. Pade 2003 discusses mediaeval and Renaissance translations of Thucydides; Willett 1999 analyses some more recent translations. More generally on the translation of classical texts, see Hardwick 2000 and Lianeri and Zajko 2008.

BIBLIOGRAPHY

Manuscripts Cited

Leiden, University Library, BPL 917: autograph manuscript of Hugo Grotius, '*De Iure praedae Commentarius*', c. 1604–8.

Paris, Bibliothèque nationale de France, Département des manuscrits, Français 17211: Claude de Seyssel's translation of Thucydides, c. 1512–14.

Bibliography

Adkins, A. W. H. (1960) *Merit and Responsibility: A Study in Greek Values.* London.

(1975) 'The arete of Nicias: Thucydides 7.86', *GRBS* 16: 379–92.

Adler, W. and P. Tuffin (trans.) (2002) *The Chronography of George Synkellos.* Oxford.

Agacinski, S. (2003) *Time Passing: Modernity and Nostalgia.* New York.

Alberti, G. B. (1972–2000) *Thucydidis Historiae* (3 vols.). Rome.

Allison, G. (2017) *Destined for War: Can America and China Escape Thucydides's Trap?* Boston, MA.

Allison, J. (1984) 'Sthenelaidas' speech: Thucydides 1.86', *Hermes* 112: 9–16.

Alty, J. (1982) 'Dorians and Ionians', *JHS* 102: 1–14.

Aly, W. (1969) *Volksmärchen, Sage und Novelle bei Herodot und seinen Zeitgenossen*, 2nd edition. Göttingen.

Anderson, B. (1991) *Imagined Communities: Reflections on the Origins and Spread of Nationalism*, revised edition. London.

Anderson, J. K. (1991) 'Hoplite weapons and offensive arms', in *Hoplites: The Classical Greek Battle Experience*, ed. V. D. Hanson. London: 15–37.

Andreski, S. (1968) *Military Organization and Society*, 2nd edition. London.

Andrewes, A. (1962) 'The Mytilene Debate: Thucydides 3.36–49', *Phoenix* 16: 64–85.

(1974) *The Greek Tyrants.* London.

Arendt, H. (1970) *On Violence.* New York.

Argyriou, A. and G. Lagarrigue (1987) 'Georges Amiroutzes et son « Dialogue sur la foi au Christ tenu avec le Sultan des Turcs »', *Byzantinische Forschungen* 11: 29–221.

Armstrong, R. H. (2005) *A Compulsion for Antiquity: Freud and the Ancient World.* Ithaca, NY.

Arnold, J. H. (2000) *History. A Very Short Introduction.* Oxford.

Arnold, T. (1835) *The Life and Correspondence of Thomas Arnold* (2 vols.), ed. A. P. Stanley. London.

(1845) *Introductory Lectures on Modern History*, 3rd edition. London.

Ashcroft, B., G. Griffiths and H. Tiffin (2013) *Post-Colonial Studies: The Key Concepts*, 2nd edition. New York.

Avery, H. C. (1973) 'Themes in Thucydides' account of the Sicilian Expedition', *Hermes* 101: 1–13.

Azoulay, V. (2014) *Pericles of Athens*, trans. J. Lloyd. Princeton, NJ.

Bacon, F. (1629) 'Considerations touching a warre with Spaine', in *Certaine Miscellany Works of the Right Honourable, Francis Lo. Verulam, Viscount S. Alban*, ed. W. Rawley. London, 1–24.

Badian, E. (1971) 'Archons and *strategoi*', *Antichthon* 5: 1–34.

Bagby, L. M. J. (1994) 'The use and abuse of Thucydides in international relations', *International Organization* 48: 131–53.

Bakker, E. J. (2006) 'Contract and design: Thucydides' writing', in *Brill's Companion to Thucydides*, eds. A. Rengakos and A. Tsakmakis. Leiden and Boston: 109–29.

Balcer, J. M. (1976) 'Imperial magistrates in the Athenian Empire', *Historia* 25: 257–87.

Baldwin, B. (1982) 'Tzetzes on Thucydides', *Byzantinische Zeitschrift* 75: 313–16.

Balot, R. K. (2001) *Greed and Injustice in Classical Athens*. Princeton, NJ.

(2014) *Courage in the Democratic Polis: Ideology and Critique in Classical Athens*. New York and Oxford.

(2015) 'Philosophy and "humanity": reflections on Thucydidean piety, justice, and necessity', in *In Search of Humanity. Essays in Honor of Clifford Orwin*, ed. A. Radasanu. New York: 17–35.

(2016) 'Civic trust in Thucydides' *History*', in *Thucydides and Political Order: Concepts of Order and the History of the Peloponnesian War*, eds. C. R. Thauer and C. Wendt. New York: 151–73.

(2017) 'Was Thucydides a political philosopher?', in *The Oxford Handbook of Thucydides*, eds. R. K. Balot, S. Forsdyke and E. M. Foster. New York: 319–38.

Balot, R. K., S. Forsdyke and E. M. Foster (eds.) (2017) *The Oxford Handbook of Thucydides*. New York.

Bann, S. (1984) *The Clothing of Clio: A Study of the Representation of History in Nineteenth-Century Britain and France*. Cambridge and New York.

Baragwanath, E. (2008) *Motivation and Narrative in Herodotus*. Oxford.

Barbour, R. (1954–56) 'A Thucydides belonging to Ciriaco d'Ancona', *Bodleian Library Record* 5: 7–13.

Barker, E. (2009) *Entering the Agon: Dissent and Authority in Homer, Historiography and Tragedy*. Oxford.

Beard, M. (2010) 'Which Thucydides can you trust?', *New York Review of Books*, 30 September.

Bearzot, C. (2004) 'Il Cleone di Tucidide tra Archidamo e Pericle', in *Ad fontes! Festschrift für Gerhard Dobesch*, eds. H. Heftner and K. Tomaschitz. Vienna: 125–35.

Beiser, F. C. (2011a) *The German Historicist Tradition*. Oxford.

(2011b) 'Hegel and Ranke: a re-examination', *A Companion to Hegel*, eds. S. Houlgate and M. Baur. Oxford: 332–50.

Bellos, D. (2011) *Is That a Fish in Your Ear? Translation and the Meaning of Everything*. Harmondsworth.

Bender, G. F. (1938) *Der Begriff des Staatsmannes bei Thukydides*. Würzberg.

Berent, M. (2000) 'Anthropology and the classics: war, violence, and the stateless polis', *CQ* 50: 257–89.

Berlin, I. (1978) *Selected Writings. Vol. I: Russian Thinkers*. London.

Best, J. (1969) *Thracian Peltasts and Their Influence on Greek Warfare*. Groningen.

Blass, F. (1868) *Die attische Beredsamkeit, I: Von Gorgias bis zu Lysias*, 1st edition. Leipzig.

Bloedow, E. F. (1973) *Alcibiades Reexamined*. Wiesbaden.

  (1981) 'The speeches of Archidamus and Sthenelaidas at Sparta', *Historia* 30: 129–43.

  (1987) 'Sthenelaidas the persuasive Spartan', *Hermes* 115: 60–6.

  (1991) 'On "nurturing lions in the state": Alcibiades' entry on the political stage in Athens', *Klio* 73: 49–65.

  (1996) 'The speeches of Hermocrates and Athenagoras at Syracuse in 415 BC: difficulties in Syracuse and in Thucydides', *Historia* 45: 141–58.

  (2000) 'The implications of a major contradiction in Pericles' career', *Hermes* 128: 295–309.

Blok, J. H. and S. D. Lambert (2009) 'The appointment of priests in Attic *gene*', *ZPE* 169: 95–121.

Blösel, W. (2012) 'Thucydides on Themistocles: a Herodotean narrator?', in *Thucydides and Herodotus*, eds. E. M. Foster and D. Lateiner. Oxford: 215–40.

Boedeker, D. and D. Sider (eds.) (2001) *The New Simonides: Contexts of Praise and Desire*. Oxford.

Bommeljé, S. (1988) 'Aeolis in Aetolia: Thuc. 3.102.5 and the origins of the Aetolian "ethnos"', *Historia* 37: 297–316.

Boone, R. A. (2007) *War, Domination, and the Monarchy of France: Claude de Seyssel and the Language of Politics in the Renaissance*. Leiden.

Bosworth, A. B. (1993) 'The humanitarian aspect of the Melian Dialogue', *JHS* 113: 30–44.

Bowie, E. (1986) 'Early Greek elegy, symposium and public festival', *JHS* 106: 13–35.

Bradeen, D. W. (1960) 'The popularity of the Athenian Empire', *Historia* 9: 257–69.

Bransby, G. (1992) *Her Majesty's Vietnam Soldier*. Worcester.

Braun, H. (1885) *Procopius Caesariensis quatenus imitatus sit Thucydidem*. Erlangen.

Brice, L. (2013) 'The Athenian expedition to Sicily', in *The Oxford Handbook of Warfare in the Classical World*, eds. B. Campbell and L. Tritle. Oxford: 623–41.

Brunt, P. A. (1952) 'Thucydides and Alcibiades', *REG* 65: 59–96.

  (1953) 'The Hellenic League against Persia', *Historia* 2: 135–63.

  (1993) *Studies in Greek History and Thought*. Oxford.

'Brutus, Stephanus Junius' (1579) *Vindiciae, Contra Tyrannos: sive, de Principis in Populum, Populíque in Principem, legitima potestate*. 'Edimburgi' [but Basel].

Bruzzone, R. (2017) '*Polemos, pathemata*, and plague: Thucydides' narrative and the tradition of upheaval', *GRBS* 57: 882–909.

Burke, P. (1966) 'A survey of the popularity of ancient historians, 1450–1700', *History and Theory* 5: 135–52.

Burns, T. (2010) 'Marcellinus' *Life of Thucydides*', *Interpretation* 38: 3–26.

Bury, J. B. (1903) *The Science of History*. An Inaugural Lecture Delivered in the Divinity School, Cambridge. Cambridge.

(1958) *The Ancient Greek Historians*. New York.

(1966) *A History of Greece to the Death of Alexander the Great*, 3rd edition, rev. R. Meiggs. New York.

Büttner-Wobst, T. and A. G. Roos (eds.) (1906–1910) *Excerpta historica iussu imp. Constantini Porphyrogeniti confecta*, vol. II. Berlin.

Buxton, R. F. (ed.) (2016) *Aspects of Leadership in Xenophon*, Histos Suppl. 5.

Cairns, D. L. (1993) *Aidōs: The Psychology and Ethics of Honour and Shame in Ancient Greek Literature*. Oxford.

(2019) 'Honour and kingship in Herodotus: status, role, and the limits of self-assertion', *Frontiers of Philosophy in China* 14: 75–93.

Cairns, F. (1982) 'Cleon and Pericles: a suggestion', *JHS* 102: 203–4.

Călinescu, M. (1987) *Five Faces of Modernity: Modernism, Avant-garde, Decadence, Kitsch, Postmodernism*. Durham, NC.

Cambiano, G. (2000) *Polis: Un modello per la cultura europea*. Rome and Bari.

Canevaro, M. (2019) 'La deliberation démocratique à l'Assemblée athénienne: procédures et stratégies de legitimation', *Annales HSS* 74: 339–81.

Canfora, L. (2006) 'Biographical obscurities and problems of composition', in *Brill's Companion to Thucydides*, eds. A. Rengakos and A. Tsakmakis. Leiden and Boston: 3–31.

Carawan, E. (1996) 'The trials of Thucydides 'the Demagogue' in the anonymous "Life" of Thucydides the Historian', *Historia* 45: 405–22.

Carney, E. (2010) 'Macedonian women', in *A Companion to Ancient Macedonia*, eds. J. Roisman and I. Worthington. Malden, MA: 409–27.

Carr, E. H. (1987) *What Is History?*, 2nd edition. Harmondsworth.

Carroll, L. (1871) *Through the Looking Glass, and What Alice Found There*. London.

Carsten, J. (2000) *Cultures of Relatedness: New Approaches to the Study of Kinship*. Cambridge.

Cartledge, P. (1993) 'The silent women of Thucydides: 2.45.2 re-viewed', in *Nomodeiktes: Greek Studies in Honor of Martin Ostwald*, eds. R. M. Rosen and J. Farrell. Ann Arbor: 125–32.

(1998a) 'Introduction: defining a *kosmos*', in *Kosmos: Essays in Order, Conflict and Community in Classical Athens*, eds. P. Cartledge, P. Millett and S. von Reden. Cambridge: 1–12.

(1998b) 'The *machismo* of the Athenian empire – or the reign of the phaulus?', in *When Men Were Men: Masculinity, Power and Identity in Classical Antiquity*, eds. L. Foxhall and J. Salmon. London: 54–67.

(2001a) 'Spartan kingship: doubly odd?', in *Spartan Reflections*. Berkeley: 55–67.

(2001b) 'The peculiar position of Sparta in the development of the Greek city-state', in *Spartan Reflections*. Berkeley: 21–38.

Cartledge, P. and P. Debnar (2006) 'Sparta and the Spartans in Thucydides', in *Brill's Companion to Thucydides*, eds. A. Rengakos and A. Tsakmakis. Leiden and Boston: 559–87.

Casson, L. (1971) *Ships and Seamanship in the Ancient World*. Princeton.

Cavallo, G. (1986) 'Conservazione e perdita dei testi greci: fattori materiali, sociali, culturali', in *Tradizione dei classici, Trasformazioni della cultura*, ed. A. Giardin. Rome: 83–172.

Cawkwell, G. L. (1978) *Philip of Macedon*. London.

(1987) *Thucydides and the Peloponnesian War*. London.

(1989) 'Orthodoxy and hoplites', *CQ* 39: 375–89.

(1997) *Thucydides and the Peloponnesian War*. London and New York.

Chambers, M. (2008) *Valla's Translation of Thucydides in Vat. Lat. 1801 with the Reproduction of the Codex*. Vatican City.

Chaniotis, A. (2013) 'Greeks under siege: challenges, experiences, and emotions', in *The Oxford Handbook of Warfare in the Classical World*, eds. B. Campbell and L. Tritle. Oxford: 438–56.

Christ, M. R. (2006) *The Bad Citizen in Classical Athens*. Cambridge.

Chytraeus, D. (1563) *Chronologia Historiae Herodoti, & Thucydidis*. Strasbourg.

(1567) *Chronologia Historiae Herodoti et Thucydidis*. Rostock.

Cogan, M. (1981) *The Human Thing: The Speeches and Principles of Thucydides' History*. Chicago.

Collingwood, R. G. (1939) *An Autobiography*. Oxford.

Connor, W. R. (1971) *The New Politicians of Fifth-Century Athens*. Princeton.

(1977) 'A post modernist Thucydides?', *CJ* 72: 289–98.

(1984a) 'Review of A. W. Gomme, A. Andrewes, and K. J. Dover *A Historical Commentary on Thucydides, Vol. 5: Book 8*', *CPh* 79: 230–5.

(1984b) *Thucydides*. Princeton.

(1985) 'Narrative discourse in Thucydides', in *The Greek Historians. Literature and History. Papers Presented to A. E. Raubitschek*, ed. M. H. Jameson. Saratoga, CA: 1–17.

(1988) 'Early Greek land warfare as symbolic expression', *P&P* 119: 3–29.

(1994) 'The problem of Athenian civic identity', in *Athenian Identity and Civic Ideology*, eds. A. L. Boegehold and A. C. Scafuro. London: 34–44.

(2017–18) 'Pericles on democracy: Thucydides 2.37.1', *CW* 111: 165–75.

Constantakopoulou, C. (2013) 'Tribute, the Athenian Empire and small states and communities in the Aegean', in *Handels- und Finanzgebaren in der Ägäis im 5. Jh. v. Chr., Trade and Finance in the Fifth Century* BC *Aegean World*, ed. A. Slawisch. Istanbul: 25–42.

Cook, M. L. (2006) 'Thucydides as a resource for teaching ethics and leadership in military education environments', *Journal of Military Ethics* 5: 353–62.

Corcella, A. (2006) 'The new genre and its boundaries: poets and logographers.' in *Brill's Companion to Thucydides*, eds. A. Rengakos and A. Tsakmakis. Leiden and Boston: 33–56.

Cornford, F. (1907) *Thucydides Mythistoricus*. London.

Crane, G. (1996) *The Blinded Eye: Thucydides and the New Written Word*. Lanham, MD, and London.

(1998) *Thucydides and the Ancient Simplicity: The Limits of Political Realism*. Berkeley.

Crawley, R. (trans.) (1874) *The History of the Peloponnesian War*. London.

Crowley, J. (2012) *The Psychology of the Athenian Hoplite: The Culture of Combat in Classical Athens*. Cambridge.

d'Andrea, A. (1970) 'The political and ideological context of Innocent Gentillet's Anti-Machiavel', *Renaissance Quarterly* 23: 397–411.

Daub, S. (1996) *Leonardo Brunis Rede auf Nanni Strozzi: Einleitung, Edition und Kommentar*. Stuttgart and Leipzig.

Debnar, P. (2001) *Speaking the Same Language: Speech and Audience in Thucydides'*
Spartan Debates. Ann Arbor.

(2013) 'Blurring the boundaries of speech: Thucydides and indirect discourse', in
Thucydides Between History and Literature, eds. A. Tsakmakis and M.
Tamiolaki. Berlin and Boston: 271–85.

Delebecque, E. (1965) *Thucydide et Alcibiade*. Aix en Provence.

Demont, P. (2013) 'The causes of the Athenian plague in Thucydides', in *Thucydides*
between History and Literature, eds. A. Tsakmakis and M. Tamiolaki. Berlin
and Boston: 73–87.

Denniston, J. D. (1952) *Greek Prose Style*. Oxford.

Derks, T. and N. Roymans (eds.) (2009) *Ethnic Constructs in Antiquity: The Role of*
Power and Tradition. Amsterdam.

Develin, R. (1979) 'The election of archons from Solon to Telesinos', *L'antiquité*
classique 48: 455–68.

Dewald, C. (1987) 'Narrative surface and authorial voice in Herodotus' *Histories'*,
Arethusa 20: 147–70.

(1999) 'The figured stage: focalizing the initial narratives of Herodotus and
Thucydides', in *Contextualizing Classics: Ideology, Performance, Dialogue.*
Festschrift Peradotto, eds. N. Felson, D. Konstan and T. Faulkner. Lanham,
MD: 229–61.

(2005) *Thucydides' War Narrative: A Structural Study*. Berkeley.

(2009) 'The figured stage: focalizing the initial narratives of Herodotus and
Thucydides', in *Thucydides*, ed. J. S. Rusten. Oxford Readings in Classical
Studies. Oxford: 114–47.

Dickey, E. (2007) *Ancient Greek Scholarship*. Oxford.

Dougherty, C. and L. Kurke (eds.) (2003) *The Cultures within Greek Cultures:*
Contact, Conflict, Collaboration. Cambridge.

Dover, K. J. (1965) *Thucydides, Book 6*. Oxford.

(1973) *Thucydides*. Oxford.

Doyle, M. W. (1986) *Empires*. Ithaca, NY.

Ducat, J. (2006) *Spartan Education: Youth and Society in the Classical Period.*
Swansea.

Earl, D. C. (1972) 'Prologue form in ancient historiography', *ANRW* I: 842–56.

Earley, B. (2020) *The Thucydidean Turn. (Re)Interpreting Thucydides' Political*
Thought Before, During and After the Great War. London.

Eco, U. (2003) *Mouse or Rat: Translation as Negotiation*. London.

Edmunds, L. (1975) *Chance and Intelligence in Thucydides*. Cambridge, MA.

(2009) 'Thucydides in the act of writing', in *Thucydides*, ed. J. S. Rusten. Oxford
Readings in Classical Studies. Oxford: 91–113.

Ellis, J. R. (1978) 'Thucydides at Amphipolis', *Antichthon* 12: 28–35.

Engel, G. (1910) 'De antiquorum epicorum didacticorum historicorum prooemiis',
Dissertation, Marburg.

Erskine, A. (2001) *Troy between Greece and Rome*. Oxford.

Euben, J. P. (2010) 'Thucydides in Baghdad', in *When Worlds Elide*, eds. J. P. Euben
and K. Bassi. Lexington: 161–84.

Evans, J. A. S. (1976) 'The attitudes of the secular historians of the Age of Justinian
towards the classical past', *Traditio* 32: 353–8.

Evans, R. J. (1997) *In Defence of History*. London.

Evelyn-White, H. G. (1914) *Hesiod: Theogony, Works and Days, Testimonia.* Loeb Classical Library 57. Cambridge, MA.

Fabian, J. (2014) *Time and the Other: How Anthropology Makes Its Object,* 2nd edition. New York.

Farrar, C. (1988) *The Origins of Democratic Thinking: The Invention of Politics in Classical Athens.* Cambridge.

Feeney, D. (1994) 'Beginning Sallust's Catiline', *Prudentia* 26: 139–46.

Ferrario, S. B. (2013) '"Reading" Athens: foreign perceptions of the political roles of Athenian leaders in Thucydides', in *Thucydides between History and Literature,* eds. A. Tsakmakis and M. Tamiolaki. Berlin and Boston: 181–97.

   (2014) *Historical Agency and the 'Great Man' in Classical Greece.* Cambridge.

Finley, J. H. (1939) 'The origins of Thucydides' style', *HSCPh* 50: 35–84. (Reprinted in *Three Essays on Thucydides,* Cambridge, MA, 1967: 55–117.)

   (1940) 'The unity of Thucydides' *History*', in *Athenian Studies Presented to William Scott Ferguson.* HSCPh Supplement. Cambridge, MA: 255–97. (Reprinted in *Three Essays on Thucydides,* Cambridge, MA, 1967: 118–69.)

   (1942) *Thucydides.* Oxford.

   (1967) *Three Essays on Thucydides.* Cambridge, MA.

Finley, M. I. (1962) 'Athenian demagogues', *Past and Present* 21: 3–24.

   (1968) 'Thucydides the moralist', in *Aspects of Antiquity: Discoveries and Controversies.* New York: 44–57.

   (1978) 'The fifth-century Athenian Empire: a balance sheet', in *Imperialism in the Ancient World,* eds. P. D. A. Garnsey and C. Whittaker. Cambridge: 103–26.

Fisher, M. and K. Hoekstra (2017) 'Thucydides and the politics of necessity', in *The Oxford Handbook of Thucydides,* eds. R. K. Balot, S. Forsdyke and E. M. Foster. New York: 373–90.

Flacelière, R. (1937) *Les Aitoliens à Delphes.* B.E.F.A.R. 143. Paris.

Flory, S. (1990) 'The meaning of τὸ μὴ μυθῶδες (1,22,4) and the usefulness of Thucydides' *History*', *CJ* 85: 193–208.

   (1993) 'The death of Thucydides and the motif of "land on sea"', in *Nomodeiktes: Greek Studies in Honor of Martin Ostwald,* eds. R. M. Rosen and J. Farrell. Ann Arbor: 113–23.

Flower, M. A. (2009) 'Athenian religion and the Peloponnesian War', in *Art in Athens during the Peloponnesian War,* ed. O. Palagia. Cambridge: 1–23.

Flower, M. A. and J. Marincola (eds.) (2002) *Herodotus. Histories. Book IX.* Cambridge.

Foerster, R. and E. Richtsteig (eds.) (1929) *Choricii Gazaei opera.* Leipzig.

Forde, S. (1989) *The Ambition to Rule: Alcibiades and the Politics of Imperialism in Thucydides.* Ithaca, NY.

Fornara, C. W. (1971a) *Herodotus: An Interpretative Essay.* Oxford.

   (1971b) 'Evidence for the date of Herodotus' publication', *JHS* 91: 25–34.

   (1981) 'Herodotus' knowledge of the Archidamian War', *Hermes* 109: 149–56.

   (1983) *The Nature of History in Ancient Greece and Rome.* Berkeley.

Forrest, W. G. (1969) 'Two chronographic notes', *CQ* 19: 95–110.

Foster, E. M. (2010) *Thucydides, Pericles, and Athenian Imperialism.* Cambridge and New York.

Fowler, R. L. (1996) 'Herodotos and his contemporaries', *JHS* 116: 62–87.

   (2013) *Early Greek Mythography. Commentary,* vol. II. Oxford.

Fox, M. (2001) 'Dionysius, Lucian, and the prejudice against rhetoric in history', *JRS* 91: 76–93.

Fragoulaki, M. (2013) *Kinship in Thucydides: Intercommunal Ties and Historical Narrative*. Oxford.

(2020a) 'Thucydides Homericus and the episode of Mycalessus (Th. 7.29–30): myth and history, space and collective memory', in *Shaping Memory in Ancient Greece: Poetry, Historiography and Epigraphy*, eds. C. Constantakopoulou and M. Fragoulaki. *Histos* Suppl. 11: 37–86.

(2020b) 'The mytho-political map of Spartan colonisation in Thucydides: the "Spartan colonial triangle" vs. the "Spartan Mediterranean"', in *Thucydides and Sparta*, eds. P. Debnar and A. Powell. Swansea: 183–220.

Fritzsche, P. (2001) 'Specters of history: on nostalgia, exile, and modernity', *The American Historical Review* 106: 1587–618.

Fromentin, V. and S. Gotteland (2015) 'Thucydides' ancient reputation', in *A Handbook to the Reception of Thucydides*, eds. C. Lee and N. Morley. Chichester: 13–25.

Fromentin, V., S. Gotteland and P. Payen (eds.) (2010) *Ombres de Thucydide. La réception de l'historien depuis l'Antiquité jusqu'au début du XXe siècle*. Pessac.

Furley, W. (2006) 'Thucydides and religion', in *Brill's Companion to Thucydides*, eds. A. Rengakos and A. Tsakmakis. Leiden and Boston: 415–38.

Gaca, K. (2010) 'The andrapodizing of war captives in Greek historical memory', *TAPhA* 140: 117–61.

Gallie, W. B. (1956) 'Essentially contested concepts', *Proceedings of the Aristotelian Society* 56: 167–98.

Garlan, Y. (1975) *War in the Ancient World*. London.

Garland, R. (1992) *Introducing New Gods*. London.

Garst, D. (1989) 'Thucydides and neorealism', *International Studies Quarterly* 33: 3–27.

Gautier, P. (ed.) (1989) *Michaelis Pselli Theologica*, vol. I. Leipzig.

Genette, G. (1980) *Narrative Discourse: An Essay in Method*, trans. J. E. Lewin, with a foreword by J. Culler. Ithaca, NY.

Gentili, A. (1585) *De legationibus, libri tres*. London.

(1587) *Disputationum decas prima*. London.

(1933) *De iure belli libri tres*. Oxford. (Citations are to page numbers of the English and Latin volumes, respectively (vol. 1, reproduction of the 1612 Hanau edition; vol. 2, trans. J. C. Rolfe).)

Gentillet, I. (1576) *Discours, svr les moyens de bien govverner et maintenir en bonne paix vn Royaume ou autre Principauté ... Contre Nicolas Machiauel Florentin*. N.p.

Geuss, R. (2005) 'Thucydides, Nietzsche, and Williams', in *Outside Ethics*. Princeton: 219–33.

(2008) *Philosophy and Real Politics*. Princeton.

Gibson, G. (2004) 'Learning Greek history in the ancient classroom: the evidence of the treatises on progymnasmata', *CPh* 99: 103–29.

Gilpin, R. (1988) 'The theory of hegemonic war', *Journal of Interdisciplinary History* 18: 591–613.

Goldhill, S. D. (2002) *Who Needs Greek? Contests in the Cultural History of Hellenism*. Cambridge and New York.

(2009) 'The audience on stage: rhetoric, emotion, and judgement in Sophoclean theatre', in *Sophocles and the Greek Tragic Tradition*, eds. S. Goldhill and E. Hall. Cambridge: 27–47.

(2011) *Victorian Culture and Classical Antiquity: Art, Opera, Fiction, and the Proclamation of Modernity*. Princeton.

Goldsworthy, A. K. (1997) 'The *othismos*, myths and heresies: the nature of hoplite battle', *War in History* 4: 1–26.

Golfin, E. (2011) 'Reflections on the causes of evil in Thucydides' work', in *Thucydides – A Violent Teacher? History and Its Representations*, eds. G. Rechenauer and V. Pothou. Gottingen: 213–39.

Gomme, A. W. (1937) 'The greatest war in Greek history', in *Essays in Greek History and Literature*. Oxford: 116–24.

Gomme, A. W., A. Andrewes and K. J. Dover (1945–81) *A Historical Commentary on Thucydides* (5 vols.). Oxford.

Gould, S. J. (1977) *Ontogeny and Phylogeny*. Cambridge, MA.

Grafton, A. (1997) *The Footnote: A Curious History*. Cambridge, MA.

Grafton, A., G. W. Most and J. E. G. Zetzel (1985) 'Introduction', in *Prolegomena to Homer, 1795*, ed. F. A. Wolf. New Jersey: 3–36.

Graninger, D. (2015) 'Ethnicity and *ethne*', in *A Companion to Ancient Thrace*, eds. J. Valeva, E. Nankov and D. Graninger. Malden, MA: 22–32.

Grant, J. (1974) 'Toward knowing Thucydides', *Phoenix* 28: 81–94.

Gray, V. J. (2011) *Xenophon's Mirror of Princes: Reading the Reflections*. Oxford.

Green, P. (2004) 'Athenian history and historians in the fifth century', in *From Ikaria to the Stars*. Austin: 67–103.

Greenwood, E. (2006) *Thucydides and the Shaping of History*. London.

(2015) 'On translating Thucydides', in *A Handbook to the Reception of Thucydides*, eds. C. Lee and N. Morley. Chichester: 91–121.

(2016) 'Futures real and unreal in Greek historiography: from Herodotus to Plato', in *Knowing Future Time in and through Greek Historiography*. Trends in Classics, supplementary vol. 32, ed. A. Lianeri. Berlin: 79–100.

(2017) 'Thucydides on the Sicilian Expedition', in *The Oxford Handbook of Thucydides*, eds. R. K. Balot, S. Forsdyke and E. M. Foster. New York: 161–77.

(2018) 'Pericles' utopia: a reading of Thucydides and Plato', in *How to Do Things with History*, eds. D. Allen, P. Christesen and P. Millett. Oxford: 55–80.

Grell, C. (1993) *L'histoire entre érudition et philosophie. Essai sur la connaissance historique à l'âge des Lumières*. Paris.

Grethlein, J. (2006) 'The unthucydidean voice of Sallust', *TAPhA* 136: 299–327.

(2010a) 'Experientiality and "narrative reference" with thanks to Thucydides', *History and Theory* 49: 315–35.

(2010b) *The Greeks and their Past. Poetry, Oratory and History in the Fifth Century* BCE. Cambridge.

(2011) 'The rise of Greek historiography and the invention of prose', in *The Oxford History of Historical Writing. Vol. 1: Beginnings to* AD 600, ed. A. Feldherr. Oxford: 148–70.

(2013a) *Experience and Teleology in Ancient Historiography. Futures Past from Herodotus to Augustine*. Cambridge.

(2013b) 'The presence of the past in Thucydides', in *Thucydides between History and Literature*, eds. A. Tsakmakis and M. Tamiolaki. Berlin and Boston: 91–118.

(2016) 'Ancient historiography and "future past"', in *Knowing Future Time in and through Greek Historiography*, ed. A Lianeri. Berlin and Boston: 59–77.

Grethlein, J. and C. B. Krebs (eds.) (2012) *Time and Narrative in Ancient Historiography. The 'Plupast' from Herodotus to Appian*. Cambridge.

Gribble, D. (1998) 'Narrator invention in Thucydides', *JHS* 118: 41–67.

(1999) *Thucydides and Athens*. Oxford.

Griggio, C. (1986) 'Due lettere inedite del Bruni al Salutati e a Francesco Barbaro', *Rinascimento* 26: 27–50.

Grissom, D. (2012) 'Thucydides' dangerous world: dual forms of danger in classical Greek interstate relations', Dissertation, University of Maryland, College Park.

Grote, G. (1843) '"Grecian legends and early Greek history": review of Niebuhr's *Griechische Heroen Geschichte*', *Westminster Review* 39: 285–328.

(1857) *History of Greece*, Vol. 5. Reprinted from the 1st London edition. New York.

(1880) *History of Greece*, Vol. 1. Reprint of the 2nd London edition. New York.

Grotius, H. (1625) *De ivre belli ac pacis libri tres*. Paris.

(1631) *De ivre belli ac pacis libri tres*. Amsterdam.

Grube, G. (1650) 'Dionysius of Halicarnassus on Thucydides', *Phoenix* 4: 95–110.

Gruen, E. S. (2011) *Rethinking the Other in Antiquity*. Princeton.

Grundy, G. B. (1911) *Thucydides and the History of His Age*. London.

Guha, R. (2002) *History at the Limit of World-History*. New York.

Hall, E. (2006) *The Theatrical Cast of Athens: Interactions Between Ancient Greek Drama and Society*. Oxford.

Hall, J. M. (1997) *Ethnic Identity in Greek Antiquity*. Cambridge.

(2001) 'Contested ethnicities: perceptions of Macedonia within evolving definitions of Greek identity', in *Ancient Perceptions of Greek Ethnicity*, ed. I. Malkin. Cambridge, MA: 159–86.

(2002) *Hellenicity: Between Ethnicity and Culture*. London.

Hamel, D. (1998) *Athenian Generals: Military Authority in the Classical Period*. Leiden and Boston.

Hammond, M. (2009) *Thucydides, The Peloponnesian War, A New Translation*. Oxford.

Hammond, N. G. L. (1952) 'The arrangement of thought in the proem and in other parts of Thucydides I', *CQ* 2: 127–41.

(1967) 'The origins and the nature of the Athenian alliance of 478/7 B.C.', *JHS* 87: 41–61.

(1969) 'Strategia and hegemonia in fifth century Athens', *CQ* 19: 111–44.

Hansen, M. H. (1980) 'Seven hundred *archai* in classical Athens', *GRBS* 21: 167–9.

(1999) *The Athenian Democracy in the Age of Demosthenes: Structure, Principles and Ideology*. Bristol.

Hanson, V. D. (1991) 'Hoplite technology in phalanx battle', in *Hoplites: The Classical Greek Battle Experience*, ed. V. D. Hanson. London: 63–84.

(1996) 'Hoplites into democrats: the changing ideology of the Athenian infantry', in *Dēmokratia: A Conversation on Democracies, Ancient and Modern*, eds. C. Hedrick and J. Ober. Princeton: 289–312.

(2000) *The Western Way of War: Infantry Battle in Classical Greece*. London.

(2001) 'Hoplite battle as ancient Greek warfare: when, where, and why?', in *War and Violence in Ancient Greece*, ed. H. van Wees. London: 201–32.

(2005) *A War Like No Other: How the Athenians and Spartans Fought the Peloponnesian War*. London.

Harding, P. (2007) 'Local history and atthidography,' in *A Companion to Greek and Roman Historiography*, ed. J. Marincola. Malden, MA, and Oxford: 180–8.

Hardwick, L. (2000) *Translating Words, Translating Cultures*. London.

Harloe, K. (2013) *Winckelmann and the Invention of Antiquity: History and Aesthetics in the Age of Altertumswissenschaft*. Oxford.

Harloe, K. and N. Morley (2012a) 'Introduction', in *Thucydides and the Modern World: Reception, Reinterpretation and Influence from the Renaissance to the Present*, eds. K. Harloe and N. Morley. Cambridge: 1–24.

(eds.) (2012b) *Thucydides and the Modern World: Reception, Reinterpretation and Influence from the Renaissance to the Present*. Cambridge.

Harrison, T. (2000) 'Sicily in the Athenian imagination: Thucydides and the Persian Wars', in *Ancient Sicily*, eds. C. J. Smith and J. Serrati. Edinburgh: 84–96.

(ed.) (2001) *Greeks and Barbarians*. Edinburgh.

Harrison, T. and J. Skinner (eds.) (2020) *Herodotus in the Long Nineteenth Century*. Cambridge.

Hartog, F. (1988) *The Mirror of Herodotus: The Representation of the Other in the Writing of History*, trans. J. Lloyd. Berkeley.

Hatzopoulos, M. B. (2011) 'Macedonians and other Greeks', in *Brill's Companion to Ancient Macedon. Studies in the Archaeology and History of Macedon, 650 BC–300 AD*, ed. R. Lane Fox. Leiden: 51–78.

Hawthorn, G. (2014) *Thucydides on Politics: Back to the Present*. Cambridge.

Hegel, G. W. F. (1861) *Lectures on the Philosophy of History*, trans. (of 3rd German edition) and ed. J. Sibree. London.

Helm, R. (ed.) (1956) *Die Chronik des Hieronymus* (= *Eusebius Werke*, vol. VII). Berlin.

Hemmerdinger, B. (1955) *Essai sur l'histoire du texte de Thucydide*. Paris.

Henderson, B. W. (1927) *The Great War between Athens and Sparta: A Companion to the Military History of Thucydides*. London.

Henry, R. (ed. and trans.) (1959–77) *Photius: Bibliothèque* (8 vols.). Paris.

Hesk, J. (2000) *Deception and Democracy in Classical Athens*. Cambridge.

Hinrichs, F. T. (1981) 'Hermokrates bei Thukydides', *Hermes* 109: 46–59.

Hirshfield, N. (1996) 'Appendix G: trireme warfare in Thucydides', in *The Landmark Thucydides: A Comprehensive Guide to the Peloponnesian War*, ed. R. Strassler. New York: 608–13.

Hobbes, T. (trans.) (1629) *Eight Bookes of the Peloponnesian Warre*. London.

(1975) *Hobbes' Thucydides*, ed. R. Schlatter. New Brunswick.

Hodkinson, S. (1983) 'Social order and the conflict of values in classical Sparta', *Chiron* 13: 245–51.

(2000) *Property and Wealth in Classical Sparta*. Swansea.

Hoekstra, K. (2012) 'Thucydides and the bellicose beginnings of modern political theory', in *Thucydides and the Modern World: Reception, Reinterpretation, and Influence from the Renaissance to the Present*, eds. K. Harloe and N. Morley. Cambridge: 25–54.

(2016) 'Hobbes's Thucydides', in *The Oxford Handbook of Hobbes*, eds. A. P. Martinich and K. Hoekstra. Oxford: 547–74.

Honig, B. (2013) *Antigone, Interrupted*. Cambridge.

Honig, B. and M. Stears (2011) 'The new realism: from *modus vivendi* to justice', in *Political Philosophy versus History?*, eds. J. Floyd and M. Stears. Cambridge: 177–205.

Hornblower, S. (1987) *Thucydides*. Baltimore.

(1990) 'Intellectual affinities', in *Thucydides*, ed. J. S. Rusten. Oxford Readings in Classical Studies. Oxford: 60–88.

(1991–2008) *A Commentary on Thucydides* (3 vols.). Oxford.

(1992) 'The religious dimension to the Peloponnesian War, or, what Thucydides does not tell us', *HSCPh* 94: 169–97. (Reprinted in *Thucydidean Themes*, Oxford, 2011: 25–53.)

(1994a) 'Narratology and narrative techniques in Thucydides', in *Greek Historiography*, ed. S. Hornblower. Oxford: 131–66. (Reprinted in *Thucydidean Themes*, Oxford, 2011: 59–99.)

(1994b) *Thucydides*, 2nd (corrected) impression. London.

(1995) 'The fourth-century and Hellenistic reception of Thucydides', *JHS* 115: 46–68. (Reprinted in *Thucydidean Themes*. Oxford, 2011: 286–322.)

(2000) 'Personal names and the study of the ancient Greek historians', in *Greek Personal Names: Their Value as Evidence* eds. S. Hornblower and E. Matthews. Oxford: 129–43.

(2004) *Thucydides and Pindar: Historical Narrative and the World of Epinikian Poetry*. Oxford and New York.

(2007) 'Warfare in ancient literature: the paradox of war', in *The Cambridge History of Greek and Roman Warfare, Vol. 1: Greece, the Hellenistic World and the Rise of Rome*, eds. P. Sabin, H. van Wees and M. Whitby. Cambridge: 22–53.

(2008) 'Greek identity in the archaic and classical periods', in *Hellenisms: Culture, Identity, and Ethnicity from Antiquity to Modernity*, ed. K. Zacharia. Aldershot: 375–8.

(2009) 'Intellectual affinities', in *Thucydides*, ed. J. S. Rusten. Oxford Readings in Classical Studies. Oxford: 60–88.

(2011a) 'Sticks, stones, and Spartans', in *Thucydidean Themes*. Oxford: 250–74.

(2011b) *The Greek World*. 479–323 BC, 4th edition. London.

(2011c) 'Thucydides' awareness of Herodotus, or Herodotus' awareness of Thucydides?', in *Thucydidean Themes*. Oxford: 277–85.

(2013) *Herodotus. Histories. Book V*. Cambridge.

Hose, M. (2006) 'Peloponnesian War: sources other than Thucydides', in *Brill's Companion to Thucydides*, eds. A. Rengakos and A. Tsakmakis. Leiden and Boston: 669–90.

Howie, J. G. (2005) 'The *aristeia* of Brasidas: Thucydides' presentation of events at Pylos and Amphipolis', *PLLS* 12: 207–84.

Hude, K. (1927) *Scholia in Thucydidem ad optimos codices collata*. Leipzig.

Hunger, H. (1969–70) 'On the imitation (ΜΙΜΗΣΙΣ) of antiquity in Byzantine literature', *Dumbarton Oaks Papers* 23–24: 17–38.

Hunt, P. (1998) *Slaves, Warfare, and Ideology in the Greek Historians*. Cambridge.

(2006) 'Warfare', in *Brill's Companion to Thucydides*, eds. A. Rengakos and A. Tsakmakis. Boston and Leiden: 385–413.

(2007) 'Military force', in *The Cambridge History of Greek and Roman Warfare, Vol. 1: Greece, the Hellenistic World and the Rise of Rome*, eds. P. Sabin, H. van Wees and M. Whitby. Cambridge: 108–46.

Hunter, V. J. (1973) *Thucydides, the Artful Reporter*. Toronto.

(1982) *Past and Process in Herodotus and Thucydides*. Princeton.

Hyland, A. (2013a) 'War and the horse: Part 1: horses for war: breeding and keeping a warhorse', in *The Oxford Handbook of Warfare in the Classical World*, eds. B. Campbell and L. Tritle. Oxford: 493–511.

(2013b) 'Part II: the development and training of cavalry in Greece and Rome', in *The Oxford Handbook of Warfare in the Classical World*, eds. B. Campbell and L. Tritle. Oxford: 512–26.

Iggers, G. G. (1962) 'The image of Ranke in American and German historical thought', *History and Theory* 2: 17–40.

(2011) 'Introduction', in L. von Ranke, *The Theory and Practice of History*. London: xi–xliii.

Iglesias-Zoido, J. C. (2011) *El legado de Tucídides en la cultura occidental: Discursos e historia*. Coimbra.

Immerwahr, H. R. (1960) '*Ergon*: history as a monument in Herodotus and Thucydides', *AJPh* 81: 261–90.

Iori, L. (2015) *Thucydides Anglicus: Gli* Eight Bookes *di Thomas Hobbes e la ricezione inglese delle* Storie *di Tucidide (1450–1642)*. Rome.

Irwin, E. (2013a) '"The hybris of Theseus" and the date of the *Histories*', in *Herodots Quellen – Die Quellen Herodots*, eds. B. Dunsch and K. Ruffing. Classica et Orientalia 6. Wiesbaden: 7–84.

(2013b) 'To whom does Solon speak? Conceptions of happiness and ending life well in the later fifth century (Hdt. 1.29–33)', in *Wege des Erzählens: Logos und Topos bei Herodot*, eds. K. Geus, E. Irwin and T. Poiss. Frankfurt am Main: 261–321.

(2015a) 'Dionysius of Halicarnassus' *On Thucydides* and Thucydides' rhetoric of the episodic', in *Tecendo narrativas: unidade e episódio na literatura grega antiga*, eds. C. Werner, A. Dourado-Lopes and E. Werner. São Paulo: 121–99.

(2015b) 'The *nothoi* come of age? Illegitimate sons and political unrest in late fifth-century Athens', in *Minderheiten und Migration in der griechisch-römischen Welt: Politische, rechtliche, religiöse und kulturelle Aspekte*, ed. P. Sänger. Paderborn: 75–122.

(2018) 'The end of the *Histories* and the end of the Atheno-Peloponnesian Wars', in *Interpreting Herodotus*, eds. E. Irwin and T. J. Harrison. Oxford: 279–334.

Isaac, B. (2004) *The Invention of Racism in Classical Antiquity*. Princeton.

Jacoby, F. (1923–58) *Die Fragmente der Griechischen Historiker*. Berlin and Leiden.

Jaffe, S. N. (2015) 'The Straussian Thucydides', in *A Handbook to the Reception of Thucydides*, eds. C. Lee and N. Morley. Chichester: 278–95.

(2017a) 'The regime (*politeia*) in Thucydides', in *The Oxford Handbook of Thucydides*, eds. R. K. Balot, S. Forsdyke and E. M. Foster. New York: 391–408.

(2017b) 'The risks and rewards of Thucydides' *History of the Peloponnesian War*', *War on the Rocks*. 6 July. Available at: https://warontherocks.com/2017/07/the-risks-and-rewards-of-thucydides-history-of-the-peloponnesian-war/

(2017c) *Thucydides on the Outbreak of War: Character and Contest*. Oxford.

Jeffreys, E. (1979) 'The attitudes of Byzantine chronicles towards ancient history', *Byzantion* 49: 199–238.

Jenkins, K. (1991) *Re-thinking History*. London and New York.

Jesse, N. G. (2014) 'Ethnicity and identity in conflict', in *Routledge Handbook of Civil Wars*, eds. E. Newman and K. DeRouen, Jr. Oxford: 93–103.

Johnson, L. M. (2014) 'Thucydides the realist?' in *A Handbook to the Reception of Thucydides*, eds. N. Morley and C. Lee. Chichester: 391–405.

de Jong, I. J. F. (2014) *Narratology and Classics: A Practical Guide*. Oxford.

de Jonge, C. C. (2017) 'Dionysius of Halicarnassus on Thucydides', in *The Oxford Handbook of Thucydides*, eds. R. K. Balot, S. Forsdyke and E. M. Foster. New York: 781–800.

Jones, C. P. (1996) 'ἔθνος and γένος in Herodotus', *CQ* 46: 315–20.

(1999) *Kinship Diplomacy in the Ancient World*. Cambridge, MA.

Jones, H. S. and J. E. Powell (eds.) (1942) *Thucydidis Historiae* (2 vols.). Oxford.

Jowett, B. (1881) *Thucydides, Translated into English with Introduction, Marginal Analysis, Notes and Indices* (2 vols.). Oxford.

Kagan, D. (1974) *The Archidamian War*. London.

(1987) *The Fall of the Athenian Empire*. London.

(2009) *Thucydides: The Reinvention of History*. New York.

Kagan, D. and G. F. Viggiano (eds.) (2013) *Men of Bronze: Hoplite Warfare in Ancient Greece*. Princeton.

Kaldellis, A. (2004) *Procopius of Caesarea: Tyranny, History, and Philosophy at the End of Antiquity*. Philadelphia.

(2005) 'The works and days of Hesychios the Illoustrios of Miletos', *GRBS* 45: 381–403.

(2007) 'The literature of plague and the anxieties of piety in sixth-century Byzantium', in *Piety and Plague: From Byzantium to the Baroque*, eds. F. Mormando and T. Worcester. Kirksville, MO: 1–22.

(2009) 'Classical scholarship in twelfth-century Byzantium', in *Medieval Greek Commentaries on the* Nicomachean Ethics, eds. C. Barber and D. Jenkins. Leiden and Boston: 1–43.

(2012) 'The Byzantine role in the making of the corpus of classical Greek historiography: a preliminary investigation', *JHS* 132: 71–85.

(2014) *A New Herodotos: Laonikos Chalkokondyles on the Ottoman Empire, the Fall of Byzantium, and the Emergence of the West*. Cambridge, MA.

(2021) 'The classicism of Procopius', in *The Brill Companion to Procopius*, ed. M. Meier. Leiden and Boston.

Kallet, L. (1999) 'The diseased body politic, Athenian public finance, and the massacre at Mycalessos (Thucydides 7.27–29)', *AJPh* 120: 223–44.

(2001) *Money and the Corrosion of Power in Thucydides: The Sicilian Expedition and Its Aftermath*. Berkeley and London.

(2006) 'Thucydides' workshop of history and utility outside the text', in *Brill's Companion to Thucydides*, eds. A. Rengakos and A. Tsakmakis. Leiden and Boston: 335–68.

(2013a) 'The origins of the Athenian economic arche', *JHS* 133: 43–60.

(2013b) 'Thucydides, Apollo, the plague, and the war', *AJPh* 134: 355–82.

Kallet-Marx, L. (1993a) *Money, Expense, and Naval Power in Thucydides' History 1–5.24*. Berkeley and London.

(1993b) 'Thucydides 2.45.2 and the status of war widows in Periclean Athens', in *Nomodeiktes: Greek Studies in Honor of Martin Ostwald*, eds. R. M. Rosen and J. Farrell. Ann Arbor: 133–43.

(1994) 'Money talks: rhetor, demos and the reserve of the Athenian Empire', in *Ritual, Finance, Politics: Athenian Democratic Accounts Presented to D.M. Lewis*, eds. S. Hornblower and R. G. Osborne. Oxford: 227–51.

Kalyvas, S. N. (2006) *The Logic of Violence in Civil War*. Cambridge.

Karavites, P. (1984) 'Greek interstate relations in the fifth century BC', *PP* 216: 161–92.

Karp, W. (1998) 'The two thousand years' war', in *The Peloponnesian War*, ed. W. Blanco and J. T. Roberts. New York and London: 400–4. (Originally published in *Harpers Magazine*, 1981.)

Kelly, D. H. (1981) 'Thucydides and Herodotus on the Pitanate *lochos*', *GRBS* 22: 31–8.

Kennedy, G. A. (1963) *The Art of Persuasion in Greece*. Princeton.

(1991) *Aristotle: On Rhetoric. A Theory of Civic Discourse. Translated, with Introduction and Notes by G. A. Kennedy*. Oxford.

Kennedy, S. (2018a) 'A classic dethroned: the decline and fall of Thucydides in Middle Byzantium', *GRBS* 58: 607–35.

(2018b) 'How to write history: Thucydides and Herodotus in the ancient rhetorical tradition', Dissertation, The Ohio State University.

Kennell, N. M. (1995) *The Gymnasium of Virtue: Education and Culture in Ancient Sparta*. London.

Keohane, R. O. (ed.) (1986) *Neorealism and Its Critics*. New York.

Klee, U. (1990) *Beiträge zur Thukydides-Rezeption während des 15. und 16. Jahrhunderts in Italien und Deutschland*. Frankfurt.

Kleinlogel, A. (1965) *Geschichte des Thukydidestextes im Mittelalter*. Berlin.

(ed.) (2019) *Scholia Graeca in Thucydidem*. Berlin.

Kleinlogel, A. and K. Alpers (2019) *Scholia Graeca in Thucydidem, Scholia vetustiora et Lexicon Thucydideum Patmense, Aus dem Nachlass herausgegeben von Klaus Alpers*. Berlin.

Knox, B. (1956) 'The date of the *Oedipus Tyrannus* of Sophocles', *AJPh* 77: 133–47.

(1957) *Oedipus at Thebes*. New Haven.

Konstan, D. (2001) '*To Hellenikon ethnos*: ethnicity and the construction of ancient Greek identity', in *Ancient Perceptions of Greek Ethnicity*, ed. I. Malkin. Cambridge, MA: 29–50.

Koselleck, R. (2002) *The Practice of Conceptual History: Timing History, Spacing Concepts*, trans. T. S. Presner et al. Stanford.

(2004) *Futures Past: On the Semantics of Historical Time*. New York.

Koselleck, R., W. J. Mommsen and J. Rüsen (eds.) (1977) *Objektivität und Parteilichkeit in der Geschichtswissenschaft*. Munich.

Kosmetatou, E. (2013) 'Tyche's force: lottery and chance in Greek government', in *A Companion to Ancient Greek Government*, ed. H. Beck. Malden, MA: 235–51.

Kowerski, L. M. (2005) *Simonides on the Persian Wars. A Study of the Elegiac Verses of the 'New Simonides'*. New York.

Krentz. P. (1985) 'The nature of hoplite battle', *ClAnt* 4: 50–61.

(2007) 'War', in *The Cambridge History of Greek and Roman Warfare, Vol. 1: Greece, the Hellenistic World and the Rise of Rome*, eds. P. Sabin, H. van Wees and M. Whitby. Cambridge: 147–85.

Krieger, L. (1989) *Time's Reasons: Philosophies of History Old and New*. Chicago.

Laird, A. (1999) *Powers of Expression, Expressions of Power: Speech Presentation and Latin Literature*. Oxford.

Lambert, S. D. (2011) 'What was the point of inscribed honorific decrees in classical Athens?', in *A Sociable Man. Essays on Ancient Greek Social Behaviour in Honour of Nick Fisher*, ed. S. D. Lambert. Swansea: 193–214.

Landemore, H. (2012) *Democratic Reason: Politics, Collective Intelligence, and the Rule of the Many*. Princeton.

Lane Fox, R. J. (2010) 'Thucydides and documentary history', *CQ* 60: 11–29.

Lang, M. L. (1972) 'Cleon as the anti-Pericles', *CPh* 67: 159–69.

(2011) *Thucydidean Narrative and Discourse*, eds. J. S. Rusten and R. Hamilton. Ann Arbor.

Lateiner, D. (1976) 'Tissaphernes and the Phoenician fleet (Thuc. 8.87)', *TAPhA* 106: 267–90.

(1977a) 'Heralds and corpses in Thucydides', *CW* 71: 97–106.

(1977b) 'Pathos in Thucydides', *Antichthon* 11: 42–51.

(1985) 'Nicias' inadequate encouragement (Thucydides 7.69.2)', *CPh* 80: 201–13.

(1986) 'Early Greek medical writers and Herodotus', *Antichthon* 20: 1–20.

(2017) 'Review of Graham Allison, Destined for War. Can America and China escape the Thucydides Trap?', *Michigan War Studies Review* 2017: 63.

(2018) 'Elpis as emotion and reason (hope and expectation) in fifth-century Greek historians', in *Hope in Ancient Literature, History, and Art*, eds. D. Spatharas and G. Kazantzidis. Berlin and Boston: 131–50.

Lawrence, A. W. (1979) *Greek Aims in Fortification*. Oxford.

Lazenby, J. (1985) *The Spartan Army*. Warminster.

(1987) 'The diekplous', *G&R* 34: 169–77.

(1991) 'The killing zone', in *Hoplites: The Classical Greek Battle Experience*, ed. V. D. Hanson. London: 87–109.

(1993) *The Defence of Greece 490–479 BC*. Warminster.

(2004) *The Peloponnesian War: A Military Study*. London.

Lebow, R. N. (2001) 'Thucydides the constructivist', *American Political Science Review* 95: 547–60.

(2003) *The Tragic Vision of Politics*. Cambridge.

Lee, C. (2014) 'Thucydides and democratic horizons', in *A Handbook to the Reception of Thucydides*, eds. C. Lee and N. Morley. Chichester: 332–51.

(2016) 'The power and politics of ontology', in *Thucydides and Political Order: Concepts of Order and the History of the Peloponnesian War*, eds. C. Thauer and C. Wendt. Basingstoke and New York: 96–130.

Lee, C. and N. Morley (eds.) (2015) *A Handbook to the Reception of Thucydides*. Chichester.

Lefkowitz, M. (1981) *The Lives of the Greek Poets*. London.

Leimbach, R. (1985) *Militärische Musterrhetorik: eine Untersuchung zu den Feldherrnreden des Thukydides*. Stuttgart.

Leone, P. (1970–1) 'Nicephori Gregorae opuscula nunc primum edita', *Annali della Facoltà di Lettere e Filosofia dell' Università di Macerata* 3/4: 731–82.

Leslie, M. (1970) 'In praise of anachronism', *Political Studies* 18: 433–47.

Levene, D. (1992) 'Sallust's Jugurtha: an "historical fragment"', *JRS* 82: 53–70.

Lewis, D. M. (1977) *Sparta and Persia*. Leiden.

Lewis, S. (1996) *News and Society in the Greek Polis*. London.

Lianeri, A. (ed.) (2011) *The Western Time of Ancient History: Historiographical Encounters with the Greek and Roman Pasts*. Cambridge.

(2015) 'On historical time and method: Thucydides' contemporary history in nineteenth-century Britain', in *A Handbook to the Reception of Thucydides*, eds. C. Lee and N. Morley. Chichester: 176–96.

(ed.) (2016a) *Knowing Future Time in and through Greek Historiography*. Berlin and Boston.

(2016b) 'Introduction: the futures of Greek historiography', in *Knowing Future Time in and through Greek Historiography*, ed. A. Lianeri. Berlin and Boston: 1–54.

(2018) '*Historia Magistra Vitae*, interrupting: Thucydides and the agonistic temporality of antiquity and modernity', *History and Theory* 57: 327–48.

Lianeri, A. and V. Zajko (eds.) (2008) *Translation and the Classic: Identity as Change in the History of Culture*. Oxford.

Liberman, G. (2017) *Les préliminaires de la guerre: prolégomènes à la lecture du premier livre de Thucydide*. Bordeaux.

Liddell Hart, B. H. (1948) *The Other Side of the Hill: Germany's Generals, Their Rise and Fall, with Their Own Account of Military Events*. London.

Lipsius, J. (2004) *Politica*, ed. J. Waszink. Assen.

Listas, F. K. (1980) 'Choricius of Gaza: an approach to his work', Dissertation, University of Chicago.

Lloyd, G. E. R. (1979) *Magic, Reason, and Experience. Studies in the Origin and Development of Greek Science*. Cambridge.

Longrigg, J. (2000) 'Death and epidemic disease in classical Athens', in *Death and Disease in the Ancient City*, eds. V. Hope and E. Marshall. London and New York: 55–65.

Loraux, N. (1986a) *The Invention of Athens. The Funeral Oration in the Classical City*, trans. A. Sheridan. Cambridge, MA.

(1986b) 'Thucydide a écrit la guerre du Péloponnèse', *Métis* 1: 139–61.

(1993) *The Children of Athena: Athenian Ideas about Citizenship and the Division between the Sexes*, trans. C. Levine. Princeton.

(2009) 'Thucydides and sedition among words', in *Thucydides*, ed. J. S. Rusten. Oxford Readings in Classical Studies. Oxford: 261–92.

(2011) 'Thucydides is not a colleague', in *Greek and Roman Historiography*. Oxford Readings in Classical Studies, ed. J. Marincola. Oxford: 1–39. (Originally published as 'Thucydide n'est pas un collegue', *Quaderni di Storia* 12 (1980) 55–81.)

Loraux, N. and P. Vidal-Naquet (1990) 'La formation de l'Athènes bourgeoise. Essai d'historiographie, 1750–1850', in *La démocratie grecque vue d'ailleurs*, ed. P. Vidal-Naquet. Paris: 161–209, 362–83.

Lorenz, C. (2013) 'Explorations between philosophy and history', *Historein* 14: 59–70.

Low, P. A. (2007) *Interstate Relations in Classical Greece: Morality and Power*. Cambridge.

(2013) 'Law, authority and legitimacy in the Athenian Empire', in *Empire and Law*, eds. J. Duindam, J. Harries, C. Humfress and N. Hurvitz. Leiden and Boston: 25–44.

(2015) 'Empire and crisis in fourth-century Greece', in *Deformations and Crises of Ancient Civil Communities*, eds. V. Gouschin and P. J. Rhodes. Stuttgart: 63–72.

Luce, T. (1997) *The Greek Historians*. London.

Luginbill, R. D. (1994) '*Othismos*: the importance of the mass-shove in hoplite warfare', *Phoenix* 48: 51–61.

(1999) *Thucydides on War and National Character*. Boulder.

Luiso, F. P. (1980) *Studi su l'epistolario di Leonardo Bruni*, ed. L. Gualdo Rosa. Rome.

Luraghi, N. (2008) *The Ancient Messenians: Constructions of Ethnicity and Memory*. Cambridge.

(2014) 'The study of Greek ethnic identities', in *A Companion to Ethnicity in the Ancient Mediterranean*, ed. J. McInerney. Malden, MA: 213–27.

Luschnat, O. (1942) *Die Feldherrnreden im Geschichtswerk des Thucydides*, Philologus Supplementband 34.2. Leipzig.

(1974) 'Thukydides (1), Nachträge', *RE* Supp. XIV: 766–86.

Luzzato, M. J. (1999) *Tzetzes lettore di Tucidide: note autografe sul codice Heidelberg Palatino Greco 252*. Bari.

Mac Sweeney, N. (2013) *Foundation Myths and Politics in Ancient Ionia*. Cambridge.

Macleod, C. W. (1975) 'Rhetoric and history (Thucydides 6. 16–18)', *Quaderni di Storia* 2: 39–65.

(1977) 'Thucydides' Plataean Debate', *GRBS* 18: 227–46. (Reprinted in Macleod 1983: 103–22.)

(1978) 'Reason and necessity: Thucydides III 9–14, 37–48', *JHS* 98: 64–78. (Reprinted in Macleod 1983: 88–102.)

(1979) 'Thucydides on faction (3.82–83)', *PCPS* 25: 52–68. (Reprinted in Macleod 1983: 123–39.)

(1983) *Collected Essays*, ed. O. Taplin. Oxford.

Maitland J. (1996) 'Marcellinus' Life of Thucydides: criticism and criteria in the biographical tradition', *CQ* 46: 538–58.

Mantena, K. (2012) 'Another realism: the politics of Gandhian nonviolence', *American Political Science Review* 126: 455–70.

Mara, G. (2008) *The Civic Conversations of Thucydides and Plato: Classical Political Philosophy and the Limits of Democracy*. Albany, NY.

Marinatos, N. (1981) *Thucydides and Religion. Beiträge zur Klassischen Philologie* 129. Königstein.

Marincola, J. (1997) *Authority and Tradition in Ancient Historiography*. Cambridge and New York.

Marr, J. L. and P. J. Rhodes (2008) *The 'Old Oligarch'. The Constitution of the Athenians Attributed to Xenophon*. Warminster.

Marsden, E. W. (1969) *Greek and Roman Artillery: Historical Development*. Oxford.

Marshall, M. (1990) 'Pericles and the plague,' in *Owls to Athens: Essays on Classical Subjects Presented to Sir Kenneth Dover*, ed. E. M. Craik. Oxford: 163–70.

Marshall, M. H. B. (1984) 'Cleon and Pericles: Sphacteria', *G&R* 31: 19–36.

Mastronarde, D. J. (2010) *The Art of Euripides: Dramatic Technique and Social Context*. Cambridge and New York.

Matthew, C. A. (2009) 'When push comes to shove: what was the *othismos* of hoplite combat?', *Historia* 58: 395–415.

Mattingly, H. B. (1963) 'The growth of Athenian imperialism', *Historia* 12: 257–73.

Maurer, K. (1995) *Interpolation in Thucydides. Mnemosyne* Supplement 150. Leiden and New York.

McCoskey, D. E. (2012) *Race: Antiquity and Its Legacy*. London.

McGushin, P. (1977) *C. Sallustius Crispus, Bellum Catilinae: A Commentary*. Leiden.

McInerney, J. (1999) *Land and Ethnicity in Ancient Phokis. The Folds of Parnassos*. Austin.

   (2001) 'Ethnos and ethnicity in early Greece', in *Ancient Perceptions of Greek Ethnicity*, ed. I. Malkin. Cambridge, MA: 51–73.

   (2014) 'Introduction', in *A Companion to Ethnicity in the Ancient Mediterranean*, ed. J. McInerney. Malden, MA: 1–16.

McLeod, W. (1965) 'The range of the ancient bow', *Phoenix* 19: 1–14.

   (1972) 'The range of the ancient bow: addenda' *Phoenix* 26: 78–82.

Megill, A. (ed.) (1994) *Rethinking Objectivity*. Durham, NC.

   (1995) '"Grand narrative" and the discipline of history', in *A New Philosophy of History*, eds. F. Ankersmit and H. Kellner. London: 151–73.

Meiggs, R. (1943) 'The growth of Athenian imperialism', *JHS* 63: 21–34.

   (1972) *The Athenian Empire*, revised edition. Oxford.

Meineke, S. (2003) 'Thukydidismus', in *Der Neue Pauly: Rezeptions- und Wissenschafts-geschichte*, vol. XV.3. Stuttgart and Weimar: 480–94.

Meister, K. (2013) *Thukydides als Vorbild der Historiker: von der Antike bis zur Gegenwart*. Paderborn.

   (2015) 'Thucydides in nineteenth-century Germany: historicization and glorification', in *A Handbook to the Reception of Thucydides*, eds. C. Lee and N. Morley. Chichester: 197–217.

Melanchthon, P. (1550) *Explicatio proverbiorum Salomonis in schola Witembergensi recens dictata*. Frankfurt.

   (1559) *Chronicon absolvtissimvm ab orbe condito vsque ad Christum deductum, in quo non Carionis solùm opus continetur, verùm etiam alia multa eaque insignia explicantur, adeo vt iustae Historiae loco occupatis esse possit*. Basel.

   (1562) *Orationes ex historia Thvcydidis, et insigniores aliqvot Demosthenis & aliorum Oratorum Graecorum*, ed. C. Peucer. Wittenberg.

   (1564) *Selectarum declamationum*, vol. 1. Strasbourg.

   (1582) *In epitomen philosophiae moralis Philippi Melancthonis*. Neustadt.

   (1642) *Epistolae Philippi Melancthonis, Thomae Mori et Lvdovici Vivis*. London.

Merrit, B., H. T. Wade-Gery and M. F. McGregor (1939–53) *The Athenian Tribute Lists* (4 vols.). Princeton.

Mikalson, J. (1984) 'Religion and the plague in Athens, 431–423 BC', in *Studies Presented to Sterling Dow on his Eightieth Birthday*, ed. K. J. Rigsby. Durham, NC: 217–25.

Miller, M. (1997) *Athens and Persia in the Fifth Century* BC: *A Study in Cultural Receptivity*. Cambridge.

   (2010) 'I am Eurymedon: tensions and ambiguities in Athenian war imagery', in *War, Democracy and Culture in Classical Athens*, ed. D. Pritchard. Cambridge: 304–38.

Mione, E. (1968) 'Bessarione bibliofilo e filologo', *Rivista di studi bizantini e neoellenici* 5: 61–83.

Mitchell, L. G. (2007) *Panhellenism and the Barbarian in Archaic and Classical Greece*. Swansea.

Mitchell-Boyask, R. (2008) *Plague and the Athenian Imagination*. Cambridge.

Moles, J. L. (1993) 'Truth and untruth in Herodotus and Thucydides', in *Lies and Fiction in the Ancient World*, eds. C. Gill and T. P. Wiseman. Exeter: 88–121.

   (1996) 'Herodotus warns the Athenians', *Papers of the Leeds International Latin Seminar* 9: 259–84.

   (1999) '*Anathema kai ktema*: the inscriptional inheritance of ancient historiography', *Histos* 3: 27–69.

   (2010) 'Narrative and speech problems in Thucydides I', in *Ancient Historiography and Its Contexts: Studies in Honour of A. J. Woodman*, eds. C. S. Kraus, J. Marincola and C. B. R. Pelling. Oxford: 15–39.

Momigliano, A. (1957) 'Perizonius, Niebuhr and the character of early Roman tradition', *JRS* 47: 104–14.

   (1966) 'Time in ancient historiography', *History and Theory* 6: 1–23.

   (1972) 'Tradition and the classical historian', *History and Theory* 11: 279–93.

   (1984) 'The place of ancient historiography in modern historiography', in *Settimo contributo alla storia degli studi classici e del mondo antico*. Rome: 13–36.

   (1990) 'The Herodotean and the Thucydidean tradition', in *The Classical Foundations of Modern Historiography*. Berkeley: 29–50.

   (2012) *Essays in Ancient and Modern Historiography*, with a new forward by A. Grafton. Chicago.

Moravcsik, G. (ed.) and R. J. H. Jenkins (trans.) (1967) *Constantine Porphyrogenitus De administrando imperio*. Washington, DC.

Morens, D. M. and R. J. Littman (1992) 'Epidemiology of the plague of Athens', *TAPhA* 122: 271–304.

Morgan, C. (2001) 'Ethne, ethnicity, and early Greek states, ca. 1200–480 BC: an archaeological perspective', in *Ancient Perceptions of Greek Ethnicity*, ed. I. Malkin. Cambridge, MA: 75–112.

   (2003) *Early Greek States beyond the Polis*. London and New York.

Morgenthau, H. J. (1993) *Politics among Nations: The Struggle for Power and Peace*, brief edition. New York and London.

Morley, N. (2012) 'Thucydides, history and historicism in Wilhelm Roscher', in *Thucydides and the Modern World: Reception, Reinterpretation and Influence from the Renaissance to the Present*, eds. K. Harloe and N. Morley. Cambridge: 115–39.

   (2014) *Thucydides and the Idea of History*. London and New York.

   (2016) 'Contextualism and universalism in Thucydidean thought', in *Thucydides and Political Order: Concepts of Order and the History of the Peloponnesian War*, eds. C. Thauer and C. Wendt. Basingstoke and New York: 23–40.

Morrison, J. S. and R. T. Williams (1968) *Greek Oared Ships, 900–322 BC*. Cambridge.

Morrison, J. S., J. F. Coates and N. B. Rankov (2000) *The Athenian Trireme: The History and Reconstruction of an Ancient Greek Warship*, 2nd edition. Cambridge.

Morrison, J. V. (2006a) 'Interaction of speech and narrative in Thucydides', in *Brill's Companion to Thucydides*, eds. A. Rengakos and A. Tsakmakis. Leiden and Boston: 251–77.

(2006b) *Reading Thucydides*. Columbus, OH.

Muhlack, U. (2011) 'Herodotus and Thucydides in the view of nineteenth-century German historians', in *The Western Time of Ancient History: Historiographical Encounters with the Greek and Roman Pasts*, ed. A. Lianeri. Cambridge: 179–209.

Munson, R. V. (2001) *Telling Wonders: Ethnography and Political Thought in the Work of Herodotus*. Ann Arbor.

(2012) 'Persians in Thucydides', in *Thucydides and Herodotus*, eds. E. M. Foster and D. Lateiner. Oxford: 241–77.

(2014) 'Herodotus and ethnicity', in *A Companion to Ethnicity in the Ancient Mediteranean*, ed. J. McInerney. Malden, MA: 341–55.

(2015) 'Natural upheavals in Thucydides (and Herodotus)', in *Kinesis: Essays for Donald Lateiner on the Ancient Depiction of Gesture, Motion, and Emotion*, eds. E. M. Foster and C. Clark. Ann Arbor.

Murari Pires, F. (2006a) 'Thucydidean modernities: history between science and art', in *Brill's Companion to Thucydides*, eds. A. Rengakos and A. Tsakmakis. Leiden: 811–37.

(2006b) 'Tucídides e o (re)acerto do fato da tirania de Hípias: alcance e limites dos indiciamentos investigativos da verdade', *Phaos* 6: 57–84.

(2015) 'The Thucydidean Clio between Machiavelli and Hobbes', in *A Handbook to the Reception of Thucydides*, eds. C. Lee and N. Morley. Chichester: 141–57.

Murray, O. (1986) 'Greek historians', in *The Oxford History of the Classical World*, eds. J. Boardman, J. Griffin and O. Murray. Oxford: 186–203.

Murray, W. (2013) 'Thucydides, theorist of war', *Naval War College Review* 66: 31–47.

Mynott, Jeremy (ed. and trans.) (2013a) *Thucydides. The War of the Peloponnesians and the Athenians*. Cambridge.

(2013b) 'Translating Thucydides', *Arion* 21: 49–62.

Nannini, R. (ed.) (1557) *Orationi militari*. Venice.

Nease, A. S. (1949) 'Garrisons in the Athenian Empire', *Phoenix* 3: 102–11.

Németh, A. (2018) *The Excerpta Constantiniana and the Byzantine Appropriation of the Past*. Cambridge.

Nevin, S. (2008) 'Military ethics in the writing of history: Thucydides and Diodorus on Delium', in *Beyond the Battlefields: New Perspectives on Warfare and Society in the Graeco-Roman World*, eds. E. Bragg, L. Hau and E. Macaulay-Lewis. Newcastle: 99–120.

Nichols, M. P. (2015) *Thucydides and the Pursuit of Freedom*. Ithaca, NY.

Nicolai, R. (2001) 'Thucydides' Archaeology: between epic and oral traditions', in *The Historian's Craft in the Age of Herodotus*, ed. N. Luraghi. Oxford: 263–85.

(2009) '*Ktêma es aei*: aspects of the reception of Thucydides in the ancient world', in *Thucydides*, ed. J. S. Rusten. Oxford Readings in Classical Studies. Oxford: 381–404.

Niebuhr, B. G. (1831) *History of Rome* (3 vols.), trans. J. C. Hare and C. Thirlwall. Cambridge.

(1852a) *Lectures on Ancient History* (3 vols.), trans. L. Schmitz. Philadelphia.

(1852b) *The Life and Letters of Barthold Georg Niebuhr*. London.

Nietzsche, F. (1990) *Twilight of the Idols and Anti-Christ*, trans. R. J. Hollingdale. Harmondsworth.

Norman, A. F. (trans.) (1992) *Libanius: Autobiography and Selected Letters*. Cambridge, MA, and London.

Nussbaum, M. (1986) *The Fragility of Goodness: Luck and Ethics in Greek Tragedy and Philosophy*. Cambridge.

Ober, J. (1989) *Mass and Elite in Democratic Athens: Rhetoric, Ideology, and the Power of the People*. Princeton.

(1993) 'Thucydides' criticism of democratic knowledge', in *Nomodeiktes: Greek Studies in Honor of Martin Ostwald*, eds. R. M. Rosen and J. Farrell. Ann Arbor: 81–98.

(1996) 'The Athenian revolution of 508/7 BCE: violence, authority, and the origins of democracy', in *The Athenian Revolution: Essays on Ancient Greek Democracy and Political Theory*. Princeton: 32–52. (Originally published in *Cultural Poetics in Archaic Greece: Cult, Performance, Politics*, eds. C. Dougherty and L. Kurke. Cambridge, 1993: 215–32.)

(1998) *Political Dissent in Democratic Athens. Intellectual Critics of Popular Rule*. Princeton.

(2009) 'Thucydides *theorêtikos*/Thucydides *histôr*: realist theory and the challenge of history,' in *Thucydides*, ed. J. S. Rusten. Oxford Readings in Classical Studies. Oxford: 434–78. (Originally published in *War and Democracy: A Comparative Study of the Korean War and the Peloponnesian War*, eds. D. R. McCann and B. S. Strauss. Armonk and London, 2001: 273–306.)

(2010) 'Thucydides on Athens' democratic advantage in the Archidamian War', in *War, Democracy, and Culture in Classical Athens*, ed. D. Pritchard. Cambridge: 65–87.

Oldfather, W. A. (1923) *Aeneas Tacticus, Asclepiodotus, Onasander*. London and New York.

Orwin, C. (1994) *The Humanity of Thucydides*. Princeton.

(2016) 'Beneath politics: Thucydides on the body as the ground and limit of the political regime', in *Thucydides and Political Order: Concepts of Order and the History of the Peloponnesian War*, eds. C. R. Thauer and C. Wendt. New York: 113–27.

Osborne, P. (1995) *The Politics of Time: Modernity and the Avant-Garde*. London and New York.

Osborne, R. G. (2000) *The Athenian Empire*, 4th edition. LACTOR 1. London.

Ostwald, M. (1986) *From Popular Sovereignty to the Sovereignty of Law*. Berkeley.

(1988) *ANAΓKH in Thucydides*. American Classical Studies 18. Atlanta.

Pade, M. (2003) 'Thucydides', in *Catalogus Translationum et Commentariorum: Mediaeval and Renaissance Latin Translations and Commentaries Annotated Lists and Guides*, vol. VIII, eds. V. Brown, J. Hankins and R. A. Kaster. Washington, DC: 103–81.

(2006) 'Thucydides' Renaissance readers', in *Brill's Companion to Thucydides*, eds. A. Rengakos and A. Tsakmakis. Leiden: 779–810.

Page, D. L. (1953) 'Thucydides' description of the Great Plague at Athens', *CQ* 3: 97–119.

Papagrigorakis, M. J., C. Yapijakis, P. N. Synodinos and E. Baziotopoulou-Valavani (2006a) 'DNA examination of ancient dental pulp incriminates typhoid fever as a probable cause of the plague of Athens', *International Journal of Infectious Diseases* 10: 206–14.

(2006b) 'Insufficient phylogenetic analysis may not exclude candidacy of typhoid fever as a probable cause of the plague of Athens (reply to Shapiro et al.)', *International Journal of Infectious Diseases* 10: 335–36.

Parker, R. (1996) *Athenian Religion. A History*. Oxford.

Parker, V. (2005) 'Pausanias the Spartiate as depicted by Charon of Lampsacus and Herodotus,' *Philologus* 149: 3–11.

Parry, A. (1970) 'Thucydides' use of abstract language', *Yale French Studies* 45: 3–20.

(1972) 'Thucydides' historical perspective', *Yale Classical Studies* 22: 47–61.

(1981) *Logos* and *Ergon* in Thucydides. New York.

(1989) 'The language of Thucydides' description of the plague', in *The Language of Achilles and Other Papers*. Oxford: 156–76.

Patterson, L. (2010) *Kinship Myth in Ancient Greece*. Austin.

Patzer, H. (1937) *Das Problem der Geschichtsschreibung des Thukydides und die thukydideische Frage*. Berlin.

Payen, P. (2015) 'The reception of Thucydides in eighteenth- and nineteenth-century France', in *A Handbook to the Reception of Thucydides*, eds. C. Lee and N. Morley. Chichester: 158–75.

Pazdernik, C. (2000) 'Procopius and Thucydides on the labors of war: Belisarius and Brasidas in the field', *TAPhA* 130: 149–87.

Pelling, C. B. R. (1991) 'Thucydides' Archidamus and Herodotus' Artabanus', in *Georgica: Greek Studies in Honour of George Cawkwell*, eds. M. A. Flower and M. Toher. *BICS* Suppl. 58: 120–42.

(1997) 'East is east and west is west – or are they? National stereotypes in Herodotus', *Histos* 1: 51–66. (Also published in *Herodotus*, vol. II, ed. R. V. Munson. Oxford Readings in Classical Studies. Oxford, 2013: 60–79.)

(2000) *Literary Texts and the Greek Historian*. London.

(2009) 'Thucydides' speeches', in *Thucydides*, ed. J. S. Rusten. Oxford Readings in Classical Studies. Oxford: 176–87. (Originally published in Pelling 2000: 112–22.)

(2012) 'Aristotle's *Rhetoric*, the *Rhetorica ad Alexandrum*, and the speeches in Herodotus and Thucydides', in *Thucydides & Herodotus*, eds. E. M. Foster and D. Lateiner. Oxford: 281–315.

Pérez Martín, I. (2002) 'Lectores y público de la historiografía griega', *Estudios clásicos* 121: 125–47.

Pertusi, A. (ed.) (1952) *Costantino Porfirogenito de Thematibus*. Vatican City.

Petrarca, F. (1996) *Trionfi, Rime estravaganti, Codice degli abbozzi*, eds. V. Pacca and L. Paolino. Milan.

Philp, M. (2012) 'Realism without illusions', *Political Theory* 40: 629–49.

Piccirilli, L. (1985) *Storie dello storico Tucidide*. Genoa.

Pires, F. M. (2007) *Modernidades Tucidideanas: Ktema es Aei*. São Paulo.

Pitcher, L. V. (2009) *Writing Ancient History: An Introduction to Classical Historiography*. London.

(2011) 'The stones of blood: family, monumentality, and memory in Velleius' second century', in *Velleius Paterculus: Making History*, ed. E. Cowan. Swansea: 253–64.

Plant, I. M. (1999) 'The influence of forensic oratory on Thucydides' principles of method', *CQ* 49: 62–73.

Podlecki, A. (1987) *Plutarch, Life of Pericles*. Bristol.

Pope, M. (1988) 'Thucydides and democracy', *Historia* 37: 276–96.

Porciani, l. (2001) *Prime forme della storiografia greca: prospettiva locale e generale nella narrazione storica*. *Historia* Einzelschriften 152. Stuttgart.

Porciani, L. (2007) 'The enigma of discourse: a view of Thucydides', in *A Companion to Greek and Roman Historiography*, vol. II, ed. J. Marincola. Malden, MA: 328–35.

Postclassicisms Collective (ed.) (2020) *Postclassicisms*. Chicago and London.

Powell, A. (ed.) (2001) *Athens and Sparta: Constructing Greek Political and Social History from 478 BC*, 2nd edition. London.

Powell, A. and S. Hodkinson (eds.) (1994) *The Shadow of Sparta*. London.

Powell, J. E. (1936) 'The Bâle and Leyden scholia to Thucydides,' *CQ* 30: 80–93.

(1938) 'The Cretan manuscripts of Thucydides', *CQ* 32: 103–8.

Price, J. (2001) *Thucydides and Internal War*. Cambridge.

Pritchard, D. M. (1998) 'The fractured imaginary: popular thinking on military matters in fifth century Athens', *AH* 28: 38–61.

(2010) 'The symbiosis between democracy and war', in *War, Democracy and Culture in Classical Athens*, ed. D. Pritchard. Cambridge: 1–62.

Pritchett, W. K. (1974) *The Greek State at War*, Part 2. Berkeley.

(1985) *The Greek State at War*, Part 4. Berkeley.

(1991) *The Greek State at War*, Part 5. Berkeley.

Raaflaub, K. (1987) 'Herodotus' political thought and the meaning of history', in *Herodotus and the Invention of History*. ed. D. Boedeker. *Arethusa* 20: 221–48.

(2004) *The Discovery of Freedom in Ancient Greece*, trans. R. Franciscono, revised by the author. Chicago.

(2006) 'Thucydides on democracy and oligarchy', in *Brill's Companion to Thucydides*, eds. A. Rengakos and A. Tsakmakis. Leiden and Boston: 189–222.

(2009) 'Learning from the enemy', in *Interpreting the Athenian Empire*, eds. J. Ma, N. Papazarkadas and R. Parker. London: 89–124.

(2013) '*Ktēma es aiei*: Thucydides' concept of "learning through history" and its realization in his work', in *Thucydides: Between History and Literature*, eds. A. Tsakmakis and M. Tamiolaki. Berlin and Boston: 3–21.

Rabe, H. (1926) *Aphthonii Progymnasmata*. Leipzig.

Radice, W. and B. Reynolds (eds.) (1987) *The Translator's Art: Essays in Honour of Betty Radice*. Harmondsworth.

Ranke, L. von. (1824) *Geschichten der romanischen und germanischen Völker von 1494 bis 1535*. Leipzig and Berlin.

(1888) *Abhandlungen und Versuche. Neue Sammlung*, vols. LI–LII, eds. A. Dove and T. Wiedemann. Leipzig.

(1973) *The Theory and Practice of History*, ed. with an introduction by G. G. Iggers and K. von Moltke, trans. W. A. Iggers and K. von Moltke. Indianapolis.

(1981) *The Secret of World History: Selected Writings on the Art and Science of History*, ed. and trans. R. Wines. New York.

Raubitschek, A. E. (1973) 'The speech of the Athenians at Sparta', in *The Speeches in Thucydides*, ed. P. A. Stadter. Chapel Hill: 32–48.

Rawlings, H. R. (1975) *A Semantic Study of Prophasis to 400 B.C.* Hermes Einzelschriften 33. Wiesbaden.

(1977) 'Thucydides on the purpose of the Delian League', *Phoenix* 31: 1–8.

(1981) *The Structure of Thucydides' History*. Princeton.

(2016) '*Ktema te es aiei . . . akouein*'. *CPh* 111: 107–16.

Rawlings, L. (2000) 'Alternative agonies: hoplite martial and combat experiences beyond the phalanx', in *War and Violence in Ancient Greece*, ed. H. van Wees. London: 233–59.

(2013) 'War and warfare in ancient Greece', in *The Oxford Handbook of Warfare in the Classical World*, eds. B. Campbell and L. Tritle. Oxford: 3–28.

Rechenauer, G. (1991) *Thukydides und die hippokratische Medizin: naturwissenschaftliche Methodik als Modell für Geschichtsdeutung*. Spudasmata 47. Hildesheim.

Reinsch, D. R. (1983) *Critobuli Imbriotae Historiae*. Berlin.

(2006) 'Byzantine adaptations of Thucydides', in *Brill's Companion to Thucydides*, eds. A. Rengakos and A. Tsakmakis. Leiden and Boston: 755–78.

(2014) *Michaelis Pselli Chronographia*. Berlin.

Rengakos, A. and A. Tsakmakis (eds.) (2006) *Brill's Companion to Thucydides*. Leiden and Boston.

[Reynolds, J.] (1624) *Vox Coeli, or, Newes from Heaven*. 'Elesium' [London].

Reynolds, J. J. (2009) 'Proving power: signs and sign-interference in Thucydides' "Archaeology"' *TAPhA* 139: 325–68.

Rhodes, P. J. (1988) *Thucydides, History, 2*. Warminster.

(1993a) *A Commentary on the Aristotelian Athenaion Politeia*, revised edition. Oxford.

(1993b) *The Athenian Empire*, 2nd edition. Greece & Rome New Surveys in the Classics 17. Oxford.

(1994) *Thucydides, History, 3*. Warminster.

(1998) *Thucydides, History, 4.1–5.24*. Warminster.

(2000) 'Who ran democratic Athens?', in *Polis and Politics: Studies in Greek History Presented to Mogens Herman M. H. Hansen*, eds. P. Flensted-Jensen, T. H. Nielsen and L. Rubinstein. Copenhagen: 465–77.

(2007) 'Democracy and empire', in *The Cambridge Companion to the Age of Pericles*, ed. L. Samons. Cambridge: 24–45.

(2008) 'Thucydides and his audience: what Thucydides explains and what he does not', *AAntHung* 48: 83–8.

(2011) 'Biaios didaskolos? Thucydides and his lessons for his readers', in *Thucydides – A Violent Teacher?: History and its Representations*, eds. G. Rechenauer and V. Pothou. Gottingen: 17–28.

(2014) *Thucydides, History, Book I: With an Introduction, Translation and Commentary*. Aris and Philips Classical Texts. Oxford.

Richards, J. (2013) 'Thucydides in the circle of Philip Melanchthon', Dissertation, The Ohio State University.

Robinson, E. (2000) 'Democracy in Syracuse, 466–412 BC', *HSCPh* 100: 189–205.

Robinson, P. (1985) 'Why do we believe Thucydides? A comment on W. R. Connor's "Narrative discourse in Thucydides"', in *The Greek Historians: Literature and History. Papers Presented to A. E. Raubitschek*. Stanford: 19–24.

Rodríguez-Piñero, L. (2006) *Indigenous Peoples, Postcolonialism, and International Law: The ILO Regime (1919–1989)*. Oxford.

Rogkotis, Z. (2006) 'Thucydides and Herodotus: aspects of their intertextual relationship', in *Brill's Companion to Thucydides*, eds. A. Rengakos and A. Tsakmakis. Leiden and Boston: 57–86.

Roisman, J. (1993) *The General Demosthenes and his Use of Military Surprise*: Stuttgart.

    (2002) 'The rhetoric of courage in the Athenian orators', in *Andreia: Studies in Manliness and Courage in Classical Antiquity*, eds. R. M. Rosen and I. Sluiter. Boston: 126–43.

    (2005) *The Rhetoric of Manhood: Masculinity in the Attic Orators*. London.

de Romilly, J. (1956) *Histoire et raison chez Thucydide*. Paris.

    (1958) 'L'utilité de l'histoire selon Thucydide', in *Histoire et Historiens dans l'antiquité, Entretiens sur l'antiquité classique*, vol. 4. Geneva: 39–81.

    (1963) *Thucydides and Athenian Imperialism*, trans. P. Thody. Oxford. (Originally published as *Thucydides et l'imperialisme athénien: la pensée de l'historien et la genèse de l'oeuvre*, Paris, 1951.)

    (1966) 'Thucydides and the cities of the Athenian Empire', *BICS* 13: 1–12.

    (2012) *The Mind of Thucydides*, trans. E. T. Rawlings. Ithaca, NY. (Originally published as *Histoire et raison chez Thucydide*, Paris, 1956.)

Rood, T. C. B. (1998a) 'Thucydides and his predecessors', *Histos* 2: 230–67.

    (1998b) *Thucydides: Narrative and Explanation*. Oxford.

    (1999) 'Thucydides' Persian Wars', in *The Limits of Historiography: Genre and Narrative in Ancient Historical Texts*, ed. C. S. Kraus. Leiden: 141–68.

    (2004) 'Xenophon and Diodorus: continuing Thucydides', in *Xenophon and His World: Papers from a Conference Held in Liverpool in July 1999*, ed. C. J. Tuplin. *Historia* Einzelschriften 172. Stuttgart: 341–95.

    (2006) 'Objectivity and authority: Thucydides' historical method', in *Brill's Companion to Thucydides*, eds. A. Rengakos and A. Tsakmakis. Leiden and Boston: 225–49.

    (2007) 'Thucydides', in *Time in Ancient Greek Narrative*, eds. I. J. F. de Jong and R. Nünlist. *Mnemosyne* Supplement 291. Leiden and Boston: 131-46.

    (2009) 'Thucydides' Persian Wars', in *Thucydides*, ed. J. S. Rusten. Oxford Readings in Classical Studies. Oxford: 148–75. (Originally published in *The Limits of Historiography: Genre and Narrative in Ancient Historical Texts*, ed. C. S. Kraus. Leiden, 1999: 141–68.)

    (2020) 'From ethnography to history: Herodotean and Thucydidean traditions in the development of Greek historiography', in *Herodotus in the Long Nineteenth Century*, eds. T. Harrison and J. Skinner. Cambridge: 20–45.

Roscher, W. (1842) *Leben, Werk und Zeitalter des Thukydides*. Göttingen.

Rosen, R. M. and I. Sluiter (eds.) (2010) *Valuing Others in Classical Antiquity*. Leiden.

Runciman, W. G. (1998) 'Greek hoplites, warrior culture, and indirect bias', *The Journal of the Royal Anthropological Institute* 4: 731–51.

Rusten, J. S. (1989) *The Peloponnesian War, Book 2*. Cambridge.

(ed.) (2009a) *Thucydides*. Oxford Readings in Classical Studies. Oxford.

(2009b) 'Thucydides and his readers', in *Thucydides*, ed J. S. Rusten. Oxford Readings in Classical Studies. Oxford: 1–28.

(2011) 'Four ways to hate Corcyra', in *Thucydides, a Violent Teacher? History and Its Representations*, eds. G. Rechenauer and V. Pothou. Göttingen: 99–113.

(2015) 'Carving up Thucydides: the rise and demise of "Analysis," and its legacy', in *A Handbook to the Reception of Thucydides*, eds. C. Lee and N. Morley. Chichester: 61–74.

(2020) 'τὴν ἐκβολὴν τοῦ λόγου ἐποιησάμην: Thucydides' chronicle in the *Pentekontaeteia* (97–117) is not a "Digression"', *Histos* 14: 230–54.

(in preparation) *Thucydides: The Peloponnesian War, Book I*. Cambridge.

Rutherford, R. (2012) 'Structure and meaning in epic and historiography', in *Thucydides and Herodotus*, eds. E. M. Foster and D. Lateiner. Oxford: 13–38.

Rutter, N. K. (2002) 'Syracusan democracy: "most like the Athenian"?', in *Alternatives to Athens: Varieties of Political Organization and Community in Ancient Greece*, eds. R. Brock and S. Hodkinson. Oxford: 137–51.

Sabin, P., H. van Wees and M. Whitby (eds.) (2007) *The Cambridge History of Greek and Roman Warfare. Vol. I: Greece, the Hellenistic World and the Rise of Rome*. Cambridge.

Said, E. (1975) *Beginnings: Intention and Method*. New York.

de Ste. Croix, G. E. M. (1954) 'The character of the Athenian Empire', *Historia*: 3: 1–41.

(1961a) 'Notes on jurisdiction in the Athenian Empire: I', *CQ* 11: 94–112.

(1961b) 'Notes on jurisdiction in the Athenian Empire: II', *CQ* 11: 268–80.

(1972) *The Origins of the Peloponnesian War*. London.

Samons, L. J. (2000) *Empire of the Owl: Athenian Imperial Finance*. Historia Einzelschrift 142. Stuttgart.

(2007) 'Conclusion: Pericles and Athens', in *Cambridge Companion to the Age of Pericles*, ed. L. Samons. Cambridge: 282–308.

(2016) *Pericles and the Conquest of History*. Cambridge.

Sandridge, N. B. (2012) *Loving Humanity, Learning, and Being Honored: The Foundations of Leadership in Xenophon's Education of Cyrus*. Washington, DC.

Saxonhouse, A. W. (1996) *Athenian Democracy: Modern Mythmakers and Ancient Theorists*. Notre Dame and London.

(2006) *Free Speech and Democracy in Ancient Athens*. Cambridge.

Scanlon, T. (1980) *The Influence of Thucydides on Sallust*. Heidelberg.

Scardino, C. (2007) *Gestaltung und Funktion der Reden bei Herodot und Thukydides*. Beiträge zur Altertumskunde 250. Berlin.

(2012) 'Indirect discourse in Herodotus and Thucydides', in *Thucydides & Herodotus*, eds. E. M. Foster and D. Lateiner. Oxford: 67–96.

Schake, K. (2017) 'The summer of misreading Thucydides', *The Atlantic*. 18 July. Available at: www.theatlantic.com/international/archive/2017/07/the-summer-of-misreading-thucydides/533859/

Schamp, J. (1996) 'La réception de l'histoire chez Photios sous bénéfice d'inventaire', in *L'image de l'Antiquité chez les auteurs postérieurs*, eds. I. Lewandowski and L. Mrozewics. Poznán: 9–26.

Schaps, D. (1977) 'The woman least mentioned: etiquette and women's names', *CQ* 27: 323–30.

Schenkl, H. and G. Downey (1965) *Themistii Orationes quae supersunt*. Leipzig.

Schepens, G. (2010) 'Thucydide législateur de l'histoire? Appréciations antiques et modernes', in *Ombres de Thucydide: la réception de l'historien depuis l'Antiquité jusqu'au début du XXe siècle. Actes des colloques de Bordeaux, les 16–17 mars 2007, de Bordeaux, les 30–31 mai 2008 et de Toulouse, les 23–25 octobre 2008*. eds. V Fromentin, G. Gotteland and P. Payen. Pessac: 121–40.

Schiappa, A. E. (1999) *The Beginnings of Rhetorical Theory in Classical Greece*. New Haven.

Schiefsky, M. J. (2005) *Hippocrates on Ancient Medicine*. Leiden and Boston.

Schlosser, J. A. (2013) '"Hope, danger's comforter": Thucydides, hope, politics', *The Journal of Politics* 75: 169–82.

(2014) 'Herodotean realism', *Political Theory* 42: 239–61.

Schwartz, A. (2009) *Reinstating the Hoplite: Arms, Armour and Phalanx Fighting in Archaic and Classical Greece*. Stuttgart.

Schwartz, E. (1919) *Das Geschichtswerk des Thukydides*. Bonn.

Seaman, M. (2013) 'The Peloponnesian War and its sieges', in *The Oxford Handbook of Warfare in the Classical World*, eds. B. Campbell and L. Tritle. Oxford: 642–56.

Sears, M. A. (2013) *Athens, Thrace, and the Shaping of Athenian Leadership*. Cambridge.

(2015) 'Thucydides, Rousseau, and forced freedom: Brasidas' speech at Acanthus', *Phoenix* 69: 242–67.

(2020) 'Brasidas and the un-Spartan Spartan', *CJ* 116: 173–98.

Shapiro, B., A. Rambaut, M. Thomas and P. Gilbert (2006) 'No proof that typhoid caused the plague of Athens. A reply to Papagrigorakis et al.', *International Journal of Infectious Diseases* 10: 334–5.

Skinner, J. (2012) *The Invention of Greek Ethnography: From Homer to Herodotus*. Oxford.

Smith, A. (1986) *The Ethnic Origins of Nations*. Oxford.

(2004) *The Antiquity of Nations*. Oxford.

(2009) *Ethno-Symbolism and Nationalism*. New York.

Smith, C. F. (1903) 'Character-drawing in Thucydides', *AJPh* 24: 369–87.

Smyly, J. G. (1933) 'Notes on Greek manuscripts in the Library of Trinity College', *Hermathena* 48: 163–95.

Soldo di Strozzi, F. (trans.) ([1545]) *Gli otto libri di Thvcydide Atheniese, delle guerre fatte tra popoli della Morea, et gli Atheniesi*, corrected edition. Venice.

Sontag, S. (2007) 'The world as India (St Jerome lecture on literary translation)', in *At the Same Time: Essays and Speeches*. New York: 156–79.

Soulis, E. M. (1972) *Xenophon and Thucydides*. Athens.

de Souza, P. (2013) 'War at sea', in *The Oxford Handbook of Warfare in the Classical World*, eds. B. Campbell and L. Tritle. Oxford: 369–94.

Spence, I. G. (1993) *The Cavalry of Classical Greece: A Social and Military History with Particular Reference to Athens*. Oxford.

(2010) 'Cavalry, democracy and military thinking in classical Athens', in *War, Democracy and Culture in Classical Athens*, ed. D. Pritchard. Cambridge: 111–38.

Stadter, P. A. (ed.) (1973) *The Speeches in Thucydides: A Collection of Original Studies with a Bibliography*. Chapel Hill.

Stadter, P. A. (1992) 'Herodotus and the Athenian *arche*', *ANSP* 3: 781–809.

(1993) 'The form and content of Thucydides' Pentecontaeteia (1.89–117)', *GRBS* 34: 35–72.

Stahl, H.-P. (1973) 'Speeches and course of events in Books Six and Seven of Thucydides', in *The Speeches in Thucydides: A Collection of Original Studies*, ed. P. A. Stadter. Chapel Hill: 60–77.

(2003) *Thucydides: Man's Place in History*. Swansea. (Originally published as *Thukydides: die Stellung des Menschen im geschichtlichen Prozess*, Munich, 1966.)

(2009) 'Speeches and course of events in Books Six and Seven of Thucydides', *Thucydides*, ed J. S. Rusten. Oxford Readings in Classical Studies. Oxford: 341–58. (A revised version of Stahl 1973.)

Stanford, W. B. (1941) 'Tzetzes' farewell to Thucydides', *G&R* 11: 40–1.

Starr, C. G. (1968) *The Awakening of the Greek Historical Spirit*. New York.

Stein, F. J. (1957) '*Dexippus et Herodianus rerum scriptores quatenus Thucydidem secuti sint*', Dissertation, University of Bonn.

Stockton, D. (1990) *The Classical Athenian Democracy*. Oxford.

Stout, J. (2010) *Blessed Are the Organized: Grassroots Democracy in America*. Princeton.

Strasburger, H. (1972) *Homer und die Geschichtsschreibung*. Heidelberg.

(2009) 'Thucydides and the political self-portrait of the Athenians', in *Thucydides*, ed. J. S. Rusten. Oxford Readings in Classical Studies. Oxford: 191–219. (Originally published as 'Thukydides und die politische Selbstdarstellung der Athener', *Hermes* 86 (1958) 17–40.)

Strassler, R. (ed.) (1996) *The Landmark Thucydides*. New York.

Strathern, M. (1992) *After Nature: English Kinship in the Twentieth Century*. Cambridge.

Strauss, B. S. (2000) 'Perspectives on the death of fifth-century Athenian seamen', in *War and Violence in Ancient Greece*, ed. H. van Wees. London: 261–83.

(2007) 'Naval battles and sieges', in *The Cambridge History of Greek and Roman Warfare, Vol. 1: Greece, the Hellenistic World and the Rise of Rome*, eds. P. Sabin, H. van Wees and M. Whitby. Cambridge: 223–47.

Strauss, L. (1964) *The City and Man*. Chicago.

Strebel, H. (1935) *Wertung und Wirkung des Thukydideischen Geschichtswerkes in der griechisch-römischen Literatur. (Eine literargeschichtliche Studie nebst einem Exkurs über Appian als Nachahmer des Thukydides)*. Speyer a. Rh.

Stroud, R. S. (1987) '"Wie es eigentlich gewesen" and Thucydides 2.48.3', *Hermes* 115: 379–82.

(1994) 'Thucydides and Corinth', *Chiron* 24: 267–304.

Süßmann, J. (2012) 'Historicising the classics: how nineteenth-century German historiography changed the perspective on historical tradition', in *Thucydides and the Modern World: Reception, Reinterpretation and Influence from the Renaissance to the Present*, eds. K. Harloe and N. Morley. Cambridge: 77–92.

Tamiolaki, M. (2012) 'Virtue and leadership in Xenophon: ideal leaders or ideal losers?' in *Xenophon: Ethical Principle and Historical Inquiry*, eds. F. Hobden and C. J. Tuplin. Leiden: 563–89.

(2016) 'Athenian leaders in Xenophon's Memorabilia', in *Aspects of Leadership in Xenophon*, ed. R. F. Buxton. *Histos* Suppl. 5: 1–45.

Tasso, T. (1982) 'Il Padre di Famiglia', in *Tasso's Dialogues*, trans. and eds. C. Lord and D. A. Trafton. Berkeley and Los Angeles: 44–148.

Thesaurus Exemplorum Medii Aevi, eds. J. Berlioz, M. Burghart, P. Collomb and M. A. Polo de Beaulieu. Available at: http://thema.huma-num.fr/about

Thomas, R. (2000) *Herodotus in Context: Ethnography, Science, and the Art of Persuasion*. Cambridge and New York.

(2006) 'Thucydides' intellectual milieu and the plague', in *Brill's Companion to Thucydides*, eds. A. Rengakos and A. Tsakmakis. Leiden and Boston: 87–108.

(2013) 'Ethnicity, genealogy, and hellenism in Herodotus', in *Herodotus*, vol. II, ed. R. V. Munson. Oxford Readings in Classical Studies. Oxford: 339–59.

Thompson, E. (1945) 'Priscus of Panium, Fragment I B', *CQ* 39: 92–4.

Thompson, H. A. and R. E. Wycherley (1972) *The Athenian Agora XIV, The Agora of Athens: The History, Shape, and Uses of an Ancient City Center*. Princeton.

Tomadakes, N. (1952) Ἀὶ παρὰ Κριτοβούλῳ δημηγορίαι Μωάμεθ Β´, Ἀθηνᾶ 56: 61–8.

Tompkins, D. P. (n.d.) 'Diplomacy, dialogue and emotion: the crisis of Spartan identity in Thucydides: 1.68–86', unpublished manuscript.

Trenkner, S. (1958) *The Greek Novella in the Classical Period*, Cambridge.

Tritle, L. (1989) '*Epilektoi* at Athens', *AHB* 3: 54–9.

Trundle, M. (2010) 'Light troops in classical Athens', in *War, Democracy and Culture in Classical Athens*, ed. D. Pritchard. Cambridge: 139–60.

Tsakmakis, A. (2006) 'Leaders, crowds, and the power of the image: political communication in Thucydides', in *Brill's Companion to Thucydides*, eds. A. Rengakos and A. Tsakmakis. Leiden and Boston: 161–87.

(2017) 'Speeches', in *The Oxford Handbook of Thucydides*, eds. R. K. Balot, S. Forsdyke and E. M. Foster. New York: 267–81.

Tubach, F. C. (1969) *Index Exemplorum: A Handbook of Medieval Religious Tales*. Helsinki.

Tucker, A. (2016) 'Historiographic ancients and moderns: the difference between Thucydides and Ranke', in *Knowing Future Time in and through Greek Historiography*, ed. A. Lianeri, Berlin: 361–84.

Tuplin, C. J. (1985) 'Imperial tyranny: some reflections on a Classical Greek political metaphor', in *Crux: Essays in Greek History Presented to G.E.M. de Ste. Croix on his 75th Birthday*, eds. P. A. Cartledge and F. D. Harvey. *HPTh* 6. Exeter: 348–75.

Turner, J. (2014) *Philology: The Forgotten Origins of the Modern Humanities*. Princeton.

Ullrich, F. W. (1968) *Die Entstehung des Thukydideischen Geschichtswerkes*. Darmstadt. (Originally published in *Beiträge zur Erklärung des Thukydides*, Hamburg, 1846.)

Underhill, G. E. (1900) *A Commentary on the* Hellenica *of Xenophon*. Oxford.

Urbinati, N. (2012) 'Thucydides the Thermidorian: democracy on trial in the making of modern liberalism', in *Thucydides and the Modern World: Reception, Reinterpretation and Influence from the Renaissance to the Present*, eds. K. Harloe and N. Morley. Cambridge: 55–76.

Usher, S. (1974) *Dionysius of Halicarnassus. Critical Essays*, vol. 1. Loeb Classical Library 465. Cambridge, MA.

(1985) *Dionysius of Halicarnassus. Critical Essays*, vol. 2. Loeb Classical Library 466. Cambridge, MA.

van Ittersum, M. J. (2009) 'Dating the manuscript of *De Jure Praedae* (1604–1608): what watermarks, foliation and quire divisions can tell us about Hugo Grotius' development as a natural rights and natural law theorist', *History of European Ideas* 35: 125–93.

van Wees, H. (2004) *Greek Warfare: Myths and Realities*. London.

(2007) 'War and society', in *The Cambridge History of Greek and Roman Warfare, Vol. 1: Greece, the Hellenistic World and the Rise of Rome*, eds. P. Sabin, H. van Wees and M. Whitby. Cambridge: 273–99.

Vasilikopoulou, A. (1992) Ἀξιολόγηση τοῦ Θουκυδίδη ἀπό τούς βυζαντινούς λογίους', *Lakonikai Spoudai* 11: 274–85.

Vasunia, P. (2013) *The Classics and Colonial India*. Oxford.

Vela Tejada, J. (2004) 'Warfare, history and literature in the archaic and classical periods: the development of Greek military treatises', *Historia* 53: 129–46.

Vernant, J.-P. and P. Vidal-Naquet (1990) 'Ambiguity and reversal: on the enigmatic structure of *Oedipus Rex*', in *Myth and Tragedy in Ancient Greece*, trans. J. Lloyd. New York: 113–40.

Vidal-Naquet, P. (1990) *La démocratie grecque vue d'ailleurs*. Paris.

(2000) *Les grecs, les historiens, la démocratie: le grand écart*. Paris.

Vierhaus, R. (1990) 'Historiography between science and art', in *Leopold von Ranke and the Shaping of the Historical Discipline*, eds. G. G. Iggers and J. Powell. Syracuse, NY: 61–9.

Villard, P. (1992) 'Constantinople et la peste (1467)', in *Histoire et société: Mélanges offerts à Georges Duby*, vol. IV. Aix-en-Provence: 143–50.

Vivian, A. (2021) 'Entanglement at the Assinarus: destructive liquids and fluid Athenians in Thucydides', *CJ* 116: 385–408.

Vlassopoulos, K. (2013) *Greeks and Barbarians*. Cambridge.

Vogt, J. (2009) 'The portrait of Pericles in Thucydides', in *Thucydides*, ed. J. S. Rusten. Oxford Readings in Classical Studies. Oxford: 220–37.

Walbank, F. W. (1972) *Polybius*. Berkeley.

Wallace, W. P. (1964) 'Thucydides', *Phoenix* 18: 251–61.

Wallinga, H. T. (1992) *Ships and Sea Power Before the Great Persian War: The Ancestry of the Ancient Trireme*. Leiden.

Walters, K. R. (1981) '"We fought alone at Marathon": historical falsification in the Attic funeral oration', *RhM* 124: 203–11.

Walton, J. M. (2006) *Found in Translation: Greek Drama in English*. Cambridge.

Walz, C. (1834) *Rhetores Graeci*, vol. 3. Stuttgart.

Wang, Q. E and F. L. Fillafer (eds.) (2007) *The Many Faces of Clio: Cross-Cultural Approaches to Historiography. Essays in Honor of Georg G. Iggers*. New York.

Warner, R. (trans.) (1954) *The Peloponnesian War*. Harmondsworth.

Warren, C. N. (2015) *Literature and the Law of Nations, 1580–1680*. Oxford.

Warren, M. (2001) *Dry Bones Rattling: Community Building to Revitalize American Democracy*. Princeton.

Wassermann, F. M. (1964) 'The voice of Sparta in Thucydides', *CJ* 59: 289–97.

Waterfield, R. (forthcoming) 'Becoming a leader in fifth-century Athens', in *A Companion to Leadership in the Greco-Roman World*, ed. S. B. Ferrario. Malden, MA.

Welch, D. (2003) 'Why international relations theorists should stop reading Thucydides', *Review of International Studies* 29: 301–19.

Wendt, A. (1992) 'Anarchy is what states make of it: the social construction of power politics', *International Organization* 46: 391–425.

West, W. C. III (1973) 'The speeches in Thucydides: a description and listing', in *The Speeches in Thucydides: A Collection of Original Studies with a Bibliography*, ed. P. A. Stadter. Chapel Hill: 3–15.

Westerink, L. G. (1986) 'Leo the Philosopher: *Job* and other poems', *ICS* 11: 193–222.

Westlake, H. D. (1958–9) 'Hermocrates the Syracusan', *BRL* 41: 239–68.

  (1968) *Individuals in Thucydides*. Cambridge.

  (1969) *Essays on the Greek Historians and Greek History*. New York.

  (1980) 'Thucydides, Brasidas and Clearidas', *GRBS* 21: 333–9.

  (1989) 'Thucydides on Pausanias and Themistocles – a written source?', in *Studies in Thucydides and Greek History*. Bristol: 1–18.

Wheeler, E. L. (2007) 'Battle: land battles', in *The Cambridge History of Greek and Roman Warfare, Vol. 1: Greece, the Hellenistic World and the Rise of Rome*, eds. P. Sabin, H. van Wees and M. Whitby. Cambridge: 186–223.

Whitby, M. (2007) 'Reconstructing ancient warfare', in *The Cambridge History of Greek and Roman Warfare, Vol. 1: Greece, the Hellenistic World and the Rise of Rome*, eds. P. Sabin, H. van Wees and M. Whitby. Cambridge: 54–81.

White, H. (1973) *Metahistory: The Historical Imagination in Nineteenth-Century Europe*. Baltimore.

  (1987) *The Content of the Form: Narrative Discourse and Historical Representation*. Baltimore.

  (1999) 'Historical emplotment and the problem of truth in historical representation', in *Figural Realism: Studies in the Mimesis Effect*. Baltimore: 27–42. (First published in 1992.)

White, J. B. (1984) *When Words Lose Their Meaning*. Chicago.

Whitehead, D. (1987) 'The periplous', *G&R* 34: 178–85.

Whittaker, G. R. (1969) *Herodian Volume I: Books I–IV*. Cambridge, MA.

Wiater, N. (2011) *The Ideology of Classicism: Language, History, and Identity in Dionsyius of Halicarnassus*. Berlin.

Wilamowitz-Moellendorff, U. von (1902) *Griechisches Lesebuch*. Berlin.

Will, W. (2003) *Thukydides und Perikles: der Historiker und sein Held*. Bonn.

Willett, S. J. (1999) 'Thucydides domesticated and 'foreignized'', *Arion* 7: 118–45.

Williams, B. (1993) *Shame and Necessity*. Berkeley.

Wilson, J. (1982) 'What does Thucydides claim for his speeches?', *Phoenix* 36: 95–103.

Wilson, N. G. (1983a) *Scholars of Byzantium*. London.

  (1983b) 'Scoliasti e commentatori', *Studi Classici e Orientali* 33: 83–112.

Wingrove, E. (2016) 'Political displacement at the point of reception', *Classical Receptions Journal* 8: 114–32.

Witt, R. G. (2000) *'In the Footsteps of the Ancients': The Origins of Humanism from Lovato to Bruni*. Leiden.

Wittek, M. (1953) 'Pour une étude du scriptorium de Michel Apostolès et consorts', *Scriptorium* 7: 290–7.

Wohl, V. (2002) *Love among the Ruins: The Erotics of Democracy in Classical Athens*. Princeton.

Woodman, A. J. (1988) *Rhetoric in Classical Historiography: Four Studies*. London.

Woodruff, P. (2021) *Thucydides on Justice, Power, and Human Nature. Selections from the History of the Peloponnesian War*, 2nd edition. Indianapolis, IN.

Worley, L. (1994) *Hippeis: The Cavalry of Ancient Greece*. Oxford.

Wylie, G. (1992) 'Brasidas: great commander or whiz-kid?', *QUCC* 41: 75–95.

Yoshitake, S. (2010) '*Aretē* and the achievements of the war dead: the logic of praise in the Athenian funeral oration', in *War, Democracy and Culture in Classical Athens*, ed. D. Pritchard. Cambridge: 359–77.

Yunis, H. (1991) 'How do the people decide? Thucydides on Periclean rhetoric and civic instruction', *AJPh* 112: 179–200.

(1996) *Taming Democracy: Models of Political Rhetoric in Classical Athens*. Ithaca, NY, and London.

Zahrnt, M. (2006) 'Macedonia and Thrace in Thucydides', in *Brill's Companion to Thucydides*, eds. A. Rengakos and A. Tsakmakis. Leiden and Boston: 589–614.

Zammito, J. H. (2015) 'Historicism', in *The Oxford Handbook of German Philosophy in the Nineteenth Century*, eds. M. Forster and K. Gjesdal. Oxford: 779–805.

Ziegler, K. (1929) 'Der Ursprung der Exkurse im Thukydides', *RhM* 78: 58–67.

Zincgref, J. W. (1619) *Emblematvm Ethico-Politicorvm Centvria*. [Heidelberg].

(2011) *Gesammelte Schriften IV, 1: Apophthegmata Teutsch*, eds. T. Verweyen, D. Mertens and W. W. Schnabel. Berlin.

Ziolkowski, J. (1981) *Thucydides and the Tradition of Funeral Speeches at Athens*. New York.

Zoido, J. C. I. (2007) 'The battle exhortation in ancient rhetoric', *Rhetorica* 25: 141–58.

Zumbrunnen, J. (2008) *Silence and Democracy: Athenian Politics in Thucydides' History*. University Park, PA.

INDEX LOCORUM

Thucydides
(1.1) 32, 77–9, 109, 304
(1.1.1) 1, 9, 35, 50, 93, 163
(1.1.2) 35, 246
(1.1.2–3) 42
(1.1.3) 143
(1.2–19) 32, 77–8, 84
(1.2.4) 167
(1.2.5) 38
(1.3) 55, 80, 163
(1.3.1–2) 163
(1.3.2) 167
(1.3.3) 39, 163
(1.4) 38
(1.5–6) 55
(1.5.3) 166
(1.6.3) 170
(1.6.4) 167–8
(1.6.6) 168
(1.8.1) 39, 55
(1.8.2) 58
(1.8.13–14) 58
(1.9) 38
(1.9.1) 57
(1.9.2) 55
(1.9.4) 57, 153, 163
(1.10) 24, 39, 199
(1.10.1–3) 55
(1.10.3) 56
(1.10.3–5) 54
(1.10.4–5) 56
(1.12.1) 163
(1.12.3) 57
(1.13.3–4) 57
(1.14.1) 163
(1.14.3) 84
(1.17) 213
(1.18) 212
(1.18.1) 163, 171
(1.18.2) 163
(1.18.2–3) 163
(1.20) 37
(1.20–2) 32
(1.20–23) 77–8, 80
(1.20.1) 27, 37, 80
(1.20.2) 25, 54–5
(1.20.3) 37, 110, 237
(1.20.3–1.21–2) 74
(1.21.1) 20–9, 37, 44, 57
(1.21.2) 31n3
(1.22) 45, 257–8, 287
(1.22.1) 53, 64, 73, 246
(1.22.2) 1, 37, 74
(1.22.2–3) 110
(1.22.3) 8–9, 20–1
(1.22.4) 4–7, 20, 23, 27, 38, 44, 74, 92, 305
(1.23.1) 35, 97, 163
(1.23.1–3) 93
(1.23.2) 93, 246
(1.23.3) 95, 114, 247
(1.23.4–6) 81
(1.23.5) 93, 110
(1.23.6) 36, 102, 143, 174, 303
(1.24–27) 93
(1.24–55) 85, 168
(1.24–65) 78, 81
(1.24–87) 78, 82
(1.27.2) 168
(1.44) 51
(1.45) 51
(1.46.1) 168
(1.46.1–2) 51
(1.46.3–50) 51
(1.51) 51
(1.52–5) 52
(1.66–87) 78, 85

Thucydides (cont.)
(1.68–71) 82, 327
(1.68.1) 169
(1.68.1–71.7) 188
(1.69–71) 212
(1.69.4) 169
(1.70) 200, 202
(1.71) 200
(1.71.2) 170–1
(1.73–9) 217
(1.73.2) 149
(1.74) 149
(1.75) 147, 303
(1.75.3) 229
(1.76) 304
(1.76.1) 229
(1.76.2) 150, 153, 229–30
(1.76.3–4) 230
(1.77) 112
(1.77.1) 230
(1.77.6) 95
(1.79.2) 188, 245
(1.80.1) 188
(1.80.1–85.2) 187
(1.80.2) 94
(1.80.3–81.4) 94
(1.80.3–81.6) 188
(1.80.141–3) 94
(1.81) 224
(1.81.6) 95, 188
(1.82.1) 95
(1.82.1–5) 188
(1.82.6) 188
(1.84) 219
(1.84.1–3) 189
(1.84.2–4) 226–7
(1.84.3) 189
(1.84.3–4) 189
(1.85.1) 189
(1.85.2) 189, 228
(1.86) 213, 228–9
(1.86–7) 200
(1.86.1–5) 189
(1.87) 228
(1.87.1–3) 189
(1.87.2) 171, 189
(1.88) 200, 213, 228–9
(1.88–118) 81
(1.88–118.2) 78
(1.88–119) 78
(1.88.1) 81–2
(1.89–118) 54
(1.89.2) 145

(1.90) 213
(1.94–5) 57
(1.95) 147, 213
(1.95.2) 144
(1.95.4) 144
(1.96) 157
(1.96.1) 144, 148
(1.97) 146
(1.97–117) 112
(1.97.2) 54, 82
(1.98) 148
(1.98.3) 145
(1.98.4) 145, 157
(1.99.2) 146
(1.100) 324
(1.100–17) 85
(1.102) 201
(1.104) 108
(1.104–103) 213
(1.109–10) 108
(1.112.5) 59
(1.118) 200
(1.118.3–146) 78
(1.119–46) 82–3
(1.119–46) 78
(1.120–4) 83
(1.120–4) 85
(1.120.1–124.3) 181
(1.120.2) 153
(1.124.3) 154
(1.125–38) 85
scholia (1.126) 83
(1.126.4–6) 54
(1.128) 213
(1.128–35.1) 57
(1.128.6–129.3) 56
(1.128.7) 164
(1.131.2) 171
(1.132.2–3) 56
(1.132.5) 56
(1.135.2) 164
(1.136.3) 167
(1.137.3–4) 56
(1.138.3) 94, 267
(1.138.4) 53
(1.139–46) 83
(1.139.4) 36, 72
(1.140–4) 72
(1.140–4) 85
(1.140.1) 95
(1.140.1–144.4) 181, 187
(1.141.3) 61
(1.142.1) 61

(1.143.1) 61
(1.144.2) 61
(1.144.4) 181
(2–5.24) 90
(2.1) 33, 70
(2.1–2) 90
(2.1–5.24) 77
(2.1.1) 12
(2.4.2) 71
(2.5.5–6) 53
(2.5.5–7) 34
(2.6.2–3) 70
(2.11.1) 190
(2.11.1–2) 190
(2.11.1–9) 190
(2.11.4) 190
(2.11.5) 190
(2.11.9) 190
(2.12.1–5) 190
(2.12.3) 116
(2.13) 51, 151
(2.13.1) 187
(2.13.2) 61
(2.13.2–6) 61
(2.13.2–9) 113
(2.14) 55
(2.15) 55, 213
(2.17.1–2) 115
(2.17.4) 61
(2.23.2) 61
(2.23.25) 61
(2.23.30) 61
(2.23.32) 61
(2.23.56) 61
(2.23.58) 61
(2.25.2) 191
(2.29.3) 56, 86
(2.29.5) 165
(2.31.2) 97
(2.34–47.1) 97
(2.34.7) 65
(2.35–46) 64
(2.35.1–3) 182
(2.35.2) 20, 182, 234n3
(2.35.3) 21
(2.36) 203
(2.36.1) 170
(2.37) 170, 203
(2.38) 170
(2.39.1) 170
(2.40) 203–4
(2.40.2–3) 204
(2.40.4–5) 170

(2.40.5) 21
(2.41) 170, 199, 204
(2.41.4) 20, 205
(2.42.1) 20
(2.42.2) 20
(2.43) 204, 207
(2.44.4) 20
(2.45.1) 20
(2.47.3) 35
(2.47.3–48.3) 114
(2.47.3–54) 97
(2.47.4) 182
(2.48) 310
(2.48.1–2) 114
(2.48.3) 50, 97, 114, 287
(2.49.3–5) 201
(2.49.8) 201
(2.50) 56
(2.50.2) 46n45
(2.51) 202
(2.51.2–3) 114
(2.51.2–4) 182
(2.52) 201
(2.52–3) 201
(2.52.3) 182
(2.52.4) 182
(2.53.1–4) 182
(2.53.3) 182
(2.53.4) 182
(2.54.2) 117–18
(2.54.4) 116
(2.55.2–58) 121–2
(2.59) 201–2
(2.59.2) 182
(2.60.1) 95
(2.60.1–7) 183
(2.60.2–4) 182
(2.61.2) 183
(2.61.2–3) 183
(2.61.2–4) 182
(2.62) 100
(2.62.1–63.3) 183
(2.62.2–3) 183
(2.62.3) 151, 182
(2.62.5) 97
(2.63) 204, 225
(2.63.1) 150, 183
(2.63.1–2) 152
(2.63.2) 155, 180, 215
(2.63.2–3) 229
(2.63.3) 182
(2.64.1) 97, 123
(2.64.2–4) 183

Thucydides (cont.)
(2.64.3) 97
(2.64.6) 183
(2.65) 21, 36, 100, 123, 154, 157, 201,
    206, 211–12
(2.65.1) 183
(2.65.1–13) 179
(2.65.3) 21, 183
(2.65.3–10) 61
(2.65.4) 183
(2.65.4–5) 183
(2.65.4–13) 192
(2.65.5–7) 98
(2.65.5–8) 179
(2.65.5–10) 225
(2.65.5–13) 245
(2.65.6–13) 83
(2.65.7) 61, 107, 150, 154
(2.65.7–8) 151
(2.65.8–9) 185
(2.65.9) 26, 179, 192
(2.65.10) 190
(2.65.10–12) 179
(2.65.11) 10–11, 104, 106, 190
(2.65.11–12) 192
(2.65.12) 98, 104, 154
(2.67) 165, 213
(2.67.2) 165
(2.68.5) 166
(2.70) 202
(2.71.1–78.4) 190
(2.72.1) 190
(2.72.2–4) 254
(2.72.3) 190
(2.73.3–74.1) 190
(2.74.2–3) 191
(2.84) 200
(2.85) 200
(2.85.1–94.4) 191
(2.87) 201
(2.89) 201
(2.91) 200
(2.92) 200
(2.93–4) 212
(2.96–8) 164
(2.98) 165
(2.100.2) 223
(2.101.5) 167
(2.101.6) 167
(3.2) 205
(3.3.1) 93
(3.10–11) 205
(3.10.1) 221

(3.10.3–4) 149
(3.11.2) 222
(3.12) 205
(3.13.3) 93
(3.17) 35
(3.22.2) 59
(3.36.2–3) 72
(3.36.6) 22, 36, 72
(3.36.6–49.1) 72
(3.37) 327
(3.37–48) 327
(3.37.1) 155
(3.37.2) 180
(3.37.3–4) 189
(3.38.3–7) 22
(3.38.4) 69
(3.38.7) 69
(3.39.3) 22
(3.40.2) 69
(3.40.4) 219
(3.40.7) 22
(3.42–58) 267
(3.42.1) 219
(3.42.2) 70
(3.43) 206
(3.45) 206
(3.47) 206, 215
(3.47.5) 221, 229
(3.58.3) 222
(3.59.2) 222
(3.66.2) 222
(3.67) 228
(3.68) 171, 213
(3.68.2–4) 32
(3.68.4) 228
(3.81.4–84.2) 267
(3.82) 198
(3.82–3) 202, 216
(3.82–4) 327
(3.82.2) 28, 223
(3.82.7) 220
(3.82.8) 221–2
(3.86) 208
(3.87) 202
(3.88) 208
(3.90) 208
(3.94–8) 166
(3.94.4–5) 166
(3.96.1) 56
(3.104) 60
(3.104.1–2) 117
(3.104.3–6) 56
(3.112.7) 166

(3.113.5–6) 71
(3.113.6) 34–5
(3.114.3) 51
(4.3–23) 58
(4.11.4–12.1) 192
(4.16.1–2) 51
(4.21.3–22.3) 180
(4.26–41) 58
(4.27–8) 58
(4.27.3–28.5) 180
(4.28.4) 58
(4.34.3) 71
(4.39.3) 180
(4.41) 213
(4.50) 112, 164
(4.55.1) 96
(4.58–65) 208
(4.59.1–64.5) 184
(4.61) 209
(4.61–3) 208
(4.62) 208
(4.64) 208–9
(4.65.1–2) 184
(4.65.4) 100
(4.70.1–73.4) 192
(4.80) 213
(4.80.2–3) 224
(4.81.1) 192
(4.81.2) 192, 224
(4.81.3) 192
(4.84) 213
(4.84.1–2) 192
(4.84.2) 69, 171, 192
(4.85.1) 192
(4.85.2) 100
(4.85.5) 193
(4.85.6) 192–3
(4.86.1) 192–3, 224
(4.86.3–4) 193
(4.86.4) 192
(4.86.6–87.1) 193
(4.87.1) 67, 193
(4.87.2) 193
(4.87.2–3) 193
(4.87.3) 229
(4.87.3–6) 192
(4.87.6) 193
(4.88.1) 68, 193
(4.102) 324
(4.104.4) 1
(4.104.4–106) 50
(4.106) 100
(4.107.3) 167

(4.108) 101, 213, 311
(4.108.2–3) 68
(4.108.4) 100, 105
(4.108.5) 68
(4.112.1) 71
(4.114.2) 194
(4.114.3) 194
(4.120.3) 194
(4.122) 53
(4.126.5) 228
(4.132.3) 52
(5.1) 60
(5.4) 208
(5.6.1–10.12) 194
(5.6.3) 194
(5.7.1) 194
(5.7.2) 194
(5.8.1–5) 194
(5.8.2) 170
(5.9.1) 194
(5.9.1–10) 194
(5.9.3) 194
(5.9.6) 194
(5.9.9) 194, 227
(5.9.10) 195
(5.10.5–6) 195
(5.10.8) 195
(5.10.11) 195
(5.11.1) 195
(5.16.2) 257
(5.16.3) 171
(5.25–116) 90
(5.26) 36, 98, 202, 212
(5.26.1) 1, 12, 90, 98
(5.26.2) 99
(5.26.3–4) 99
(5.26.4) 99
(5.26.5) 1, 50
(5.32.1) 60
(5.65–82) 101
(5.65.2–3) 54
(5.68) 171
(5.68.2–3) 54
(5.84) 101
(5.84.3) 229
(5.85–8.1) 77
(5.85–113) 327
(5.85–114) 101
(5.87) 229
(5.89) 207, 221–2, 229
(5.90) 229
(5.91) 229
(5.91.2) 229

Thucydides (cont.)
  (5.92) 207
  (5.95) 207
  (5.97) 207
  (5.100) 207
  (5.101) 207, 229
  (5.103) 311
  (5.104) 272
  (5.105) 207, 213
  (5.105.1–2) 304
  (5.105.2) 229
  (5.105.4) 171, 229
  (5.107) 229
  (5.111) 207, 229
  (5.116.3) 229
  (6–7) 86
  (6.1) 36
  (6.1.1) 102, 104
  (6.2–5) 169, 209
  (6.2.3) 162
  (6.2.6) 162
  (6.4.2) 162
  (6.6.2) 162, 167
  (6.8–26.1) 72
  (6.8.2) 28–9
  (6.9–14) 72
  (6.9.1) 162
  (6.10) 210
  (6.10.5) 162
  (6.11.7) 162
  (6.12–13) 210
  (6.13) 210
  (6.13.1) 102
  (6.14) 210
  (6.15) 26
  (6.15.1) 73, 185
  (6.15.2–4) 36
  (6.15.3) 103
  (6.15.4) 103
  (6.16.1–3) 180
  (6.16.1–18.7) 185
  (6.16.6–17.1) 180
  (6.16.18) 73
  (6.18) 210
  (6.18.1) 162
  (6.18.2) 170
  (6.19) 210
  (6.19.1) 162, 180
  (6.19.2–26.1) 181
  (6.20–3) 72
  (6.23.1) 103
  (6.24) 210
  (6.24.3) 152

(6.25.1) 73
(6.25.2) 73
(6.27.1) 60
(6.27.3) 60, 103
(6.28.1) 60
(6.28.2) 60
(6.30.2) 103
(6.31) 311–12
(6.32) 211
(6.32.3) 73, 185
(6.32.3–41) 86
(6.33–4) 211
(6.33.1) 185
(6.33.1–34.9) 73, 184
(6.33.2) 185
(6.33.3) 185
(6.33.4) 185
(6.35.1) 185
(6.35.2) 185
(6.35.2–40.2) 73
(6.38) 211
(6.39–40) 211
(6.41) 211
(6.41.1–3) 185
(6.41.2) 185
(6.41.2–4) 73
(6.41.3) 185
(6.46) 24, 29
(6.46.3) 162
(6.53) 212
(6.53–4) 211
(6.53–9) 211
(6.53.1) 60
(6.53.2) 27
(6.53.3) 27
(6.54) 211
(6.54–9) 25
(6.54–69) 36–7
(6.54.1) 25, 37, 55
(6.54.5) 223
(6.54.6–7) 56
(6.55) 86
(6.55.1) 56
(6.55.1–2) 56
(6.56–8) 86
(6.59.3) 56
(6.60) 211
(6.60.1) 27, 60
(6.60.2–5) 54
(6.61.1–3) 60
(6.70.3–4) 185
(6.72.2) 185–6
(6.72.3) 186

(6.72.3–5) 186
(6.72.4) 186
(6.72.5) 186
(6.73.1) 186
(6.76.4) 149
(6.79.2) 169
(6.82) 72, 170
(6.83.1) 149
(6.83.4) 152
(6.85.1) 155
(6.99) 212
(6.102.2) 225
(6.105) 103
(7.14.3) 180
(7.14.4) 180
(7.15.1–2) 180
(7.18) 212–13
(7.18.2–3) 228
(7.18.2–4) 172
(7.18.3) 172
(7.21.3) 186
(7.21.3–5) 186
(7.21.5) 187
(7.27.3–28.4) 103
(7.28) 213
(7.28.3) 100, 104
(7.29–30) 151, 174
(7.29.4) 165, 174
(7.29.5) 35
(7.30.2) 165
(7.42.5) 103
(7.44.1–2) 54
(7.44.4–6) 72
(7.44.6) 175
(7.48) 212
(7.48.4) 226
(7.50) 174, 212
(7.55) 212
(7.55.1) 175
(7.55.2) 168, 172
(7.56) 212
(7.57.1) 168
(7.57.4) 169
(7.57.5) 162, 168
(7.57.9) 168
(7.59–71) 212
(7.66–7) 212
(7.69.2) 170
(7.73) 212
(7.73.1–4) 187
(7.74.1–2) 187
(7.77.2) 225
(7.80.4) 226

(7.86) 212
(7.86.5) 225, 245
(7.87) 212
(7.87.5) 35, 172
(8.1) 154, 214
(8.1–2) 104
(8.1.1) 71
(8.1.2) 172
(8.1.3) 104, 172
(8.4) 214
(8.9.4) 104
(8.15) 214
(8.24.4) 104, 172
(8.24.5) 104
(8.24.6) 172
(8.25.5) 172
(8.27.5) 106
(8.40.2) 172
(8.45–97) 214
(8.53) 214
(8.61.1) 239
(8.66) 327
(8.67.4) 106
(8.68.1) 223
(8.68.1–2) 36
(8.68.2) 106
(8.68.4) 106
(8.74.3) 106
(8.82) 105
(8.86.4) 105
(8.87) 54
(8.89) 214
(8.89.2–3) 59
(8.89.3) 107
(8.96) 213
(8.96.1) 107–8, 172
(8.96.5) 107–8, 172, 175, 327
(8.97) 213
(8.97.1) 172
(8.97.2) 36, 107
(8.106.2–5) 108
(8.107) 108

Other
  Aristotle
    Poet. 1455a22–4: 71n28
    Rh.
      1358a36: 75n33
      1358b13–18: 75
      1365a 29–32: 65n10
  [Aristotle]
    Ath. Pol.
      23.5: 144–5

Other (cont.)
26.4 with Irwin 2015b: 112
Athenaeus 896P 25
Diodorus Siculus
7.11: 58
12.39–40: 113
12.58: 117
12.58.6: 60, 117
Dionysus of Halicarnassus
Pomp. 3.3–4: 5
Thuc.
8: 2–3
11: 81–2
16: 73
18: 64n6, 65n11
20: 79
24: 9
42: 65n7
Eupolis, K-A fr. 303, vol. 5, 474: 162
Hecataeus, *BNJ* 1 F1: 37n17
Herodian, 1.1.4: 246
Herodotus
4.147–58: 174
5.32: 57
5.42: 174
6.57.5: 37n16
7.139: 163
7.151–2: 112
8.144.2: 160
9.106: 145
Hesiod, *Op.* 240–3: 118
Homer
Il.
2.638–44: 166
5.63: 116
11.604: 116
22.16: 116

Horace, 2.1.11.ll. 156–7: 261
Isocrates, *On the Peace*, 8.85–6: 156
Libanius, *Orat. ad Antioch.* (16) 50–1: 116
OR 160 = *IG* I³ 369: 61
Plato
Grg.
483cd: 221
483d: 219
491e–2a: 221
Leg. 693d: 214
Prt. 322c: 221
Resp.
1.348c12: 219
352c4: 221
Plutarch
de glor. Ath. 347a: 24
Nic. 1.1: 71
Per. 35: 120
Polyb.
12.25d.1: 61
12.25i.2: 61–2
12.27.3–4: 62
12.4c.4–5: 61
Quintilian, *Inst.* 10.2.17: 233
Sallust
Cat.
8.1–4: 233
53: 245
Socrates, *Phaedr.* 261e–62b: 124
Solon 36.4 W: 115
Sophocles, *Phil.* 1440–4: 222
Xenophon
Hell.
2.2.10–11: 119
2.2.3: 102
2.2.20: 154
[Xenophon], *Ath. Pol.* 112

SUBJECT INDEX

Acanthus/Acanthians 68, 192, 228
accuracy 2–3, 43, 48, 74, 110–11, 287–8
  and translation 325
  see also truth
Aelius Theon 83
Aeolians 168
Aetolia
  ethnicity 166
  suffering in battle 140
Africanus, Julius 255
Agacinski, Sylviane, *Time Passing* 282
Agamemnon 38, 57
  and divine anger 116
agon
  and Cleon 21–5
  Pericles' speech 20
Akarnanians 165–6
Alcibiades 185, 279
  characterization of 36
  Chytraeus on 269
  compared to Pericles 181
  as informant 52
  Melancthon on 268
  and the Mysteries and Herms scandals 26,
    37
  recalled as general 108
  restrains Athenians at Samos 105
  Sicilian Debate 209–10
  and the Sicilian Expedition 73, 103, 170, 180
  in Xenophon 196, 239
Alinsky, Saul 314–15
Allison, Graham 301, 310
allusion, of historiographers to Thucydides
    236–7
alternative versions of events 34, 53, 150
Altertumswissenschaft 289–90
Ambraciots 34–5, 71, 141, 166
Ameinocles of Corinth 57–8

Amiroutzes, Georgios 261–2
Amphilochia/Amphilochians 34–5, 141, 166
Amphipolis 100, 165, 170, 173, 195, 324
analepses 90, 98, 107–8
analyst/separatist approach 10, 78, 90
anarchy 303–4, 306
andrapodization 141
Andrewes, A. 22–3, 59
Androcles 106n62
Antiphon 36, 106–7, 223
Aphrodite Erykina, temple 162
Apollo, and divine anger 116–17
Apostoles, Michael 252
Appian 241–2
Aratus of Sicyon 236
Archaeology 38–48, 79–84
  first empire 151
  and Greek ethnicity 167–8
  terms used for confirmation 55
Archedice of Lampsacus 56
Archelaus 223
archers 133–4, 136, 140
Archidamian War 96–101, 134
  see also Peace of Nicias
Archidamus 245
  and leadership 187–91
  prolepses 94–5
  on Spartan virtues 226–8
argumentation 40–1n89, 42–3, 46
Aristocrates 59
Aristogeiton 25, 36–7, 86
Aristotle
  Poetics 71–2n164
  Rhetoric 65, 75
Armstrong, Richard 293
Arnold, Thomas 297
Artabazus 56
Artaxerxes 56–7, 164

Asclepius 120
Aspendus 54
Assinarus massacre 141
Astyochus 106n59
Athenagoras 73, 185, 211
Athenaion Politeia (Aristotelian) 144
Athens
  alliance with Corcyra 51–2
  character of 229–30
  democracy 200–14, 327
  early history of 55–6
  empire and imperialism 143–4, 147–9,
      158–9, 303
    Delian League 144–8
    end of the empire 153–8
    explanation 149–53
  ethnicity/stereotyping 169–72, 175
  leadership 177–9, 327
  mutilation of the Herms scandal 25–7, 60
  navy 35
  patriotic stories 18, 20, 38–9
  portrayal of aggression of 81–2
  speech at Sparta 149, 217–18
Augustus, speech in Cassius Dio 245

Bacon, Francis 277
Bann, Stephen 292
barbarians 160, 162–7, 175
Barker, Elton 69
battle
  Aetolia 140
  Delium 139–40
  Epipolae 71–2, 140, 175
  Great Harbour 168–9, 181, 187, 209, 212
  Mantinea 54, 101, 139
  Platea 18, 32–4, 53, 59, 137, 140–1, 174,
      190–1, 228
  Sybota 140
  types of 132
  see also Sicilian Expedition
Berlin, Isaiah 328
Bessarion 252
Bible, translations 324–5
biographical information (Thucydides) 1, 60,
      129–30
biography 252–3
Blass, Friedrich 63
Bloedow, E. F. 190
Boeotians 57
boundaries, violation of 102
Brasidas 52, 67–9, 96, 138, 142
  and Acanthus 228
  and Amphipolis 173, 227

on Athenian troops in Amphipolis 170
  character of 223–4
  on the Illyrians 228
  and leadership 191–5
  and Scione 53, 68
  and Torone 71
  un-Spartan qualities 171
Brauro 167
Brodsky, Joseph 319
Bruni, Leonardo 266
Brunt, P. A. 52
Bury, J. B. 288, 290–7
Byzantium, transmission in 249–64

Callias 112
Callicles, in Plato's *Gorgias* 219, 221
Calvinists 270–2
Carians 39, 55, 57
Carr, E. H. 3
  The Twenty Years' Crisis, 1919–1939 306
Carroll, L., *Alice through the Looking Glass* 317
Cassius Dio 245–6, 256–7
Catalogue of Ships (Homer) 54, 56–7, 166
Catalogue of Women (Ehoiai) 166
cavalry 133–6
Chaereas 106
Chalcidians 100–1, 105, 122
chance (*tuchē*) 58, 94–5, 328
character, moral 223–6
characterizations 36
Chians, revolt 104–5
Chinese history 296
Chorikios of Gaza 253
chronology 89–91, 321
  and summers/winters 12, 33, 77, 90–1, 103
  see also analepses; historical consciousness;
      prolepses
Chrysoloras, Manuel 266
Chytraeus, David 268–70
Cicero 274
circumvallation 137
citizenship
  laws 112, 165n16
  Plataea 173
  Spartan 171n33
Clearidas 52, 194
Cleon 58, 142
  on *agon* 21–5
  on the Athenian Empire as a tyranny 155,
      225n33
  and Brasidas 194
  characterization of 36, 180
  Chytraeus on 269

on democracy 327
Justus Lipsius on 273
Melancthon on 268
and the Mytilenean Debate 69–70, 72, 180,
    189, 205, 218n10, 219
Cochrane, Charles, *Thucydides and the
    Science of History* 41
Collingwood, R. G., *An Autobiography* 324
colonization, Sicily 54
conflation 244
Plutarch 120–1
Connor, W. R. 192, 310
constructivism 306
Corcyra 82, 85, 216, 218–19
Athenian alliance with 51–2
Athenian intervention 85
civil war 202, 222–3
and Corinth 57–8, 78, 168
ethnicity 172–3
Gentillet on 271
and greed 221
stasis 28, 93, 141, 267, 327
Corinth/Corinthians 82–3, 85
on the Athenians 154, 200
and the Battle of Sybota 140
and Corcyra 57–8, 78, 168
on the Spartans 327
speech to Spartan assembly 169–70
Cornelius Sisenna, L. 235
Cortes, Ernesto 315
courage 186–7, 204, 218, 227
Cratippus 73
Crawley, R. 321–2
Ctesias, *Persian History* 257
cultural distance 323–4, 328
Cylon 54, 82–5
Cyzicus 108

Darius II, peace with 112
Debnar, P. 63–4n5, 189
Decelea 103, 138–9
deception 274
and democracy 206–7, 210
deeds see *erga/ergon* (deeds)
Delebecque, E. 52
Delian League 117, 144–8, 151, 157
deliberative oratory 66, 74–5
deliberative rhetoric 75
Delium 96n30, 137, 139–40
Delos 117
Delphi
amphictyony 59–60
and Cylon 54

democracy 198–9, 212–14
Athenian 200–7
Demodocus, in Homer's *Odyssey* 18–19
Demosthenes 58, 70, 103, 142, 226
Dewald, Carolyn 31, 86–7, 90
Dexippus 256–7
Dii 165
dikē 218
Diodorus Siculus 2n2, 58, 321
on Hagnon's campaign 122–3
on the plague 117
Diodotus 22, 70, 72, 96, 205–6, 215, 219,
    221, 267
Chytraeus on 269
Justus Lipsius on 273
Melancthon on 268
Dionysius of Halicarnassus 5, 9–10, 252, 321
on the *Archaeology* 79–80
paired with Thucydides 251
on Thucydides' speeches 64–7, 73
on Thucydides' style 9–10, 78–9, 84n17
on veracity 2–3
Dionysus, theatre of in Athens 23
direct discourse 63, 68, 72–3
disjunction 86–7
divine anger 116–17
documents, source 50–3
Dorians 57
and the Dorian Argives 168
ethnicity 172
foretelling of war 117–19

earthquakes 96n33, 246–7
Egestans/Egestaeans 24, 28–9, 72
ethnicity 162–3
Egyptian history 295, 298–9
Electoral Palatinate of the Rhine 272n30
elegy 18
enargeia 24, 71, 89n1
ending 11, 89, 108
Ephorus 2n2, 113, 117
Epidamnus 82, 85, 93, 174
Epidaurus 120–3
epigrams, and Byzantine Thucydides 251
Epipolae (Syracuse) 71–2, 140–1, 175
erga/ergon (deeds) 12, 24, 45–8, 53, 58–9,
    67–70, 202–3
and Archidamus 189–91
and Brasidas 192–5
and Hermocrates 186–7
and new political realism 315
and Pericles 120–3, 181–3
and the plague 124

erga/ergon (deeds) (cont.)
  speeches as 67–70, 74
  and Sthenelaidas 189
  see also *logos*
ethics 308
Ethiopia, and the plague 114, 116, 124
ethnicity 160–2, 173–6
  Egestans/Egestaeans 162–3
  Greek 167–73
  Persians 163–4
  Sicilians 162–3, 169
  Sparta 169–72, 175
  Thracians 164–5
  Trojans 163
Euboea, revolt of 108, 145, 239
Euesperides/Euesperitans 174
Euphemus 149, 152, 170
  on the Athenian Empire as tyranny 155
  Justus Lipsius on 273
eusebeia 222–3
Eusebios 255
eutaxia 132–3
evidential discourse 44, 46–8
Excerpta (*Constantinian Excerpta*) 256
exile 50, 202

fear, as cause of imperialism 149–53, 155–6
'Fifty Years' see *Pentecontaetia* ('Fifty Years')
Finley, J. H. 50n1, 218
First Punic War 241, 243
Five Thousand 36, 59, 107
forensic oratory 42
foresight 100, 175
  Pericles on 97, 100, 326
Four Hundred 58–9, 106–7, 214
Frederick V 272n30
freedom 215
  and democracy 203–5, 207, 210
Fritzsche, Peter 292
Funeral Oration 19–21, 65–6, 83, 97, 170–6,
      182, 233–4
  and democracy 203–5
  and Dionysius of Halicarnassus on 64
  and human suffering 139–40

Gallie, W. B. 283
Garnett, Constance 318–19
Garst, Daniel 306
Gela, speech by Hermocrates at 184, 209
gender, and ethnicity 167
Gentili, Alberico 274–5
Gentillet, Innocent, *Anti-Machiavel* 270–2
Georgios the Monk 255

Geuss, Raymond 307–10, 312–13
Gilpin, Robert 304
glosses, narratorial 92, 94, 97, 100, 104–5
Gomme, A. W. 50n1, 59
good judgement (*euboulia*) 218–20, 227–8
Great Harbour battle 168–9, 181, 187, 209,
      212
greed (*pleonexia*) 221
Greek Anthology 250–1
Gregoras, Nikephoros 254
Gribble, David 31
Grote, George 297–8
Grotius, Hugo 275–7
Guha, Ranajit 298
Gylippus 211

Hagnon 122–3, 195
Hannibal 239
Harmodius 25, 36–7, 86
Hawthorn, G. 217n7
Hecataeus 37
Hegel, G. W. F. 285, 291, 299n80
Hellanicus 2n2, 25, 112
  Atthis 54
Hellen (son of Deucalion) 167
Henderson, Bernard 7
Hera, building of inn and temple to
      32–3
Heraclea 59–60
heralds see messengers/heralds
Hermocrates 73, 149, 183–7, 202–8, 211–12
  in Xenophon 239
Herms, mutilation of the 25–7, 60, 103
Herodian 246–7
Herodotus 8, 57, 82, 237
  anecdote of Thucydides hearing 253
  in *Bibliotheke* (Photios) 256–7
  on Callias 112
  criticism of 54–5
  ethnicity in 160, 164, 175–6
  Euesperitans 174
  imitation of by Laonikos 260
  and 19th-century historiography
      293–4
  oral presentation of work 18
  Prolegomena 77
  self-presentation 31
  superlatives 240–1
Hesiod 56, 118
  Catalogue of Women 166
Hesychius of Miletus, *Onomatologos* 252
Hipparchus 25–6, 55
Hippias 26, 56

historical authority 31–2
  and the *Archaeology* 38–48
  and the Thucydidean narrator 32–8
historical consciousness 173, 282–3, 291,
    293–8
historical method 40, 42–3n36, 80–1, 282,
    290, 293, 295, 298
historical science 283–6, 290–3
historiographers
  19th century 282–300
  Greek and Roman 233–5, 248
    adaptation 244–8
    amplification 240–4
    anonymity of Thucydides 235–40
historiographic genres 80–1, 84–6
history, as a genre 17–18
Hobbes, Thomas 265, 277–80
  translation 312, 319–23, 325
Homer 39, 175
  19th-century historiographers on 292, 297
  Iliad, Catalogue of Ships 54, 56–7, 166
  Odyssey, Demodocus 18–19
  in Pericles' funeral speech 20
  on the Trojans 163
Homeric Hymn to Apollo 56
Honig, Bonnie 313–14
  Antigone Interrupted 314
honour, as cause of imperialism 149–53,
    155–6
hope 100, 310–12
hoplites 131–6
Horace 234, 261
Hornblower, Simon 33, 50n1, 51–2, 54–5,
    59–60, 83, 220, 222–3, 237n22,
    322
human condition 4–5, 7, 92
human nature 27–8
Hyperbolus 106n62

idealism/ideal theory 307–8
Illyrians, Brasidas on 228
imitation 258–60
imperialism
  Athenian 143–4, 147–9, 216, 229–30
  cause 149–53
incorporative rhetoric 181–2, 188, 193
indirect discourse 63, 68, 72–3
Industrial Areas Foundation (IAF) 302–16
influence/persuasion 327
informants, as sources 52
inn 32–3
inscriptions, as sources 56
international politics 303

international relations 7, 301–2, 305–6, 319
intratextuality 12
Isocrates, *On the Peace* 156–7

Jaffe, Seth 301
javelin throwers 133–4, 136, 140
Johnson, Laurie 302
judgements, political 326–7
justice 215–30, 320–7
justifications, moral 320–7
Justinianic plague 262–4

Keohane, Robert 305–6
Kerkyraika 168, 174
kinship see *sungeneia* (*xungeneia*) ('kinship')
Konstantinos VII Porphyrogennetos, and the
    Excerpta 255–6
Koselleck, Reinhart 285
Kritoboulos 251, 259, 261–4
Kyriacus of Ancona 251

Lacedaemonians *see* Sparta/Spartans
Laches 208
Laird, Andrew 63–4n5, 67
Lamachus 142
Lane Fox, R. J. 52–3
Laonikos 260–1
Lattimore, R. 321–2
leadership 177–9
  Archidamus 187–91
  Brasidas 191–5
  'good' 195–6
  Hermocrates 183–7
  Pericles 178–83
Lebow, Richard Ned 306
Lee, Christine 315
Leon the Mathematician 251
Leontini 208
Leslie, Margaret 303
letters 56–7
Libanius 116, 253
Lichas 53
lies/deception, and democracy 206–7, 210
light infantry 133–6
Lipsius, Justus 272–4, 278
logographoi (orators) 18, 37, 294
  criticism for 74 *see also* oratory
logos 12, 24, 45–8, 58–9, 67–70, 73–5, 92,
    202–3
  and Archidamus 189, 191
  and Brasidas 192–5
  and Hermocrates 186–7
  and new political realism 315

logos (cont.)
  and Pericles 181–3
  on the plague 115, 123–4
  and Sparta 213
  and Sthenelaidas 189
  see also *erga/ergon*; speeches
Long Walls 138
Loraux, Nicole 7
Lorenz, Chris 288
Lucretius 236
Lutheranism 268
Lygizos, Michael 254

Machiavelli, Niccolò 270–2
Macleod, Colin 67
Malalas, Ioannes 255
Mantena, Karuna 307
Mantinea, battle 54, 101, 139
marginalia 250
Markellinos 252–3
masculinity 135
master narrative 284, 286
Megara 97, 113, 116, 139
Megill, Allan 284–5
Mehmet II 261–4
Melanchthon , Philip 267–8
Melos/Melians 102, 141, 176, 207, 216, 272
  in Herodotus 176
  and the IAF 314–15
  and justice 222
  Melian Dialogue 66, 101–2, 171, 174, 221,
    229, 304, 306
  Dionysius of Halicarnassus on 64–5
  and realism 310–12
  and translation 322
    moral justifications 327
Mencius 325
messengers/heralds 70–1, 141
meta-history 18–19
  Cleon on *agon* and spectatorship 21–5
  Pericles' funeral speech 19–21
  the tyrannicide 25–7
methodology, reflection on 246
Methone 191
Minos 38
modes of historical writing 84–6
Molossia, queen of 167
Momigliano, Arnaldo 282
monosandalism 59
monuments, *Archaeology* compared to 44–5
morality 215–30, 320–7
Morgenthau, Hans, *Politics Among Nations*
  303

Morley, Neville 302
Morrison, James 66
Muhlack, Ulrich 283
Murari-Pires, Francisco 287
Mycalessus 35, 141, 151, 165, 174–5
Mycenae 39
Mysteries scandal 25–7
Mytilenean Debate 21–5, 69–70, 72, 180, 327
Mytileneans/Mytilene 149, 205–6,
    215–16n2
  ambassadors 221–2

narrative style
  glosses 92, 94, 97, 100, 104–5
  and historical authority 31–2
  use of messengers 71
narratives
  grand narrative 284–6, 293–8
  master narrative 284, 286
  metanarrative 284, 290, 295–6, 298
narratological theory 12
naturalisation 165, 173
naval warfare 136
Naxos 145, 148, 157
new political realism 307–16
'New Simonides' see Plataea
Nicias 58, 72–3, 103, 170, 212, 245
  Chytraeus on 269
  compared to Hermocrates
    185
  compared to Pericles 180–1
  Melancthon on 268
  moral character of 225–6
  Sicilian Debate 209–10
Niebuhr, Barthold Georg 41, 285, 287,
    289–99
Nietzsche, Friedrich 307–8
nightingales 56
noise of war 71–2
novellas 85

objectivity 4–5, 287
Oedipus, and divine anger 116
oligarchs/oligarchy 106–7, 214
  Antiphon 36, 106–7, 223
  see also Five Thousand; Four Hundred
On Ancient Medicine 85
oracles
  and the occupation of the Pelargikon
    115–16
  on the plague 117–18
orators (*logographoi*) 17–19
  and deception 206–7

oratory 327
  and the *Archaeology* 46
  and Cleon 21–5
  deliberative (sumbouleutic) 66, 74–5
  epideictic 19–21
  forensic 42
  incorporative rhetoric 181–2, 188, 193
  training/education, Byzantium 252–4,
    258–9
organization 77–9
Ostwald, M. 218

Paean 72
Palatinus (Heidelberg) graecus 252 (E) 257
Pandion 56
Panionios of Chios 241
papyrus 51, 250
Parry, Adam 304, 312
patriotic stories/myths 18, 20, 38–9
Pausanias the Regent 56–7, 82–5, 164
Peace of Callias 112, 146
Peace of Nicias
  Athenian violation of 103
  prolepses 96–101
Peisistratids 26–7
  see also Hipparchus; tyrannicide
Pelargikon 115–16
Pentecontaetia ('Fifty Years') 54, 83, 85, 108,
    112
performance of Thucydides' work 9
Pericles 36, 61, 142
  Chytraeus on 269
  and foresight 97–8, 100
  in Hobbes 279
  and leadership 178–83, 192
  Melanchthon on 268
  moral character of 224–5
  'obituary' 151, 154
  and the plague 119–24, 182
  and political judgement 326
  speeches 83, 85
    on Athenian Empire as tyranny 155, 158,
      215, 225
    on Athenian resources 51, 94, 99–100,
      113
    chance (*tuchē*) 94–5
    Funeral Oration 19–21, 65–6, 83, 97,
      170–6, 182, 233–4
      and democracy 203–5
      Dionysius of Halicarnassus on 64
      and human suffering 139–40
      and honour 150, 152
      warning against acquisitiveness 151

Persian Wars, and the Delian League 147–9
Persians, ethnicity 163–4
persuasion/influence 327
pessimism 199, 309, 313
Petrarch 266
Peucer, Caspar 268
Phaeax 208
phalanx 131–3
Pharnabazus, in Xenophon 239
Philistos of Syracuse 2n2
philology 289–90, 292–3, 295–6
Philp, Mark 307
Phormio 191, 200–1
Photios, *Bibliotheke* 256–7
Phrynichus 105–6
phusis/nomos contrast 58
Pindar 234
  Euesperitans 174
Piraeus 191
Pisistratus 55–6, 223
place-names, and translation 324
plague 21, 35, 50, 55–6, 201–2, 216, 263,
    310
  in Herodian 246–7
  in Kritoboulos 262–4
  in Procopios 259–60
  and prolepsis 93, 95–7
  and truth 113–24
Plataea
  citizenship 173
  and messengers 70
  and the noise of war 71
  siege/fall of 18, 32–4, 53, 59, 137, 140–1,
    174, 190–1, 228
  Spartan treatment of 171
  see also Gregoras, Nikephoros
Plato
  Euthyphro 222
  Gorgias 219, 221
  Laws 214
  Menexenos 21
  Protagoras 221
  Republic 219, 221
Pliny, *A Fine Aufidi Bassi* 238
Plutarch 6, 320
  in the 18th century 287
  Pericles 4n9, 120–1
  on Thucydides' *enargeia* 24, 71, 320
poets/poetry 37, 44, 56–7
  criticism 74
political realism 302, 307–8
political theory 250, 307–8, 313, 319–20, 326
political thought 7, 319–20, 328

politics, attitude to 60–1
Polybius 61–2, 236, 238, 242–4
    in the 18th century 287
    'possession for all time' 4, 20, 23, 27, 44, 269,
        305
    and modern international relations 302
Potidaea 78, 122–3, 202
power, and empire 151–3
Procopius, Bruni on 266
profit, as cause of imperialism 149–53, 155–6
Procopios 259–60
    Secret History 260
    Wars 260
Prolegomena
    chronological interruptions 79–84
    disjunction 86–7
    and modes of historical writing 84–6
    organization 77–9
prolepses 109
    Archidamian War/Peace of Nicias 96–101
    Book 1 92
        actors' 93–5
        implicit/'ironical' 95
        narrator's 92–3
    Book 8 104–8
    'obituary' of Pericles 151, 154
    Sicilian expedition 102–4
Propertius 236
prose writers, as sources 57–8
Psellos, Michael 260
publication 9
Pylos 58, 96, 100, 191–2

Quintilian 233

racism 161, 173
Ranke, L. von 17, 41, 286–8, 290, 297
Raubitschek, A. E. 218
Rawlings, H. R. 4–5n10
Rawls, John 308
reading Thucydides 8–12
realism 301–16
reason 284–5
recklessness 102, 104
Reinsch, Diether 261
relevance, and translation 317, 323–5, 329
religion, attitude to 59–60, 222–3
resilience, Athenian 100, 105, 172, 202
reverence (to hosion) 218, 222–3
Reynolds, John 278–9
rhetoric see oratory
rhetorical history (term) 63
'ring composition' 80, 86

Romilly, Jacqueline de 40, 42
Rood, Tim 293–4

Sadokos 165, 173
Said, Edward 293
Sallust 233–6, 244
    Bellum Catilinae 233, 235, 244–5
scholia 250 see also Tzetzes, Ioannes
'scientific' (term) 40–3
Scione 216
    and Brasidas 53, 68, 194
Sears, M. A. 68n20
self-control 155–6, 218–20, 226–7
self-presentation 31–2
    and the Archaeology 38–48
    and Thucydides' narrative style 31–8
separatist/analyst approach 10–12, 78, 90
Serpent Column 56
Seyssel, Claude de 267
shame (aidōs), sense of 218, 220, 227–8
Sicilian Debate 209–10
Sicilian Expedition 10, 24, 28–9, 35–6, 72–3,
        100, 213, 216, 239
    and ethnicity 172, 175
    and profit 152
    prolepses 102–4
    and realism 311–12
    and tribute 151
Sicily
    in Appian 241–2
    ethnicity 162–3, 169
    Greek colonisation 54
    war against 86
siege warfare 137
significance, historical 240–1
Sikeliots (Sikeliōtai) 162
simplicity (to euēthes) 220
slingers 134, 136
snobbery, and war 135–6
Socrates 124
sophistry, and Cleon in the Mytilenean
        Debate 22–4
Sophocles, Philoctetes 222
sources/evidence 50–62
    criticism 39–40
Sparta/Spartans
    characterization of 200
    ethnic stereotyping 169–72
        government 171
    kings' votes 37n16
    leadership 147, 187–95
        see also Archidamus; Brasidas

regime 212–13, 327
and Sphacteria 71
virtues/moral character 223–4, 226–9
see also Archidamus; Brasidas
spectatorship, and Cleon in the Mytilenean
Debate 23, 25
speeches 63–7
as action 67–70
on *logos* 73–5
and messengers/heralds 70–1
soundscape of war 71–2
as sources 53
'suppressed' 72–3
see also *logos*
Sphacteria 71, 139–40
Stahl, Hans-Peter 26, 311
stasis 327
Athenian 106
in Brasidas 193
Corcyrean 28, 93, 141, 327
translation by Melanchthon 267
Stears, Marc 313–14
stereotyping, ethnic, Athens and Sparta
169–72
Sthenelaidas (ephor) 189–90, 200, 228
Melancthon on 268
Stout, Jeffrey 315
stratēgoi 178
unnamed Syracusan 185
Stratonike 167
Straussian school 8
Stroud, R. S. 50
structural realism 303
style 322–3
Suda 252–3, 256
suffering, human 139–42
summers/winters, and chronology 12, 33, 77,
90–1
sungeneia (*xungeneia*) ('kinship') 161–2,
168–70, 173–4
superlatives 34–6, 124, 179, 240–1
Sybota, and the Corinthians
140
Synkellos, Georgios 255
Synoecia 55
Syracuse 327
Athenian expedition against
54, 139
Epipolae 71–2, 140–1
debate 86
democracy 207–12
ethnicity 175
Great Harbour battle 168–9, 181, 187

Tacitus 241, 272
tekmēria 80–1, 84–6
Teres (king of Thrace) 56
Tereus 56, 86
theatres, Dionysus (Athens) 23
Thebes, on Plataea 228
Themistios 253
Themistocles
death of 53
excursus on 82–5
Hermocrates compared to 187
letter to Artaxerxes 56–7
and the Molossian queen 167
prediction of 94
Theopompus of Chios 148n15, 256
Theramenes 59, 106
Theseus 55, 213
Thirty regime 107, 109
Thirty-Years' Peace 115, 117
Thomas, R. 42–3n36, 46n46
Thomas (scholastikos) 253–4
Thrace, ethnicity 164–5
Thrasyllos 239
Thucydidean Germans 41
Thucydides, biographical information 1, 60,
129–30
'Thucydides Trap' 301, 310
Timaeus 61–2, 242–3
Tissaphernes 54
title 321
Torone 71, 194, 216
tragedy 17–18, 216, 310
translations 10, 249, 267–8, 317–29
transliteration 250, 324
transmission, Byzantium 249–64
treaties, as sources 51
tribute, Delian League 117, 145n6, 151
Trojans, ethnicity 163
'truest cause' 81–2, 149, 303–4
truth 2–3, 9, 43, 53, 74, 288
labouring for 37–8, 110–12, 123–5
and Athenian growth 112–13
and the plague 113–23
and *logographoi* 20–9
modern historiography 290
and Pericles 19–21
tuchē (chance) 58
Tucker, Aviezer 287
typhoid 124
tyrannicide 25–7, 36–7, 86, 211
tyrants/tyranny 213, 215
admiration of 223
Athenian Empire as 154–8, 215

tyrants/tyranny (cont.)
  Vindiciae, contra tyrannos 271
Tzetzes, Ioannes 251, 257–8

unitarian approach 10–11
usefulness 27–9, 74

Valla, Lorenzo 266–7
Velleius Paterculus 233, 235–6
veracity *see* truth
Vergerio the Elder, Pier Paolo 266
Vergil 236
Vindiciae, contra tyrannos 271
virtues 218–20

Waltz, Kenneth, *Theory of International
        Politics* 303
war/warfare
  art of 131–7
  autonomy of 130–1
  cost of 139–42
  military career of Thucydides 129–30
  Sparta and Athens as opposing forces
        137–9
Warren, Mark 314–15

Welch, David 305
Wendt, Alexander 306
West, William 63
Westlake, H. D. 52
White, Hayden 299
Wilamowitz-Moellendorff, U. von. 82n10,
        83n13
Williams, Bernard 308–9, 313
Wingrove, Elizabeth 313
Wolf, Friedrich August 289–90
Woodman, A. J. 41–2
words and deeds, see *erga/ergon*; *logos*
Wylie, G. 193

Xenophon
  and Gentillet 270
  Hellenica 154, 196, 237–40
        Thucydides paired with 251
Xerxes 84n15
  and Pausanias 56–7, 164
xungeneia see *sungeneia*

Zincgref, Julius Wilhelm 272
Zonaras, Ioannes, *Epitome
        of Histories* 255

Cambridge Companions To ...

AUTHORS

Edward Albee edited by Stephen J. Bottoms

Margaret Atwood edited by Coral Ann Howells (second edition)

W. H. Auden edited by Stan Smith

Jane Austen edited by Edward Copeland and Juliet McMaster (second edition)

James Baldwin edited by Michele Elam

Balzac edited by Owen Heathcote and Andrew Watts

Beckett edited by John Pilling

Bede edited by Scott DeGregorio

Aphra Behn edited by Derek Hughes and Janet Todd

Saul Bellow edited by Victoria Aarons

Walter Benjamin edited by David S. Ferris

William Blake edited by Morris Eaves

Boccaccio edited by Guyda Armstrong, Rhiannon Daniels and Stephen J. Milner

Jorge Luis Borges edited by Edwin Williamson

Brecht edited by Peter Thomson and Glendyr Sacks (second edition)

The Brontës edited by Heather Glen

Bunyan edited by Anne Dunan-Page

Frances Burney edited by Peter Sabor

Byron edited by Drummond Bone

Albert Camus edited by Edward J. Hughes

Willa Cather edited by Marilee Lindemann

Catullus edited by Ian Du Quesnay and Tony Woodman

Cervantes edited by Anthony J. Cascardi

Chaucer edited by Piero Boitani and Jill Mann (second edition)

Chekhov edited by Vera Gottlieb and Paul Allain

Kate Chopin edited by Janet Beer

Caryl Churchill edited by Elaine Aston and Elin Diamond

Cicero edited by Catherine Steel

J. M. Coetzee edited by Jarad Zimbler

Coleridge edited by Lucy Newlyn

Coleridge edited by Tim Fulford (new edition)

Wilkie Collins edited by Jenny Bourne Taylor

Joseph Conrad edited by J. H. Stape

H. D. edited by Nephie J. Christodoulides and Polina Mackay

Dante edited by Rachel Jacoff (second edition)

Daniel Defoe edited by John Richetti

Don DeLillo edited by John N. Duvall

Charles Dickens edited by John O. Jordan

Emily Dickinson edited by Wendy Martin

John Donne edited by Achsah Guibbory

Dostoevskii edited by W. J. Leatherbarrow

Theodore Dreiser edited by Leonard Cassuto and Claire Virginia Eby

John Dryden edited by Steven N. Zwicker

W. E. B. Du Bois edited by Shamoon Zamir

George Eliot edited by George Levine and Nancy Henry (second edition)

T. S. Eliot edited by A. David Moody

Ralph Ellison edited by Ross Posnock

Ralph Waldo Emerson edited by Joel Porte and Saundra Morris

William Faulkner edited by Philip M. Weinstein

Henry Fielding edited by Claude Rawson

F. Scott Fitzgerald edited by Ruth Prigozy

Flaubert edited by Timothy Unwin

E. M. Forster edited by David Bradshaw

Benjamin Franklin edited by Carla Mulford

Brian Friel edited by Anthony Roche

Robert Frost edited by Robert Faggen

Gabriel García Márquez edited by Philip Swanson

Elizabeth Gaskell edited by Jill L. Matus

Edward Gibbon edited by Karen O'Brien and Brian Young

Goethe edited by Lesley Sharpe

Günter Grass edited by Stuart Taberner

Thomas Hardy edited by Dale Kramer

David Hare edited by Richard Boon

Nathaniel Hawthorne edited by Richard Millington

Seamus Heaney edited by Bernard O'Donoghue

Ernest Hemingway edited by Scott Donaldson

Hildegard of Bingen edited by Jennifer Bain

Homer edited by Robert Fowler

Horace edited by Stephen Harrison

Ted Hughes edited by Terry Gifford

Ibsen edited by James McFarlane

Henry James edited by Jonathan Freedman

Samuel Johnson edited by Greg Clingham

Ben Jonson edited by Richard Harp and Stanley Stewart

James Joyce edited by Derek Attridge (second edition)

Kafka edited by Julian Preece

Keats edited by Susan J. Wolfson

Rudyard Kipling edited by Howard J. Booth

Lacan edited by Jean-Michel Rabaté

D. H. Lawrence edited by Anne Fernihough

Primo Levi edited by Robert Gordon

Lucretius edited by Stuart Gillespie and Philip Hardie

Machiavelli edited by John M. Najemy

David Mamet edited by Christopher Bigsby

Thomas Mann edited by Ritchie Robertson

Christopher Marlowe edited by Patrick Cheney

Andrew Marvell edited by Derek Hirst and Steven N. Zwicker

Ian McEwan edited by Dominic Head

Herman Melville edited by Robert S. Levine

Arthur Miller edited by Christopher Bigsby (second edition)

Milton edited by Dennis Danielson (second edition)

Molière edited by David Bradby and Andrew Calder

Toni Morrison edited by Justine Tally

Alice Munro edited by David Staines

Nabokov edited by Julian W. Connolly

Eugene O'Neill edited by Michael Manheim

George Orwell edited by John Rodden

Ovid edited by Philip Hardie

Petrarch edited by Albert Russell Ascoli and Unn Falkeid

Harold Pinter edited by Peter Raby (second edition)

Sylvia Plath edited by Jo Gill

Plutarch edited by Frances B. Titchener and Alexei Zadorojnyi

Edgar Allan Poe edited by Kevin J. Hayes

Alexander Pope edited by Pat Rogers

Ezra Pound edited by Ira B. Nadel

Proust edited by Richard Bales

Pushkin edited by Andrew Kahn

Thomas Pynchon edited by Inger H. Dalsgaard, Luc Herman and Brian McHale

Rabelais edited by John O'Brien

Rilke edited by Karen Leeder and Robert Vilain

Philip Roth edited by Timothy Parrish

Salman Rushdie edited by Abdulrazak Gurnah

John Ruskin edited by Francis O'Gorman

Sappho edited by P. J. Finglass and Adrian Kelly

Seneca edited by Shadi Bartsch and Alessandro Schiesaro

Shakespeare edited by Margareta de Grazia and Stanley Wells (second edition)

George Bernard Shaw edited by Christopher Innes

Shelley edited by Timothy Morton

Mary Shelley edited by Esther Schor

Sam Shepard edited by Matthew C. Roudané

Spenser edited by Andrew Hadfield

Laurence Sterne edited by Thomas Keymer

Wallace Stevens edited by John N. Serio

Tom Stoppard edited by Katherine E. Kelly

Harriet Beecher Stowe edited by Cindy Weinstein

August Strindberg edited by Michael Robinson

Jonathan Swift edited by Christopher Fox

J. M. Synge edited by P. J. Mathews

Tacitus edited by A. J. Woodman

Henry David Thoreau edited by Joel Myerson

Thucydides edited by Polly A. Low

Tolstoy edited by Donna Tussing Orwin

Anthony Trollope edited by Carolyn Dever and Lisa Niles

Mark Twain edited by Forrest G. Robinson

John Updike edited by Stacey Olster

Mario Vargas Llosa edited by Efrain Kristal and John King

Virgil edited by Fiachra Mac Góráin and Charles Martindale (second edition)

Voltaire edited by Nicholas Cronk

David Foster Wallace edited by Ralph Clare

Edith Wharton edited by Millicent Bell

Walt Whitman edited by Ezra Greenspan

Oscar Wilde edited by Peter Raby

Tennessee Williams edited by Matthew C. Roudané

William Carlos Williams edited by Christopher MacGowan

August Wilson edited by Christopher Bigsby

Mary Wollstonecraft edited by Claudia L. Johnson

Virginia Woolf edited by Susan Sellers (second edition)

Wordsworth edited by Stephen Gill

Richard Wright edited by Glenda R. Carpio

W. B. Yeats edited by Marjorie Howes and John Kelly

Xenophon edited by Michael A. Flower

Zola edited by Brian Nelson

TOPICS

The Actress edited by Maggie B. Gale and John Stokes

The African American Novel edited by Maryemma Graham

The African American Slave Narrative edited by Audrey A. Fisch

African American Theatre by Harvey Young

Allegory edited by Rita Copeland and Peter Struck

American Crime Fiction edited by Catherine Ross Nickerson

American Gothic edited by Jeffrey Andrew Weinstock

American Horror edited by Stephen Shapiro and Mark Storey

American Literature and the Body by Travis M. Foster

American Literature and the Environment edited by Sarah Ensor and Susan Scott Parrish

American Literature of the 1930s edited by William Solomon

American Modernism edited by Walter Kalaidjian

American Poetry since 1945 edited by Jennifer Ashton

American Realism and Naturalism edited by Donald Pizer

American Travel Writing edited by Alfred Bendixen and Judith Hamera

American Women Playwrights edited by Brenda Murphy

Ancient Rhetoric edited by Erik Gunderson

Arthurian Legend edited by Elizabeth Archibald and Ad Putter

Australian Literature edited by Elizabeth Webby

The Beats edited by Stephen Belletto

Boxing edited by Gerald Early

British Black and Asian Literature (1945–2010) edited by Deirdre Osborne

British Fiction: 1980–2018 edited by Peter Boxall

British Fiction since 1945 edited by David James

British Literature of the 1930s edited by James Smith

British Literature of the French Revolution edited by Pamela Clemit

British Romantic Poetry edited by James Chandler and Maureen N. McLane

British Romanticism edited by Stuart Curran (second edition)

British Romanticism and Religion edited by Jeffrey Barbeau

British Theatre, 1730–1830 edited by Jane Moody and Daniel O'Quinn

Canadian Literature edited by Eva-Marie Kröller (second edition)

The Canterbury Tales edited by Frank Grady

Children's Literature edited by M. O. Grenby and Andrea Immel

The Classic Russian Novel edited by Malcolm V. Jones and Robin Feuer Miller

Contemporary Irish Poetry edited by Matthew Campbell

Creative Writing edited by David Morley and Philip Neilsen

Crime Fiction edited by Martin Priestman

Dante's 'Commedia' edited by Zygmunt G. Barański and Simon Gilson

Dracula edited by Roger Luckhurst

Early American Literature edited by Bryce Traister

Early Modern Women's Writing edited by Laura Lunger Knoppers

The Eighteenth-Century Novel edited by John Richetti

Eighteenth-Century Poetry edited by John Sitter

Eighteenth-Century Thought edited by Frans De Bruyn

Emma edited by Peter Sabor

English Dictionaries edited by Sarah Ogilvie

English Literature, 1500–1600 edited by Arthur F. Kinney

English Literature, 1650–1740 edited by Steven N. Zwicker

English Literature, 1740–1830 edited by Thomas Keymer and Jon Mee

English Literature, 1830–1914 edited by Joanne Shattock

English Melodrama edited by Carolyn Williams

English Novelists edited by Adrian Poole

English Poetry, Donne to Marvell edited by Thomas N. Corns

English Poets edited by Claude Rawson

English Renaissance Drama edited by A. R. Braunmuller and Michael Hattaway (second edition)

English Renaissance Tragedy edited by Emma Smith and Garrett A. Sullivan Jr

English Restoration Theatre edited by Deborah C. Payne Fisk

Environmental Humanities edited by Jeffrey Cohen and Stephanie Foote

The Epic edited by Catherine Bates

Erotic Literature edited by Bradford Mudge

The Essay edited by Kara Wittman and Evan Kindley

European Modernism edited by Pericles Lewis

European Novelists edited by Michael Bell

Fairy Tales edited by Maria Tatar

Fantasy Literature edited by Edward James and Farah Mendlesohn

Feminist Literary Theory edited by Ellen Rooney

Fiction in the Romantic Period edited by Richard Maxwell and Katie Trumpener

The Fin de Siècle edited by Gail Marshall

Frankenstein edited by Andrew Smith

The French Enlightenment edited by Daniel Brewer

French Literature edited by John D. Lyons

The French Novel: From 1800 to the Present edited by Timothy Unwin

Gay and Lesbian Writing edited by Hugh Stevens

German Romanticism edited by Nicholas Saul

Global Literature and Slavery edited by Laura T. Murphy

Gothic Fiction edited by Jerrold E. Hogle

The Graphic Novel edited by Stephen Tabachnick

The Greek and Roman Novel edited by Tim Whitmarsh

Greek and Roman Theatre edited by Marianne McDonald and J. Michael Walton

Greek Comedy edited by Martin Revermann

Greek Lyric edited by Felix Budelmann

Greek Mythology edited by Roger D. Woodard

Greek Tragedy edited by P. E. Easterling

The Harlem Renaissance edited by George Hutchinson

The History of the Book edited by Leslie Howsam

Human Rights and Literature edited by Crystal Parikh

The Irish Novel edited by John Wilson Foster

Irish Poets edited by Gerald Dawe

The Italian Novel edited by Peter Bondanella and Andrea Ciccarelli

The Italian Renaissance edited by Michael Wyatt

Jewish American Literature edited by Hana Wirth-Nesher and Michael P. Kramer

The Latin American Novel edited by Efraín Kristal

Latin American Poetry edited by Stephen Hart

Latina/o American Literature edited by John Morán González

Latin Love Elegy edited by Thea S. Thorsen

Literature and the Anthropocene edited by John Parham

Literature and Climate edited by Adeline Johns-Putra and Kelly Sultzbach

Literature and Disability edited by Clare Barker and Stuart Murray

Literature and Food edited by J. Michelle Coghlan

Literature and the Posthuman edited by Bruce Clarke and Manuela Rossini

Literature and Religion edited by Susan M. Felch

Literature and Science edited by Steven Meyer

The Literature of the American Civil War and Reconstruction edited by Kathleen Diffley and Coleman Hutchison

The Literature of the American Renaissance edited by Christopher N. Phillips

The Literature of Berlin edited by Andrew J. Webber

The Literature of the Crusades edited by Anthony Bale

The Literature of the First World War edited by Vincent Sherry

The Literature of London edited by Lawrence Manley

The Literature of Los Angeles edited by Kevin R. McNamara

The Literature of New York edited by Cyrus Patell and Bryan Waterman

The Literature of Paris edited by Anna-Louise Milne

The Literature of World War II edited by Marina MacKay

Literature on Screen edited by Deborah Cartmell and Imelda Whelehan

Lyrical Ballads edited by Sally Bushell

Medieval British Manuscripts edited by Orietta Da Rold and Elaine Treharne

Medieval English Culture edited by Andrew Galloway

Medieval English Law and Literature edited by Candace Barrington and Sebastian Sobecki

Medieval English Literature edited by Larry Scanlon

Medieval English Mysticism edited by Samuel Fanous and Vincent Gillespie

Medieval English Theatre edited by Richard Beadle and Alan J. Fletcher (second edition)

Medieval French Literature edited by Simon Gaunt and Sarah Kay

Medieval Romance edited by Roberta L. Krueger

Medieval Women's Writing edited by Carolyn Dinshaw and David Wallace

Modern American Culture edited by Christopher Bigsby

Modern British Women Playwrights edited by Elaine Aston and Janelle Reinelt

Modern French Culture edited by Nicholas Hewitt

Modern German Culture edited by Eva Kolinsky and Wilfried van der Will

The Modern German Novel edited by Graham Bartram

The Modern Gothic edited by Jerrold E. Hogle

Modern Irish Culture edited by Joe Cleary and Claire Connolly

Modern Italian Culture edited by Zygmunt G. Baranski and Rebecca J. West

Modern Latin American Culture edited by John King

Modern Russian Culture edited by Nicholas Rzhevsky

Modern Spanish Culture edited by David T. Gies

Modernism edited by Michael Levenson (second edition)

The Modernist Novel edited by Morag Shiach

Modernist Poetry edited by Alex Davis and Lee M. Jenkins

Modernist Women Writers edited by Maren Tova Linett

Narrative edited by David Herman

Narrative Theory edited by Matthew Garrett

Native American Literature edited by Joy Porter and Kenneth M. Roemer

Nineteen Eighty-Four edited by Nathan Waddell

Nineteenth-Century American Poetry edited by Kerry Larson

Nineteenth-Century American Women's Writing edited by Dale M. Bauer and Philip Gould

Nineteenth-Century Thought edited by Gregory Claeys

The Novel edited by Eric Bulson

Old English Literature edited by Malcolm Godden and Michael Lapidge (second edition)

Performance Studies edited by Tracy C. Davis

Piers Plowman by Andrew Cole and Andrew Galloway

The Poetry of the First World War edited by Santanu Das

Popular Fiction edited by David Glover and Scott McCracken

Postcolonial Literary Studies edited by Neil Lazarus

Postcolonial Poetry edited by Jahan Ramazani

Postcolonial Travel Writing edited by Robert Clarke

Postmodern American Fiction edited by Paula Geyh

Postmodernism edited by Steven Connor

Prose edited by Daniel Tyler

The Pre-Raphaelites edited by Elizabeth Prettejohn

Pride and Prejudice edited by Janet Todd

Queer Studies edited by Siobhan B. Somerville

Renaissance Humanism edited by Jill Kraye

Robinson Crusoe edited by John Richetti

Roman Comedy edited by Martin T. Dinter

The Roman Historians edited by Andrew Feldherr

Roman Satire edited by Kirk Freudenburg

Science Fiction edited by Edward James and Farah Mendlesohn

Scottish Literature edited by Gerald Carruthers and Liam McIlvanney

Sensation Fiction edited by Andrew Mangham

Shakespeare and Contemporary Dramatists edited by Ton Hoenselaars

Shakespeare and Popular Culture edited by Robert Shaughnessy

Shakespeare and Race edited by Ayanna Thompson

Shakespeare and Religion edited by Hannibal Hamlin

Shakespeare and War edited by David Loewenstein and Paul Stevens

Shakespeare on Film edited by Russell Jackson (second edition)

Shakespeare on Screen edited by Russell Jackson

Shakespeare on Stage edited by Stanley Wells and Sarah Stanton

Shakespearean Comedy edited by Alexander Leggatt

Shakespearean Tragedy edited by Claire McEachern (second edition)

Shakespeare's First Folio edited by Emma Smith

Shakespeare's History Plays edited by Michael Hattaway

Shakespeare's Language edited by Lynne Magnusson with David Schalkwyk

Shakespeare's Last Plays edited by Catherine M. S. Alexander

Shakespeare's Poetry edited by Patrick Cheney

Sherlock Holmes edited by Janice M. Allan and Christopher Pittard

The Sonnet edited by A. D. Cousins and Peter Howarth

The Spanish Novel: From 1600 to the Present edited by Harriet Turner and Adelaida López de Martínez

Textual Scholarship edited by Neil Fraistat and Julia Flanders

Theatre and Science edited by Kristen E. Shepherd-Barr

Theatre History by David Wiles and Christine Dymkowski

Transnational American Literature edited by Yogita Goyal

Travel Writing edited by Peter Hulme and Tim Youngs

Twentieth-Century British and Irish Women's Poetry edited by Jane Dowson

The Twentieth-Century English Novel edited by Robert L. Caserio

Twentieth-Century English Poetry edited by Neil Corcoran

Twentieth-Century Irish Drama edited by Shaun Richards

Twentieth-Century Literature and Politics edited by Christos Hadjiyiannis and Rachel Potter

Twentieth-Century Russian Literature edited by Marina Balina and Evgeny Dobrenko

Utopian Literature edited by Gregory Claeys

Victorian and Edwardian Theatre edited by Kerry Powell

The Victorian Novel edited by Deirdre David (second edition)

Victorian Poetry edited by Joseph Bristow

Victorian Women's Poetry edited by Linda K. Hughes

Victorian Women's Writing edited by Linda H. Peterson

War Writing edited by Kate McLoughlin

Women's Writing in Britain, 1660–1789 edited by Catherine Ingrassia

Women's Writing in the Romantic Period edited by Devoney Looser

World Literature edited by Ben Etherington and Jarad Zimbler

World Crime Fiction edited by Jesper Gulddal, Stewart King and Alistair Rolls

Writing of the English Revolution edited by N. H. Keeble

The Writings of Julius Caesar edited by Christopher Krebs and Luca Grillo